Celebrating
What Is Important to Me

Grades 4-6
Fall 2007

Creative Communication, Inc.

Celebrating What Is Important to Me
Grades 4-6
Fall 2007

An anthology compiled by Creative Communication, Inc.

Published by:

CREATIVE COMMUNICATION, INC.
1488 NORTH 200 WEST
LOGAN, UT   84341

Printed in the United States of America

ISBN: 978-1-60050-140-1

Foreword

A few years ago there was a series of books of photographs that recorded a day in the life of the country. It was insightful and refreshing to see how people lived, worked and experienced their world. Along the same lines, this anthology is a day in the life of our youth. The essays that are recorded between these pages reflect the perceptions of our youth as they experience their world. These essays tell a story about global warming, relationships, and hundreds of other topics that are important to students today.

We are proud to have recorded these perceptions. Without this anthology these essays from our youth would have been lost in a backpack or a locker. We hope you enjoy the enclosed essays as much as we have in recording them.

Believe in our youth. They have much to offer our world.

Thomas Worthen, Ph.D.
Editor
Creative Communication

WRITING CONTESTS!

Enter our next POETRY contest!
Enter our next ESSAY contest!

Why should I enter?

Win prizes and get published! Each year thousands of dollars in prizes are awarded in each region and tens of thousands of dollars in prizes are awarded throughout North America. The top writers in each division receive a monetary award and a free book that includes their published poem or essay. Entries of merit are also selected to be published in our anthology.

Who may enter?

There are four divisions in the poetry contest. The poetry divisions are grades K-3, 4-6, 7-9, and 10-12. There are three divisions in the essay contest. The essay division are grades 4-6, 7-9, and 10-12.

What is needed to enter the contest?

To enter the poetry contest send in one original poem, 21 lines or less. To enter the essay contest send in one original essay, 250 words or less, on any topic. Each entry must include the student's name, grade, address, city, state, and zip code, and the student's school name and school address. Students who include their teacher's name may help the teacher qualify for a free copy of the anthology.

How do I enter?

Enter a poem online at:
www.poeticpower.com

or

Mail your poem to:
Poetry Contest
1488 North 200 West
Logan, UT 84341

Enter an essay online at:
www.studentessaycontest.com

or

Mail your essay to:
Essay Contest
1488 North 200 West
Logan, UT 84341

When is the deadline?

Poetry contest deadlines are April 8th, August 14th, and December 4th. Essay contest deadlines are July 15th, October 15th, and February 17th. You can enter each contest, however, send only one poem or essay for each contest deadline.

Are there benefits for my school?

Yes. We award $15,000 each year in grants to help with Language Arts programs. Schools qualify to apply for a grant by having a large number of entries of which over fifty percent are accepted for publication. This typically tends to be about 15 accepted entries.

Are there benefits for my teacher?

Yes. Teachers with five or more students accepted to be published receive a free anthology that includes their students' writing.

For more information please go to our website at **www.poeticpower.com**, email us at editor@poeticpower.com or call 435-713-4411.

Table of Contents

Essays from Canada are included in this edition
as well as essays from the following States:

Alaska
Arizona
California
Colorado
Idaho
Illinois
Indiana
Iowa
Kansas
Michigan
Minnesota
Montana
Nebraska
Nevada
New Mexico
North Dakota
Ohio
Oregon
South Dakota
Texas
Utah
Washington
Wisconsin
Wyoming

Fall 2007 Writing Achievement Honor Schools

* Teachers who had fifteen or more students accepted to be published

The following schools are recognized as receiving a "Writing Achievement Award." This award is given to schools who have a large number of entries of which over fifty percent are accepted for publication. With hundreds of schools entering our contest, only a small percent of these schools are honored with this award. The purpose of this award is to recognize schools with excellent Language Arts programs. This award qualifies these schools to receive a complimentary copy of this anthology. In addition, these schools are eligible to apply for a Creative Communication Language Arts Grant. Grants of two hundred and fifty dollars each are awarded to further develop writing in our schools.

Argyle Middle School
Argyle, TX
Jamie Tomlinson*

Barrington Elementary School
Upper Arlington, OH
Clay Bogart*

Camellia Avenue Elementary School
North Hollywood, CA
Anne Tichenor*

Challenger School – Ardenwood
Newark, CA
Rebecca Arnold*

Cheyenne-Eagle Butte Upper Elementary School
Eagle Butte, SD
Jessie Keckler*

Covington Elementary School
South Sioux City, NE
Kris Vondrak
Diane Woodford
Mrs. Zediker

DeQueen Elementary School
Port Arthur, TX
Gwen E. Simmons
Maybelline Washington

Dingeman Elementary School
San Diego, CA
Leigh Morioka*
Paige Wilkens

Divine Infant Jesus School
Westchester, IL
Lucille Perry*

Dr F D Sinclair Elementary School
Surrey, BC
Cheryl Andres*
Mrs. Aylett
Mrs. Davies
Mrs. Gill

Gateway Pointe Elementary School
Higley, AZ
Samantha Collins
Jennifer Hawkins
Joyce Lewis
Christine Rice

Greenwood Elementary School
Plymouth, MN
Tami Arvig*

Imagine Charter School at Rosefield
Surprise, AZ
Tracie Petrie*

Irma Marsh Middle School
Fort Worth, TX
Mikie Smith*

Isaac Newton Christian Academy
Cedar Rapids, IA
Lorraine Potter*

Isbell Middle School
Santa Paula, CA
Mark Lopez*

Kinsey School
Kinsey, MT
Beth May*

Liberty Elementary School
Victorville, CA
Patty Morentin*

Linfield Christian School
Temecula, CA
Pat Heckert*
Desirae Jesse*
Kimberly Legg*
Dr. Ruth Young*

McMonagle Elementary School
Flint, MI
Mrs. Bradshaw*
Mrs. Fischer
Diane Richards

Menchaca Elementary School
Manchaca, TX
Mary Jane Ledesma
Madelyn Reiner

Mendocino Middle School
Mendocino, CA
Pamela Duncan*

Milltown Elementary School
Milltown, IN
Holly Barron*

Nishna Valley Community School
Hastings, IA
Paula McGrew*

North Oaks Middle School
Haltom City, TX
Carolyn Hedgecock*

Oak Crest Intermediate School
San Antonio, TX
Monica Franco*
Karen Garza

Our Lady of the Rosary School
Paramount, CA
Sr. Ellen Mary Conefrey*
Sr. Brigid Mary McGuire
Maricruz Soto

Pike Christian Academy
Waverly, OH
Charlotte Saltzman*

Pomerene School
Pomerene, AZ
Karen Troncale*

Round Valley Elementary School
Bishop, CA
Ms. Morales*

Santo Niño Regional Catholic School
Santa Fe, NM
Heidi Schmidt Alcaraz*

Snake River Montessori School
Idaho Falls, ID
Mrs. Mikkelson
Carolyn Neblett*

Southport 6th Grade Academy
Indianapolis, IN
Anne Manning*

St Matthew Catholic School
San Antonio, TX
Kathy Dylla*
Laurette C. Kirby*
Sharon Pirro*

St Monica Catholic School
Converse, TX
Lisa Jordan*

The Academy
Milwaukee, WI
Martin Gutnik*

The Study School
Westmount, QC
Elana Agulnik
Isabelle Fahmy
Edna Reingewirtz*

Thomas Jefferson Charter School
Caldwell, ID
Mike Sasaki*

Westview Elementary School
Jackson, OH
Pam Steele*

Winona Elementary School
Winona, TX
Marsha Hutson*

Language Arts Grant Recipients 2007-2008

After receiving a "Writing Achievement Award" schools are encouraged to apply for a Creative Communication Language Arts Grant. The following is a list of schools who received a two hundred and fifty dollar grant for the 2007-2008 school year.

Acadamie DaVinci, Dunedin, FL
Altamont Elementary School, Altamont, KS
Belle Valley South School, Belleville, IL
Bose Elementary School, Kenosha, WI
Brittany Hill Middle School, Blue Springs, MO
Carver Jr High School, Spartanburg, SC
Cave City Elementary School, Cave City, AR
Central Elementary School, Iron Mountain, MI
Challenger K8 School of Science and Mathematics, Spring Hill, FL
Columbus Middle School, Columbus, MT
Cypress Christian School, Houston, TX
Deer River High School, Deer River, MN
Deweyville Middle School, Deweyville, TX
Four Peaks Elementary School, Fountain Hills, AZ
Fox Chase School, Philadelphia, PA
Fox Creek High School, North Augusta, SC
Grandview Alternative School, Grandview, MO
Hillcrest Elementary School, Lawrence, KS
Holbrook School, Holden, ME
Houston Middle School, Germantown, TN
Independence High School, Elko, NV
International College Preparatory Academy, Cincinnati, OH
John Bowne High School, Flushing, NY
Lorain County Joint Vocational School, Oberlin, OH
Merritt Secondary School, Merritt, BC
Midway Covenant Christian School, Powder Springs, GA
Muir Middle School, Milford, MI
Northlake Christian School, Covington, LA
Northwood Elementary School, Hilton, NY
Place Middle School, Denver, CO
Public School 124, South Ozone Park, NY

Language Arts Grant Winners cont.

Public School 219 Kennedy King, Brooklyn, NY
Rolling Hills Elementary School, San Diego, CA
St Anthony's School, Streator, IL
St Joan Of Arc School, Library, PA
St Joseph Catholic School, York, NE
St Joseph School-Fullerton, Baltimore, MD
St Monica Elementary School, Mishawaka, IN
St Peter Celestine Catholic School, Cherry Hill, NJ
Strasburg High School, Strasburg, VA
Stratton Elementary School, Stratton, ME
Tom Thomson Public School, Burlington, ON
Tremont Elementary School, Tremont, IL
Warren Elementary School, Warren, OR
Webster Elementary School, Hazel Park, MI
West Woods Elementary School, Arvada, CO
West Woods Upper Elementary School, Farmington, CT
White Pine Middle School, Richmond, UT
Winona Elementary School, Winona, TX
Wissahickon Charter School, Philadelphia, PA
Wood County Christian School, Williamstown, WV
Wray High School, Wray, CO

Grades 4-5-6

Note: The Top Ten essays were finalized through an online voting system. Creative Communication's judges first picked out the top essays. These essays were then posted online. The final step involved thousands of students and teachers who registered as online judges and voted for the Top Ten essays. We hope you enjoy these selections.

Top Essay Grades 4-5-6

Don't Judge a Book by Its Cover

Equality is really important. The Golden Rule is that you should always treat people how you want to be treated. You shouldn't make fun of someone because of the way they look or what skin color they have. These are just the things they were born with, but they can't help it. Those are just the simple traits that make them who they are. Without those traits we would all look the same and looking the same wouldn't be good. Everyone should get the same amount of respect.

If you make fun of someone you should try to step into their shoes and think about how bad they must feel right now, what if that was you? Think of the Golden Rule and follow it all the way through your whole life!

Taylor Ellis, Grade 4
Maple Avenue Elementary School, WI

Top Essay Grades 4-5-6

911 Tribute

When I think of September 11th, this comes to my mind:

I was a little girl coming home from school one day. All of the grown ups I saw were looking so sad. My mom came to pick me up. I remember it was quite windy and pretty silent. When I got home, I arrived with the news blaring. I went to my dad, sneaking up so he could tickle my belly, but instead I got a different reaction. He just sat there with a dead stare on his face facing the television. I didn't know what was going on! I looked at the television and all I saw was big buildings. I looked at my mom and she was staring at me. I didn't understand. I felt my world had just disappeared and the only one left was me and my thoughts. Then after I powered over my tears, I got the nerve to make a statement. I opened up my lips, but nothing came out! I finally broke the silence. I felt like a steamy pot of boiling water pouring out words and not able to stop. My parents said there was a plane crash in the Twin Towers in New York. I stopped. I felt like a drop of water frozen in the air. I wondered that night how all those people felt and all the pain they all had. I will pray and stand tall for the victims of that fateful day.

Leanna Gordon, Grade 4
Norwich Elementary School, OH

Top Essay Grades 4-5-6

Walking in My Shoes

I am a survivor. Having been born prematurely weighing only two pounds, six ounces, I faced an uncertain future. But I continue to beat all odds, just as did one of my biggest heroes and inspirations, Dr. Brunstrom.

She and I started life out the same way. She also has beaten all odds, just as I plan to do. She heads the top clinic in the nation for children with cerebral palsy, and is a professor at Washington University, in St. Louis, Missouri. Dr. Brunstrom is an author of many medical books, as well as having graced the cover of many magazines. She heads up an organization of parents, my father included, called *"Reaching for the Stars,"* which has lobbied Congress seeking funding for cerebral palsy.

Every six months I go to St. Louis for my regular check up. She and I love to argue, but the truth is, I know she knows best. Dr. Brunstrom has already walked in my shoes and succeeded. She tells me my future is bright. She believes in me and has been a great inspiration in my life.

I will someday own a business, run oil wells, and farm. I *believe* I can do anything I want. Dr. Brunstrom has proven if I *believe, I can achieve.* As I continue *Walking in My Shoes,* I know the sky's the limit. I will overcome my challenges and reach my life goals, thanks to one of my many inspirations, my doctor, Dr. Brunstrom.

Zach Hamilton, Grade 5
Westview Elementary School, OH

Top Essay Grades 4-5-6

A Family Death

I stared out the window until I got bored. Six whole hours is way too long to be sitting in the car. We were on our way to Chowchilla to visit my papa (grandpa) who had prostate cancer. "I hope he'll be okay," I thought to myself.

As soon as we arrived, I saw Papa lying in his hospital bed. His face had no expression. It was like he was in agony and constantly moaned. It was hard to communicate with him. He could barely speak and almost everything came out as a mumble. When my nana started talking to my dad and my brother turned on the TV, I felt a little bit more at home because of the comforting noise.

Our plan was to stay for four days. Four days later, I walked into the TV room. I noticed that Papa and his bed were no longer there. I asked my mom where he went and she said that he passed away in the middle of the night.

I remember how much fun we had together before he died. We picked the harvested fruit, played cards, built the garage, played and made up games and read stories together. These activities were probably some of the most fun things I've done in my whole life. I wish I could relive these moments over and over again.

The house got quiet and our eyes started to sparkle and sting with pain. Papa still is very special to me and I feel weird when I think about him. It's sad because he died, but happy because he's with God up in heaven. Sometimes I feel like I can only see him in my dreams, but I know that's not true because he'll always be in my heart.

Elaine Hughes, Grade 5
Dingeman Elementary School, CA

Top Essay Grades 4-5-6

Discrimination No More

Discrimination, many children face it every day. Not for race, ethnicity, or gender, but for religion. Catholics and Jews are some of the religions that face religious discrimination all the time. Public schools are one of the culprits. The Pledge of Allegiance says "one nation under God." George Washington believed in God, Abe Lincoln believed in God, I believe that God kept our union together and was more than a humongous help in the end of slavery.

Many public schools do not allow religion, except for an occasional Christian Club. They do not allow references to God unless you're learning about Moses in social studies. They don't allow you to promote what you believe in.

Schools say that students need to welcome differences, Christianity should be included. Religion is an important part of our culture, it is one of the things that makes our country so diverse. If people read the Bible they would see that there are many answers that solve confusing issues.

People are smart; if they had common sense they would see in an instant that religion should be allowed in school regardless of the school being public or religious. When people see a problem they think of a solution. I see a very clear solution: that schools should include religion as long as students don't beat other religions down. Religion is extremely important to society, too important to forget about. CATHOLIC AND PROUD.

Mikaela Maneely, Grade 6
Prescott Mile High Middle School, AZ

Top Essay Grades 4-5-6

You're Unique, Embrace It!

Unique. A word so special and important to people. But if you practically live in the shadows of popular boys and girls who tease you just because you're different, they usually don't call you unique. Weirdo, freak, geek and loser are just some of the names that kids can call you in elementary and high school. Sadly, being unique or different in school can make kids feel like they are almost drowning and the popular kids aren't even throwing life rafts. In the classroom, one laugh, snicker or giggle can make the walls and windows start making fun of another child's insecurities. I believe no unique child should have to go through all of that torment and ridicule. Being super smart, obese, in a wheelchair, or someone with a prosthetic arm are not things to be made fun of, but things to embrace! Eventually all kids will learn that teasing hurts and they should never laugh at people without getting to know them. I think different people have different qualities that make EVERYONE unique. When you laugh at someone who is different, it's exactly like people laughing at you because you're all the same. Kids should think before they act because they might not know if they hurt someone. No matter what, there will always be people who tease and victims with insecurities. But let us all remember one extremely important thing. You are unique. EMBRACE IT!

Joelle Mariano, Grade 6
Immaculate Conception, BC

Top Essay Grades 4-5-6

Your Imagination Is Powerful

Have you ever got caught daydreaming in class? I know I have, but sometimes daydreaming can be a good thing, as long as you don't do it during school. When you're daydreaming you're using your imagination.

I think that imagination is the key to success. When you use your imagination, you're unlocking a whole new world. You can come up with all kinds of different things. You can exercise and strengthen the mind. As you grow up, your ideas can become actions. The things you are daydreaming about now can change your future. The flying machines, trips to Jupiter, and all of your wildest dreams can come true. Our imagination can challenge us to achieve the most we can.

If kids didn't daydream and use their imagination, nothing new would be invented. If kids wouldn't use their imagination, things like the light bulb, the television, and the computer, would not have been invented. All those things started out as ideas.

Daydreaming is not the only way to use your imagination. You can use your ideas in drawing, painting, music, dance, drama, and any other form of art. Paintings like the *Mona Lisa* and *Starry Starry Night* started out as ideas. You can use your imagination to build things also. Buildings like the Eiffel Tower, the Empire State Building, and the Brandenburg Gate, were all just ideas the architect had. Many novels that were written started out as ideas also.

As you can see, your imagination is a very powerful thing.

Jacob Sellers, Grade 6
Fort Branch Community School, IN

Top Essay Grades 4-5-6

Hate

Many people would ask the simple question, "What is hate?" The answer is not so simple. Hate is a complicated feeling of extreme dislike that has the potential to do harm. When put into the soul of anyone, hate can change a person forever.

The first question leads to another question, "What can hate do?" Hate can do many things. All of them come out badly. Hate can destroy a person's sense of logic, cause utmost stress, and destroy a person's innermost willingness to do good. In a community hate will spread, by harmful deeds and influencing children. In a group of states, hate will completely demolish a region's or even country's sense of morals.

Another question may be asked, "What message does hate send to our youth?" The message tells children to hate everyone they see, and they shouldn't like anyone they see. It also tells them to physically, emotionally, or any other way they're capable, to hurt someone for no reason at all.

Then we ask another question, "What is an example of hate?" An example of hate is racism, like segregation. There used to be different water fountains for different races, and they couldn't use each other's water fountain. Jews were also persecuted, in World War II. They were forced to live in ghettos, and tortured and killed.

Thus we conclude, "What can we do about hatred?" Kids cannot stop adults from doing bad deeds, but kids can stop other kids and themselves from hateful acts.

Mikah Semon, Grade 5
Hillel Academy, WI

Top Essay Grades 4-5-6

Heaven's New Star

"At the end of our lives, we will not be judged by how many diplomas we have received, how much money we have made, or how many great things we have done. We will be judged by I was hungry and you gave me to eat. I was naked and you clothed me. I was homeless and you took me in." This quote is from a woman who became a symbol of untiring commitment to the poor and suffering. The "living saint" made a difference in this world. Mother Teresa, probably the most admired woman, brought light to poverty, injustice, indignity, and disease that have showered our planet.

Mother Teresa's life experiences can teach us many lessons. She, my inspiration, devoted her life to helping promote understanding of the needs of those who are less fortunate. Her efforts demonstrated that one person can make a positive influence on the lives of millions across political, geographic, religious, and cultural boundaries. Now more than ever, I believe that if I try I, too, can make a difference in people's lives. Through her teachings, I have learned to appreciate all the important people in my life and the benefits of living in the United States. Mother Teresa inspires us to aid the world by helping and giving to the less fortunate. Her work helping the poor, sick, and dying will forever remain her legacy. In her death, Heaven gained another star which shines light to the world.

Kestine Thiele, Grade 6
Challenger School – Ardenwood, CA

Top Essay Grades 4-5-6

Several Sweet Seasons

I love the outdoors. When people ask me what my favorite season is, I say, "I don't have one." In my opinion, every season is exciting!

In spring, the annual flowers flourish like rainbows and the grass grows a vivid emerald. Trees grow brilliant coats, and lakes and ponds restore their life again. Spring is the time to start on a clean page, for you will have company as the world around you starts over too.

Summer is when you can hang out at the pool or beach and enjoy the warm sun, the humidity rising with it every day. Summer is a time to meet and renew friendships, and bond with family.

Lying in the cool grass, the zephyr washing over me, and rustling the dry, brilliant leaves, I can tell that fall is here. Fall is a calming season to enjoy beautiful weather before snow and frost arrive.

Finally, the eventful winter is here. The snowflakes dance around in the fierce winter wind like ballerinas, and the air nips your cheeks. Winter is a bittersweet season, the sharp air lingers everywhere, but the fun times in the snow make vivid memories. I would be miserable living in some areas where people may live their whole life without ever meeting snow.

I love the outdoors with the variety of seasons, each with special qualities. I can never decide which one is my favorite, for I love them all.

Amanda Urke, Grade 5
Greenwood Elementary School, MN

My Family

According to the dictionary, family is "a group of people that live together." But to me, family is so much more. My family is very important to me and I am very thankful for them because of all the love and support that they give me and how they've helped me grow. I can always count on them being there for me.

I can't imagine what my life would be without any of them. I wouldn't have any of the love that my family has or any of the sincere warmth that we have for each other. The love that my family gives to me is so unconditional.

My family is made up of my mom, dad, my brother, and myself. I also have a cat. Each person provides something different that is very special and unique in our family. My mom plans many special family outings, my dad and I share a love of sports and both of my parents help me be the best student I can be. I can always count on my brother when I want to play with somebody. And, I can always count on my cat Tazz for big kisses.

I like to think that all of the families out there have the same kind of love ours does. And I hope that your family is as close as ours is, and has as much love as ours shares.

Kyle Tornow, Grade 6
Greendale Middle School, WI

Henry Ford: The Hardworking Engineer

Many people do not know about the famous automobile engineer, Henry Ford. Ford, born in Dearborn, Michigan in 1867, showed a dislike for farm work and an interest in mechanical objects. Because of this, when he turned sixteen, he traveled to Detroit to work as an apprentice machinist.

In 1888, the Edison Illuminating Company hired Ford, and by 1893, he was promoted to Chief Engineer, giving him time to work on his experiment with internal combustion engines, and of course, his fascination, automobiles. After many experiments, Ford tried to make his own automobile company, but only succeeded in 1903. During the period from 1903-1932, he created the first automobiles, Model A, Model T, and in 1932, he created the first ever car with a V-8 engine.

Ford also had a political and charitable side. During World War I, he and 170 other people went to Europe for a pacifist expedition, but failed. He also ran for U.S. Senate, but failed at that too. Finally, he succeeded in created the Ford Foundation for education, research, and development. After his death in 1947, Henry Ford II succeeded him.

Henry Ford has inspired me to study hard because that is the way I can turn out to be a great automobile engineer like him. He has also inspired me to be informed about the activities in the world, because that is the way I can become an ace politician and possibly a better politician than him. Henry Ford is really a great, admirable person.

Amogh Pershad, Grade 6
Challenger School – Ardenwood, CA

Animal Cruelty

Have you ever heard about animal cruelty? Ok, it's any act of violence or neglect towards animals. Cruelty is illegal in all fifty states, it's considered a felony in forty three. People who injure animals might also injure people too! So stop cruelty today for everyone!

Animal cruelty includes many varied cases and forms. It could be a dog in a puppy mill having litter after litter of unhealthy puppies. A tiger or an elephant being forced to perform for a circus crowd. A helpless raccoon being tortured by the hands of teenagers for "fun." It could be your neighbor's dog not having enough food, water, attention, or shelter. Or an unlucky dog or rooster being thrown into a pit and killing each other. Whatever the case this unbearable activity needs to end.

If you suspect any abuse trust your instincts. If you're feeling guilty because it's a family member don't be. This animal needs you now more than ever. Don't let it fight by itself, until it becomes too fragile and exhausted. Report it!

Think of all the chaos these animals encounter day after day. So help the animals and stop cruelty today!

Ashleigh Graham, Grade 6
Concord Ox Bow Elementary School, IN

Get Ready for a Disaster!

If there was a disaster I would need many supplies like, food, water, and a first aid emergency kit.

What I have in my emergency kit is money, cotton balls, alcohol, Band-Aids, and more. I would have more than one emergency kit. Then place the emergency kits in different places.

Where I will escape is through the window of my room. I wouldn't care if I sprained an arm or leg just to be safe. If I could I would go through the front door. My big brother can get out through his window in his room.

If a disaster happens we will meet at my aunt's house, because it is close to my house. We will go wait at the mailbox and call my aunt to let her know we are on the way.

I learned to be prepared for a disaster for when something happens. I need to make a plan before it happens.

Yessica Arellano, Grade 5
Liberty Elementary School, CA

Tera'ney's Story...

I'm Tera'ney and my life is a little difficult right now. It's hard because I think about a lot of things that make me cry. Sometimes I share some of the things that bother me with my teachers. It makes me feel better to talk.

Sometimes I try to talk to people. I have decided to write a story and hope it makes me feel better. A lot of times after I finish my work I write a story.

My sister and my Mama both tell me to write a story when I need to express what I am feeling. I know I'll be all right... but right now life is difficult.

Tera'ney Turner, Grade 5
DeQueen Elementary School, TX

Who I Admire

Do you have someone you really admire? The person I really admire is my brother, Luis, because he cares about me. This summer I fell and got hit on the back of the head. He ran and told my mom, then said I fell. I turned out to be ok.

Another way he helps me is my homework every time I need help on it. Last time he helped me on my vocabulary. He also watches to see if I really read every day. He also helps me on my spelling and comprehension.

The last reason I admire Luis is because he is fun. Like last time we rode our bikes and took turns using the computer. We also play the PlayStation 2. We play outside and make funny jokes every day.

In conclusion, he is funny, he helps me on homework, and he cares if I get hurt.

Juan Sanchez, Grade 5
Camellia Avenue Elementary School, CA

Why It Is Important to Do Good Deeds

Deeds are very important; they keep the world clean and organized. Many deeds make you remember many tragic and happy things. You can help the world by doing good deeds.

Good deeds are good things you can do without people telling you. People can do many simple deeds, such as recycling paper, cans, plastic, and newspapers. Some good deeds you can do on special occasions like on tragic days like the "Attack on America."

"Attack on America" happened on September 11, 2001 and it will be remembered forever. Police officers and firemen sacrificed their lives for others. Many big and great deeds were done on that day.

Deeds are important in life. Some deeds can help others, some help yourself and some help the Earth. Remember a good deed a day keeps the world from going astray.

Aleesha Cutler, Grade 6
Snake River Montessori School, ID

Don't Smoke

Here is a healthy tip for everyone, don't smoke! Cigarettes have a very additive drug called Nicotine. One cigarette may have you addicted for life. It fills your lungs with black gunk and makes it harder for you to breathe. It is very hard to quit smoking and people that smoke are at bigger risk of getting cancer, emphysema and other illnesses that can kill you.

You may not want to know this, but in cigarettes there are the following gross ingredients: Nicotine, which is a deadly poison, Arsenic, which is used in rat poison, Methane, which is a component of rocket fuel, Ammonia, which is found in floor cleaner, Cadmium, which is in batteries, Carbon Monoxide, which is in car exhaust, Formaldehyde, which is used to preserve body tissue, Butane, which is used in lighter fluid, Hydrogen Cyanide, which is used in gas chambers. These are just a few sickening things in cigarettes. If you still smoke after reading this I think you are totally crazy, but it's your life choice.

Nicole Spence, Grade 5
Woodside Elementary School, WI

Never Give Up

Never giving up is the most important thing in one's life. People who start a project should always finish it. For example, when I do my 4-H project, I start from the beginning. I get my two-to-three-week-old calves, and bottle feed them daily for two months. I clean their stalls, make sure their bedding is clean, and provide fresh water.

Next, I start brushing them and talking to them and getting them used to me. The trying part is getting them accustomed to a lead halter and teaching them to walk beside me without dragging me through the field.

After months of leading, cleaning, washing, feeding, and spending quality time with them, it's Jackson County Fair time. I arrive with my calves on Sunday. Monday and Tuesday are spent tending to them and getting ready for my Dairy Market Feeder Show on Wednesday. When Wednesday morning arrives, I'm at the fairgrounds at 6:00 A.M., grooming and bathing them both.

Showtime arrives, and I enter the show arena with a smile and do my very best. This year I won three 3rd place ribbons.

Friday is the livestock sale, and I sell my dairy market feeder. That completes my project, which has taken seven months. It's sad to sell the calves, which have become good friends. But if I didn't follow through, I wouldn't have reached my goal. Every time I start something, it's rewarding to finish.

Joseph Wines, Grade 5
Westview Elementary School, OH

My Future Is Important to Me Because…

My future is important to me. The reason being is because my goal is to go to the Performing Arts College in Beverly Hills. I have to get good grades to go there. Part of the reason I want to go there is because I want to get discovered. Now, I know it's going to be a while until I get to that point; still, it is a part of my future.

Now, back to reality, in the close future, all I have to do is get through my first year of middle school. It's not too hard, but it's not real easy either. My family will help me get through it, but they can't do my homework for me, so I need to do most of it on my own. Down the road, I will need to buy my own car. My parents will pitch in, but they can't just buy me and my brothers' cars. That's just too much money, to buy a car for each of us. I know I'll get through this but only with God's help.

But there's more to my future than buying cars, going to college, and getting through middle school. There's being acquainted with the Lord. I'm very excited and a bit nervous for what God has planned for me. There's one thing for sure: God will be with me every step of the way!

Alexa Feddema, Grade 6
Linfield Christian School, CA

My Sister Being Born

My sister being born was kind of gross, but after a minute or two, I was like WOW, this is actually happening. I was lucky to be old enough to be in the room. At the time, I was 10 but now I'm 11 1/2. I got to hold her first, then my mom. When I first saw her, I burst out crying because she looked exactly like me! She had brown hair, blue eyes, and a tiny nose. After everyone got their turns holding her, I read her a book. Then I curled in a ball with her and just sat there, retaking what had just happened so far. For the next couple of weeks my family was really emotional. I cried a lot and I really don't know why. Then I just started being lethargic. But then I was better about being active. After that, things just got better and better. I met new friends, moved to California, etc.! But that brings us to now. My sister is 1 1/2, fun and energetic. She goes to daycare and I go to school. She loves me and I love her!

Hannah O'Kelly, Grade 6
Akers Elementary School, CA

My Name, Nicole

My name means little girl, but it also means happiness. When someone says my name, it sounds like opening a soda can because it snaps. Sometimes it reminds me of a sunflower, because of that, it reminds me of summer. My name is like the number 6 because it is fun to write. My name reminds me of the color aqua because when it rains, I can hear my name. I have only known one person with my name but I didn't really know her at all. All that we had in common was that we lived on the same street. Now it's a different story when it comes to nicknames. People call me Nikki, Me-me, or the shoe brand, Nike. But it's ok. Some people have my name as their middle name, it's cool!

Nicole Garcia, Grade 6
North Oaks Middle School, TX

Israel

Israel is a nice place. It's much safer than places like New York or Los Angeles, but it wasn't always safe. Thousands of years ago there were many wars over Israel, but the Jews always won. There has been a recent war. It was called the Six Day War.

When the U.K. controlled Israel they couldn't handle it, so they gave it to the Jewish people. The Arabs weren't happy, so they declared war on Israel. David ben Gurion, the Prime Minister of Israel at the time, fought back.

Israel is very important to the Jewish people. We believe that God promised us the land of Israel. We also believe that when our messiah comes he will be in Israel.

There is a Jewish monument in Israel. It is called the Kotel or the Western Wall. Israel is in a war. Some parts of Israel are destroyed, but most of it is still safe. Israel is a very beautiful place. In Israel there are beautiful places like the Red Sea, the Dead Sea, and the Mediterranean Sea. Israel is a beautiful place.

Daniel Gaudynski, Grade 5
The Academy, WI

Remembering You

When it comes down to the most important thing, it's family. My grandma, Nana, we used to call her, died right before I was born. She was my mom's mother. She died of cancer. Not breast cancer, though she did have it. My mom said that Nana's stomach would swell up because of all the fluid inside her.

My mom and dad were there when Nana took her last breath. If the doctors had caught it sooner, she would probably be here right now. She was about 69 when she died. My grandpa, Tata, was Nana's husband. Tata is still alive and he's turning 90 on October 20, 2007. I'm pretty sure, like my mom always says when this subject turns up, that she is still watching over us from heaven, like a guardian angel. Sometimes, I would look up at the starts and tell myself that she's the brightest star in the sky. Other times, I think Nana is the sun, the sun that lights the world, or the mountains that block the sun when setting. Sometimes, I see her in my dreams or sitting next to me. Someday, I know it, I will see her on Earth or in heaven, maybe not today or tomorrow, but maybe, just maybe, I'll see her.

Mariana Murphy, Grade 5
Kyrene Monte Vista School, AZ

Yukon Territory — Land of the Midnight Sun

Many people assume that the Yukon Territory is just a barren land, but actually it's a surprisingly diverse place. The land, people and resources of the Yukon, make this land unique and beautiful.

The total area of the Yukon is 483,450 km2 with more than half as forested land. The capital city is Whitehorse. Although most of the year you'll find snow, in the summer where the land is tundra, tough grasses, moss, and small shrubs grow. Still, the soil is frozen, making it difficult to grow crops. In the winter there is a period with no daylight and in the summer the opposite is true.

The Yukon has a population of about 32,000. Over 70 percent live in Whitehorse. About 24 percent of the people are aboriginal with fourteen First Nations speaking eight different languages. The people still retain many of their customs. They hunt, fish and trap. The fur trade and the Klondike gold rush brought many non-aboriginals to the Yukon.

The largest industry in the Yukon is mining, (gold, lead, zinc and silver). There is drilling for oil in the Beaufort Sea. Tourism is a major resource with people visiting the Yukon to hike, rock climb, camp, fish, and hunt. Fishing and trapping are also other resources.

The Yukon is a beautiful territory with so much to offer. The uniqueness of the land, the people and its diverse resources, makes the Yukon a special place in our country.

Kailyn Smith, Grade 6
Immaculate Conception, BC

Being on a Boat

I arrive at the boat and down goes the plank. On board the ground isn't stable. The engine begins to roar and the boat starts moving. Then the big roar fades away.

In the morning I'm awakened by the waves and the boat tipping. I put on my clothes and go to eat breakfast. Outside I can feel the morning dew collecting on my face. The sun is just rising and the sky is orange. Suddenly I hear, "Good morning." I turn around and it's the captain. I tell him my name. He leaves. I go to wake up the rest of my family. They go eat breakfast.

We finally pass through the Caribbean Sea. The rest of my family meets in the room and plays cards. It's time for lunch so we eat. We look over the side of the boat and see a bunch of fish. The captain comes out and meets my family. We talk for a little while. We have dinner and watch a movie in bed.

The next morning we are awakened by the sound of the waves crashing over and over again and the boat tipping from side to side. We have breakfast and go on the deck, but the motor isn't running any longer. It is time to get off. They put down the plank and we walk off.

We get in our car and drive home thinking about our wonderful boat adventure. When we arrive home we are glad we went.

Ashley Fallon, Grade 4
Country Montessori School, CA

Crud War

Every summer I go to a camp called Pine Cove and this year we did Crud War. It is one of the most disgusting and exciting things I have done!

The campers were divided into two teams. The war began when a horn was blown and I ran onto the field throwing the flour at my enemies. The field looked like a powdery, white cloud. I had flour in my mouth, which tasted disgusting and my clothes were a mess.

The second round was shaving cream. I had the shaving cream squirted into my hands, and then I heard the horn and sprinted onto the field. I smeared it onto people's backs. I ran back to my side and reloaded my ammunition then I ran back to the field to slather my next victim. I was a gooey glob of cream.

The third round was the most disgusting. We used horse food. The food was brown, slimy, and smelly. I scooped it into my hands and got ready to throw. The horn blew, I ran onto the field, and threw it. People were wiping it in my hair and over my clothes. I was the dirtiest out of my cabin.

The Crud War was fun and very stinky. You would probably enjoy doing it if you like to be dusty, white, brown, gooey, and smelly. If you participate in the war, you need goggles!

Sydney Austin, Grade 6
Argyle Middle School, TX

A Real Role Model

Have you ever felt that someone has done something that means so much to you, but you can never repay them? I feel this way to Mr. Anup Kumar Nayak, a computer engineer, an MBA student, and my father.

My dad greatly excels at math and science and types at a phenomenal speed, maybe eighty or ninety words per minute. My dad works as a chip designer and an MBA student. He wakes up at 4:00 AM to study without getting disturbed. He helps me with my homework, along with studying for tests. Although my dad always helps me in my work, he is the top student in his own class.

I have always wanted to be like my dad. He tries to do everything as flawlessly as possible. Watching my dad, I am encouraged to study hard, focus, concentrate, and be responsible. I am inspired to do better in my studies so I can go to an Ivy League college. I will follow my dad and be exactly like him.

Akaash Nayak, Grade 6
Challenger School – Ardenwood, CA

Vince Young One of the All-Time NFL Players

At age 24 Vince Young was setting records at Texas, his college. He started his college season as 6'5" 230 lbs. At this point in college he had a 5 star ranking, one of the best in college. Then, in his last year, 2005, he was named MVP of the Rose Bowl against the USC Trojans, they won the game.

Then in the NFL draft, he was picked 3rd overall. Then his first year in NFL he was named Rookie of the year. He finished his rookie year with 184 passes out of 357, along with 12 touchdowns and 2199 yards. Along with passing he is a very talented runner as well as finishing his rookie year with 552 yards rushing and 7 touchdowns.

I like him because I believe he will become one of the best NFL players. It is his second year this year so we'll have to see if he improves any.

Alec Haughian, Grade 5
Kinsey School, MT

How Smoking Affects People

Every year hundreds of thousands of people die from diseases caused by smoking. The strain put on your body often causes years of suffering from emphysema, which is an illness that slowly rots your lungs.

Smokers get more colds, flu, bronchitis, and pneumonia than a nonsmoker. Smoking also restricts blood vessels and can prevent oxygen and nutrients from getting to the skin, which is why so many people that smoke look pale and unhealthy.

Lung cancer is another effect smoking has on people. It is caused by the tar in tobacco smoke. Smoking causes around 1 in 5 deaths from heart disease.

This year alone Ohio has collected nearly $1 billion in taxes from smokers which shows smoking also costs a lot and seems to be a big problem in Ohio.

Gaige Roe, Grade 5
Westview Elementary School, OH

Guitar

The first guitar was called a Sitara which came from ancient India and Central Asia. The modern guitar is descended from the Roman cithara brought by the Romans to Hispania around 40 AD and further adapted and developed with the arrival of the four-string oud. Then there was the six string Scandinavian lute, which gained popularity in areas of Viking incursions across Europe.

There are many types of guitars, but they are narrowed down to a few main types—acoustic six stings, acoustic twelve strings, semi acoustic six strings, semi acoustic twelve strings, electric six strings, electric twelve strings, and the bass guitar. Guitars can also have six, seven, eight, ten and twelve strings. There are many styles of guitars; all have different shapes and sizes. There are different types of picks too. There are thin, thick, large and small but mainly are all the same.

Guitars are used for almost every type of music, probably because the sound style matters on how you play so it can sound classical to heavy metal. They are the most common instrument in rock bands because of this.

A slide is used in blues and rock to create a glissando or "Hawaiian" effect. The necks of bottles were often used for this in blues and country music. Modern slides are constructed of glass, plastic, ceramic, chrome, brass or steel, depending on the weight and tone desired. An instrument that is played exclusively in the manner, (using a metal bar) is called a steel guitar or pedal steel.

J.J. Weston, Grade 6
Charles Beaudoin Public School, ON

My Heroine

My heroine isn't Superwoman, Elastagirl, or anyone like that. It's my aunt, Teresa Leighty. Aunt Teresa lives in California, so her visits are very special to me, especially if she stays at my house.

My aunt LOVES dogs, like me. She has one named Dio. He's a Weimaraner/Doberman mix. I think Aunt Teresa is Dio's heroine too, because she got him from a rescue center, even though he did have a few minor problems. I don't think anyone else would have done that.

Aunt Teresa looked like me when she was young. She also loves to read, like me. Having her be like me makes me feel closer to her.

The main reason she's my heroine, though, is karate. She is a black belt. I really look up to her for that because I do karate, too. I'm only a white belt, but someday I want to be a black belt, like her.

To have a hero or heroine means that you want to be like someone, and this is the same way with my feelings for my aunt, Teresa.

Mel Leighty, Grade 4
Stilwell Elementary School, KS

Zebras

Zebras are cool. They are magnificent animals. Zebras are very unusual creatures with their black and white stripes. Many people believe that the stripes are for camouflage in the herd. People also think they are a way to stay cool and warm with the changing seasons. Animals such as lions hunt zebras. Zebras are art of the horse family. They are fast runners; this helps them escape from lions. The Zebra's population is decreasing just like many other African animals. Many people want to save the zebras from hunters who hunt them for their skins. Zebras are awesome.

Taylor Romanowski, Grade 6
St Monica Catholic School, TX

Sanibel Island

When you arrive at Sanibel it is beautiful. The way to get to Sanibel is by flying to Ft. Myers Airport and driving 45 minutes. Before you reach the island you have to go over the causeway. Even though Sanibel got hit by the tip of Hurricane Katrina it is still beautiful.

Across the Gulf of Mexico is Captiva Island. You can see it best from the north end of the island. Also on the north end is the lighthouse. It is close to the old drawbridge, that still works!

The beach is very relaxing. All you can hear is the waves crashing against the shore and the seagulls. One of the many things you can do besides relaxing is going on a walk and looking for some of Sanibel's amazing shells. One of my favorites is looking for dolphins in the ocean.

When the day is over you can check into one of their amazing hotels. To finish off the day you can go and have dinner at one of their awesome restaurants.

All of those great things are only some of the reasons why Sanibel is the number nine beach in the U.S.

Alyssa Tedesco, Grade 5
Barrington Elementary School, OH

My Favorite Place

My favorite place is my nana's house. She gives me a lot of comfort at her house. I go there when I can. I have my own room in there which is the guest room. When I get scared I ask my mom to go over there. My room has games and puzzles in there. It has my own bed. It has covers and pillows. Me and my mom play in there on the bed. My nana lets me spend the night with them. One time I spent two whole nights with them. I love to play in my nana's house. Pawpaw plays with me in the house. I love my nana's house. It has books I can read. I love it because it has a lot of room. Me and my Pawpaw always roughhouse. Me and my baby cousin work on her walking. Me and Nana always take pictures. My pawpaw will always throw pillows at me and I throw them back. My nana will get furious sometimes. My nana will take a lot of pictures. We go there a lot and I love to spend the night there. It is so comfortable. My nana's house is the best place ever.

Jordan McHam, Grade 4
Winona Elementary School, TX

Music Is My Hero

Who is your hero? Do they have extreme super powers? Do they have immortal enemies? My hero doesn't, because it's music.

The kind of music I listen to is alternative rock such as: My Chemical Romance, Three Days Grace, The Red Jumpsuit Apparatus, and so on. I don't really care what other people think about the music I listen to, as long as it makes me feel good, it's good with me.

I don't ever go a day without listening to music, it's my favorite thing to do. It gets me through stressful times, so when I'm stressed I go to my room and turn up the radio. The only way I can completely calm down is to listen to my music.

I think you can tell the character or personality of a person by the music they listen to.

Music keeps me out of trouble (most of the time). And also it helps me with my schoolwork. For some messed-up reason, I always get my work done faster when I'm listening to it. Only a few friends like the same kind of music as me. And some people hate me for it, but I still listen to it.

So, just because someone downs you or thinks you're weird because of what you listen to or what you do, just ignore their rude comments and walk away. But most of the time, you will have a couple of good friends there to back you up.

Timber J. Collins, Grade 6
Milltown Elementary School, IN

Be Drug Free

There are many reasons to be drug free. Doing any kind of drugs is extremely bad for a person. People who do drugs will lose their real friends and will also waste a lot of money buying drugs.

Drugs are extremely bad for the human body. Smoking makes lungs get weaker. When playing sports a person won't be able to keep up. Smoking can also cause lung cancer. Drugs mess up the brain so getting good grades is much more difficult.

People who smoke and do drugs will lose their real friends. Hanging out with bad people who smoke and do drugs will cause true friends to stop hanging out with you. Hopefully true friends would convince a friend to stop doing drugs.

Buying drugs wastes a lot of money. Cigarettes are very expensive. In fact, they cost $3.75 a pack at the local gas station.

All drugs are very bad for the human body. Drugs will cause a person to lose their true friends. Also, a lot of money is wasted buying drugs. I hope I have convinced people to be drug free!

Andrew Herner, Grade 6
Southport 6th Grade Academy, IN

A High Sky Day

I was at the airport one day to see the Blue Angels. We sat in the car and waited for the show to start. The show began when the Blue Angels started their engines. Then they went up in the sky and flew. My favorite thing that they did was one went up, one went left, one went right, one went on top, and one went on bottom so the made a diamond shape. About twenty minutes later it was over. It was hard getting out of the crowd, but we got home.

That day was so much fun. I love the Blue Angels. I saw them in Washington state, but it wasn't as nice because there were so many trees. In Bozeman it was so much better because they were in midair, and you could see them. When I got home that day, I looked at my Blue Angels model of #4 Blue Angel. I played with that toy for 1 hour because it was so much fun. Then I got tired so I put it up in my room. Today is sits on my night stand by my bed. I still play with it today, but I would rather keep it as a sculpture to keep for the rest of my life. I tell people about the Blue Angels.

Taylor Twofeathers, Grade 6
Monforton School, MT

Dogs

This essay is all about dogs. A dog's life-span is 9 to 12 years. In our world there are many different kinds of dogs. My favorite is the American Bulldog. There are other types of dogs. For example, sporting, hounds, working, herding, terrier, and non sporting dogs. All dogs need regular exercise to keep them fit. Dogs need to run with their owners in the morning and afternoon.

Dog behavior resembles their wild relatives such as coyotes and wolves. A good understanding of dog behavior and communication can help most people avoid dog bites. If a dog jumps right at you, thrust your knee upward into the dog's chest.

Wow! This report is great for me because I learned a lot about dogs. Dogs are wonderful pets. I bet your parents will let you keep one. Dogs are the best.

Christian Segura, Grade 5
St Patrick's Catholic School, WA

Who I Admire

Who do you admire? I admire Ms. Tichenor because she is very fun. And she is also funny.

Another reason is she is smart. She knows her multiplication really quick. She could remember what she has to do. When we are doing math she makes the lesson very fun.

Another thing is that she is helpful. She helps me with my homework. She also helps other kids in the class. In math she helps us a lot.

When I graduate I am going to come and help her class. Also when the class graduates I know everybody is going to miss her. I couldn't have gone this far if Ms. Tichenor hadn't pushed me hard and made me keep my head in school.

Jannet Rocha, Grade 5
Camellia Avenue Elementary School, CA

Achieving

Why does achieving help you be successful in your life? Let me tell you. It makes you feel better when you win an award. Then you know that you have achieved something in your life. If you go to college, that might be something that you will want to accomplish. I bet you wonder what I want to pull off someday?

Something I want to achieve is to go to the NFL and be a superstar. If anybody is reading this I want him or her to say one thing that you would like to achieve someday. If you do not know what achieving means it is to accomplish something.

Achieving something feels really good because I know how it feels. The first thing I accomplished is a Covington Pride Award. I felt proud when I got it. This is how achieving helps you in your life in many ways.

Joseph Prescott, Grade 5
Covington Elementary School, NE

School Uniforms

I think that schools should not have uniforms because school would be awkward because everyone would look the same. It would be hard to find each other.

One other thing is that it would be expensive for the school to buy them. I think that schools shouldn't have uniforms. You couldn't tell who was who.

The worst thing is that some families couldn't afford them. One thing if schools had uniforms most people would not buy their kids' clothes from JC Penny, Mervyns and Target, etc. Then the clothing industry would fall like a rock! My opinion is schools should not have uniforms.

James Pahlow, Grade 6
Round Valley Elementary School, CA

The Beach

The thing that I love is the beach, and why I picked it is because it's a nice place to be with your family, and I love how God made the water. The most part I like is the horizon. I sometimes watch it with my cousins and family. Sometimes I bring my board and go surfing with my dad. My dad and I sometimes race and see who can get to shore faster. He always wins, but someday I might beat my dad. My sister and I play on the sand and sometimes we build a sand castle.

One time we buried my dad in the sand, then when the water came the sand went away. I also love when my cousins come to visit. Then we ride our bikes, find clams, swim or go out on the boat. When we ride our bikes, we race or ride down on the beach with our mom and dad. Also we love to find clams. One time, my cousin Talia found a pearl inside her clam! It was a gold one, and it was beautiful. My most favorite is swimming and going on the boat. On the boat we like to sit in the front and when my dad drives the boat, he goes super fast and my cousins and I hold on to each other because we get scared that we might fall off. I love my family and my best cousins.

Sarah Haddadin, Grade 6
Linfield Christian School, CA

It Couldn't Be True

"No! This couldn't be true!" I said. Was this a nightmare I was living? Was this me getting dressed for her rosary?

The day was December 31st, 2006, the second saddest day of my life. The first saddest day of my life was two days before, December 29th, 2006 when I heard the news that my grandmother had died. At the rosary, she arrived in a closed casket. When people arrived the slide show began. My cousin's band played beautiful music.

"Will the sadness end?" I said. I couldn't believe I was going to *my* grandmother's funeral! The day was January 1st, 2007. That's right, New Year's Day! The last day I would *ever* get to say goodbye to her! Once seated, my Uncle Bobby sang "Ave Maria." Tears flowed down faces! The pain I felt was horrible. I could only imagine my mom's pain. Next my cousins and my brothers read the prayers of the faithful. Now my uncle told all about my grandma's life. After that my cousin and I read a poem that talked about my sage grandma not wanting us to cry because she is now with God! Suddenly I saw my serene grandpa crying even after being divorced for 24 years. It touched my heart. We ended this emotional day with a celebration at my aunt's house.

Yes, the incomprehensible nightmare *was* true! My grandmother sadly did leave me on December 29th, 2006.

Haley Kirby, Grade 6
St Matthew Catholic School, TX

What Fun We Had

Last summer of 2007, my mom, dad, brother, and I took our traditional trip on Sunday to South Padre Island, Texas. Monday was sunny and clear, the perfect beach weather. My family and I headed to the beach after breakfast and enjoyed a great day on the beach.

On Tuesday, Grandma Esther, Great Grandma Perez, Aunt Kim, Aunt Veronica, Uncle Randy, cousins, Josh and Jon, joined us in a condo at the Saida as well. We all stayed inside my grandma's condo and watched movies that day due to the rain. It rained hard that day. We couldn't even go out for dinner since the weather was so bad.

My favorite day was when I went on an early morning horseback ride on the beach with my aunts and cousins. It was my first time riding a horse on the beach at South Padre. I rode a big brown horse. His name was Jake. It was kind of weird to ride a horse with the same name as me because it was funny calling him, "Jake." My horse would go fast only if you told it to. We rode the horses by the water for two hours that morning. My horse, Jake, was friendly to me.

I said, "I did not know that horseback riding could be so much fun on the beach." Next year, I hope to have a better time on South Padre Island, especially now that I know we can take a horseback ride family excursion.

Jacob Marsalis, Grade 6
St Matthew Catholic School, TX

A Challenge

A month ago I learned a lesson when I was playing basketball with my brother and I won!!! So I started making fun of him because I had never beat him and he had never lost to me. Dakarie got mad and he stumped in the house and told my mom and she said "what I need you to do is go back outside and ask Daminique to play another game and this time you will win." Dakarie came back outside and asked me and I said "yes." So me and Dakarie flipped a coin and I said "heads" and it was heads so I went first. When we first started I was winning but Dakarie started stepping up his game and I lost. Dakarie started making fun of me and calling me names. I ran in, went up to my room and then my mom came in and I told Dakarie sorry and he told me sorry. That's when I had a challenge with my brother and learned a lesson.

Daminique Price, Grade 5
McMonagle Elementary School, MI

The Unbelievable Day

"Please mom, please! Can we get him please?" I pleaded. My brother, my sister, and I were on our knees begging. It was a bright, sunny day in the shining sea of green grass in someone's backyard. There were puppies scattered all over the place jumping at our legs. They looked like little brown puff balls with reddish pink tongues full of saliva hanging out of their mouths. The adorable puppies were all sprinting and wrestling around. Every time we tried to plead, our mom would say "I don't know, it will be a lot of work." Although one of the dogs sat in the palm of my hand while my grandma picked tons of little black nibbling fleas off of one of the adorable puppies. All of the dogs were dark, dark brown except one. We finally decided on him. He had thin tan fur with a white spot on his tail and his whole belly was white. We had to go out to this big, giant store full of stinky animal food and squeaky toys and we bought a tiny jail for him. This changed my life because from then on, Jack always slept in my bed with me. That was an unbelievable day!

Josh Fish, Grade 5
Dingeman Elementary School, CA

Straight A's

"Wake up," my mom said. "It's the first day of school!", she added. I was very excited but scared. I had teachers from third grade telling me that it was going to be ok. My teacher's name was Mr. Ortiz, but I called him Mr. O. He was not mean at all, but he gave us a little too much homework. That actually helped us. I tried extra, extra hard to do better. In my two semesters I got all A's. What surprised me the most was that I was the only one in my class to get straight A's. My parents were so proud of me that for my birthday they got me a baby sister. Mr. O. was so, so proud of me! My prizes for my effort were candy and pens. I also got to leave early from school as a reward for my grades. Hopefully I'll do good and keep my grades up this year.

Paola Maya, Grade 5
Bagdad Elementary School, TX

Coco Bunny

I opened the door to the pet shop. I scanned the shop until I saw that mysterious creature, Coco Bunny. Did you know Coco Bunny is a pet? He has white and light brown fur. It is small, but very fast. Can you guess what it is? If you guessed a bunny then you are… wrong. It's my hamster.

Coco is a male hamster. He is really fast so I can never put him on the ground. If I tried, he might be on my bed when I wake up!!

Having a hamster is a big responsibility. You must clean its cage every week and play with it. If you don't, your hamster would get very grumpy.

Coco likes to bite on things. When I tried putting him on my desk, he kept on shredding up my papers. I forgot that I had chocolate on my desk so Coco nipped it open, but he was smart enough not to eat it. Coco is also really energetic. At night when I'm sleeping, I can hear his hamster wheel making sounds as the wheel turns in the cage.

I love playing with my hamster because he's cute and cuddly. Coco likes to run around the house in his hamster ball. My hamster is very important to me so I take good care of him. Even when I'm not there, Coco is still by my side.

Cathy Wong, Grade 6
Northwood Public School, ON

I Love…My New School!

Oh, my gosh!! I LOVE my new school. It is DeQueen Elementary where there are the BEST teachers, BEST principal, BEST students, BEST parents, BEST classrooms and GREAT P.E. classes!! Oh, my gosh!! It's a new building and I LOVE it!!!

There are a lot of GREAT things about DeQueen too. They have GREAT lunches, GREAT cheerleading and a GREAT drill team. Since I like it here so much…so will my family. I love it so much that I would like to stay here all day long! Oh, that's right…I do.

One day when I am older, have finished school and gotten a car I will come back to DeQueen to visit! I really will. If I can I will bring my entire family to show them around the school. It will be good to see all my old teachers: Ms. Simmons, Mrs. Washington, Ms. Fisher and Mr. Taylor. I love all my subjects.

I wish I could stay at DeQueen for the REST of my life! It's just that GREAT! Everything's perfect at this school. If you don't believe me, come and see just what I'm talking about!! Seeing is believing.

DeQueen is BEST! It's the school where I have GREAT friends, family, fun and GREAT times, too. I love my school, DeQueen Elementary. It is the BEST of all schools in the world. That's how much I LOVE DeQueen.

Oh, guess what… I LOVE DeQueen!! I really, really do.

Shairell Landry, Grade 5
DeQueen Elementary School, TX

My Phenomenal Idol

My cousin, Neeti Desai, stands as the person I think of as my inspiration. Once you know her, it is obvious why I think of her as influential. From kindergarten throughout high school, my cousin received only a few B's on her tests, and in all of her report cards she received straight A's. Neeti, chosen as valedictorian when she graduated from high school, decided to enter a college in Boston. She chose to enter this college because she wishes to become a dentist. Her college has been considered as one of the best throughout the country. This also happens to be Neeti's first year in college.

I consider Neeti as my role model because she has inspired me to achieve my goals. When it comes the time for me to attend college, I wish to attend a medical college and obtain a scholarship. In the future I strive to reach the top and become a successful doctor. I shall forever remember the inspiration my cousin, Neeti, gave to me.

Supriya Kazi, Grade 6
Challenger School – Ardenwood, CA

Step by Step

Marie Curie the only lady who won a Nobel Prize and discovered new radioactive elements inspires me because of her perseverance, self-confidence, excellent study habits, and the need to strive for perfection.

Marie's self-confidence remained throughout her life because she always believed in herself. She rigorously continued her experiments in the dim light. Staying up late at night, she studied until she understood the concept. Her excellent study habits earned her student licentiateships in mathematical and physical science.

Due to her perseverance, she discovered three radioactive elements. Even though numerous people stopped their financial contributions, Marie continued working with determination and managed to extract minute amounts of radioactive material from pitchblende. Finally, when Marie collected her radioactive samples, they were concentrated enough for an experiment and she derived three new elements, polonium, uranium and radium.

Marie Curie always strived to be the vest and practiced what she learned at school to the real world, and she finally succeeded. She relentlessly worked on her experiments and applied her full potential to all her endeavors. She stated: "Life is not easy for any of us. But what of that? We must have perseverance and above all confidence in ourselves. We must believe that we are gifted for something and that this thing must be attained." Thanks to her, I am determined to study harder and set a higher expectation level for myself. She taught me that everything is possible if you try. I am improving little by little, step by step.

Yao Guang Hoh, Grade 6
Challenger School – Ardenwood, CA

The World's Deadliest Creatures

The world is filled with animals. Among these animals we find deadly creatures.

Tigers are carnivores. They are the largest cats in the world and the only kind with stripes. These stripes help them blend in the tall grass and surprise its prey. Tigers can grow 9 to 10 feet and weigh 800 pounds. A tiger's eye sight is six times better than a human's.

Great Whites are carnivores. They eat seals, fish, other sharks and sometimes even humans. Like all other sharks, Great Whites have sandpaper like skin and a perfect sense of smell. The Great White can grow to 21 feet and weigh 3000 pounds.

Crocodiles are carnivores. A crocodile mostly eats fish, wild boar, antelope and humans. Crocodiles move on the water like floating logs and when prey gets close, the crocodile quickly drowns the prey and feeds underwater. A full grown crocodile can grow 20 to 25 feet.

Octopi are carnivores. Some are microscopic and some are as big as double-decker buses. Most octopi are venomous in the suction cups on their tentacles. The largest Octopus is the Giant Pacific Octopus which grows to at least 25 feet long and 6 feet long tentacles.

People try to kill them out of fear but deadly creatures can be more scared of you than you are scared of them. Therefore, instead of just killing them, first find out and learn all the animal's interesting features.

Tobias Duerr, Grade 4
Trelawny Public School, ON

Goals

It was a glorious day in Genesee, where my team's first soccer game was. "All right!" my dad, the coach said. "Claire, you're at goal." "Yes!" I thought, as I rushed to the goal. Playing soccer teaches me many things, and it is also a life long activity.

By playing soccer, I am learning more than just kicks and turns. Teamwork is a huge part of soccer. Being able to work as part of a team takes an enormous amount of practice and dedication. Playing soccer teaches me how to be physically fit. I have to work extremely hard to succeed. To beat my opponent to the ball, I must hustle and give one hundred percent. The harder I work, the better I'll get, the more athletic competitions my team and I will win.

By playing soccer, I am believing in myself. Through soccer, I am working hard as a team member to win championships and earn trophies. Playing high school soccer could possibly lead to a scholarship in college. If I have an outstanding college career, it could lead to a position on a women's professional soccer team. If I am committed to playing soccer and always give it my best effort, I could make it to the Olympics! When I get older, I could become a soccer coach for young people. Soccer isn't just a sport to me. It is a life long activity that is teaching me to follow my dreams.

Claire Birk, Grade 4
Maple Avenue Elementary School, WI

All About Polar Bears

One animal that I have become close to over the recent past is the polar bear. Do you know that they're closely related to the brown bear? The only difference is their color.

Polar bears live mostly by the North Pole and in that area. Throughout the entire year, the bear lives on the ice of the Arctic Ocean. They walk westward moving from one ice pack to another. Polar bears can swim for miles to reach another ice pack.

Once polar bears are four to five they can start having babies. Their newborn cubs are not very big though, they are only the size of a mouse and weigh close to one pound. Can you imagine seeing one of those newly born babies?

Female polar bears can be as little as four times smaller than the male bear. Adult males can be up to ten feet tall and weight up to 1400 pounds! The most that a female weights is 650 pounds! Polar bears eat mostly seals. They catch their prey by waiting at a hole in the ocean and catching the seals when they come up for air.

As you can see polar bears are a very intriguing animal. I do so enjoy seeing them in the zoo, I think they should be free. I hope to see a bear in the wild sometime soon.

Courtney Smiley, Grade 5

Bye-Bye Meg

"Come on Meg, let's get some ice cream!" I yelled up to my sister.

"I can't, I have to pack!" she yelled back.

"Why do you have to pack? We aren't going anywhere." I said as I walked up the stairs.

"Well Shea, I hate to tell you, but it's almost time for me to go to college," Meghan said.

"Oh," I said sadly and walked away to my room and stayed in there until it was time for dinner.

"Shea, it's time for dinner," I heard from downstairs.

"Coming," I said back.

As I walked downstairs I had a feeling that my best friend, Meghan, would leave and not come back for a while. When I got downstairs I saw the rest of my family already eating, "So Meg when will you come home?" I asked in a soft voice.

"Every 3 weeks," she said back.

"It will be that long," I said back.

"Yah, I am really sorry," she said back.

The next morning when I got out of bed I went into Meghan's room to see if she was gone yet but she was standing right behind me ready to leave, "Are you leaving right now?" I said in a really sad voice.

"Yes,"

"I will miss you Shea," she said and kissed me good-bye and left. As I watched her leave I felt tears rolling down my face. It felt like a hundred bees were stinging me all at once.

Shea Donahue, Grade 6
Haslett Middle School, MI

I Call This Room

Our white townhouse on Santa Catalina was becoming very small. My middle brother, Nathaniel, had just been born. With only two bedrooms in our house, it was an indisputable fact that we were in desperate need of space!

We called our resourceful real estate agent and friend, Susan. Finding the right home was an elusive dream for the first month that we house-hunted. Eventually, we found an immense red brick home in a gated community called Finesliver Ranch.

My dad rented a U-haul truck for the big move. My aunt, burly uncle, grandma, crotchety grandpa, cousins, and my cousin's sluggish friends helped us to move. However, our helpers just threw things in boxes without following a logical order. As we were getting ready for church the following serene Sunday morning, my mom couldn't find any of her shoes. She had a wistful look on her face as she asked, "Has anyone seen a box with my shoes?" Moving wasn't fun that morning.

The one fun thing about moving was that I was able to pick my own bedroom from the two upstairs bedrooms. "I call this room!" I shouted. I painted my room lavender and I bought a new comforter and pillows to match my new bedroom theme.

I sometimes miss our old white house. Now I know that moving was the best decision because I now have a new rotund baby brother, Dominic. We have plenty of space even with three children in our family.

Lianna Pais, Grade 6
St Matthew Catholic School, TX

The Best Birthday I Ever Had

Last April 5th was the best birthday. On April 5th in the morning I was so excited because it was my birthday. At school I saw three of my friends who were smiling at me. Then one said, "Happy birthday Aye!" I was happy they knew it was my birthday. Then I realized that they are going to give me my birthday punch. I tried to run away but another one caught me. I was hoping that they would not punch me too hard. Finally they stopped.

I had a great time at recess. At lunch time I told one of my friends to come with me to the teacher. I asked the teacher if I could give candies to everyone because it's my birthday. My teacher smiled and told everyone that Aye is going to give everyone candies because it's her birthday. Then we will sing the happy birthday song after lunch. I felt weird that everyone was going to sing for me. It was a pleasure giving candies. Then I realized that there are some candies left. But others asked me for more candies. So I gave it to them. I was relaxed that there's still a bag of candies left for the teacher. Everyone sang a birthday song for me. I was delighted.

That day was terrific. After school I was very excited because of my surprise present. That is why that day was the best birthday I ever had.

Aye Oo, Grade 6
Dr F D Sinclair Elementary School, BC

The Age of Dinosaurs

Millions or even billions of years ago, creatures called dinosaurs roamed the Earth. Some dinosaurs are as gigantic as a ten-story building. But some aren't even as big as humans. Once you hear these unbelievable facts about these creatures from the past, your eyes will pop out.

Just one of the many types of giants, Diplodocuses were about 82 feet in length, 13 feet in height, and could reach 17.6 tons. But even larger was Sauroposeidon, which could reach 98 feet in length, 55.7 feet in height, and weighed up to 65.5 tons! It was probably the biggest creature to walk on Earth. Diplodocuses and Sauroposeidons were both herbivores (grass-eaters).

One of the biggest carnivores (meat-eaters) was Tyrannosaurus. Tyrannosaurus Rex was about 48 feet long. It's nothing compared to the herbivores, but it is to other carnivores. Tyrannosaurus Rex is bigger than 95% of other types of dinosaur carnivores and smaller than 95% of types of dinosaur herbivores.

One of the smallest dinosaurs ever discovered was Eoraptor, which was only about 3 feet long and 2 feet tall. Eoraptors lived in what is now Argentina. One eerie thing about these tiny dwarves is that they had both carnivore teeth *and* herbivore teeth.

These unbelievable facts about dinosaurs are just *so* amazing. I really wish I could see them before my eyes. Oh, and if you have noticed, your eyes did pop out.

Joe Sun, Grade 4
Stone Ranch Elementary School, CA

My Ski Trip

On my tenth birthday, I went skiing with my dad. It is a tradition in our family that when a kid turns ten years old, they go skiing with just dad. I had mixed feelings about this trip. I was excited but also a little apprehensive.

We flew from the Peoria airport to Denver via Minneapolis on the United Airlines. In Denver we rented a Hummer to drive to Keystone which is a ski-resort approximately one hour away from Denver. That night we stayed at a bed and breakfast inn. It was nice except there was no television or Internet access in the room.

In the morning, I was ready to go early before the slopes got crowded. We got our ski equipment and took the gondola up in the mountains. We skied the whole mountain down. It was an exhilarating experience. The next day, when I woke there was a blizzard outside. The ski lifts were still open though. I stayed real close to my dad. The wind gusts had to be more than fifty miles an hour.

On our last day, my dad took me snowboarding. Snowboarding is easier on the knees and so much cooler. Unfortunately, I was not able to complete my lesson since we had to catch the flight back to Peoria. I am looking forward to finishing my snowboarding lessons on my next trip.

In conclusion, it was an incredible tenth birthday. It's given me many memories and I learned how to snowboard.

Sahil Sabharwal, Grade 6
Peoria Academy, IL

Peyton Manning: Road to NFL

Peyton Manning, quarterback for the Indianapolis Colts, led his team to win Super Bowl XLI. He was awarded Most Valuable Player of the game. People say he is a 6 foot, 230 pound throwing machine! I say he is one of the best quarterbacks in the history of the National Football League.

Football runs in Peyton's family. Born and raised in New Orleans, Peyton's father was the quarterback for the New Orleans Saints. The saying "like father, like son" is very true for the Mannings, as Peyton was the starting high school varsity quarterback as a freshman. He had a record of 34-5 as a starter, and ended his high school career with a total of 92 touchdowns!

Peyton was the number one recruited quarterback in the nation. He accepted a football scholarship to Tennessee, where he continued paving his road to glory. He had fans going insane with 11,201 yards of passing! He had defenses crying with 863 completions and 89 touchdowns! He threw 33 interceptions in 1,381 attempts, the lowest of all-time! Peyton finished his career as the all-time leading passer. He holds 42 NCAA, Southeast Conference and Tennessee records.

Peyton graduated with a degree in Speech Communication and went on to become the number one NFL draft pick. Peyton continued his leadership on the field, leading the Indianapolis Colts to their first ever Super Bowl victory! Given his history of achievements, I have a feeling his first Super Bowl win will not be his last!

Colin Padalecki, Grade 5
Oak Crest Intermediate School, TX

Honesty

"We tell lies when we are afraid...afraid of what we don't know, afraid of what others will think, afraid of what will be found about us. But every time we tell a lie, the thing we fear grows stronger." Tad Williams

I was swimming with my friends and playing Marco Polo. I was Marco. I finished counting and while underwater I opened my eyes to look for my friends. When I tagged someone they asked if I had looked. I said "No." This was a lie. I had lied because I did not want to be found out. I felt bad lying to my friends. My friends said, "We won't be able to trust you if you don't tell us the truth."

When someone lies to me I feel like it changes my friendship with them. Their lie causes me to wonder if I can trust them. I feel like they could lie to me again.

I learned about honesty from my mom, dad, and sister. They taught me that it was right to be a truthful person, and that lying causes consequences. These consequences are not feeling good about myself, and losing people's trust. This is why honesty is important to me. I want to feel good about myself and feel that others can trust me.

Olivia M. Patterson, Grade 4
CORE Butte Charter School, CA

Disaster Plan

If a disaster happens I will need different objects like water, food, and a first aid kit.

My family will have 5-7 days worth of water and food. You should also have flashlights if it was night or the electricity came off, walkie talkies to say in touch, extra pair of clothes and shoes, batteries, a map.

For the escape route, I would go from my brother's window because it leads to the front yard. My room is difficult because it leads to the backyard also my parents' room the same thing and the dining room. The guest room leads to the front yard too.

Where would you meet your relatives? I will meet my parents at my auntie's house. And the Liberty Park because they're far away but not that far.

I learned that when there's a disaster you got to be ready there's no time to get ready during the disaster.

Donia Alamas, Grade 5
Liberty Elementary School, CA

Surfing

Carlsbad California is a wonderful place to surf! Carlsbad is a beautiful beach located near San Diego. The hot sand mixes perfectly with the 75 degree water. It is amazing. The waves rise from 4 ft. to 10 ft. and are wonderful for beginners because of the white waters in the low tide. It is also great for the advanced surfers who just love to go into the deep ocean. I am sort of a beginner; I learned how to surf two years ago. I just love feeling that mist hitting your face. I borrow my brother's board. The company that made it is named N.S.P., and the color of the board is a blend of orange and yellow.

My brother Anthony helps me with everything especially my foot work. Anthony is very good at surfing. He likes to go out deep. But I do not because I think I will get eaten by a shark. Sometimes the sand gets so steep. I will fall. Also when you're in the water you might step on a fish or stingray, or you might get stung by a jellyfish. It hurts A LOT! I love to surf and anyone who does.

Austin Hall, Grade 6
Linfield Christian School, CA

No Gangs + No Violence…Good!

Just think if we didn't have violence in our world? We wouldn't even have to wear school uniforms because no one would fight you for your clothes or shoes. We wouldn't be fearful of being shot or even killed. When I play outdoors, I ask God to please keep angels around me.

When I go to Houston, TX for a football game I pray not to be murdered as we leave the games. I hope every day that violence was not a part of my life or this world.

I hope one day…soon…this world will change and we won't have gangs or violence. It would be so cool if the gang members changed and decided to go to church someday.

No gangs…no violence…that's GOOD.

Ronald Gray, Grade 5
DeQueen Elementary School, TX

My Family Reunion

This is a story about my family reunion. My family reunion took place in the Lyndhurst Community Park. My tall skinny dad, my two cousins, my two siblings, and I got to the park first. When we got to the park my cousin, Stormie and my sister, Ryan ran straight to the playground. After a while my Uncle Dirk, Aunt Kim, my mom, and my granny came with the food. I ate a juicy hot dog. Everybody was coming. Before I knew it, I saw my five uncles, my three aunts, my cousin. My grandma and grandpa were coming through the gate.

We were all about to go swimming before we saw that big pan of juicy steaks. So, before we went swimming we sat down to a delicious meal. We had tender steaks, sweet baked beans, juicy hot dogs, tasty chicken, some awesome greens, last but not least, some hot flavored Georgia sausage. After we ate, we went to the pool. It was a really big pool.

After we got out of the pool we went back to the picnic table and ate some more of that delicious food.

Then we had a water fight. My grandma told me to take the water gun from my Uncle Harold, so I did. But then my uncle took the water gun from me and got me soaking wet. So after that we had to go home. But I will always remember my family reunion at the Lyndhurst Community Park.

Ja'Rai Skinner, Grade 5
Prospect Elementary School, OH

The Best Day Ever

Have you ever had a time when you thought wow what a great day that was! It was July 15, 2005 at the Three Bears campground. My friend Sarah was visiting for the weekend. There was a scavenger hunt that afternoon, guess who came in first place, Sarah and I. That evening we went to bingo to try our luck. Guess what, I won the 6th game along with the jack pot. I ran to my trailer to share the excitement with my parents, they were happy for me and said what a great night for a walk.

The campground section had a very special trailer to me, it was blessed with 6 beautiful bouncing cocker spaniel puppies. How my heart ached to own one of those puppies. I would sit on my dad's lap and beg and plead for one of those puppies he always said no. Even though the answer was always no I would return to that trailer day after day. My favorite one had big dark brown ears. As we walked onto their lot that night there was something different about that brown eared puppy. He was wearing a red collar with an owner's tag which meant he was sold. My heart sank as he ran up to me. My parents said check his tags, the tags read, "Silverado belongs to Kayshia Lemieux, Hampton NB." Tears filled my eyes my wish had come true. There we were girl and her best friend. What a day!

Kayshia Lemieux, Grade 6
Hampton Middle School, NB

Being Fit

Exercise, diet, and not smoking are the three factors in keeping a person fit. Being fit is really good for your health. People look up to you when you are fit. If you are overweight, it is called obese.

If you are fit, you have less of a chance of having a heart attack. You also have a lesser chance of having diabetes, stroke and high blood pressure. When you are fit, you can participate in activities with your children. You feel better at normal day activities. You feel good about yourself when you are fit.

If you have children, they are more likely to be overweight if you are overweight. They will learn to eat fatty foods and not a well-balanced diet. If you do not exercise, your children will probably not exercise. If you smoke, your children are at greater risk to smoke.

Smoking can greatly increase the chance for lung cancer and other lung diseases. Smoking cuts your lung capacity and makes it difficult to breathe during exercise and can cause dizziness. Therefore, people are less likely to exercise.

If you don't exercise and eat right, it's not too late to start. If you smoke, it's not too late to stop. Being fit can change your life in a positive way.

Justin Roepsch, Grade 5
Norwoodville Elementary School, IA

My Family

My family is very special to me.

My mom is a stay-at-home mom. She works very hard. My mom cuddles with me and helps me. She makes me feel better when I'm sick. She makes her famous soup and gets me ginger ale. My mom is a very good cook. She makes good eggs and desserts. I love her pasta. She is special.

My dad works in the air force. He is a MSgt. He works very hard. He loves to have fun with me. We like to play hockey, football, and he jumps on the trampoline with me. My dad wakes me up and sometimes tucks me in. Dad and I like to wrestle. My dad also helps me on the computer. I love to be with my daddy!

My sister and I fight but we still have lots of fun together. She is also very special! My sister helps me a lot. She is also very smart. She taught me how to write cursive and helped me with times. My sister and I like to play Bratz and Polly together. We also like to dress our stuffed animals and turn our music very, very loud, and downstairs our parents yell for us to turn it down. I love my sister very, very much! My sister also helps me with things like cleaning. Even though my sister and I fight we still have fun together. Together my family has lots of fun. We love to ice skate, play in the woods, travel, and many other things. My family has lots of fun!

Lexi Hauptman, Grade 4
Finger Lake Elementary School, AK

Life Without My Daddy

My life without my Daddy is very difficult. I lost my daddy on June 30, 2004. We buried my father on July 3. He was 37 years old at the time of his death.

My daddy, Tommy, would take us on vacations and outings. I really miss my Daddy's presence in my life. My brother and I let balloons go in memory of our daddy.

I have other family members. I have an aunt in Alaska, great cousins, and an uncle in Houston, TX. They are nice to have and I'm grateful for their presence in my life also. However, when my head is down and I'm not talking to anyone that means I'm missing my Daddy. I was very young when Daddy died.

That's my whole story about missing my Daddy.

Ashley Forward, Grade 5
DeQueen Elementary School, TX

Exciting Adventures

The thing I enjoy doing the most is playing with my friends. My best friend is Justin S. He is very fun to play with. Every time I go to his house, he always asks me if I want to play Xbox. I say "YA!" So we go upstairs and we play "HALO" and "HALO 2." It's very fun to play.

I first met Justin at the big park in our neighborhood. I asked him if he wanted to play with me, and he said "Ya! Sure!" After that we started playing together every day, and we became good friends. We don't just play XBOX. We like to play at the park, doing stuff like baseball or basketball, tag, pretending to be army soldiers, and other fun things.

Playing with Justin is a lot of fun, but it's also good for me. I like to run to his house, and when we play we do a lot more running, so it helps me build muscles and be strong. That's what Justin and I do every day, and that's why I enjoy it the most.

Alex Vidaca, Grade 4
Gateway Pointe Elementary School, AZ

Stitches

One day we were going to a baseball game. When we got there my brother wanted a water bottle. My mom gave me money to go buy one for him. I waited in line then I got one. I ran back, a metal sign was sticking out from the fence and cut my arm.

My friend's mom saw I was bleeding, she put a bandaid on it. My mom and I ran to the car because she was going to take me to the hospital. We waited almost 40 minutes! When we got into the room, the lady lifted up the bandaid and she said it was a deep cut. After we went into a different room and the lady stuck a needle through my skin to numb it. I was moving so much that the nurse had to come in and calm me down.

When we were done I went to the bathroom. I had to go to a different baseball game. I went home to get ready for the other game. Before we got out of the car my mom put on a bandaid. My arm felt a lot better after that.

Lillie Dixon, Grade 5
Bang Elementary School, TX

Mary Edwards Walker

Mary Edwards Walker was a very important person in the Civil War.

She was born on November 26, 1832 in Oswego, New York. Her birth place is now made a historical landmark. Mary grew up in her home town, Oswego, New York. She graduated from medical school.

Mary married a fellow student named Albert Miller at the age of 21. He was a doctor also. Her marriage ended in divorce in 1869.

Mary was a doctor for the army. She was not hired because they wouldn't hire female doctors. Mary was a surgeon and some say spy. She was arrested many times for wearing men's dress. Mary spent the rest of the war practicing in Louisville, Kentucky.

She set up office in Rome, New York. After her service in the Civil War she became a writer and lecturer. She traveled the U.S. and Europe giving speeches.

Mary was the only female to win the Medal of Congressional Medal of Honor. Mary's medal was taken away for unusual circumstances.

She died on February 21, 1919 in Oswego, New York.

Mary Edwards Walker was so supportive in the Civil War you would want to talk to her about the Civil War.

Julia Arpan, Grade 5
Cheyenne-Eagle Butte Upper Elementary School, SD

Saving the Earth

The Earth is so beautiful; it might not stay this way if people keep littering, not recycling, and cutting down trees. Don't you want a clean and healthy place to live? I do! There are *so* many things that humans don't do to help keep the Earth clean. I think we should do something about it!

The thing that I hate the most is when trees are cut down! Don't people realize that by cutting down trees we're losing oxygen? It's one of the main things that we need to live. People cut down trees for *useless* buildings and places! I hope they know that cutting those trees down means less and less oxygen for us! Another thing that makes me mad is when humans cut down trees that animals are living in. These animals are becoming endangered! Here's another thing people should think about, if all of the trees get cut down that we have, imagine how weird and different Earth would be!

The thing that also makes me angry is when people *don't* recycle! By throwing trash on the ground, having it taken to a landfill, or burning it, is *not* good for the Earth! I want a wonderful, clean, beautiful, healthy, and nice place to live! *Recycle*! Don't you get tired of seeing that trash?

I hope this made you think about what's going on in the world. Maybe you should do something about it? I know I will. Save the Earth! It's easy!

Emily Bradley, Grade 6
Southport 6th Grade Academy, IN

Baseball

I started playing baseball when I was three years old. I chose baseball because I like baseball. I like playing baseball because it keeps me active. I like to run and keep moving.

The one game I remember was when we played the Blue Jays team. We were tied and we had to play an extra inning. It was exciting. The final score was 16 to 17, we won! This is how we beat the Blue Jays. The Blue Jays were in last place. My team was in 4th place, but we were happy. I like the feeling of winning, especially in baseball.

Matthew Sosa, Grade 4
Our Lady of the Rosary School, CA

The Person Who I Admire

The person who I admire the most would be my mom. My mom always understands my problems and she never tells anyone. That's why I love her so much.

Here is another thing about my wonderful mother. Whenever I am sick my mom always takes care of me. My mom gives me medicine to make me feel better.

My mom is really smart. The reason why my mom is smart is because she always helps me on my projects. Last time I got a 4 on my project it was because my mom helped me on the project.

I admire my mom because she is funny, sweet, and smart. I love my mom because she is the best. My mom is sweet and nice. All those things that I said about my mom are true. I love my mom so so much because she is wonderful.

Jasmin Anglade, Grade 5
Camellia Avenue Elementary School, CA

Baseball

Baseball is known to almost everyone. It is like the number one sport. All the teams are aggressive. People are crazy at games. Remember, don't sit in front of someone that has pale ale, because we were spilled on at a game with beer.

Baseball was started in the Civil War as a game. Then after the war, they needed money and made it into a sport. They sold tickets and food, etc. They made a lot of money because it was entertainment and fun.

Most of the teams were strong in the game. Some had gotten better records than others. Some fans got disappointed during the end of the year. If their team did not get enough money to pay for the field, etc. they would have to quit and make another team.

In these days of baseball, there are divisions and two leagues. The two leagues are National and American. The divisions are west, central, and east in both American and National leagues. The wild card is sometimes considered a division. These divisions are hard if you do not have a good team. It will probably become harder every day.

There are divisions and leagues. Baseball was started in the Civil War. The teams are aggressive in the game. Baseball is a great sport to play.

Harrison Hillis, Grade 6
Imagine Charter School at Rosefield, AZ

Smiles

Smiles make me feel better when I am sad. They are one of the greatest gifts. Smiles are symbols of happiness. They can be very uplifting. Smiles are really great to share. I think a smile can come from anyone. A smile can change a person's heart. Never doubt that a person might smile at you today. Smiles make all the difference. We should smile to keep our hopes up, to make someone happy, and more! Smiling shows your emotion is happy. One of the best ways to share a smile is to talk to people. Smiles are great. Smiling makes your troubles go away. I love to smile!

Baylee DePugh, Grade 5
Pike Christian Academy, OH

My Secret Place

My secret place is under my sister's bed. I cannot fit under my bed but I can under my sister's bed. I also hide under there when we play hide and go seek. I like that game. My sister can never find me there. That is why I never tell anybody. I also go there when I am sad. What I have under there is: a flashlight, a fan sometimes, something to do like a game, a journal, a pencil, a blanket and a towel. Sometimes I take my baby doll under there. I like playing with my baby doll. She is so cute. And I guess my sister does find me under there but not all the time. Sometimes when my mom lays down on the bed I try to push her up. After that she finds out where I am. I tell her "Do not tell my sister." She does not. Oh, I forgot to tell you something about my sister. Sometimes I scrapbook under there and my sister says "Can I come in?" I say "Do you see any room?" I like it when my sister wants to go into my secret place. I like my secret place.

Cassie Speer, Grade 4
Winona Elementary School, TX

Tea Parties

My grandma and I used to go out to a flea market or a little store and look at the teacups. We would find the most unique one and make sure that they didn't have anymore like it. Then once we made sure that it was the right one we would buy it, take it home, and clean it up. A couple weeks later we would call my cousin Gabbie and ask her if she would like to stay the night at my grandparents house with me. She would reply and often with a yes.

Once she got there we would make cookies or my grandma would have scones out. We would set the table very beautifully and then we would go pick out our teacups. Almost always Gabbie grabbed one with a violet on it since her last name is Violet and I would pick out a different one each time. We would then order our tea from my grandma and she would go get the kettle ready. Gabbie and I would tell each other our secrets and once grandma returned she would bring out the cookies or scones. Then we put as many sugar cubes in our cup allowed and a little bit of milk. We always had fun at those tea parties.

Elizabeth Orgon, Grade 6
St Anne School, CA

Having an Imagination

Imagination is a very important trait for a person to have. What would the world be like without it? There wouldn't be light bulbs, technology, or even television! Everyone who invented these amazing items would have had to imagine these things being used in the future. If we didn't have the amazing art of imagination, our world would not have any signs of God's superior creations. But because we have imagination, our world is full of living things, story books, technology, beautiful attractions, and many simple inventions and machines.

Everyone who invented things, had imagination. It is one of the most important traits that changed our world over time, like, Thomas Alva Edison, started imagining himself being a famous scientist, and look what he has done to change the world! People like him all start by imagining things like that when they are children.

It is so important to raise children to have an exploding imagination. But imagination comes natural, and it is not a special gift to certain people. If you imagine a peaceful world with no drugs or violence, go for it. Use the imagination you have and change the world. Don't think that famous inventors and artists were just lucky, do whatever your imagination tells you! Know that you can use your imagination to do what you dream of doing. Put your dreams, wishes and imagination together, and you are unstoppable. Make the world a better place with your imagination.

Hannah Hubbell, Grade 5
Maple Avenue Elementary School, WI

All About My Family

I am Brianna and I have five people in my family. I have one brother, one sister, a mom and a dad. My sister's name is Kayla and my brother's name is Matthew.

A family to me is a group of people who help each other. Whenever I need help with something, my family is always there to help me. My mom helps me with a lot of things like my homework, cooking and baking muffins.

My family has a family business. It's called Matt's Custom Signs and Graphics. We all have different jobs to do to help the business. Matthew, Kayla, and I have to cut vinyl and clean up the shop.

When I really don't know what to do, I play with Kayla or Matthew. Matthew just started school, so I get to teach him things he doesn't know yet. I also help Kayla with her homework. She also wants me to teach her how to braid hair.

My family is the most important thing to me. I love them very much. I like my family the way it is and I would like it to stay that way forever.

Brianna Armijo, Grade 4
Gateway Pointe Elementary School, AZ

Dogs

Dogs rule! Do you think so? Here is some amazing facts about dogs! Dogs come in many different breeds and are all awesome! Every kind of dog has their own personality, are all unique and are almost exactly like people.

Taking care of dogs is a very important concept. When you take care of your dog, you need to care for it. You should give them fresh food and water each day. At occasional times during the day or even once a day, it is good to take your dog for a walk so they can see new places, have some fun, and get good exercise.

It is very important to love your dog. When you get a dog, right away you should love it. It its good if you fit in time for cuddling and playing. At night your dog may make noises and get tired of being outside, so a good idea is to let them inside and maybe turn the television on so your dog can see and hear something.

So remember, love your dog, care for it and be a great owner! Dogs are all unique. Try to teach them new tricks so they can have some fame too. Dogs are great! Now we know more on how to take care of our wonderful pets!

Megan Zimmerman, Grade 5
St Patrick's Catholic School, WA

My Dog

My dog's name is Sandy Cheeks. She got her name from SpongeBob the cartoon. My dog knows tricks. The first is she can sit and shake. Last is she can roll over! My dog is the best. She listens to me when I call her. If I did not have her, my life would be changed. I would have no one to play with. She sleeps in the room with me at night. In the morning she wakes me up. I like to take her for a walk. She likes to bark at other dogs. We like to take her camping and on special travels. Sometimes she gets a little annoyed and so she chases me. My dog is now about 10 years old. She is a Beagle. A funny story about my dog is when I was about 5 years old. I was taking her for a walk. We were camping at the time. She saw a squirrel and started to chase it. She pulled me off my feet and started dragging me around the campground. My dad had to stop her. I hope my dog lives for a long time.

Gino Dotson, Grade 4
Santo Niño Regional Catholic School, NM

To Try Your Best

"Shoot for the moon, and if you miss you'll still land among the stars." — Anonymous.

I think this saying is important because it says that if you try really hard, you will always succeed in some way. If you don't get exactly what you want, you can still be very close if you just look.

This saying means a lot to me when I feel like I didn't succeed to the highest point; it tells me that I still went somewhere. "Shoot for the moon, and if you miss you'll still land among the stars" is a phrase that everyone should go by.

Caroline Bailey, Grade 4
Addison Elementary School, CA

Why Cats Chose Us

Why Cats Chose Us is a nonfiction book about cats and their history. There are more to cats then meets the eye. This book explains how cats are special and different from other animals!

Why Cats Chose Us tells us why cats are special. For example, they are the only animals that are domesticated but not far removed from lions, tigers, and other feline animals. It is said that the Egyptians were the first to have domesticated cats. The cats were sacred to the people of Egypt. Today's Siamese cat is said to be the descendant of Egyptian cats. There are many different types of cats. Some are stranger then others like the European wild cat which is untamable no matter if it is raised from kithood or straight from the wild. There is also the Ragdoll cat. It is the most unusual cat. It's body is limp and when you pick it up, it dangles in your hand like a rag doll.

There are many cats in the world. Some stranger than others. Cats are fascinating animals with all the different breeds.

Emma Sinclair, Grade 6
St Theresa's Catholic School, TX

Road to the NFL

Eli Manning is a quarterback for the New York Giants. He is six foot four inches tall and can throw like a machine. Manning achieved many football awards and had fantastic stats in college while he played football.

Eli Manning was born on January 3, 1981, in New Orleans, Louisiana. When he was young, he played football with his brother Peyton Manning. He also played football at Isidor Newman High school in New Orleans, Louisiana. When he was done with high school, he started to play football at the University of Mississippi. Manning became a magnificent quarterback in college. By the end of his college years, Manning had a passing rating of 137.7, 81- touchdown passes, and 10,119 passing yards.

While Manning was in college, he earned four awards. He earned the Conerly Trophy in 2001 and 2003. In 2003, he won the Johnny Unitas Golden Arm Award and the Maxwell Award.

Manning overcame two obstacles in college. The first one, in 2002, was when he was named to the American Football Coaches Association. Manning's greatest year was probably in 2003 because he led the Rebels to a 10-3 record and a 31-28 victory in the Cotton Bowl.

Finally in 2004, Manning was drafted to the New York Giants. He was the first person drafted. Manning played with Tiki Barber and Jeremy Shockey on his team. Eli Manning is still playing for the New York Giants. He is one of the best quarterbacks in the NFL.

Collin Real, Grade 5
Oak Crest Intermediate School, TX

My Dream Horse

I owned a sorrel Quarter horse. He was the best riding and 4-H horse. Before we got him his name was Tramp. Since he was my horse I decided to name him Hunter because he was a great hunting horse. He was about 16 years and about 16 hands high.

He was a spectacular riding horse. He stopped when I asked him to and did everything he could.

Hunter's behavior was magnificent. He would even follow me around while I picked up rocks! That showed that I had good leadership over him.

I did 4-H and riding lessons with him. The first time we went to 4-H he was acting crazy because he didn't know where he was. The more we went he became more used to it.

I also did lessons with Hunter. After about six lessons he was doing superbly. Every Tuesday I had lessons.

Hunter had gotten a lung infection after about a month that we had him. I kept coming back after we thought it was gone.

One night when my dad went out to feed the horses, Hunter started acting woozy. After about ten minutes he fell over. My parents called the vet as fast as they could, but it was too late. It was very tragic while he was being buried. We buried him by his favorite eating spot. (The tree.)

As you can tell Hunter was very important to me. I will never forget my best buddy.

Sierra Myers, Grade 6
Thomas Jefferson Charter School, ID

I Admire

I admire my sister Amy; who do you admire? My sister is fun to play with because we go outside and play soccer, volleyball, and Uno. When we play I feel so happy and proud. When I want to play and she is busy, I say, "Ok, I understand." I say it with a sad feeling. Then 10 minutes later she tells me "Let's go play." After she says that I get so happy.

My sister is fun because she tells me her secrets and I tell her my secrets. She and I are very close to each other. We are like the sun and rainbow. I love her because she is the best. She is so pretty and smart. She is like my best friend. I like being with her. I am so glad she is my sister.

She is also the best because she helps me with my homework, my problems, and with my chores. I love when she helps me because I feel that I have magic because I understand. I like it because she explains everything.

I like to be with my sister, Amy, because she is all of these things that I said about her. I would really like to be with her forever because she is the best. I love her in all ways. I am so lucky to have a wonderful sister like Amy. I love her a lot.

Julia Joaquin-Gomez, Grade 5
Camellia Avenue Elementary School, CA

My Great Cousin*

My brave and determined cousin is fighting in Iraq for our proud nation. During the summer, my cousin was fighting for our country, while we were having fun in the sun at the beach or at the pool swimming. Our nation's real heroes are our U.S. troops that are fighting in Afghanistan, Iraq, Pakistan, and Baghdad. I'm proud of them. They are great. My cousin flies helicopters, and he has been shot before. He kept fighting the war. He is brave and noble. My cousin is a proud trained soldier. He has fought many wars, and this is his last. He is going to sign out of the U.S. Army.

Bryce Dunlap, Grade 4
Burchett Elementary School, TX
*Dedicated to my brave cousin fighting in Iraq.

Call of Our Times

"I want to be a doctor. I want to be an actor. I want to be a vet." That is the world around me. Girls and boys all want prominence, ease, and to be known. I would like to be something, but what, I do not know.

Is it so essential to have distinction? Perhaps in this life that is so unsure. Is there ever ease? Never, however sweet a thing may seem, there is a price. Is fame so necessary to honor? I think not.

Life is not to be taken for granted. We live on the precarious edge of the present times. We must grasp opportunity at the first chance; we cannot hang back and let the world pass.

What we take from Earth, we must recompense. Some people give very little, but make themselves seen. Yet, some give everything and remain invisible.

Whatever I may become, I will be sure to help — seen or unseen, paid or not paid, known or unknown — and give the world my all.

Sandra Vadhin, Grade 6
George Ellery Hale Middle School, CA

I Want to Go Back

It's the best place in the whole wide world. It's magical. I would go there every summer if I could. And yet, we couldn't make it last summer. Wonderful magical Disney World.

We couldn't afford to go last summer because we built a huge amazing pool. We thought it would be worth it because we could swim all through the sweltering summer. But, it's not done yet! I'm back in my strict challenging school, and my 6th grade teacher is making me write about it, which would have been a lot more fun if I could have written about my Disney vacation or my summer in the swimming pool. Instead, I have to write about how I didn't get to do either.

There were several factors that caused the scheduling delays on the pool project. "There was too much rain," said my mom. "The annoying home owners' association wouldn't let us use propane to heat it," said my dad. So, I gave up going to Disney World for a dangerous dry hole in the now messed-up backyard. Oh, how I want to go back!

Eriq Tobias, Grade 6
St Matthew Catholic School, TX

Theodore Roosevelt

"Speak softly and carry a big stick; You will go far." — Theodore Roosevelt.

Theodore Roosevelt was born on October 27, 1858 in New York City. He was also called T.R. or 'Teddy' to the public. T.R. had always been interested in politics and the government, but his first claim to fame was when he led one of the largest battles held in Cuba. Because of this achievement, Teddy became governor of New York in 1898. But Teddy did not stop there.

In 1901, the 'truth buster' was elected vice president. That same year, William McKinley, the current president, was assassinated, which booted Roosevelt up to current president. Theodore was the youngest man to become president at age 42. Roosevelt was concerned with the environment. Roosevelt started the Department of Natural Resources, or DNR, which prevents poaching and increases wildlife population. One day, Teddy was alerted that a young girl was sick. As a gift, he gave her a small toy bear filled with cotton, which later came to be known as the teddy bear. Roosevelt liked to hunt. During one speech, T.R. had been shot and spoke for an hour before being rushed to the hospital. He plainly stated "I will deliver this speech or die, one or the other." One night, at age 61, Teddy went to bed and didn't wake up. One news reporter said, "Death had to take him sleeping, or there would have been a fight." Roosevelt died in 1919.

Nick Dolan, Grade 5
Norwoodville Elementary School, IA

Animal Cruelty

Why? How could somebody do that? What can I do to help? All of those things are rumbling in my mind when I think of animal cruelty.

I feel very strongly about animal cruelty. The number one animal cruelty is abuse. People starve their pets, and physically hurt them on purpose. That's just horrible.

The second most common animal cruelty is hoarding. Hoarding is when someone clearly has too many pets and can't properly take care of them, causing them disease, hunger, and maybe even death. Most hoarders have a mental illness, but that's still no reason to hurt that many innocent animals.

Another animal cruelty that people are not even aware of is the keeping of wild animals, such as big cats. People think awww they're so cute, but little cubs will soon turn into big cats. When the animal grows into adulthood, no untrained person will be able to properly take care of the animal.

I hope you take animal cruelty as seriously as I do, and hopefully do something about it. Together we can make a stand against animal cruelty!

Riley Hajicek, Grade 6
Concord Ox Bow Elementary School, IN

Fright Flight

"Thank you for flying Continental Airlines. We will be flying to Washington, D.C. It will take 2 hours and 30 minutes to arrive. We will be taking off shortly." I didn't care about that; the only thing I cared about was getting there without being hurt. I mean I didn't know what to expect it was my first time ever to fly.

"Time to take off," is what my mom said. I sat in my seat and put on my seat belt. We took off; this was the best part of my flight experience. We were half way through the flight and when the food cart came around it was lunch time. I had a ham and cheese sandwich and a Sprite with some chips. It was about 45 minutes left in the flight I did what any other 5-year-old would do, I took a nap.

I woke up to a loud voice it was the pilot saying that we would land in 5 minutes, and for everyone to put their seat belt on again. The landing felt like we were falling to the ground. My parents got our carry-on luggage while I thought about the amazing adventure.

Jennifer Alvarado, Grade 5
Aloe Elementary School, TX

The Heroes of 9-11

I'm sure we've all heard of September 11, 2001. How two planes flew into the World Trade Centers, how one plane flew into the Pentagon, and how one plane crashed in Pennsylvania. We thank the heroes of 9-11 for saving as many lives as they could. I believe the heroes of 9-11 are the firemen, the policemen, and those aboard the plan that flew down in Pennsylvania. I believe the firemen were definitely heroes during 9-11. They helped people on the street find safety. But I believe the biggest heroes of all were those passengers aboard the airplane that crashed in a field in Pennsylvania. When the plane was hijacked, they fought to turn it around. The hijackers were planning to fly the aircraft into the capitol, but as the passengers fought, they caused the plane to fly down and they lost their lives. As the plane was flying down, the passengers called their families on their cellphones and told them goodbye. September 11, 2001, was a sad time for America, but we should thank the heroes for saving lives, and they should always be honored.

Michael Jayne, Grade 5
Pike Christian Academy, OH

My Favorite Place

My favorite place is my room where I can draw and play games and watch TV. It is quiet, really quiet. I watch TV, and play army games. My favorite part about it is that I can play in my room for a long time. My mom lets me eat popcorn and drink water when I watch a movie. I can play under my bed, I even use my imagination to play games. It is just the beginning of what I can do. I can stay up all night and my mom won't care. But when it's a school night, my mom will tell me to go to bed. I can eat and drink in my room on special occasions like movies. My room is my favorite place.

Clayton Johnson, Grade 4
Winona Elementary School, TX

The Great White Shark

The Great White Shark is probably the most fearsome creature in the ocean. Its identifying features include 5 gill slits, a torpedo shaped body, a pointed snout, and a white underbelly. It has 3,000 saw edged, razor sharp teeth. As their teeth are lost, broken, or worn, they are replaced by new teeth that rotate into place.

The diet of a Great White Shark has a great variety. A young Great White Shark's diet consists of mostly fish, rays, and other smaller sharks. Older Great Whites eat bigger prey, such as pinnipeds (which is a fancy name for sea lions and seals), small toothed whales like Belugas, otters, and sea turtles. Great White Sharks do not chew their food. Their teeth rip the food up and it is swallowed whole.

In finding food Great White Sharks primarily use their sense of smell, followed by the sensing of electrical charges. Sensing changes in water pressure, eyesight, and hearing are less important. The sensing of electrical discharges (for an example, muscle contractions) are accomplished in a series of jelly-filled canals called the Ampullae of Lorenzini. These sensory canals can detect an electrical current as small as 0.005 micro volts.

Most Great White Shark attacks are not fatal. Four people are killed from Great White Shark attacks every year. About 4,000 Great Whites are killed every year and are decreasing in large numbers. They are now a protected species along the coasts of California, the USA, Australia, and South Africa.

Kole McKay, Grade 5
Ray E Kilmer Elementary School, CO

Help Save the Ozone Layer!

What is the ozone layer? Ozone is a form of oxygen. One ozone molecule contains three oxygen atoms. Ozone is found in a layer of the upper atmosphere where it absorbs the sun's harmful ultraviolet rays. Ultraviolet rays can cause skin cancer and other health problems for humans.

But something is destroying the ozone layer! That something is a group of chemicals called chloroflurocarbons (CFCs). CFCs are gases that contain atoms of chlorine, fluorine, and carbon. In the upper atmosphere, the sun's ultraviolet rays break CFCs into atoms. The chlorine atom attaches to an ozone molecule, stealing one oxygen atom and destroying the ozone molecule. Scientists estimate that one chlorine atom can destroy up to 100,000 ozone molecules. That's a lot of ozone!

CFCs are used in many different products like air conditioners, refrigerators, and hairspray. CFCs have been banned in most countries, but some people are getting rich by illegally selling CFCs. It costs a lot of money to replace products that use CFCs, so some people would rather keep buying illegal CFCs and destroy the ozone layer than spend money.

So help save the ozone layer! Replace your old air conditioner, refrigerator, and hairspray. You too can go the extra mile and help save life as we know it today!

Kathryn Baldauf, Grade 5
Dishman Elementary School, TX

Catherine Bach, SD Actress

Catherine Bach made South Dakota famous. She is one of few actresses from the state, and she is well known in all states. Catherine played in a lot of movies.

Catherine was born in Warren, Ohio in 1954. Her real last name is Bachman but she took part of it off. She has relatives in Eagle Butte and Faith, South Dakota. Some of them go to school where I go at Cheyenne Eagle Butte School.

She spent her high school years in Rapid City, South Dakota. Catherine had been dreaming about becoming an actress since she saw her uncle act.

When Catherine was done with her high school years she flew to California for an acting career. In the 1970s she had small roles in *Matt Helm*. She appeared in the movies *Thunderbolt* and *Lightfoot*.

In 1979 Catherine was Daisy Duke. She was the female of the Dukes of Hazzard. The series was a success. Catherine's shorts were named after her. They were cutoff blue jeans.

After the Dukes, she appeared on *Canonball Run* and *Nut House*. She also appeared on *Midnight Man*. Her next role was Melody in 1974.

Catherine Bach had been dreaming about becoming an actress since she was little. Her dreams came true.

Amanda Lance, Grade 4
Cheyenne-Eagle Butte Upper Elementary School, SD

A Great Summer Trip

A great, awesome summer trip is going to Branson and Arkansas. The drive is long but worth it in the end. Dallas was our first stop on the way and we got to see my aunt and uncle. Our second trip was to Fort Smith. We went to my great-grandma's grave. Then we stopped at Harrison. When we got there we got to see my other aunt and uncle. Our super cool cousins Nolan and Bethany came over and then my cousins Abby Joe, Maggie May, and lil Glen. We got to ride in a Jeep on a dusty dirty road. We went real fast and made a lot of dust.

Then we went to Branson in the "Show Me State," Missouri. We went to the best amusement park called Silver Dollar City. We rode a lot of rides, but the thing that I remember most is a phenomenal, awesome funnel cake. We got the cake and put the powdered sugar on, then we put raspberries, fried ice cream and whipped cream. The next day we went to the Titanic museum. At the beginning they have a super cold iceberg and they give you cards with a name on it and you see at the end if your person lived or died. They have this bowl that you can stick your hand in and it is about as cold as the water was when the Titanic sank.

Unfortunately we had to return home from that great summer trip.

Nicholas Medellin, Grade 6
St Matthew Catholic School, TX

The Heroes of 9/11

September eleventh is remembered as one of the most horrifying events in the United States history. More than five thousand people witnessed an act of war, and more than 15,000 children lost at least one parent. Many people were harmed, but let's not forget the heroes. They gave all their energy and some, even their lives, to save others. When everyone wanted to escape they faced the tragedy and saved people no matter what. With fire and dead bodies falling from the sky, they had only one purpose in mind, to rescue those trapped inside the colliding towers. It took courage and effort to save lives. Police officers, SWAT members, and people like you and me were useful. They needed all the help they could get. That is why all these people are remembered with respect, as the heroes of September eleventh.

Georgina Chavez, Grade 6
Sanford Fritch Jr High School, TX

Miley Cyrus

Did you know that my idol is Miley Cyrus? Well she is because she isn't afraid to get up on stage and give it her all.

Miley Cyrus' birth name is Destiny Hope Cyrus but she is also known as Hannah Montana or Miley Cyrus. She is an American actress, singer, and songwriter. Miley is best known for staring Miley Stewart on Hannah Montana.

She was born on November 23, 1992 in Franklin, Tennessee and grew up on her parents' farm in the backwoods of Nashville. Miley's first guitar was a Daisy Rock. She's won a 2007 winner of the favorite TV actress: comedy. And lots of others. Miley became interested in acting at age 9 when the family briefly lived in Toronto, Ontario, and Canada.

She has an older half sister, Brandi and two older half brothers, Christopher Cody and Trace. She also has a younger brother, Braison and a younger sister Noah Lindsey Cyrus who is also an actress. Miley is the goddaughter of country music star Dolly Parton. She has lots of pets including horses, dogs, cats, fish, and chicken. Miley Cyrus is friends with costars Emily Osment and Mitchel Musso.

So that's all about my idol, Miley Cyrus.

Jordan Wight, Grade 5
Oak Crest Intermediate School, TX

What Do You Think of Peace?

I picture peace as a token of friendship. My hand in yours, tightly gripping each other's. Peace represents an empty beach waiting and waiting. Peace is like a field of flowers slightly blowing in the breeze. Peace looks blue, it's full of people treated equally. In other words, peace is freedom. Peace is when you feel comfortable walking down the street and you know you can trust that there won't be any war going on. I think of peace as a partially cloudy day because it's quiet and most of the time it's raining gently in the hot sun. It's what we need. That's what I think of peace. What do you think of it?

Michellie Thurman, Grade 5
Foothills Elementary School, CO

My Most Memorable Moment

The most memorable moment of 2006 was when my grandmother passed away from lung cancer. I had to miss school for almost three weeks so I could see her the last time. When we got to my grandparents' house in Iowa, it was midnight and we had to be really quiet because they were sleeping upstairs. The next morning, Grandpa made a great breakfast and we said hello to Grandma with lots of hugs and kisses.

On Friday, October 13th, my grandma passed away late at night. We went to her funeral and cried a lot. Then we left the grave and cried more (a lot more). I will never forget her and she is in heaven, a much better place. I love her with all my heart. She was very talented at cooking and I will never forget her apple pie. It was the best, especially when she let me help her make the pie crust. My grandma was funny and cool. I really liked it when she did the "Grandma dance" after she won a game of Uno. She would also sew me very cute clothes for my birthday and Christmas.

At Christmas we visited Grandpa. All her grandchildren got pillows made out of her sweatshirts. Her best friend Willy made them for us. That's how we remember her. My mom, her sister, brothers and my grandpa got quilts made out of her sweatshirts. We will always remember her and we love my grandma.

Abby Clark, Grade 4
Kerr Elementary School, AZ

Manatees

Manatees are mammals and their closest relative is an elephant. Manatees have paddle shaped tails and have wrinkles on their faces with whiskers on the snout. The Manatee is a plant eating animal also known as a herbivore. The adult Manatees can be found in shallow salt water in South America that is moving slowly. The Manatee spends most of its time eating and resting. When resting, Manatees have been known to stay under water for 20 minutes. They have almost 10-15% of their body weight from eating plants that grow under water (a lot of the time). The Manatee can't breathe under water so it has to come up every 3-5 minutes to take a breath. When Manatees are using a lot of energy, they may have to go to the surface to take a breath as often as 30 seconds. Manatees live to be about 60 years old. Female Manatees are not sexually mature until they are at the age of 5 or older. One calf is born every 2-5 years. The gestation is about a year long.

Mothers nurse the calves for 1-2 years so a calf may remain dependent on its mother during that time. There are only about 3000 left of the West Indian Manatees in the United States. That's why people should bring no harm to these somewhat cute animals that bring *no* harm to us at all!

Emily McKee, Grade 6
Tosorontio Central Public School, ON

Being Healthy

Being healthy is important, and one way to maintain good health is to be active each day. It is not healthful to lead a sedentary lifestyle. A good way to get some necessary exercise is to ride your bike or jog. You should play outside at least an hour a day to take in fresh air, enjoy the sunlight, and exercise your body. If you play video games or watch TV, you should watch or play for only thirty minutes at a time.

Besides making sure that you exercise each day, good nutrition is also important. There are a couple of alternatives to eating junk food. Instead of soft drinks, mix some unsweetened fruit juice with sparkling water and a slice of orange. Instead of fried potato chips, eat baked ones. Keeping frozen grapes in the freezer is a good alternative to candy. They are sweet, crunchy, fun to eat, and loaded with antioxidants.

Did you know that on the average, children between the ages of eleven and nineteen eat at fast food restaurants twice a week? Is it any wonder that in the six through nineteen-year-old category, over nine million Americans are overweight? If you are overweight, try eating at home where meals are likely to be more nutritious, and remember to exercise each day. Those who take care of themselves by being fit and eating right enjoy the best health they can give to themselves.

Sebastian A. Deak, Grade 4
Birchwood School, OH

The Best Tradition

Well, to start it off, I love my grandparents. I have so many cherished moments with them. To me, I think traditions are very important, and they should be to everybody else.

Every year, my grandparents and I have been going to San Francisco. In San Francisco my grandparents take me to mostly all of my favorite places. Those places they take me to are Caesars, an Italian restaurant, the Exploratorium, and they used to take me to the zoo. Years ago I would go by myself, then I went with my sister one year, and this year I went with my sister, brother, and two of my cousins.

The trip to San Francisco is my favorite tradition, but I also have more. We stay at my grandparent's house in Novato for three days, we still do more! The first day we go see a movie with my grandmother, then we come back and have either hamburgers or spaghetti. Occasionally, we go to the beach (Bodega bay) if it is nice enough. Before we go, we pick up the best pizza in the world, Old Chicago pizza which is located in Petaluma, CA.

I love our trip to San Francisco and my grandparents so much. I know they love me, care about me, and they would do anything for me.

Kara Salvestrin, Grade 6
St Anne School, CA

Riding Bikes

Riding bikes are fun because you can go fast. If you go too fast the chain will break. Riding a bike is good exercise too. Bikes are fun to ride if you know how to. Every time I break the chain my brother or dad fix it for me. To ride a bike you have to know how to turn and peddle. You also have to be careful and not fall off. You need to tie your shoes so you will not fall off. Once you start to ride a bike it will be fun all the time. To ride a bike you have to know how to peddle with your feet. You also have to know how to turn. To ride a bike you have to be able to turn and peddle together. Riding a bike is fun because the wind is in your face. Trust me. It feels good! Riding a bike takes responsibility. If you're riding a bike, you always have to be careful when you are on a bike. A bike is fun to ride.

Joe Marsh, Grade 4
Winona Elementary School, TX

My Life's Work

My passion, my dream, is basketball. Even though I've only played one year, it is my life's goal. When I'm older I want to be a woman's basketball coach.

Basketball is a wondrous thing. My favorite thing about basketball is playing defense, because I love to be aggressive. Another kick is I love to run!

When I play basketball, the whole time I play I think "Eyes on the prize." I don't know what you think the prize is, but "my" prize is the ball.

Something else that's cool about it is it keeps me healthy. When I play basketball I run constantly. When I run, it's good for my heart. Now, you know about my passion, my dream, basketball.

Madison Womeldorf, Grade 5
Westview Elementary School, OH

Home Sweet Home

The smell is pleasant, the sound is quiet, and the taste is wonderful. What am I talking about? I'm talking about my home. It's my favorite place in the whole world! Why? Well because that's where my family is and it's where I spend most of my time sleeping, playing and doing other things.

Every time I come home from a place, I like to walk around and smell the scent, listen to the sounds and imagine what it would be like to be here all the time. That would just be wonderful.

Sometimes it could smell very good, because my mom is cooking up something in the kitchen. But most of the time it smells like fresh laundry.

My house has a living room, four bedrooms, a kitchen, a dining room and a family room. My favorite room is my room because that's where all my stuff is. I like looking out my room's window. Because I get to watch all the cars that go by, the birds up in the sky and more.

If I could explain my house with only 3 words, they would be "Home Sweet Home."

Kim Nguyen, Grade 6
North Oaks Middle School, TX

Splash!!!

The wind rushed on my face, excitement filled my beating heart. I gasped for a breath right before I hit the water. I was at the Poway Pool with my two best friends, jumping off the high dive. As I glided smoothly through the clear, chlorine water I felt a wave of courage rush over me. I thought about how I was trembling with fear on the edge of the diving board and people yelling, saying "Hurry up." But I couldn't hear them. Everything was a mute around me. Everything was rushing through my head. "What if this diving board broke with me on it?" I kept thinking to myself. I was petrified. I never had jumped from this high.

Two seconds later I plunged from the bottom of the crystal clear pool. I thought to myself, "That wasn't scary, that was so much fun." That day I kept on jumping off the wobbly diving board, the whole time I was there. Now whenever I go to the Poway Pool, the first thing I do is go off that wobbly diving board. Now I am not scared of the Poway Pool diving board. It was a great experience and one I would do over again.

Caroline L. Rouch, Grade 5
Dingeman Elementary School, CA

Lance Armstrong

I think Lance Armstrong is a great American.

Lance was born as Lance Gunderson on September 18, 1971 in Plano Texas. His father left when he was a baby. His mother married Terry Armstrong, who adopted Lance giving him his new name, Lance Armstrong.

His first Olympic qualification, held in Barcelona, Spain, was when he was a senior in high school. It was after the Olympics that he turned professional.

I think that Lance is great because he overcame cancer when he was only 25 years old when he was first diagnosed, he was given only a 50% chance of survival. He didn't give up, but fought his cancer. He continued to ride his bike during his treatment. During his treatment he created the Lance Armstrong Foundation. About 55 million people in the world wear a yellow LIVESTRONG wristband to support people living with cancer.

Following his cancer he entered the Tour De France. Many felt he couldn't win it. Lance Armstrong not only won but went on to win it a total of 7 times. This set a new world record.

I think that Lance Armstrong is a great American leader because he had a strong work ethic, he defeated cancer through medical treatment and by educating himself about his disease. With confidence, he beat the disease and became a world champion.

If we choose to have a positive attitude like Lance, we can fight, we can succeed, we can LIVESTRONG.

Jacob Schafer, Grade 6
Nishna Valley Community School, IA

Living with Asperger's Syndrome

Asperger's Syndrome is a form of autism. People with Asperger's have a hard time making friends. They have a hard time looking people in the eyes. Sometimes their voices sound different, like a robot.

Many people with Asperger's have problems with their senses. They can be picky eaters because of how food smells or tastes. They don't like to be messy. They can be sensitive to sounds.

Another difference about people with Asperger's is the way they communicate. They flap their hands and make strange noises. When they are mad they yell loud and cry easily. They have a tough time controlling how they feel.

My family is affected by Asperger's Syndrome, my little brother has it. He doesn't have many friends. He only likes to eat noodles, pizza, and crackers. He doesn't like being messy. He spins things and lines up his toys. He is hyper and gets wild. Even though he has Asperger's he is very smart, he is really good at math. He is fun to hang out with. He makes me laugh.

Just because you see someone act different, don't judge them, they might not be able to help it. Don't be afraid or embarrassed to be their friends, try to understand them. They are very special people once you know them, my brother has taught me that. Sometimes I get asked what it is like to live with a brother that has Asperger's Syndrome. My answer is, sometimes difficult but also very interesting and fun.

Ericka Rickards, Grade 5
Sunset Elementary School, WA

A Long Hard Battle

I remember that day just like it was yesterday, we were together laughing and having fun. Before we knew it there was a setback and then he was no longer here with us on earth, but he is in a better place which is with our Lord.

My beloved wonderful grandpa Frank Garza was diagnosed with terminal lung cancer about 3 1/2 years ago. We had gone to many chemotherapy treatments but they just made him weak. So all we had left was the power of prayer. That seemed to help.

Unfortunately on New Year's Eve he left us. Worshipping our Lord, holding hands, and many sad tears were rolling down our hurt faces. We watched him take his final breaths. In front of our eyes, he died.

My beloved grandpa was my best friend and still is. I knew the funeral was going to be a sinister time, but all of us managed to cope through the whole thing. The ceremony was long and nice. I knew my grandfather would have just loved it, it was everything he wanted.

There isn't a day I don't think about him; we all miss him so much. He fought a long hard battle and in the end he was gone. Although he is not physically here on this wonderful and filled earth, he is always going to be in my big joyful heart.

Celeste Garza, Grade 6
St Matthew Catholic School, TX

Wrestling

I'm in Isbell now and I started to wrestle. Mr. Lopez is my coach and my avid teacher as well. So far I've only wrestled in three tournaments, I've only won 1 and lost two. I'm a beginner. Today, 10/10/07, I'm going to wrestle, Isbell vs Robert Jake Frank. One day in practice I flipped Welch and I took the air out of him.

If I want to keep on wrestling, I have to keep my grade point average 2.0 or higher. If your grade point average is lower than 2.0, your off the team. Today, 10/15/07, I got my report card, and my grade point average is 3.0, and that's good. My grades are, C+, B-, B, B, A+, and A. They give a report card every 6 weeks.

We've have only wrestled two schools, and they are balboa (twice) and Robert Jake Frank. So far we've wrestled in two away and one home. For the rest of the year we will wrestle home. We wrestle every Wednesday, and we always have practice on Tuesdays and Thursdays.

Christopher Romero, Grade 6

Good Deeds and Why We Do Them

On September 11, 2001 almost three thousand people died because of the terrorists that had attacked the Twin Towers in New York City and the Pentagon. Some people think terrorists attempted to attack the White House. There was also a plane that crashed in Pennsylvania.

Many of the people that died were policemen and firemen who lost their lives to save others. We honor the people that died that day by doing good deeds, especially on September 11. We also honor the people that they think saved the White House and everyone in it. Even though they themselves died in the plane crash they saved many people.

Since 9/11/01 we have done good deeds on September 11. It is called "Good Deed Day" to honor all the people that died to save others on September 11, 2001.

Dalley Cutler, Grade 5
Snake River Montessori School, ID

Spirit

This is a story about my horse Spirit. She got her name from the Walt Disney movie *Spirit*. My aunt Gina, Cecil, my mom, and my dad all put in some money to buy me a horse. When she first came to live with me she was very spooked and scared. After we gave her the first five days to calm down, I started to ride her every day. She was the best horse I ever had, until my mom and dad got a divorce and no one would help me ride and saddle her up. Today she is very mean and runs away from me and is stubborn. She is only like that because nobody messed with her for a long time. Back when my mom and dad were still together, my dad took her to have a baby. After 9 months she had a baby on a dark rainy night, when I was sleeping. When I heard that Cecil said he saw her I jumped out of bed and ran outside. I also named her from the movie *Spirit* and she is now three years old. That story is about my horse Spirit.

Jordan Goodner, Grade 5
Aloe Elementary School, TX

Lady Sovereign

Lady Sovereign is my favorite singer. She sings by herself. Lady Sovereign's real name is Louis Harmon. She participated in a contest called Battle of the Bands. She wrote a lot of her own songs and she won the contest. I know all of her songs like "Love Me or Hate Me," "Blah Blah," "Fiddle with the Volume," "Hoddie," "9 to 5," "Gatheration," "Those Were the Days," "Tango, Random," "Public Warning," "My England," "The Broom," and "A Little Bit of Shh."

Louis Harmon also acted in a movie she made in England. That is where she got started. It was so cool. She's also been on TV. She was talking all about herself, like what she does for a living and what she likes to eat. Louis Harmon also likes to keep her hair to the side. I think it looks real cool. She puts all of her music videos on YouTube.com. Some of the music videos are just pictures of Lady Sovereign with music. Lady Sovereign learned to play songs from Miss Dynamite. That is why she is so good at playing music. Lady Sovereign has written thirteen music videos and songs. I wish I could meet Lady Sovereign at her house or somewhere on the street or at her concert. Lady Sovereign is twenty years old. I remember when Lady Sovereign was singing but no one was cheering for her but she never gave up. Now she is selling lots of records.

Marcelo Garner, Grade 4
Menchaca Elementary School, TX

My Dog

One morning I saw a dog in my backyard. It was a dog with black and white fur, and he didn't have a collar. I went to school, when I got home I went directly to see the dog. He had beautiful green eyes. He looked so cute. I touched him and his fur felt like dandelion mixed with cotton. I asked my mom if I could keep him, she said yes. We went to the store and bought him dog food. My mom called the veterinarian to make an appointment. It was scheduled for the following Wednesday.

On Tuesday, when I came back from school, my mom told me something terrible that my dog ran away. We looked for him, but we couldn't find him. The appointment was canceled. I was sad, very sad. Then one day my dad went to my uncle's house and he saw my dog. When he came home, he told me. I couldn't believe I was going to see my dog I was amazed and happy. In two days I went to my uncle's house and he told me my dog wasn't there anymore. I figured out that he ran away again. This time I felt sadder than the last time, because I was really happy to see him. The next day when we were going to visit my uncle, we found my dog, but dead. Now, I was more sad than before. He was my dog Peluchin.

Jaquelin Miramontes, Grade 6
Los Padillas Elementary School, NM

A Name to Love

My name means little in English but in Vietnamese it means Einstein. My name is a number 2 because its my favorite number. The name Chris is a color blue because its bright, and I'm a bright person. My name reminds me of my sister because her name is Christina and Chris and Christina are kind of the same. The name Chris makes me feel awesome. My friends like my name but they say too many people have it. My name reminds me of people screaming because when they hear the name Chris they know trouble is here. My friend Chris has the same name as me he is funny, cool, smart he is awesome. I like my name a lot but if I had to change I would change it to David because David is a cool name.

Chris Le, Grade 6
North Oaks Middle School, TX

My Secret Place

My secret place is at home in my bedroom. It is silent so I can turn on my radio. I can lay there all day long. It is nothing fancy. It is just a silent place for me so I can lay there. I love my room. It is clean. I can adjust my old slingshot to hit trees. I have everything I need. I have books, stereo, TV, sofa, and a doll table. Sometimes when I am bored I make a big tunnel through my bedroom. I can make up anything like fighting a samurai or something. I also play like I am in World War II. It is so cool. You just go to set your mind to it. I like how I imagine it. Also if I wanted to close my eyes and daydream I can. It is cool. I have a lot of creative ideas. I make up fun games and I have a fun imagination. I also have a sense of humor. I have a lot of ideas but I can only have one in my secret place — my bedroom.

Karrie King, Grade 4
Winona Elementary School, TX

The Dolphin

Darting through the sea, catching fish, leaping out of the sea: the dolphin.

First, if you were wondering if dolphins had gills and can breath underwater, I have the answers. Dolphins actually have no gills like fish. Also dolphins can't breathe under water but they hold their breath for several minutes.

Second, what do they eat? Dolphins primarily feed on fish, squid and crustaceans. Dolphins have filters called mysticetes using their baleen to strain plankton and other tiny organisms from the water.

Finally, I want to tell you where dolphins live. Dolphins live all over the world as well as some freshwater lakes and rivers. So you can find dolphins just about anywhere.

I also wanted to tell you about a rare dolphin, the Vaquita. The Vaquita is one of the rarest and endangered cetaceans. It is poorly known even on official surveys around its home in the northern sea of Cortez. Darting through the sea, catching fish, leaping out of the clear blue sea: the dolphin.

Damien Lee Richards, Grade 6
Pomerene School, AZ

The Man

One day, at my grandma's, there was a man on a motorcycle who had the cops chasing him. His motorcycle got out of control. He slid into my grandma's yard. He got off the bike and ran into the backyard. My grandma has woods at her backyard and a swamp. So he ran into the backyard and tripped over a log, and fell into the swamp, and broke his leg. When he tried to crawl out, he crawled over a bees' nest. The cops were trying to get the man. The cops were stung by bees trying to catch the man. My grandma used to have a motion detector that spits out water. My mom said it would be funny if it were on. I told my grandma that she should have made popcorn, and gone out to sit on her deck and watch a free movie. My grandma said you can still see the marks of the bike handles in her front yard. I wish that I could see them. My grandma said that it was scary, but I said that it would be funny. I really hope that it would happen again, but this time when I am there. I still remember that story from this day forward. There are still some questions that have not been answered yet. One is did the man get in jail and for how long?

Mary Lautar, Grade 4
Hardin Central Elementary School, OH

Do They Play Nice?

Some people think animals are "nice" like people, yet others think differently. They think animals are acting on instinct, and some people don't know what to think! I have discovered stories about animal kindness. But is it kindness? It is up to you to decide.

A forest elephant needed help. He caught his trunk in a sharp trap, and while tearing away he had torn a piece of his trunk too. Until the pain eased he could not eat or drink. As if to explain to another, he lumbered up to an African savanna elephant and placed his trunk into the savanna elephant's mouth. The sympathetic savanna elephant uprooted a small acacia tree and stuffed it into his new friend's mouth. This may have been an act of compassion.

Another example of animal kindness is this extraordinary hippo. He liked to play with the crocodiles. He would sunbathe, play, and lick the dung off of their scales. That's why it was surprising that he saved a monkey from being eaten by them. The monkey, who was looking for something to eat by the water's edge, had no clue about the crocodile waiting silently in the murky depths waiting to spring. Suddenly, the hippo sprang up and chased away the crocodile from his prey.

You still might disagree about animals being nice, but elephants don't just randomly help other elephants eat, and hippos don't just save monkeys from being eaten. Why did they? We don't know; we can only guess.

Rachel Ormsby, Grade 5
Spicewood Elementary School, TX

Focusing on the Things That Matter

Everywhere, in the comics and on the news, you hear all about the illegal immigrants coming here from Mexico that we need to keep out. That's bad enough, but it's even worse because the government is worrying about this more than they are worrying about global warming and Americans killing themselves by smoking.

I have been interested in this ever since I read about what they're doing to stop illegal immigrants in *Times*. What they are doing is unfair and needs to be stopped! What has happened to "Give me your tired, your poor, your huddled masses yearning to breathe free, The wretched refuse of your teeming shore, Send these, the homeless, tempest-tost (storm-tossed) to me!"

Around 500,000 deaths each year are caused by lung cancer in the U.S. You may not think that that is a lot of people, but imagine that many people dying every year. Smoking is banned from almost every public place now, and here there is a new law that bans cigarette commercials. I'm hoping that they will make smoking illegal.

At this rate, because of global warming, I believe that we're likely to drown ourselves before we develop advanced enough technology to survive the melting of icebergs. I think that the government should be working harder to at least slow down global warming.

The government is focusing on the wrong things. They should be focusing on the things that matter. Global warming and smoking are things that matter now, and should always matter more.

Stefanie Maier, Grade 6
Southport 6th Grade Academy, IN

Leadership

What does leadership mean to you? Leadership is the guidance of others. It has many synonyms including direction and guidance. When you set an example for others you are a leader.

Leadership is seen all around us. For example, George Bush is a leader because he can guide us in what to do. He is the leader of our country in good and difficult times. At school we follow the leadership of our principal and teachers to learn and make good choices. When I watch the sports channel, I see all the teams who have leaders. It could be the coach or the team captain. They lead their teams to play hard and fair.

Do you show leadership? I do because I think younger kids should know what is right, and what is wrong by our examples. I walk my sister safely to school each day. I am a leader to her because I cooperate with my parents at home.

Leadership is not always easy, but it is a great quality to have.

Nathan Keeton, Grade 5
Covington Elementary School, NE

Alligators and Snakes

Alligators and snakes are both reptiles. Reptiles are cold-blooded, scaly animals. Most reptiles live on land, some live in water.

Alligators and crocodiles are reptiles who live in the water. They eat big animals such as buffalo, deer, and big fish. They attack by letting their prey see their back to make them think it's only a log. It swims slowly closer to its prey. Then it springs into action and eats the animal.

Snakes are reptiles who live on land. They eat little animals such as rabbits and lizards. Some snakes are poisonous, such as Anacondas, so stay away from them! Snakes attack by hiding behind objects, so they can sneak up on their prey. Finally, they have a meal.

I think reptiles are cool. They are very good hiders, too. So watch your back, and beware of reptiles.

Sanaam Callahan, Grade 4
Louise Foussat Elementary School, CA

Family

My love for my family is very important to me. First, my dad got me into a wonderful school. He always works hard for my brother and I to get into a great college. He always helps me with my math homework and even studies with me! Every time he comes home from work, he brings a smile. I like that about him. He takes very good care of me. I love him so very much.

My mom. There are so many words to describe her: loving, caring, generous, kind, and beautiful. She always helps me write my essays, and also studies with me too. She also cooks for me. Her food is the best food I have ever tasted. She also helps me to prepare to go to the best college in America. I love her so very much. She will always be in my heart. There will never be a better mother than her.

Last but not least is my brother. He is very kind to me. He always looks out for me, he is the best. He always shares with me; like when I have no snack to eat he shares his with me. I love him so very much. He is the best. No one can replace him. This is how much I love my family.

Eduardo Sanchezdiaz, Grade 6
Linfield Christian School, CA

Learning to Be Disciplined

When I learned something is when I decided to go to karate. When I went to karate I thought it would be like the movies, but there was more to karate than I thought. You had to be a little flexible, be disciplined, powerful, and a good listener. I wasn't very disciplined, not very respectful, so it took me a while to learn it. On my first day it was hard, but the class went easy on me. After that it was even harder on. I started to learn how to be disciplined, and to be respectful. If I was disrespectful the class and I had to do 25 push ups. Like if I talk back or if I said "I can't" it was like a cuss word. These are some things I went through to learn my lesson about discipline.

Eric Rogers, Grade 5
McMonagle Elementary School, MI

Seasons Come, Seasons Go

Seasons are like snowflakes. They come and they go. Each different season has a particular smell, sight, and sound. Each unique and refreshing.

Fall. Fall has the sweet and sour sound of the wind blowing rapidly through the almost bare trees, the smell of pumpkin, apple and bumble-berry pies baking in the oven of every house across America and the sight of electric fireplaces being turned on with brilliant, blazing hot flames.

Winter. Winter is cold and bitter with a hint of frostbite. Sounds of plastic shovels scraping against driveways, smells of fiery hot cocoa being slurped down furiously, and snowballs rotating through the air like baseballs.

Spring. Spring has a different feel to it; the pitter-patter of rain tapping on the window, 1-100 year olds splashing puddles and the sweet smell of brand new spring flowers blooming slowly.

Summer. Summer, most kids' favorite time of year…School's out! Kids are outside screaming and moving at hypersonic speed, bees are buzzing and watermelons are as juicy as ever.

Seasons are like snowflakes; they come and they go.

Molly Grosser, Grade 5
Greenwood Elementary School, MN

Never Trust a Saleslady

"Come on, let's go in here," my mom said.

"Okay," said my grandma and I as we followed my mom into Bath & Body Works. I always liked going into that store even though my mom takes forever in there smelling things. But for some reason at this particular store, there were a lot of salespeople everywhere. Even when you just touched or looked at something, the salespeople HAD to tell you all about the lotion you were smelling. I had just finished smelling Spiced Apple when I looked up to see a saleslady just about to corner grandma.

"Oh, Wild Cherry," the saleslady said (slightly TOO happily). "My favorite. Did you know that the people who make this actually HAND PICK the cherries?"

"Really," my grandma said sounding fakely interested.

"You should try it." the saleslady replied. So grandma reluctantly stuck out her hand so it could be moisturized. Unfortunately, the saleslady had bad aim and the lotion got all over the front of her shirt and jeans. "Ohmygosh!" the saleslady wailed. "I…am…so sorry! Let me get you a towel." There was a big puddle of lotion on the floor. As soon as the lady left, we burst out laughing. My grandma smelled more cherry-ish than usual. As soon as we left the store, all the dogs outside started smelling grandma. Now we look back on that day and laugh. We all decided NEVER to trust a too-happy saleslady ever again.

Meredith Ray, Grade 6
St Anne School, CA

What Thanksgiving Means to Me

Thanksgiving means a lot to me. It means turkey and stuffing, you go hunting to get a turkey and make decorations. You can do lots of things. I love Thanksgiving.

Thanksgiving started when the Indians helped the pilgrims. The pilgrims are the best. Think about some of the Indians. When you start a meal do you pray? I do, and do you think Thanksgiving is about football? It's not.

It's about giving thanks. So this Thanksgiving give thanks to people who made it possible for us to be here, and anything or anybody who have helped or did something for you.

Joseph Cherry, Grade 4
Scipio Elementary School, IN

Bats

People think bats are blind, but no they're not blind. They just don't have good eyesight. But they have echolocation to help them see better. Echolocation can tell them where an object is at and how big or small it is. Bats live under bridges, in chimneys, forests, farms, buildings, hollow trees and houses. Often people think bats drink blood, only, but there are different types of bats. Fruit bats eat fruit, pollen, and nectar, but vampire bats eat blood. They also eat small fish, insects, and small lizards. Bats eat up to five hundred mosquitoes in one hour. They can reach speeds of forty miles per hour. The longest bat to live had lived up to forty years old. Bats have different colors of fur. They have brown, gray, gold, black, and white fur. Bats are killed because people misunderstand them, but I really don't have a problem with them. I think bats are amazing creatures and helpful in the world. I enjoy being close to them. I hope they're better understood in the future.

Francisco Cardenas, Grade 4
Burchett Elementary School, TX

Smoking and Chewing Tobacco

Smoking tobacco is bad for people's bodies. When people smoke they paralyze cilia in their throat that collects dust and dirt. Cilia can't collect smoke that people inhale, so the smoke turns people's lungs black. When people smoke they also shorten their life.

Lots of people start smoking because their friends are doing it and they say it's the cool thing to do. Others just say, "I'll try it," and when they do, the get addicted to nicotine. Nicotine is a chemical that is very addictive. Then there are some people who try it and don't like it. Other people just say "No." In my opinion that is what people need to do.

Chewing is just as bad as smoking. When people chew tobacco they just put tobacco in their mouth, inside of the cheek. People can get cancer in their mouth, their throat, and their gums. People don't swallow tobacco, they swallow some of the juices. Chewing can stain people's teeth and make their breath bad. People usually have to keep spitting in something like a spittoon. I hope you make the right choice and say, "No" to drugs.

Jennifer Dean, Grade 6

My Grandma's Porch

My favorite place is my grandma's porch. One reason why my favorite place is my grandma's porch is because when I am swinging on her porch swing, the chains on it wriggle against each other. Another reason is because I can see the eye-appealing, glistening sunrise in the morning. In addition, I can smell the aroma of the oak trees. Additionally is when I'm swinging on her porch swing it sounds like finger nails scratching across a chalk board.

Last but not least is I can feel the splinters from the wood come closer to the palm of my hand. Those are some of the reasons why my grandma's porch is my favorite place.

Cassie Garcia, Grade 5
Neosho Heights Elementary School, KS

My Grandpa

My grandpa I loved him so very much. He was a generous man in my life and soon later he started feeling sick. He had a lot of sunburns in his life. One day he went to the doctors, the doctor said my grandpa had skin cancer. He took his medication and he passed away one and a half years ago. So we went to his funeral and that is a man that is significant in my life, my grandpa.

Before he passed away he did a lot of hunting in his life. He and my dad went hunting a lot and when my dad was a kid he almost shot my grandpa a couple times. My grandpa has a lot of guns and he gave them to my dad and one time when I was 8 years old we camped out and we were in my grandpa's truck on a field and then we saw a deer and my dad almost shot it. And I remember this other time when we went out back and we shot some jack rabbits and we got about seven of them and now he's just gone and I'll never see him again and that just hurts my dad so much.

John Roster, Grade 6
Round Valley Elementary School, CA

Getting Shots

Would you like to hear about one of the times I got shots at the doctor's office? Well it's coming right at you.

One morning at 5:30 my mom woke me up and told me we have to go somewhere, so I put on my clothes and got in the car. We were going to the doctor's office. We pulled up at the parking lot in the hospital. When we entered the building we went up an elevator on the side of the hallway. I knew I was going to get three shots, so I told myself "Think of good thoughts." The nurse that worked there took us to a small room at the end of the hallway. She said "the doctor will be here shortly." When the doctor came in he started to interrogate my mom. When he was done taking care of my mom, he checked my blood pressure. When he was done checking my blood pressure, he pulled out something sharp that had a needle on it. He started to point it at me, I started to scream. I tried to think of good thoughts, but before I could it was over. I was so happy when it was over and the doctor gave me a lollipop and my mom and I left.

Junior Charles, Grade 5
Bang Elementary School, TX

Harley

My uncle had a dog named Harley. Harley was awesome! I would go to my Grandma's house where my uncle lived and just lay with Harley on the sofa. I would talk to Harley and sometimes I would think he was talking back. I would whisper in his floppy ear.

When I was little, I was sometimes lonely and when I could have the time to talk to Harley I would pour my heart out.

Harley was with me all my life until I was seven. When I was six my uncle noticed a lump on Harley's stomach. When they took him to the vet they said it was "nothing" and sent him away.

About a year later Harley was slowing down. My uncle took him to the vet again and they looked at the lump again but this time they didn't say it was just "nothing." Harley had a lump. The lump had a tumor in it.

My uncle had two choices. He could let Harley suffer and die or he could put him to sleep. My uncle would not let Harley suffer so a couple of months later they put him to sleep.

I was crushed. I cried for hours. It is now four years later and I still miss Harley.

My uncle is in college now and has a dog named Holly who will never replace Harley.

Rebecca Lothspeich, Grade 5

The Courageous Night

Have you ever thought that you were going to die of a medical condition? Sometime in the beginning of June 2007, I thought I was going to die of appendicitis. This was a memorable event because I was so scared I could jump out of my skin. I remember the shock, the comfort, and how I was "The Courageous Knight on the Courageous Night."

First, we got to the doctor's office because my parents thought I had food poisoning. I actually thought my parents had an edge on this one. Then, the doctor brought out the bad news; I had appendicitis and had to have surgery. I was as shocked as a mosquito in a bug zapper. I said "What?! Am I being punked?"

I cried into mom's shoulder. Could you blame me? I was about to have a surgery. When I got to the hospital, some nurses were acting in loco parentis (Latin for 'in the role of the parent'), even though my mom was there. Nurses must know how kids feel, that's when I started to feel okay.

At last, I was ready to be "The Courageous Knight on the Courageous Night," at one in the morning the doctors started the operation and soon it was over, I was still alive!

This event taught me a lesson. I learned to never be afraid of what you don't know will happen. I am glad I took a risk and got healthier in the process.

Vincent Macareno, Grade 5
Willow Glen Elementary School, CA

Caring

Caring means to feel interest or concern for something. I think that this is very important. For example, people donate food or clothes for others who need it. People should always care about others when they need it and help them out. Another example for that would be when Hurricane Katrina came. People watched over and cared for the ones that lost their homes.

Personal events of caring are very important to me. When someone in my sister's class was stealing her school supplies, I told our mother so that she could report it. Another time I cared for my little sister, Kaitlyn was when a boy kicked her in the face at the park. When it happened I told him not to do it, and also ran to our mom. Then she took us home. I love Kaitlyn so I try to care for her.

Everybody in the world should care about others. If everybody care life would be easier.

Allison Agee, Grade 5
Covington Elementary School, NE

Pocohontas

Pocohontas was the daughter of an American Indian Chief, Powhatan, and is a great leader and role model to the world. When Pocohontas was born her mother was one of the many wives of Powhatan and sent away after her birth. Pocohontas' name meant playful one, but the name that her tribe called her was Matoaka. She didn't know how to write so most of the information that we have is from other people's point of view.

Pocohontas was taken hostage in 1612 when she was staying with the village of the Patawomecks that the Powhatans did some trading with. The chief of the Patawomecks was Japazaws. One day two English colonists saw Pocohontas and with Japazaws' help they tricked Pocohontas into captivity. She was kept at Henricus while in captivity. During her stay at Henricus she met John Rolfe who she later got married to on April 5, 1614.

For a few years they lived together on Rolfe's plantation. They had a child Thomas Rolfe, born on January 30, 1615. In the spring of 1617 Rolfe and Pocohontas boarded a ship to return to Virginia. Pocohontas became ill on the boat and later died. Her funeral was on March 21, 1617.

Hannah Packer, Grade 6
Thomas Jefferson Charter School, ID

A Life Lesson

My cousin fell asleep by the pool. He fell in a 4 ft. pool head first. He couldn't get his head out of the water because his lifejacket wouldn't let his head out of the water so he drowned and he died. It was a nice hot sunny day. A little later my mom and Aunt Lynda just got home from school. Then they found him in the pool! He drowned at the age of four. We all miss him still. My cousin dying was a lesson to stay in my heart forever. That's how I learned a lesson not to fall asleep on or in a pool. This story is a life lesson.

Phillip Couch, Grade 5
McMonagle Elementary School, MI

Music's in My Life

You can find music anywhere. Outside, in a restaurant, even the background music during the movies! Just turn around, you'll probably find the music. To me, music's in my blood, and in my life every day.

Some people wake up in the morning by just waking up. Others use an alarm. Me, I'm the alarm type of person. When I wake up each morning, no bells wake me up. The songs do! So, my days always begin with the soft melodies.

Right after school, I do my homework. When I'm solving problems and writing definitions I get really bored. Not because it's actually homework, but there's no flow. What did I do? I crank up the tunes! The music starts playing and I start to flow. In a few minutes, I'm finished with a tune-filled smile.

During the summer, I played a lot of sports. Especially volleyball. I always needed some kind of rhythm to get me going. Right when I hear the music, I start to spike the volleyball with an intense pulse. My bumping skills increase with agility. With music playing during a game, I can spike, bump, dive, and serve without a problem!

As you can see, music is a huge part of my life. Even if I don't hear it in every place in the world, it doesn't matter. All I have to do is listen to it in my mind. You know why? The music's in my soul, and always in me.

Naomi Caridad, Grade 5
Jefferson Elementary School, MI

Who Knew Playing Basketball Would Be Fun

I didn't want to play basketball at first for my 5th grade team at school. I thought I would not be a good basketball player and did not want the kids to laugh at me. My parents really wanted me to play basketball because they thought it was good for me to get some exercise. So even though I didn't want to, I signed up for the basketball team.

At first I hated basketball because I didn't really like my coach. He yelled a lot and made me feel like I wasn't any good. I asked my mom if I could quit and she said no. I was very unhappy.

Then we had our first game. I found it was a lot of fun to compete with the other kids my age. When I play football, I have to play with the older kids because of my size and sometimes that is hard. Playing with kids my own age gave me more confidence.

I played center and I got to start in many games. I also got to do the tip off. That is one of my favorite parts of the game. I also worked hard at my timing and blocked a lot of opponents' shots.

I'm glad that my parents pushed me to sign up for basketball. I learned a valuable lesson. Don't knock something until you try it. Playing basketball is fun.

Justin Hunter, Grade 6
Divine Infant Jesus School, IL

My Special Brother

My brother has Fragile X, which is a syndrome of X-linked retardation. My brother's name is Noah; he's twenty-two and he plays as the starting quarterback for Elkhart County Special Olympics. If you had the chance to meet him you would realize he's just a regular kid in a man's body inside and out. I play on the Concord All-Stars baseball team and all my friends love him and always remind me to tell him they said, "Hi."

Noah's brain doesn't function like a normal person, as a matter of fact he can't read or do any math and he never will be able to. He lives at home with our family and as my parents get older they hope to establish a living foundation for mentally retarded kids.

As I said earlier that Noah's the starting quarterback for the Elkhart County flag football team. My brother, however, does seem to have the ability to memorize plays. I involve myself with the team by dedicating my time to help the team out with their weaknesses. If you came to a game you would see the true meaning of, "For the love of the game."

As I was discussing what I was going to write about with my dad all of the sudden my brother said, "I think you should write about Monday." Well I hoped you liked it, but I'm running out of words so I have to go, see you later.

Andrew Sandlin, Grade 6

Western Chokecherry

The western chokecherry is a shrub or small tree. It reaches 3 to 20 feet tall and occasionally as tall 30 feet tall in some areas. The bark is smooth to scaly and dull red to grey. The trunk may grow up to be 20cm in diameter. The leaves are oval and rounded at the base or slightly heart shaped. They're 1 to 3 inches wide. The leaves are smooth or slightly hairy with finely toothed margins.

Chokecherries are too bitter to eat raw, though some people find them tasty, especially after the berries have aged a while. Jellies and wine making seem to be the most common uses for chokecherries, yet chokecherries are still used for juices, syrups and jams.

The western chokecherry is used not only for humans but for animals. Some deer and elk eat the berries and leaves. Bears, many species of songbirds and pheasants, eat the fruit. Chokecherries also provide shelter and food for birds and small animals. The leaves of the chokecherry serve as food for caterpillars.

The western chokecherry can be found in Alberta, BC, Manitoba, Ontario and combining states in the United States of America.

This tree is Latin and is called PRUNUS VIRGINIANA MELANOCARPA and is native. The western chokecherry is also called bitter cherry and blake chokecherry.

Madison Macaulay, Grade 6
Our Lady Of Fatima, AB

Facing a Challenge

Wow, I can't believe it, my first day in gymnastics. It's just me and some other children. My mom is here to watch me perform.

Facing that challenge was very hard with all the moms watching me. The balance beam was so high, the parallel bars were so far apart, and all the other girls looked like pros. That made me feel nervous, afraid that I would fall and be laughed at, but I looked at my mom and remembered she said, "Always do your best, never give up, keep on working at it, and I love you!" I felt like the little engine that could.

I didn't care what the girls said. Now that I've conquered that quest I believe in myself, and if the girls laughed at me, at least I tried and did my best.

I was four years old then. I stopped going when I turned eight. Now that I have faced that challenge, I know I can do anything.

Ja'Toria Ware, Grade 5
Seminole Academy, MI

Teamwork

Did you know that the work or activity of a number of people acting together as a team is teamwork? I would like to tell you how I am good with teamwork. My first example is that I help my sister with all her chores after school. Next, I help my mom clean the whole house, and watching over my little brother and sisters. All of these show teamwork because I am working with my family to help them out.

People in the world show teamwork by helping their communities with cleaning up the cities by recycling and donating their time to help others in need. All in all, teamwork is not just doing things for yourself, but working with others.

Gabriela Medina, Grade 5
Covington Elementary School, NE

September 11th

One day in 2001 on September 11th in New York, two planes were hijacked. The planes crashed into the Twin Towers and over three thousand of innocent people, not knowing what was happening, died because of some terrorists. The Twin Towers were centered and crashed into a bunch of other buildings. We thank the policemen, firefighters and many more who tried saving as many people as they could.

I was four when it happened and I don't remember it well. I've been told about it, and every time I help someone I think about September 11th sooner or later and all the people that died and what happened to them.

One time in 2007 it was around July, we went back East and one of the places we went was New York. I learned a lot more about September 11th. We got pictures that they were selling of September 11th. I got to see the platforms of all people that died. I also saw some workers working on a new building. I think everyone should remember that September 11th is important.

Sephra Miller, Grade 4

How to Treat a Friend

Do you have a good friend or two? If yes, do you know how to treat them? If not then read this! Treat a friend with kindness, give as much support as you can. There are a couple of steps to treat a friend with kindness and support.

Number 1: When your friend is going to be in something big, like a science fair, or a speech contest, don't be jealous! And if your friend is nervous about their big event, then you really don't want to be jealous! Being jealous too much, can make you behave in a different way.

Number 2: No ditching! Ditching is absolutely not acceptable. If you ditch your friend(s), think about how they're going to feel? Here's what the results could be after ditching someone: your friend won't talk to you anymore or your friend will find a new friend. Last result is you will be left, hurt inside, because you ditched a friend. That might not be a lot that could happen, but if it happens to you, it will make you feel bad.

Number 3: Have fun with your friend. If you don't play or talk with your friend, what kind of fun will you have? That's like playing tag by yourself! Try to play what your friend would mostly like to play. I hope you have learned a lot after reading this. And remember this, be a super great friend!

Kirandeep Deol, Grade 6
Dr F D Sinclair Elementary School, BC

My Trip to the Big House

"The Big House" was a place I had only seen in pictures and on television until a few weeks ago when Dad surprised my brother and me with a trip to Ann Arbor, Michigan. In case you don't know about "The Big House," it is the stadium where the Michigan Wolverines play football. When my dad was getting directions to the stadium, he was told to just "follow the other 112,000 people."

When we entered the stadium we were surprised to see that about 70 rows were below street level. It was interesting to see the sea of maize and gold, and the uproar of 112,000 people crammed into one stadium.

Shortly before kickoff both bands played their fight songs which really got the crowd fired up for the great match-up between Michigan and Joe Paterno's Penn State Nittany Lions. Coach Paterno has been the Lions coach for 48 years. The fans cheered as the Wolverines came out of their tunnel. They ran toward the end zone and jumped to touch the field goal cross bar before heading out for pre-game warm-up.

The game started and for the next few hours I got to see two of the greatest college football teams play in one of the loudest, biggest stadiums in college football. The game ended with the Wolverines on top with a score of 14-9. It was the most exciting football game I have ever seen and I will never forget it.

Jack Vickery, Grade 6
Argyle Middle School, TX

Number 33

Bulldozer was my 2nd calf and 1st steer. We got him from a friend. The first year went well until his first bath, when he saw the new animals at the fair, and the two times he got out. The first bath we gave him was an experience. We were using the blower, and Bulldozer got scared. We turned it off, and then turned it on again. Then he started to buck and kick me right in the arm! We decided we were done for the night.

Well the new animals and fair are combined. It all started when we got in the ring he would not move! We think the only reason why he didn't move is because he was so happy to see other steers!

The last experience we had with Bulldozer was when he escaped twice. He got out the 1st time he ran 4 miles down the road. It took 2 hours to get him home! Then he got out the second time and went to our friends feedlot across the road.

At last, it was time to say good bye. I was bawling so much my brother had to lead him in the trailer! But I still got to keep his ear tag: Number 33.

Bailey Naylor, Grade 6
Kinsey School, MT

Leopards

Leopards live in more areas of the world than any other big cat. Leopards are found in parts of Africa, southern Asia, China, and Korea. They live in rainforests, jungles, mountains, grasslands, and even cities and towns. They roam from sea level to the highest mountain.

Leopards are shy animals. They are mostly nocturnal. They like to hide in trees or bushes during the day. Leopards are tan and have many dark spots.

The spots help the leopards hide. Some leopards that live in thick jungles are black. Leopards are predators, which means that they hunt other animals. They hunt by stalking their prey.

They can't run very fast for very long. They must be very close to an animal to catch it. A leopard kills by leaping from a hiding place and knocking the animal down with its front legs.

The leopard grabs the animal's throat and bites down hard. The animal can't breathe and soon dies. They eat insects, reptiles, birds, monkeys, small mammals, and larger grass-eating animals. An average leopard weighs around 100 pounds.

It can kill an animal that weighs almost 300 pounds! Some leopards carry their food up into trees. A leopard hangs its food in a tree so other animals won't eat it, leopards have many enemies.

Baboons, lions, and hyenas will attack a baby leopard. These animals will also kill an adult leopard if they get the chance. Pythons also eat leopards. People, though, are the leopard's greatest enemies. In conclusion I love learning about leopards.

Joeisha Leon-Guerrero, Grade 4
Louise Foussat Elementary School, CA

Julius Caesar's Assassination!

Do you know the story of Julius Caesar's murder? Believe it or not, his murder was plotted by his so called friends in the Senate! If only he had listened to his family, he probably would have had a longer life!

After all of the places Julius Caesar had conquered, he was considered a massive threat. That's why the Senate felt they must murder Julius. The murder of Julius was not going to be a breeze. What do you think would be the best way to kill Caesar? This question was difficult for the Senate to answer. A vote among the conspirators would decide.

The first option was to push Julius off a bridge during the elections. The second was to kill him while he made his favorite walk. The winning plot was to murder him while he sat in the Senate. On March 15, 44 BC it was time to have a meeting with the Senate.

Julius had heard that bad things were planned for the meeting, but he was persuaded to go to the meeting anyway. When Julius arrived he sat in his seat. When the Senate was standing around him they made their vicious move. Julius was taken by surprise.

Julius was wounded more than 23 times, by 16 known killers. Three of them were Marcus, Gaius and Gaius Trebonius. I think of his 16 killers as cruel cowards. Although, I think of Julius Caesar as a very brave and powerful man.

Hannah Cooper, Grade 5
Oak Crest Intermediate School, TX

My Favorite Kinds of Dogs

Dogs make excellent and loyal pets. There are all kinds of dogs. My favorite breeds are Bulldogs, Boxers, and Golden Retrievers.

Bulldogs are short and heavy. They can be very mean. I should know since I own one. When they bite their under jaw locks with their upper jaw.

Boxers are medium sized dogs. They can weigh from 60-75 pounds. Boxers have been used in wars for protection as well as guide dogs for the blind.

Golden Retrievers are also medium in size. Golden Retrievers are the nicest kinds of dog I know. They also weight up to 60-75 pounds just like the Boxers.

The Bulldogs, Boxers, and Golden Retrievers are my favorite because they are fun, playful, sometimes nice, and energetic.

Anthony Perez, Grade 5
St Patrick's Catholic School, WA

Farming

There are all different types of farming. There is dairy farming, grain farming, hog farming, and tons and tons more. If we did not have farmers, it would be harder to survive. We could not go to the local store and get what we wanted or how much we wanted. So the next time you go to the store, remember the hard working people that supply our food.

Tom Benner, Grade 6
Pike Christian Academy, OH

Pizza Time!

This story is about someone I love; my grandmother. She cares for me and my siblings, all six of us. One day, she asked if I could come over to spend time with her because she missed me. I obviously said yes and we were both very happy. When I got there we had some snacks and sat down for a little while. She then told me we were making a pizza! I was so excited, but I thought it would be simple, it turned out that we were making it from scratch! She had so many ingredients on the table laying there all ready for us to use!

We were trying to make the best pizza we could for my family. We mixed the ingredients and we did everything by hand. We tried to throw them up into the air and catch them as fast as we could. It was so fun!

Then, my family came and we all had such a good time! We told them how we made the pizza and we talked and talked. It was so much fun for everyone in my family! Me and my grandma had such a great bonding time. I'm so glad I spent that time with her. I will remember that moment forever!

Cristina Herrera, Grade 6
St Anne School, CA

Penguins

Have you ever seen an emperor penguin? Well if you ever see one the odds are he'll be as tall, if not taller, than you!

The penguin population is huge, but the global warming is affecting the polar bears and penguins. So, the population has gone down a lot.

Penguins are very fun animals. Sometimes after they catch their fish they play tug of war with them for fun. They also slide down hills on their bellies to have a race.

Pairs of penguins have to work together to stay warm and feed their young. So to work together they must take turns making trips to the ocean for food. Then must return to their family to feed their young and let the others go for food.

When it gets very cold, the penguins huddle together to stay warm. So if you looked at them from above they look like one big black dot.

When a penguin is looking after their egg, if the egg falls off its feet it's immediately dead. Because the ice is so cold the egg can't withstand the temperature for more than one second.

A penguin's skin and/or feathers are so smooth that if you run your fingers through its feathers, it will feel like your desk top with water on it.

If you're ever in a cold part of the world and you see something in the distance it could be a penguin. Just be careful, because it very well could be a bear.

A penguin is a very cute and interesting animal. That's why it's my favorite.

Emily Sun, Grade 4
Butterfield School, IL

Every Summer Vacation

Every year I always do the same thing over and over again. Some of my vacation I am busy because I have to go to America, to somebody's wedding or visiting my grandam. Those things I did over the summer when my parents were on vacation. Mostly we have to blueberry pick every day from seven o'clock in the morning to eight-thirty and the best part is that I get to have a slurpee every time when blueberry picking is over. After I get home from blueberry picking my brother always tells me to do things I don't want to do. I always tell him "NO." Every time when we go to Cultas Lake we kids eat ice cream but that only happens when we go back home.

A day after I went camping with my mom's friends they told Stephanie and I to take care of our brothers because they are troublemakers. My brother is two years older than me and a year younger than Stephanie. Her brother is a year older than me and is a year younger than my brother. All we did was sit there and do nothing until our parents came back. Simon, Jimmy and I tried to make a fire with only a portable stove and papers. We tried so hard but it kept going out so we decided to stop. I have great memories of my summer vacation.

Rita Seng, Grade 6
Dr F D Sinclair Elementary School, BC

Whooping Crane

The Whooping Crane is the biggest, most beautiful bird in North America. The weight of a male Crane is 16.5 pounds and for a female 14.3 pounds. The Whoopers may weigh differently, but they both are 5 feet tall and 7.5 feet in wingspan. Full-grown Whooping Cranes sport flashy red crowns on their heads, wings that look like they were dipped in ink, and snow white feathers.

These beautiful birds migrate to Texas, colliding into power lines, leaving us with a count of 149 Cranes left. In the 1800's there were 1,500 Whoopers in the United States and Canada.

Cranes fly to Wood Buffalo National Park for the breeding season. They fall in love with one another, it is for life. When they start to breed, they display odd actions such as jumping, bobbing, weaving around and calling to each other.

The female lays two eggs and each parent takes turns keeping the eggs warm. The adults kick the second child out so it can starve to death.

Cranes eat the bottoms of plants, fish, snails, and other animals that live underwater. They eat leeches, baby bugs, and rats. They look for dead ducks, swamp birds, and muskrats.

Whooping Cranes live to be 24 years old. In 1975, the Canadian Wildlife Service started a project to save them. Other projects were in Kissimmee, Florida, and near the Mississippi River.

In 2001, they added birds to the population. In 2006 a storm killed some of the birds.

Janae Barner, Grade 4
Menchaca Elementary School, TX

Saving Lives

When I say that I want to save lives, do I mean human lives? Do I want to be a doctor? No, I mean animal lives. Of course, people are important, but animals are, too. Endangered species such as pandas, hawksbill turtles, elephants, and whales need help. Hawksbill turtles are stolen and killed for their shells, which are used to make jewelry, earrings, and the outer parts of combs. Elephants are killed for their tusks. If this goes on, endangered animals will not only be endangered, but also extinct! They need help to save them from human beings.

I would suggest government laws to stop poaching, but this had already been done. So why do animals continue to disappear? People poach animals illegally. If this is not stopped, animals like pandas and whales will become a faint memory. I know we do not wish for that to happen, so some people have set up national preserves where it is illegal to poach, and animals are kept under watch.

Because all animals are important, we must help them to stay alive. Please try to help in any way you can. You could put flyers up and form organizations. These are only a couple of the ways you could become involved. Remember, endangered animals are very important, but without your support to save them, they will soon disappear.

Naomi Wu, Grade 4
Birchwood School, OH

Longing for a Pet?

Have you ever had a pet? Did you ever long to have a pet? Did you ever think of what responsibilities you would have once you adopted a pet? If you didn't, you made a huge mistake.

Once you adopt a pet a bond forms between you and the pet. For example, if your pet dies, gets hurt, is ill, or if you need to put it up for adoption again because of other issues, you would become sad, grumpy, and depressed. That is when the bond comes in. It makes you care for each other.

My pet dog, Windy, is a two year old female. She is very playful and extremely active. Windy is a Beagle and Shepherd mix, with brown fur and a line of black fur along her back. Her name is Windy because whenever we take her out for a walk, instead of walking she runs!

Windy is a great pet, but the problem is my grandma is coming to stay in three years. If you're wondering how can that be a problem… my grandma is allergic to animal fur! Which means she is allergic to Windy! I'm trying to delay my grandma from coming in three years to five.

I'm trying to reason with my parents to keep my dog. I hope I can keep my dog.

Me and Windy have a bond that can last for a lifetime. I care for her and she cares for me.

Gordon Duzbou, Grade 6
Northwood Public School, ON

A World of Danger

Why are there so many horrible things that happen every day? Houses are dilapidated because of catastrophes, not to mention several deaths caused by them. Poor children are dying from cancer and other disease in hospitals. Malaria is killing more than 1,000,000 children per year. Policemen are allowing terrorists to slip away over and over causing more massacres. Why are there endangered animals, and so much pollution in the air? Why can't Lindsay Lohan, Paris Hilton, and Nicole Richie start with a clean slate? Why is tobacco popping out of the earth in the first place? Murderers and scammers lurk the Earth, doing something to hurt someone every day. There are inappropriate music videos on YouTube.com! There are anti-people striking against unique and sweet people. There are bad influences and bullies in schools. There is war. There are people who use hurtful words. Think of infants, children, teenagers, and adults, wandering around in the dangers of the Earth completely unaware of what is going on around them. People are not vigilant enough because sooner or later, they become the victim. Why can't people realize they need to save Mother Earth, the people, the environment, the communities, and the animals? Wouldn't the world be beautiful and healthy if people saw the importance of taking care of our Earth? Earth is all we've got. So stop checking your emails with M&M's in your lap! Come help me SAVE THE EARTH!

Ashley Stern, Grade 5
The Shlenker School, TX

My Grandfather

My grandfather is a great man. His name is Fred Gossman. He served in World War Two. He grew up in Bridge Water, South Dakota. My grandfather's mom and dad's name were Lorena and John Gossman. His wife and he met in Emery. Her name is Rita. And they have eight kids.

When he grew up, he lived in Bridge Water, South Dakota. He and his siblings went to St. Steven's Catholic School. He was the oldest. His dad died when they were all very young, so he had to help raise them. He had one brother and eight sisters. There was Luella, Marilyn, Rita, Barbara, Rose, Pat, Joyce, Betty, and Paul.

When my grandfather was about eighteen years old, he joined the War. He was an Army Engineer. He went from New Guinea, to the Philippines, to Japan, and then back to the United States. His first leader was Sullivan.

He is eighty-one years old. He lives in Rapid City, South Dakota with his wife, Rita Gossman. They met at a dance in Emery, South Dakota. They live in a log cabin in the Black Hills. They have eight kids. There is Fred, Tim, Kathy, Teresa, Steve, Jack, Mary and my mom Nancy.

Tori Swope, Grade 6
Kinsey School, MT

Rocket Fly

First, I want to tell you about rocket fly. The rocket was for science. It had wings and a nose cone. It was made out of construction paper with pink white red and green flames.

When I shot my rocket off it was up, up and gone. The rocket flies up into the beautiful sky. It was 4.20 seconds long. It landed on the bleachers and it smushed the top of the nose cone. My rocket stayed in the air the longest and Damon's was in second.

Damon's rocket was orange, white, and black. When I was making the rocket I thought it was going to be the worst rocket. It wasn't the worst one; it was the best one because it had the longest air time.

I wish we could do another science project about rockets and space shuttles. I wish that because it was so fun to make it, especially when we spray painted it. Wouldn't you want to make one?

Tyler Hamilton, Grade 6
Lynnville Elementary School, IN

Who I Admire and Respect

The person who I admire is my big sister, Lizette Cardenas. I admire her because she is cool. For example, she lets me do whatever I want as long as I don't make a mess. If I do make a mess I have to clean it up.

Another reason why I respect her is because she respects me. For example, she does not hit me or tell me what to do.

One other reason why I admire and respect Lizette is because she is smart. For example, she gets good grades most of the time.

In conclusion, I admire and respect Lizette because she is so smart, respectful, and cool. Either way I still love her.

Amber Cardenas, Grade 5
Camellia Avenue Elementary School, CA

The Person I Admire

The person I admire is my mom because I was born from her stomach. She does nice things, like helping me do my homework. I love it when she helps me.

I admire her because she cleans with me and gives us five dollars each Sunday. When she does that she tells me that I'm the coolest girl and I tell her she's the best mom ever.

The cool thing about her is that she's my mom. She does fun things like baking cakes. If she changes I'll be sad.

She should have more fun with our family and never let go of her job with me. When I was writing about her it reminded me about a rose that blooms in our garden. She is the moon that my cousins like. My cousin says that she is the mother of the Lord. I invite my friends to meet my mom so they could know that's my mom. My friends even want her to be their mom.

She smiles and I smile too! We both are happy. I admire her because she's never mean to me, she's nice, she cooks, we both spend time together, and we paint a lot. I love her a lot.

Dayanara Pineda, Grade 5
Camellia Avenue Elementary School, CA

Drug Free for Me

People ask themselves about the importance of not taking drugs. Some on a daily basis. Others are not affected at all because they do not listen to bad influences. Staying drug free is important to me because it destroys your body. People should not take them if their friends say it is okay. If someone is trying to make you take drugs, you should tell them NO!

Kids are pressured by their peers all the time. They ask them to do things that are not always what is considered the right thing to do. If someone asks you to do drugs with them, they are not your true friend. If someone threatens you if you don't try their drugs, you should tell someone that you trust and ask them for help.

Don't let your friends put you into a bad situation. For example, if they invite you to their home and their parents are not home, you should not stay because the obvious might occur. Drugs could be involved especially if you know that other kids are going to be there that think that doing drugs are cool.

Don't go around people that you know are doing drugs because adults might think that you are a drug person and you don't want people to think bad things about you. Be a positive role model. Show people that you have pride in yourself and that you love yourself. Always be drug free.

Marisa Alloway, Grade 6
The Arts Academy School, OH

Friends

Friends are the life link for you when adults are not around. You have your best friends, your friends, and people you don't really hang out with. Friends always have your back no matter what. Sometimes you get mad at each other and don't talk for awhile and you think you will never be friends again. In the end when it comes down to it you realize how silly you were being and you make up.

It is fun to look back on your mistakes and fights you've had and laugh. Last year my friend got mad at me because I poked him with a pen and he overreacted and yelled out loud. The teacher overheard and I got in trouble. In the end we worked it our and are friends today. Another time was when I hit someone with a ball too hard, now anytime I throw I try to remember to throw slower.

It is frustrating for me because a significant amount of my friends go to a different school. At my current school I only have 3 or 4 real friends. All the other people just pretend to act nice to me. I really can't wait until I go to middle school as I can reunite with my friends.

Friends have been with me through everything. I am just getting over a broken elbow and they were with me through that. I love my friends, I couldn't live without them.

Jenson Carlgren, Grade 6
La Mariposa Montessori School, NM

My Trip to Wild Horse Canyon

I went to Wild Horse Canyon for four days because my dad was the camp doctor. Jack, my brother, was his first patient. He broke his arm skateboarding. We had to drive to the hospital. It took two hours to get there because we were out in the middle of the desert. When I got out of the car, my legs felt like Jell-O. I could barely walk, that's how long it took.

There were tons of things to do at Wild Horse Canyon. One thing was Blobs. I didn't go on them, but it was fun watching people. There's a tall tower over a giant inflatable blob in the water. One person sits on one end and the other person jumps off the tower onto the other end and sends the first person flying "splash!" into the water.

Also there is a zip line, a pool, an awesome sports center, and a place where you can have meals. Also in the evenings there is a club where you sing. There are games on the stage and a skit. I thought "wow this is the coolest place ever!"

Annabelle Geisler, Grade 5

The Day I Was Born

Hi my name is Matthew Wilson. I was born May eighth of nineteen ninety eight. I was born in Houston Texas, that was a great day for me. It was a very long day for my mom! Meanwhile, my grandpa was taking care of my brother in our old apartment as my grandma was with my mom, signing her in at the hospital. My grandma helped answer questions and got my mom water when she needed it. My dad even came all the way from Oklahoma to pick up my brother and grandpa so they could see me. My mom couldn't have anything to eat. She was very upset but Doctor White took me out of my mom's stomach and picked me up so my mom could see me. My mom saw me. She was happy, and thought I looked handsome. The nurses took me so they could clean me. They also took my temperature. After they were done, they took me back to my mom. As my mom passed me around, I kept on crying, but when I came back to my mom I stopped. It was our first night together and no one could ruin it.

Matthew Wilson, Grade 4
Burchett Elementary School, TX

My Favorite Place

My favorite place is a little room. My dad built it for me. Only it is a cool little room to do my homework in. It was supposed to be a bathroom but that was a long time ago. Every night on the weekends I sneak back there and do all kinds of stuff. But sometimes my sister wakes up and follows me back there. I tell her to go back to sleep. I always hang out in the room. I like to be by myself. Sometimes I do activities for my sister. I have fun in it. I do all kinds of stuff like draw, color, and paint. It is so cool. My sister likes to come and paint, draw, and color with me too. I mainly do my homework in there but other stuff too. Every day I get home from school I check to see if anybody's been in there.

Whitney Russell, Grade 4
Winona Elementary School, TX

Anne Frank

Once upon a time in 1942 the city of Amsterdam. There lived a girl named Anne Frank and she is 13 years old and she is Jewish. She has to wear a gold star. They can't get entertainment.

They and another family called the Van Daans are hiding from the Nazis because they are going to kill them by gassing them in a concentration camp. They are hiding in a old office building called the "Secret Annex" for almost three years.

The other people that were there were Dussel, Koophius, Kraler, and the Van Daans. Mr. Van Daan is very fat and is in the meat and spice business.

Anne Frank was killed in 1944 at a concentration camp. Otto Frank which is her dad was the only survivor.

Ian Ramos, Grade 4
St Luke Catholic School, TX

My Nana

My favorite person is my Nana. She is so good to me, she is like my mommy sometimes.

Nana will yell at me. She won't really yell at me; she just tells me to mind.

She always cares about my school work or if I've done my homework. She makes sure I have my room clean before I go anywhere. She knows my volleyball schedule and makes sure I'm there on time. Nana takes great care of me, and I'm so lucky she does. She loves me with all her heart; I know that for a fact.

She loves to be with her grandchildren all the time. She takes me places, like her work, Walmart, and shopping.

In October we get to carve pumpkins. We don't do it alone; we do it with my Papa, cousins, and my Uncle PJ.

Nana gets me off the bus even though I'm 10 years old and I'm in 5th grade. I tell my Nana sometimes I'm going to grow up very soon and that just breaks her heart. She is my favorite person because I love her and she loves me so very much.

Kayla Rose, Grade 5
Westview Elementary School, OH

Savannahs of the World

Do you want a new cat? I know what cat you should get, a Savannah! They are great cats. The Savannah's name came from the plains its ancestors, the African Serval roamed.

They are fun loving and energetic cats. They weigh more than 20 lb. when they are full grown. Savannahs can also stand up to 15 inches when full grown.

Savannahs are a mix of the African Serval and a domestic cat. Savannahs are basically a smaller replica of the Serval.

They are literally addicted to water. If you are really their friend, they will lay their head against yours. Savannahs can jump very high.

If you want to learn more about Savannahs go to www.savannahcats.com or www.savannahcatbreed.com.

Zoe Brantley, Grade 5
Oak Crest Intermediate School, TX

9-11 Heroes

There were many people who died on one of the saddest days in our country, 9/11/01. Some of those people were firefighters who risked their lives just to save the lives of other people. If you don't already know about this disaster it took place in New York. It wasn't all bad really because sure there were a lot of deaths but there were also people who survived.

Many soldiers who did live didn't consider themselves as heroes. They just said they were doing their job by rescuing people but they are wrong. They are heroes who have definitely accomplished modesty, charity, and humility. They show modesty by not bragging and calling them great when they saved those people in the towers. They were charitable when they went in to save people. They were humble when they weren't thinking of themselves. It wasn't just firemen it was also policemen and rescue workers. You can obviously see that the world isn't all evil but it is also filled with people who care about each other and help. I am so thankful for those firemen, policemen, and rescue workers who care about us.

Carrie Melson, Grade 6
St Gertrude School, OH

Juan Rodriguez Cabrillo

The place and date of birth of Juan Rodriguez Cabrillo is unknown. What we know is that he was a brave soldier.

In his youth, he was a Spanish soldier and settled the new world. Cabrillo joined the Spanish military expeditions; he defeated the Aztecs in southern Mexico, Guatemala and San Salvador.

By the middle of 1530 Cabrillo led the citizens of Guatemala's town named Santiago. After 10 years there was an earthquake that destroyed Santiago. Meanwhile, in the year of 1532, Cabrillo traveled to the country of Spain.

In Spain he met a beautiful lady named Beatriz de Ortega. In that year they married and returned to Guatemala where Beatriz gave birth to two boys. As their family grew their reputation and wealth as a ship builder also grew. The ships of Cabrillo in use for the trades for Guatemala were constructed and built in Spain. Some of theses ships played a vital role in Spain's early efforts to explore the Pacific.

Pedro de Alvarado the Governor had selected Cabrillo to build a ship that he needed to explore the Pacific, because of his skills as a leader and businessman. They also asked him if he would want the two expeditions to go and explore the Pacific. Cabrillo then accepted the proposal and set out for the exploration of the north and west coast of Mexico. The other expeditions set out to the Philippines.

Cabrillo was a soldier as well as a successful businessman.

Esmeralda Rodriguez, Grade 4
Our Lady of the Rosary School, CA

My Friends

My friends like to play with their pets, shop, and swim. We like to hang out at my house and play Wii or air hockey. We like to make cool stuff to eat and watch a movie or two. But when it comes to friends, we have twenty-twenty vision. We would have to be the best of friends. Me, Kali, Kaitlin, and Sydney. It's oh so true. But I have other friends not from school like Maki and Megan and Hunter, Carly and Jen, but at the end of the day I have one special friend who honestly I've never met face to face, that special friend is God. He goes with me wherever I go. He's sweet, kind, and gentle. Before I wrote this, I thought nobody liked me. Now I look, and think. Now it feels like I have a lot of friends.

Andi Cole, Grade 5
Pike Christian Academy, OH

Church...Gotta Have It

What kind of world would we have without church? Without church, people would curse because they didn't have God in their lives. They would fight all the time. The things they'd fight over would be about stuff that's not even important. The world would be messed up if we didn't have church.

Our world would very likely be out of control without church or God. Everyone would be screaming, panicking and poor children would be in the middle of all the confusion. They might be lost in the angry mob!! Life just might be what you could call, "a disaster."

Without church, life would be bad...it wouldn't be good at all.

Cheyanne Jones, Grade 5
DeQueen Elementary School, TX

Shopping

Don't you just love cell phones and computers or shopping at the mall? Back in the day, people used antique phones where you just talk in the microphone piece and listen from the receiver that is attached to the phone by a wire.

Now we have cell phones and computers. If you are not familiar with them, (but I bet you are) I will name a couple of things: texting is very fun, journaling, schedules, there is also videos (can be or are) funny. You can video tape many events like at Halloween, sleepovers, and the best is Christmas.

Computers are the best! On iTunes you can listen to music like Kelly Clarkson, the Jonas Brothers and other singers. You can also play games online. With the right equipment you can instant message and e-mail.

Now let's go to shopping. I love to shop. Shopping is the best thing in the world — in my opinion. The things I like to shop for is nail polish, lip gloss and really cute clothes. I shop for fun things too like Build A Bear. When you first walk in the light is so bright and makes you feel excited. The food is the best part! The churros and soft pretzels.

Sydney Jordan, Grade 6
Imagine Charter School at Rosefield, AZ

People Do Not Quit

Everyone has someone special in their life. Michael Jordan is my inspiration. Michael turned into a basketball player that has played for the Chicago Bulls. Michael retired in 1994 and played a year of baseball. Michael soon realized that basketball was his passion so he quit baseball and rejoined basketball.

Young Michael did not quit. Back in high school Michael started to play but then the coach cut him from the team. That did not stop him because he continued to play and made it into a college team. Michael Jordan had joined the North Carolina Tar Heels. Later he was drafted to the Chicago Bulls and he played a few seasons there.

Michael could shoot from all around the court and managed to make the winning shot in a championship game. He also broke the single-season scoring record in the whole NBA. Michael led his team to two Olympic titles and five NBA Finals championships.

What inspired me about this young man? He never gave up and had the determination to accomplish his goal. I have loved the sport of basketball. When I was ten I broke my arm and thought it was the end of the world. Luckily for me I read the story of Michael not giving up so that gave me the hope. I wish all people will always have hope and persevere in their dreams.

Jonathan Xu, Grade 6
Challenger School – Ardenwood, CA

Camp Interlaken

I woke up on a Saturday morning very happy. This would be my last day in Madison until I went to Eagle River for a summer camp I had been looking forward to for moths. Camp Interlaken would be the first time away from my parents for two weeks. I needed a break from my crazy house. I was going to live with 10-year-olds!

For my last home-cooked meal, Mom made a fabulous dinner of steak and mashed potatoes. Yum! The next morning, I got up really early, had a quick breakfast, and got all the stuff I needed for camp. My bag was so heavy, I would never be able to carry it myself. I could almost fit in it!

Soon, I was on a really nice bus. Kids were crying and hugging their parents. I was not crying at all, but of course I was hugging my parents. I would really miss them. One girl was so sad she didn't want to go, but she did.

Soon we drove out of the area and sat on the bus for four hours until we reached Camp Interlaken. We walked into a big room and found our cabin mates. It took us a while, but soon we found them all in the back of the room. We introduced ourselves and went off to our cabin. We had the smallest cabin on campus, so unpacking was not easy. This was just the start of an amazing, friend-making two weeks!

Hannah Joseph, Grade 5
Huegel Elementary School, WI

Texans Game

Once I went to the Texans game. My dad takes me to a bunch of football games. We were going against the Colts, they were the champions ever since they won the super bowl.

At first the Texans were winning. Later, we were tied. We had to try. They went for the 3 points it was now 8 to 15. We scored a Touchdown, 14 to 15. Texans got the field goal 16 to 15. Touchdown Colts 16 to 21. Man! We had to win.

Touchdown Texans! I knew we could catch up we were one point ahead. Touchdown Colts 22 to 27. I had faith in the Texans. Colts got the 2 points 22 to 30. Suddenly, it was the 4th Quarter. Texans were 1 Touchdown from winning. We lost, with 10 seconds left. We lost by one touchdown!

We stayed and waited for our friends to come out of the stadium. We almost won the game. We would have won if it wasn't for that last touchdown. I really wanted the Texans to win but we were close to winning at least because it could have been 30 to 0. We played a good game. Who knows, maybe we could win next time. Well good game, right? I hope you thought it was a good game. It was the best game I ever saw in a long time…

Jacob Paz, Grade 5
Bang Elementary School, TX

The Declaration of Independence

One July morning in 1776, in the Pennsylvania State House, a group of political leaders were planning their future and the future of all the Patriots. Britain and the Patriots have been fighting for more than a year. The members of the Second Continental Congress must decide to declare their independence or not. This decision was risky because if they lost the fight with Britain they would be arrested. Britain has been steadily raising taxes and tightening its control over the colonies. In April of 1775, the Patriots started with the battles in Massachusetts in the towns Lexington and Concord. The Second Continental Congress first met in Philadelphia in May of 1775 and began to operate a national government. The government addressed military issues because they had no formal military. George Washington would lead the continental army. Five committee members were asked to make a document that explained why they were at war with Britain. The committee members were John Adams, Roger Sherman, Benjamin Franklin, Robert Livingston, and Thomas Jefferson. When they met they decided that Jefferson should write the Declaration of Independence because he was considered to be a good writer. Jefferson showed his draft to the committee. Adams and Franklin wrote notes and Jefferson added their comments. On June 28, the committee turned in their declaration to the congress. The debate started on the afternoon of July 1. On July 4, the Second Continental Congress approved the Declaration as we know it today.

Daniel Zou, Grade 4
Butterfield School, IL

My Woods

Do you have a special place that you love to be in? Well I do and it's in my own backyard. My favorite place to be is in my woods. It makes me feel hidden and unseen.

The smell of leaves with dew on them and fresh air all around me makes me excited. Green and brown trees rise above me like towers. Tall yellow grasses are great to hide in.

I hear cheerful little birds chirping and singing. The wind blows through narrow branches on the trees and sounds like quiet whispers.

The dead trees that litter the ground make great stools, except the ones covered in rotten mushrooms. I stay for hours in my woods and when I leave, I know I can always come back to my tree covered hide-out.

Madelyn O'Brien, Grade 5
Kimball Elementary School, MN

Memories of My Dad

My dad passed away when I was nine years old. I have preserved many memories of him. I remember when my dad would come home from work and I used to jump into his arms and give him a big hug. At night he used to sing a song to me called "My Little Sunshine" to help me fall asleep. After school, he would pick me up and take me to his work called "U.S.A Computers." He taught me how to put a computer together, take it apart, and put it back together again.

One time I was jumping on my couch and fell on this lamp that had sharp fake metal leaves. I impaled myself, and my dad held me, blood and all! I had stitches inside and out. I still think about him to this day, and sometimes I still even cry. It was hard for my mom to get back on her feet, but she did it, she's so strong! She still sometimes breaks down and cries, and I know that she has a lot to worry about. She has to take care of me, to love and to support, with a full time job.

Rachel Hanson, Grade 6
Linfield Christian School, CA

Responsibility

Responsible means being the one who answers or account for something or being able to be trusted. The most responsible person I know the whole world is my mother. This is because she is responsible for taking care of my family. She does this by working hard to make money for the family, she buys our food and clothes, and cares for us when we are sick.

I show that I am responsible by watching and taking care of my possessions. I also make sure that I am always doing what is right. When someone tells me to do something, I do what I am told.

Finally, being responsible is one thing you will have to do for the rest of your life. You will accomplish many successful things by doing this.

Alexis Camarillo, Grade 5
Covington Elementary School, NE

Water Park

One hot summer in Louisiana my brother and I were there including our mom. We were sitting on the water hose. It was really hard. It would splash on your head, and hurt. But it was fun. After awhile I felt something in my toe. It was a blister, it didn't hurt, also it didn't come out so I just kept playing.

I was watching my brother Marcus after I sat down next to my mom.

One hour later I started to play again. But this time I almost slipped because it was more slippery than last time, other than that I was perfectly fine.

After a while people started to go home, but not us. We stayed because we didn't go to school until one year. Anyway me and Marcus kept on playing it was a blast!

It was getting dark, but we still weren't tired. But it was time for us to go home, it took a while to get dried. Then we got in the car and drove all the way home. It was a long long way to get home.

Then finally we made it to Houston from Louisiana. But it took four hours to get home, so we went to sleep again. When we got home we had to change and then eat. Then we had to go to bed. But that's not all check out my next story "Skate City in Louisiana." See ya next time!

Shayla Harbor, Grade 5
Bang Elementary School, TX

The J. O. Journey

This is a story about how I conquered my fears, and you can too. I am a martial artist, but didn't like to spar even though I get to wear tons of protective gear.

Last year my older brother Zach sparred in Junior Olympics and it looked really cool. So I wanted to do it. J.O.'s is when martial artists from around the country compete against each other. I decided to try it, but figured out that it was a lot harder than I thought.

It was time for the qualifying tournament in Kansas City. I lost when I sparred, but still got a silver medal because my division was small. I wasn't scared at Kansas City because it was a small tournament and I knew I could qualify.

This is how my story ends. When my training had ended, it was time for the very big tournament. It came time for sparring and I was so scared I cried until I couldn't cry anymore. I prayed and my coaches and teammates got me through. Although I sparred very well and lost, I still felt like I had won on the inside.

I found my strength from God and my inspiration from my teammates and coaches. So remember, if you're scared, have faith and you will succeed. Just draw strength from those close to you. You are special and can win. So if you have a fear, face it head on and you will conquer it. I know, I did.

Christian DiSalvo, Grade 5
Shepherd of the Hills Christian School, CO

One Brave Day

The day my family and I went to Cedar Point I was scared out of my mind. All of those huge roller coasters that I knew I had to go on were freaking me out. This was going to be the ride of my life.

We got in line for Top Thrill Dragster, the second tallest roller coaster in the world. The wait in line was even scarier because I was thinking about how high and fast it went. It shoots up straight at one hundred and twenty miles per hour in two seconds. After the ride was over, I decided it wasn't very scary.

My first upside-down roller coaster was Millennium Force. The one bad part was going slowly up this gigantic hill, but when it was over I thought it was fun. When I got off the ride, I could not believe I had just done that. My mom and I were extremely proud.

When we had to leave, I was sad, because I wanted to have more fun. I had done every ride except one that the adults did. I couldn't believe I had missed out on upside-down roller coasters before I went to Cedar Point.

The next time I go to an amusement park I will not be afraid of anything. The more I don't do, the less fun I have, is the motto I use now. Remember, being brave is hard, but it is wonderful.

Kaitlin Powers, Grade 6
Southport 6th Grade Academy, IN

My Family

I have five people in my family and I will talk about them all. I have a brother, a sister, a mom, a dad, and me!

The first one is my sister. Her name is Mallory Christine Ehlinger, and she is eight months old. Her birthday is January 18, 2007. She is very chubby. She is heavier than my 10 month old cousin! She is cute, even though she is chubby like I said she was.

The second one is my brother. His name is Cyle James Ehlinger, and he is two years old. His birthday is February 26, 2005. He is tall for his age. He looks like he is five, but he is not. We're trying to potty train him and teach him how to talk at the same time. It's very hard.

The third one is my mom. Her name is Maria Estelle Ehlinger, and she is twenty-eight years old. She is not my biological mother; she is my step mom. She is very tall and skinny. She is the biological mother of my brother and sister.

The fourth one is my dad. His name is Dustin Corey Ehlinger, and he's twenty-eight years old. My step mom and everyone else calls him Corey because he doesn't like his first name.

The last one is me. My name is Alexis Nicole Ehlinger and I'm nine years old. My nickname is "Lex." When I was little, people used to call me Shorty; I still am kind of short but the brains are all that matter. I got those from my dad!

Those are all of my family members and I am of course the oldest one out of the bunch. I know they look up to me but I don't mind. That's the role of being a big sister!

Alexis Ehlinger, Grade 5
Desert Trails Elementary School, CA

Don't Play with Fire

I remember a time last year when I was playing with fire at my house because my mom and my family had gone to the beach without me and I was at home with my sister. I was in my room. I had some toilet paper, some water, and a lighter. I lit the toilet paper and I had poured some water on it to put it out. Then I did it three more times, then my momma, my sister, and Reggie came home. My momma smelled smoke and ran upstairs and looked behind the blind and saw burnt paper and I got grounded for a week, and if I wanted to go outside I had to stay in the yard. The lesson I learned was never play with fire.

Willie Jackson, Grade 5
McMonagle Elementary School, MI

A Life Without Violence

A life without violence is better than a life with violence because you stop hearing guns going off wondering if someone was getting shot at or if someone got shot.

I want to know how violence came to the world? How violence came to be? Who made up violence? I want to know everything about it. I wish violence wasn't even a word. I wish the word was violence free. I wish we didn't have to wonder if they were going to die or live every day. I wish they didn't have to wonder if they're going to die.

I wish people could live their life without going to jail for killing someone. I wish people could live their lives freely and not have to wonder when their loved ones are getting home, wondering if they'll ever see them again. Why can't the world be violence free, why do we have to have violence? Every day when I pray, that God watches over me and my family, keeps us safe from hurt, harm and danger. I just wish the world was violence free.

Rolonda Polidore, Grade 6
DeQueen Elementary School, TX

The Coolest Dad

My father started motorcycling at the age of 14. He raced TT and flat-track. His father owned a motorcycle shop in the late 50's and early 60's. My dad raced at the Owyhee Motorcycle Club. When he was young, he raced in Idaho at Pocatello, Idaho Falls, and Mountain Home. As he got older, he developed skills. Every year he competed in the Owyhee Club's national race. He raced at the amateur level until he was old enough to go professional. In 1969, he moved to Longview, Washington. While living there, he rode for Kawasaki Motors. My dad raced in Oregon and Washington. He became 2nd in the nation in the amateur class. Ike Reed was first at that time.

After that he turned professional and rode for Triumph Motorcycles. He raced all over California, including at Ascot Speedway. But in order to compete with the top ten racers, you had to travel the country and he didn't have enough money. He still managed to place 13th in the nation in TT and flat-track.

Alex Lawrence, Grade 6
Thomas Jefferson Charter School, ID

Who I Admire

Who do you admire? The person that I admire is my older sister Brenda. I admire my sister because she is truthful. For example, one day we were playing ball inside the house. When she threw the tennis ball it hit the lamp. It wobbled on the table until it fell. My mom came and furiously asked who hit the lamp. My big sister told the truth and said that she did it.

In addition, I admire my sister because she is very kind. One day I was trying to teach myself how to ride a bike. I kept falling, falling, and falling every time I got on. I was about to give up. My sister came and told me never to give up. So I got back on the emerald green bike, rode it, and I wasn't falling! So now, thanks to my sister, I know how to ride my new luminous blue bicycle.

Another reason I admire my older sister is because she is smart. She gets pure A's and B's on her report cards. Sometimes she helps me with my homework. She even teaches me things I never knew about.

The last reason I admire my sister is because she is fun. Whenever I have nothing to do she starts to play with me. That's why I admire my older sister.

Daniela Sandoval, Grade 5
Camellia Avenue Elementary School, CA

My Emergency Disaster Plan

My disaster plan would be for an earthquake, house flood, flash flood, tornado, and a twister like getting under the table for an earthquake. Jumping out the window or getting in the basement for a tornado or twister.

In my supplies I will have a flash light, lighters, band aids, medicine, alcohol. Also talking about where my escape route meeting place.

My emergency supply kits would have band aids, shots, medicine, casts, batteries and flash lights. I would keep each supply and discuss with my parents so the emergency kit can be in every bathroom, closet and car. Just in case if they're taking a shower and getting dressed or riding in the car. Another supply is a box of clothes. Also a gallon of water and boxes of food.

My escape route would be a door or a window because my house is full of windows. In case of a fire I can get outside by jumping out the window or out the door.

Also my meeting place would be at Liberty Park because members of my family live near there and the fire station's near there so I can go there. I would go there for 20 minutes and then run to the fire station or to a family member's house.

These are the things I would do and get for any type of an emergency, but maybe for a tsunami or hurricane it would be different because you can't really do anything about that.

Marc De La Torre, Grade 5
Liberty Elementary School, CA

The Meaning of Friendship

FRIENDSHIP. A word with a meaning so powerful, that it can save some, but rip some apart.

Friends can tear people apart, make them ache for days, even months. Friends can be nasty, wicked and drag you down to the pit of despair, make you feel like dying. Friends can be hidden as nice, good-natured people, but in the end they turn out to be wicked monsters. I once knew two girls and I thought that they were my friends, but in the end, they wrote me a cruel note.

Friends can be trusted in, and help you with your worst nightmares, boost you up when others are against you. I have a best friend, and she has helped me through everything imaginable. Last year when the girls wrote me that note, I knew that I could tell her what happened, and she would support me.

Friendship is what holds us together, the world together. It is a beautiful thing, and at the same time, it is a hardship that we go through. It is a terrible thunderstorm, but at the same time, it is a calm, sunny day at the beach. It is our friend, for without it, we would all surely perish.

"A friend is one who walks in when others walk out."— Walter Winchell

"Everyone is a friend, unless they prove otherwise."— Steve

Lily Kay Gabriel, Grade 6
Spring Creek Elementary School, WY

Don't Forget to Say I Love You!

I remember that summer very well when my cousin Danny got very sick. All his life, he struggled being handicapped, but it was last summer when it got worse. I remember when my mom said Danny wasn't doing well. I was very scared but I kept on praying. It was a month later when it got so bad that the doctors wanted to cut off his oxygen. My Uncle Jim said NO! After awhile, he got better, but he wasn't well enough to go home, so he stayed in the hospital. Three weeks later, he got real sick again. He was worse than ever before. He could even die any day. The whole family went to the hospital.

A few days later we heard the bad news, Danny died, but he didn't die on his own. My Uncle Jim was rocking him and decided it was time to let him go. At the funeral, my cousin sang for him. She wrote a song how he would be happy in Heaven.

I remember when I would walk by his room and he was sleeping in his bed. I always said "Hi Danny," or "Feel better," but I never said "I love you." It made me feel bad because he will never get to hear me say "I love you." Be thankful of the people you have while you have them, and most important don't forget to say, "I love you."

Rachelle Weyerbacher, Grade 5
Kinsey School, MT

A Russian Princess

You may ask who she is, where's she from, and is she dead? Well I will tell you that in the following below. Anastasia was born on June, 18, 1901. She is the youngest of all her brothers and sisters. Anastasia has 1 brother and 3 sisters. Her brother's name is Alexei Nikolalevitch and Anastasia's sisters' names are Grand Duchess Ogla, Grand Duchess Tatlana, and Grand Duchess Maria. Anastasia's parents name's are Nicholas the second of Russia and Alexandra Fyodorovna. They lived a happy life for a long time until the Bolshevik execution. They killed Anastasias family. People say Anastasia and one of her sisters escaped the execution. One person named Anna Anderson is the most famous person to claim she was Anastasia. Anna was found in a hospital with only cuts and bruises. She says she lost her memory. Anna lived, talked, and acted like Anastasia would have. Some people say they've seen a resemblance between the two (in their pictures.). People say Anna was really insane. Medical reports said that they took the DNA off of Anna's and Anastasia's bones but, they weren't a match! Some people say it's impossible for her to escape the execution with only a few cuts and bruises. I think it probably is possible for her to escape with only a couple wounds.

Unfortunately Anastasia was only 17 when she was said to have died. Could it be possible that Anna Andersen is really Anastasia? Scientists are still trying to solve this mystery. Could it stay a mystery? Who knows? Maybe.

Selina Andersen, Grade 5
Dr F D Sinclair Elementary School, BC

Lady Sophia

Lady Sophia is the best dog in the whole world. She's supposed to be my brother's dog and mine, but prefers my parents instead. Yet she still is my baby doll.

We got her from a Schnauzer Breeder last Christmas here in Miles City. Her fur coat is a salt and pepper color. The breeder sold Sophie's parents, she got new brothers and sisters! They are so cute!

The one thing in the world she must have, is her clothes. Because in the mornings, she gets really cold. It is almost winter and my mom shaved her skirt so she gets really cold. And with one of her robes that has a turtle on it my mom got her matching turtle slippers! They are so cute! She has a bikini she wears for contests. She won a trophy for hottest dog!

She also knows some tricks too. And all the tricks she knows I taught her. She knows sit, come, and stay. Then there is this one trick I started with her to where she won't eat from the dogcatcher. It is so hilarious! She is the best dog I have ever had out of the two we used to have.

Hailey Smith, Grade 6
Kinsey School, MT

Cheerleading

There are many fun and interesting facts about cheerleading. There is everything from cheers and chants to competitions and so much more. There is a lot more to cheerleading than meets the eye.

Cheerleading chants and cheers are a big part of cheerleading. Ways to keep your voice in tiptop shape are to drink lots of water, warming up your voice before you cheer, and cheerleading while you are exhaling. Cheerleaders yell chants and cheers to encourage the crowd and the team if they are winning or losing.

Cheerleaders wear the same uniforms throughout that certain squad. Most squads also have matching pompoms and when they go to competitions, they usually do their hair and make-up the same way. It is important that cheerleaders look the same so they appear as one.

Before you start cheerleading there are different stretches you need to do so you don't strain or pull a muscle. Here are some good stretches to do before you start. You can do the middle or right and left leg splits. Another good stretch is the bridge but make sure you roll your wrists and ankles first. My favorite stretch is the arm circles, either forward or backwards.

Cheerleading has a competitive side too. Cheerleading squads around the world compete in competitions. Cheerleaders work in their spare time to perfect their routines and on their tumbling to get ready for competitions. So really cheerleading is more than meets the eye.

Maddie Stewart, Grade 5
Concord Ox Bow Elementary School, IN

The Healer

Why does Jennifer Logan inspire me? Jennifer Logan is an average high school girl. One day she was watching a show about Africa and how people are suffering. She sat on her bed that night and just thought of how she would have felt in that position, not going to school, or never having seen a pencil before. After about twenty minutes she got the idea that she would send all her money to Africa. Today she has a million dollar company called Join the Tree and she got a chance to meet Bill Clinton and Oprah Winfrey. When she was on the Oprah show a man generously donated half a million dollars to Join the Tree. However the man wanted to remain anonymous. She has also got her whole school in on the act. She is not too big yet but I know she will be. To follow her example I will do my best to help anyone and everyone. I will also try raising money to help the homeless. I want to be just like her and help our environment and all that inhabit it. I hope now you understand why Jennifer is my source of inspiration and I hope you can see what kind of person I am as well.

Parinaaz Boparai, Grade 6
Challenger School – Ardenwood, CA

Teamwork

Have you ever helped someone before? Well if you have you probably did a little teamwork. First of all, teamwork is the work or activity of a number of persons acting together as a team. For example, if you help a neighbor with a project or chore, that is teamwork. My football team showed teamwork when we beat a team called Lawton. We showed teamwork by getting those tackles and touchdowns. If we wouldn't have used teamwork we would not have won our game. Another example in history showing teamwork was when Lewis and Clark went on their big expedition. Native Americans helped the expedition out by trading with them, and feeding the men. They all had teamwork in helping each other out. This shows that there is teamwork going on in the world and has been for a long time.

Last but not least, if you see someone that needs help, just go up and give them a hand. Think of how wonderful you would feel helping them out.

Certainly you can see many people to this day use a lot of teamwork all the time.

Nolan Nelson, Grade 5
Covington Elementary School, NE

Molly and Me Forever!

Molly, one of my best friends, is my hero!

Who's Molly? Molly is the family's attractive dog. She is a Border Collie mix. Her coat is all black except for a white chest. She's loyal, protective, and brave. Once she scared away a thief. I found my window screen slit open. Somebody tried to break in my room and Molly probably barked to get our attention. So the thief turned and ran.

She also scared away my ex-friend. We were gone and a girl went past the NO TRESPASSING sign and over the fence. Molly ran and bit her kneecap. By the way, she knew we were gone. The girl was sent to the hospital and Molly was put in the garage to see if she had rabies.

Molly is definitely MY HERO.

Jenna Frisch, Grade 5
Nisley Elementary School, CO

The Big Splash

I was walking home one day when I got a phone call. It was my mom calling, to tell me to cook dinner. That's when it all happened. I got home, and I took out a pan. Then I started to cook dinner. My friend called and distracted me. When I went back to the kitchen, the noodles were boiling over. The water was coming over the top, noodles were all over the floor, and the flames were sizzling.

I got a mop to clean it up. I started to clean up the water when my mom called again. She said she'd be home soon. I finished cooking dinner and cleaning everything up. She never found out that it happened. There was only one downfall. The carpet was completely soaked. I'm still a free man luckily, but she always wondered why the carpet was so wet.

Tye Ehlers, Grade 6
Monforton School, MT

Chihuahuas

The characteristic of Chihuahua is a very individualistic breed. They each have their own unique personality, so only a few generalizations can be made. They are commonly referred to as a "Chi." They are energetic, graceful, and display a human-like expression. Their life span is the longest of any size dog.

The Chihuahua is the smallest of all breeds and has the distinction of being the oldest breed in America. They were named after the Chihuahua region in Mexico. It is believed that this breed descended from an ancient breed that was larger in size and highly prized by Aztec royalty. The Chihuahua of today has a very fine bone structure.

The Chihuahua is deeply devoted and fiercely loyal. They typically become extremely attached to one or two people. They are bold, fearless, and highly protective of their masters. They thrive on a lot of amounts of attention. The Chihuahua is by nature, gentle, loving, and sweet-tempered. They are wary of strangers and make excellent watchdogs. This breed is not well suited for children or other pets. However, they are sociable with their own kind. Chihuahuas are excellent companions in the right circumstances when needed.

Alan Millan, Grade 6
Isbell Middle School, CA

Most Feared Sharks

There are many varieties of sharks that range from non-threatening to man-eating. The Great White Shark is most feared by humans and most threatening to many creatures. The Great White on average is 12-16 feet, but can grow to over 22 feet, and weigh over 7,000 pounds. It can have as many as 3,000 teeth that can grow to 3 inches in length. Old or broken teeth are replaced by a row of new teeth. It eats seals, sea lions, dolphins, big bony fish, and even penguins. They do not usually attack humans, though they are known to be man-eaters.

The second most dangerous shark to humans is the Tiger Shark. Tiger Sharks are as long as 20 feet and can live up to 30-40 years. They have a very strong, large mouth, and powerful jaws. Their teeth are triangle-like with saw-like edges that can slice through any object. Tiger Sharks have very good eyesight which allows them to often hunt their prey at night.

The Bull Shark is in third place for being the most dangerous to humans. Bull Sharks live near or in coastal areas, but are also found in rivers and freshwater lakes. Every season they are known to travel from the upper Amazon River to the sea, which is a distance of 2,300 miles. Bull Sharks can grow up to 11.5 feet, females are longer in size than males. They have a life expectancy of up to 14 years.

Brandon Nylen, Grade 5
Dishman Elementary School, TX

The Triceratops

The Triceratops was a plant eater. Triceratops could chew with their cheek teeth unlike most dinosaurs (dino). Triceratops were hunted and eaten by Tyrannosaurus Rex (T. Rex). Triceratops walked on four short legs and was very slow. many fossils have been found, mostly in western Canada and the United States. There was a fossil that was accidentally identified as an extinct buffalo. About fifty Triceratops skulls have been found and some partial skeletons. Triceratops was a rhino-like dino. It walked on four strong legs and had three horns on its face. It had a big bony plate, one little horn on its mouth, and two by its eyes which probably kept it safe from predators. It also had a huge skull that was ten ft. long, ten ft wide, and weighed up to six to twelve tons. It had a small tail and it was immense. It lived in the late Cretaceous period almost 72-65 million years ago. When threatened by another animal it might have charged the threatening animal for its safety. The Triceratops' mind was probably very intermediate — in other words it was stupid.

Christy Sue Anderson, Grade 6

Is It a Good Idea to Do Good Deeds to Remember 9/11?

I think it is a good idea to do good deeds to remember 9/11. I think we should do good deeds to remember 9/11 because it's very sad because so many people died.

I think some good ideas to remember 9/11 are by helping other people and maybe donating money so we could rebuild the Twin Towers and make them nice again. A lot of police and firemen died saving people and that's why I think police and firemen should get a lot of respect.

Jared Marsden, Grade 5
Snake River Montessori School, ID

My Dog Shang

I walked into the living room. There lying before me was a dead cockroach. I was in my house, and before my feet was my new Pekingese puppy, Shang. He had rolled over on his back and was acting like a dead cockroach. Shang is playful, but calm. I love Shang a lot.

Shang is a very playful puppy. When I get home from school, every day he jumps on me and makes me pet him. When I pet him, he makes me pet his belly. When I try to pet his back, he nips at me. Every morning when I go to school, Shang wants me to pet him. When I don't, he barks at me. If I don't respond to barking, Shang will jump on me. I will be branded with hair from Shang.

Shang can be calm and sweet, though. After we are done playing, Shang always snuggles up with me. He lets me hold him and pet him. Sometimes when I don't want to sleep on my bed because my stomach hurts, he comes and licks my face. Finally, when I am tired, he goes to sleep next to me.

Shang is an excellent dog to have. He's playful and sweet. I know I will have more dogs in time, but I know Shang will always be one of my favorites. Shang is the best dog.

Marrissa Morrisseau, Grade 5
Joseph M Simas Elementary School, CA

Good Deeds

A lot of people wonder if what they did was a good deed or not. A good deed is something somebody does that maybe will help somebody or something else. It's not a good deed to throw your trash on the ground because it will help create global warming.

It is a good deed, though, to pick up trash that somebody else threw out and to recycle. If you pick up trash it helps not only global warming but also the animals all around the world. If you do a deed it could make a BIG DIFFERENCE!

Even if you pick up a small piece of trash maybe the person who would have stepped in it, will not, because you threw it out. That is what a good deed is.

Cooper Sailer, Grade 6
Snake River Montessori School, ID

Honesty

Honesty is a special value important in all of our lives. Honestly is being truthful and never lying.

There are many other words that mean the same. First is being fair. If you have a friend and there is only one cookie, you can split it and that's being fair. Another word related to honesty is being truthful. This is never lying to your friends, family, or teacher. Being open is also being honest. You would never steal or cheat a friend or be mean to them.

I can show honesty in many ways, at home, school or in my community. To begin with I don't litter and follow the laws, like wearing my seat belt. At school I respect others' property and do my own work, even when it is hard. At home it is important to be honest to my parents. I tell them what I am doing or where I am going.

These are some things about honesty. What does it mean to you?

Joanna Soto, Grade 5
Covington Elementary School, NE

A Biography of Harriet Tubman

Harriet Tubman was a strong girl growing up in slavery. She was born in 1819 or 1820 in Maryland. At around the age of 5 she started to work. At night she heard her parents talking about how some people were free up north. When she was 12 she was blocking a runaway slave when his master threw a block of lead at the slave. Instead it hit Harriet and she got a wound in her head.

When she was 25 years old she married John Tubman, a free African American. When she told him that she wanted to go up north to be free he said, "I will not go and I will tell your master." One night, though, she started to go north with her two brothers but she did not go far before they went back. She did not tell her father because he never told a lie so if her master asked, "Do you know where Harriet is?" he could honestly tell him he did not know. She did go up again by herself and followed the North Star. She got up to Canada using the Underground Railroad. After doing that and getting up north she helped over 300 slaves to be free.

Stella Crall, Grade 5
Santa Catalina School, CA

Animals in Need

Think of how many dogs and cats are in animal shelters. These animals are having to be put down every day.

If you have spare money you could donate some to your local shelter. It would help the caretakers buy food and beds for the animals. Pennies and nickels that you find around the house helps. If you happen to have cat or dog food you're not using, donate it, along with no longer used beds and toys.

Some of the reasons dogs and cats are in animal shelters is because their owners don't keep track of them. I've seen poor dogs wandering around on streets without a collar. Some starve because they can't find food. If your dog can jump over the fence in your yard, put up an electric fence. Please don't let your animals wander around loose.

If you've never had a cat or dog, think about adopting one. Some people are clean freaks (take me for instance), but getting an animal wouldn't hurt. Think about adopting an animal, they are really special.

So please help the animals in need.

Amelia Yarborough, Grade 6
Round Valley Elementary School, CA

Towi

I have a dog named Towi. He is a toy poodle. He is funny, silly, cute, and sometimes annoying. He's also little, but tough. My dog is four years old, which means he's twenty-eight in dog years. He's going to turn five on September 27, 2007.

My dog can do only four tricks. He can jump, stand, sit, and spin around while jumping. Every time he does a trick, I give him a doggy treat.

Towi's favorite doggy treats are chicken sticks, beef flavor jerky strips, and Beneful. He also likes eating bones, cookies that look like bones, cookies with a picture of a toothbrush, mozzarella string cheese, and Kraft cheese.

Towi is a naughty dog. He almost runs away when my grandma opens the door to take out the garbage bins. Towi either runs away to the end of the block, or to the park across the street. When he comes back from wherever he came from, my grandma shouts at him, but he just wags his tail at her, thinking it's all a game.

When Towi first came to my house on Christmas morning, I was really happy! My dream had come true! I had always wanted a puppy. When he came, the first thing he did was chase me around the house. My sister was afraid of him so she climbed up a chair. We told her that he wouldn't bite her, because she was afraid that he would.

The first night he stayed with us, he had to sleep with me in my bed. When he came on my bed, he saw my stuffed dog and started playing with it. From that day on, that dog was his. That was his first Christmas present from me to him!

Monica Lazo, Grade 6
Corpus Christi School, CA

Four-Wheeling with My Cousins

My cousins and I have had a lot of awesome times together. Like when we went to a place called Sun Ridge. It is where you can ride four wheelers, it is so cool. My older cousin taught me how to drive the black four wheeler. I like going very fast. When you go fast it gets kind of hard to turn that's why I like riding down straight paths so I can go as fast as I want.

Before I learned how to ride a four wheeler I would ride on the back of my grandpa's white four wheeler. I think the white one is more fun though because it goes like five thousand seven hundred sixty two miles per hour, no just kidding, it goes about one hundred miles per hour. The black four wheeler only goes about negative fifty two thousand miles per hour; kidding again, it only goes about fifty miles per hour. It is still fun to free ride in but if you want to race you should definitely use the white one because it is the second fastest one they have. The fastest one they have is the red one. I can't ride it yet, but when I go up there again I definitely want to learn how. I enjoy spending time with my cousins and riding four wheelers.

Kyler Bender, Grade 4
Gateway Pointe Elementary School, AZ

Listen to Your Parents

One hot day on August 16, 2007, I went to work with my mom because I did not want to go home. My mom was talking to her friend Lisa. She was talking about my new school. I was annoying her so she told me to go play in traffic. So I yelled "Okay" then my mom yelled "Zachary, come back here," but I did not listen. I was like the chicken crossing the road, and I almost got hit! And I got in big, big trouble. The lesson I learned was listen to your mom.

Zachary McCuaig, Grade 5
McMonagle Elementary School, MI

Music and Me

There are several reasons why I love to sing. The first reason is that I hear my sister on her clarinet playing in the house. The second reason is that I just love to sing. Also, whenever I sing, I also dance around the house.

I love to hear my sister on her clarinet. Her clarinet is a black instrument about 2 1/2 feet long. It is like a recorder except it has reeds and buttons. My sister practices every day after school. I love to hear her play.

I just love to sing. I can sing for hours and I know lots of songs. My favorite songs are the ones that I hear my mom humming. When I hear them, they get stuck in my head and I just want to sing them.

I also dance around the house all the time. Whenever I hear music, I just start dancing and singing along. Sometimes people complain that I am being too loud, but I just can't stop myself. Singing makes me want to dance around the house.

Those are the reasons why I love to sing!

Kamryn Turley, Grade 4
Gateway Pointe Elementary School, AZ

My Eighth Birthday Party

My eighth birthday party was the most memorable birthday, because it was my last birthday with my mom. The morning of my birthday, my mom and I were preparing for the party. We ate breakfast and started decorating the room and cooking food. My mom prepared different dishes such as spinach chicken, goat meat, salad, rice, Indian bread, and bought Indian sweets. My mom's friend bought a cake that said, "Happy Birthday, Girima!!!" with roses all around it and sprinkled nuts on the sides. My mom's other friend brought CDs and a table for the cake to be placed on when we were going to cut it. I blew lots of balloons and my mom helped me put them around the room. My mom invited her friends while I went to my friends' apartments to invite them. While I was gone, my mom ironed our clothes and took a bath. When I got back, I took a bath and put on my pink Indian dress which was a skirt, top, and shawl. The next thing we noticed, it was 5:00!! Time for my party! My party was in my apartment in Los Angeles, CA. All my friends were there and I was in a room full of people that loved and cared about me. My mom, my mom's friends, my friends and their families were all there. We talked, ate, danced, and had fun! It was the best party and I'll never forget it!

Girima Bhalla, Grade 4
Fleming Public School, ON

Don't Do Drugs

Hey, are you doing drugs? If you are STOP. If you're not, well that's really cool.

Doing drugs or smoking can cause damage to your body.

If you smoke, please stop. Smoking can cause lung problems and very bad things can happen. You can even die.

If you use tobacco, please stop. Tobacco can cause brain damage, lung damage, mouth and throat cancer and can even cause your body to shut down.

The last thing I am asking you not to do is drink alcohol. Please stop if you are drinking and driving. Alcohol is a type of poison. It causes liver damage, brain damage, and can cause your body to shut down completely. A lot of people die every year because of drinking and driving.

There are many ways to say "NO" to drugs. If a stranger gives you candy, don't eat it. It might be a drug. If a stranger asks you to smoke, say "NO." If a stranger asks you if you want some pills, say "NO." You do not want to die.

If you don't do drugs you are cool. If you do, boo to you!

Never think that drugs will help you in life. Because they won't and they never will.

All I am trying to tell you is don't do drugs. And if anyone asks you to do them, just say "NO."

Don't do drugs, because you are not only hurting yourself, you are hurting everyone around you.

Jessica McNelly, Grade 5
Oak Crest Intermediate School, TX

Me and the Amazing Things I Do

I'm Morgan Burkhart. I am an athlete, gymnast, love to run and my hobbies are playing softball and basketball. I am an athlete because I usually play sports like most athletes do but also instead of sports I am a gymnast and I trampoline too. At McNair Elementary School in Winnebago, Illinois we have to run a mile at school that is where we have to run four laps around 4 cones spread out far — far away from each other in the shape of a square or we have to run around the Winnebago High School and Middle School track in the shape of an oval.

One of my hobbies is softball because my mom loves it and played it all her life and I love it to and particularly played it all my life so far too. Our family together all go around the states to what is called a tractor pull. It is when we have a big tractor called Git-R-Done. It is named that because my dad Scott Burkhart likes a comedy guy called Larry the Cable Guy. When you tractor pull it is where you take a big tractor, hook the back of the tractor up to what is called the Terminator or can be called many other names too.

My teacher this year is Mrs. Lehne. She is the best teacher ever. The amazing things I do are *fun and crazy*. I love them.

Morgan Burkhart, Grade 5
Jean McNair Elementary School, IL

Help Save the Trees

My name is Elli Sanchez, and I think we shouldn't cut down so many trees. Also, we should be more careful with tree-made items.

My first reason we should conserve trees is we don't even need to use so much paper. We certainly don't need to waste as much paper as we do. We should put more paper in the recycling bin so we don't waste trees.

My second reason we should conserve trees is that the trees give us oxygen, and if we waste all of the trees we could die because we wouldn't have enough oxygen to breathe.

My third reason we should conserve trees is that we don't want to waste such a beautiful part of nature. Animals or insects might live in the forest, as well as many other animals.

My fourth reason to conserve trees is we grow these wonderful plants for many reasons. Just think how beautiful the world looked before we cut down so many trees. I know we need to cut trees down, but I think we should cut down less. I also think if we cut down trees, we should cut down trees that grow faster. That way we can replant those trees, and they will grow back more quickly.

I don't want people to feel bad about using a lot of paper. I want people to think about what they are doing before they waste or throw away so much paper. Thanks.

Elli Sanchez, Grade 4
Lincoln Elementary School, WA

Muddy Madness

Yesterday I washed my pants until they were perfectly white, but when I came home it was a whole different story. At my football practice it was massively muddy so when I heard a "splat!" it wasn't a good sign. I like to get muddy so it wasn't a big deal until I got hit by a mud ball. I could feel the soggy goo running down my back. My team scrimmaged the Oakwood team and we beat them twenty-eight to zero and everybody got down in the mud. So when I got home my pants were pitch black! Not even one white spot on them! My mom screamed, "What in the world happened?" All I mumbled was oops. A while after that my mom said, "Do you want some brownies? Brandon made them." Once I saw the brownies, I thought of that foul taste of mud in my mouth and I yelled NO!

Brett Alan Smith, Grade 5
Greenwood Elementary School, MN

My Boy Rocky!

There he is in my back yard, he's all mine and my best friend. Can you guess who he is? He's my horse Rocky. Rocky My Boy is what I call him. He's a dirty chocolate palomino with a mangy mane and scars, but that's ok because I love him anyway. People don't think he's the prettiest horse in the world but I do.

I have owned Rocky for a year and a half and it's been great, I've been training him for a long time. He used to be one of my mom's client's horse. The first time they brought him over was when my mom was going to train him for her client Jay's oldest daughter. When I saw him it was love at first sight. After a few months, I was able to ride Rocky while my mom was training him. After Jay saw how much we all loved him, he sold Rocky to us for $800.00. I was so happy that I finally had my own horse that I could love and take care of. I will always love, My Boy Rocky!

Kylee Wyant, Grade 6
Thomas Jefferson Charter School, ID

Tazz the "Fat" Cat

Tazz is a fat cat. Tazz lives with my sister Chelsey, my dad, and my grandma. He follows me everywhere I go, except when I go back to my regular home. When I'm at my dad's house and I don't pay any attention, Tazz gets on his hind legs and begs for attention.

Tazz is important to me because he won't come to anyone else, but me. Tazz is probably the fattest cat in Illinois. He is also important to me because my dad found him in Oquawka, IL, at Delabar Park. So, he brought him home, now Tazz and I are best friends. Tazz used to be very skinny. Now he's really chubby, because he's ten pounds.

In conclusion, Tazz is fat and happy cat, that loves to be petted. He also has a nice family that loves him a lot. Tazz is always happy and any time you're sad he'll cheer you up. He loves anyone that comes into our house. Tazz is fat, happy, and cute. I'm happy my dad found him.

Ashley Carnes, Grade 6
West Central Middle School, IL

All I Know About Archimedes

Archimedes was the smartest person I know. He wrote things that you can't understand. He wrote things that would have sent astronauts to Mars by now, but he is gone now. He was born a long time ago in around 212 B.C. When we was fifty years old, he wrote a lot of fascinating things that would have sent us to another planet by now (Mars, Jupiter, Mercury). He was the smartest of them all, but he died.

He attended school at Alexandria. His mathematical contributions are still used to this day. He is also known for inventing the catapult. It helped the Romans fight wars and conquer countries. Archimedes was also known for his work in geometry and astronomy. His father was an astronomer. Archimedes wanted to follow his father's footsteps.

Another remarkable work of his was a sandreckoner. That is where he starts a number system capable of expressing numbers up to 8 x 1016. He says this method can help count all the grains of sand in the world.

One day he was working in his house, and a soldier came to his house and murdered him. He was only seventy years old when he died. He counted how many grains of sand it would take to cover the world. I think it was .000013 of the grains of sand it took to cover the world. His famous words were, "Don't disturb my circles."

Arslan Bhatti, Grade 5

How the Color Gray Makes Me Feel

Gray is not one of my favorite colors. Whenever I see the color gray, I can feel downright bored. Gray is a very depressing color to me.

On rainy days, there is the color gray everywhere. Gray clouds come in overhead, and I just know something bad is going to happen. When the gray clouds hang for awhile, it starts to rain, and then it pours. A thunderstorm approaches and then I can get very scared.

Sometimes I dislike the color gray even more, especially when it comes to sports. In sports, there is one team that has obvious gray in their uniforms. The team with the color gray in their uniforms is my favorite sports team's rival. In sports, I detest the color gray!

Sometimes the color gray can make me change my plans. I'll do nothing on gray days. I'll just sit in bed on weekends, but when I go to school, I tend to sit there and daydream. Gray is such a boring, spiritless color. It sometimes even affects how I do in school.

Whenever gray overwhelms me, I seem to not care about anything. It can even spoil my day. Whenever it ruins my day, that is discouraging. On weekends, the color gray can ruin my plans.

On a scale from one to ten, the color gray scores a perfect zero to me, in terms of excitement.

Luis Wright, Grade 6
Corpus Christi School, CA

How I Met Mary

A long time ago I was walking and I accidentally ran into Mary. I said: I'm so sorry. She said: I forgive you. Then after that we went to go get some hot chocolate. After that I asked: Do you want to come over to my house? She said: sure for a little while because I have to get ready for tomorrow. I said: okay at least you can come over. We got home we had grapes, salad, and a sandwich. She said to me: That was great. I said bye and she said bye back. So I went to my room and I took a shower and went to bed.

Cynthia Ibarra, Grade 4
St Luke Catholic School, TX

Entering Your Imagination

Where I really like to go is my mind. My mind is a wonderful place where I can think whatever I want.

What I can do in my mind is unlimited. I can imagine Pokemon like Blaziken and Turtwig to battle with. I would also think about my mom because I loved her so much.

I also think about what to do in a video game. In Halo 3, for example, I would choose if I would want to snipe my enemy, stick him with a plasma grenade, or assassinate them in the back with an energy sword.

You basically can think of whatever you want, Pokemon, video games, etc. Without a mind, you are nothing.

Think about a test, you need the mind to think of the answers, but you can't get the answers if your mind is in la-la land. Essays are also things you need to focus on.

A mind is an imaginary world you can go into almost anytime you want.

In conclusion, think about whatever you want.

Zachary Trumbaturi, Grade 6
North Oaks Middle School, TX

My Good Deed

I got out of the car. I had just gotten back from football. What I saw was bad. There were only a few places of visible grass because garbage had covered the whole yard.

Someone's trash can had tipped over! It was a cold day and I had a short sleeve shirt on. It was very cold. I decided to pick it up knowing it would help a lot. I picked it up even though it took a long time. I had to run way down the street to get some trash that had blown farther away. It was worth it. I knew I did a good job.

It felt good to do a good deed. My good deed felt good because I know I helped the Earth. If more people would try to be "Earth friendly" may be the Earth would be a better place.

I think good deeds are good to do. They should be done a lot more often. If you do a good deed such as walking to school, if you can, instead of driving a car it would help a lot. You can pick up trash that you see on the ground. Good deeds like this can help others and yourselves. I think doing good deeds is great! I know it felt good doing my good deed. I hope you do good deeds too.

Conner Corbridge, Grade 5
Snake River Montessori School, ID

Ups and Downs of Life

Has there ever been a time in your life when you felt so hurt inside? Thinking that life itself was worthless now that a very special someone has passed away? Well, you're not the only one who has experienced this type of pain.

It was the year of 2001 when the phone rang. During that time I was reading a book, when my mother answered the phone call. I sat there curious, wondering what the problem was when my mother started to sob. I asked why she was crying. She sobbed a little more then told me that my grandpa was really sick and the we needed to go to the Philippines.

About 24 hours passed by when we arrived at the Manila Airport. It was in the afternoon when we arrived at my grandpa's house. Each step I took toward the bedroom, the sound of weeping family members grew louder because right when my mom and I walked through the door, my grandpa had already passed away.

The day passed by with much sorrow. The sun was setting when I stood in front of the window, thinking of memories that reminded me of him. But the most special memory was when he would hug me close and tight. These thoughts helped me to understand that even if I wouldn't be able to see him anymore, life is still worth something because he is in my heart. My grandpa will always be an important person in my life.

Alyssa Acha, Grade 6
Northwood Public School, ON

Elephants

An elephant is a really big animal with a really strong trunk. An elephant is an animal that eats grass. They drink water through their trunk. Some elephants can eat a whole watermelon in one big bite.

Elephants have long floppy ears that protect them from the sun. They also have strong trunks that can lift up a tree trunk. An adult elephant can weigh about six tons, and when baby elephants turn six they weigh up to one ton. Some elephants are grey and some are brown, but they are all hairy.

Elephants are very big animals with big feet and big footprints. They are the largest animals on land. They live seventy years longer than any animal on land. They are mammals. Some elephants have tusks.

The most interesting thing about elephants is that they can eat a watermelon whole. They can also lift up a tree trunk with their strong trunk. Asian and Indian elephants have similar ears and the female elephants don't have tusks. In the African species both male and female elephants have tusks.

Lastly, Latin female elephants don't have tusks. Greek female elephants don't have tusks. I think that they are very good animals, because they are the biggest land animals. Also because they live longer than any other four-legged animal on land.

Emily A. Matias, Grade 5
Desert Trails Elementary School, CA

Alaska

I've been all over the United States, but my favorite state is Alaska. My family and I go on a yearly cruise. My grandma lives in Baltimore, Maryland, and we live in Menasha, Wisconsin. We don't see each other too often. Cruising to Alaska together was the perfect thing to do.

I will tell you about my favorite port as well as about the nature and wildlife in Alaska. My favorite port was the time we spent in Juneau, Alaska. Our plans were to go whale watching! We got on the boat which had about twenty people on it. After about five boring minutes, I saw a white and black fin in the distance! Then, out of nowhere, huge killer whales started leaping out of the water! Next, amazingly, a gigantic humpback whale surfaced. Some of the whales were less than ten feet away from us! It was great!

Next, I will tell you about our trip through the glacier pass. Everybody was rushing toward the deck. All I could see were dozens of huge glaciers. Some were big, small, and even collapsing. Most were a beautiful bluish color.

Throughout the cruise, we could see snowcapped mountains, waterfalls, eagles, glaciers, and even totem poles! We also saw whales, dolphins, and sea otters in the ocean.

Alaska is truly an amazing place! Did I mention we are all going back there next year? I can't wait!

Jared Skarsten, Grade 5
Trinity Lutheran School, WI

Christian Youth Theater

Cinderella, Annie, Treasure Island!!! These are the three CYT plays I have been cast in. CYT means Christian Youth Theater. CYT is one of my favorite hobbies because I have time to sing, dance, and just be myself. The only things I ever need to worry about are my singing, dancing, memorizing my lines, and auditions. Otherwise, I don't care about anything else except the show.

Cinderella was my first experience with CYT; well it was my first show.

I tried out and was honored and surprised to get two roles! I was a mouse and a towns person. I didn't have any speaking roles, but was in three scenes!

The next play was Annie; I tried out and made it again! I was in the NYC chorus, and was a hobo. It was funny because for our hobo scenes had to pretend it was the dead of winter. (It was very hot onstage because of all the people and the lights!) We'd pretend to shiver, but we would be sweating bullets from the winter clothes we were wearing. I also had a speaking role. I spoke to the apple-seller, Al. I said, "Hey, how'd it go today, Al?"

In winter 2007, the show I was in Treasure Island. I tried out, and made it!! I got the role of a pirate. I was happy because I got to be in eight scenes! I love CYT!!!

Nicole Johnson, Grade 6
Linfield Christian School, CA

Nintendo Wii Safety Rules

Have you ever played a Nintendo Wii? If you have, you probably know they're dangerous. Some safety rules are: always wear the wrist strap, never play when somebody is behind you, and never throw the controller. Here is why.

There are a lot of reasons why you need to wear the wrist strap. If you don't wear the wrist strap, you might let go and hit the TV! That's why you need to wear the wrist strap.

You should make sure nobody is behind you for two reasons. You might hit somebody and hurt them. And, if they're practicing you might hit their controller and break it.

Finally, you never want to throw the controller. If you throw it the controller might hit the wall and shatter your eyes. It might also bounce back at you.

In the end, the Nintendo Wii is dangerous. I hope you now see why they are. So next time you play the Wii, don't forget to wear the wrist strap, make sure nobody is behind you, and never throw the controller.

Taylor Grafton, Grade 6
West Central Middle School, IL

My Dad

My dad is 42 years old. His job is an officer in the U.S. Army. He is a 1st Lieutenant in a Civil Affairs unit. He lives in Chicago, Illinois. I live in Plymouth, Minnesota. My parents are divorced, so that means that I do not see my dad that much. It is very sad and frustrating when your dad isn't around. He has a squad of six soldiers that he is in charge of. He is responsible for their safety. If one of his soldiers gets hurt he would have to make sure that they do not die. He'll get in trouble if one of his soldiers dies. He has to go to Iraq in December 2007. Then he will have a two week break in July 2008. That makes me happy. Then he goes back to Iraq until December 2008. Then he comes home. I'll be excited when he will finally be home from the war! Then he is done with the war. It is very sad and stressful to have a family member in Iraq, especially when it's your father. I think most people don't understand how hard it is. I think that people should support the troops and their families more, especially kids like me.

Patrick Butler, Grade 5
Greenwood Elementary School, MN

Horses Through Time

Long ago horses roamed the prairies, some tamed but most wild. They varied from different sizes — Shetlands all the way up to Clydesdales. They ran free across wide open, glades of wild flowers and splashed freely though rushing streams. As time wet by, farmers started using horses for plowing fields and pulling covered wagons. Soon horses started being used for pleasure riding as well as being used by farmers.

Now, as you drive through the countryside, you see tons of equestrian (riding) stables or barns. Now you know horses came through time!!!!!!!!!!

Emma Schmelzle, Grade 5
Forest Hill Public School, ON

A Man of the Ages

Do you know six languages? What about printing with type? Benjamin Franklin, though schooled for two years, became a successful printer and a Congressman. Benjamin excelled in reading and writing. Even though his schooling ended, he believed the "Doors of wisdom never shut." He taught himself math, navigation, logic, grammar, natural and physical science, Latin, French, Italian, Germany, and Spanish. Because of his skill in literature, he read books during most of his leisure. He worked with his dad creating soaps and candles, and after became the apprentice of his brother James, a printer, because he detested his father's occupation.

After numerous years, he ran away from home and started a print shop, in Pennsylvania. His neighbor commented "The industry of Franklin is superior to anything I ever saw…I see him still at work when I go home from the club; and he is at work again before his neighbors are out of bed." Contributing to being a scientist, he invented the lightning rod and improved several lives.

To me, Benjamin Franklin is a "man of the ages." His accomplishments protect and educated us. One day, in his 30s he strived for perfection, and made a list of feats he should accomplish. The next day, he attempted to remember his goals but failed. Learning from this failure, I will accomplish my goals if I try. Benjamin Franklin made the most of what he received and encouraged me to do my best in tasks I perform.

Shravan Grandhi, Grade 6
Challenger School – Ardenwood, CA

Honor

Do you know what the word honor means?

Honor has many different definitions and synonyms. First of all, it means to show respect and praise. Other words associated with honor include reverence, pride, and tribute.

Some examples of honor include the President because he helps us and the world. He helps when areas have been destroyed by weather disasters and war. We should show our parents honor because they protect us and help us to grow in different ways.

Many people in the world don't know how to follow and live by honor. Here are a few suggestions. First, always show honor when you receive something like a gift. Secondly, you should follow others YOU think deserve honor. Third, is to never forget what honor stands for.

Many kids think of honor in different ways. Some may think of honor as glory, fame, or getting things. Although, real honor means being proud and thankful.

Honor is very important, and I hope to live this value the rest of my life.

Alexandria Conley, Grade 5
Covington Elementary School, NE

Don't Smoke

My noni and grandpy were great! But when I was little, my grandpa died of cancer. He got cancer from smoking. Before my grandpa got sick, my noni and grampy used to both smoke. When my grandpa died, my noni stopped smoking right away.

I remember when I was eating spaghetti and it was all over my face! My grandpa would hide behind the table and jump out and kiss me on the cheek. When I was about one, my grandpy brought me a huge bunny (stuffed, of course)! I'm not so sure what I used to call my bunny, but now I call him Grandpy.

I remember when my grandpy was sick and he was lying in a hospital bed in my noni's family room. I was holding his hand, not sure what was going on, since I was so young. My mom was looking like she was going to cry, and everyone else looked sad too. Now that I'm older, I understand why everyone was so sad. I miss my grandpa a lot. My noni has remarried an old friend of hers, named Rudy. I really enjoy him. Now I know, DON'T SMOKE!

Taylor Newman, Grade 6
St Anne School, CA

Leadership

Leadership is an important quality in the world. George Washington was an Army general who led Americans during the Revolutionary War. He was well-known and well-respected. The people elected him to be the first president of the United States of America. That is how he became the father and leader of our country.

Martin Luther King, Jr. started out as a pastor like his father and grandfather before him. He led Americans in a bus boycott in 1955 which lasted over a year. He went on to receive the Nobel Peace Prize at the age of 35 for leading a nonviolent, peaceful revolution that changed history. He taught boys and girls, blacks and whites, to be friends and live in harmony. He was a great leader.

The sixteenth president of our country was Abraham Lincoln, a great leader. During his presidency, he led the Northern states in an effort to keep the country together. He told the Northern states, "We work together to finish what we started."

Leadership comes into this world in many ways. I follow this by having a positive body posture, or I have a tendency to back down. For example, in fights I stand up proud for myself. I follow leadership in football because I lead my team in tackles. Also, I demonstrate it by doing what I am told.

There are many examples of leadership. Do you step up to be a leader? These are prime examples of leadership to follow.

Noah Uhing, Grade 5
Covington Elementary School, NE

My Little Sunshines

Riley and Ava bring a bundle of joy to my life. Riley is the one that is goofy and can't wait to see me. Ava, on the other hand, loves me but doesn't come running to greet me. Every Sunday at church, Riley comes running to the early childhood room yelling "Krista! Krista for a hug!" She lights up my heart every time I see her. Ava always has a little joke for me. She makes me laugh every time I see her.

These two girls are best friends. They are both two years old. I love them so much. It's like I'm their big sister. I've always wanted to be a big sister, so they are like my little sisters. They've been in my life ever since they were born at the hospital. I was actually at the hospital as soon as they were born so I could see them. Riley is at my house almost every day. She is so cute! Riley has long brown hair and sparkling brown eyes. Ava has curly blond hair and big brown eyes. I love Ava so much. Her big sister Hayden is so cute too! She is six years old. No one could be cuter than Riley and Ava. They're the best.

Krista Harvey, Grade 6
Linfield Christian School, CA

What Is Teamwork?

Have you ever worked together with someone to accomplish something? If you have, this is called teamwork. Teamwork is the best! You get to share and work with others. Teamwork is when you and others want to get a job done. I have teamwork in my class. We work together and discuss how to solve different problems. It is a lot of fun.

All in all, teamwork is knowing how to work with others and getting along.

Andrea Pulido, Grade 5
Covington Elementary School, NE

He Smelled Like Dirty Socks

I wanted to watch TV but to do that I had to help my dad first. I started to help him but he smelled horrible, worse than an old dirty sock. So I wouldn't get my clothes dirty or wet I wore one of my dad's t-shirts. It was dirty, ugly, and old, but it smelled worse than him. On the t-shirt it said "THE GUY GAME." I started to help him so I could watch TV. The best part was that the work really paid off because my aunt asked me if I wanted to go to Schlitterbahn. My dad and mom said, "yes!" because I was working hard. We went and it was really fun. I didn't get to watch my favorite show, but Schlitterbahn was better. At first, I was scared because I didn't know how to swim very well but my aunt's sister showed us how to float. We went on the lazy river which went all over the park. I was still a little scared, but I did it any ways. For the second ride we went on Crystal Water. Next we went on a water slide. Then we went on a ride that had big waves. It was similar to the one called Crystal Water, but with waves. It was late and we had school the next day so we went home to eat and rest. I never had to smell my dad's shirt again that day.

Delia Castillo, Grade 6
Chapa Middle School, TX

My Dogs

I love my dogs very much! More than you can imagine. They are both Labradors, but the oldest dog named Bailey, gave birth to 10 puppies on March 8, 2007. We kept one. And she is six months old, and her name is Kenzie. When things happen in my family that make me sad, Bailey will come up to me and lick my face! She also will put her head up against mine. Kenzie on the other hand, will attack me furiously. I still love her though.

When I get bored, I walk into the kitchen, and there they are staring at me in amazement. So, I take them outside and throw the ball to them. They keep me very active and that is how I stay fit and healthy. Every day I take them on a walk, and people think they are so cute. They take pictures and pet them. Bailey is actually on the cover of a magazine with me that was published across the world. She is very lucky to be in my family.

Have you ever seen the movie Air Bud? Well, if you haven't, that is how people treat my dog. Saying hello or petting them. After a while it kind of gets really annoying. My dogs are so spoiled it's amazing! So if you are around, stop on by and say hello!!

Katie Merrill, Grade 6
Linfield Christian School, CA

2 Amazing Heroes of 9-11

"Lets roll!" with these words, Todd Beamer and other heroic passengers rushed the hijackers of United Airlines a passenger jet, Flight 93, the last of four planes hijacked on the horrible day of 9-11. One hero is passenger Richard Guadagno, the only law enforcement officer on board. The nasty people never reached their target, thought to be the White House or Capital Building. The heroes on Flight 93 saved many lives, but gave up their own. The jet crashed in a field in Pennsylvania.

Richard had many talents like guitar, scuba diving, surfing and botany. He was a fearless man who was armed with only a pen light, subdued a man that was shooting a sign in a refuge.

Terrorists ended his life but did not end his legacy. Richard's name stands proudly on the Memorial Wall in Washington D.C.

Even when Clinton Davis was a kid playing cops and robbers, he was always the cop. After serving his time in the Air Force, Clinton joined the Port Authority and helping others by using his skills he was called to 9-11 and was assigned post by ground floor when the first plane struck. He stayed to rescue many others.

Richard says, "I ain't afraid of dying, Lord; it's the living that scares me to death." At his funeral his son said "I'm glad you are free now, Dad, and in a better place."

Lauren Spankowski, Grade 5
Marcy Elementary School, WI

The Big Move

We were moving to San Antonio! After I found out that I was moving the next step was telling all of my amiable friends. My friends were so disappointed, but after I told them that I would be closer to my family they understood. A few weeks later, the school year ended and we had to put our unique house on the market. With a helpful realtor we put our house on the market. A little while later, people started to look at our house and we always had to keep it clean. My mom decided that if we left the house while people were looking at it, that they might feel more comfortable. We ended up being out of our house more than we were in it. Later, we had to start packing everything we could. I disliked that so much mostly because I hate to clean. A few weeks later, people started to get serious. Two families wanted to buy our house. We agreed to one of the gainful offers. My family started packing everything.

I remember the immense house we looked at for fun. It was cool and eerie at the same time. The house had an elevator but it had leaks everywhere. A few days after though, we found the right, suitable house. It took a while to unload everything and we still have boxes to this day, but I don't think it was that bad of an idea after all.

Logan Glick, Grade 6
St Matthew Catholic School, TX

The Girl Who Saved a King's Family Tree

Have you ever wondered who Ruth was? What did Ruth do? Why do we remember Ruth?

Ruth's story has been told for a long time in the Bible. This is what the Bible says about her. Ruth married a man whose parents were Elimelech and Naomi. Ruth had one brother-in-law. All of the men in her husband's family. Elimelech, Ruth's husband, and her brother-in-law died suddenly.

After the death of these men, Naomi told both her daughter-in-laws to return to their Moabite land. They argued because they wanted to stay with Naomi. Naomi told her daughters-by-marriage that she could no longer have any children. Orpah, Ruth's sister-in-law, left, but Ruth stayed because she was faithful to Naomi. Ruth told her that she wouldn't leave her.

So, they decided to return to Naomi's homeland, which is Bethlehem. Once they arrived in Bethlehem, Ruth asked Naomi's permission to pick up leftover grain from Boaz's field. Boaz let her collect the grain after his reapers gathered their harvest. Boaz liked Ruth and did other nice things for her and Naomi, by telling his men to allow her to reap in his fields. Ruth never left his fields empty-handed (without grain). Boaz loved Ruth and decided to marry her.

Although Ruth was a Moabite, she still helped save Jesus' family tree. She loved her mother-in-law, stayed with her, and obeyed God.

In conclusion, Boaz and Ruth saved Jesus' family tree by marrying and having a son.

Amy Greeb, Grade 6
Isaac Newton Christian Academy, IA

Why Is It Important to Go to School

It is important to go to school and get good grades in order to go to college. In school we have to learn many subjects for example: math, reading, English, science, and religion. We need to go to school not just for a future job, but for our daily life.

In our daily life we use many of the things we learn in school. For example: we use math when we buy things at the store. We also use English when we write an e-mail to a friend. Another subject we always use is reading. Reading is used for bills, food menus, T.V., computer, driving and maps. The most important subject is religion because we learn about God. God created us and He is always with us.

The high school I want to go is Saint Matthias. I want to graduate from high school and go to a good college. When I go to college I want to study to be a veterinarian. I want to be successful in school and life.

In conclusion, it is good to study and go to school because you will feel very good about yourself that your hard work has paid off.

Yahaira Velasco, Grade 6
Our Lady of the Rosary School, CA

Being Short

I am short. It can be annoying to be short. It's annoying that my little brother is taller than me. Most of my friends are taller than I am. I sometimes like being short.

Being short can be fun. The good thing about being short is being able to get in small places that other people couldn't get in. I like being short, but it sometimes can be bad.

The bad part about being short is that you can sometimes be teased. It is also bad because a lot of people are taller than you are. What can be really bad is that people think you are younger than you actually are. Being short can be bad and good at the same time.

People make fun of short people like they did to the darker skinned people. They should just live with it. They should also be nice to short people.

Being short can be good because in games like dodge ball you are a smaller target. It can be bad sometimes people treat you like a little kid. They also do things for you when you did not need help. I like being short, and I also don't like it.

Sam Goodwin, Grade 6
La Mariposa Montessori School, NM

Floating Islands

What I liked about the islands was how the people made the islands and how it cleaned their ponds. I'm really excited to go back next year so we can go in that underwater observation room. It looks interesting. Last time I wanted to go in it. It's cool looking! When we go again, I hope to see more frogs. Also what amazed me was that the worker could build some islands in one hour. That big pond will probably have a lot of islands to keep all that water clean.

Ian Kline, Grade 6
Billings Educational Academy, MT

Parents

We all have something in common…parents. They are the reason we are here. Parents think that they are always right and usually are. They get on your nerves sometimes by telling you what to do or by punishing you. Parents might make you mad when they punish you in some way whether it is by restrictions, grounding, or spankings. Parents make you do chores like: take out the trash, clean the house, or do the dishes and you might get mad at them but try to remember that they are trying to make you a responsible young adult. During all this don't forget that they love you. We need to be more grateful towards them; they provide for us and care about us. They almost always know what to say or do. You can tell them anything and even if you don't they'll find out someway, somehow. Strict parents aren't bad they just want to protect their children from making mistakes and to follow the rules. All kids have at least one thing they don't like about their parents, but usually there are other things that they do like. Just remember parents are here to help through the good times and the bad. They are here to be supportive and to guide us in our young lives to help mold us to be the person we will be in the future.

Stephen Harris, Grade 6
Tri-West Middle School, IN

Tea, Anyone

After the British Military was defeated in war they had a big debt to pay off. To pay off the debt the British decided to tax all imported goods in the Colonies. The Colonists were not happy with the British government but no one was plotting rebellion yet. The stamp act of 1765 was the first time the British government taxed American made items. Things went along more peacefully but none of the Patriots liked the taxes. By 1767 most of the Colonists stopped buying English goods. The taxes were too high for many families.

On March 5, 1770 some colonist insulted British soldiers and the soldiers got very angry and started shooting around. The soldiers killed 4 men and a young boy. This incident is remembered as the Boston Massacre. In April 1770 the British removed the taxes on all items except tea because no one was buying any British goods. Many colonists started to buy a few British items but many people still drank cheaper tea from Holland that was smuggled in. On December 16, 1773 many apprentices, blacksmiths, carpenters, and farmers and very few wealthy colonists disguised them selves as Mohawk Indians. After everyone discussed the plan, they headed to the British ships in the harbor. 342 chests of tea were hoisted on to the deck, smashed open, and heaved overboard. Tea piled up like stacks of hay in waters 2 feet deep.

Colleen O'Neill, Grade 5
Woodside Elementary School, WI

Disaster at Mount St. Helens

An eruption that killed 57 people and badly damaged or destroyed 2,000 homes, 185 miles of highway, and 15 miles of railway can be nothing less than horrific. Mount St. Helens did this and more when she erupted on May 18, 1980, her most famous eruption.

This catastrophic Plinian eruption began on March 20, when Mount St. Helens experienced a 4.2 rated earthquake. On March 27, she started venting steam. By the end of April, the north side of the mountain was starting to bulge.

On May 18, at 8:32 Pacific Daylight Time, the north side of Mount St. Helens collapsed, triggering the largest debris flow in history. Some of the debris mixed with snow and ice to form lahars, volcanic mud flows. The magma inside the mountain burst forth in a huge pyroclastic flow, flattening buildings and vegetation covering over 230 square miles.

For more than nine hours, the eruption continued. The column of ash and cinder eventually reached 12 to 16 miles above sea level. The eruption reduced Mount St. Helens' height from 9,677 feet to 8,365 feet — 1,312 feet less! It left a crater one to two miles wide and half a mile deep.

The eruption of Mount St. Helens is certainly one of the most significant natural disasters in recent North American history. The effects of this event are still visible to visitors to the mountain, and atmospheric and climactic changes may still be felt around the world.

Anna Rubsam, Grade 6
Isaac Newton Christian Academy, IA

The Most Important Person in My Life

He is the most important person to me. When I was born, he was excitedly waiting. I have pictures of him feeding me. He also helped me take my first steps. I never felt alone because he was almost always around.

When I was three, I was terrified about daycare, but he reassured me. Once after we came home from the store, my mother left me in the car, and he reminded her. When I did not know how to read, he brought me pictures books.

He was always helpful. When I went biking, he made sure I did not fall off. When I took swimming lessons, he waited for me. I never missed having playmates, because he was my friend.

I was never alone while I waited for the school doors to open each day. During breaks, he sometimes came out to play with me. Even now he helps me with my homework. I never have any trouble with my computer because he is a wizard with them. I am never alone when my parents yell at me either.

He gets me the best birthday presents, and he shares whatever he has with me. We have dinner together, and on the weekends, we watch movies. I do get into arguments with him, but he always yields to me and spoils me.

I am scared about next year, because for the first time, I will not have him around me in school. He is my wonderful older brother.

Dhweeja Dasarathy, Grade 4
Birchwood School, OH

My Favorite Place

My favorite place is my tree swing. I love to do almost everything that starts with an s — swing, swim, sing. Swinging in my swing is very fun. I love spinning in it. I could do it all day. It is so fun. When I swing in my swing I feel like the birds flying above me. I feel like a flying bird so free. I am so free to do whatever I want. My dad built my swing last year when I was at school. I was so amazed at what he did. I had been asking him to build it. He finally did. I fancy swinging in it. I adore pushing my little niece in it. The first thing she does is run to swing and says, "Push Please." I play Peter Pan in it. That's when you put the swing on your stomach and swing and try to keep your balance. I fell out of the swing before because someone pushed me too hard. I hit the ground so hard it knocked the wind out of me. I could not breathe for a minute or two. Before long I had scars and bruises and bumps on my head. Finally I got through it and all the wounds went away. I was OK. But there is a lesson to be learned here. When you get knocked down, get up and try again. Never give up without a fight. Try again and again 'til you get it right.

Destiny Keith, Grade 4
Winona Elementary School, TX

Being Physically Fit

How long do you want to live? If you aren't physically fit you won't live very long. How do people get overweight? How can you prevent kids from getting overweight? Most importantly, how can kids get healthier? That's what you are about to learn.

Kids can get things such as diabetes from eating high calorie foods. Mostly from fast food restaurants, baked goods, and vending machine snacks. Also eating too much candy, desserts, and soft drinks can cause kids to be overweight.

How can we prevent kids from getting overweight? If they already are overweight how can they help themselves? Kids need to be active. Sports can help because you are being active. Being active and getting exercise helps your body in so many ways. When you are active, it makes your heart, lungs, and other muscles stronger.

Also eating healthy foods will help you get healthier. Try eating a variety of fruits and vegetables. Before you go to grab a bag of chips, think what would be healthier, a bag of chips or an apple? You decide what's best for your body.

I have family members that have diabetes. Usually your family members try to set a good example, but having diabetes is not a good example. Did you know that this will be the first generation of kids to have shorter life spans than their parents because of obesity? We should really do something about obesity soon.

Cassandra Del Castillo, Grade 6
San Elijo Middle School, CA

My Hero

Do you know any famous political leader who spent about a third of his life in prison? Nelson Mandela, famous for fighting apartheid in South Africa, was imprisoned for about 28 years. Apartheid is the policy of racial segregation practiced in South Africa. Even though his body was imprisoned, his ideas weren't. After released, he eliminated apartheid from South Africa and was treated as a hero from the citizens of South Africa. Soon after, he was elected the first black president of South Africa and president of the African National Congress.

Nelson Rolihla Mandela entered our world on July 18, 1918 in Qunu near Umata. His father was the chief of the Tembo tribe. Instead of following in his footsteps, Mandela prepared himself for a legal career. He attended the College of Fort Hare and Witwatersrand University. For his great work, on apartheid, he received the Nobel Peace Prize.

Nelson Mandela influences me and my actions. I think a second time before giving up because of him. If I get a bad grade in school I persevere and try again and get a better grade. Whatever challenges are thrown at me, I face them how Mandela would, with dignity. Whenever I give up, I question, this is not as hard as going to prison for 28 years. I look up to this great hero and persevere to be just like him.

Aditya Kotecha, Grade 6
Challenger School – Ardenwood, CA

Special Things

I am thankful for my 4 friends, my family, and my dog. My four friends' names are Brayden, Devin, Jacob, and Zach. I like Brayden because he is funny and he always makes me happy. I like Devin because he is very athletic and smart. I like Jacob because he is very smart and whenever I have a question, Jacob is there for me. I like Zach because he is hilarious; sometimes he is serious and sometimes you just can't stop him!

My family is important to me because I can always count on them. I like my dad because he is a really funny guy and he likes to play Game Cube with me. I like my mom because she'll help me with anything. I like my little sister, McKenzie, because she'll play anything I want.

I like my dog, Cooper because he always cheers me up. Even if I'm not in a good mood, he will always play and listen to me. If my sister doesn't want to play with me, he'll come in there and play with me. If my sister is in a good mood we'll all play together.

There is a lot to be thankful for like food, water, and my Game Boy. The things that I'm the most thankful for is my great family, my awesome friends, and the greatest dog in the world. These are my special things and for that I am very grateful.

Justin Harding, Grade 4
Gateway Pointe Elementary School, AZ

Who I Admire a Lot

Who do you admire the most? Well, the person who I admire the most is my cousin, Carla. She is 13 or 14 years old. She lives in Arizona with her mom and baby brother. We have a lot of family over there. I admire her the most because she defends me from our older cousin because she is always accusing me of things.

Another reason why I admire her a lot is because she can be very nice at times, and even mean because she has a lot of problems. So I help her with them.

One other reason why I admire her is because she can be my role model and teach me a lot of good things to do. I admire Carla because she is so much fun, and funny, even weird — but she is so smart. I'm glad to have her as a cousin. Who do you admire?

Jazmin Perez, Grade 5
Camellia Avenue Elementary School, CA

Man's Best Friend

There's a saying that dogs are a man's best friend. I agree with that because I have had dogs my whole life. I have two bloodhounds, Duke and Duchess. Duke, the male, is one year old, and he is my best friend. We go for long walks, we ride in the car together, and we play fetch.

Duchess is the female and is two years old. She will lie next to the fireplace all day. She likes to play fetch with me and sleep all day long.

I used to have a Chihuahua and he would always curl up in my lap while I was watching TV. I also had a German Shepherd, and he used to be a police dog that sniffed out bombs before I got him.

My dogs make our family laugh all the time, because they will play for hours, jumping, running, and sliding. A lot of times when I was sick or not feeling good, they would always make me smile. They would lick my face or run around the house and jump up and down.

I like taking care of my dogs, like giving them baths and grooming them. I take them to the vet about twice a year for their shots.

I have had dogs my whole life and I couldn't imagine what it would be like without them. My dogs have definitely been my best friends.

Adrian Thompson, Grade 6
Nishna Valley Community School, IA

Peace Inside of Me

Peace is what you call a sunset on a warm beach, next to the cold tattered water. It feels as relaxing as laying on a sauna bed! It's about NO bad battle being fought, or nobody getting hurt. Sunflowers, on a perfect sunny day, in the field, that's what I'm talking about. So, when you're playing on the grass, stop and admire the beauty of the blue sky up above. You will think to yourself and say, "Yep, it's just like heaven, it's just like hearing Christmas bells." Peace is my life, I live in it. We all must.

Natalie Guttman, Grade 5
Foothills Elementary School, CO

The Huge Move

When I went back to school for 5th grade, I felt like it was my greatest year at Rolling Hills Academy yet. It was the best year because I got to play basketball and run cross country with the older middle school teams. I won the school spelling bee that was a competition for grades 4th through 8th. Then I was selected to enter the PSIA (Private School Interscholastic Association) competition. I was chosen to represent the school for Number Sense, Dictionary and the Mathematics Competitions. I won 3rd place in the city for the Dictionary Competition and 2nd place in the Number Sense Competition. Because I placed 2nd, I got to go to Fort Worth, Texas to compete in the state finals for the Number Sense Competition. Although I did not place in the state finals, I had a very good experience.

After the challenging state competition, my mom told me that we were leaving Rolling Hills; I told her I was not happy with this. It did not come as a total surprise for me but I was still very sad about me leaving.

After a long summer, I attended the middle school orientation at the very large St. Matthew's Catholic School. I met new people and made some good friends. I have been doing well in school and my good parents are happy about that.

I am growing to like the school more than I thought I would. I am sure one day I will feel the same way about the big move to St. Matthew Catholic.

Joshua Villarreal, Grade 6
St Matthew Catholic School, TX

Bullies

I hate bullies because they are always hurting small kids. They pick on kids every day. It makes me want to hurt them. I have gotten into fights with a bully before.

I think that kids should stand up to bullies. We should start a group that is really brave enough to stand up to bullies. We will teach the bullies not to mess with us. There will be no more Mr. Nice Guys.

Bullies are doing things that are almost close to what criminals do. They take kids money which is stealing. They beat kids which is assault. They charge kids to go to the bathroom and that is embezzlement.

Parents should check with the teachers to see if their child is bullying kids. Teachers should check in the halls to see if kids are bullying other kids. If kids are, then they should write them up. Bullies might grow up to be criminals.

Without bullies, schools will be a safer place to learn. Kids will not have to go around thinking that they will be bullied every day. There will not be a lot of problems for the principal to solve. Parents will not have kids coming home hurt.

Johnathan Adair, Grade 5
Starms Discovery Learning Center, WI

The Amazing André Rieu

"We are practically married my orchestra and me." Those are the words of a violinist that is not only my favorite, but world renowned. The violinist is André Rieu. He travels the world playing beautiful music. He plays this music on a 1667 Stradivarius. He describes Stradivarius as "Undoubtedly the best and most famous violin builder of all time."

André never performs without his orchestra. When he first started his amazing career, he built an orchestra of 12. This very orchestra has 43 members at the present time. This orchestra still has its original name of The Johann Strauss Orchestra.

His career touched millions, starting many into the realm of music. He inspired me to take up violin. Now I'm even thinking about a career with my magnificent instrument. His music will touch millions more, as he shows no sign of stopping.

Although they only make him happy to know that so many enjoy his music, he has won 64 musical awards. Two of these are the World Music Awards he won in 1996 and 1998. I think he should get an award for speaking the most languages, as he speaks a total of 6 languages! What a linguist!

André Rieu hated not being able to laugh at concerts. Therefore he makes sure everyone in the audience gets a good laugh. He believes in playing music lightheartedly. He does crazy things at his concerts. At one, he even threw sausages into the crowds! That's an amazing musician.

Mark Fuller, Grade 6

The World's Favorite Sport

Soccer is one of the world's favorite sports. I like it because it's challenging and good exercise. I started liking soccer when my dad took me to see a real live game. There was noise everywhere you went. It sounded as though you were in the middle of a battle with rocket launchers and planes soaring all over the sky. Even though it was noisy, I enjoyed it very much

Soccer is played all over the world. In poor and rich countries it's played such as Asia, Mexico, USA, Europe, and Africa. There are a lot of tournaments and trophies; the most popular is the World Cup. Every country dreams of winning the World Cup, the last World Cup was won by Italy. The countries with the most World Cups are Brazil, Italy, France and Argentina. Brazil has five, Italy has five, France has four, and Argentina has three.

I have three favorite soccer players; number one Hugo Sanchez, number two Ronaldihno, number three, I only know his last name is Pele. Although Brazil is the best team in the world, England invented soccer. It was invented in the early 1800's. Soccer wasn't invented by adult athletes, but by school kids who played it at recess. Soccer is called futbol in every country, but US.

Now that you know about soccer, ask your friends to play or join a team, because soccer is fun, you won't regret it.

Miguel Rodriguez, Grade 6
Irma Marsh Middle School, TX

My Hike

I went camping with my brother, Connor, my dad, and his friends Frank and Paul Mocker. We went to Sand Point. I knew we were almost there because I could smell and taste the sea air. We had fun on the way hiking to Yellow Banks. Connor and I swam really far out in the ocean. We went so far out that we got sucked in too far and then a wave shot us back ten feet.

Later we started a fire on the beach. Then Dad, Connor, Paul and Frank pitched rocks to me as I hit them with a big stick. One time when Paul pitched to me I hit a line drive and almost hit my dad in the head. After awhile we put out the fire and hiked up a cliff. Frank scared everyone when he misstepped and almost fell off the cliff.

Later that night we put on our headlamps and went to the watering hole to find "Capa Lava Man." We were disappointed when we couldn't find him. The locals told us that ten years ago "Capa Lava Man" drank unfiltered water at the watering hole every day. Rangers told him he would get sick if he continued to drink it. One day rangers went to find him and when they got to the stream he wasn't there. They heard crying and slurping up stream. Every day at the same time rangers heard these same sounds.

On our way back from the watering hole, we heard strange sounds in the bushes. We were scared. Then we looked back at Frank and he was gone. Paul went to find him and he was at the Ranger Station. We thought "Capa Lava Man" took him, but he was reporting to the rangers that we had an encounter with "Capa Lava Man." It was an exciting day.

Collin Hoag, Grade 5
Eugene Christian School, OR

Brothers and Sons

I have many things that are important to me, but one of them is my dogs Biscuit and Gravy. Biscuit is a yellow Labrador Retriever with brown eyes. The other one is Gravy and he is a fat brown Labrador. Gravy has these beautiful brownish yellow eyes. They are both boys, but not brothers. Both are three years old. They are very calm, but love to play. I love them both so dearly. I do not know what I would do without them. I do a lot of things with them. I go swimming with Biscuit a lot. I don't go swimming with Gravy because he will drown or Biscuit will drown him. We love to go on hikes. Even though they look like they are dead when we get back! They are very good at listening to commands. I love to teach them tricks like play dead and bowing.

I tell them everything, like who I like, or what I am thinking, or what grade I got on a test. When I am sad, and if I start crying and cannot talk to anybody without crying, I can always talk to them and be ok. When I have a bad day at school, I always know that when I get home, they will be in my face giving me kisses and licking my lotion off my legs.

My dogs are very important to me and I love them very much!

Milia Gibbel, Grade 6
Linfield Christian School, CA

World Trade Center

Long ago in New York City in September 11 the World Trade Center had been crashed into by two hijackers. I was at home when I heard the news. A lot of people were in the Twin Towers. I ran outside and something even more terrifying! Both of the Twin Towers were in flames! Suddenly without any warning the first Twin Tower collapsed! Just then I heard about Flight 93.

Then it was the saddest thing ever the second tower collapsed! I was very sad that the hearts of so many people were broken. I walked home crying in depression. That night I had a nightmare that I also was in the World Trade Center. Just then I realized it was just a dream. Still I hope the Lord will never ever let it happen again.

I really wanted to get some sleep so I ducked down and said a prayer. "Lord please make everything better guide life to protection of the world in Your hands and You make things better. Lord please help us. Amen." The next morning I woke dad was having his morning coffee but undressed for work. "Don't you go to work Dad" I asked him. "No today they have to clean up." "Oh yeah," I said "well at least maybe something like this will never happen again." Even something just like flight the still people were sinful but God will keep His faith.

Antonio Vasquez, Grade 4
St Luke Catholic School, TX

A Curious Kitten

The first time I saw Gizmo, I knew we'd be friends for life. He was smaller than my hand, his eyes were closed. His umbilical cord was attached to his belly button, and he was drinking his mama's milk. When he was eight weeks old, he was ready to come home with us.

Gizmo is a very adventurous kitten. For example, when he awakes, he follows me around, eagerly watching me brush my teeth and hair. After I go to school, he runs over to my mother and watches her prepare his *tasty treat*. Although, he is still a kitten, he can climb up on top our TV.

Right now, he weighs approximately three pounds, and is about the size of a quart of milk. His black and white fur is silky with a fuzzy touch to it. His golden eyes are always wide with curiosity. Even though his claws are small, they feel like needles when he climbs up my legs.

The old cats, Honey and Sweetie, do not like to play with him, but Honey does like to cuddle up with him and take naps. I have to keep him busy by using my hands as toys. He also eats a lot, more than both other cats put together. I always have to keep filling up their food dish. At the end of the day he cuddles up under the blankets and sleeps next to me. Now, I can't imagine how my life would be without Gizmo.

Alexandra LaBrie, Grade 6
Spring Creek Elementary School, WY

Desirae's Story...

I'm Desirae Whitmore and I was born in Blue Springs, Missouri. When my Mom had me we were a happy family. I have a brother, David and a sister, Davisha. My brother is the oldest...sister's in the middle and I'm the youngest.

When I was 6 years old Mom and Dad divorced. We packed a couple of things and moved to Texas where my Grandmother lived. If only you knew how I felt. I can't put into words how I really felt. I just wanted to run away... and fast!! Over the years, I've grown up and gotten smarter.

I'm 10 years old now and go to DeQueen Elementary School. I love cheerleading at my school. I love it mostly because I am the Captain. I have to say that I'm a nice captain. The girls on the cheerleading team are all cool and so I like that!!

I really do like my life now and the way that I live it. Well, now I have told you my life story. Desirae Whitmore signing off...

Desirae Whitmore, Grade 5
DeQueen Elementary School, TX

Washington D.C.

Once upon a time, last year to be exact, it was the summer of 2006. I went to Washington D.C. with my family to visit my aunt. My aunt was going to show us around. Our first stop was the Washington Monument.

I was a boy named Robert. I was there to take a vacation because we were off of school. I saw many neat things like the Washington Monument, and the Lincoln Monument and a lot of other neat stuff. I heard a lot of guides talking about a monument or something else.

I met just one famous person like the President of the United States, George W. Bush. I met him by taking a tour around the White House. It meant a lot to meet him because he is the President of the United States.

I made it home by taking a plane to Houston then to San Antonio. It was a long way home but I had a lot of fun. When I came home I went straight to my bed and when to sleep.

Robert Elizondo, Grade 4
St Luke Catholic School, TX

9/11 Good Deeds

Good deeds are important to do on 9/11 because think of what all the fireman and policeman did trying to save as many lives as they could, trying so hard to get everybody out of the Twin Towers. Think of all the people that died because of the terrorists in the planes wanting to destroy all the buildings and hurt so many people.

So, in remembrance of 9/11, I think everybody should do good deeds. Well, you should do good deeds every day. Some good deeds to do are picking up trash out on sidewalks, around schools and other buildings. Or, doing your chores without being asked and helping out around the house.

Christian Simon, Grade 4
Snake River Montessori School, ID

The Great Days of Hanna-Barbera Cartoons

What cartoon production company is responsible for creating some of the most famous cartoons in the United States? That's Right...it's Hanna-Barbera Cartoons!

Hanna-Barbera, an animated cartoon production company, ruled television animation during the second half of the 20th century. The company was formed in 1944 by William Hanna and Joseph Barbera.

Two of their most well known cartoons include *Scooby-Doo* and *The Flintstones.*

William and Joseph first teamed together in 1939 while working at the Metro-Goldwyn-Meyer animation studios. Their first directorial project was *Puss Gets The Boot* which is now known as the *Tom And Jerry* series.

Hanna-Barbera was the first animation studio to produce animation especially for television.

When William Hanna died on March 22, 2001, an era ended. The last official Hanna-Barbera cartoon was *Scooby-Doo And The Cyber Chase.*

You can summarize this story in four sentences: Hanna-Barbera is one of the most well known animation cartoon company. They teamed up in 1939. William Hanna died on March 22, 2001. The last Hanna-Barbera cartoon was *Scooby-Doo And The Cyber Chase.*

Skyler Engelmeyer, Grade 5
Newburgh Elementary School, IN

My Hawaiian Trip

"Is it already morning?" I groaned. Then I remembered what today was. It was the day we would travel to Hawaii! I was so excited that at that moment I lost all the tiredness and jumped out of bed. We had to hurry because our flight left at 6:40 a.m. So we packed our luggage and scurried to board the plane. It was a long trip but we finally arrived.

When we went to pick up our rental car, it was a Lincoln Town Car, not the car I would have chosen. Our friends got a Mustang convertible for the same price. Despite the grandpa car we went to our hotel, the Sheraton. Our room was rather small but it didn't matter because we were only in there to sleep. The hotel had an amazing breakfast consisting of fresh pineapple and other various things. For lunch and dinner we would eat out somewhere except on the last day. That day, we went to a little beach with no one there and ate hotdogs and smores. Then, we played on some huge sand dunes. Another thing we did was take a catamaran voyage where we snorkeled, drove the boat and raced the dolphins. One day we went to a beach where you can't swim because of the thrashing waves. There was even a sign that said 83 people had already been killed, but we survived.

All in all, we had the greatest trip ever. We might even go again next year.

Matthew White, Grade 6
Argyle Middle School, TX

A Halloween Nightmare Comes True

My mom's hands went up. Her eyes and mouth opened up wide. She let out an ear piercing scream. I ran to help. Wouldn't you? I got more scared as I approached her. She yelled, "Stand back!" I was frozen. "Run! Run, back to the swings!" my mom commanded. I couldn't move. "Run!" my mom cried again. I found myself running as fast as I could. I kept telling my legs to run faster, but they wouldn't.

When I got to the swings I was breathing hard. My mom busted out, "There's a huge black widow on the window!" My heart stopped. At any other time I would be delighted to see a big spider, but a black widow's different. I knew it was the most poisonous spider in the world.

My mom ran away. She got smaller and smaller until she disappeared into the garage. SLAM, she was in the house. I was as scared as a mistreated dog. I was too worried to speak. SLAM, she was back outside.

Suddenly one of our neighbors approached. She started instructing my mom. Mom zoomed inside and rushed back out. When she came back out I almost started laughing. She was wearing a long sleeved shirt, tennis shoes, long pants, long yellow gloves, and was carrying a golf club.

Smash! The spider was gone. Every time I see a spider now, I'm scared. Even though the spider is gone this Halloween nightmare will stay in my mind forever.

Meghanne Clark, Grade 5

Football Season

Last football season I played for the Chiefs. We were awesome, we went for an eleven and one season. It was so cool. I'm going to tell you about that season.

Our first game was a scrimmage. We weren't very good. Our defense stunk. I got put in a position that wasn't right for me, so I stunk. We didn't keep score.

Our next game we played the Redskins. They destroyed us in the first half, so our coach called us "girls" and said that if we didn't redeem ourselves he'd bring dresses to the next practice. We did what he said and redeemed ourselves. Our defense shut them down. The offense scored four touchdowns in one half.

They got the ball first and they scored a touchdown. Then we got the ball. After that we fumbled. They returned it for a touchdown. I'm going to skip to the fourth quarter. They were saying, "It's all over." I was mad. That next play I smashed through the line and sacked the QB. That was our one and only loss.

This is our most impressive win. We were playing the Vikings. They were five and none and we were four and one. I'm only going to tell you the important things. The other defensive end on my team nailed the running back so hard, it was cool. Lastly we won. The rest of the season rocked.

Carter Capuano, Grade 5
Barrington Elementary School, OH

Hole in One

One day my Dad wants me to come and play golf with him so I did. When we got there we got a golf cart and rode to the hole. Then we started to play. My Dad went first and he hit it far away, then it was my turn and I did not hit it very far. We walked where my golf ball landed then mine went past my Dad's ball so it was my Dad's turn.

When he was up, he made it in the hole so it was my turn and it took me a while to make it in the hole. After I made it we went to the next hole and my Dad made a hole in one.

When it was my turn I did not make a hole in one, then I was sad because I was not good at golf. Then we went to the other hole. Then I hit the ball, still I did not hit a hole in one, my Dad did.

Then at the last hole I made a hole in one. Then I wanted to keep playing. But we had to go home.

We went home and ate supper and went to bed.

Christian Lynch, Grade 5
Bang Elementary School, TX

Being a Kid

Being a kid is an adventure. One of the adventures is getting to play a lot of sports and you get to have summer vacation!! You have to go to school and at the end of summer you get to go to the fair.

During the summer you get to do a lot of exciting things. For example, I get to go swimming, you can go camping, and there isn't school!! During the summer, I get to go to my grandma's house and see my uncles, my grandpa, and a whole bunch of friends. It's very exciting. I'm so glad I get to go up there.

When the school year starts the homework begins. A couple of other things start also such as riding the bus and getting to have recess. Also, basketball gets underway and a new 4-H year begins.

At the end of summer we participate in the fair. During the fair we can enter things, be judged, and get premiums, and money for our 4-H projects. We get to go on carnival rides. It is so exciting. This summer I got to go to the Demolition Derby. It was LOUD!!! This is the end of another exciting year.

Harley Dowse, Grade 5
Kinsey School, MT

Animal Testing

I think animal testing should stop. I think this because there are a lot of animals that are killed or hurt. According to Wikipedia, people have estimated 50-100 million vertebrate animals from zebra fish to non human primates are used and then they die. Rodents used often are guinea pigs, hamsters, gerbils, rats, and mice. 1,910,100 mice are used. 464,727 rats are used. 37,475 other rodents are used for animal testing. Beagles are used a lot because they are friendly and gentle. 7,799 of 8,108 dogs used in 2004 were beagles. I think we should stop testing products on animals.

Emily Gard, Grade 4
Lincoln Elementary School, WA

A Trip to Another World

I dove into the ice-cold water when I found myself face to face with a barracuda! It was scary when I felt it slide by my leg with its rough and slippery skin. That was probably a once in a lifetime experience. That was the start of my snorkeling adventure.

I went down in the cold water. I found myself in a whole different world. All the beautiful, colorful fish and corals. You could see all the little fish together and the big fish alone. They came in all different colors. You could see from a clown fish to a shark!

I went down even further. I saw a lion fish. As you know those fish are poisonous. I went back to the surface really scared. I told my dad and he said, "Are you sure you want to go down again?" I said, "Yes, I want to see more beautiful things!"

I went down once more. As I was going down I felt some kind of slippery rough skin touching my leg. I said, "It must have just been a fish." Then I turned around when I saw some red shiny eyes looking straight at me. It was a barracuda! I was scared to death! I swam slowly back to the surface. I told my dad about the adventure, he laughed. That was the first time a barracuda had ever touched me. It was a once in a lifetime experience.

Andrea Biaggi, Grade 6
St Matthew Catholic School, TX

Mary Edwards Walker, Civil War Doctor

There are men that we think of in the Civil War, but Dr. Mary Edwards Walker did great things too.

Mary Edwards Walker was born in November 26, 1832 in Oswego, New York. Mary grew up in rural, New York with four sisters, Aurora, Luna, Vesta, Cynthia, and one brother, Alvah.

Mary was the only woman in her class to join the little number of female doctors in the nation. Mary graduated from Syracuse Medical College.

Mary was married to Albert Miller. She was married only thirteen years.

Mary Edwards Walker fought against tobacco and alcohol. She fought against gender discrimination of her time. Also she was a published author.

Her medal of honor award was revoked, but she refused to return the medal and wore it until her death. But, thanks to her granddaughter, President Jimmy Carter signed a bill in 1977 reinstating her medal. She was honored in the newly, dedicated Women in the Military Service for America, memorial in October 1977.

Mary Edwards Walker died February 21, 1919.

Mary Edwards Walker was not well known, but she was still important.

Melody Semon, Grade 5
Cheyenne-Eagle Butte Upper Elementary School, SD

Got Mail?

Older folks like getting handwritten letters in the mail. Who doesn't? People who hand-write letters are becoming rare.

I think it is important to keep this tradition going. The ease and speed of e-mail is endangering the Postal Service. If we don't hand-write more letters the Postal Service might go out of business!

A handwritten letter is like an artifact in a museum. It is a historical record. You can put it in a journal or up on a bulletin board. If people who write letters become extinct, a part of our history will become extinct.

Handwritten letters are an important piece of our history. The Postal Service relies on people who write letters to stay in business. Getting a handwritten letter brightens everyone's day. Don't let the tradition go extinct. Write some letters today!

Laura Kromrey, Grade 5
Moose Pass School, AK

The Okapi: An Endangered Animal from Africa

Have you ever researched an endangered animal? If you have, you would find that there are not as many animals left as you might think. A specific endangered animal is the Okapi. An Okapi is a cousin to the giraffe and has long legs, large eyes and a short brown mane on the back of its neck. The Okapi is an interesting animal because it has multicolored legs, two short horns and large ears. The Okapi's fur is a reddish brown and it has stripes on the top of its legs. The Okapi is found in the rain forest of the upper Congo River Basin. The Okapi is an herbivore and mainly eats berries, fruits and shoots. Guess what? They swallow their food without chewing it! Something you may not know is that the Okapi is nocturnal. That means it is mostly active during the night. The Okapi is also very heavy. It weighs 450-550 pounds!

There are a lot more endangered animals, this is only one. Animals that aren't known very well are very interesting!

Nicolette Pridavka, Grade 5
Woodside Elementary School, WI

All About Me

My name is Kennedy. I have blue eyes and dirty blonde hair. It takes me forever to get dressed, but it pays off because I am very stylish. My skin color is lightly tanned. I live in Leduc, Alberta which is found in the country of Canada.

My family is awesome!!! My mom's name is Diane and my dad's name is Stan. I have one sister, and her name is Brooklyn. I also have a dog named Pete. I love my family!!!

The things I like to do most are Irish dancing and ballet. They are such fun dances. More things that I enjoy are animals. I want to work with animals when I grow up. I love animals so I want to keep learning more about them!!!!!

That's all about me!!!

Kennedy Neustaeter, Grade 4
Linsford Park School, AB

The Person I Admire

The person that I admire is Ms. Tichenor. I admire Ms. Tichenor because she is a great teacher. Also because Ms. Tichenor likes to be a very organized person. She likes to have a lot of fun with all of her students. Ms. Tichenor has a very great personality and she is a very sweet person.

Second, Ms. Tichenor is a very smart person and she is a very great writer. Ms. Tichenor likes to tell the truth and she likes people to be honest. If you don't tell her the truth you will be in big trouble. She is a very honest person and when she promises she does it. Ms. Tichenor likes to finish all of her work.

The reason I admire Ms. Tichenor is because of how smart she is and how great she is. She loves all of her students that she has each year. Ms. Tichenor is the best teacher I've ever had.

In conclusion, I think Ms. Tichenor is the best. She is the most fun teacher in this school. When I finish 5th grade I'll miss her.

Sireni Galindo, Grade 5
Camellia Avenue Elementary School, CA

Strange Ideas…Pop…Up!!

It's often surprising how many places strange math ideas pop up!! You need it from physics to medicine to law and just in your everyday life. The more you know, the better your chances for job opportunities.

So basically, the idea here is that if you learn math now when you are confronted later in life you won't have to worry about it.

Kiara Jacobs, Grade 5
DeQueen Elementary School, TX

The Vaccination Man

"Eureka," one of the greatest scientists in the world shouts in his laboratory. Louis Pasteur made many accomplishments such as: becoming a scientist and making a vaccine to prevent and cure rabies. Also, he was involved in the experimenting of spontaneous generation and biogenesis, but these are only a few reasons why he inspires me.

Consisting mostly of microbiology, Pasteur's research has saved countless lives. Working long hours, Pasteur came up with numerous theories about bacteria and how life came to be. He found diseases were spread by bacteria from one person to another. There came a time when he was paralyzed, but he did not stop conducting his experiments. Contributing to the chemistry and industry businesses, he formed the process of pasteurization.

The scientist has inspired me to keep going toward my dreams, though there are setbacks, I should never give up and should treat my studies seriously. No matter how many setbacks he had like being paralyzed or having experiment after experiment fail, he still worked hard. With that, he has inspired me to go toward the path of being a scientist or a similar career like his, but like him I will not give up!

Samie Azad, Grade 6
Challenger School – Ardenwood, CA

The Dog That Meant Everything

My mom and I were cleaning the mess in the small garage. An odor wafted in the air, dark and musty mixed with the dim light overhead. My mom stuck her hand in a box and pulled something out. White with brown sparkly eyes. A smile crept out and snuck on my face.

I laughed and carried it, dashing out of the hot garage, forgetting my cleaning. I felt like running my fingers over its soft back, feeling like rumpled fur from a dog. I sped upstairs to my room and pulled out something pink with shiny rhinestones.

While putting it on the dog's neck, I decided to name it. I had a HUGE list in my mind. I felt like my mind was going in big circles. Just think of an easy name that begins with the letter on the bracelet! The rhinestone bracelet had a pink "S." Suddenly, my brain felt like a light bulb popped out. That's it! This is a name that no one else would have. The name is Spangle like the Star Spangled Banner. Yeah, I know it's weird but I liked it. It's a name like no other.

Spangle is like my best friend. My mom played with her until she outgrew stuffed animals. Spangle is my American Flag in my heart. She is mine and I know that we will be together until the end.

Rhea Bae, Grade 5
Dingeman Elementary School, CA

Benjamin Franklin

Benjamin Franklin was a great person. Ben Franklin was the type of person that I wish I could say we were related. I'm not any relation to him but I do appreciate everything he did in his lifetime. Many things that Ben Franklin were involved in are still part of our country today.

Ben had many jobs and titles throughout his lifetime. He was an author, printer, politician, scientist, inventor and showed great leadership.

The 1783 Treaty of Paris, which ended the Revolutionary war was written with the help of Ben Franklin. He also signed four very important documents that are history of the USA. These four documents are: The Declaration of Independence, Treaty of Alliance, Treaty of Peace, and the Constitution of the United States of America. These documents are still being used by me and the citizens of the USA.

Being the scientist and inventor that he was, Ben invented the bifocal glasses, the Franklin stove, and many more things. One of the most important discoveries that he had that we use all the time in our lives, is electricity.

I feel Ben Franklin was an important man in history because with his leadership, the colonists created the ideas that became the basics of a great, new democratic country, (my country), the United States of America

Molly Bolton, Grade 6
Nishna Valley Community School, IA

My Favorite Place

My favorite place is at Janeth's house. Her room is my favorite place because it is adorable and because her bed is soft. Her room is medium and she has a lot of jewelry and a VCR. Her bed is the softest bed that I've ever sat on. Her bedroom is cool. She has a big mirror that's brown. Janeth's house is beautiful and I like it. Her closet is not that big. Janeth has three rooms in her house. This big squared thing is where she has covers and pillows in there. Her room is comfortable and it is not that cold or hot, it is just fresh. I like to sleep on her bed and eat and watch the TV. You should go to Janeth's house!

Griselda Rosas, Grade 4
Winona Elementary School, TX

Strangers

Encountering a stranger is very scary. You might hear your Mom say "Don't talk to strangers," but mostly you'll hear it on Halloween.

A stranger can be many things to many people. For instance, someone from the South may think a stranger is someone they have not met in their life. Someone in the North might think a stranger is someone who they do not enjoy being around. One thing that you might look for is a kidnapping stranger. A kidnapping stranger might call on the phone and say to meet them somewhere. They also might try to do it at night.

At school do you have a duck-and-cover drill? A duck-and-cover drill is for your own safety if a stranger walks onto your campus. I have had a stranger walk onto the campus of my school once. I was not there that day but I heard that it was really scary.

If your parents say "Do not talk to strangers," it is for your own safety. Remember…a stranger can be anybody!!

Caiden Permenter, Grade 5
Stone Ranch Elementary School, CA

Our Beloved Backyard

It is a wonderful fall day as I'm sitting here on our family's swing set. School bus wheels are screeching to a halt, and crows are squawking. I can hear a dog bark in the distance. The clouds are growing larger and grayer. Birds are chirping and boy, do they have a lot to say today. An airplane passes above me, hovering and melting farther into the gray clouds. Our cat is looking for something to do, and noticing he has done most of that stuff today; he lies down and takes long, hard licks at his back. This backyard has history in it. It holds tremendous catches in a football game, jammed fingers and the crash of plastic Star Wars light sabers in it. It is starting to get a little windy now, and about ten or twenty leaves out of thousands skitter along our yard. Those leaves are the coolest right about this time. They consist of bright colors like sandy tan, dusty gold, sunshine orange and crimson red. The other thousands of leaves just sit still like they have for a long time.

Christopher Johnson, Grade 5
Greenwood Elementary School, MN

Bullying

If you ever witness a person getting bullied you should take action. When I say take action I don't mean fight or start to be a bully too. I just mean go get a teacher or something. Don't just let them fight helplessly against the bully.

Bullying starts when the bullies have no friends. Sometimes they can be raised badly and take their anger out on other people. Bullies may also have a bad childhood.

The bullying can also start when someone thinks they're cool so they start talking trash. When it gets to "your momma," jokes someone pushes the other person's buttons. Then somebody swings at the other person and soon after that a fight breaks out.

If a bully wins that fight they will keep picking on you until someone stands up for you. Most likely if a person won't stand up for you the bully will kick you, punch you and other things like that. Some bullies even take your lunch.

When a bully picks on someone they are mostly younger kids. Some are smart kids or weak people. When you get bullied or see someone get bullied you should tell because you would want someone to tell if you were getting bullied. Do the same for others.

Isaiah Booker, Grade 6
Starms Discovery Learning Center, WI

Women for President

Women play an important part in our nation. Presently, we have a woman as Secretary of State, Speaker of the House, and nine governors. Girls are inspired to believe that they can become whatever they want. I believe that a woman should become president of the USA within the next decade.

Women don't jump to conclusions immediately, but listen and think about what they've heard. Women would listen to many opinions from the citizens of the USA. This would make people feel they are not invisible.

A president is like a parent. Women are caring and usually have children, and they want their kids to have good lives. So a woman will do whatever she can to make the world a better place to live. A mother treats each of her children as individuals, and would treat people the same way. A good leader should also stand her ground and does whatever she believes in. For instance, if a child wanted to do something bad, she would try to stop them.

Women also keep their promises, and that is one of the most important qualities of being president. Sometimes candidates keep their campaign promises, but I think that a woman would be more likely to keep her promises than a man.

People should vote on qualities, not on gender. It is often asked "Is it a woman's turn to be president?" The answer to this question should be a firm "Yes!"

Lizzy Hall, Grade 5
Highlands Elementary School, KS

My Thoughts

While I walk under the waving leaves of the cottonwoods, I let my mind wander. I can feel the familiar weight of my fly rod in my hand and the pull of my binoculars around my neck. I glance up at the rustling leaves above my head. Fall is coming and they are in full glory, casting orange shadows on the path before me.

This makes me sad, yet when I think about it, it makes sense. The older you get, the more elaborate you become. I feel slightly sorrowful, for I know that it will not last long. Within the month, the leaves will fall and suddenly the trees will be bare, like skeletons stripped of their splendor.

This structure of life and death is repeated all throughout nature. Salmon, which spend their whole life working up to the moment they can travel back to their birthplace, mate, and lay eggs, die after their lifelong goal is completed. One famous poet, by the name of Hokusai, was known to have said that the older he got, the more centered and wise he became, both inwardly and outwardly.

Suddenly I am aroused from my thoughts by the sound of the creek. I hear a Dipper call, and I smile, knowing that I am about to have a great day of fishing.

Jeremy Brooks, Grade 6
La Mariposa Montessori School, NM

Lost Homes

Have you ever thought about what the world would be like if there were no trees or plants? One summer morning, I was on my way to summer camp, and a short distance from our subdivision, I drove past "The Forge Club," a local restaurant. I noticed something different — the color? — the sign? Nope. Suddenly, I saw it, and I was shocked. Right next to the restaurant, what seemed like a forest yesterday, now was a big, open, dirty field. I couldn't believe it!

You might ask, "What's the big deal about some land being cleared?" First of all, it makes "The Forge Club" look bad. Secondly, they are destroying animals' homes. Even the pond is almost drained; birds and fish love that pond, now it's wrecked! Thirdly, they cut down all those trees for commercial buildings. Birds nest there. Deer live there, and now they've taken away their homes!

Following that, I started to notice something around our own neighborhood. There were many more squirrels, deer, hawks, owls, and road kill nearby. And when I talked to my neighbors, they were noticing things too! Sometimes the animals don't know where to go, so they die out, and some may be endangered species!

Don't let them do this! If we keep this up, our town would be a deserted area with no life, just buildings. Stop cutting down animals' homes! Let's be more responsible about developing with nature in mind.

Sara Ploch, Grade 6
Daniel Wright Jr High School, IL

Stealing Something You Want

One time I learned my lesson from stealing. I stole some candy and toys I really wanted. I stole them out of John's store. It was a Bratz collection and sour gum and they glow in the dark. I got caught and I had to put them back. My aunt caught me stealing them. They cost 1.99 and 5.99. When I had to go in my room and think of what I did, I learned my lesson from stealing something you want. You ask for it.

Tianna Edward, Grade 5
McMonagle Elementary School, MI

My Favorite Place

My favorite place in the whole wide world is the farm. When I go to the farm, once my dad stops I jump right out of his truck. I used to run up to the dog, but Shadow died. Anyway, I jump out and I run right inside. And I would go into one of the guest rooms. I go to this little gambling machine. It does not take quarters. It takes these tokens. The tokens are sitting there waiting for you. They are saying: "Play me, play me before you leave! Please!" When I play for like an hour I turn it off and I go to the television. But since we don't have cable we have dish network. When I turn it on I watch Hannah Montana. Then I change into my hunting clothes, grab my gun, and I take a spin on the mule to go to check on the oil machines. The reason I put on my hunting clothes is because when I am driving, if I see a deer or a hog, I can shoot it. So I went back to the farm and I got a drink of Mountain Fizz.

Sara Bass, Grade 4
Winona Elementary School, TX

The Best Family Ever!

My family is important to me because they love me and I love them. My Dad is 43 and he is a doctor. My Mom is 44 and she is so nice. My sister Danielle is nine and she's your typical (annoying!) little sister. My dog Koda is two and he's a chocolate lab. My family likes going on walks together. We also like eating together and talking too. Danielle and I sometimes play games together, but mostly we stay away from each other. When I play Hockey my family supports me. We visit amusement parks and we always have fun because we go on all the rides together and have fun.

I got my dog Koda at a Starbucks Coffee shop when my mom and I saw a man trying to sell him. He looked so nice, so I talked mom into it and she gladly got him. Koda and I love to wrestle and play fetch. Koda also likes to go on walks, and He loves swimming. Koda also enjoys being chased and playing tug-of-war.

My dad is so cool! He always takes me to fun places and he is really nice. He makes me work hard at hockey and encourages me to do my best. He also takes me to the skate park and that's cool. He always lets me go to friends houses and I always have fun. My family loves each other and we always will.

Adam Ardigo, Grade 6
Linfield Christian School, CA

Alexander Ovechkin
The Greatest Hockey Player in History!

I know what you are thinking…who the heck is Alexander Ovechkin? Well if you would like to find out, read on. Alexander Ovechkin otherwise known as Alexander the Great, is one of the greatest hockey players who ever lived. I bet you can guess why they call him Alexander the Great. It's because of his magical moves. He can deke defenders with ease and he scores plenty of goals. He's also an entertainer. He scored some of the greatest goals in NHL history and he always has good goal celebrations.

Goal scoring isn't all he can do. He had forty eight assists last year and fifty four the year before. Ovechkin has also had the honour of being on *EA Sports NHL '07* video game. He won the Calder trophy in 2006 as the NHL's Top Rookie. He joined the Finnish flash, Teemu Selanne, as the only two rookies in NHL history to get at least fifty goals and one hundred points (goals and assists). Selanne had seventy-six goals and one hundred and thirty-two points while Ovechkin got fifty two goals and one hundred and six points.

The last thing I'm going to tell you about is his commercials. He has done numerous commercials. Well actually he's made two, but that's a lot for a hockey player. I hope you think Alex Ovechkin is the greatest hockey player in the world now, if you didn't already think so.

Harman Dhillon, Grade 6
Dr F D Sinclair Elementary School, BC

The Winning Goal

The first day of my soccer tryouts was on July 14, 2004, that day was my sister's birthday. I was so happy because I made it to the team. My family and I went out to eat that afternoon. My brother ate so much that he got sick so we had to go to the doctors. He got sick because he could not resist eating too many french fries. Sunday was my first game. It was my chance to show off all the great soccer moves I knew. That day we won with a score of 3-1. We were getting near to the finals, it was the last game to win the heavy, but big trophy. I was about to make a goal when just then a friend from the opponent's team that I used to go to school with, kicked me.

It really hurt, I got out of the game to rest a while. Then I got back in, I was feeling much better. I made the final goal, my mom said, "WAY TO GO MIGUEL!" I felt really good about myself. The thing I didn't like was that our coach got to keep the trophy. My mom and I did get a little mad because the team members did not get anything. But at least I kept myself proud about winning and trying my best. After we won I stopped playing because I started to do badly in school. Then I improved my grades and entered a different soccer team, Nuevos Valores.

Miguel Sepulveda, Grade 6
Our Lady of the Rosary School, CA

Six to Remember

I was eight years old and in the third grade. It was my second year playing for Jackson Red Pee-Wee football. It was a year I will remember the rest of my life.

It was a nice day on October 1, 2005, playing against the Southeastern Panthers. The size of their team players made our players look like runts. I was playing running back, eager to get the ball.

The play had been called, I-right-R-four-lead. That was my play to run the ball. We were down on the 40 yard line.

The ball was snapped and handed off to me. The entire defense was coming after me as I was dodging them. Then suddenly all I saw was an open field.

I was running as fast as I could and hard as I could. I ran for 40 yards, and scored my first touchdown. I couldn't believe what had just happened.

My heart was beating so fast, and I was so excited! Everyone was giving high-fives to me. Since that day, I've been unafraid to get the ball, and *now* I *want* the ball to score 6 points!

Chase Spires, Grade 5
Westview Elementary School, OH

Don't Give Up

This is a story about when my sister taught me how to ride my bike. One day I asked my sister if she can teach me how to ride my bike. She said ok Alyssa, I will help you learn how to ride your bike. Let's get going. So we went outside to ride my bike and we got going and the first try I fell over and the bike went tumbling over on top of me. Are you ok my sister asked? I said yes but it did hurt a little bit but not too much. I don't think I will ever get to ride a bike because I am so bad at it I said. Don't worry you will get it some day my sister said. I said how about if we go inside and take a break? I have an idea…How about the next time we try it I will have my sister give me a little push and maybe that will get me going on the bike longer than two or three seconds. We decided to give it another try and my idea worked! I FINALLY learned how to ride my bike! Yeah!!! I thanked my sister for all of her help in believing in me and know that since I did not give up that I could do it. If you will believe you will succeed and if you succeed you will achieve!

Alyssa Ventresca, Grade 4
P H Greene Elementary School, TX

Friends

A friend is a very special person. They can make you feel better with a simple hug. A friend brightens up even the darkest days just by being there for you. They go the extra mile just for you. But, there is a friend that is perfect, one who words cannot describe. John 15:13 says it all: "Greater love has no one than this, that he lay down his life for his friends." That is what Jesus Christ did. I praise God for giving me good friends, but most importantly, I'm thankful that He sent his Son for our sins. He is the ultimate friend!

Bailey Patrick, Grade 5
Pike Christian Academy, OH

My Secret Place

My secret place is in the woods. One day when I was at my cousin's house we were bored. So me and my cousin asked our mom if we can go outside, and they said yes. So we got some boards, nails, chains, and a hammer. We got a red wagon and put everything in it. Then we went into the woods. We found a big tree and started to build. Our clubhouse is brown and tan. The tree that it is in is dark dark gray. It also has white spots on it. After we put it up we put a laptop, flowers, and books, in it. We also put a chair and a desk and windows. We also have a ladder that you go up to the clubhouse. When we get up in the tree house we pull the ladder up, and we shut the door. We also have some games up in the clubhouse. So when we get up there we can play our games. We play tons of games. We also have a TV up there so we can watch TV.

Autumn Granberry, Grade 4
Winona Elementary School, TX

Being a Good Friend

Friends are nice to have. If you want to get to know them you have to greet them, talk to them, hang out with them and help them do things. You could play with them and tell them secrets because you trust them. Your parents can also make friends with their parents.

You can go on trips with them. For example, you can go to Disneyland with your friends. Or on field trips, you can sit next to each other. Or when you're on the field trips you can stay next to each other.

You can also help each other with homework. You can take each other to places your friend doesn't know. He or she can take you to places. You can stick together, like a team.

Jose Luis Solorzano, Grade 4
Our Lady of the Rosary School, CA

The Unpredictable Ocean

The ocean is very exciting and breathtaking. Sometimes the ocean can be scary. When I go out really far, I don't know what is in the water.

When I go to the beach, the best things about it are the sand and all of the sea shells. I like the feel of warm sand between my toes.

Once I went to the ocean and I saw a huge, dead sea turtle. It was sad. The tide had washed it up to the seashore.

The ocean is very pretty when the sun sets and when it rises. A few years ago I went to the ocean, but we had to leave because Hurricane Charlie was coming. It was on my birthday and I was glad we left. It was frightening.

It takes such a long time to get to the ocean from Jackson, Ohio, you think you'll never get there. But the trip is worth it.

Sometimes the ocean can be calm and pretty. Other times it can be stormy and scary. But regardless, the ocean just continues to call my name.

Kyle Shasteen, Grade 5
Westview Elementary School, OH

The Power of Imagination

Everyone should use their imagination frequently because when you use your imagination you can help yourself and others become better. You can also help the world become a better place.

A strong imagination leads to great creativity. We need creativity for art, music, drama, stories, and information. These things can help you get to know yourself better. They can help you be yourself and let your imagination fly! Then you will know you can do whatever you want.

Using imagination will help you create all kinds of inventions. Some people make inventions that help themselves and others. Someone that helped millions of people was Alexander Fleming. He invented antibiotics. Antibiotics made a huge impact on our lives.

Uniqueness is another quality of imagination. Uniqueness helps us be ourselves. It shows off how you are special from other people. Being strong helps when others try to put you down. We should all be free to let our light shine. Follow the voice inside you instead of those around you. Imagination lets you be proud of yourself!

Imagine that you are somebody that tries to use imagination to make a difference! You could make a huge discovery, make up your own story, or help someone or something be better. Let your light shine and your imagination fly!

Hannah Dobrowski, Grade 5
Booth Tarkington Elementary School, IL

My Sister

Having a little sister is hard. Trust me, I have one. Her name is Anika. I call her Ani and so do my parents. I also call her a Tasmanian devil but my mom doesn't like it when I call her that. Her birthday is on June 11th and she's really funny and also very annoying too.

Like when we eat dinner she uses her hands instead of her spoon and fork. She also spills her drink on herself and yells when we are eating at the table and then starts laughing because for some reason she gets the idea that it's funny and does it over and over and over until she either gets yelled at or spanked and then starts crying.

There are only a couple things I don't like about her crying. The first reason I don't like her crying is that it's extremely loud when she cries. The second reason I don't want her to cry is because when most people cry they only cry for like 4 minutes tops. Anika cries until she gets attention. For Anika that means either my mom or dad talks to her and says that they are sorry and stuff like that. Then Anika slowly stops crying. It takes forever which is annoying, because that means that I have to listen and stuff. Even though Anika is annoying, I love her anyway.

Avery Ellis-Byerly, Grade 4
Menchaca Elementary School, TX

Scotty

Scotty is my dog. He is a German Shepherd, part wolf. Scotty is three years old and his birthday is March 3. He is the best dog I have ever had.

He is white and on his back, ears and head he is an apricot color. Scotty has humongous ears. He is about three feet tall, but when he is on his hind legs Scotty is about five foot six inches. He has a really long tail that can sweep the floor. I love Scotty.

Scotty comes whenever I call him. I taught him to play tag, be my horse and ride in the truck. I have been trying to teach him to sit ever since I got him.

The weird thing about my dog is, whenever my dad gets out of a vehicle Scotty barks at him. Also, when he wants his belly scratched he lays on his back and sticks out his tongue until you leave or scratch his belly. When my mom's car alarm goes off Scotty howls until the alarm is turned off.

My dog is the best guard dog ever! Once a mean stray dog came to my house. The dog was really scary. Scotty was mad that the dog was on his territory so he barked and fought the dog until he left. He saved me from getting bit. I love my dog, Scotty.

Shanna Skousen, Grade 6

No More Drugs

Illegal drugs? Why do they even make them? All they do is kill people! I think the people who make them, should stop. The number of people hooked on drugs is amazingly high. My opinion is everyone selling drugs should be punished. Those who are addicted need medical help.

There are many types of drugs: tobacco, opium, speed, marijuana, cocaine, meth, uppers, downers, and ecstasy. There are so many drugs, they lead people into temptation. Once people start drugs, they keep wanting more and more. Some people abuse drugs so much, they die from it.

Drugs. Who needs them? Not me, and I hope, not you!

Andrew Triona, Grade 5
Westview Elementary School, OH

Disasters

What I would do during a disaster is use my escape plan. I would also get my safety supplies. To get out the window I will tie a rope to the bed then the other side of the rope to my leg or arm. Then jump out the window.

I would need lots of supplies to survive in a disaster. I would put them in a box. It will have can openers, 3-5 days worth of food, 5-7 days worth of water, and more. I will put them in the living room.

I can escape through my door or window. It would be good to know you have something to land on like a soft bed. But getting hurt is better than dying. I would choose to meet close to Christian's house because he's my second best friend. He lives 3 blocks away on Dahlia Drive. I think I would have to go in with him after about 20 minutes.

I learned that it is important to be safe and that it's not easy to survive a disaster.

Donovan Jones, Grade 5

The Ranch

My family's ranch is a wonderful and exciting place. There are all kinds of animals to enjoy and take care of.

Our days at the ranch are filled with fun and a lot of hard work. Starting at dawn and working 'til dusk is our everyday life on the ranch. In the morning, we begin by feeding the livestock and many pets. Then, we move on to cleaning up after the horses and smaller animals. While we are cleaning, we make sure that all the animals have fresh and full troughs of water. Next, we sweep out the barn aisle of any excess dirt or sawdust. In the mornings we never have "nothing" to do.

Interacting with all of the different species of animals on our ranch is entertaining. The afternoon is our time to ride and do extra ranch work. First, I ride Pablo, the pony that I started myself. Pablo has a lot of personality and is extremely pleasurable to ride. Rookie, an incredibly fancy and cute pony, is the next horse I ride. I am training him to rope cattle and jump. Rookie has his own personality and a little bit of an attitude. There are also other colts I ride to help my step-dad. It is cool to have the opportunity to ride different types of horses.

Living on a ranch is hard work, but is also extremely exciting.

Noah Cornish, Grade 6
CORE Butte Charter School, CA

Got Pets?

I have seven pets. Their names are in order Sandy, Chilly, Trixy, Scuttles, Bob and Tom, and Ginger Snap.

First, there's Sandy. Sandy is my Australian red healer. She is a very energetic dog. Sandy loves to play catch and likes to bark at other dogs when taking a walk. Sandy is my favorite pet I have.

My second and third pets are my chinchillas. My first chinchilla is Chilly. She is always willing to go in her ball. Chilly like to make noises while you are sleeping like my other chinchilla, Trixy. Trixy, like Chilly loves to go in her ball. She loves to chew on everything but rabbit food.

Scuttles is my beta. He is Chinese colors. It's funny to watch him try to fight himself with a mirror in front of his glass jar.

My fifth and sixth pets are my sister's two mice. Their names are Bob and Tom. Bob and Tom are feeder mice. Bob is the lazy one and black and white. Tom loves to run in his ball and is gold and white.

My last pet is my one-year-old snapping turtle. Her name is Ginger Snap. Ginger is fun to play with when you put your finger in front of the glass and she tries to bite it. It makes me jump.

Now you know a little about my pets Sandy, Chilly, Trixy, Scuttles, Bob and Tom, and Ginger Snap.

Marissa Lange, Grade 6
West Central Middle School, IL

A Blind and Deaf Inspiration

Have you ever felt like something is impossible to do? Imagine how hard life was for blind and deaf Helen Keller. She possessed determination and perseverance, which led her to fulfill her dreams. She accomplished many tasks that people thought unbelievable for someone in her situation.

What are some of the goals she achieved? She actually attended a regular school, with only her governess to help her. Growing older, Helen signed her signature for thousands of people. Society at her time thought she would not even be able to attain that. Also writing a book called *The Story of My Life*, Helen changed many people's minds. All these were accomplished only because Helen Keller tried her very best. She showed determination to try to do what every body else could and, bit by bit, she achieved that dream.

Helen Keller has inspired me in many ways. First, she has inspired me to do my best in school, or at anything I do. No matter the situation, I should never give up. Even when my goal seems unattainable, I will try to fulfill it. If Helen Keller achieved it, so can I.

Shivani Chandrashekaran, Grade 6

The Green Flash

One day my Mom was driving in the car at 90 mph. Then I said, "Mom hurry tonight might be 'THE Green Flash.'" I was trembling with excitement just thinking about the possibility of seeing THE Green Flash in real life. "Hey Mom, look there's the perfect parking spot." We slammed the doors to the car and scrambled down the beach stairs through the warm grains of sand. I noticed as I was sitting there on the beach that there was an unbelievable silence in the air.

So there I am sitting with my Mom and we are anticipating what we pray to see for once in my short little life. What was happening in the moments of waiting was not anything I could have anticipated. The sea gulls were swirling around us. The beach sounded so calm like it knew that IT was going to happen tonight. My Mom and I held hands and were peaceful together which doesn't happen a lot with us. Ever since my parents got their divorce things have been chaotic. So at last we felt peace because we had hope. Hope always brings butterflies inside your stomach and that feels good. Now we watch the blazing sun say its good-byes until the morning. "Mom, it's about to happen." I slowly counted down 5, 4, 3, 2, 1, 0. I waited for a moment and promised I wouldn't blink no matter what. Then we saw it. IT happened! The Green Flash happened. It seemed like it was going so fast that it would travel around the whole world in the snap of a finger. From that day on, I have a treasured memory that will never leave me. Remember don't blink, life might pass you by!!

Molly Milford, Grade 5
Stone Ranch Elementary School, CA

Heroes

I think everybody needs a hero. My hero is my Dad. There are three reasons my Dad is my hero. They are: Number 1 he is the bravest person I know; Number 2 he was in the Army; number 3 he works at the scariest place I know of (prison). The reason he's the bravest person I know is because he really works at the crazy prison place anyway! Also, because he's not afraid of anything. He had to chase a prisoner and shoot him with a taser gun. Anyway, I can't believe he works at the crazy place! He says the people are dangerous. The last reason is he went in the Army!!! Who in their right mind would go there?! Well, that'll be my Dad. Even though he did some crazy things, he's my Dad and he is my hero.

Hannah Brabson, Grade 6
Pike Christian Academy, OH

The Rain Forest Is Calling You

Did you know that most of the Earth's oxygen comes from the rainforest? Without the rainforest, our lives would change. We need to save these tropical places!

Each minute 30 acres of land are destroyed, which is used for paper, building materials, and firewood. If you chop down the rainforest, you won't have a very good variety of medicine. Most tropical plants produce lots of medicine! Farmers burned down a lot of this land for grazing and farmland. Without all this land, the rain forest is falling apart and so is the air we breathe.

You can save the rain forest by recycling cans, bottles, motor oil, scrap metal, etc. It would also help if you reuse bags and Tupperware. Always turn off electric devices when you leave a room. Set your water temperature at 130 degrees. Turn down your heat and wear a sweater instead.

With everybody doing their share, it will increase the chance of our rainforest being saved!

Olivia Boucher, Grade 4
Maple Avenue Elementary School, WI

My Special Cat

My cat is named Snickers because he is the colors of the candy bar. I like to call him Snicker Picker. Snickers is special to me because he is kind and gentle, he is also adventurous because he hides and bounces on his toys.

Snickers keeps me company while I watch TV. He never complains about what I watch. I like to spoil him with treats and toys that I buy with my own money. He's very sad when I'm leaving to school. When I come home he is happy to see me. His baby blue eyes sparkle and he smiles with joy.

Snickers was my Easter present from my mom and dad. He was born on November 23, 2004 at 6:03 p.m. He is a Siamese Blue Seal. He got attached to me very quickly. I knew we would be best friends forever. He teases me by taking something I'm playing with and runs off. His toy is a mouse on a stick. Snickers can jump two feet high to catch it. That is why Snickers is important to me.

Kylene Archuleta, Grade 4
Santo Niño Regional Catholic School, NM

Dance Is My Life

One thing I enjoy doing is dancing. There are many reasons why dance is important to me. I have the opportunity to learn different styles of dance, make new friends and go to dance competitions.

There are different types of dance. I have been learning tap, tumbling, ballet and jazz. Tap is fun because I can hear the sound the tap shoes make when I dance. In tumbling we learn new moves like a one-handed cart wheel. Ballet is important for a dancer to learn. Ballet helps build core strength and flexibility. The other style of dance I enjoy is jazz. My jazz classes are fun because I can use my personality to act out the dance. Each style of dance helps me learn to be a great performer.

The great part about learning all about dance is the competitions I attend. The costumes I wear have lots of rhinestones on them to make me sparkle on stage. When every dancer is done dancing they give out the awards. The awards let me know I am doing a good job.

Dance is an important part of my life. I will never give up on dance. Learning in class, making friends and competing make dance great for me.

Ciara Steinbach, Grade 4
Gateway Pointe Elementary School, AZ

Horses

Do you have a horse? I don't, but I still love horses. Horses are fun to play with and they're my best friends. When I ride horses it makes me feel relaxed and calmed. If I move to the country I will buy my grandparents' thoroughbreds, Cash and April.

It's a big responsibility, so if you do get a horse you will need to tend to it properly and get the right supplies like, brushes, feed, saddles, blankets, etc. There are English and Western saddles. Western saddles have horns that you hold on to, and English saddles don't.

Health is important too; if your horse is acting bizarre don't ignore it! If you do it may lead to fatal injuries. Take your horse to the vet regularly. After long rides on scorching hot days you should give your horse a rubdown with soapy water and a hose or it smells like rotten eggs in 100 degree weather! "P.U."

Which one is for you? What you plan to do with the horse, will probably determine what kind of horse you get. If you would like to enter your horse in a contest you'll need to train your horse. Maybe you just want to have a horse for company.

Some people don't want to spend hours upon hours caring for a horse but that would be their opinion, not mine. Horses are very enjoyable. Now after reading this wouldn't you like a horse?

Kylin Grubb, Grade 4
Stilwell Elementary School, KS

My Dogs Rani and Maya

I like dogs because they're soft and cozy. I have two dogs named Rani and Maya. They love to lick my face and my hands.

My dogs were born in a quadruplet family. They're both Pomeranian dogs, born in captivity. I don't know where their mom was born but she was born in captivity. Their parents were show dogs. My parents got them three years after they were married. After I was born my two dogs started getting jealous.

One time when my dog was outside one of my dogs ran away through the gate. When we went to let the dogs in the other one was by the door barking. My mom didn't know why the dog was barking until she realized Maya was gone. She looked down at Rani and said, "That's why you were barking!"

These days they are slow-going and old, but they're the healthiest dogs the vets have seen. Whenever we have a party they run around and have fun. They love their two sisters. If we mention their names, Rani's and Maya's ears will go up. If I say they're dogs they'll bark at you. If I squat down she'll come to me. Sometimes they'll misbehave and run away but they always come back.

My parents told me that when I was not even two years old, I was sleeping with my dad. The dogs jumped up onto the bed when I was sleeping. One of them lay down next to my feet and the other one curled up right in front of me. I woke up from my nap and the dogs were surrounding me. The dogs were right next to me and I baby patted them and they both woke up.

If I want a pet dog, I prefer the Pomeranians!

Mallika S. Parlikar, Grade 4
Country Montessori School, CA

Space Mountain

We were in a big room from the future. Conner and I were next to each other. Finally we were there. We sat down and got ready. We moved. We were on Space Mountain. I readied myself by grabbing the bar in front of me. Lights flashed. I looked at Conner. He said, "Are you ready?"

I said, "Yes."

We came to a room filled with stars. It was dark. We came to the top of a hill. The countdown began. 5, 4, 3, 2, 1. I gripped the bar, but we didn't move. The music began like we were supposed to be going really fast.

The music stopped. I looked at Conner and said, "Is this supposed to happen?"

"No."

Well at least we had a good view. Then the light turned on. It was a plain room with green carpet. We took some pictures, and my dad video recorded us. It was so cool. We got to see what Space Mountain looks like inside. The people who work at Space Mountain had to come and get us off the ride one by one. After that we went on a ride again hoping we would get stuck, but it was a once in a lifetime deal.

Ashley Noel, Grade 6
Monforton School, MT

Marvelous Max

I have long brown hair and huge brown eyes. My skin is tan in color and I have two big front teeth. On my feet I wear size three and a half shoes, and I am pretty tall. Max is my name and I am a nine year old boy who is in grade four.

For fun, I like to play video games. I also like to keep active by playing soccer, baseball, and running in races. At recess I enjoy playing with my friend Trent. He is an athlete too.

I love my family, even though I always fight with my older sister. My mom cooks for me when I am hungry. My dad plays video games with me. They love me too, even my sister, although she might not always admit it.

Thanks for taking the time to read about me, Marvelous Max!

Max Ohlmann, Grade 4
Linsford Park School, AB

An Education in a Child

Everyone knows that an education is very important in life. When you go to school, you can do anything. You have better choices for work and you can understand so many things that most people who do not have an education cannot. An education can help you do many things in life.

Now, I will tell you about my education. My mother tongue is English but I go to a bilingual school. Therefore, I had to learn French. I learned it pretty quickly, but I was not perfect. My parents decided to get a French tutor. I liked the idea of it, but not the homework part. So as the years go by, I have more and more homework, but the homework is getting more and more fun; it was getting more fun not because she gave me things that were easy, but because, as the years went by I had not noticed that I started paying more attention to my homework and I got used to it. So that is why it is fun.

For most good jobs, you need to have an education; you must know how to read. If there are 100 jobs out there in the world, 100% of them are related to reading. There is also something called a résumé; a résumé is a list of all your education and accomplishments. So when you are a kid an education might not sound important, but when you grow up, you realize that it is.

Emily Nolan, Grade 5
The Study School, QC

Fighting Cancer

My Uncle Craig has cancer, and he's still battling it. September was his last month for chemotherapy. He is cancer free for right now, but he still has leukemia. He is brave, and has never given up. He is so courageous.

Uncle Craig is forty-eight years old. He is just ten years older than my mom. My mom will give him her bone marrow, when he needs it, to get better. She's very special too.

Though he has been dealing with cancer since March of 2007, Uncle Craig continues to inspire me every day.

Chelsea Moon, Grade 5
Westview Elementary School, OH

Americans Share

Americans share many things. All of them are great! Let me tell you about them, I know you will love them!

Did you know that Americans share rights? Well we do. We share many rights for example we have the right to say what we want about the government. And we have the right to worship as we please. Everyone has different ways so we can't make them do things the way we want them too.

Also we share responsibilities. They are very important. You should always obey traffic signs. Otherwise you might get in a crash. Another responsibility that is important is to treat others fairly. You might hurt someone's feelings if you are not responsible for that.

Another great thing that we share is freedom. We have freedom of speech, freedom of religion, freedom of where we live, and freedom of where we work. What a great country we have!

So, as you can see we have an amazing country with many rights, freedoms, and responsibilities! GO USA!!!!

Mikayla Karloff, Grade 4
Rohwer Elementary School, NE

Furry Friends

Bears, bears, and more bears. It's all about bears (and other animals) at Build-A-Bear. This store is filled with many different creatures you can create in your own special way.

Have you ever wondered how you make a Build-A-Bear? Well...

Step 1: Selecting your Build-A-Bear: Pick out an empty stuff animal.

Step 2: Stuffing your Build-A-Bear: You have an option of adding a voice box and putting in a heart to make your Build-A-Bear real (make sure you make a wish, spin three times, and then kiss the heart before you put it in!), put some fluff in, and then lace it. You'll soon be able to give your Build-A-Bear a big bear hug!

Step 3: Next, my favorite step — dressing and accessorizing your Build-A-Bear: Make sure you pile on the accessories! Your Build-A-Bear will love this, (I do!).

Hey, do you know who "Bearemy" is? Well, it's Build-A-Bear's sweet mascot. Bearemy was born August 21, 1998, one year after Build-A-Bear was founded by Maxine Clark in 1997. Bearemy is nine-and-a-half paws tall, and "beary" cute!

I took a survey of my class to see how many people have Build-A-Bears. Eighteen (!) out of 28 have Build-A-Bears! Even one of my teachers has one! You can tell Build-A-Bear's popularity has grown throughout the years.

Build-A-Bear is a wonderful place. I hope everyone will be able to go to Build-A-Bear; because truly, it's "Where best friends are made!"

Lora Blanco, Grade 5
Oak Crest Intermediate School, TX

My Best Friend Maryann

Hi, my name is Kaitlin Dobesh and I am writing about my dog Maryann the best dog in my life. Maryann is a medium size Black Labrador with a little bit of white hair. She is really soft and loves to be petted. Maryann and I are both 9 years old. Though she is 9 years old I say she is a puppy. Though from my eyes she is the prettiest animal I have ever seen.

Maryann is the best friend I have ever had in my life. When I am sad she will comfort me. When I need a friend she will be my friend. Every day when I get back from school, she's really happy. I say she thinks she is a puppy. Maryann has never growled or tried to bite me. She is great and very nice to me all of the time.

My mom always tells people that when I was younger and I would cry Maryann would come and sit or lay by me. My mom said that after she came I would pet her and stop crying.

I call Maryann my second mom. My mom calls her my nanny. I say she is my baby girl.

Kaitlin Dobesh, Grade 4
Santo Niño Regional Catholic School, NM

Who I Respect

I respect my brother Joe, because he is older than me so that means I need to listen to him but sometimes I don't. Sometimes I respect him when he buys me something like ice cream, candy, and video games.

My brother and I like to play a lot of sports with our friends. I always want to be on his team because he's good. That's another reason I respect him.

Mostly I respect him because he's my brother. He cheers me up when I am bored. I also respect him because he helps me with my homework.

I respect him because he's someone I can look up to. He's really cool because when I do something bad, instead of giving me a lecture or screaming at me, he helps me out. If I didn't have my brother at my side I would probably be lost because he comes and shows me the way. These are all the great reasons why I respect and love my brother.

Anthony Palomares, Grade 5
Camellia Avenue Elementary School, CA

A Gentle Moment

A gentle breeze blows across my face. The breeze shakes the tree's leafs, making a rustling sound. Some clouds are cotton white, like a huge piece of fluff. Others are grey.

I can hear grasshoppers chirping away. If you tilt your head back, you could see light blue skies and clouds floating lazily around.

Green grass grows in my family's front and backyard quickly. There might be a rabbit hiding in the wetland, though I'm not sure. A few birds might be hiding in a big tree in-between my neighbor's backyard and my family's backyard. This is what it's like on a peaceful, gorgeous day when a gentle breeze blows across my face.

Bennett Lee, Grade 5
Greenwood Elementary School, MN

Two Days in Michigan

I have two friends named Michael and Teresa. We have been friends for a long time. Then one day, their mom, Deana, invited us to their grandma's lake house. They lived in Ohio and then they moved to Michigan. So we all drove to Michigan, me, my two ants, Michael's sister and her baby Chelsea. We had put our suitcases up in our rooms. I slept with Michael, Teresa and Chelsea. Titi slept with my other aunt Vanessa. In the morning, I went in the garage to see what Michael and Teresa were doing. They were getting their life jackets to go swimming in the lake. I went with them and then we got really bored, so we asked to go to the water park. We got our paddle boat and Nikki and Vanessa paddled us to the water park. When we got there we went down the water slide like one hundred times, which was a lot of fun and when we got bored we paddled back and played Monopoly. Michael won the game and then we rented Madea and ate ice cream. We went to bed after that and then woke up early. We ate cereal for breakfast and packed up to get an early start back home. We said goodbye to everyone first and then left. When we got home, I felt like we'd been gone for ages. It was nine o'clock, we all took a shower and went to bed.

Julissa Younkin, Grade 5
The Arts Academy School, OH

My Fabulous Dog, Lady

My dog, Lady, has a very interesting story. She started out as someone else's dog, but now she is my dog! How is that you may ask? Well here's how her story goes:

One day as my grandma was inside her house, she noticed a dog wandering the streets. Now this didn't happen just that day, she had been seeing this dog wander for days now! One time the dog was at her doorstep, but when she tried to carry the dog inside, the dog ran away! This happened for many days. In the next couple of days the dog came back. This time my grandpa sliced a hot dog into pieces and tried to lure the dog into the door and close the door as soon as the dog walked in. This time the plan worked! My grandparents were happy.

After the capture, my grandma waited for 2 hours before she bathed the filthy dog. The dog was named "Lady" because she acted like one. Lady lived with my grandparents for awhile, because they found out she was abandoned. In a couple of years my dad went over to my grandparents house in Las Vegas for a business trip. My dad told them if they could give one of their dogs to me, the daughter. Their answer was yes.

As soon as my dad came back he told me the good news. In a year they gave me Lady! I was glad for the first time in my life!!!!

Angelica Justine A. Reyes, Grade 5
Cameron Elementary School, CA

Giraffes

Once when I was a child, I went to the Hogle Zoo in Salt Lake City. I saw many big creatures, but one in particular caught my attention. It was the giraffe! I went to the cage and it licked my hand! I became fascinated and ever since then I have loved giraffes.

Giraffes can be an amazing 17 feet tall and can weigh 3,000 pounds! A giraffe's heart can pump 20 gallons of blood per minute. Each stride a giraffe takes is 15 feet long! A giraffes' 22 inch long tongue can help reach leaves on tall trees. The largest giraffe on record was 19 feet tall. Their closest relative is the rare Okapi which is the last big land animal found on Earth.

Giraffes only live in Africa. They live in many countries like, Sudan, Zaire, Niger, Senegal, Chad, Kenya, Uganda, Tanzania, Zambia, and Angola. The largest female giraffe on record was 17 feet tall.

You would think that because their necks are so long giraffes have hundreds of bones in their neck, but they only have 7 huge bones. One giraffe is usually born at a time. Twins are very rare. In 1827 the first giraffe was put in a zoo. People wore "giraffe" hair that represent the horns of a real giraffe. I am glad I got the opportunity to see them at the zoo, but I would love to take a real African safari, when I am older.

Alexander Quinn Fisher, Grade 6
Thomas Jefferson Charter School, ID

Bullies

Bullying has been a big problem in schools. I've been a victim of bullying. If people don't want others to bully them then why would they bully somebody else? Bullying is an unacceptable behavior.

I think bullying is an unacceptable behavior because I've been bullied. Every time I was bullied I would be terrified, scared, and afraid. I would tell my mom or dad that somebody had been hitting me or messing with me. They always told me to push them back. I'd try but I'd get too scared.

The other reason why bullying is a big problem is because bullying can cause violence, or cause people to use weapons. Most bullies are bigger than the people getting bullied. That's why bullying needs to stop. There are lots of kids getting killed because of bullying.

Do you know how to stop bullying behavior? Well schools can hide video cameras in their building to video tape bullies so people can see who is getting bullied and who's doing the bullying.

This is a major problem. That's exactly why bullying needs to stop because people can get killed and in trouble. If I don't do it why should you?

Davis Dana, Grade 5
Starms Discovery Learning Center, WI

No Smoking: Or Pay the Price!

You've seen it everywhere: smoking. It causes cancer and diseases. It even kills! Why do people continue to smoke?

Here in America, many people smoke. They are just killing themselves, and us, too! You know what's in a cigarette? Poison with added nicotine to get you addicted!

I love it when I see that nobody is smoking in a restaurant. I can enjoy my food in peace. I can't imagine why smoking was invented. Who could ever have created such a foul-smelling, unpleasant practice? But alas, someone did.

I'm glad some people are taking a stand by setting up campaigns to stop smoking, but smoking still hasn't stopped. If we work harder, we just might make it happen.

Phillip Hedayatnia, Grade 4
Birchwood School, OH

Our Earth!

The Earth is the only known planet that supports life, but soon we may not be able to live here anymore. Why? Because of Global Warming. Ice caps are melting, endangering polar bears and other arctic animals. Some parts of the world are beginning to flood and in other parts, people are suffering from droughts.

As kids, we must take action NOW! If we all conserve water and electricity, recycle and reduce waste, we may be able to save this planet. Turning off lights when you are not in the room, carpooling or biking or walking to school are just some examples of how you can help. Remember, one person can make a difference and together we can save the planet.

We all share this magnificent planet and to keep our dear earth, we all must clean up this big mess on it. Conserve, recycle, and don't pollute. Everyone of you can help to save this priceless planet. What are you waiting for? The planet's future lies in our hands, so get to work!

Neha Mannikar, Grade 6
Cupertino Middle School, CA

Don't Put Your Finger in a Dog's Mouth

One day me, my sister Taya and my mom were playing outside in the backyard playing with my puppy. I received my puppy on August 20th which was my birthday. My mom asked me what are you going to name her? I said, "Coco." My sister and my mom agreed that Coco was a good name for the puppy. When I called the puppy Coco, she came to me. Coco wanted something to chew on. So I gave her my finger. First Coco was just sucking on it. I said, "Coco is a nice puppy." My mom and my sister agreed. Coco was trying to bite me a little bit, but I took my finger from her and said, "That is not nice." Then I gave her my finger back. Then she really started biting me. I said, "Ouch! That hurt!" My mom and my sister said, "Are you all right?" My mom said now you know not to put your finger in a dog's mouth. That is when I learned my lesson.

Isis Brown, Grade 5
McMonagle Elementary School, MI

A Mother's Fuel

Marion C. Garretty once said, "Mother love is the fuel that enables a normal human being to do the impossible." My mom's fuel inspires and motivates me to multitask, persevere, and make valuable decisions.

She performs a great job of multitasking by being both a caring mother and an experienced clinical laboratory scientist. Even with her arduous job, she possesses a rush of enthusiastic excitement and looks forward to her next responsibility after an exhausting day. As a dedicated mother, she meets our needs with ease. By emulating my mother's ability to multitask, I excel in both academics and extra curricular activities.

My determined mom always perseveres. If either frustration or failure occurs, she displays determination. With my mother's constant support and encouragement, I have learned tenacity by working hard and never giving up. Perseverance enables me to overcome perplexing math concepts.

In addition, my mom always decides wisely. Many people find making decisions challenging, but I have learned from her to make great judgments. Whenever I have a choice, I weigh the pros and cons and form a decision by selecting the one that would assist me in the future. So when deciding to perform a community service, I elected junior life guarding as it teaches commitment, sacrifice, and endurance.

A mother like no other makes me feel special. I incorporate inspirational qualities to pursue my goals. Thank you, mom, for being a great role model and my inspiration.

Ashley Wong, Grade 6
Challenger School – Ardenwood, CA

Who I Look Up To!

Who do you look up to? I admire my brother, Jorge. I bet you're wondering why I admire my brother. I admire my 13 year old brother because he is good at sports, especially soccer. He has many shirts of soccer teams because he was on so many soccer teams. Right now he is on Team USA. He teaches me lots of soccer tricks so I can juke people (to do tricks that fool or confuse them). That's one of the reasons why I admire my brother.

Another reason I admire Jorge is because he taught me lots of things before I started school! When I was in kindergarten I knew my numbers 1-50. Also if this gets published I'll thank him for teaching me how to write. But also I'll thank Ms. Tichenor and the publisher(s).

The third reason why I admire my brother is because he gives me money when I need it, like when I have overdue library books. So, in conclusion, if my brother wasn't here I wouldn't be who I am today, and my life wouldn't be how it is today.

Ignacio Solorio, Grade 5
Camellia Avenue Elementary School, CA

Puppies

Have you ever seen a puppy? If you have, aren't they so cute! They look like a lost baby that is trying to find a way home. So when you see that lost face, help it find its way home. So get a puppy. They are so friendly and harmless!

Another reason to get a puppy is if you are lonely there is no reason to say that you are sad and bored. Puppies are so full of energy! They will play with you from sunrise to sunset. When you tell them it's time for bed they'll say, "no it's time to play!" That's another reason!

Sometimes they are hard to train. Like when you tell them to do something they look at you like you are totally coo coo. But it is all worth it. You can do anything with it like take it on a walk without a leash and you will stop getting complaints from neighbors!

They are also like a sheep that follows you everywhere! Like when you get lost it will sniff you out of bushes and if it gets lost it will sniff you out even if you are in another town. Have you heard that dogs have the best noses? Well they do!

So get a puppy, see what it's like, they'll be like a stuffed baby monkey to you!!!!

Allison Berhost, Grade 4
Santo Niño Regional Catholic School, NM

Lauren

My name is Lauren, it means glory. Probably, the most normal thing about me is my origin, American. My name is yellow. It is bright and flexible, and tries to strive high. My name is a masterpiece. It is a delicate piece of art that is unique in its own way. It is colorful, because I can do many things. My name is determination; To be unlike anyone else. My name is eleven. Eleven is two, together, the sticky glue that keeps everyone from falling apart. My middle name is from a princess, Princess Caroline, because my parents think that I am as beautiful as her. My name is splashes in water. The air bubbles bursting up with ideas and decisions. I have met one other Lauren, but we are all different. If I could have another name it would be Chrystal; A unique balance of courage and beauty, but I'll stick with Lauren, because that's who I am.

Lauren Loeffler, Grade 6
North Oaks Middle School, TX

September 11

September 11, 2001. What kind of person would kill other people to prove a point? What horrible, horrible, person would do such a thing? Not all people are bad, in fact, most people are good. Here are a few examples.

Walter Reed defeated Yellow Fever, a disease that hadn't been defeated for 400 years and "Little Bad Legs" the boy who would not give up, Dr. Martin Luther King, Jr. helped bring peace between two races and YOU!

You can make a difference, even if you think you can't, even if you want to roll over and say "whatever." There's a difference only *you* can make!

Amber Griffin, Grade 5
Snake River Montessori School, ID

The Snow Leopard

The Snow Leopard is endangered because many people hunt them for fur coats. There are only about 2,500 of them left. They are found in Eastern Asia. During the 1960's a Snow Leopards pelt was worth a lot of money.

The Snow Leopard has grey and white fur with numerous spots on it's neck. A Snow Leopard's tail is striped, and can grow up to 90 cm long. A Snow Leopard weighs 35-55 Kilograms (77-121 lbs.).

A Snow Leopard is known for its very beautiful fur, and spots. The life span of a Snow Leopard is 15-18 years, but in captivity, they live until they're 20 years of age.

I like Snow Leopards because they are very beautiful creatures of God, and shouldn't be so mistreated. With Snow leopards on the endangered list, it makes me feel so sad because they're just like us but with fur (and we need pretty things in life).

Ashley Gaydosh, Grade 6
The Arts Academy School, OH

Football Practice

The first day of football was excruciating because we had to run for two hours straight. I was drenched in sweat like a pig in the sun. I was as nervous as a chicken about to have its head cut off. I wanted to make first string. But I didn't think I could because it was my first year.

The tryouts for positions were on the second week of football. I tried out for D-Line. I got the positions! I was as happy as a monkey about to get fed a banana. But I didn't make first string like I predicted. I still held my head high, I did make second string. I am glad I made second string and not third string.

At the end of practice I was glad that I made second string. I went over to one of my friends and asked him, "What position did you tryout for?" "The quarterback," he replied.

Cameron Strawn, Grade 5
Dingeman Elementary School, CA

Foreign Language

I think people should teach more foreign languages in school. Most schools teach at least one foreign language, but my school doesn't teach a foreign language. I surveyed thirteen people and four people wanted to learn French; one person wanted to learn Swedish; three people wanted to learn Latin; three people wanted to learn German; and one person wanted to learn Irish. Honestly, people really want to learn foreign languages. At first, this survey was loaded with different languages, but I had to just lower it down to one language. The most popular is French. Lots of people have friends or family members that could teach them a foreign language, but some don't have that luxury of people teaching them a different language. These people would need to learn the language in school. To really sum it up, more schools should teach more languages for students to learn.

Hannah Levine, Grade 4
Lincoln Elementary School, WA

A Problem

Do you remember when you were little and your hero was Superman? Here's the problem. Today's heroes are people like me. Older people. Little kids do everything you do. They probably don't think "cool" people like you, me, and my friends say babyish things like please and thank you. You may not notice, but I do, that little kids look up to you and watch everything you do each and every day. They see you walk down to the office because you got in a fight. You think okay, no biggy, I do this all the time. But what you don't think about is what that little kid thinks when he sees you do that. He's thinking that if my hero goes down to the office then so should I. If you wear your hat to the side and pants past your knees then they think, "I should cut holes in my jeans and sag them so I can look like my hero." If you don't say thank you, then you're pretty much telling that little kid, "Why should you say thank you? I don't. It's not cool." Today kids are forced to say excuse me because they didn't learn when they were young or that one older kid taught them wrong. You could go anywhere and you will find at least five kids that say thank you without being brainwashed into doing it.

I hope this tells you something about the world's problem and loss in manners.

Hannah Huxford, Grade 6
Concord Ox Bow Elementary School, IN

The Life of a Dog

First off, the dog is born. There are many different kinds of dogs, Shepherd, Husky, Labrador and Pugs. But those are just a few of the different kinds of dogs.

When the dog is ready to leave his or her mother, they are either sold or given to the kennel. In the kennel they are fed and taken care of. Often people come and go along with the dog.

By now the dog will be adjusted to this world of people and will now be part of your family. If you have kids you will want a quiet little dog, or maybe you want one just for you. Perhaps you may want to teach your dog tricks or not; it's your choice. If you want to get a second dog or pet I think you need to remind yourself of these things.

1. Is your dog settled in?
2. Will your dog be able to get along with another dog?
3. Will you and the animal get along?

If you don't get along then you might take it out on the dog. If the dog gets really mad it might run away or take it out on you or anybody else around.

If your dog is sick take it to the vet. Try a variety of vets to see which one you and your dog like best. Try bonding with your dog. Buy treats and take it for walks. That concludes The Life of a Dog.

Jaden Jack, Grade 5
Forest Hill Public School, ON

When I Think About September 11, 2001

I feel really good when I do good deeds. That is why good deeds are important because it keeps everybody happy and it makes me happy too. When I do a good deed, I think about September 11, 2001. That day was the day when the Twin Towers in New York were destroyed by terrorists.

Lots of men and women did good deeds that day. There were policemen and firemen that rescued people and put out the fires. There were businessmen and women who lost their lives to save other people.

I really think that is a really good deed. When I do community work like picking up trash in the park or whitewashing walls from graffiti, I think about all of the people who lost their lives on September 11th. I even think about all of the men and women in Iraq fighting and I think that's a *great* deed. They are losing their lives for us.

I'm really glad some people are great enough to do great deeds. That's why I think doing good deeds are great and great deeds are marvelous.

Steffany R. Snell, Grade 6
Snake River Montessori School, ID

Reading

When I read I become part of the story. I could be Harry Potter battling the dark Lord Voldemort, or Eragon riding Saphira. When I read it's like the world we're in doesn't exist. Reading is my porthole to a new world. When I read, I sword fight from the safety of my house. If books were no more, I think I would be a lifeless blob lying on the floor.

Half the intelligence I have, I gained from reading. When I feel down, I read and cheer up. Reading helps me learn how to do different activities, like making a bow and arrows, finding flint, and making a homemade flash light. When I find a good book I'll read all day until I finish. When I was in third grade, I started reading *Captain Underpants*. Then I started reading more and more. My reading skill improving whilst I did so. That's why reading is important to me.

Danny Radosevich, Grade 6
Spring Creek Elementary School, WY

Friendship

There are many values to live, and friendship is an important one. To be a friend you enjoy sharing many things. When I think of friendship, these words come to mind: love, fairness, understanding, fellowship, and good buddies.

There are different ways to show friendship. One example is sharing possessions or time with another. You can play with friends when they are alone. Friends don't lie or steal from each other.

I have learned many things about friendship. I see it at school when we get along and don't fight. We help each other when someone is hurt. At home, we are friends by sharing things, working together on chores, and telling the truth.

Friendship is an important value to your life.

Fermin Saldana, Grade 5
Covington Elementary School, NE

3 Types of Racing Popular in Europe

Le Mans is one of the racing types popular in Europe. The rules of Le Mans are: the maximum amount one driver can drive before switching (in a normal race) is one hour and if you cause damage to an opponent car you will receive a penalty; sometimes it can cost you the whole race! The most famous race in Le Mans is the Le Mans 24 hour race where each driver drives for 12 hours total in this big event. Some teams are Aston Martin (Aston Martin DBR9), Risi Competitionizone (Ferrari F430), White Lightning Racing (Ferrari F430), Compuware (Corvette Z06), Advan (Callaway C12) and Viper (Viper Gtsr).

Formula One is another popular racing league in Europe. The rules of Formula One are the same as that of Le Mans except that they happen more often. The most stressful track in F1 is Monaco because it has lots of tight turns. Various teams are: Ferrari, BAR and McLaren.

One of the most popular racing leagues in Europe is the World Rally Championship (WRC). The main objective of a rally race is to try to get the least amount of time on a rally course. The Monte Carlo rally is the biggest and very first race of the season. It is worth a lot of points because of the snowy roads. Some teams are Subaru, Mitsubishi, Citröen and Peugeot.

Ian Shafer, Grade 5
Barrington Elementary School, OH

Smoking

"P.U! What is that smell?"

"I don't know. It's not me."

"Hey look! Someone's smoking!"

You know, smoking is a deadly thing to do. It's so addictive once you try it. It means you won't feel better unless you smoke. But people only start smoking because they don't fit in, they're depressed, or because of peer pressure. Peer pressure is when someone mentally forces you to do something. Each cigarette also shortens your life by 7 minutes. Imagine what you could do with all this time. 7 multiplied by 81 years = 567 minutes! 567 minutes x 2 cigarettes a day = 1134 minutes. You could accomplish many things in 1134 minutes. If you smoke, you have more chances of getting lung cancer. If you smoke often, eventually you'll get very sick.

Second-hand smoking is just as bad. It's when you smoke and someone else breathes in that polluted air and you could die earlier in life. Or you could get lung cancer even if you don't smoke from second-hand smoke.

Smoking is not healthy and it is just stupid! So for people who do smoke, you should think about what you're doing to yourselves and the environment. Those people who don't smoke, you've protected your health.

Adam Shen, Grade 6
Northwood Public School, ON

Fun Campin'

"Help!" I shouted. I was running on granite as fast as I could. My best friend and I were playing a game of tag as usual. I ran up a big slope, crisp green leaves whooshed by my ear. I turned my head only to see Shane right behind me. I hesitated; I hadn't jumped off this piece of granite before. Shane was gaining on me so I jumped. I overbalanced landing in the softly crackling dead leaves and I crashed into a soft bag in my tent.

Shane crashed down on top of me. I jumped up, flinging Shane on his own sleeping bag and put my foot on top of him triumphantly. He didn't seem bothered that I had won play fighting. It was hard not to be optimistic on a morning like this. "Duncan," Shane gasped, "We should take a break now."

"Ok," I panted.

I noticed that a grey light filtered through the tent flaps. It was still morning. I laughed at Shane; he was backwards in his sleeping bag. "Let's go see if breakfast has been made yet!"

I jumped up and watched Shane try to escape his sleeping bag. When he got out we raced to the camping table. "I smell pancakes and eggs!" I yelped. Our hair streamed in all directions as we sprinted, homing in on the great smell. Soon we were eating hungrily. In that moment I realized that Shane will always be my best friend, whatever happens.

Duncan Klug, Grade 5
Dingeman Elementary School, CA

University of Northern Iowa Panthers

University of Northern Iowa is off to a great start this year. So far they are 4-0. They played the Iowa State Cyclones, South Dakota State, Minnesota State, and Drake.

The Panthers are one of four teams in Iowa. There are the Iowa Hawkeyes, Iowa State Cyclones, Drake Bulldogs, and the UNI Panthers. The Panthers are the "unofficial champions" since they beat Drake. The Panthers beat ISU Cyclones, and ISU beat the Iowa Hawkeyes. Now they are the "unofficial champions." They beat Iowa State 24-13, Minnesota State 41-14 South Dakota State 31-17, and Drake 35-7.

Next, they have homecoming at the UNI dome, Sat. Oct. 13. They are going to be playing the Southern Illinois Salukis. So far they are ranked 2nd in their division. I got tickets so my family and I are going to the game, but they aren't very good tickets. We got our tickets two weeks before the game and now they are all sold out. The last sold out game was in 1995. I think the Panthers are going to be really good, but the thing I don't like is that on "NCAA 08" a game, the Panthers aren't good. I can't wait to see their record at the end of the year. GO PANTHERS!

Michael Kuntz, Grade 6
Orchard Hill Elementary School, IA

Hard Work

It started when I saw my report card laying in front of me. I just couldn't believe my eyes. I took a quick look at it and I was so amazed because I got really good grades. I was so proud of myself because I knew that I made such a strong effort. In order to become a very good student here are some steps you need to follow.

Number one, when you are going to have a test it is best to study every single night and don't goof around. Number two, when you have homework you need to be responsible for getting it finished and turned in on time. Number three, if you have a job you need to be a hardworking person and you need to show that you care.

Today is a great day to become a hard worker. You can do it!

Maria Gonzalez, Grade 5
Covington Elementary School, NE

Shopping

The sun was beaming down on downtown South Carolina when all of the girls in the family were shopping just for fun. Everyone wanted a drink and lunch. So we went to eat lunch at a place called The Purple Lobster. After we ate lunch, all of us looked inside the market. Emily and I got stuffed animals. Emily got a puppy and I got a hippo. Our moms got us crystals with light-up stands to put them on at night.

The next morning, we all got up and went to Quicksilver/Roxy to get a couple swim shirts and suits for Emily, Delaney, and I. So we got our stuff and left the store. Then we went to the baby doll store. I got a blond baby doll and Emily got a toddler that had strawberry blond hair. We also got outfits for them. After shopping at the baby doll store we went home. That's how my summer shopping spree went!

Carlyn McKee, Grade 5
Barrington Elementary School, OH

How I Got My Pets

I want to tell how I got my pets. My first pet is Buster, I found her in my Grandma's yard. How she got her name is because she likes to knock things over. She is a Calico.

My second pet is Susie. She ran in front of my mom's car; she looks like a Susie, and she is a Wheaten Terrier.

My third pet is Casey. I found him at Safeway so I call him Safeway kitten. I really like that name, he is a Tabby.

My fourth pet is Alex, he was a housewarming present. I like that name, he is a Belgian Malinois.

My fifth pet is Lady. How I found her, she was walking in the street. How I got her name is because she is an old lady, she is a Springer Spaniel.

My sixth pet is Sammy, I found him on my front porch. How I got his name is because he'll disappear. He's a wild tabby.

My seventh pet is Willy. Willy was kicked out by neighbors so we took him. His name was already Willy.

Kimberlyn Lorance, Grade 4
Gateway Pointe Elementary School, AZ

Million Dollar Goals

Do you have really big goals that you dream of achieving someday? I do. They almost sound impossible to do unless you're a millionaire! My goals seem impossible, but I know that if I get a good education like I'm getting right now, I know that they'll be a piece of cake!

I want to be a veterinarian when I grow up. I know that I'll have to go through a lot of college, but it'll be worth it! I love studying animals and learning new things about them. My favorite animal is a horse, and I want to have *lots* of those once I'm older.

I'd like to begin my career by having my own, small office. I'll work to get my scholarship and graduate college, then, I'll start by building a *large, beautiful* home. I'd like to have a veterinarian's office to be attached to half of my house. I'd like to have lots of children and animals, and eventually start my own veterinary clinic. On my farm, I'll have tons of animals. After school, my children will do their chores on the farm, then play basically all day! I call that living the life! My goals sound pretty much impossible, but if I work hard enough, I know that they can be achieved.

If you have large goals that seem impossible, I encourage you to work on them until they're achieved. *Nothing is impossible!*

Mariah Hassard, Grade 6
Thomas Jefferson Charter School, ID

Smoking

A high percent of teens begin smoking early in their life. Smoking destroys your life in so many ways. It would take a long list to tell all the ways smoking could kill a person. Taking one of those ugly, white, hot things and putting them in a person's mouth starts shortening their life right then.

Smoking destroys a person's lungs by not allowing them to breathe. They may be told that smoking makes them cooler, but it really narrows their chances of living long. Smoking also messes up your brain cells, too. Smoking destroys everything in your system.

Your life is shortened a whole lot from smoking cigarettes. When a person smokes it slows them down in sports and also thinking. IT makes your life not worth moving around. This is a major life-ending thing to do.

When cigarettes are put in your mouth, it is like setting a bomb off in there. It blows up so many important parts that are needed for your system to work. Smoking would change your life forever. It will destroy everything in its path.

Smoking can also be very gross. It can turn a person's fingers and toes blue. Tobacco is said to have bird poop in it. It has also been said that it has worms in it, too. I would never in my life smoke and so can you. For God gave you a brain, so just don't light up!

Andrew Clevenger, Grade 6
Southport 6th Grade Academy, IN

Mrs. Saltzman

Mrs. Saltzman is my favorite teacher, and there is not enough good I can say about her. I'll start with her qualities. She is sweet, and kind, loving, understanding, peaceful, caring, a good teacher, fun, and Godly. That is why I love her so much! She helps me and makes learning fun. She is always there ready to hug me when I need her, or just need someone. I will be so sad when I leave this school because I will not get to see her. Her love is always in my heart, and I will never let it leave because I hold it so dear. She seems as if she is the perfect teacher, and I have no doubt she is. She is always there for me, and I will always do the same for her no matter what.

Kali Cool, Grade 5
Pike Christian Academy, OH

My Baby Sister and Me

I remember when my baby sister was born. She was so pretty. I liked to feed her. I would give her milk from a bottle. I would play with her and my uncle's daughter. I use to be the baby-sitter on the weekend.

On Monday I would watch T.V., and play my games after I ate my oatmeal. Sometimes I would read to my baby sister, then some days we would watch movies. One day we watched a show named Nature, then I played Nature on my game. My baby sister is growing up, but I still feed her and play with her. Some days we have pizza and hamburgers and we tell stories. I like to tell stories and I like to write stories. I like to do a lot of things. Some times I skate on my skateboard and I play with my friends. My friends are Joe, Brittany Jones and Sunny Jones. I like to ride my bike and I like school. I like to go to the zoo with my friends. But I am me and I like taking care of my baby sister.

Sonnie Lewis, Grade 6
Prospect Elementary School, OH

I Have the Sword and Shield

My Bible I value very much. It helps me learn more about Jesus Christ. I love to read my Bible whenever I have time. It helps me understand how Jesus died on the cross for our sins. The Bible helps me to be a better person. It especially helps me understand life, like how it's so hard and tough. My mom encourages me to read the Bible and to pray to God. When I read the first sentence in the Bible I was amazed. How God created the Earth and how he created Adam and Eve, and how they were the first humans on Earth. But my favorite chapter in the Bible is Psalms. Psalms helps through difficult challenges in my life. The verse that encourages me to do the right thing is Psalms 23: 1-6. That verse inspired me to do the right thing even more when I read it. So when I'm doing wrong I think of that verse, and it help me. I'm so thankful for the Bible and what it teaches me. The Bible helps me in life so it should help you. So pick out a verse that you like and that helps you relax, and use it when you're mad.

Jeremiah Bailey, Grade 6
Linfield Christian School, CA

9/11 Good Deed Day

September 11th is a day that we should do good deeds to show respect for the people who died. Good deeds are opening the doors for somebody or helping somebody that needs help. You can help to feed poor people. You can visit people in a retirement home and sing Christmas carols to them.

If you don't want to help in those ways, you can do other things too. You can pay attention to your teacher, and listen in class.

It is important to do good deeds because it makes you a good person and it's a nice thing to do. Good deeds make me feel great. It will make you feel good too.

Matthew Goriup, Grade 4
Snake River Montessori School, ID

One of the People I Admire

Have you ever had a person you admire? Well, I do, my dad. One reason I admire my dad is because he helps me with my homework. He helps me on math and spelling. He also signs my reading log or I ask my mom.

Another reason I respect my dad is because he's always nice to me. He's always helping me on projects. On my mission project he helped me build the Santa Inez Mission. I'm pretty sure he's going to help me on my state report and neighborhood map.

One more reason I respect my dad is because we always go to the park. When we are at the park we always watch people play soccer. Sometimes we even play together. Sometimes it gets so hot we leave.

I admire my dad because he helps me with my homework, he always helps me on projects, and we always play soccer.

Henry Santos, Grade 5
Camellia Avenue Elementary School, CA

I Believe

I believe in a lot of things. One of the things that I believe in is peace. Peace can mean a lot of things, it can mean inner tranquility or it can mean the opposite of war. The type of peace that I am talking about is the opposite of war.

I believe that a perfect world would be a world without war, a world in which everyone could get along. We could still have different opinions and disagreements about things like slavery, or the draft, but not fight over them. War only happens because people have a lack of imagination. If people could make up a nonviolent alternative like civil disobedience, a protest or just working it out with words, a lot of pain would be saved. One example of civil disobedience was Martin Luther King's boycott. His boycott was for the equal rights of African Americans in the U.S.

I believe that the killing of people is wrong, and that there is always another way. Sometimes I think that world leaders just start wars as an easy way out. Leaders who start wars are not serving their country the least bit. This is my view on war.

Ceryn Schoel, Grade 6
La Mariposa Montessori School, NM

Hunting

The first deer I shot was an eight point buck at my grandparents' ranch in Schroeder, Texas on November 8, 2005.

That day it was about 39 degrees outside. I was wearing my camouflage clothes and boots. As the sun started to peek out from behind the enormous oak trees, I heard leaves crunching. My dad spotted two coyotes coming towards us. I slowly raised the gun, cocked the bolt and released the safety button. POW!! I got one! This was probably a good thing since coyotes kill baby deer and baby calves. My dad and I waited patiently for another five minutes or so, and I saw something move out of the corner of my eye. There he was standing behind two young does. This was the deer we had been scouting for since deer season began. I started sweating and shaking a bit, but then I paused for a few seconds to get myself together. Once again, I slowly raised the gun, cocked the bolt and released the safety button. I carefully examined the buck as I aimed the crosshairs on his thick neck. POW!! I missed the first shot. POW!! "Yes," I yelled. He dropped to the ground. I put the rifle back on safety and placed it in the back of my grandpa's 4x4 John Deere Gator. We tagged the deer and loaded him up in the Gator. What a great hunt!

Garrett Stockbauer, Grade 5
Aloe Elementary School, TX

The Tragic Night of 1912

"Extra, extra, read all about it!" The R.M.S. Titanic, the unsinkable ship, hit an iceberg at 11:40 pm on April 14th, 1912, and has sunken to the bottom of the icy cold Atlantic Ocean. She struck the iceberg about 400 miles off Newfoundland, Canada. The holes that were made by the iceberg were only the size of a refrigerator! She was fully sunk to the bottom of the ocean at 2:20 am, April 15th, 1912.

Titanic was taking its maiden voyage from Belfast, Ireland to New York. She sunk 12,050 feet in two hours forty minutes to the bottom of Davey Jones' Locker at her final resting spot. Seven hundred and five out of two thousand two hundred eight perished that night. Some of the passengers were rich, some were poor, and some were even famous. The majority of survivors were first class passengers especially women and children. The lower classes didn't survive as well as the first class passengers did because their rooms were located closer to the water so it came in their rooms first.

There were many needless deaths on the Titanic that tragic night. The chaotic atmosphere was worsened by the lack of lifeboats. Most of the lifeboats left the Titanic without their full capacity of people. Despite all of the new technology of the day, the unsinkable Titanic did not survive.

Patrick McGibben, Grade 4
La Costa Heights Elementary School, CA

Cat

After my pet Bailey died my whole family was in pain, except for my little sister had no clue what had made everyone cry. We knew we had to get a new cat fast. My dad was the first one to find the new kitten. He was a Siamese apple head kitten. Just like Bailey!

We had to drive all the way to Wisconsin to get him. We would meet at McDonald's. We got there first and had to wait in *suspense*; after what seemed like forever a car pulled up next to us. A woman came out with something under her coat…suddenly a kitten head popped out of her jacket. The moment that fuzzy head popped out I knew he was purrrfect. We rolled down the window; she gave us the kitten. We named him Koko because of his tan cocoa colored fur. We put a "K" instead of a "C" because we thought "C" was for a girl and "K" was for a boy. Right now he is just teeth and fur but he is turning into a fine cat. No cat is as good as Bailey, but he is pretty close!

Lexie Ogdahl, Grade 5
Greenwood Elementary School, MN

Herlinda Magana

My grandma was one of the sweetest women I have ever met, she was 52 when she died, she died on February 1, 2006. I had barely come home in the best mood ever and then my mom told me that she had died. I overheard my dad talking to my mom saying that he was going to go to Mexico with my big sister and that he didn't want to take the whole family because they where going to go with my uncle. My grandma's name is Herlinda Magana; she died of cancer.

My Nina was driving her to the hospital because my grandma was having a hard time breathing and halfway there she passed out. My nina still kept going to see if they could do something to her but it was to late. My Nina called all my family members that live in Mexico and they all hurried to the hospital. It was a very sad day for us and it was especially sad for my dad because she was his mom. It was very hard for me to let her go and it still is but I know I will never forget her and neither will any of my family members because we all loved her very much and as my dad says the only place we could find her is in our hearts.

Anays Magana, Grade 6

How to Be a Friend

Have you ever had a new friend? It's not easy. To begin, you have to be a fun, nice, and respectful person. Next, I have an example of helping people with work in the classroom. If you ever find anyone alone you should ask him or her to be part of your learning group. If you are one of those people that are always shy, just go up to a new person and say, "Hi." Probably, you just made a new friend. A friend is always there for you. If you are in a bad time, a friend is always going to be there for you. Everybody has classmates to make into friends. So be happy!

All in all, that is how to be a friend.

Herlinda Magana, Grade 5
Covington Elementary School, NE

My Inspirational Hero

"Yes! Congratulations, woo hoo," the fans yelled.

Lance Armstrong, perhaps the greatest man to ever pedal a bike, had won his first Tour de France. The Tour de France is the biggest and more important biking event in the world. It consists of twenty-two grueling stages across two countries, France and England. In 1996 Lance Armstrong was diagnosed with testicular cancer, but he still continued to stay in shape at this time. In 1997 he recovered from his cancer and in 1999 Lance Armstrong won his first Tour de France. He continued to win six more for a record of seven in a row.

Born in Texas, as a young boy Lance Armstrong continued moving around in the state. He participated and tried to win many triathlons, but liked biking the best and pursued his dream of becoming a professional biker. Lance Armstrong is an unbelievable inspiration to athletes and kids just like me. He fought cancer and was still able to win seven races. When accused of taking performance-enhancing steroids, he defended himself bravely, and nothing was proven against him. He never gave up and that is what I would like to do, never give up. This is what I would like to do when I grow up; to always do my best, not matter what the obstacles.

I'm already practicing this when I play as goalkeeper for my soccer team. I also try to beat my own statistics in all the Presidential Fitness exercises we do in school.

Nirav Murthy, Grade 6
Challenger School – Ardenwood, CA

Thanksgiving

Today is Thanksgiving and I look forward to this day every year! There are many things about this day that I really enjoy and things that I am thankful for.

One of the many things I really like about Thanksgiving is the Thanksgiving dinner. It makes the kitchen smell good for the whole day. At dinner my family has turkey with gravy and cranberry sauce, butternut squash casserole, green peas, stuffing and mashed potatoes. For dessert we have pumpkin pie. I help make the pie and, if there are any extra pieces of dough, I bake pie dough cookies with them. The dinner tastes delicious and it's hard not to eat too much.

I also like the celebration of the holiday. There is a long weekend and my grandparents usually come to our house for dinner. I get to see my grandad who lives in St. Catharines, which is approximately an hour away, and my grandmother who lives in downtown Dundas (my town) but can't drive.

I feel thankful that I live in Canada, a secure country that is relatively rich compared to some countries in the world. I have nutritious food, good shelter and safe water. Another thing I feel thankful for is having excellent teachers at school. Most of all I feel thankful that I have a family that loves me and cares for me.

Travis Stoddart, Grade 6
Sir William Osler Elementary School, ON

Maccabia

When I go to an overnight camp we play a game called Maccabia. Maccabia is a Jewish athletic event, like the Olympics. The games begin usually with a skit which turns into questions about Maccabia. Next 8 counselors run onto the stage wearing red, yellow, blue, or green. It is never announced and is a surprise for the whole camp.

There are 2 days of competition with the first day being sports. Some of the sports are tennis, flag football, basketball, swimming, softball and dodge ball. At night everyone goes to the cafeteria and wins points for singing/participation. On the second day the teams make cheers, songs and even anthems to get their team fired up for the triathlon. For the triathlon you swim a lap around the lap pool, ride your bike around to the oak tree where you then have to sprint all the way to the finish line. After the triathlon there is an all camp race. For example we had to eat doughnuts off of trees and do a puzzle with peanut butter and honey on our fingers.

When everyone is in the theater we all listen for the events we played. The camp divides the age groups into 8-9, 10-12, and 13-15 years old. Each group wins points for each of the sports. At the end of the games the points are rounded up and the team with the most points wins. This is one of the most favorite and competitive camp activities for everyone.

Tyler Gibson, Grade 6
Argyle Middle School, TX

The Day My Little Sister Was Born

One day my mom was lying on the couch, she was eating potato chips. She was expecting to have a baby real soon. I told my mom to call me when the baby kicked. She called me, "T.T. the baby is kicking." I ran in there and started to rub my mom's stomach. I said, "All this is my baby sister!" I saw her kick. I said "Wow!" She kept kicking, I said that the baby was mad because she was feeding her those nasty potato chips. The chips were spicy, but my mom really liked them.

I left my mom on the couch and went to the porch because she did not really feel good.

My mom and I had been staying with my aunt and would be there until we bought a new house. But it was fun living with my aunt.

While my grandma was in the bathroom getting dressed and singing. My aunt Lilly was in the kitchen cooking breakfast when she heard my mom saying that her stomach was hurting. My mom started to really complain about her stomach hurting. When I went into the living room to see my mom I said, "I love you." My mom said, "and so do I, and I will love you forever no matter what." I started crying. Then my mom screamed, "My water broke!"

The next day I had a brand new beautiful little baby sister!

Tautianna Robinson, Grade 5
Prospect Elementary School, OH

Knights

When a knight's boy becomes six or seven he is sent to a castle. Then, he'd be trained by the lord, or king, to become a knight. First, he is a paige. He plays a variety of training games that include wrestling, piggyback wrestling, and sword training with blunt wooden swords and tiny round shields called bucklers. A paige rarely ever learned how to read because it wasn't thought to be very knightly. The ladies of the manor taught him manners. Last, sometimes they got trained at arms with squires.

At around the age of 14 a paige must show promise to become a squire. A squire is kind of like a knight's servant. If a knight needs weapons or armor the squire brings him some. Unlike the paige the squire plays with real weapons! They play games with real knights too! If they got through all of that, they got knighted or "dubbed."

Robert Mansour, Grade 5
Cameron Elementary School, CA

The Day My Life Changed

The day my life changed is when I had a decision to make that caused life or death. I chose life.

It happened on December second, two thousand and four. I felt like a hero.

I had to make a decision quickly. I grabbed latex gloves, warm water, and a towel. I was going to save lives.

Treasure, my dog, was having puppies, and couldn't get them out. Seeing her in pain made me cry. She was bleeding and wouldn't stop. I pulled out seven when she was howling. I waited on her for awhile and then started again. I pulled out another ten when she got stuck. I panicked trying to think. I tried remembering what to do when it hit me. She must have a runt. So I have to get it out slowly or she'll die.

I saved eighteen puppies that day and it turns out there were 4 runts, Arwen, Cleopatra, Ceaser, and Titian. I felt great saving the puppies and their mom. I wish I had a license to save dogs every day. I'm glad I was brave and was able to do the try.

Alexandria Melton, Grade 6
Milltown Elementary School, IN

Poody, My Cat

My cat's name is Poody. I know that you are probably thinking that it is a weird name, but it's his name. He is 18 years old. When he walks he is very slow. Every time you pick him up, he is so bony! Cats are very sneaky. One time, at my nanny's house, we almost lost him. We thought he ran off when he was in the garage the whole time! Another time, my grandpa chased the cat all over their property. My grandpa finally gave up and went back in the house. He was on his way in and he saw Poody in the window! The cat that he was chasing was the wrong cat. Cats are really tricky. When my mom brought him home, she called him Hamlet. Then she decided to call him Poody. I enjoyed writing this about my cat.

Ivy Taylor, Grade 4
Burchett Elementary School, TX

Friendships

Why is friendship hard to get? First it is hard to get because you can't just barge in and say, "You are my new friend." You have to get to know each other first. For example, my friends Silvia, Andrea, Alicia, and Elizabeth and I are friends because we understand each other and we got to know each other first.

Maybe if you want a friend you could probably invite them to play or to a birthday. It would be nice for them and you to make pals. Then when you are friends, she or he might give you gifts when you are sick in a hospital or for your birthday. Sometimes they even give you cards that say, "Buddies Forever." Pals always help each other for everything. Sometimes you want to be friends and you try to get along. It may not turn out like you want it to be. But sometimes you still want to try to go for it. It might work next time. Maybe you could be like my friends Silvia, Andrea, Alicia, and Elizabeth and I and just get along and never break each other's friendship.

To bring the memory back, friendship is real hard to get. So next time, try really hard just to get at least one classmate friend to trust.

Evelyn Avila, Grade 5
Covington Elementary School, NE

Ingredients for a Great Teacher

"T.E.A.C.H.E.R." spells out what makes a great teacher. "T.E.A.C.H.E.R." represents these good traits and qualities: Trustful, Enthusiastic, Accommodating, Challenging, Helpful, Encouraging and Reasonable.

First of all, having a trustful teacher means that both the teacher and the student can trust each other completely, so the students have no fear in expressing themselves. Secondly, students need an enthusiastic teacher who loves and enjoys teaching; otherwise, if the teacher talks in a mono-toned voice for hours, the class would be falling asleep. Next, when a teacher is accommodating and understanding to special circumstances, it can really brighten up the student's very worst school day. In addition, you must have a teacher who challenges and stimulates your mind in learning, because you don't want to learn something as easy as your A-B-C's in sixth grade. Subsequently, I think a helpful teacher is like a Swiss Army Knife, who knows exactly which tool to use on assisting each individual student. Next, learning minds really need an extra push to explore and learn new things, and an encouraging teacher would know exactly how to guide them. At last, a great teacher needs to be reasonable in the classroom because all students want to be treated fairly and equally and not get excluded. Boy! I am very blessed that all my teachers contain the seven important traits of "T.E.A.C.H.E.R."

Dragon Siu, Grade 6
Miraleste Intermediate School, CA

The Important Lesson

I learned an important lesson the time I went to my friend Keondra's house, even when my mom told me that I couldn't. It was a hot sunny day and my mom said I could go outside, so I did. While I was outside Keondra came along and she asked if I could go to her house. I said hold on, so I could go ask my mom if I could go. When I asked my mom she said no, so I got mad and slammed the door and told Keondra that I could go to her house. Then at Keondra's house we played games, after three hours I called my mom. She answered the phone and she sounded really mad. She asked me where I was and I told her I was at Keondra's house, and then she said "okay come home." I went home. When I got home, I could tell I was in a whole heap of trouble. Guess what, I was! My mom told me I was on punishment for two weeks. I was sad. That day I learned a very important lesson. That lesson was to respect your parents and do what they tell you to do.

Kianna Brown, Grade 5
McMonagle Elementary School, MI

Soccer

Soccer is fun and good exercise. You can get hurt in soccer by getting hit in the stomach. You can make lots of goals if you work together. Sometimes you have to bring snacks for the team. In soccer you can't pull on somebody or kick them. Yerimi and me are on the same team. Sometimes at the end of soccer we play flag soccer or tag. You can get tired at the end of soccer. I might be a champion. You should try soccer some day, you never know if you are a champion too.

Daniel Brokaw, Grade 4
Santo Niño Regional Catholic School, NM

Animal Friends of the Valley

L.E.A.F., A.S.P.C.A, and A.F.O.T.V. Those are some of my favorite veterinary organizations. Vets are important to me because I think we can make a difference in abused animals' lives. What I want to do when I grow up is to become a vet to save many of those poor animals' lives. I always watch this television show called Emergency Vets. It comes on at 6:00 in the evening and 8:00 in the evening.

My mom always says, "If you have a dream, follow it." She lets me watch the show because I can learn a lot from it and it is part of my dream right now. The show is about vets who take care of emergency animal situations. In order to become a vet, I need great math and science grades. Right now, I have solid A's in both of those classes. My mom is very proud of me that I have been chasing my dream for four years now, and I am not giving up!

My dream college is UC Davis, because it is a really big veterinary school. I have even learned a type of skin cancer. It's called ringworm, but when people think of ring worm, they think of worms. But it is really a type of sore. I hope I never quit until I have achieved my goal.

Miranda Schulz, Grade 6
Linfield Christian School, CA

My Favorite Place

My favorite place is the lake. One reason I like the lake is that when you're in the woods you can hear the birds singing beautifully. You can hear the fish splashing in the water, and at sunset you can see dim colors of pink, red, purple, and orange reflecting off the horizon. At midnight you can hear whistling noises from my grandpa's RV watching the football games. You can hear the waves striking the giant rocks. I feel safe there because I'm surrounded by people who care about me. That is why the lake is my favorite place.

Kel Yeoman, Grade 5
Neosho Heights Elementary School, KS

The Week of a Lifetime

I enjoyed going to Canada with my Dad to fish for one week. When we landed in Vancouver I said to myself, "It's unusual how it took us eight airplanes to get here." When we checked in, the flight accountant said to us, "You're going to have to take a helicopter to get to the resort." We would normally have to take a seaplane, but the rain gave us no choice but to take a helicopter.

As we arrived at the resort, we were amazed at how big it was! The next day, we met our counselor Doug. He was a very nice guy, I knew I was going to like him. During the end of the week, we saw some porpoises and a whale!

As we left the resort, I was waving to the friends I had made during that week. "This was the best week of my life!" I shouted excitedly.

As we got back to Ontario, I promised myself that I would never forget that week. "There will never be an adventure like that one." I thought. As we got home, I was still in awe about things I saw, the things I did, and I knew I would never forget.

Jake Callison, Grade 6
Linfield Christian School, CA

The Best Dad

Who do you look up to? I look up to my dad. I look up to him because he has taught me everything I know. For example, he taught me how to multiply and divide when I was in third grade. When I was in fourth grade he taught me how to find the average of things.

I also look up to him because he's understanding. Whenever something is bothering me, I tell him. One time I remember I had bad grades. I told him and then I started getting better and better grades every year. Sometimes I wonder where I'd be without him.

Another reason I admire my dad is because he is really nice. One time I was really bored, then my dad started to tell me jokes, it was extremely fun. Yesterday my dad and I started to play cards with my friends and we had a lot of fun. My dad is really nice and funny. I love him.

I think my dad is the best because he is different from other dads. He helps me, he teaches me, and he is really, really funny. I wonder where I'd be without him. I love him.

Jose Garcia, Grade 5
Camellia Avenue Elementary School, CA

2005 Soccer Season

Practicing forever then finally getting to take a break. Sure I don't like going to practice but hey? What sport would I be playing if I wasn't playing for Santos.

My name is Julia Anderson and I play travel soccer for the TVSA Santos. Soccer is one of my favorite sports ever. Between tournaments, games, and practice, it can be very busy.

I remember the first time I tried out for Santos, I was so nervous if I'd make it or not. But when I heard the news I made it, I was filled with joy.

Right before our first game in 2005 I was excited and full of energy! And we won! And as the games went on we got more amazing than ever! Then finally our first tournament came, the Mossi tournament; we knew we could win this. We were doing really well, when we knew for sure we were in the finals we all screamed with happiness. When we started our final game we were scared what the results of the game were going to turn out like.

When it was almost the end of the game we were all exhausted. Finally the referee blew the whistle and Santos won! When the awards came we were so excited to see them. When our name was called up it was like getting an award for winning the Super Bowl. And now we've won three out of five tournaments and we're still not done yet!

Julia Anderson, Grade 5
Barrington Elementary School, OH

Fly Cave Adventure

Have you ever been inside a cave before? Well when I was almost three years old, I was with my parents and Hart and Karen Krumrine. We were on our property in Colorado getting ready to enter Fly Cave. Before we left, we made sure that everyone had a coat and a flashlight. As we entered the cave, we entered a small cavern filled with flies, for that is why it was called Fly Cave. From there, we slid down a steep, slippery tunnel, where we saw a few bats fly around our head as we entered into another cavern. That cavern had a very large rock we had to climb over. After the rock, I was excited about what would be next on our journey. My mom had told me the next part in the cave was very dangerous. Then we came to the most dangerous place in the whole cave, my parents called it "Fat Man's Fright, Skinny Man's Delight" because it was very narrow. After we got through there by maneuvering through it on our backs, we finally entered the bottom of the cave. The whole trip down took only about thirty minutes. Then we had to get back to our house, so we went back through "Fat Man's Fright, Skinny Man's Delight," over the rock and then the hardest part about going up, the steep, slippery tunnel. When I went in the cave, I had fun and it was exciting.

Shakota Dilley, Grade 6
Ashby Public School, NE

Spelling Bee

One day me and my cousin Amiya we were playing spelling bee at my house in the living room. It was just for fun. I lost by one point, I was very upset. My mom told me it was going to be okay, I felt better about losing. Amiya started teasing me because I didn't know how to spell important. I was okay because she did not win anything. The lesson I learned is never to think of yourself as a loser.

Mia Williams, Grade 5
McMonagle Elementary School, MI

Re

Have you ever had the feeling that one thing is connected to another? The feeling that you love two things and want to make them one can overpower you. Not a day goes by that my heart and mind aren't singing. Not a day goes by without hearing the voices of my family.

First, I hear *Do*…the deep voice of my doting father.

Followed by *Re*…the warm and comforting melodies of my mother.

Continuously *Me*…my own inner voice, as constant as the Wyoming wind.

From a distance, I hear *Fa*…the wacky wisdom ringing in on the telephone line from my grandparents far away.

Silently sneaks in *Sol*…the imaginary sound through the eyes of my puppy.

The laughter of *La*…the lighthearted La, La, La from my little sister.

Now it's time for *Ti*…the high, polite teachings from my great-grandmother.

So now the circle joins again when I begin a new day with *Do*. "I live, I love, I sing."

Kristen Hess, Grade 6
Spring Creek Elementary School, WY

Mysteries at Fort Peck

Let's go to the time of your life at Fort Peck. I went to Fort Peck and had the time of my life, and you can too.

"Going fishing" is our specialty. We usually troll, which is a little motor on the back of our boat. It is very slow. We usually catch (10-1 fish but it's better than a kick in the pants) walleye, or northern pike; yum, nothing like fried fish with pepper and lemon juice. We're usually out fishing for 2-4 hours, sometimes more.

Now we're going on a hiking adventure. My brother and I enjoy hiking. Whenever we get the chance we would go. We would go wherever. And what we saw was amazing! We saw mule deer, white tail deer, wild flowers, footprints of almost everything. And, too many things to count.

Night is so mysterious. I usually sleep in the boat, where it rocks me back and forth, back and forth to sleep. I can hear the fire crackle, and my parents mumble softly to each other. The wild is at peace and the fish are having a bug buffet.

So I hope you enjoyed Fort Peck; I know I did.

Laina Raisler, Grade 5
Kinsey School, MT

No More Sore Throats!

As I got into the car with my dad all I thought was if something went wrong I could die! The drive was 30 aggravating minutes. While we waited I told my dad, "My tonsils are fine," even though they were too big. The nurse called my name, I didn't want to get up, my dad forced me to, it was time. In the room I changed into disgustingly, gross scrubs. The gave me cold IV sedation to numb me. I thought it took all day but it was only an hour.

After the surgery, I screamed, "I WANT MY MOM!" The doctor tried to calm me but I paid no attention and kept yelling, at least not until they let my mom in. They released me from the hospital within the hour afterwards.

At home I couldn't talk so my throat could heal. I ate Jell-O, mashed potatoes, and anything soft but nothing too thick like ice cream or pudding. That same day my mom picked me up from my dad's and we went to Luby's. I didn't talk until my sister, Carol pointed out that if I didn't start talking it would be harder for me to talk when I went back to school in a few days.

All in all my surgery was an experience I'll never forget, but I've never had a sore throat since.

Mercedes Mercado, Grade 6
St Matthew Catholic School, TX

Angkor Wat

The Angkor Wat was first found by Jayavarman the 7th. This temple was built to honor the gods of the people of Angkor. It is one square mile long and has at least three other buildings inside of it. The Angkor Wat is one of the world's most beautiful and amazing sights to see.

Suryallarall and his building crew built this beautiful temple. The amazing Angkor Wat is located in the city of Angkor, Cambodia. The Angkor Wat was built in the 12th century. It was discovered by the French explorer, Henri Mouhot in the 1860s. The Angkor Wat was made of sandstone. This beautiful creation is more than four centuries old.

The city of Angkor, Cambodia where Angkor Wat is located, had more than a million people at the time. That was more than any European city in the 1800s.

The place of the Angkor gods was a mountain called Mount Meru. The Angkor people built structures like Angkor Wat to please their gods and make them happy.

An army of Thais attacked the city of Angkor. The army took control of the city in 1431 and left in 1432. The temple was left alone for centuries. It became overgrown with trees and bushes. After it was discovered in 1860, it was restored to the way it looked when it was first built.

Angkor Wat is amazing! Today, it is used for worship and as a tourist attraction. I wish I could travel there.

John Rupar, Grade 5
St John of the Cross Parish School, IL

Bullying

Bullying is something that bigger kids do to little kids. They like to take things that they have. When the people that do the bullying get out of hand they start hurting the kids and adults. Just like a little girl was playing basketball and an older girl took it away and ran.

Let me tell you who gets bullied. Usually a kid that is younger than a bully gets picked on. Also parents can get bullied. They can be threatening or talked about or either be stalked or get hurt badly. Things can get stolen away from them.

If I witnessed somebody getting bullied I would tell the teacher. If a teacher cannot do anything about it I will try to break it up. I will tell the bully to stop. If that doesn't work I will tell the principal to do something.

If I ever got bullied I would do anything to stop it. If that person does not stop after I tell them to, I will tell my mom or my guardian. I will tell the boy or girl that what comes around goes around and this might happen to her or him.

I think that schools should watch out for bullies in every school. I would tell people to supervise everyone that looks like they are going to hurt or bully somebody. Also the bullies should go through a stop bullying program. I think the schools should suspend all the bullies.

Eugenia DeCou, Grade 5
Starms Discovery Learning Center, WI

My Furry Friend

My very best friend has four legs, a tail and fur. Her name is Lulu. When I'm at school, I can't wait to get home to see her and play with her. Each day, without fail, she's waiting at the door for me when I get home. She is always excited to see me.

We got Lulu when she was eight weeks old. She was a surprise for my sister and I after our fifteen year old Yorkie died. She sleeps on my bed every night. She loves to play ball in the backyard too. She is very smart! When she's hungry or thirsty, she lays down in front of her food and water bowls until we notice that she needs something.

Lulu is very afraid of storms. One night there was a huge thunderstorm and the power went out. While we were waiting for the power to come back on, we heard a scratching sound coming from upstairs. We discovered Lulu standing in the bath tub scratching at the wall, quivering and whining.

My dog does some crazy stuff that makes us laugh. When I turn on the TV she runs in and plants herself on the floor in front of it. Her favorite channels are ESPN, the tennis channel, and the hunting channel. She barks at the animals and goes behind the TV to look for the baseballs when there's a baseball game on. Life would be so boring without Lulu!

Jared Bogosian, Grade 6
Argyle Middle School, TX

Guam!!!!

Guam is an island located on the Western Pacific Ocean. Guam is an organized unincorporated territory of the United States 3/4th of the way to Hawaii and the Philippines. Guam is three times the size of Washington D.C.

The "chammorros," Guam's indigenous inhabitants, first populated the island approximately 6,000 years ago. It is the largest and southernmost island of the Mariana Islands. The capital is Hagatana, formerly Agana. The economy is mainly supported by tourism (particularly from Japan, Korea, and Taiwan, the United States armed force bases). Guam was ceded to the U.S. by Spain in 1898 and captured by Japan in 1941. The U.S. retook it three years later. In Guam, it's generally warm and humid. It's moderated by northeast trade winds. Dry season is January to June. Wet season is July to December, little seasonal temperature variation. The island's famous flower is the pink, yellow, or red hibiscus. The island's famous bird, the ko'ko', is tall with brown feathers and black stripes that make it look like a half zebra. Guam's flag is blue on the outside and red inside. In the middle, it has white and an oval-like shape.

You could see white sand and a bright green palm tree with a little blue sailboat (my dad has a tattoo of it). My mom grew up in Guam, and my dad, also. My mom was from Tamuning and my dad Merizo. Merizo is pretty far from Tamuning.

Mikayla Santos, Grade 4
Burchett Elementary School, TX

On the Internet

The Internet is fun. You can play games, have an online chat, and watch clips or movies. You can even search for important stuff or read. I like going on nick.com, ytv.com, and miniclips.com.

On nick.com you can sign up. You have to get lots of nick points by playing games and finding points. By signing up you can go on nicktropolis. Even if you don't sign up you can still play games. So if you're looking for funny stuff nick.com is a great place.

On ytv.com you can play games and sign up for a sidekick. A sidekick is a round robot and has an antenna on top. There is a special chip that goes into your sidekick. The chip has a surprise that makes your sidekick put on cool things. So if you're looking for great stuff ytv.com is the place to be.

On miniclips.com you can play a lot of games and watch clips. You can't sign up for anything. But the games are in alphabetical order. Miniclips.com is really awesome. And if you're looking for really neat and smart stuff go to miniclips.com.

Once I saw a clip of *T.D.I.* and *Scooby Doo*. They were both awesome and funny. But the clips were all on teletoon.com. Once I saw *Lord of the Rings: Return of the King* on the Internet. It was really amazing and cool. I think the Internet is really cool 'cause of the fun and neat stuff.

Lojang Geremiah, Grade 5
St Gerard School, MB

Friends

My friends are very important to me. I have female and male friends. I have laughs with them. They cheer me on. We make jokes about each other. We never get mad at each other because we know that we are kidding. We know that they are trying to make each other happy.

My friends look out for each other if there is a problem they are trying to help me with. They would do anything for us so we will not get in trouble. They would even lie to save us.

We tell each other if it is right or not. We tell each other that we should not do drugs. If they are doing it, we try to help them so they would not get addicted.

We encourage each other if we're playing sports. We cheer for one another, too. If they are embarrassed I get embarrassed with them.

We tell each other our secrets. I know they will not tell anybody. I know that we can trust each other. We will not tell anybody if we do not want him or her to.

For my friends and me we're like a family. We sometimes fight, that makes each other a family. That's what families do. Then we get back together and we are a family again.

That's why everyone should have a friend. They keep you company. They make you feel better. You can know that they are going to be by your side.

Dania Monzon, Grade 6

Times at Paramount Academy

Times at my former school Paramount were tough. My friends' were there to pick me up. Paramount was a fun and boring school. When it was fun there was always something to do. Everyone had fun and cooperated with each other.

Friends are important especially during hard times. Football was one of the school's favorite sports. The entire fourth and fifth grade played soccer. That was a major sport throughout school. If you do not like basketball, leave the school! Everyone and I mean everyone loved kickball. You would instantly be popular if you kicked a homerun, but it was hard since the seventh and eight graders were so tall.

The lunch there was gross most of the time. That is one of the reasons why I wanted to leave, but now I regret it. Nacho and pizza day was the best days of hot lunch ever. On special days you paid five dollars for an extra small box of pizza with any toppings. The fun times eating hot lunch is when we ate outside and when we were done eating we picked up our trash and went to go play.

Computer art was fun everyone played it. Online games were the most popular on the computer. Research reports were fun. I researched the wolves on our animal report. Computer essays are also fun, even though we hardly did them, but it was fun while it lasted.

Timothy Taylor, Grade 6
Imagine Charter School at Rosefield, AZ

Why Did My Dad Die?

Every day I think of my dad. It makes me cry sometimes. My father was very nice to me. He loved to draw and paint. I now know how to draw just like my dad. He's an artist to me. I loved spending time with my dad. But I want to know, why did my dad die? That's what I really want to know.

My dad died from a weapon. It made me cry when I found out. How do you think I feel? I'll tell you. I feel SAD!!!! I know you wouldn't want your dad to die either.

I bet it would make you cry, too. I love my dad and I bet he's thinking about me right now. I love you dad. My dad loved me, too. But WHY did my dad die?

A Letter to Daddy…
Dear Daddy,

I just wanted to know if you are in Heaven? My heart is pounding right now because I am wondering if you really are in Heaven. Daddy, could you talk to me from Heaven if you are there? I hope so. If you can't, I want you to know that you will always be in my heart.

Love, Your Daughter
Tanisha

Tanisha Thomas, Grade 5
DeQueen Elementary School, TX

Good Deeds

I think it's not a good idea to do a good deed in remembrance of September 11th. In New York City there were some buildings that caught on fire and collapsed because terrorists flew a plane into them. Some people were still alive and firemen tried to save them from the buildings and when the firemen put out the fires some people got hurt and doctors tried to help them stay alive. It was sad, so I think it's not a good idea to do good deeds in remembrance of 9/11.

People might have relatives that died during 9/11. They might not want to remember because it's really sad. I think it's a good idea to just do a good deed for someone just to be nice to people. Doing a good deed means you are being good to people and responsible every day and that you care.

Lelan Skinner, Grade 4
Snake River Montessori School, ID

My Dog Rowdy

My dog Rowdy is probably not like most people's pets. He is a great dog, but he is blind. The cool thing about him is he can still *navigate* through the house. He is a dark red Chow. He weighs about 70 pounds and is 2 feet tall.

We have two houses that Rowdy has to navigate. If we move any furniture Rowdy would probably hit his head. He sometimes doesn't know his way around the houses. He likes to stay by people so he is not alone.

Rowdy used to be playful but now he sleeps a lot. We help him find his way around the houses when he takes a wrong turn. He is 8 years old. I hope he lives 'til he is at least 10. I hope he has a great life.

Matthew Despain, Grade 5
Desert Canyon Elementary School, AZ

My Dog "T"

When I was nine months old, my mom and dad got a Yorkie. Yorkie's are small dogs, so we named him "T" short for Terminator II. My dog is cool because he is black and gold. We play fetch, I throw him a teddy bear and he brings it back to me.

He is cute. T is 63 in dog years, but in human years he is nine years old. In dog years they go by seven.

I love my dog T because he always is happy to see me after school. He runs up to me and licks me. I love him, too, because he protects my family and me by barking loud.

Christopher Baca, Grade 4
Santo Niño Regional Catholic School, NM

Purr-fect Cat Facts

Hey! Do you know cats are a mysterious breed? Come with me to a journey of amazing cat facts. It will be fun, you'll enjoy it!!

Some cats are fussy and finicky. Some cats are cute and cuddly and some are just unsocial and downright snooty. Cats sometimes leave us bewildered by their behavior. They scratch, they hiss…they eat grass, then have the nerve to turn up their noses at our dinner plates.

Purring is a rumbling sound that cats make deep down in their throat. It's their way of letting us know they're happy as clams — or rather, cats! If a cat rolls on his or her back and shows you their bellies that means they think you're the cat's pajamas! They can be cute!

Cats claws are retractable. Also, some girls just adore cats, like me! But some girls hate cats. Did you know cats are nocturnal? I know, it's amazing! Whenever you're asleep all a cat wants to do is play, play, play!

Now you see there are so many facts about cats. Thank you for taking a journey with me!

Carmela A. Danao, Grade 4
Louise Foussat Elementary School, CA

My Thoughts on Smoking

I don't smoke because I can't breathe around smokers. Some people do. If you ever thought of smoking, this is what might happen.

In the U.S., 1 out of 5 deaths are caused by smoking. There are 40,000 chemicals in cigarette smoke, and 43 are known to cause cancer. That cancer can be in your kidney, bladder, lip, tongue, lung, stomach and other organs. Smoking affects every organ in your body. If you smoke, you increase your risk of lung cancer by 24% and heart disease by 25%. It causes 85% of all lung cancer deaths.

Secondhand smoke comes from being around smokers and breathing their smoke. You can get sick too, and you didn't smoke. Cancer is the second cause of death linked to smoking.

As you can see there are a lot of things that can happen when you smoke. None of the things listed are good; that is why I don't like smoking, and why I don't smoke.

Ben Rice-Hawkins, Grade 5
Westview Elementary School, OH

My Grandpa

I think there are a few good grandparents out there but I think I know one of them, my grandpa. His name is Dennis Rivinius, he served in the navy, and he is the ultimate grandpa. He can be funny but serious. I remember when he would always take my brothers Brandon Warmerdam and Brett Warmerdam and myself Brock Warmerdam golfing. He is the one who taught me how to swing a golf club and how to learn to concentrate on the ball. When he would hit a bad ball he would always say "Oh my back's killing me!" That was his catch phrase. Sometimes we will still go golfing, but we won't play a full 18 we would play 9 or so.

When I was about 5 or 6 he had a fart machine and I always thought he actually farted until he said did you just step on a frog! He still has it but the batteries are dead. Just a few days ago when I was looking at the machine I saw his old dog tags and asked him about them. He told me that when you get those they are the only numbers you can remember, he said you can't even remember your own birthday! I didn't believe him so I asked him what they said and he told me word for word and number for number. That's only 3 reasons why he is the best grandpa ever!

Brock Warmerdam, Grade 6
St Anne School, CA

My Cat's Soul

My cat Mojo is still a kitten, but she has the soul of her ancestors…the cheetahs! When she goes outside, her turquoise eyes turn to bright yellow! She runs like a cheetah, darting down the bleak grasslands, springing for her prey, while gliding in the air and elegantly landing on her leather-like paws. Slowly and happily she laps up the water from the crisp blue pond, while carelessly stirring her paw around in the water. She knows that the sun and moon are shifting, and her enemies will soon be hunting her. So she catches her last meal for the day and enters her den (our house). Slowly, her amazing eyes calm to their relaxing turquoise for the night. She lies against me and knows she is her kitten soul once again.

Still in kitten soul, she begins to wake up and get ready for her 7:00 a.m. prowl. She slowly begins to look around her den, listening for any signs of movement. Zzzz…Mojo freezes…zzz…it's food! She runs down the hallway to find me opening a can of cat food. She eats it up as soon as the plate touches the ground. As the sun comes up, so do her yellow eyes. She dashes through the door and begins her day…soaring like a hawk, prancing like a deer, and happily doing what she does.

My cat's soul is special because it's hers and hers only. To me she is love, hope, kindness and bravery. That is my cat's soul.

Kelsey Larson, Grade 5
Country Montessori School, CA

My Parents Are Special

My parents are very special to me. They have total control and take care over me. My mother is as organized as the president. She takes me to school every day. She also picks me up after school. She cooks delicious, nutritious meals, mainly dinner. When I am sick, she comes back from work and gives me care. She doesn't leave the house until I'm healthy and I'm not sick anymore. That is how important my mom is.

My father takes me to all of my ice-skating lessons, private lessons and practice. He has such enthusiasm in me in all of my classes. When I fail, he says, "Don't give up, I know you can do it!" Now you can see how important and caring my mother and father are.

Ivy Li, Grade 4
Addison Elementary School, CA

How to Make My Secret Place

My secret place is at home that I am going to build after I get home from school. I am going to need staples and a staple gun, a glue gun and some cardboard boxes. It is going to be about ten yards long and about 20 inches wide. I'm going to decorate it with glitter glue markers, crayons, magazine words, pictures and numbers. I will cut doors and windows out and put lights in it. I am going to call it clubhouse mansion. It is going to be by my bed. I'm going to do my homework in it and read in it. I'll play video games in it. The bottom is going to be made out of pillows. I'm going to write in it. I'm going to write on the walls about my life in it. I want to hang ornaments in it. I'm going put all my secret writing in it. I'm going to have a code for it. I'm going to play with toys in it. Play with my dogs in it. I am going to create some things to put in it.

Leland Norman, Grade 4
Winona Elementary School, TX

Thanksgiving

Every Thanksgiving we have a feast. Just thinking about all the food, I can smell it and my mouth gets watery, and my stomach gets bigger. I can just see the mac-and-cheese, the corn on the cob and I won't get started on the pork and desserts. Every Thanksgiving we go to Orlando, Florida. We always rent a house near my uncle's house. My uncle has a swimming pool in his backyard. It is protected by a glass shield.

On Thanksgiving Day we all sit at the table together, my granny, my aunts, my uncles, a lot of cousins, my mommy and my twin sister Deja. We eat and eat. Then we play. I like to shoot pool with my cousins and uncles. I always beat everybody except my oldest cousin. He's good.

The next day we get up early and go to Universal Studios or Walt Disney World. Last year we went to "Holy Land." It is a really great experience. We saw plays and all kinds of fun things. I can't wait for November to come. I can hear my family smacking and saying, "Yum, yum!"

Andrea Abrams, Grade 5
Prospect Elementary School, OH

Damp, Dark Day

The rain dripped down from my over-soaked hair to the hairs on the back of my neck. "Whoa, look at those stairs cut out from a log!" I yelled enthusiastically.

"Amazing," my brother Alec said, rolling his eyes. We finished the first mile of our three mile hike. We waited under a pine for our twenty-two aunts and uncles. I decided to sit between my cousins, Kyle and Fritz.

Ten minutes later, I went down the log stairs and finally saw the adults. I yelled to the boys, "They're coming!"

The next mile we walked soaking in silence. Finally we reached Lake Agnes. It reminds me of my wonderful grandma named Agnes. I found a nice spot under the protection of another pine. We were walking five minutes later down an ATV trail. The crimson and cherry colored leaves squished beneath my feet. By this time, the rain water has already drowned my ankles. I was cold and miserable. Following my Uncle Jim, we could see the road up ahead. I ran as fast as I could. Finally, we reached the parking lot.

Back at our condo, the rain stopped. We built a blazing campfire.

The deep dark waves of Superior crashed against the rocks. The waves sounded like thunder. We were all huddled around the campfire. I was warm in my mom's jacket. "It turned out to be a great day after all," I thought. Just then, I saw lightning. Here we go again!

David Trenda, Grade 5
Greenwood Elementary School, MN

Family Love

Family is so important to me. Even though we may have our ups and downs together, I would never trade them for the world. My family makes me cry and laugh.

My mom and dad are so important to me, because they provide food, shelter, advice and love. They make sacrifices for me. My parents do so much to keep me happy, and I love them for that. My two brothers, Mikey and Marvin are also the best. They are the best brothers a sister could ever have. Giving me advice and help, I could never imagine my world without my brothers. Brothers will get you through everything! Brothers will take the blame for you, if they want to. My brothers set good examples, and made mistakes, but I learn from them. We respect each other a lot. My family made me who I am today. As I grow I will make mistakes too, and they will always guide me right from wrong.

Whenever I get scared, they try to calm me down. Whenever we cry, we give each other a shoulder that we soak with our tears. When we laugh together, we make each other stop breathing until we can't take it anymore. They have inspired me to go to infinity and beyond. Family is so loving and they will be there for me throughout my life.

Melody Mallari, Grade 6
Linfield Christian School, CA

A Normal School Day

Every weekday I wake up and say, "Oh boy! Another day of school." I get dressed and eat; we leave for school at 7:59. Because I arrive early the "Before School Care" room is where I go. We build toy cars for fun. At 8:10 we head for our different classrooms. I see Miss Koehneke and my classmates. Our daily routine is always mixed up, but we definitely have religion first. The other subject that is for sure is Social Studies with Mr. Boettcher at 11:10. Following Social Studies we have recess and lunch. When afternoon classes end at 3:00 we prepare our backpacks, then clean the room. Our class pet Buster gets special care. We say prayers, the bell rings and Miss Koehneke dismisses us. Some kids head for the bus and others go to the parking lot doors to wait for their parents. When Mom gets there I usually ask for time on the playground with my friends. Sometimes she says it's okay. Sometimes we need to go right away. Either way is good with me; I'm glad to be done with another school day. On the ride home we talk about my day. If I have homework that gets done first. Then I play for a while, eat dinner, and play again. I clean up and get ready for bed about 8:00. Most of the time I read a book or watch part of a movie before falling asleep. One of my dogs usually crawls in just after the lights go out.

B. A. Zimmermann III, Grade 5
Trinity Lutheran School, WI

The Place for You!

As I stepped foot into the 3 story high building my jaw dropped and my smile grew bigger and bigger! It was the cutest place I have ever been to. It was the American Girl Place!

We started on the first story. My sister got the "Girl of the Year" doll Niki. Our family friends and I got some outfits for our dolls! We went to the second level and there one of the little girls got a historical doll named Kit. She also got the accessories to go with Kit like the basset hound and some clothing. We headed to the third level and there we all got a bunch of outfits like gala dresses, pajamas, and so many more. They have the biggest selection of historical dolls such as Kit, Samantha, Molly, Josefina, and too many more to mention. They have so many different types of clothing to choose from also. My friend got a doll named Emily! She is my namesake and I have her too! On the third floor they have a doll salon and a doll hospital. They also have a theatre, a café, and a photo place.

One night we had dinner at the café. At the dinner you bring your doll with you and they have a little dinner too. We had the greatest time there! Best of all was the decor of the café. The whole café was pink, black, and white! We all had the greatest time and we all hope to go back.

Emily Ingram, Grade 6
St Matthew Catholic School, TX

My Years Playing Baseball

I was waiting, the ball was coming I swung "cling" I heard and started running. I had made it home safe, and then I noticed that nobody had the ball. I finally heard "you made a home run" by my coach. I was proud of myself because it was my first home run. Later we won the game.

I started playing baseball when I was eight years old. At first I was bad, but I got better later on. My team and I don't like getting hit by the pitcher. I like batting because it makes me feel good when I hit it out of the park.

I play a lot of positions, like second base, third base, short stop and left field. Second base is my favorite position. People say first base is the hardest, but I think short stop is the hardest. I hope one day I can play in the major leagues; I would play second base because it is my favorite position.

I have won a lot of trophies. Last season my team and I got second in district. I will never forget last year's season. I hope this season will be as good as last season.

Juan Gomez, Grade 6
Irma Marsh Middle School, TX

Soccer

Soccer is a popular sport in USA and Canada. It plays all over the world. In some countries soccer is called football. It is a team sport. There are some rules for soccer, no one can touch it with their hands except the goalies. Each team has eleven players. It is good exercise. People should be physically fit and active in order to play this sport. There is no height limit for this sport like basketball. Sharp mind and quick movements are important in soccer. One should know where and when to kick the ball. It should be done in seconds so opponents don't take the ball away from you.

I started to play soccer at the age of five. I still play soccer; it is one of my favorite sports. I would like to be a soccer player when I grow up. I love soccer!

Harveen Sanghera, Grade 5
Micro Education and Consulting School, BC

My Friends

My friends are Yermi, Daniel, Alejandro, and Jared. Yermi is nice to me every day, he is nice to me at the special places we go to. He is nice to me at recess, he helps me up when I am hurt on the play ground. At lunch he sits with me when I am alone at a table.

Daniel is respectful because he is quiet and tells me not to get in trouble. He is a nice person to play with at recess. Daniel and I play Goosebumps, the book at recess. He is fun to talk to at the beginning of the day, we talk about what we are going to play at recess. Daniel is respectful, he is nice too. He is a big friend with Yermi, and so am I.

Alejandro is caring; he likes to play tag at recess. He also likes pepperoni pizza for lunch every day. He likes to play basketball, his favorite is soccer. He also likes to eat salads too, he likes to go to 6 Flags. He likes math a lot. His favorite thing to do is to play his Wii.

Robert Lopez, Grade 4
Santo Niño Regional Catholic School, NM

Doing Our Part for the North American Songbird

Many animals are harmed by the use of backyard pesticides especially the non-migrating songbirds of North America. While these chemicals can kill birds directly, more often it hinders their ability to reproduce effectively. Common backyard pesticides are used to kill mosquitoes and other disease carrying insects. What is often forgotten is that insects are an important part of our ecosystem and part of a bird's well balanced diet.

There are many ways to get rid of pests without using dangerous chemicals. Eliminating breeding grounds for mosquitoes and other disease transmitting insects by changing the water in bird baths daily is a good start. Ponds can be made unfavorable for mosquitoes by adding a fountain and fish. Allowing bats to take up residency is another way to reduce mosquito populations naturally.

A lot of people do not understand the harmful effects of common backyard pesticides on North American songbirds because it is not always as obvious as finding a dead bird on the ground. Much of the harmful results of pesticide use is measured by bird population growth. Harmful pesticides can cause a bird's egg to be thin and unable to provide the protection a developing bird needs. Many of the birds are born unhealthy and do not survive.

By making educated decisions about pest control for our lawns and gardens everyone can do their part to help the earth and especially the songbirds of North America. Even though humans do not eat mosquitoes, we are still part of the same ecosystem.

Noah Tolan-Combs, Grade 6
Southport 6th Grade Academy, IN

My Pet Pudgy!

My pet is Pudgy. Pudgy is a pug/Chihuahua. When I just got him he was as small as the palm of my hand. He started liking me, and sleeping by me. He was just a little thing and drank out of a baby cup full of milk. He was so cute. Days passed and now he is one.

We do lots of things together. We play tag, and hide-and-go-seek. He plays with me every day! I get dressed for school. After I get dressed I go eat breakfast. I tell Pudgy good-bye and go.

After I come home from school he comes running to the door wagging his tail. After, I do my homework and get dressed into play clothes; we go outside and play.

Whenever a big dog comes by me Pudgy will bark very loud. When I fall he will sit by me until I get up. We even sometimes go on a walk around the block. When I go inside to get a drink he comes and laps a whole gallon of water.

At night I eat dinner, I brush my teeth, and we lay down in bed. Pudgy wakes me up every day. Pudgy is the best dog in the world.

Amelda M. Maynes, Grade 6

How to Do a Cake

I love to make cakes a lot. My mom showed me how to make different kinds of cakes. First you put the mix thing in a bowl. Then you put the oil and two eggs and a cup of water. Then you mix it and when you are done mixing it good you put it in a little tray. Then put it in the oven. Then when it's ready you let it get a little bit cold. Then you can eat it and you can save it for tomorrow. That's what I do when we make cakes. We make different kind of cakes. There are strawberry, chocolate, vanilla, banana and there are brownies. The brownies are really good. My mom makes me some brownies because I can't make the brownies. My mom makes them really good. My mom said she is probably making some for my birthday. I'm going to help my mom do them, so I can know how to make them. My mom said that she is going to make some tomorrow for a birthday party, it's going to be my cousin's birthday party. So we get to go to the party. We are going to have some cake and brownies and ice cream. First we are going to eat. Then break the piñata and then have the cake and candy bags.

Glenda Lozano, Grade 4
Winona Elementary School, TX

My Favorite Place

My favorite place is in my bedroom because I get my reading time. In my bedroom I get to read my Harry Potter books. I get some alone time from my sister Marian. She's always getting on my nerves. So my room is my favorite place to because I can read and get away from my sister. Also in my bedroom I get to play in there. I also like to play games in my room and usually it is real quiet. I almost never leave my room.

Alexis John, Grade 4
Winona Elementary School, TX

Linfield O Linfield

I picked Linfield because it is one of the most important things in my life. I feel safe in the atmosphere of Linfield. It is a wonderful place to go to school. The teachers are nice and the students are as well. It is a great place to bond. We have middle school sports such as football, flag football, basketball, baseball, softball, and soccer. Sometimes the teachers give us candy!

We even have a pond in the middle of our campus. Linfield has an elementary, middle, and high school. They are even working on a preschool. It almost looks like a college campus. It's that big! If you are a new student, you would feel comforted the first day of school. Your friends here are almost like your second family. When I came in fourth grade everyone was very nice to me. They asked me to play certain games, asked if I needed anything to eat, or if I needed an escort to P.E., or the office.

All of the teachers were very nice to me as well. They had lots of thing to do at break, I played basketball most of the time. Linfield is one of the most important things in my life.

Cody Coyle, Grade 6
Linfield Christian School, CA

On the Mississippi River

This summer I went to the Mississippi River. I was so excited when we got there. I saw all of the boats, trees, birds, and fish. Then Pa John rented a boat to us for the day.

Soon Pa John started the boat and we were off on the Mississippi River! We saw a lot of ducks in the no wake zone. Then we stopped and did a little fishing, but we didn't catch anything. Then we just drove for a while.

It was so amazing looking at the river and trees. "Like to drive the boat?" I was like, "You're kidding!" He said nope. So I started to drive the boat. I honked the horn at all of the people I saw.

Then we had lunch. It was fun and funny. We ate sandwiches. I gave ducks some of my bread it was so funny, how they eat and swim. Then we fished some more. Pa John soon got a fish, but it got away.

Soon we headed back to the boating dock. I was sad that the trip was over, but Pa John said we will come back soon. Then we went for some food at Pizza Hut.

Tyler Brooks, Grade 5
Bang Elementary School, TX

Learning a Lesson

One day on Monday at Merrill School I got into a fight. This boy pushed me so I pushed him back then he hit me then I started beating him up. We were in the hallway after we got done fighting. We went in the office. My mom came and picked me up. I went home. I was in trouble. My 2 big sisters were laughing at me because I was in trouble. So when I was done my sisters asked me what happened, I got into a fight at school. He pushed me so I pushed him back. So he hit me so I beat him up. The my mom said you are grounded. No games and no TV and no going outside. I learned my lesson. Then my mom said be nice to people and they will be nice to you. I am never going to get kicked out again.

Jalen Fykes, Grade 5
McMonagle Elementary School, MI

Inedible Pizza

Bump! We rolled into my cousin's driveway. "Bye Mom!" I said. I was at my cousin's. My sister, my cousin Anne, and I were staying home alone. "I think we should put it on a pan!" we argued. The decision was final. We put the pizza on a pan and popped it into the oven. Fluffy thick crust here we come! We stumbled down the stairs to watch a movie. Anne and Kjirsten (my sister) brought a timer downstairs. With our tummies rumbling louder than thunder, we waited anxiously for our yummy pizza. "Beep, beep, beep!" The timer went off. Anne and Kjirsten trampled upstairs like a herd of buffalo. Thick smoke like fog rubbed against their faces. Funny aromas filled the air. Once the smoke cleared out of their faces, they saw black gooey strands running off the pizza. The pan was not a pan at all, it was a cutting board!

Katrin Ree, Grade 5
Greenwood Elementary School, MN

My Summer at Camp

This summer I went to Camp Harlow for three nights and four days. When we got there we checked in and waited for my friend Courtney. I asked my mom, "When will she be here?" Then she arrived. After that we went to the wagons. Then we met our counselors, Sadey and Jello. They were happy to have us. When we got inside the wagons they smelled good and clean.

Next we had to choose our bunks. We chose the top bunks. After that we got settled in and said bye to our parents. Then two other girls arrived named Rachel and Amber. They are sisters.

Then we had lunch and it was good. Next we had quiet time. After that we had free time. That is when we get to do things like drive go-carts, or bumper boats, rock climb, swim, do crafts, ride horses, play on the playground, swing on the tire swing, play in the game room, golf, or canoe.

At dinner we would open mail from family. Then we put on warm clothes and bug spray for Camp Pastor time. That is when a pastor comes to talk to us. Then we had cabin time. That is when we talk and answer questions. Next we had a snack. After that we would do a night game or campfire. Then we went to bed. I had so much fun at camp!

Hannah Horton, Grade 5
Eugene Christian School, OR

Mary Edwards Walker

Mary Edwards Walker did great things in the Civil War. She wasn't a soldier but she was important.

Mary Edwards Walker was born in November 26, 1836 in New York. She lived with her parents, five sisters and one brother.

Mary Edwards Walker was educated. She went to medical school. Mary Edwards Walker set up an office in Rome and New York. Everything changed because she married Albert Miller. They had a daughter but it did not go well. After 13 years they divorced.

Mary Edwards Walker did a lot of things, like she became a nurse because during the Civil War they would not let women in the army.

During the civil war she was a spy. She got caught. She was greatly pleased that when they released her, she had been traded man for man.

One other thing Mary did was she became a writer and made a book and it was published. They put her on a stamp and it was worth 20 cents.

Mary Edwards Walker was the first woman to get a Medal of Honor. They tried to take it away but she refused. Thanks to her granddaughter, Jimmy Carter signed a bill in 1977 reinstating her medal.

Mary Edwards Walker died on February 21, 1919.

Traci Bagola, Grade 5
Cheyenne-Eagle Butte Upper Elementary School, SD

My Dog

Hi my name is Valerie. I think my dog is special to me because he cares for me when I am sad. When he is sad I make him feel better. He is my best friend forever. I will never forget about him, because I love him and he will always care for me, so I have to care for him. Because he is small, but he will always love me, and care for me because I told him to bark at strangers because he is strong and everything. He can knock strangers down because he knocks my mom down. He is stronger than me. So he can do that for me. Then I will give him a treat. He respects other dogs. But only his size of dogs. Not big dogs, he hates big dogs because he is afraid of them. He is afraid of them because he is afraid they might eat him or something else that I don't know about.

Valerie Sosaya, Grade 4
Santo Niño Regional Catholic School, NM

Responsibility

Responsible is being the one who must answer or account for something. I've been responsible because I've been handing in my work when the teacher tells us it's due. I am responsible when I listen to the teacher and obey her. So, for being responsible I got chosen to go to Wayne State College to represent Covington Elementary for a leadership day. Also, I show responsibility when we have a pep rally by listening and looking at the person who is talking.

Having responsibility means that you obey, listen, and follow directions. I have to obey my older siblings. I am also responsible for taking care of my younger siblings.

All in all, I have told you what being responsible means and how you can show that your being responsible.

Diana Amador, Grade 5
Covington Elementary School, NE

The Table Saw

I have had many injuries. Some of the worst ones were when I cut my head open, got stitches in between my toes, broke my finger, and last but not least, when I broke my wrist. I could list pages of injuries that I've had but I'll tell you about one.

When I was 4 years old my mom went to Washington. My dad was watching us for the weekend. He was also fixing something in the kitchen, so the table saw was in the kitchen. I was just a little girl, and I didn't know what the table saw was, so I hung on the bars. It didn't tip over on me the first couple of times, but it tipped over me eventually. I just laid there until someone came in. Finally, my sister came in, and then raced to my dad. He hurried into the kitchen. He leaned the table saw back up, and then he and I went to the car. Ashley grabbed our shoes and came. My dad took off his shirt and held it on my head. We went to the emergency room. I got glued back together and everything was fine. My mom called that night and I answered the phone. I told her the story and she said, "Let me talk to your father!!"

Beth Sutter, Grade 6
Kinsey School, MT

Florida Panther

I researched the Florida panther. It is one of the most endangered animals in the world. They have been endangered since 1967. They are endangered from cars, accedes, and ill infections.

The Florida panther's habitat is related to humans. For example, it has trees for shade, water to drink also, space to run, and fresh air to breath. The Florida panther's habitat is called its range. Its range is in southern Florida. Some live east of the Mississippi River. Panthers, especially young males, may travel great distances for their needs. For some reason they can only mate within their range. The loss of habitat to the Florida panther is a great threat to it.

The male panthers weight is about 150 pounds and lives in a big range. One-fourth or less may live today. They travel and hunt at night. They may be subspecies of the mountain lions. They need large wilderness for their survival. It also has a great bite. It is a very uncommon event to see a Florida panther. The Florida panther cannot climb trees. They can only hang from the branches to hide from hunters. They are part of the cat family. The number one thing they eat is white-tailed deer. It also has a very loud and scary roar.

Michael Medrano, Grade 4
Menchaca Elementary School, TX

Sssss

It was a hot sunny morning, and I was camping with my dad. "Wow, this looks like a good day for walking around," I exclaimed. A friend's dad showed up with a gigantic mountain bike. "Is it okay if I can ride that bike," I asked. "Sure thing," he said. I jumped onto the bike and glided down the street. As I went down the street, I dodged cars and kept going. The sun was very, very strong, and I sweated a lot. My hair blew in the wind as I kept riding down the street. "Oh man, I think that I should get back to the campground," I thought. I could not turn well on the bike because it was too big for me. I tumbled over the bike and I felt big pain.

Meanwhile, a Pacific Diamondback rattlesnake slithered by. "Snnaaake," I screamed! The snake continued across the street, glaring at me. Later on, a car came by. "Maybe I should stop the car," I thought. I stood in the middle of the street, stopping the car for help. "There is a rattlesnake right there! What do I do," I exclaimed. "Did the snake rattle or threaten you in any way," the man asked. "No," I replied. "Umm, it glared at me."

Suddenly, my dad came by. "Are you okay," my dad asked. "I'm fine," I replied. "Well, get into the car," my dad instructed. After that we decided to get back to the campground. From now on, I will always remember that incident.

Ricky Bialick, Grade 5
Dingeman Elementary School, CA

My Family Camping Trips

The scent of fresh pine needles brings my family closer. About every other month, my family and I take a trip to the woods and enjoy the great outdoors.

Usually, we go on a hike after we arrive. We don't exactly know where the trail takes us. Most of the time, we end up by a stream or a river. There is plenty to do on a river bed. My dad and I can look for fossils, race boats made out of twigs, and sometimes catch crawdads or mini lobsters.

Although my dad loves to hike, he is terrible at roasting marshmallows. Luckily, my mom isn't. You would never believe how perfect my mom roasts marshmallows. The sweet creamy marshmallow melts in your mouth, and your taste buds go to heaven. It's amazing that my mom never burns a marshmallow.

Although my mom is the marshmallow roaster, she never cooks on our camping trips. My brother is the chef in the great outdoors. His specialty includes hot-dogs and corn. Over all, my brother has achieved the rank of a four star chef.

While camping, all of my family members have responsibilities, including me. At the end of the camping trip, I carefully inspect the camp site for anything that we might have left behind. I love my family camping trips. I can't wait to go again.

Carmela Chaney, Grade 5
Kyrene Monte Vista School, AZ

Friendship

There are many values in the world, but friendship is the true value everybody needs to experience. To begin, friendship means the condition of being friends. Friendship includes fellowship and companionship. A famous poet once said, "A real friend is someone who walks in when the rest of the world walks out." The famous poet who wrote this was Walter Winchell. He is a newspaper writer and a radio commentator. To me this wonderful quote means when you have a friend, they will step up and help you when nobody else wants to. In friendship you sacrifice for another.

Friendship is easy. Here are some special people who live this value. For instance, principals and teachers show friendship in school by guiding and helping us. Your parents may also show friendship by praising you and helping you make good choices. There are many famous people who showed friendship. For example, Lewis and Clark had friendship because they cooperated together and had teamwork to be successful in their expeditions.

Even though there are many ways to live this value, I am special in ways myself. First, I show it by being nice to people and helping them when they are sad. Because of this, I have many friends in return.

In fact, friendship is very important on a daily basis.

Kaylee Gill, Grade 5
Covington Elementary School, NE

The Importance of Education

I think that education is important. One reason is that you need it to get a good job. Another reason is that people will insult you if you don't have it. Another reason is that people will cheat you.

Education is important. You need it to get a good job. If you want to be a doctor or fireman or police or anything you need some education. Any job you have you need education.

Education is important for people. People will insult you if you don't have it. They would call you stupid and idiotic and retarded all because you don't have an education. Everyone would laugh at you.

Education is important. If you don't have it people will take advantage of you. Someone might charge you something $20 instead of $10. They would talk about you and make snide comments.

Education is important. You need it to get a good job. People will insult you if you don't have it. People will take advantage of you. This is why I think education is important.

Harish Atluri, Grade 5
Indus Center for Academic Excellence, MI

My Cabin in Flagstaff

My family and I have a cabin in Flagstaff, Arizona. We usually go up there every other weekend. It's a two hour drive from the house that we live in. In the winter, it snows and I go sledding down my favorite hill. It took four years to build our cabin and we're still not done with it! A feature in our cabin is its big deck in the back. I always like to look over the edge and watch birds eat seeds and talk to each other. On a special occasion, I may see a gray squirrel scurry up a tree to find a pine cone to munch on. I even made a birdhouse and hung it in a tree for a bird to fly and nest in. We also have a huge backyard that's fun to play in. Towards the top of it, there are some enormous rocks that you can either climb, or find crystals. There's also a big ditch that's fun to walk down and find sticks. Well, no matter what you can do up in Flagstaff at my cabin, it's always fun!

Kyle James Koleber, Grade 4
Kyrene Monte Vista School, AZ

Following Your Dreams

Hi I'm Lainie, and I'm trying so hard to follow my dreams of singing. One day I hope to become a famous singer. So I want you to follow your dreams of anything because it just feels great and I know how you feel. You just feel like you have control and can do what you want. So if you have my same dream, join a choir or something so that people can hear you sing.

The people that hear your voice can tell others about your amazing voice. I bet you that you become a famous singer one day. All I'm saying is follow your dreams and have fun with it! If you are doing something else still do the same. Again and most important FOLLOW YOUR DREAMS! I forgot to tell you to sing from your heart.

Lainie Serna, Grade 4
Santo Niño Regional Catholic School, NM

The Football Field

It's 4th and 7. Coach has you running the ball. You line up behind the fullback. The anticipation is building. You're on the 39 yard line. The score is 31-28. You have 7 seconds left. The clock is stopped. It's the fourth quarter. The QB yells. You're in motion. The ball is tossed to you. The only thing in your mind is run. You're past the offensive line. WHAM! You're hit, but you break the tackle. You rush past a defensive player and spin around the LB. It's total silence. Nobody is in front of you. The ones behind won't catch you. It's you and the open field. You cross the goal line. An explosion of noise fills the stadium. Your teammates jump you. The score is 34-31. The clock is out — you just won the Super Bowl.

This is my favorite place. The football field. That's what it's like for me to be on the field. Every time you score, you get a great feeling that pushes you to do it again. You feel unstoppable. Football is my favorite sport and I don't know how I'd live without it. The feeling of winning is so great and knowing you have to come back and do it again is even better. This is why I love football, and that is why my favorite place is the football field.

Jake Rainey, Grade 6
North Oaks Middle School, TX

Marie Antoinette

Marie Antoinette was born in Vienna, Austria, on November 2, 1755. She was the most stunning and youngest daughter of Francis Stephel and Maria Theresa. Her full name was Maria Antonia Josepha Johanna. At age twelve she became an archduchess.

Her mother, Maria Theresa, was the Empress of the Holy Roman Empire. Her father, Francis Stephel, died when she was only nine years old. Her sister, Maria Christina, married Albert of Saxony. Her favorite sister, Maria Josepha, was married to Ferdinand, King of Naples.

Marie Antoinette was to wed Louis XVI. It had been planned from when she was nine years old. At age fifteen, she married him. Together they had four children; Marie Theresa, Louis XVII, Sophia Helene, and Louis Charles.

In 1789, a mob descended on the palace at Versailles and demanded that the royal family move to the Tuilerie Palace inside Paris. From then on the King and Queen were virtual prisoners.

When Austria and Prussia declared war on France, she was accused of passing military secrets to the enemy. On August 10, 1792, the royal family was arrested and imprisoned. On January 21, 1793, King Louis XVI was executed on the guillotine. She followed her husband to the guillotine on October 16, 1793, and she was executed. She was only 37 years old.

Dea Boyadjiev, Grade 5
La Costa Heights Elementary School, CA

My Favorite Place

Most people might not think that a best friend's house is a favorite place, but to me it is the best place in the world. Over the summer and on the weekends I go over to my friend Justice grandma's house. It is fun to go over. Sometimes I even like to go over when she is not there. Once over the summer when I went over, she had a sleepover and boy did we have fun! We stayed up all night long and ate popcorn. We drank soda and watched a movie called *Sleep Over*. It was about four girls and this one cute boy that they were after. They were so crazy about him that they got dressed up in dresses, high heels, and makeup and followed him to this place. It was some movie!

Kevonica Erwin, Grade 4
Winona Elementary School, TX

Imagination

My imagination is big. I like my imagination. Just think if everybody had a good imagination, we would be happy. But all of us have a different imagination. It would be cool if our imaginations came to life. "Run!" that's what everybody would say. But all of us don't have a good imagination. I would think that I was a cartoon character. Somebody else would imagine that he was king of the world. That would be scary. His friend would think we're the Simpsons. I call Bart after she imagines it. Just in case somebody imagines Harry Potter I am you, Harry Potter. I am your Siamese twin. Just kidding, but I do look like him. What if we were a board game? I would call it "Shew, Shew." That would be very funny. Another kid, oh no he imagines he will destroy the world. I know what my sister will imagine — a sister. Everybody in the world knows what I want. My imagination says I want a motorcycle. Is he correct? Yes he is the champion. My mom kind of doesn't have an imagination. But I still love her very, very, very much and so on. I am just asking. What if the world was a flashlight? This is what you would hear, "I'm melting!" I am so sorry but if you can please exit to the right young man. I am sorry wrong exit, but I'm finished.

Miguel Morales, Grade 4
Burchett Elementary School, TX

My Exciting Dog, Sophie

My dog, Sophie, was rescued by my family from the pound. We saw many other dogs, but it seemed obvious Sophie was the one.

When we took her home, all she did was play with my brother and me! She's very energetic.

Sophie is a tannish-brown, short-haired collie. She's very well-behaved, and very protective of my brother and me. Sophie's only about a year old. Her birthday is a couple weeks before Halloween, so we always get her a new costume!

I'm very lucky that we rescued Sophie, the world's greatest dog!

Parker Davis, Grade 5
Westview Elementary School, OH

My Grandma

My grandma grew up in Illinois on a farm. Her name is Sharon Schwin, and she had an awesome childhood! She also has a great adulthood.

Here are some things she did as a kid to make it awesome. Sharon's favorite memory as a kid was getting together with her cousins and the rest of her family. With her cousins she would play baseball and a card game called *Flinch*. She also rode her cousins' horses.

During her everyday life she enjoyed playing in the hay bales and helping on the farm. She also liked taking care of the animals and playing sports.

Sharon's favorite animals are sheep. She showed sheep in the County Fair and she won five consecutive years for Champion Fat Lamb. She liked leading them, because she put her arm around them and they would follow her.

One of the sheep Sharon owned had triplets. Then the mom died so Sharon bottle-fed the babies by putting a bottle between her legs and one in each hand.

As a kid she loved to do sports like high jumping and basketball.

Now she enjoys feeding birds and decorating and redecorating her house. Her favorite color is burgundy, which she has a lot of in her house.

Her favorite job was being a nurse for cataract surgery. Her favorite part was giving intravenous injections. Now she's retired and lives in Eugene, Oregon, and lives a very happy life.

Makeesha Boyum, Grade 6
Thomas Jefferson Charter School, ID

LBE

My mom, dad, and sister Emilee are my awesome family members. I love them so much. Even if they're mad at me! It's hard not to love them. They're like a super family! If I'm sad they're there to wipe away my tears. If I'm mad, they're there to calm me down. If I need a hug they're there with open arms. No matter what, all day and every day, they're caring, loving, and happy. They are extremely important to me.

When I have a bad day, the first people I look forward to seeing at the end of the day is my family. To me, my family is terrific, phenomenal, and excellent. They'll never miss any important event and they always remember my birthday! Plus they always cheer me on too. Whether I'm bad or good. My family is like a mixture of happiness. My dad, Brian, is always cracking jokes. Lisa, my mom, always laughs at my jokes. She even understands.

Last but not least, my sister Emilee is always watching me. Say I'm playing soccer, volleyball, the piano, or even competing in a swim meet, she's there watching me and cheering me on. But if they can't all come, my parents never send me alone and send me with someone else. One of my family members is usually always there. I love my family because they always love me no matter what.

Madison Mason, Grade 6
Linfield Christian School, CA

Oh, No! Are We Stuck?

We started our turkey hunt with a mud puddle at the bottom of a hill. My mom put the truck into gear, and we churned through the mud. At first it was going well, but when we got to the middle of the puddle, we got stuck. My mom tried to go further, but nothing happened. So she tried going back where we started. My mom had a bucket of butterflies in her stomach. She was going through the mud like it was an obstacle course that lasted two seconds or you were out. We were halfway through the course when the front tires grabbed onto some dry dirt. The tires held on like they were climbing a cliff. The tires climbed and climbed until we had a little way to go. In less than 10 seconds we were out. We were all relieved to get on top of that cliff that we conquered.

About an hour later, we found some turkeys at the bottom of the hill. We let our friend, Kendal, take his shot. He ran down the hill as fast as he could. We saw him crouch down. Within seconds, we heard the gun fire. Then he cheered like never before. He ran up that hill like he was racing a jet to show us that fine turkey. That year I had an awesome time, and I can't wait until next year.

Tana Spaid, Grade 6
Monforton School, MT

The "Cherry" on Top

My story is about a person who made a difference in my life. That person was my Aunt Lorraine. She was significant to me, because she always pulled the family together.

I have many memories of times spent with my aunt. In the summertime, my grandma Hart would always take my friends, my sister, and I to go swimming in Wray, Colorado where my aunt lived. After we went swimming, we would go to my aunt's house for snacks. My aunt had awesome snacks for us.

Every Easter, my aunt would invite all the family for dinner. Her specialty to me was her deviled eggs. They were very appetizing! The highlight of the day involved the children receiving an Easter basket. The baskets were hidden and found during her annual Easter egg hunt. We always had a great time!

The last time I was with her, she did something very special for my sister and I. My grandma Hart took my aunt, my sister, and I to a restaurant for lunch. Upon returning to my aunt's house, she made me the best banana split ever!

I will never forget the day I found out she was in the hospital. My parents took my sister and I to see her. The hardest thing I ever had to do was to say "good-bye."

Today, the banana split bowls sit in our cupboard. These banana split bowls represent my aunt as being, "The Cherry on Top."

Ashley McFadden, Grade 6
Haxtun Elementary/Jr High School, CO

My Sister and I

My life before I had my sister was nice, but there was something wrong. My mom I guess, kind of knew what was wrong, but I didn't. So one day my mom asked me if I wanted a sister and I said yes.

The feeling I had before my sister was okay. I was very lonely. One reason why I was so lonely was, if my parents were busy I had nobody to play with and no one to share my thoughts with. So I felt bored and lonely. Now I do have a sister. It's great because I can do all those things now!

Amber is my best friend. She will be in my life forever. I don't ever have to be lonely. My mom was home by herself when she was little, and she didn't want me to feel that way at all. I am very thankful that my mom and dad made this decision.

Amber thinks of me as a role model; I know because I asked her. Amber wants to be a veterinarian when she grows up just like me. Now, unlike me, she takes after my dad and I take after my mom. We are very opposite.

Amber is my heart and I will always be here for her no matter what she does. That's what sisters do.

Gabriella Parks, Grade 5
The Arts Academy School, OH

What I Enjoy

What I enjoy most is going on a trip. It is so fun because people might be different there and you might get to experience how they feel around people. Like one time when I went to Cabo people spoke a different language and looked different, too. But it was fun to be in a different country. When I went to Hawaii people were different too. I enjoy being with my relatives too even though they live far away I still LOVE to. It is so fun to be with them because they are funny, smart, and really fun to play with a lot.

Morgan Pinckard, Grade 4
Gateway Pointe Elementary School, AZ

Me, Myself, and I

I'm Trent. I have extremely dark luscious brown hair and dark skin. My eyes are a light chestnut color with a hint of really dark brown. I have a slim build and crooked pinky fingers. For a nine year old boy, I am quite tall.

My hobbies and talents are singing, video games, soccer and school. My favorite subjects are math, gym, and computers. It is important to me to get good marks on my report card. I am a dedicated student and a proud Canadian.

My family consists of two older brothers, a mother, a father and of course me. We are a happy family and care for one another. Two other important family members are our two Newfoundland dogs. One is named Bishop and the other is named Lucy. Lucy is Bishop's mother and she howls a lot. Bishop is really playful and entirely black in color, while Lucy is white and black. Both of their coats are thick and glossy. Together with my pets, parents and brothers we are a complete family.

Trent Williams, Grade 4
Linsford Park School, AB

Standing Up for Freedom

Have you ever thought about war? I wouldn't. That is because war is absolutely horrible, people die and family's then have to suffer from their loss. War is heartbreaking and deadly! But of course there is always a reason for everything. Just like there is a reason for war. In 1776 the Revolutionary War began. Women and mothers said their good byes to sons and husbands fearing that they may never see their loved ones again.

Close your eyes and imagine. Imagine America's peaceful, quiet land that stretches across America farther then a man could see. Then without warning a loud "BAM, BAM" that interrupts our peaceful land. Men take aim and suddenly fall one by one, then two by two. Smoke raises making it hard for anyone to see and then as quick as the battle started, it ends, still more to come though. As all of you may know we did win our right in freedom, but only because of the brave solders that fought for it. We should be thankful for all the men that died for us and all the men that fought for us.

Our flag represents our country, it represents the land that we fought for and its stars represent each state that we fought for. Our flag represents our homeland, America!

Breanna Herbert, Grade 5
Maple Avenue Elementary School, WI

My Growing Pain

My doctor said, "By the time I count to ten, you'll fall asleep."

"O.K.," I said. As he got to eight, he pulled out one of his sharp, scary surgical tools. At that moment everything went dark. I must have either fainted or fallen asleep.

I am Joshua Kutsch and have O.I. (Osteogenesis Imperfecta). I have brittle bones; so, I need stable rods in my legs to support my weight better. After my annual checkup, my nightmare had come true. I needed surgery on my right leg because the rod was too short and needed to be replaced. Once I arrived at the hospital, I was weighed, measured and given horrible tasting sleep medicine. It tasted so bad, I couldn't swallow at all; so, I spit some out. As I was being rolled into the operating room, my eyelids were feeling heavy.

After the surgery, I woke up in the cold, uncomfortable post-op room. I ate a red, cold Popsicle that tasted so good to my empty, starving stomach. Next, they moved me to a private room for observation while I recovered. After a few days, my doctor released me to go home. I couldn't wait! Once I was in the car on my way home; I said, "It's finally over, yeah!"

Although the surgeries are not desired, they're a must. They are part of my growing pains. My first surgery happened when I was two years old; and I've had more than I care to remember.

Joshua Kutsch, Grade 6
St Matthew Catholic School, TX

How to Care for a Rabbit

Rabbit care is simple. All you have to do is make sure you give it plenty of exercise and clean out its cage once a week. Just make sure that you don't give it too many treats. That would make your rabbit sick.

Rabbits love fruits and veggies, so make sure that you give them something every day. Just be careful what you give them because they can't handle citrus fruits. Another thing that they love is timothy hay. It's always good to give your rabbit hay because it helps their digestion. Make sure that you include a salt lick for the rabbit because they do not get enough salt out of a regular diet.

Rabbit pellets also make up a rabbit's diet. They are a good supplement for grass, but I'm sure no rabbit would say no to some fresh grass. Just make sure that you don't give too much.

Something that I find interesting is that rabbits can be potty trained. They may not always use it, but the majority of their feces and urine will end up in the litter box. It's all very easy. Just find out where the rabbit goes the most and then stick a litter box there. Make sure that the first time you put it in, there is a little bit of their feces in the box. Soon they will learn to go there. Don't forget they need a house! Wood is the best kind for them.

Heidi Van Valkenburgh, Grade 6
South Suburban Montessori School, OH

Nature

Nature provides recreation for me, an outdoors kind of guy. Being in nature is my favorite activity. I like to ski in the winter. The mountains let me go fast down the slopes — so fast that my nickname is "Blue Trail Skier Boy." I ski through the glades and ride on the ice.

Nature also allows me to go camping with my family. My favorite place is the Smoky Mountains National Park. My dad uses wood to build a campfire so we can roast marshmallows and hot dogs. When we are camping in nature, we leave the TV at home and spend quality time together. We ride bikes, go fishing and canoeing, and just have fun together.

I also go hiking in nature, one of my favorite places being Clifton Gorge. We walk on a historic stagecoach trail and pass an old paper mill. We also see plants such as jewelweed. When you squeeze the seeds, they explode.

One last reason why nature is important to me is because I can ride my bike. During the summer, we ride in the metro parks. I like the smell of woods as I speed along the trail. I also ride with my grandpa on the Rails to Trails path near his house. We usually ride four to six miles at a time. We have fun talking and racing. Nature is important because I can learn, get some exercise, and spend time with those I love, all while I am having fun.

Jorgen Kerens, Grade 4
Birchwood School, OH

Losing a Pet

Hi my name is Angelica and I want to tell you a story about a family pet. My sister Ivette used to have a cat named Midnight and he had black fur and green eyes. When my sister got her cat I had realized that the cat was different from its sibling and mother. I guess that's why my sister chose that one particular cat. Its family had light brown and white fur. I wanted to get its sibling for my own pet. We took the cat home and my sister named it Cookie. But then she thought that was too funny so she thought of Midnight. I thought that was ok because Cookie didn't really fit for a black cat. I was hoping for a name more like Black Cobra or Darkness. But anyway, we went to the animal store and got the cat a food bowl and other cat stuff.

I got a little bit jealous of my sister having a cat and not me but I got over it. One time Midnight threw up in my room and I had to pick it up. But it wasn't that gross. My dad just couldn't stand the cat so we had to let my grandma take care of it. She was having a bit of trouble so my dad decided to give it away and we were all sad because he was sold without us saying good-bye.

Angelica Martinez, Grade 4
Menchaca Elementary School, TX

My Name

My name means kindness. To me it means the number 7 because it's my favorite number and it makes me feel lucky because I have a lot of people that love me. It gives me the feeling of happiness. Blue because it makes me feel calm and cool. It reminds of a waterfall flowing swiftly. My mother named me this because she liked it she thought it would fit perfectly. My family and friends say it's a pretty name. It doesn't remind me of anything. I've never met anyone with the same name as me. If I could change my name it would be something unique and different.

Marissa Picon, Grade 6
North Oaks Middle School, TX

Responsibility

Being responsible in your life is important because if you are not responsible you could have trouble.

When you are responsible at school it means a lot because if you are not accountable you might have bad grades. The word responsible means being the one who must answer or account for something. If you are responsible at school you won't get into trouble. For example, getting your work done on time is good and shows responsibility.

Doing your chores is another example of being responsible. What if your mom went to the market and you were asked to take care of your brothers and sisters, what would you do? If you were a responsible person you would take care of them until she came.

Therefore, being responsible makes you a better person in your life.

Leonardo Velazquez, Grade 5
Covington Elementary School, NE

The Truth About Smoking

Tar, nail polish, paint thinner, formaldehyde. What do these things have in common? They can all be found in…cigarettes. Yes, those nasty things that thousands of Canadians have in their hands. As you read, thousands are suffering.

Smoking causes cancer, emphysema, and heart disease, but thousands of Canadians smoke. Why? Addiction. Cigarettes contain nicotine which is a highly addictive drug. Your body get used to it, so you need it to feel normal. Cigarettes have all sorts of other chemicals in them, such as oil and factory disposals. You could spend up to about ten thousand dollars a year for these nasty things rolled into a tube. Smoking sure has become difficult.

Most people start smoking, not because they want to, but because everyone else is. This is called peer pressure.

Research shows that a person who smokes will die ten years earlier than a healthy person who doesn't. If only it was just your health you're harming, but it isn't. Secondhand smokers have just as much a risk in developing lung cancer as firsthand smokers. Even if a smoker smokes out the window it might blow back into the house. Little kids who have never smoked a second in their lives are paying just because their parents smoke.

Personally I think poisoning yourself is stupid. Poison that turns your lungs black and fills your body with tar and diseases. Too many have lost a loved one through first or secondhand smoking. Help stop smoking and you could help save lives.

Aparajita Bhandari, Grade 6
Northwood Public School, ON

All About Kelly Jean Dorff

Kelly is about 38 years old. This woman is my mom. She was born in Green Bay. She has two beautiful kids. Their names are Ashely and Kayla. She works at Hardee's and Lou's One Stop too. She gets a lot of money from both jobs, so she has enough money to last her for the week.

My mom is a very tough woman. She will not stop at anything. She goes and goes and keeps on going! My mom is so amazing to everyone around her at work and at home. She cares so much for others.

My mom cooks tasty food for me, my family, and last but not least, my sister, Ashley too. I love my mother so much! My mom listens to country and soft rock music. She listens to it on the radio a lot. My mother is also crazy, because she will get on a bar and start dancing. I love that about my mom.

Well that's all I have to say about my mom, Kelly Jean Dorff. She is a wonderful mom and I wish everyone could have a mom like mine! I love her so much!

Kayla Dorff, Grade 6
Edison Middle School, WI

The Car Crash

It all started like a normal day, the sky was blue the birds were singing, it was a typical summer day. My mom had to take her car in to get her brakes fixed so my brother and I went with her and my dad took his car so he could take us home after my mom dropped off her car.

We were driving along the freeway about to exit when, CRASH! We hit the car in front of us. It took me awhile to finally realize what happened, we had gotten into a car accident. But as quick as a blink, my brother jumped out of the car.

My mom yelled "Joseph! What do you think you are doing? Get back in the car!" But he ran to the car in front of us and helped the little girl out. She had a small cut on her forehead and it was bleeding a little so he told her to hold her forehead.

As he helped the last person out, the paramedics arrived. They rushed to the people and then two more men went to help us. They asked a couple of questions and gave me a Band-Aid because the impact of the crash ripped my scab off that I got a couple of days earlier. No one in our car had broken anything…except for my mom's glasses we were all okay. The paramedics thanked my brother and they left. I'll never forget that day, even though it was four years ago! What a day that turned out to be!

Lauren Salazar, Grade 6

Being a Good Friend

Being a good friend is someone who encourages you when you go to a baseball game. A good friend never lets you down. A friend helps you when you are hurt and sick. My friends and I like to play games after school like tag, freeze-tag, and hide-and-seek. We also go to summer camp and swim in the pool. We are best friends and we will be best friends forever. My best friend is nice, kind and funny. We like to hang out in his dad's barber shop. His name is Angel Floras and he is my best friend forever.

Stephen Cervantes, Grade 4
Our Lady of the Rosary School, CA

September 11 (a.k.a. 9/11)

September 11th is a day for Americans to remember that people risked their lives to save others, when the Twin Towers fell in 2001. In remembrance of them; we are asked to do a good deed. A good deed is something that comes from the heart and what you think of. A good deed is not something that someone asks you to do, ever!

It is a good way to remember, September by doing a good deed. There are a lot of good deeds out there and most of them are as simple as cleaning your room without being asked or holding a door for someone. A good deed is very easy to do.

In conclusion it's very easy to do a good deed. I've given you some examples of some good deeds that are easy to do…so do them!

Connor Serr, Grade 6
Snake River Montessori School, ID

Perseverance

A lesson I learned from someone was the day I was running a race. It all started when my family and I went to our family reunion in Louisiana. We stayed in Mississippi but the family reunion was in Louisiana. We stayed in hotels for six days. One warm day my cousin Dazjah and I decided to have a race for $1.00. My cousin Kizzy was the judge. Before we started the race we drank lots and lots of water. She said we had to run around the hotel five times. Each lap we ran she counted out loud. I started getting tired and slow. Kizzy didn't see me coming around the corner, so she came around to me and asked me what was wrong. I said, "I can't do it." "Yes you can, you can do it. Don't give up," she said. I said, "You're right, I can do it." I started supporting myself and stopped giving up, I started running like it wasn't anything, and guess what, I won the race because I persevered. That is a lesson we all should learn, and who knows how perseverance might surprise you.

Acajah Bowman, Grade 5
McMonagle Elementary School, MI

My Great Father

My humorous dad inspires me because he makes comical faces and creates humorous dances. He also makes incredibly funny comments about any subject my family discusses at dinner.

My dad plays billiards, hand tennis, and basketball well. I mostly play with him because I like a challenge and I get it from him. I really wish I could be better and beat him more than I can right now.

My dad cooks wonderfully and makes tasty food for my family. Although my mom could cook, my dad is faster, a better chef, and has more experience. I hope to be a great cook like him when I grow up.

But the best part about my dad is that he cares, loves, and does wonderful things for me. For instance, whenever I get hurt or sick, he gives me the right type of medicine. He never shouts when I accidentally do something bad. He protects me in any way I need protection. My dad is my inspiration because I am trying to follow his good steps.

Nimish Saxena, Grade 6

Susie, My Little Angel Friend

I admire someone very special. Her name is Susie. She's my angel friend, because she's honest, friendly, and touching.

She is everything to me. We were friends, 2nd-4th, now we see each other in the morning. I wish that we can be in every single grade together.

Her honesty is like a diploma, or a parent signature for your reading log.

Susie is touching and friendly. If she tells you a poem, she'll make you cry. She'll be a friend if you need one.

We are the same, were meant to be friends forever. That is why she's my angel friend.

Do you have a special person that you care about?

Marylyn Chavez, Grade 5
Camellia Avenue Elementary School, CA

The Human Body

Many people think that the human body is old news. Well I think it is what we should give attention to. We have so much technology to find cures but it is not easy to find all those cures. Well let me tell you about the human body. The human body has so many cells that we humans are called walking cells instead of earthlings. The human body has a lots of organs. The most important ones are the brain and the heart. If you are reading this then you will know what the important organs in your body are.

The heart has four chambers. The heart is always circulating the blood from the lungs when it comes back from the body. When the blood comes back to the heart, the heart refilters the blood then it pumps it to the body. When the blood is finished going around the body and is gone to the lungs, the lungs send it back to the heart and the process starts all over again. There are two different cells in your body. They have different colors. The colors are red and blue. The blue ones carry the oxygen and maybe food. The red cells are for carrying blood. Did you know there is a disease that gives you a darker skin color splotches? That disease is called the fungus. At first they did not have the cure. Never be scared to go to the doctor because it's for your health.

Fatima Fatima, Grade 6
Dr F D Sinclair Elementary School, BC

J.K. Rowling

My favorite author of all time would be Joanne Rowling (J.K. Rowling), author of the *Harry Potter* series. She was born on July 30, 1965, in Gloucestershire, England. From a very early age, she enjoyed writing fantasy stories, and came up with the idea for the *Harry Potter* series on a train ride to London. In 1994, she moved to Edinburgh, Scotland, and began writing in nearby cafés while her young daughter was sleeping. Her first novel was originally published as *Harry Potter and the Philosopher's Stone* in 1997, and was then published in 1998 as *Harry Potter and the Sorcerer's Stone* by Scholastic in the U.S. The final four books in the series were the fastest selling books in history, with the final novel being the fastest selling. Rowling is not planning to publish an eighth book, but is planning to write an encyclopedia of the wizarding world. She currently owns houses near Aberfeldy in Perth and Kinross, Scotland, and Marchiston and Kensington, West London, England, and lives with her husband and children. Rowling is my favorite author because of her style of writing. Once I started reading *Harry Potter*, it became a sort of obsession of mine. I own every book and movie available to the general public, and have seen or read each one about twenty times each. My current favorite novel in the series is *Harry Potter and the Deathly Hallows*.

Suzie Knuppel, Grade 6
Argyle Middle School, TX

My Lovely Mother

What kind of mother do you have? My mom is very trustworthy. You can tell her a secret. If you tell her secrets she will keep it locked up in her mouth and never say it to anyone. If you feel bad about something she will make you feel better. She made me feel better when I was young and I thought that I was going to be robbed. She also knows how you feel.

My mom is very nice because she helps me in things that are very hard. She is also very nice by buying me things. She says that if she buys us something kind of expensive the thing that she bought me will be our Christmas gift. She also is very nice by letting us go and get an ice popsicle.

My intelligent mother is so smart that she helps me with my homework by explaining to me very good. She can do a lot of things quickly. When I'm stuck in something she moves the thing in front of me and I get out. She is such a loving person.

In conclusion, I admire my mom because she is good in many things. What can your mother do?

Janice Contreras, Grade 5
Camellia Avenue Elementary School, CA

My Secret Place

My secret place is in the woods, way back in the woods, in a tree…a very high tree. My secret place is a tree house. It took me weeks to build it because no one knew about it. The tree house is about 16 ft. tall and 16 ft. long. It has 6 windows on each wall and on the roof. I climb up the ladder when I am up there. It is real neat. I have a bed in there, a couch, a TV, a PS2, and an Xbox. Me and my friends like to hang out in there.

Cody Couey, Grade 4
Winona Elementary School, TX

Recycling

Every Monday I take the recycling bin out to the driveway. It is a chore I do not particularly enjoy, but I do it because I like to help the environment by recycling. Do you like to recycle? Here is some information that may inspire you to get involved.

Recycling began in 1922 in England and has continued ever since. During World War II, people were especially encouraged to recycle because of supply shortages.

Many things can be recycled in our daily life. These things include glass, aluminum, asphalt, iron, textiles, and plastics. People recycle because it saves energy, and less trash is produced. If we recycled more paper, we wouldn't have to cut down as many trees, and the environment would be a better place in which to live.

Teaching people to recycle is a very important practice. Why? Because recycling is a major piece in the jigsaw puzzle of protecting the environment. Knowing that recycling is important, it is our duty to carry out this activity as much as we possibly can.

Peter Abou Haidar, Grade 4
Birchwood School, OH

Education

You're never going to get a good job if you don't get a good education. In order to get the job you want you must go to college.

For instance I want a good paying job to support my family, not a job where you just hold a flag and sit on the road. If I were you, I would go to college right after you get out of high school and start training to be a math teacher. But if nothing worked out I'd just move on to something else.

Besides, if you think about it, if you get a good paying job and when you retire you'll get so much money.

Honestly, if you are looking for a football college, the one with the best football program is USC.

Besides, if you get a job with a good education that fits you, you just might make some new friends, but you never know.

Oh and about earlier, I forgot to tell you that when you get into high school, you might want to start saving up money for college.

Seth Fell, Grade 6
Milltown Elementary School, IN

Flight 19

"We have liftoff!" the pilot shouted over the radio. The plane engines roared with ferocity while they lifted off the ground. At about 2 p.m. on December 5 of 1945, five torpedo bombers had just departed from Fort Lauderdale, Florida on a navigational bombing mission. They were to bomb an island and return to Florida, right on the edge of the Bermuda Triangle.

A radio message intercepted at 4 p.m. from the leader of the Flight 19 was the first indication that Flight 19 was lost. The leader reported that the compasses were malfunctioning and they had no idea where they were. Suddenly, the radio stopped working and they were no longer able to contact land.

This was the last message the leader transmitted to the control tower and his other bombers, "All planes close up tight…we will have to ditch unless landfall…when the first plane drops below ten gallons of fuel we will all go down together."

After dark, two seaplanes were directed to perform searches for Flight 19. The search planes never returned and were never heard from again. The crew or wreckage from Flight 19 were never found.

The leader of Flight 19 didn't know it, but the crew had just flown right into the middle of the Bermuda Triangle. Today, it remains a mystery as to why so many planes and ships disappear in that area. Some say a black hole exists there and others say you disappear from alien abduction. The Bermuda Triangle is one of Earth's biggest mysteries.

Cole Love-Baker, Grade 5
La Costa Heights Elementary School, CA

My Pet Python

My pet python Buddy, is a 30-inch long baby ball python. I think Buddy is a really cool pet to own, because Buddy doesn't eat your normal food, he eats live mice. I think it's interesting to watch him eat, because he'll bite his prey voraciously, then he coils around the victim's body and asphyxiates his prey until it suffocates to death.

Buddy is a neat pet to have, he's low maintenance and he's just plain cool. I say one of the most interesting things about Buddy is that when you touch his scales, they feel like beads.

After I read a book about ball pythons, I wanted a ball python. When I got Buddy he was wrapped up in a little ball. He did this for quite some time, but once he got used to me, the ball started to slowly unravel.

Buddy is mostly called a ball python, but he is also called a royal python. The reason he is called this is that long ago Cleopatra wore the snake as a bracelet.

Buddy is still the mouse killing king, but every day he seems to change in some way. Buddy will change by length, width or even look, but some days he just stays the same.

Aaron Meek, Grade 6
Spring Creek Elementary School, WY

Neptune

Exploring space is every child's dream. Perhaps someday, people will be able to live on planets. Neptune would be an interesting place to live.

Neptune was discovered in 1846. It was discovered by scientists when they noticed that something was pulling Uranus. It was being pulled in the opposite direction of the Sun's pull of gravity. Neptune is the eighth planet from the sun. Neptune sometimes overlaps Pluto which makes Neptune the last planet. Neptune's orbit is slow. It takes 165 years for Neptune to orbit the Sun.

Neptune has many interesting features. Like Earth, Neptune has water. Neptune also has rings, four in fact. Neptune has the fastest winds ever recorded. Winds have been up to two thousand kilometers per hour. Neptune also has great storms. Neptune has dark spots like the Great Red Spot on Jupiter. These spots appear and disappear because they are caused by atmospheric pressure. Compared to Earth, Neptune is much bigger.

Neptune's moons are a unique feature. Neptune has 8 moons where the Earth only has one. Triton is the biggest moon. The coldest temperature ever measured in the solar system is -230 Celcius on Triton. Naiad is the smallest moon. The others are Thalassa, Despina, Galatea, Larissa, Proteus, and Neried.

Neptune is still a mystery. But who knows, maybe someday people will live there.

Alex Scott, Grade 4
Norwoodville Elementary School, IA

What's Happening

"Noooo!" What's happening? I yelled, running to my room crying! I didn't know my puppy was having a seizure.

When my puppy, Jessica, has a seizure her brain takes over, her eyes roll inside out, her legs get stiff and, she slips and falls. My mom and I were in my living room when Jessica slipped and couldn't get up. My mom held her 'til she could walk again. I told my mom I was scared, ran to my room and shut the door.

This mostly happens when someone is over, she meets someone new, gets too hot or, gets too excited. I never want her to have another seizure! It's sad too, I hope your dog doesn't have epilepsy (seizures).

Her longest seizure lasted about 45 min. My dog's name is Jessica, is brown and white, she has green eyes. She is a cocker spaniel, jack russel terrier and a little bit of lab and springer spaniel.

It's sad and if she dies I will remember her. I never want her to have another seizure again.

Marissa Jacobs, Grade 5
Bang Elementary School, TX

The Lake

Usually going to the lake is a good thing but not last summer vacation. It was a perfect summer until I went to the lake that is when it all went wrong. I was on my knee board and I just got out of the wake. I stayed on the longest ever and broke my record. I was so happy. I fell very hard and got hurt. I had the taste of lake water in my mouth. But I still stayed on until I got to the dam. I pulled back up to the boat and grabbed a football of mine and started to pass it around. My friend tossed it back to me and he missed when I was on the boat and it went in the water. I was going to jump over the edge of the boat and grab the ball but my foot got stuck in the chair in the back and I fell forward and broke my teeth. It scared me more than it hurt. It chipped the boat and it smelled like rotten teeth for a long time and the boat still had a mark since I saw it. That is why it was not a good thing to go to the lake last summer.

Cole Farrell, Grade 5
Desert Canyon Elementary School, AZ

Fall Leaves

The leaves danced around the yard daintily when the wind blew. They look like they're hopping sometimes. The leaves fall like swirling tornados. There are many different shapes, colors and sizes just like different people all around the world. They sit on the trees at night like sleeping people. It seems like they love to jump in the pool during the summer with the hot steamy sun shining on them. The leaves glistened from the summer sun and waved to me when I passed by. I love the smell, not too hard but still not too light. I walked along the sidewalk enjoying the sound of the crackling leaves as my friends and I walked by on the sidewalk.

Shauna Setzler, Grade 5
Greenwood Elementary School, MN

A True Wish

I bet many of us have not seen beggars running towards us for food and money in America, but I have — in India. It didn't affect me much when I was younger, but it bothered me during my trip this summer.

Trips to India are always tiring but fun, because I get to meet my family. The sad part is seeing poor people with children at train stations, temples, and even homes! I usually ask my mom for money to give them, but many times, too many beggars crowd around us.

My grandparents have been following a tradition of cooking food every Saturday for the poor and giving it to people. During this trip, I went with them to see what it was like. After I came back, I felt depressed. Those people had no homes, no food, and no money. When I saw little boys running towards our car for food, I was so thankful for what I had.

When I came back to America, I thought about how I could help more. I started collecting clothes, toys, books, and games, and donated them to charity organizations. I am happy to share my things with people who need it more than I do.

Poverty isn't just in India, it's everywhere in the world, even in our wealthy nation. I wish the world could be poverty-free. We can make this happen by giving things to people who need it more than we do.

Anirudh Viswanathan, Grade 6
Daniel Wright Jr High School, IL

Moving

"You know the house we've seen?" my dad asked. "Well, we're going to buy it!" he said. We had seen the house three times and now we were going to move in!

I felt happy to move to a nice new house but also sad that I was leaving our old house and neighborhood. I'd lived in this house since I was a baby and I was going to be leaving my friend Alyssa who lived across the street.

When the movers came and piled all the stuff into the truck, Alyssa came over to say goodbye; that was a little sad. We had been friends since Kindergarten!

When we looked at our old house after the stuff was in the truck it looked so empty as if we'd never lived there!

I have great memories of living there, like sliding down our big hill, turtles laying eggs and the eggs hatching into tiny baby turtles (they were so CUTE!), grandparents coming from England, birthdays, decorating for holidays, jumping in leaves and swimming in the pool in the summers. There were many fun times.

The first night in the new house I walked in my sleep and ended up in the spare room!

I've made new friends and still see Alyssa on weekends. I love the new house now!

Savannah Strudwick, Grade 5

My Life Without My Parents

It's hard to imagine what it would be like without my parents. I wouldn't really have that much as I do now for example: shoes, expensive clothes, a lot of other stuff like that. Sometimes it's good to have parents, sometimes not. One day you might need your parents because it might be a serious emergency. My life without my parents would be a very painful time for me. Not that many people can live that long without their parents when they're really young. Most people in the world do. But I really don't think I could live without my parents. I just want to say I love my parents and I can't live my life without them.

Kyra Odom, Grade 5
DeQueen Elementary School, TX

The Lost Race

One day before the drag races we went to get our car dynamometered. We had a really old car, a 1972 Camaro. We had just put a new engine in it, and it already had 300 miles on it. Later that day we finally got to Dynojet (that's the shop where we dyno our race cars.) Now it was about 10:00 P.M. and we were hungry, really hungry. So we went inside to get a piece of pizza. We ate and then it was time to get the car off of the trailer. It was about 2:00 P.M. and we finally got ready to start the dyno. My job was to watch the time. We started 3000-5000-7500 rpm's. BOOM! Antifreeze poured out on the headers. Oil was all over the floor. It was a mess. The motor was gone. It had blown! My mom said, "Well it's a lost race!"

Dylan Jones, Grade 6
Monforton School, MT

Benelli Days

Have you ever been to Benelli Days? That's when Tom Knapp comes to Ace's Guns in Kentucky. Benelli Days only happen once every four years.

This year I went for the first time. There were so many hunting supplies, guns, and ammunition. If you paid a dollar you could shoot a gun with three shots of your choice. I ended up doing that 4 times, trying a different gun every time. We went into Ace's Guns and looked at over and under shotguns, a couple of hours later I ended up with one of my own. It's a Kahn 20 gage shotgun. It is my favorite gun!

At 1:00 p.m. Tom Knapp came out to get ready for his show. Tom did all kinds of things such as he threw up 9 clay pigeons and shot them with an 8 shot shotgun. He shot at golf balls to the left, right, and the center. He got kids out of the audience and let them throw eggs in the air while he shot them. He made potato salad by shooting potatoes and lettuce at the same time. For the grand finale he shot cans of powder, filling the sky with red, white, and blue.

On our way back we stopped at the Tell City McDonalds and ate ice cream making my day complete. I had so much fun! I can't wait until four years from now when Benelli Days returns!!!

Nikolaus Greulich, Grade 6
Nancy Hanks Elementary School, IN

Global Warming

Hi my name is JuanCarlos and I'm going to talk about global warming. If you are wondering what it is it's a temperature increase causing the ice caps to melt and sea level to rise. Global warming can be stopped. We could carpool every day. That slows down the process of global warming.

People are being affected by global warming. There are more floods. In the future Florida might be half covered in water. The west is not getting enough rain, which causes droughts. Water restrictions are being made. That is what global warming is doing.

JuanCarlos Armijo, Grade 4
Santo Niño Regional Catholic School, NM

Drinking and Driving Don't Mix

Beer and wine are popular drinks but when lives are threatened it becomes a serious matter. At most adult parties wine, beer, or liquor are a choice of drink, but sometimes things can get out of hand. If adults go too overboard with drugs or have a glass of wine right before they leave, driving home is dangerous. Not only are the drunk drivers risking their own lives, but they are also risking those in the cars around them. Thirty percent of all Americans have or will be involved in a car crash because of a drunk driver. So far there have been over sixteen thousand car crashes because people have been drinking. If you don't think sixteen thousand is a lot think of next year, the year after that. The amount of drunk drivers is growing so much each year. I think the drunks are very irresponsible. Every adult is responsible for managing how much they drink. If they can't they are risking more than they are allowed to risk. (Other peoples lives.) Drinking and driving don't mix! Adults need to stop because more than their own lives are at stake.

Remi Lassiter, Grade 5
Marcy Elementary School, WI

JRT

Do you like dogs? I'm dog crazy! Now, I will tell you about the Jack Russell Terrier. The reason I chose this breed is because not everyone knows about this dog. The Jack is a friendly guard dog. I know when you hear guard dog you think of mean. Nope that isn't the Jack. The Jack is a very energetic breed. They love to play twenty-four seven. They have two sizes tall and stump. They also have three types of coats smooth, rough and broken. If you have a Jack you may see a round colored circle close to his tail that is his trump mark.

If you live in the city well, no Jack for you because they were bred to get animals out of underground burrows. Did you know they race in dog races? They usually live to be sixteen or older. They love to cuddle with you. The Jack is in the Terrier group. Here are some usual colors of the Jack white, black and brown. Well bye or what the Jack would say "woof."

Danel Graham, Grade 4
Scipio Elementary School, IN

The Time I Almost Passed Out!

I was nervous but filled with excitement. I couldn't wait for my first cross country meet to start. Coach said, "This is rough terrain, there are going to be hurdles, a hay jump into watery mud and a big log you have to jump over." Before the race I prayed and tried to motivate myself to finish unhurt.

Boom! I heard the loud gun and I took off. I was dripping with sweat. I was really thirsty and I wanted to douse myself with cold water. I jumped over the tall hurdles, and I said to myself, "Two more obstacles to go!" I heard many people cheering for me, including my parents, so I scanned the crowd for them. I jumped over the hairy hay and landed into a deep puddle of mud! I almost tripped going over the big log! I only needed 100 meters to go. So, I sprinted with every bit of stamina I had left. Yes, I finished, almost seemed instantaneous.

They announced my time, I ran two miles in 22.15 minutes. I felt like an oaf. My dad said, "I'm happy you finished the race." I almost passed out; I was so famished and out of breath. I felt like my body was withering. I was mad because I got 96th out of 107 kids! I felt sheepish about my time. "That's what practice is for," Dad said. I made a plight that day to practice and do better at my next meet.

Rudy E. Bonilla, Grade 6
St Matthew Catholic School, TX

Sargon the King

Sargon was the king of the Akkadians. In 2340 B.C., Sargon conquered all of Mesopotamia. He then set up the world's first empire. He ruled his empire for more than fifty years. His empire lasted for more than two hundred years. In the centuries following the fall of Sargon's empire, Asher would become a new empire. The land of Asher would become Assyria.

In 1792 B.C. King Hammarabi conquered nearby cities. Hammarabi became powerful by controlling the Euphrates River. He built a dam to control its flow. By 1750 B.C. Hammarabi controlled all of Mesopotamia. Hammarabi took what he believed was the best laws and put them into one code that contained 282 laws. The Assyrian army was well organized at its core were groups of foot soldiers armed with spears and knives. Other soldiers were good at using bows and arrows. The army also had soldiers on horseback and on chariots. This was the first army to use four weapons. Iron was first used for tools but was too weak to use for weapons. Then the people called Hittites developed a way to make iron stronger. The Assyrians tunneled under walls and climbed over them when they attacked. They used trees as batting rams to knock down city gates. The Assyrian ruled for many years and built the mighty city of Babylon.

David Tanksley, Grade 6
Round Valley Elementary School, CA

My Favorite Place

My favorite place is my grandma and grandpa's house. My favorite room is my room. I love my room 'cause it has all my stuff. I have pictures in my room and drawings. Even some of the things are my grandpa's. Every time I go there I go straight to my room and start to play games. Then when night time is here I go back to my room. Then I go to sleep until the morning. My room is a great place to ask friends to come and visit me. My grandma and grandpa love to come in my room. One time me and my mom slept in the room together cause there was a storm and the electricity went off from the storm. Me and my niece Destiny normally go in there to play with all my stuff. She loves to be in my room 'cause all the decorations. Even some of her toys are in there with my toys. Once me and my sister went into my room just to talk to each other. We had a good time talking to each other. It is so fun too.

Chase Wallace, Grade 4
Winona Elementary School, TX

Linfield

Jesus, God, the Bible, math, English, friendship, and love are some of the things I learn every day at Linfield. Linfield is a good school because I get to learn about Jesus, the Bible, and all the many subjects.

I have a locker, so I don't have to lug all of my books around classes all day. It's a lot easier to have lockers for my books and to store my belongings for P.E.

Sometimes, I get candy too! It is the best. My parents have to pay a lot because it is a private school, but it is worth every penny. I also get to go on field trips. Some field trips are to Washington D.C., Astrocamp, Legoland, Sacramento, and Rawhide Ranch. Rawhide Ranch was the best field trip ever. I got to go horseback riding and got to play archery. I think archery was the best thing to do. My second favorite field trip was Sacramento. Sacramento was fun because I got to go to the State Capital. I can't forget the eight person bike. It was fun! Linfield is important to me because I get to have freedom at this school. I will go to this school till 12th grade. Linfield is the best!!!

Ryan Reed, Grade 6
Linfield Christian School, CA

What I Like to Do

I Matthew O., like to play video games, computer, I like to play sports, I play basketball, soccer, baseball, and football. My favorite sport is football. I also like to read books and to swim. I like to play instruments. I'm good at guitar, piano, and drums.

I play baseball at Northwest Little League. We have 0 loses and almost 6 wins. Baseball is my third favorite sport. Soccer is fun because you are with your friends. For soccer we have 0 loses and 10 wins. We are undefeated for baseball and soccer. The only problem in soccer is not all my friends are on my team.

Matthew Overton, Grade 4
St Luke Catholic School, TX

I'm Improving Myself

From the time I walked in the fourth grade class, I was struggling and I didn't try. But they gave me a chance and placed me. I passed, so then I was in fifth grade and I was working a bit harder. It wasn't hard enough, so I quit. Then I got placed in sixth grade.

It all started. I said to myself, I think I am actually going to try. And I'm going to get A's, B's, and C's. I really want to get all A's and B's and get honor roll. It probably won't happen, but you never know. I never got below an A or A- this year on math tests.

I think I'm doing one hundred percent better this year, but my sister is saying "The beginning of sixth grade is so easy," and she said "Just wait, it will get harder." I said it probably won't be too hard or you would have gotten held back. I personally think I have the brain to get good grades this year, but I'm just saying I will never know.

Mrs. Holly is one of the nicest teachers ever. I love that because it makes a big difference on my report card and in my life too.

My uncle said if I have time to goof off I have time to do good in school.

If I work hard anything is possible. I'm even thinking about going to college. So all I have to do is work hard and try and excel.

Austin May, Grade 6
Milltown Elementary School, IN

Getting to Know Me

My name is Emma. I have light blond hair and sparkling blue eyes. My favorite colors are blue and green. Monkeys and dogs are both my favorite animals.

I have a mom, a dad, and a very annoying brother, named Benjamin or Ben for short. I'm lucky to live on a farm because there's always lots to do. Sometimes I help my dad with chores and I like to bake with my mom. Living in the country is great for kids!

The pets that I have are two dogs named Freddy and Lizzie. I also have four puppies that are very cute and they are named Peter, JoJo, Karly, and Jane. Sadly we will have to give the puppies away, but they are sure playful to have right now.

In school I am in grade four. I have lots of work to do, especially on Mondays but I always get it all done. At recess I like to play outside with all of my friends. On Sunday after church, I love to go to my friend Chloe's house. Chloe does not go to my school, but that is okay because I get to see her on the weekends. Friends have a lot of fun together!

I have a wonderful life and I hope you enjoyed getting to know me!

Emma Kern, Grade 4
Linsford Park School, AB

Imagination, My Key to Fun

Imagination is wonderful! It can take anyone any place, it makes life so much fun, and it makes every day better! Without imagination I am sure life would be dull. I am not sure if I could even live without imagination.

Imagination takes the mind so many different places! I have been a princess living in a splendid castle, and even Laura Ingalls Wilder when she was a girl, but I only went those places because of my imagination. I have also been poor, an adult at work, even a nurse and a teacher, but only because I use my imagination.

Imagination makes life so fun because no matter what season it is imagination is always available and amusing. Without imagination most of the games I play would not be near as fun. Life would be incomplete if I did not have my imagination along with me.

Imagination makes every day better because it gives an individual something to do even while doing homework! Perhaps the chore is to pick up the sticks or mow the lawn; a person could pretend to be a worker for the emperor, or maybe the king! Everyday chores could become fun too if imagination is used. Using imagination will make the day go by faster.

I love imagination it is fun, creative, wonderful, and even inspiring. It makes life a lot more interesting, imagination makes the day amazing, and takes me anywhere I want to go! I cannot wait to use my imagination again!

Anna Laws, Grade 6
Southport 6th Grade Academy, IN

Being a Drug Free Person

Do you ever wonder how good it is to be free? Just think, you wouldn't really be able to do very many things. You couldn't do any work really. Being drug free is so nice.

If you took drugs, you would be a very bad person. Everyone has their own choice, but you're the one to make that choice. You are the person that controls your body.

You might think that since your friends are doing it, it is fun or cool. But you're just doing that to be cool. You don't realize it, but you're practically killing yourself. I have never had a friend that does this, but I know what it does to you.

If you do a lot of sports right now, that is great. But if you get stressed or mad, no matter what you think is best for you, don't do drugs. It would be really good if you have all A's on your report card but that's not going to happen if you take drugs.

I am a drug-free person and I am great. When I get mad or have one or two bad grades, I try to do better. You can work it out. Being a drug-free person is the best you can do for yourself.

Bailey Fidler, Grade 6
Milltown Elementary School, IN

The Electrifying One

Barry Sanders is a Hall of Fame and Heisman Trophy winning running back. Sanders was born July 16, 1968. He was ranked 3rd in all-time rushing yards in the NFL with 15,269. He also rushed for 99 touchdowns in ten years. Also he was five feet 8 inches tall and weighed 203 pounds. Sanders played all ten years with the Detroit Lions. He wore number twenty all ten years.

Every season he played he rushed over 1,000 yards. In his rookie year he rushed for 1,470 yards and got 14 touchdowns. In his career he made it to the Pro-Bowl all ten years. In 1997 he broke 2,000 yards and rushed for 11 touchdowns. After all his years, he had an average of 5.0 yards per carry. His longest touchdown run was 82 yards. Sanders had seventy-six matches with a hundred yards or more. His retirement year was shocking in the 1999 season.

Joshua Stiltner, Grade 5
Desert Trails Elementary School, CA

Don't Litter

Have you ever been to an ocean? Have you seen litter or trash inside the ocean? Well I'm telling you right now if you have you should pick it up or if you have any trash or garbage throw it away! Litter and trash can cause a lot of bad things to fish and other creatures living in the sea. If a fish swallows some garbage it might choke and die. Some people can even die if you litter. They could accidentally swallow or get a piece of trash caught around their neck. A sea boat could get some trash stuck on its rudder and make it not go anywhere. If fish keep on dying we won't be able to eat as much fish anymore and their population will go down. My final thing to say is just not to litter and just throw trash away if you see it on the ground or in the water or anywhere! Just pick it up and throw it in the garbage.

Austin Mottl, Grade 5
Maple Avenue Elementary School, WI

July 20th

It all started on July 12, 2007 when I went to Santa Cruz Island. I went on a two day trip with my friend. He and his mom invited me to go over there. It all started on a Saturday morning. I woke up that morning and brushed my teeth. After I brushed my teeth I ate breakfast and changed my clothes. Then I packed my clothes for the two day trip and called my friend Jack to pick me up. We left from my house and went to the Ventura Harbor. That night I slept on a boat and it felt kind of weird. The next morning we ate breakfast and got ready to unpack the supplies for the two day trip. My friend Jack and I were the people that unpacked mostly all the supplies but we got a little help from the adults. They were mostly all teachers except Gorgy, Jack, and me. We were on a boat with teachers that we all knew. We left the harbor around noon and we got to the Santa Cruz Islands around five o'clock in the afternoon. The islands were a very beautiful sight when we got there.

Rafael Medina, Grade 6
Isbell Middle School, CA

Ferrari Enzo

There are more than 15 kinds of Ferraris in the world. But if there's one car that they say it was a super car, it would be the Ferrari Enzo, named after the founder of all the Ferraris, the person who led this car to the future, with astonishing figure and power.

This super car has a 660 horse power engine. Horsepower is how much power a car has. 660 horsepower is good because that is very quick. It is super quick, it can reach from 0 to 60 in three seconds. It has a V-Twelve engine and the gears are on the side of the steering wheel. A disadvantage is that it only gives eight miles a gallon. It's top speed is 200-miles-per-hour. They only use carbon fiber so it's lightweight and fast. This is a good racing car because it is very lightweight. The back wing is lifted by a computer in the car, with the wing you can go faster. To make this car, they used technology from formula 1 such as the whole body. The price of the Enzo goes over $630,000. The last one was sold on June 28, 2005 for over $1,200.000.

They only made 400 of these Enzos. These cars were made in the year 2003. This car is rated number four in the top ten cars in the world. All of the cars are awesome. That's why the Enzo is number on my list.

Oliver Ortega, Grade 5
Oak Crest Intermediate School, TX

My Dog Mo

When I was a little girl I had a cat named Cici. She died when she was eight years old. At first I did not believe my mom when she told me. After she died, I really wanted a puppy.

We looked everywhere for a puppy. One of them we looked at was a black Lab but we did not get it because it kept jumping on me. About a week later my parents saw an ad in the paper about Dachshunds for sale. So my parents talked it over and they decided to get one. The next day we went to get a puppy where the paper said it was. The one I picked was a girl. I picked her because she was the last one left. We named her Mo. Now she is six years old. That is about forty-two years in dog years.

Four months later my parents entered Mo in the Buda Wiener Dog Races. The first year she came in 4th place out of about 125 dogs. There is a dog that wins almost every year.

When Mo was a puppy she had a big black spot on her side. Now she is all brown. Since she is old, she has gray around her mouth. She weighs about 17 pounds.

Mo is still racing. There is Buda Wiener Dogs Races once every year at the end of April. Most of the time, Mo has come in at least 1st, 2nd, 3rd, or 4th.

Kaylee Hodnett, Grade 4
Menchaca Elementary School, TX

Hard Work

When you devote yourself to a goal what does that mean? It means that you try your best. The most important thing is that you put your hard work into it. That is how you do great in school. Also you put effort into it. So you do your best. Hard work takes a plethora of time to get every single question right.

Hard work takes so much time to accomplish. The goal is to do your best in school. You practice your spelling words and the hard work will get you good grades on your test. That is how you endeavor to accomplish your work. Try to complete your work on time. Aim for the top so you can achieve your goals. When you achieve it is like reaching the highest peak of a mountain. Why do you need to devote to hard work? You devote yourself to hard work because it leads you and me to good grades in our schools.

Mike Mogensen, Grade 5
Covington Elementary School, NE

Friends

Having good friends is very important in life. My friends are very important to me and they mean a lot to me! My friends help me out when I need help, support me when I'm sad and my friends will always care about me! I love having all of my friends!

Some people have just one best friend. I have many best friends because it is so hard to choose just one best friend. I can trust all of my best friends and I can tell them anything and I know they won't tell anyone else! My best friends are also very important to me!

Sometimes, you think that someone is your friend but they aren't. That is why you have to find true friends. True friends will always be there for you and never let you down.

Friends…real friends should be able to support you when you really need it. Also, they should be able to make you feel happy when you're sad. Real friends should care about you and always be there for you.

Friends are very nice to have in life and everyone should have true friends in life. True friends should be there for you when you need them the most. Friends are awesome!

Alexis Ward, Grade 6
Southport 6th Grade Academy, IN

My Life Without My Parent

My life without my parents would be hurtful, because I wouldn't have anyone to give my attention to. I would not have anyone to say goodbye in the morning. I wouldn't be able to ask for money for my lunch at school. I wouldn't have anyone to hug. If my parents weren't in my life I would cry and I would not stop because it would hurt badly. I would even have soft feelings if my parents weren't in my life.

I wouldn't have anyone to help me with my homework for school. But I am happy to have my parents in my life!! I wonder what would happen if there was no one in my life. I would be sitting up looking at everyone with their parents.

Lynneisha Battiste, Grade 5
DeQueen Elementary School, TX

Fly with the Angels

Angels are always by us, through the bad and the good. They got our backs no matter what happens. They're faithful by not giving up on all of us, even if we're sad they get us back up on our feet and happy. They will be our light through the darkness, even if we are scared they will help us. They will help us no matter what we say or do, they're always there watching over us. We're all in this together, through the end of the world, because we are a big happy family.

They will be our friends and our family. They are in the big blue sky flying over us all the time. The angels are our saviors. They are everything to me. Angels are my guide through everything no matter what happens. They are my bright light that guides me through the night. They are nice, kind, sweet, and a loving friend. They are my life and my best friend 'til the end of the world. They may be anyone around you so don't be mean, be a friend to everyone around you and be a loving and caring person to everyone. Angels rock the world!

Latysha Archuleta, Grade 4
Santo Niño Regional Catholic School, NM

My Favorite Baseball Player

Yadier Molina is my favorite baseball player. Why? Well it's because his team, the Cardinals, won the World Series last year. Molina is an awesome player. He plays catcher. I have never seen him miss a ball. If you go down the streets of St. Louis banners with pictures of him on the light posts show him yelling with joy when they won the World Series. I personally, have been to the St. Louis Cardinals Stadium and saw him play. It was so exciting. Molina bats too. He hit home runs both times I saw him play. Molina hit six home runs this season, and made thirty runs. Even though Molina is number four, three seems to be his lucky number. He has the third longest hitting streak. Molina is the third catcher under twenty-five to go to the World Series twice. He is the third brother from his family to become a Major League Baseball catcher. Think his number should be three? I like Molina so much I have his bobble head and his T-shirt. I would strongly recommend you to be a Molina fan. See you at the next game!

Sarah Hoshaw, Grade 5
Mary Morgan Elementary School, IL

Friendship

There are many tips for making a great friendship. You have to be nice to the people at school and wherever you go. To be a great friend you have to play with them in a kind way. That is what being a great friend is all about.

When you play with friends, play whatever they want. Play with friends and enjoy yourself. Whenever you talk to your friends say something nice about them because if you do they will like you and talk to you. That is what having a friend is all about. If you always are nice you will have a lot of friends and you will have fun with them.

Alicia Nuno, Grade 5
Covington Elementary School, NE

My Experience Getting Hit by a Car

One day my auntie Kateri picked me up to go to her apartment. Then my auntie Joy was hungry so I went to Wendy's with her which was across the street, so we went into Wendy's to buy our stuff and when we came out of the store we were starting to cross the street. My auntie Joy said "Run!!" and I looked to my left then CRASH! My auntie Joy said "I flew eight feet." Then she said to my mom and dad that "It was like I was in slow motion and I was being carried by hands." It was a mini van that hit me, my auntie Joy screamed and a guy came running out and gave my auntie Joy his cell phone so that she could call 911 and my other auntie Kateri and Chantel that was at the apartment. The guy who lent the cell phone to my auntie Joy was a paramedic so that was good. Then the ambulance came and my auntie Kateri was sitting in the front and my other auntie Chantel was in the back.

When I got to the hospital around 10:15 p.m. my mom and dad were crying by my side. I was covered in bruises and scrapes on my left side. When all my family heard the news they all rushed to come and see if I was ok. At 1:00 a.m. they had to do a CT scan on me. After that my family was at the hospital crying. The next day all the bruises were gone. That was my experience of getting hit.

Brendan Phillips, Grade 5
St Gerard School, MB

Best Summer Ever

Every year my best friend invites me to Michigan to have lots of fun with her and her family. By the second day I'm there we're already tubing in the best lake in Bellaire, Michigan. As we roar five feet over the huge whitecap waves the pressure of the air is trying to shove us backwards off the twelve seater tube. As we land in the water with a *thud* we all try desperately to hang on.

Besides tubing we also go cherry picking. We always fill up at least ten buckets full of different cherries. The cherries are so ripe and fresh that when you pick them you just have to eat them! The first cherry that we pick we always end up eating it and when we do eat it, it practically explodes in our mouth and on us. There are yellow, red and really dark red cherries, but my friend and I always just pick the dark ones because those are our favorites. You can use huge wooden ladders or you can climb. Here's no surprise, we climb! Whenever we climb the trees one of us always gets stuck and I really mean *stuck!* Sometimes when the ladders are taken up and there are cherries hanging on a limb and we really want them, we get on that limb and pray that it doesn't *snap!*

I always have the best time in Michigan and can't wait to go back next summer.

Kelsey Peiser, Grade 6
Argyle Middle School, TX

Rat Terriers

Rat Terriers were originally bred to kill rodents such as rats and mice. To kill the rodent in a burrow, obviously, the dogs would crawl into the rodent's den and kill it in the little space it has. What's remarkable is there are even annual races to see which Rat Terrier can kill the rat the fastest. What's also remarkable is that they're all held underground. There are also obstacles or dead ends, gates, and scent markers.

My Rat Terrier is a full size Terrier, which is unusual. Rat Terriers are bred in three sizes; small, medium, and full size. Rat Terriers are usually very uniform in color. What I found weird about my dog was that she has spots, on her tongue! My dog also has a bad habit of turning things into pancakes. We have field mice in our back yard so she goes out and "hunts" them. When she's done with it she displays it like a trophy.

As you can see, I love Rat Terriers.

Tyler Roth, Grade 6
Franklin Phonetic Primary School, AZ

Why Little Brothers Are Big Pains

My baby brother drives me up the wall! He never listens to me! When I was baby-sitting him, he would not even go sit down when I told him to. He did the exact opposite. When I tell him to pick up his toys, he doesn't. So I'm stuck picking up his toys and always cleaning up his mess.

My baby brother never, I mean never, leaves me alone!! Sometimes when I want to go to sleep, he doesn't let me.

All my little brother does is blame everything on me. He says that I bite him. One day at his daycare he got bit and he told my mom that I bit him. I was not even there!!! He also tells my mother that I yell at him. First of all I would not yell at a two year old. At my house we were playing and as soon as my mom came in, he said I hit him.

I would never give my brother up because I love him so much. He always cries for me when I'm gone. I miss him when he goes with his father.

Although he can be a pain, I would never give him up.

Kirsten Tutt, Grade 6
Orchard Hill Elementary School, IA

Learning How to Make a PowerPoint

One day in February 2007 we were writing our reports for Black History month. One day Miss Johnson said today we were going to the computer lab. That is when I learned how to make a PowerPoint presentation.

I was doing a report about Rosa Parks. What I learned about Rosa Parks is that she started a bus boycott. I also learned that she did not give the white man her seat. Instead she said, "No." Then she went to jail.

Slide 1 was the title page, I put my title. Then I put my name on it. On slide 2 I put Rosa Parks did not give the white man her seat. So it started a bus boycott. Then Rosa Parks went to jail.

Olivia Spanke, Grade 5
McMonagle Elementary School, MI

My Peppy Puppy Pepper

Pepper is about one year old and weighs 9 lbs. She is black and gray and really fluffy. She is a Malti-poo and maybe a little Bichon or Havaniese. Pepper's nicknames are: Boo, Muffinhead, Pupsters, and Fuzzy Furball.

Normally, dogs are really expensive, but not this one! My mom and dad own a dental office and they were in a meeting when this little fluffy dog ran through the open door. We decided to call her Pepper until we could find her real owner. Of course, that darling, well-groomed puppy had to have an owner, or so we thought. Three weeks went by and still nobody claimed her. Finally we were able to keep her.

We got her puppy shots, we got her spayed, and we got her microchipped. Even though we try our best to keep her quiet, she still has separation anxiety (that's where she whines and cries when we leave her). She is too afraid of being abandoned again.

Just like some dogs and cats, mine don't like each other. They claw, scratch, bite, swipe, and bark. One thing Pepper loves to do is give lots of kisses. Pepper also likes to climb up in my lap in the car and look out the window. Car rides, play times, and treats are some of her favorite things.

Pepper is really energetic and runs one to four miles every day. I think Pepper is the best dog in the world!

Sydney Mastrovich, Grade 5
Country Montessori School, CA

The Best Vacation Ever

It was July 7th when my uncle Jaime, who was going to marry my gorgeous and amiable aunt Selene, invited me to go bay fishing. Since there was too many of us to fit in one sluggish and small taxi, unfortunately we had to walk. I was still tired, so the short walk felt like a thousand miles and of course I was complaining.

When we got there the two jovial men assisting us boarded all of us onto their medium-sized boat called La Madre De Dios. We paid them and we were off to the blue bay of Puerto Vallarta. We arrived at our destination point in minutes, but it felt like seconds to me because of the cool and gentle winds rubbing against my face. We began to notice ripples in the water. I was exasperated when I saw a huge whale plunge out of the water and it wasn't even whale season! "Wow, it's gigantic!" I yelled out. It almost tipped over the whale watcher's banana boat! "Thank God the whale didn't cause that much upheaval," I told my uncle Jaime.

At the end of this long and exciting fishing trip, we caught a total of 84 fish between us 6 men. We invited all the guests that were here for my aunt's wedding to a restaurant where they would cook all the fish. In a few hours all the fish we had caught were eaten and that was the best vacation ever.

Christopher Davis, Grade 6
St Matthew Catholic School, TX

I Didn't Know

"Yay! We have a party today," I cheered. I was four. I always liked parties.

My friend and I had all sorts of fun. We played follow the leader, ditch the leader (a game my friend and I made up), and other games until…we saw the big kids playing on a pay phone.

As little ones we follow our elders, so I went to the phone and my friend followed in a very nervous state. He looked so nervous that it looked like he couldn't speak to himself in a mirror. I think it was because he knew what I was going to do.

I picked up the phone. "It's not going to go anywhere," I told him in a very confident voice. I thought about the number I should call. Finally, I chose…911!

I dialed in the numbers as slow as a turtle would walk a mile. My friend, well, he was a nervous wreck. Then after I called I hung up. My friend was about to faint when… WWYYYOOOW WWYYOOOW. It was the police sirens. A lump formed in my throat when two police officers walked in. The lump in my throat grew bigger. My friend fainted. My dad came. Luckily, he explained everything because I couldn't talk the rest of the day.

I think I learned three important things that day. One, 911 can work on pay phones. Two, don't follow your elders. Three, if your friend is a nervous wreck, stop what you're doing.

Rohan Sinha, Grade 5
Greenwood Elementary School, MN

Grandpa Dale

My Grandpa Dale always thought about work. He was either at the ranch or at his business, Ro-Tile. He never sat down, kicked back, and relaxed. But after he had two strokes, he settled down. Whenever we visited him, he would be sitting in the same chair in the kitchen. He never got up, walked around, or did anything. He wasn't alone in his chair, though, my grandma would be standing next to him. My grandpa was getting sick and very, very weak. He was in such bad shape that he couldn't talk. I don't even think I remember his voice. Though he was sick, he still played games with us. We would play really old games like Blockhead and the Marble game (which my grandma made up). I thought it was so nice when he put out an effort to make my brother and me happy. But when my Grandpa was sick he regretted working all his life. He wanted to spend more time with his children and his grandchildren. My Grandpa Dale died 4 years ago, but when he was here with us he taught me and other members of my family a very important lesson. Family first, work second.

Paulina Hanna, Grade 6
St Anne School, CA

My Favorite Place

My favorite place is in my living room. My living room has a TV. I adore it because I watch my favorite shows. It is in the front part of my house. It has three couches. They are green. They look so elegant. They are also comfortable. They have a couple of pillows on them. I have a secretary on my living room. It is brown and black and three doors on each side. It has a chair on it and a TV and a big radio. I also have a lot of pictures in there. Actually this weekend we put some more with a family picture. Well, anyway I love my living room! It's just so gorgeous! The TV on the secretary is large. We have another TV to watch shows. Where the TV that we watch shows is we have a cabinet. We have pictures there. It's brown. We have a white table and I eat there sometimes. My favorite thing is the TV. When I don't go nowhere that's what I do. Watching TV, well, how can I tell you I love it!

Janeth Tarango, Grade 4
Winona Elementary School, TX

Disaster Plan

In my disaster plan I would have a lot of materials. These are reasons how I would solve my problem if a fire would happen.

In my supply kit I would have flashlights, matches, walkie talkies, batteries, camp supplies, food and water bottles, also two gas masks. I would keep all these things in a trash can in the closet.

My escape route would be really easy. I, Siri live in a one story so we could escape out of the window. (But you never know if you can put the fire out yourself.) We have about ten windows and doors in all.

Our meeting place would be in the middle of the street, Liberty Park or the fire station. We chose those places because we live nearby those places and are safe. We have to stay there for about ten minutes if the family is not there we need to go and get help.

Disaster plans are very important to have because anything at any time could happen. That's the important thing to do, is to have a disaster plan.

Siri Osborne, Grade 5
Liberty Elementary School, CA

B.M.X.

B.M.X is a cool ESPN sport you do all sorts of tricks like superman and 360 back flips. I like it because it is fun. I am not very good at it but I try. It's dangerous.

Because if you don't do the trick right you will crash. You don't want that to happen. There's rules like no breaking windows or hitting people with your bike.

Grinding is hard if you don't know how to do it. B.M.X grinding is cool and hard, grinding off a rail is not that easy you just have to know when to jump on the rail and jump off the rail and land it perfect. B.M.X riders practice and practice a lot every day for three to four hours a day.

Anthony Soto, Grade 6
Irma Marsh Middle School, TX

George Armstrong Custer in the Civil War

George A. Custer was a well known person, but not many people knew he played an important role in the Civil War.

Custer was born in New Rumley, Ohio on December 5, 1839.

Before the war, he went to West Point in 1861. He had a wife named Elizabeth Bacon Custer.

He played an important role in the Civil War. During the Civil War he was an active and daring officer during that time, but he did unexpectedly well during the war. He returned in 1862 for cavalry duty as lieutenant.

Custer was in many different battles. The Battle of Gettysburg, Battle of the Bull Run, and Five Forks were only some of the battles he was in. He surrendered at Appomattox. Custer was the one who accepted a flag called the Confederate Flag of Truce.

Custer's last stand came after the Civil War was over. His last stand was at the Battle of Little Bighorn where he was killed. He died in the year of 1876 on June 25.

Custer was not only known for his last stand. He also played an important role during the time of the Civil War.

Braylan Benoist, Grade 5
Cheyenne-Eagle Butte Upper Elementary School, SD

Memories of My Life

This paper will be based on my past, present and future. However, I will only tell you the important things in my life. My life contains many memories, dreams, and places I want to go to. There are many things that are incomplete in my life.

When I was three years old, I cracked my head open by jumping off a flight of stairs. Ever since then, I could not remember anything before or around that time. About a month later, I cracked my head open again by running into a corner of a wall. My early years were great, especially the holidays. Such as New Year's, Easter, Halloween, and Christmas. My birthdays were also great. I used to live in Anaheim, also known as Down the Hill. A couple months after my 7th birthday, I moved to the high desert, enrolled into a new school, and made new friends. However, that doesn't keep me away from my family.

I have many dreams of going places, being famous, and having a good life. When I grow up, I want to be a professional soccer player. I want to play in the World Cup with millions of people surrounding me. Of course, I will be traveling around the world during my career. That means I might be performing different customs of different countries and eating different types of foods, but before all of that, I want to receive a good education at a good university and be able to benefit from that.

Joseph Gudino, Grade 5
Desert Trails Elementary School, CA

Chui

I have a cat named Chui, whose name means leopard in Swahili. She is eighteen years old and doing fine. Her birthday is March 27th. Chui has a brother named Pounce, who does not exactly like to pounce; rather, his name comes from Sir Pounceville.

Chui's mother became pregnant unexpectedly after she was allowed outdoors. Chui was the only female in the litter. She and her brother are domestic shorthairs. She is a target tabby and has the markings like a bull's eye on her sides. Chui's fur is very soft, but the little pads on her feet are, unbelievably, even a little softer.

Chui likes to sleep in my parents' bedroom, in my bedroom, in the sun in the living room, and sometimes in my lap. She can walk without a sound, and she likes to get petted, to sleep, and to meow. Chui is my favorite cat in the house. Although she does not catch mice anymore, she does tamper with their minds by cornering and scaring them. Chui also likes to listen to reading.

Chui gets sick often but not seriously. Because of food allergies, she eats a special diet, and the only milk she can have is lactose free milk. She doesn't eat meat; she only sucks on it.

She is fearless and not even afraid of dogs. All of these qualities make her extremely special to me. I really do...*love Chui very much.*

Jamie Schmidt, Grade 4
Birchwood School, OH

Discus Throwing

Discus is a very interesting and unusual sport. Not many kids age ten throw it. Discus is a unique sport and similar at the same time. It is a common sport because you throw something. It is a unique sport because you spin around, sort of like a top.

It is actually a very ancient sport. The discus thrower statue, or Discobolus, is the symbol of the Olympic games. The shot put, javelin, and discus were weapons of the early wars, and that is why they were events of the ancient track and field games.

Track and field events are the basis of almost all athletics. It is where you develop the speed and strength to be used in major sports such as football and basketball. You need to be very athletic, flexible, and you have to practice a lot for this sport. Most athletes practice at least four times a week. Most throwers have to watch what they eat, work out, and lift weights. The ages for this sport are about ten to seventy.

To throw a discus, bend your knees, bring your left leg around to about a one-hundred-eighty-degree angle. Then take your right leg, and spin around to the left. You are now in the "Power Position." Your elbow is now pointing at the sky. You should feel the stretch in your upper arm. Then release.

I hope everyone would try to throw a discus, to see how difficult, but fun it is, and see how much practice it takes.

Kiana Phelps, Grade 4
Kingsley-Pierson Community School, IA

Follow Your Dreams

Following your dreams means never giving up. Believing in yourself is important. Following dreams is important to me because I know someday my dreams will come true. Think about all the great people on Earth who became great because they never stopped following their dreams.

If you have some kind of disability you should try to forget about it because on the inside you are just like everybody else. You should keep on believing even if you think it will never come true. Look in your heart and you will find the way for anything to come true. You should also stay true to your own dream because it is important to YOU, and not to anyone else. No one should tell you what to dream about.

Sometimes you have dreams about things that are not real and that is okay, as long as you have a dream to follow. Maybe dreams will lead you to a new discovery. Maybe they will make you the happiest person on Earth!

Who knows what you will find or get when you keep on dreaming and believing? Something good, for sure! Keep on dreaming and you will always be happy!

Katherine Warzocha, Grade 5
Booth Tarkington Elementary School, IL

Fishing

Fishing is a fun sport. 36 million people fish in the world. It requires patience and time. Fishing is a very popular sport in many places. Some people catch the fish for money and some catch the fish just for the fun of it. Most people around the world have fish at the market. Deep sea fishing is the most popular type of fishing. There are sport fish, fish you can eat, and some bad fish. All fish must be a certain length for you to take home. People can fish almost anywhere. People can fish in fresh water and salt water, and there is game everywhere in the water. Many kinds of fish live near tunnels and caves, be careful when going near caves and tunnels because your line may get stuck.

Clarisse Sandoval, Grade 6
St Monica Catholic School, TX

Friendship

To show kindness is to be a friend. To show relationships and to share likes is friendship for many reasons. My friends are probably the most important success in my life. At school I have tons of friends. There are so many that I can't even name them all. Also, I have more friends than just school chums. I have sporty friends that play sports with me. They are mostly my age but some of them aren't. Sometimes I have a few middle school friends. That is all right though. Being as nice as I can be is an example of me.

Complimenting is one of my keys. Trying to compliment makes more friends and then you learn to be nice. After you compliment someone they want you to be their friend. After you do all of these things you will be the best friend in the whole world. If you want to be a great friend then you have to be nice. You will also have awesome friendships and life.

Allie Verzani, Grade 5
Covington Elementary School, NE

About My Bikes

When I bought my new bike the tire was flat. I was mad at first because my dad wouldn't pump my tire up. Then my dad said okay. I was happy. When I came back to my house I was upset again because my helmet wouldn't fit. It did not fit because it was too tight. So my dad fixed that too. The brakes on the bike were stuck. So my dad fixed it.

When I bought my other bike I kept on putting my seat up. It kept on going down. It was a little bit big for me but I grew and then it was not so big after all. That bike was the best bike I've had so far. I wanted a new bike but my dad and mom said, "NO!!!!" I made a plan to pop my tire so my parents would buy me a new bike. My dad said, "Now you have no bike to ride."

After two or three years went by I got a new bike again. This bike was a gear bike, but I did not know when to change the gears. My friend told me that you can change it any time you want to go fast. The hand brakes were a little bit hard to help me stop. I am getting better at riding bikes. I love to ride bikes. Now they are my favorite activity. You now know about my bikes. Soon I will be a pro.

Kenraj Saran, Grade 5
Dr F D Sinclair Elementary School, BC

Super Bowl

It was my second year of football when our team won the super bowl. That was the first time I had ever won a super bowl. It was one of the greatest days of my life.

I was on Argyle Red that year. We weren't that big, but we were fast. Our head coach was Coach Kuketz and the assistant coaches were my dad, Coach Phillips, Coach Dryden, Coach Katzen, and Coach Sadler. The coaches were very good and so were the players. The players on our team were very athletic. We practiced very hard before our first game of the season. Our first game that we played was against Northwest Red. We beat them twenty-six to zero. We were very glad that we won and couldn't wait until the next game.

After our first game we kept on winning. We won our next game and the next couple of games after that. We were doing amazing. There was another Argyle team and they were Argyle Black. They were undefeated like us. Near the end of the playoffs, our fullback/middle linebacker broke his elbow. He was one of our key players. Even though he was out for the rest of the season, we still won our last playoff game.

Now we had to face Argyle Black in the super bowl. We were extremely nervous before the game but the final score was us winning thirty-two to sixteen. I will remember that game for the rest of my life.

Jon Michael Pucciarello, Grade 6
Argyle Middle School, TX

My Faith in Immanuel

My faith in God is very strong because I had a heart transplant. It is one of the most important things I'll ever have. When I was born I needed a new heart. So when I was four weeks old I got one. I would have never made it this far without God. Because of my heart problem I have a low immune system. That means I can't have a pet because of their diseases. I've always wanted a pet ever since I knew what one was. I have prayed for years that I could have one. But because I might get sick if I have one, I know it's more important to stay healthy.

Then one day while I was at Wal-mart, my mom called the doctor to make sure I couldn't have one. But what do you know? He said I could! I could have a dog or a rodent. God had answered my prayers. I was so happy, and praised God a lot. I'm very thankful that God let me have a hamster. His name is Dusty. God is so great. I became a Christian at the age of five. And I was baptized at age seven. God has helped me in many great ways throughout my life. I love Him so much. I can't wait for what God has in store for me next.

Evan Schneider, Grade 6
Linfield Christian School, CA

Gone to Grandma's

The best place for me to be in this world is at my Grandma's and Papa's house. I love going there and I can go there a lot because it is only a 25 minute drive. I love going there because my Grandma and Papa are always nice to me. When I go there I always smell the sweet scent of apple butter. My Grandma makes apple butter a lot. It is kind of like jelly but it is different and it is way better. I also like going there because my grandma always makes something good to eat.

Another reason I like going there is because my Papa has a lot of BB guns and he lets me shoot them a lot. He also was in the war at Vietnam so I like to see all the things he got there. He has a spear, a bow, an arrow, and a drum. He even gave me some of his coins from Vietnam. And that is why my favorite place to go is my Grandma and Papa's house.

Colten Nix, Grade 6
North Oaks Middle School, TX

Crazy Friends

My friend, Kayla, and I were looking at my go-cart one day, when my dad walked outside.

He said, "Would you like to ride it, Kayla?"

She was glad to. She got on it and my dad said to go "around" the trampoline and swing set because the cart didn't have brakes. He told her to avoid the hill below the trampoline.

Kayla did not listen, and she went down the hill screaming! She hit a huge tree and started laughing her head off! She wanted to go again.

My dad said, "Sorry girls. No more go-cart adventures until we fix those brakes."

Karleigh Atwood, Grade 5
Westview Elementary School, OH

My Imagination Square

This favorite place of mine is my own community, a place where my imagination can be free. I have books at one place, sports, and dancing in another, art up high in the walls of these places. And a place where my animal and I may take our nightly rest. Also grass and sky, with a streamy blue river.

This place is my room. Walls of green like grass and blue of skies. A warm, comfy, soft bed were my animal and I can catch a good nights rest. As 'animal', I mean dog.

I have a huge bookshelf, with all kinds of books. Artwork hanging all over the walls. I have picture and trophies on a shelf for dancing and playing sports. And the 'streamy blue river' is my soft blue carpet.

I also have a place were I can have adventure, go on quests, be different people, and beat high scores! My shelf with over 15 video games!

Also I have a place where I can decide who I want to be every day. My dresser and vanity. In the middle of all of this, I have a place where I can burst in to a new dance. Sometimes I just grab a book, or some paper and let my imagination reach outer space, into an unknown place.

My room is a great place to be me. I love my room and everything about it, and that is why it's my favorite place.

Rebekah Sandoval, Grade 6
North Oaks Middle School, TX

Ziggy, My First Dog

My dog Ziggy is a yellow Labrador but he is white in color.

We got Ziggy when he was only one year old back in 2002. He lived with a family that had a small yard and the only child was going off to college.

The first time we saw Ziggy he was very excited and I was small. That resulted in me landing on the floor several times because of his swooshing tail. Ziggy's previous owners wanted to make sure he was going to a loving, caring family so they came to our house first to see our yard and meet our family. They must have liked us because they gave him to us for free.

Apparently, Ziggy didn't know what a pool was. When he went charging into our back yard, he ran directly into the pool, twice. He was very surprised and hasn't done it since.

Ziggy is very smart. When it is 9:00 pm he knows that it is time to go for a walk with mom. He even knows what "walk" means, so sometimes we spell it so he doesn't get excited. But now, I think he even knows what we're talking about when we spell w-a-l-k.

All the neighbors know Ziggy because somehow he always gets out of the back yard and goes up to them to be petted.

I'm glad we have Ziggy for a pet. He really is much more than just a pet; he is part of our family.

Chase Dale Gregory, Grade 4
Country Montessori School, CA

Being Loyal and Trustworthy to Your Best Friend

Do you have a best friend, or a BFF? If you do then you can say all these things. You can say you're loyal to them, but are they being the same way? Are they being trustworthy? That's what I think best friends should be like.

When you say you have a BFF can you say you're loyal to them, or do you gossip? I know people don't mean to gossip about their BFF, but it can happen. I sometimes gossip about mine. It happens when you get mad at them, but you should try not to. People should be loyal, because if they aren't they're not being a best friend.

Not only do you have to be loyal but also your BFF needs to be trustworthy. Can you tell your best friend things and not have doubts about them? If you have doubts about them your best friend isn't being trustworthy. I have a good best friend and I trust her with anything, she doesn't even tell her twin sister. Your best friend needs to be trustworthy because if they aren't they're not being a best friend back to you.

Being loyal and trustworthy are both very important in friendship. If you are loyal you are an excellent BFF. If your BFF is trustworthy they are being an awesome one too. You both are equal. That's what I've found in my BFF, and I have a great one.

Hannah Sullivan, Grade 6
Southport 6th Grade Academy, IN

My House

My house is perfect for me and my family. It is nice, cozy and big enough for all five of us. The yard is about six hundred feet, two hundred yards, from the street to the fence in the back of the woods. One word, fun!

My house is always warm in the winter, and cool in the summer. I guess my dad does a great job of keeping it cozy. The house is not ridiculously big, either. It is just big enough for us. A few years ago, we turned the attic into bedrooms. My bigger brothers, Matt and Ben, live up there. My bedroom is downstairs still.

The yard is about the length of two football fields, two hundred yards, and the width of one. Parties are awesome here. We usually play football here on Thanksgiving and the yard is perfect for it, despite a few trees in the middle of it. When my friends come over, we usually have small games too. The parties are obviously mostly held in the yard. The parties inside are great too. Almost all of the kids have some sort of contests like how many of the younger kids you can lift. The parties are extremely fun.

My house is perfect for my family. It is not too big, nor too small. It is nice all seven days of the four weeks in all twelve months in the years of all of our lives. It is just perfect!

Alex Darland, Grade 6
Southport 6th Grade Academy, IN

Freedom

Boom, that is the thundering sound of men and women fighting for our freedom! Freedom is a special thing the USA has.

One of our freedoms is to vote. When you vote someone will give you a ballot and you will go to a little area so people can't see your vote. But don't put your name on it. You may be voting for mayor, governor, or president like George W. Bush. Did you know that some countries don't get to vote?

Another freedom is to worship. A lot of people go to church to pray. Some people put their hands together or they fold them. Some close their eyes.

Our last freedom for today is we get to wear what we want to wear. I sure wouldn't want people picking out my clothes for me. Would you?

As you can see we have a lot of freedoms. Each one is special to the USA. Can you think of ten freedoms?

Logan Lichter, Grade 4
Rohwer Elementary School, NE

Isbell

When I was going to start to go to Isbell Middle School I felt scared because I was going to go to a new school and I was going to meet different students and teachers. The first day of school seemed strange to me the moving of class to class and getting 4 teachers instead of 1 like in elementary. The school seemed huge to me but now it doesn't seem so big because I got used to it. When I first came to school all I wanted to do was meet my teachers and see the gym. I wanted to see the gym because it looked so big and it was new also because I never had a gym at school but now I am going to have a gym at school.

Now that I met all my teachers they seemed very friendly and I think that I am going to have a great year. I hope that I get to meet more teachers and make lots of friends. I think Isbell is not so bad and that it is a great school to go to because it has some very good and nice teachers to count on for help. I am definitely going to have a great time at Isbell.

Daisy Duran, Grade 6
Isbell Middle School, CA

First Deer

When I was 9 years old, last November, I shot and killed my very first deer. It was a 4 point buck, I used a .222 Magnum rifle. I was very happy. I shot and killed it on my first try. I was so excited that I called my mom and grandpa as soon as we got back to the truck. We took pictures so we could show all my family and friends. They were excited for me. My mom sent the pictures of my first deer to everyone she could think of. My nanny saved it as a screen saver on her computer. They were happy for me and called me to tell me congratulations for shooting my very first deer. My grandma took the pictures of my deer and my brother's 10 point buck and had it put in the paper where she lives. After the friends saw it in the paper, they called to congratulate me.

Coby Schunka, Grade 5
Aloe Elementary School, TX

Camping

Have you ever been to Shadow Rim Ranch (Payson)? Have you ever seen wild turkey? Well, I have done all those things and it's hard packing. The whole time it was raining. I went with Girl Scouts. I saw a lot of girls from school.

The main thing to me is preparation. First you need to pack clothes, food (for the ride) and a sleeping bag. For the sleeping bag you need to pack a certain kind, like 40°F. Just in case it gets really cold.

On the way you should have packed things to do like CDs or movies. When our troop got there we signed in. It started to rain. But, the next day, we did all kinds of activities. The most fun was archery. It started to rain. So we didn't have that much fun.

On the way back we saw a fire. A car had crashed and caught on fire. We just barely made it through. Everyone else got stuck in traffic. When we drove past it the car started to get warm. One kid almost threw up. We think it must have been food that we ate at camp. Next year my mom is setting up camp. I just hope my mom picks a camp better, and it doesn't rain.

Louise Garcia, Grade 6
Imagine Charter School at Rosefield, AZ

My Dad Deserves to Be on a Postage Stamp

My Dad "Mohammed Yousuf" deserves to be on a postage stamp. Why? Not only he is my dad, but he also helps other people besides my family.

When my dad was 2, he became sick and got polio. By the time he recovered, the polio left him unable to walk. Doctors didn't recognize the illness that handicapped my dad's legs.

My dad says he remembers counting cars passing, as his siblings went to school. When my dad was 11, his grandmother enrolled him in school. He couldn't carry his shoulder bag so Grandmother hired a helper for him. Because of his love for math and science, he skipped 4th grade and soon finished high school. He fulfilled his and his father's dream of becoming an engineer. He came to the USA, did masters in Wayne State University, and got a job. He went India and married my mom.

On May 1st, 2001 he established the Help Handicap Foundation which helps people with disabilities in India and helped over 1000 people.

I cry when I hear or tell my dad's story. I really love my dad, he's special and he deserves to be on a postage stamp more than President Bush or any dad in the world. The one who encouraged my dad was my great-grandmother, Sara. She died before I was born but my dad's memories hang with her, hence I am named after her, one great lady.

Sara Yousuf, Grade 4
Kenbrook Elementary School, MI

The Day I Saved a Baby Squirrel

One day I was strutting through the woods after my neighbor cut down a dozen trees so he could make a cow pasture. Suddenly there was a "squeak!" I found a baby squirrel on a pile of leaves. He curled up in my hands and I took him inside my house. I fed him a small bottle of milk and I showed my mom the baby squirrel.

I asked her if I could take it to the animal shelter in Dubois County and she said yes. I got my bike out of the shed and rode him over to my grandma and grandpa's house. I asked my grandpa to take the squirrel and me to the animal shelter. When we got there, we showed them the squirrel. They said the squirrel had a bone that broke when the tree fell.

The people at the animal shelter said the squirrel would have suffered if I hadn't brought him to them in time. My grandpa and I asked them when they thought the squirrel would be able to be let go. They said, "After he is treated and well enough to go back where he was before. Come back in 3 weeks and we will see if he will be ready."

We went to the animal shelter after 3 weeks and we found out the squirrel had healed and was ready to go. We took him home, set him free, and that is the last we saw of him.

Cayden Allen, Grade 5
Nancy Hanks Elementary School, IN

Isis, Mother of Life

Egyptian history is filled with unique culture, religion, and customs. Mythology was a big part of Egyptian history. Isis, considered the "Goddess of all Goddesses," is known by many names in Egyptian Mythology. One name Isis is well known for is the "Mother of Life."

Isis was born into royalty. Her father was named Geb, a Pharaoh that later retired. Isis' mother was the Ennead, or known as "Gods of Egypt." Isis had two brothers, named Osiris and Horus, and a sister named Nephthys. As customary in Egyptian royal families, Isis married Osiris.

Isis was known as the "Mother of Life" because she performed magical acts on her husband, Osiris. The magical acts were brought on when Set, an enemy, had poisoned Osiris.

After poisoning Osiris, Set placed him in a coffin and threw him into the ocean. Isis found her husband in Phoenicia under a tree. Isis brought Osiris back to Egypt where she hid him in a swamp. However, Set discovered where Osiris was hiding and dismembered him, or cut him into parts.

Using magical powers, Isis gathered the pieces of his body and put them together, though she couldn't find one of his body parts. Isis breathed into Osiris and healed him with her wings.

Although she is known by many names for the amazing things she did as a Goddess, Isis showed she was caring and loving to her husband, Osiris. Her act of bringing Osiris back to life gave Isis the name "Goddess of Life."

Kaitlyn Denson, Grade 5
Oak Crest Intermediate School, TX

The Full Moon Festival

Every year there is a holiday for kids. The festival can be in the street, at a church or temple, and even at home. The holiday is called the Full Moon Festival or in Vietnamese, Tet Trung Thu. The festival started around 15 to 20,000 years ago celebrating the full moon. There is always entertainment, such as dragon dancing, music, and games, just to name a few. There is lots of food like noodles, rice, and especially the sweet moon cakes. At the end, everybody lights up candles and puts them in multicolored lanterns that are different shapes and sizes. After everyone fires up the lanterns, and the night is bright as day, the dragons then come and walk to the huge temple. They perform their routines and finish off the night with colorful fireworks, and everyone puts out their lanterns and goes home.

Mikah Campbell, Grade 4
Burchett Elementary School, TX

Think About It

One of the best ways to remember the people involved in 9/11 is to do good deeds. So just take a minute to remember what they did for our country to save people's lives and the Twin Towers.

Think about how many people died on that day. Sometimes you cry and sometimes you feel angry but if you were in a situation like that what would you do? Would you save people's lives and risk your life for others or would you save yourself and let other people die a very painful death?

Think about it and make your decision about what to do. You can do good deeds to remember someone you loved that died. You can help someone by offering to carry something or help your mom do laundry. There are many things you can do, just think about it.

Charlie Gougar, Grade 5
Snake River Montessori School, ID

Koalas

Called a Joey at birth. Eating Eucalyptus trees that are poisonous to others. The amazing Koala. I know what you're thinking. It is that cute bear. Wrong! Koalas are cute, but that's the only reason it's called a bear. People said they looked like teddy bears, but they're actually related to the Kangaroo family.

Another reason their name is Koala is because they eat Eucalyptus trees which have lots of water in them. So they hardly take a drink of water. Koala means, "no drink."

Pretty much the only thing they eat are Eucalyptus trees. If they can't find one, they won't eat at all. They are very picky, as you can see. (Well actually, you hear me not see.)

The history of the Koala dates back to 1798 on January 26: The first record of a sighting of a Koala. They were called many things back then, but they finally came to Koala.

I hope you learned things about the Koala and remember: Don't feed them other things except for Eucalyptus trees. They probably won't like you.

Sarah Harper, Grade 6
Pomerene School, AZ

Friendship

The lesson I learned is about friendship.

I got into a fight with someone. She was demanding, mean, and was not truthful at all. I never liked her much. When we were friends nothing went right.

First of all she and my best friend got into a fight.

Both of them then wanted me to choose who to be friends with. So then I chose my most best friend. I was very pleased me and Chloe are not friends anymore.

Chloe was very frustrated and did not like who I had picked.

She would scream and yell, I couldn't take it anymore so I smart mouthed at her. She rode away on her bike. So did her brother.

Chloe was as mad as a bull.

Soon she got over it and hung out with her other friends. We get along but are still not friends. Both of us have our own friends.

A whole other lesson that has been learned.

What I learned is to choose friends more wisely and carefully. So remember your friends are special in every way. Just about every single person in this world should learn the lesson I have learned.

Cameron Day, Grade 5
McMonagle Elementary School, MI

My Ambulance Ride

I could hear my frantic and hysterical mom saying "Call 911!" I was trying to hear what was going on. I went to my sister's room and she was sitting on her bed wheezing and gasping for air, she couldn't even talk. My fast-beating heart fell. I wanted to cry but I tried to keep cool and calm. I could see red flashing lights outside my little sister's window.

Within seconds there was a barrage of EMS, fire, and policemen in the room. I could tell by the look on my mom's worried face she was really scared and nervous. They suggested taking her to the hospital. This would be my first ambulance ride.

They constrained my little scared sister on a long metal stretcher and we walked to the big white ambulance. We got into the eerie ambulance. Once we were in the ambulance he hooked her up to a plastic oxygen mask. The white fluorescent light in the ambulance was very bright. It hurt my eyes and you couldn't even see outside.

The ambulance was cold and quiet. The ride was smooth, it felt like we were not moving. I felt like I was in a dream. The EMS man was really nice; he kept us all calm and pacified by talking to us. We were at the hospital in minutes, I felt so relieved. This was my first ambulance ride. My sister is fine now and I hope this will be my last ride.

Gaby Moro, Grade 6
St Matthew Catholic School, TX

Dogs

Do you like dogs? Well I do. I mean who wouldn't like dogs? They are so cute! You might have a cat but I prefer something more sophisticated. One of the biggest dogs are Great Danes. One of the smallest dogs is the Chihuahua. Dogs can grow to be really, really big like Great Danes! They could drink out of the sink if they wanted to. I have a Great Dane, her name is Satie. Even though she is a dog, I call her a horse.

Anyway there are many types of dogs. Like Beagles, Jack Russell Terriers, golden Retrievers and St. Bernard's. There are many other types of breeds too. Bernard's can almost take care of themselves. Great Danes can't take care of themselves because they are so big. Any way dogs are the most energetic besides Cheetahs. All of my dogs are fast. I have three dogs. Most dogs are brown but not all dogs. I love dogs so much. That's why I wrote about them.

Brianna Breidenbaugh, Grade 4
Scipio Elementary School, IN

Save Our World

Our oceans: an unimaginable beauty or a hazardous waste dump? We've done it for years; throwing garbage into the rivers. We think it's not going to hurt anything, but it does. All rivers lead to the ocean.

Lake Erie, one of our Great Lakes, was at one time called the "dead" lake because of all of the dead fish that washed up on shore. The fish died because of all the chemicals dumped in the lake.

Our president has cut funds that America needs for our environment. We need these to stay on top; clean and unpolluted. These funds are crucial to keeping us, our land, and our oceans healthy.

If people would listen to an eleven-year-old girl like me, we would be able to save our world.

Avery Walke, Grade 5

Doing a Good Deed

On September 11, 2001, a very tragic thing happened, two or three planes crashed into New York City's Twin Towers and firemen sacrificed their lives so other people could live. I decided to do a good deed in remembrance of September 11th. My good deed is being nice to people I don't know and family members. I held the door and I was kind and loving to my friends when they were being mean to me. When I was nice to them, they were nice to me.

Sometimes I think a lot about September 11th. I have a book at home that I sometimes look at. My dad told me all about what happened. This is important to me because my grandpa was in the Air Force at the time. He didn't die because he wasn't flying any of the planes, but if he was he would of probably died. I love my grandpa because he is funny and nice. I am glad my grandpa did not die. So, on September 11th, you should always do a good deed and write about one.

Victoria Langley, Grade 4
Snake River Montessori School, ID

Boys and Girls

Have you ever wondered what girls and boys like to talk about? Have you ever wondered what they talk about in their room with their friends or what they talk about on the phone or cell phone? If you have...then get on to reading!!

Girls talk about gossip like those he said/she said stuff, having a job or career, having a family, sports, High School Musical, boys and what they do, what favorite animals are, and lastly Britney Spears and her strange and unusual ways.

Girls gossip because it's probably a fun thing to do. Sports because that's what they do after homework and school. High School Musical because it's popular. Animals because sometimes they are cute and cuddly. Boys because girls sometimes girls think they're cute or handsome. They talk about Britney Spears because of her strange and unusualness (I think).

Boys talk about loads of things, that I'm about to tell you. When they come back from physical education, they talk about how the girls pass the ball to their friends. They don't talk about how terrible they were themselves!

One time I had to scream "be quite" to the others, because they found out that I liked this girl, and I denied it (I felt terrible when I said this!) But I really do like her! But if girls (or boys) find out you like them they will pester you until they get bored! I know this because it happened to me once!

Ricky Mehrmann, Grade 6
Imagine Charter School at Rosefield, AZ

The Disaster!!!

Have you ever experienced a disaster in your life? I have. It happened in Lagoon. My clogging team had won first place on all our dances, so we got to go to Lagoon and compete there.

We had just finished our first dance when I looked down, and saw that my taps were hanging by a thread of glue. If I had continued to clog I'm sure they would have flown off and hit someone in the head. I was so worried about this. Then I was even more worried when I found out my teacher had forgotten the emergency bag that had all the glue in it. Miss Becky (my teacher) quickly hunted around for someone who could lend me some shoes. She finally came back and said that a little girl said I could borrow her shoes. I was so glad when I tried them on and they fit. My class ended up winning first and third place.

I was so happy that there was a young lady willing to let me borrow her shoes. Recently, I bought some clogging shoes that have the taps nailed in so hopefully I will never go through this again. I still love clogging and hope to be able to clog for many more years.

Madison Heaps, Grade 6
Thomas Jefferson Charter School, ID

Mrs. Legg

"Stand up and jump two times!" Mrs. Legg said. I got up right away and jumped twice. Mrs. Legg is my favorite teacher. After lunch, I can't wait to go to English. I pack my back pack and run to meet her inside. And I cannot forget to give her a hug! I wish period five were a little longer! Mrs. Legg makes English so much fun!

Mrs. Legg sets a great example to me and the school. She saved so many children and taught them God's word. And she gave them hope. When I'm older I want to be a missionary like her. It seems like fun to help all those children.

On the first day of school I was very nervous. But once I came to English I felt different. I had a lot of fun. I was laughing and I felt more like myself. English soon became my favorite subject.

To me it doesn't matter how much money you have or what clothes you wear. It just matters how nice you are. And how many friends and family you have. Mrs. Legg made me feel like the richest person in the world. Thank you Mrs. Legg!!!

Breanne Arnold, Grade 6
Linfield Christian School, CA

Leopards

Have you ever gone to the zoo and seen a large spotted cat? If so there's a good chance that it was a leopard!

Many people get leopards confused with jaguars. For the most part there is only one difference between the two. The difference is that in the black circles on a leopards fur there is only one black spot. Jaguars usually have two or more spots inside the circle. Leopards are about six to seven feet and ranging from 100-160 pounds. Leopards are also very slim. Leopards are beautiful creatures!

Leopards sleep for a lot of the day. They also have to hunt. Leopards hunt birds, zebras, rodents, and gazelle.

Leopards live in both Northern and Southern parts of Africa. They live in a habitat called a grassland. The grasslands in Africa were very hot and humid.

Leopards usually hunt and live alone. They do not live in packs like lions. When it is hot out, leopards usually sleep in trees because it is shady. They are like house cats because they like to sit and sleep in high places. Leopards are very strong and have claws that can grip on to trees very well. Leopards are excellent climbers.

When a leopard is done eating it's "meal" it pulls it all the way up a tree to save it for later. They do this so other animals don't find and steal their food. Leopards are very clever creatures.

I hope you learned a lot about leopards.

Kaitlin McKernan, Grade 5
Butterfield School, IL

Teamwork

Do you know what teamwork is? First, teamwork is the work activity of a number of persons. I show teamwork with others by playing soccer and how we pace the ball back and forth to each other. Next, our class shows teamwork by raising our hands and not shouting out answers at the teacher. Lastly, teamwork can be helping someone do a project and not having them struggle on their own. Working together to get the job done. All of these things show teamwork.

Fabian Huerta, Grade 5
Covington Elementary School, NE

Disaster Drill

I will be needing to get ready for a disaster like an earthquake, a power outage, or a mud slide. I will have to know escape routes out of my house and meeting places if the house burns down. I will probably need supplies like a first aid kit when a disaster occurs.

The supplies I will probably be needing are: fire extinguisher, a bike, 3 to 4 days of food, 6 to 8 days of water, a flashlight, batteries and a first aid kit. (We should use the supplies the way we need to use them.) We're not going to play around with these supplies. If we do we will probably die in confusion.

The meeting places I could probably go to are: Liberty School, or five blocks away. Then I could go to a clear place (if there is one). It's good to make a meeting place because you can find out what happened to family members all around the world. When you make the meeting place make sure it's not close to a fire or any other disaster.

There are escape routes I know and they are the backdoor, the windows, the gate and the door.

I learned wherever you are, always be prepared for a disaster.

Christian Tinajero, Grade 5
Liberty Elementary School, CA

My Pet, Bingo

My pet dog, Bingo, is black and white. My pet dog is a pit bull. Bingo is a big dog. Bingo is a nice and sweet dog. My dog Bingo likes to play a lot. I like to play with Bingo. Bingo will chase me on my four-wheeler. Right now he is chained up. Today me and dad are going to put a fence up. So we can let Bingo off the chain. Then he can play with my other big pit bulls. You know what's weird, he won't fight other dogs. Bingo is a very good dog and he's so friendly with people. But if he has to protect us, Bingo will. He's a funny dog when we were popping firecrackers and Bingo was going nuts. We would get real close and then pop back really fast. A while back Bingo got hurt really bad because a dog fought him. He bled and got cuts all over him. Bingo always will get tangled up. He's bad at that but I still love him even if he is a little messed up in the noggin. Well, that's all I know about my dog, Bingo.

River Gordon, Grade 4
Winona Elementary School, TX

My Family Sticks Together Like Glue

My family is made up of great people who care about one another deeply. My family consists of my dad, my mom, my sister, and my brother.

Whenever I have problems of any kind, I go to my mom. My mom always has such great advice for me. When I'm ill, my parents are there for me. They try anything they can think of to make me feel better.

Every kid who has parents should appreciate them very much! I appreciate my parents because they work their whole lives to provide food and shelter for my siblings and I, and they also spend time with us when they have it.

Having a family that sticks together and never separates is something that one should really be thankful for. There are many kids in the world that do not have a family. Also, there are many kids who are not lucky enough to be part of a loving family.

Another great thing about having a family is that you never have to be alone. You will always have company with you. I know that my sister is very small and does not like to play the same things I do. Then I just play with my brother. He is closer to my age and we have so much in common!

I love my family, and so should you. Appreciate anything and everything that your family has. I think my stuck-together family is the best I can have!

Carolina Figueroa, Grade 5
Booth Tarkington Elementary School, IL

The First Perfect Spring Day

I am sitting in the most perfect place in the world, looking around, and I realize the wonderful creation that has been made. It is 1:24 p.m. on a gorgeous Tuesday afternoon, and I'm admiring all the sights, sounds, smells, and feelings I have on this special day.

I'm thinking, "OH, look at that bird fluttering its wings! And the airplane, humph, leaving a white tail." As I look to my right, I see a car cruising by as slow as a turtle. I'm sitting here and I scream because I just saw a bee zigzagging by my ear. I freeze, hoping it will go away, and I whisper, "I'm not that tasty. Go find a flower!" I was enjoying all that I was seeing when my dog came over and, panting, drooled on my arm. But, I still love my dog. I close my eyes and can still hear the leaves rustle from last year's fall. I feel an attractive breeze that is not too light, but also not too hard. I hear a meow and look to see my cat prowling, and the dog chewing a bone. My favorite part is the sun — yes, the warmth of the sun. It is all so refreshing! Now, where could that most perfect place in the world be? Could it be my front porch? Yes, I wish every day could be like this one. It is surely the first, PERFECT spring day!

Kellie Stanton, Grade 5
The Options School, CO

Bullying

I was outside when I saw a little girl get bullied. She was getting bullied by a bigger kid. The bully was choking her. I tried to help her. I tried to pull her away but that did not help any.

Bullying is when someone messes with you for no apparent reason. It could be because they don't like you. Bullying could be hitting. It could also be taking things from you. That's what bullying means.

The people that get bullied are little kids and kids who are quiet. Kids who are taller and bigger do the bullying. They do that because they might not like you. The bully might not like your siblings or any other relative.

If you or someone else is getting bullied you should call for help. When you and the other person call for help and no one helps you should send for someone to tell an adult. You should tell your parent. Your parent should come up to the school and talk to the principal.

Schools can prevent bullying by organizing groups about not bullying. The person who gets bullied on all the time can take a self defense class. Try to stand up for yourself. STOP THE BULLYING!!!!!!!!

Jatayvia Carson, Grade 6
Starms Discovery Learning Center, WI

Captain Edward John Smith
Captain of the "Unsinkable" Titanic

Edward John Smith, the captain of the luxurious Titanic, was born January 27, 1850, in Hanley, England. He attended the Eturia British School until the age of 13, then began his career at sea by apprenticing on a clipper ship. Smith fell in love with the sea and decided that he wanted to be a captain. In March 1880, he joined the White Star Line as a Fourth Officer and after several promotions, he received his first command in 1887.

In 1887, Smith wed Sarah Eleanor Pennington. Two years later, Sara gave birth to their first and only child, Helen Melville Smith.

In 1888, Smith earned his Extra Master's Certificate, and later joined the Royal Naval Reserve. In 1899, the Boer War started and, under Smith's command, the Majestic transported troops to Cape Colony. Smith received the "Transport Medal" from King Edward VII for his wartime service.

Smith eventually became a Commodore, such that other captains reported to him. He also developed a reputation among wealthy English passengers, many of whom would only sail under his command. In 1911, Smith became captain of the grandest ship ever built, the Titanic.

On April 14, 1912, the Titanic was steaming across the Atlantic on her maiden voyage. Suddenly, the peaceful evening was disrupted when the ship struck an iceberg, killing 75 percent of the passengers. Smith, who refused to abandon the sinking ship, perished at sea. We will always remember his courage and bravery.

Emily Blair Marcus, Grade 5
Valley Beth Shalom Day School, CA

My Horrible Story

I hate the way my Dad was taken away from me. Here's my story… I was just 2 years old when this happened. But I remember it as if it were yesterday.

See, Mom needed some money and my Dad loved her very much. So he had to do ONE bad thing. He tried to rob the bank. But it didn't work. He got caught and went to jail. He has never come back.

I still write notes to him… and that's my horrible story.

Cierra Fentroy, Grade 5
DeQueen Elementary School, TX

My Seizures

When I was little I had seizures. It was very scary for my family and me. I can hardly remember what it was like because I was still little. I can only remember one; it was around February. My brother was outside with his friend, riding bikes, and it was still slippery out, but right then and there I had a seizure. Thank gosh I stopped having seizures when I was 7. I kind of enjoyed the hospital. The reason I enjoyed the hospital is because all day I got to lie in the hospital bed and eat ice cream and popsicles. All of the doctors and nurses were really nice. My mom said that when I had my first seizure that the doctors gave me medicine that I was allergic too (but they didn't know that), and now my eyes change colors. I'm so glad that all of that is over.

Bailey Henderson, Grade 6
Haslett Middle School, MI

Cooking 101 with My Noni

My grandmother, Noni, has taught me a lot about cooking. One of our favorite things we have made together is the secret family recipe for ravioli sauce that was handed down from my great-grandmother. Our sauce recipe takes all day to make but is worth all the trouble. My great-grandmother never wrote down the exact measurements for anything we put in the sauce. Finally, with a lot of trial and error, Noni has come up with the right combination of ingredients that makes the sauce delicious. Every Thanksgiving our family cannot wait to sit down for dinner and dive into the wonderful raviolis and sauce.

Another thing we like to bake is cakes. For some reason, there is always a problem with the way our cakes turn out. When Noni opens the oven, I always cross my fingers, hoping there is nothing wrong with the cake. It always has a tiny crack in the middle, but by the time the cake cools down it looks like an earthquake has hit! Noni and I don't worry about that though because the frosting acts like glue and holds the cake together. Everyone thinks they are normal cakes and they taste delicious, but little do they know what lies under the frosting.

Spending time with Noni means a lot to me because I am learning and carrying on a family tradition of cooking. It also allows me to bond and make memories with Noni that will be with me forever.

Breanne Sabbatino, Grade 6
St Anne School, CA

M&M's

M&M's are known for their chocolatey taste, and their melty goodness. Many people know them for their famous phrase, "The candy that melts in your mouth, not in your hands." Just thinking about M&M's makes me want to grab a mouthful. People of all ages can eat M&M's, so can you!

The M&M first started when two men named Forrest Mars and Bruce Murries wanted to create a food which had turned out to be the "M&M." Do you know why they call it the M&M? Both of the inventor's last names began with the letter M. Amazing right? It would be so cool to name a candy after you or me! Back then when the M&M was first created, the M&M was black with just plain old milk chocolate. The types of M&M's we see today are colorful and have many different types of chocolates.

From 1950 to 1995, M&M's have changed the most, which has made them how good they are today. In 1950, M&M's were still black, and didn't have the letter M on it until 1950. In 1960 three new colors were added: red, green, and yellow. In 1976, the orange M&M was added to the clan. Finally, in 1980, M&M's had spread all over the globe…all because of their great taste. M&M's have grown over the years, with their success of making them better than ever. Which do you prefer, milk chocolate or M&M's with nuts?

Madison Schultz, Grade 5
Oak Crest Intermediate School, TX

Moving

My family has been wanting to get a house for a while. Then last year we found our dream house, until I found out that I had to change schools. That day I was so confused because I wanted to stay at my old school but I didn't want to stay in my old small house. What I am trying to tell you is that moving is never easy. It was so hard when we moved that I got a teacher from my old school to drive me from school to my house because I didn't want to leave my friends from my old school. But unfortunately my teacher could not drive me forever so my mom and the teacher talked and they said that when winter break comes I will go to my new school.

When that time came, I came to Menchaca Elementary. I felt so scared because I would not know anyone there and if they were nice or mean. Also if I would get a mean teacher or a nice teacher. Then when I went to my new school called Menchaca Elementary, I met this girl named Abby Stanfield and she showed me the school and who the principal is and the vice principal. I felt happy that I had someone there at Menchaca Elementary to help me. After all of this happened everything turned out okay. As you can tell from my story moving is never ever easy.

Tarika Nath, Grade 4
Menchaca Elementary School, TX

Outstanding Outside

The outside is very amazing. It is an open place for the world to grow. It is very interesting to see, smell, hear and feel. I love to see the wind blowing the leaves in the trees like a person blowing their hair out of their face. The outside smells wonderful too. The smell reminds me of fresh pine trees in your house at Christmas time. When I stroll down the walkway I can smell the roses that welcome me home every afternoon, following a fun day at school. My favorite thing to hear in the outdoors is the birds chirping like they are singing a pleasant melody. In the winter and fall the air feels very chilly like a fan blowing in your face on a warm day spent in the sun. I hope every day will be as beautiful as today.

Amy Erickson, Grade 5
Greenwood Elementary School, MN

Honesty

Honesty is the quality or state of being honest. People that are honest are people who don't lie, don't steal, and do their own work in school when they're supposed to. An example of a person being honest is my dad Jerry. He is honest because he doesn't lie to me and he is the most honest when he tells me he loves me. When he says that we are going to do something, we do it.

I believe it is best to always be honest. If you are honest to people, they will respect you. When you are honest you don't do bad things, don't lie, and you don't cheat off of other peoples papers.

These are the qualities of being honest. If you are honest it is a big responsibility. If people believe you aren't honest they will not believe you. That is why I think it is best to be honest.

Gabriel Barrera, Grade 5
Covington Elementary School, NE

Volunteering at the LaSalle Bank Chicago Marathon

When I volunteered for the Chicago Marathon, I did a lot. First, I had to wake up at 4:45 A.M. I got ready and my family and I met with the rest of the volunteers. Everybody got set, and we went to Chicago in our vans. There were 9 people in the van that I was in.

When we got to Chicago, we had to wait 2 hours until we got set up! That was because we were between the 24 and 25 mile marks. Before we got set up, we were nice enough to help set up the chip mats. The way we did that was we spread out the mats, and just put cords underneath. We watched the wheelchair racers go by, and then set up our tables for water. Since we had our water station set up only for the fastest runners, we didn't have to stay for the whole race.

As soon as the fast runners passed by, we had to hurry up and take down the tables. Once we were done, we watched a little of the race, and then got in the van to go home. It was really fun, and I would like to do it again next year.

Lauren Wajda, Grade 6
Divine Infant Jesus School, IL

Otters

Otters live just about everywhere in the world. Different species live in different parts of the world, such as the Pacific coasts of North America, Iraq, Europe, and South America.

Otters have soft fur under their long thick guard hairs. They also have elongated slim bodies, short legs, webbed feet, and most have claws. The average river otter grows about three feet in length and will normally be 10 to 30 lbs. A sea otter grows to be about six and a half feet in length and can weight up to 65 lbs. That makes the sea otter about twice as big as his fresh water cousin. The sea otter has about 1,400,000 thick hairs per sq. in! There is also an even bigger species called the giant otter! Otters do not have a layer of insulating blubber like other aquatic mammals such as seals.

River otters need to eat 15% of their body weight daily (about four and a half pounds). Sea otters require the nourishment of 20 to 25% of their body weight (about three and one fourth pounds). In water as warm as 50°F the otter must catch 5 1/2 lbs. of food, and if the otter doesn't catch that much it will die. Otters eat fish, frogs, crayfish, crabs, and some otters can eat shellfish by cracking the shell on rocks.

Most people love otters because of their playful nature. I however am intrigued by the many things you can learn from them.

Samuel Gotthoffer, Grade 5
Ray E Kilmer Elementary School, CO

Best Friends

What are friends to me? Everything! I look forward to spending time with them in my free time. This always gets me motivated to finish my school and chores. Sometimes it's hard to make new friends, but for me it's usually easy. Almost all my friends are Christians. I'm glad God has blessed me with so many best friends.

When I go to church all of my friends are there, this helps me feel comfortable. The first time I went to church on Saturday I felt shy, but when I met all the people there I was happy to become their friend. We all have strengths in different areas. One friend helps me with self-discipline, while another encourages me with kindness and patience. I'm glad, and so are they, that we're always supportive of each other.

We are faithful friends. We will not let an innocent friend take the blame for something someone else has done. For example, if a teacher asks us to "stop talking," the person that started the conversation will own up to being the initiator instead of allowing someone else to take the blame.

Being able to see my friends at church and play has helped and strengthened my life skills in so many ways.

Whitney Hayes, Grade 5
CORE Butte Charter School, CA

Spitting Cobras

Have you ever heard of a "spitting" cobra? If you have, then did you believe it? If you didn't believe it then I guess I'm here to convince you that it's true. I'll start by explaining to you how they "spit." Spitting cobras don't actually spit. They have small holes at the end of their fangs. Their fangs have tubes that connect to their venom glands which carry venom for killing prey. The venom is then forced out of their fangs with such force that the venom sprays in a jet of over 10 feet. Spitting cobras have very accurate aim and they aim directly for the eyes. They only spit venom to defend themselves. Spitting cobras will spit at an animal with hooves to keep from getting trampled. If venom gets in an animal's or person's eye it will burn and sting severely because it burns the sensitive cornea. If the venom is not washed out quickly, then it may cause temporary or permanent blindness. A drop of this venom is powerful enough to kill a human. A very strange fact is that the baby spitting cobras are more dangerous than adults because they have no control over how much venom they inject, so when they bite they inject a full dose. Now that you know about spitting cobras, do you believe that they are actually real?

Brandon Thompson, Grade 6
Thomas Jefferson Charter School, ID

Mummies of Ancient Egypt

When you think of a mummy what comes to mind? Most of us usually picture an Egyptian mummy wrapped in bandages and buried deep inside a pyramid. While the Egyptian ones are the most famous, mummies have been found in many places throughout the world, from Greenland to China to the Andes Mountains of South America.

A mummy is the body of a person (or an animal) that has been preserved after death. Normally when we die, bacteria and other germs eat away at the soft tissues (such as skin and muscles) leaving only the bones behind. Since bacteria need water in order to grow, mummification usually happens if the body dries out quickly after death. The body may then be so well preserved that we can even tell how the dead person may have looked in life.

Mummies are made naturally or by embalming, which is any process that people use to help preserve a dead body. Mummies can be dried out by extreme cold, by the sun, by smoke, or using chemicals such as Natron. Some bodies become mummies because there were favorable natural conditions when they died. Others were preserved and buried with great care.

The ancient Egyptians believed that mummifying a person's body after death was essential to ensure a safe passage to the afterlife.

Danica Kloes, Grade 6
Granite Falls Middle School, WA

My Dad

My Dad is awesome he is also cool and funny. My dad is fun to play with. My dad likes to hunt and so do I. My dad does landscape and he owns a lawn care and landscaping business. My dad is my hero. I love to help my dad work. He also likes to go camping and fish a lot too. My dad likes to play a lot too, sometimes he will play two whole basketball games. That is an essay on my dad.

Chase DeHaven, Grade 6
St Monica Catholic School, TX

Life Is Going to Be Great!!!

My family is really important to me because I know that they love me no matter what. My mom, dad, and grandma take care of me and do really fun things with me!! My mom is the best mom in the world, she takes me everywhere I need or want to go and she makes me dinner every night!!! My dad is the coolest dad on earth, he loves me very much and he does a whole lot of great things with me!! My grandma is also very important to me because she takes me places and she loves to just hang out with me!! My grandma even drives in circles around the mall just to hang out with me!

My family loves each other very much. We love to go places, like Disneyland, Sea World, Wild Animal Park, San Diego Zoo, horse shows, beaches, or even just to church! We have a lot of fun no matter where we go. My mom drives my family wherever we decide to go, and she makes our drives fun, relaxing, and short. My dad makes everything funny and he makes my entire family laugh!! My grandma makes our times together fun and memorable, plus she buys me everything!! My family goes everywhere together. I love my family very much and they're the best family that you could ever dream of!

Makala Phillips, Grade 6
Linfield Christian School, CA

My Family

My family is important to me because they take great care of me. My family is also important to me because they cheer me up when I am down. I know when my parents say no, it's for a good reason to help me, or protect me from danger. I love my family dearly and I would not trade them in for anything in this galaxy.

There is another part of the family and his name is Leo. Leo is a cute Labrador Retriever. He is two years old, and in dog years he's 14. My sister Marissa is nine and in 4th grade. My sister and I get in to arguments a lot, but we still love each other very much. There are some things in my family that I regret, like saying hurtful things that could just break a heart and or doing things that I shouldn't do. If I could go back in time and stop myself from doing bad things, I would. But you can't change the past. I can change the future and form it just right. My family and I have fun every holiday, like Christmas when we put up the Christmas tree and decorate it with ornaments and lights.

Nathan Lamonte, Grade 6
Linfield Christian School, CA

Don't Be Afraid of Chores

Almost every child in the United States of America hates doing chores. If you are one of those rare people who actually like doing chores, then call me. Most people try to avoid doing chores, but don't succeed.

My mom sets the vacuum out in the living room. And when we get home, she says in delight: "The vacuum! I wonder who put that there!" Anyone who heard that would get the hint. My dog Pearl is terrified of the vacuum, and squirrels, so we don't mind.

I don't think we should have to clean our rooms. Only because it's our own special place. When I finally got my own room, I had to clean it. When I only spent three minutes there, and when I finally got it the way I liked it.

When I was little, every other Tuesday was "sock day." I hated matching socks. And I cried and wailed every time the basket was set out. Now that I look back on it, I realize how easy it was.

What I am saying is, if you realize you have a messy house, pick up that sock that has been gathering dust since you were three. And before you go jumping off a bridge, make sure that your room is semi-clean. It will make a big difference. You will get it out of the way, so next week, when you are supposed to be partying with some movie star, you won't be cleaning your room.

Maddy Muff, Grade 6
West Central Middle School, IL

How Bears Live

People might not know what bears eat. Healthy bears eat a lot more than a person. They don't eat and last for at least two hours. They're always hungry. All bears eat different depending on their diet. For example grizzly bears eat grass and roots, sometimes they even catch fish underwater. People might not know that they also eat little animals underground. Grizzly bears eat about 30 pounds of food a day. It could take us about two weeks to eat that much. They all eat that much because they're big. Some of the bears weigh as much as ten adults. Polar bears eat a lot so they could keep warm. These kinds of bears eat many kinds of food, especially seals. Polar bears may also eat walruses, fish, and whales that have died. Everybody knows they live in a cold habitat. The thick layer of fat also helps them stay warm. That's what bears eat.

Bears find food by the help of their snout, also known as nose. The bears snout gives them a great sense of smell. It helps them find food.

When they stand up they're very tall. Bears stand up to fight their enemies. Mostly all bears travel far to find food. That is how bears live.

Elizabeth Ramos, Grade 5
Desert Trails Elementary School, CA

My Favorite Place

My favorite place is my tree house. It looks beautiful. It takes a lot of work to build it. It is made of a lot of wood, a couple of blankets, metal and carpet. The top is made of metal and the floor is made of carpet. It took me a long time to put in the carpet. I had to get my daddy to do it. Then I had to build an enormous box out of wood. I had to get my daddy, brother, and my uncles to get it up there. Then my daddy let me paint it with all different colors. My daddy had to cut out two blocks of wood to make windows. When it rains I will hang up the blankets by the windows and anything that is open. Every once in a while I will put a TV in there, chairs, and a table with chips. When I have nothing to do I will ask daddy if I can go to my treehouse. I would go ask Sara (a friend) if she would like to go inside. For 24 hours me and Sara would play, laugh, and watch TV. Sometimes we will bring my dog in there, his water and toys. So that is my favorite place to go. It is the best you can ever imagine.

Lydia Crow, Grade 4
Winona Elementary School, TX

My Dog NaBoo

My dog, NaBoo, is the dumbest pet ever. One time a long time ago I threw my dog's ball and it bounced off the wall. But she didn't stop. She kept on going and ran smack into the wall.

My pet looks like a coyote, but she is so cute. Every time anyone looks at her weirdly, she barks and howls.

My dumb dog, NaBoo is the best pet ever.

Kierstyn Smathers, Grade 5
Westview Elementary School, OH

Hannah

I'm thankful for my family because they're always there for me. My cousin Hannah is the same age, and has the same last name. We were born very close together because Hannah was born on the 27th and I was born on the 15th of March. So I'm older than she is by a few days. We were both born in Chandler Regional Hospital. Even the hospital got us mixed up, because they sent my parents her hospital bill!

I'm thankful we have some things in common. We like to fix our own hair, and enjoy dressing up in costumes. We both like animals and the zoo. Both of us swim like fish. Starbucks and Dairy Queen are two of our favorite places.

I love Hannah so much, but I'm also thankful that she's not exactly like me. That would be boring! Hannah has two sisters; while I'm an only child. You could tell the difference between me and Hannah in photos. Hannah would be holding a soccer ball, and I'd be smiling wearing fancy clothes. Hey, we still get along great even though I'm hyper and she's not. I love my cousin Hannah. Hannah is my favorite cousin because she treats me like a sister. Her parents are getting a divorce. I haven't talked to her in a while. I bet she isn't too happy right now. Hannah probably is going to need a friend to talk, and I'm a good listener.

Skylar LeMans, Grade 4
Gateway Pointe Elementary School, AZ

What a Day

As the sun peeked through my window I woke up. It was morning. It was my birthday. I thought there was only going to be a cake and piñata. I put on my brown shoes, my jeans, and my shoes. My mom drove me to the park. I was thinking, "The same old birthday kid running around people that I know." Then I saw it. It had a red nose, big shoes, and blue hair! It was a clown!

I came up to him and he said, "My name is Bob. Are you the birthday boy?!?" He magically turned a piece of paper into a five dollar bill! After he made me and my friends balloon animals, he painted our faces. We had water balloon fights, and got all wet. One really fun game was when we hit a SpongeBob and a Hulk piñata. We got a ton of candy. I was the first one to whack the piñata.

I at a Chicken Little cake. It was a chocolate cake. There also was pizza. We played all kinds of games. A lot of my friends came to the party. At night it was time for everyone to leave. It was the best birthday I ever had!!!

Alex Gonzalez, Grade 5
Dingeman Elementary School, CA

5 Star Hotel

The last three days I went to SeaWorld in Florida we went there by Caravan. When we got there the first thing I won was a poster of a clown the second prize was an X box and two games and six action figures. My brother won twelve comic books and a PSP. My sister won the whole collection of Harry Potter books.

Then when the day ended I thought we were going to go home our aunt told us we were going to rent a five star hotel room. When we got to the hotel everybody had their own room. It was cool. The room had a big bed and a flat screen TV. There were a lot of pillows and on the floor was a carpet the color of the sky. The next day we went to the pool for three hours. Then we went back to the hotel, my aunt told us to get our stuff ready to go home.

Mark Perez, Grade 6
Chapa Middle School, TX

My Summer

My summer has been a wild one. I had friends over to swim. They weren't friends from school, they were a neighbor and the housekeeper's daughter. We went swimming and played Sea Creatures.

Then my family went camping with me. We had fun camping. I went tubing, arrowhead hunting, swimming, snorkeling, fishing, and wakeboarding. I did a lot of face plants, but I managed to get up twice, and fall down again. After all, I was a beginner.

Then we went home for two days and played on my computer. Then we went back camping and did the same things.

I liked my summer so much that I don't want to go to 5th grade.

Sam Meakins, Grade 5
Eugene Christian School, OR

Webkinz

One of my favorite things to do during my spare time is Webkinz! I imagine you're wondering what a Webkinz is. If so, I will tell you!

A Webkinz is a virtual pet online. You have to have the stuffed animal to be able to make the account because the Webkinz has a special code attached to the leg. You cannot create the account without the code. Once you create the account, you need to keep the code in a safe place just in case you forget your password. When you log on to Webkinz, your pet will become an animated creature.

There is a program on Webkinz called Quizzy's Corner which teaches you all the basics of the subjects. It is like a game show your pet participates in. First, you choose your age group. Second, you choose a subject. Third, you start answering your questions. You get a limit of 20 seconds for each question. If you get a question wrong you lose money. Every set of questions is called a series and a series is 50 questions.

I got into Webkinz because my friend Madysen's nana purchased her and her brother Maverick a Webkinz. When I went to her house we went to the Boutique in Burnet and I purchased a Lil' Kinz Golden Retriever.

Webkinz is a really cool place to play during your spare time. I hope this will get you interested in being part of the Webkinz community!

Callie Levine, Grade 5
Spicewood Elementary School, TX

The Importance of God and My Family

God and my family have done so much for me in my life, like giving me three younger sisters that I always hang out with. I'm also privileged to go to Linfield Christian School. I love coming home to a family that loves me and that I can love back. I'm glad I'm allowed to have a wonderful family by my side, all the time.

God has always been working in my life to save it from despair. Once, my mom wasn't feeling good and one day she had a minor "heart attack." At that moment, I never felt so scared in my life. I prayed for my mom to get better. When I came home one day I saw my mom lying in her bed. I felt overjoyed that my mom was okay and that God had answered my prayers. A few months later, I found myself in the hospital. I prayed to God. I found out that I had a type of heart problem. Doctors barley even knew the disease I had. I was afraid to die, but I knew God was watching over me. By the end of the week, I was feeling a lot better. Still to this day, I'm grateful that He had saved me and my mom. I guess I'm lucky to have God and a wonderful family. This is why God and my family are so important to me.

Taylor Lindsay, Grade 6
Linfield Christian School, CA

Tankers

I have a puppy, and he is super small. My dog is a Chihuahua, and his name is Tank. Tank has light tan fur and big brown eyes.

Tank loves to play, well sometimes. If he is being good he lets us play with him by hitting him softly on his nose. He growls at us. It is so funny. Tank isn't allowed on the couch because he sheds a lot. When he is allowed, we put a blanket on the couch so he can sit up there.

Tank doesn't like sirens at all. One time we were watching *Barnyard*, and sirens came on. He got scared and started howling, so I took him to the back of the house. Sometimes Tank gets in trouble because he doesn't do what we say. He has to go in his kennel and he doesn't like it. I love my dog Tank. I enjoy him very much.

Kelsey Sellers, Grade 4
Burchett Elementary School, TX

Disaster

If there was a fire in my house I would be prepared with every item I need, like food and water and most of all a first aid kit.

I would have a first aid kit with bandages and big bandages and emergency items like a map, cellphone, some walkie-talkies, food, water for about 5-7 days or one week. The food and water would be in the garage.

I think my escape route would be the window because it's faster and easier to get out of the house. But I better close the window because if I don't the oxygen would go faster.

We decided that our meeting place would be the gasoline station because it's the closest place to our house. And if no body showed up in one hour I had to go to my grandma's house.

This is real, my family really plans on doing this if there was a fire.

Rodrigo De La Torre, Grade 5
Liberty Elementary School, CA

My Disaster Plan

This essay is about how I can be ready for a disaster. This is what I would do if there was an emergency.

In my supply kit I would have a first aid kit and fruit snacks because they don't go rotten. I would also have canned food for about five to seven days and bottles of water for about three to four days in my supply kit.

If there was a fire I would run to my mom's room and jump out of the window. If there was an earthquake I would try to get my dog and go out the front or back door. I would put my dog on the roof and climb up our porch's overhang if there was a flood.

My family's meeting place would be at the gas station down the street or school down another street. Maybe it could be at a neighbor's house across the street too.

In conclusion that is what I would do if I were in a disaster. Hopefully I will never be in a disaster.

Andrew Navarro, Grade 5
Liberty Elementary School, CA

Performing Arts

5, 6, 7, 8! When I count like this, I'm usually dancing. I love dancing! Don't try and tell me dancing isn't a sport. Dance requires concentration, practice and creativity. If you don't have those, sign up for a dance class. Dancing isn't just for girls either. Dance and music go together very well. Some dances can go without music but I prefer them with music, it helps me stay on rhythm. Sometimes I even sing along, but not on stage. No! Wrong key!

Singing to me is great! One fun thing you can do is write your own songs like musical writers do. Music has changed a lot over the years. Some styles are rap, opera, country, pop and so many others. I believe music will always be changing. "Quiet on set! Action." Those are sometimes the words of a director. Acting is one of my favorite things to do! Imagination is one of the key things you have to remember in acting. You're not always going to have what you need so make something up. Make your character someone different, make them stand out! Some tips on acting are; don't be afraid to look stupid! Always stay in character. Speak loudly and don't look directly at the audience, they could throw you off. Those are some tips on acting. Acting is a great way to have fun, read, and meet new people! These are my favorite things.

Kazmiere Brown, Grade 6
Orchard Hill Elementary School, IA

Living in a Bush Village

I live in an Alaskan bush village. Some of the things I like to do are go on four-wheeler rides and help my dad in the hangar. I work at the hangar and I get paid $8.00 an hour. At the hangar I usually help degrease the bellies of the plane, put oil in the plane, or sweep the floor, but most of the time it is just doing whatever I'm told.

In the winter my dad, my sister, and I go to a frozen lake in a plane and set up a wall tent. We trap martins, wolverines, lynx, fox, and other small animals. This year we are going to get beaver. Their hides are neat, and we can sell them for a lot.

We like playing at home or at a friend's house. At a friend's house we go outside and we play paintball, air soft, and sometimes we sword fight. Those are the fun things to do out here in the village. We also like hiking, biking, hunting, and going on walks.

The difficult part about living in the bush village is that sometimes during winter we get frozen pipe lines and my dad has to fix them. Sometimes it's difficult getting to Anchorage when the weather's bad. Once our sewer system busted and my dad had to fix it. Even though life sometimes is hard I still love life in the bush village!

Joel Natwick, Grade 5
Tanalian School, AK

Constitution

I am so happy to have freedom, aren't you? Well, the Constitution tells us all of our freedoms, rights, government, and responsibilities.

First government is very important to us because if the government couldn't provide special services for us we wouldn't have our fire fighters, policeman, or a rescue squad to save us. But we also have to pay the government our taxes to help pay for those special services.

Next, freedom is also very important to us because some people don't have the freedom we have. It is very valuable to most people. Some people unlike us don't have the freedom to live where they want to live, to wear what they want to wear. Some people aren't even allowed to go to school. We are very lucky to have all of our freedom from the Constitution.

Thirdly, our rights and responsibilities come from the Constitution too. Some of the responsibilities we have are to obey the traffic signs, go to school, and not to break the law. Some of the rights we have are to vote, say what you want about the government, and worship. Everyone has the right to a fair trial.

Things like rights, freedom, government, and responsibilities all come from the Constitution that we are really, really, really, lucky to have.

Anna Palmesano, Grade 4
Rohwer Elementary School, NE

The Game Room

My favorite place is the game room. One thing I like about it is its grass green color. I see my skin-tone carpet, my grass green walls, my books stacked high and ready to read, with book marks sticking out of them. My foosball table is crooked by my blue, high, bent back chair which faces my tiny gray-silver, and white TV. My trophies stare at me while I play my black PS2 in my other gray, low, soft bent back chair, and I am reminded of my first soccer goal and my winning of the Cub Scout Derby.

The room is cool because it's air conditioned and I can smell the fresh air. When I am in the room I can hear the video games and the rumbling of the cars within the game. The TV plays the upcoming weather forecast. The sizzle of the pancakes my dad makes beneath are hitting the skillet and makes me hungry.

Although many sounds surround me, in my own world, there is a silent hush that makes the room very quiet. I love being able to escape reality and go to my own world, cut off from everything. It is the best feeling ever. I feel like I am separated from the real world here, and I can do whatever I want.

Boone Bufkin, Grade 5
Neosho Heights Elementary School, KS

My Dance Life

My name is Ana Elizabeth Cherry. I was born on November 21, 1997. When I was born, I was gifted naturally with a singing voice. My parents didn't know I could also naturally dance until I took my very first dance lesson. I started dance when I was three. At that time, I only wanted to take dance lessons because my friends were taking lessons. I was happy for the first few weeks but I wanted to take a break for a while.

I returned to dance lessons when I was five, and am glad I did! I've had many great experiences in dance! I've won two national dance championships in Las Vegas! Competitors were there from all over the country. My group took first place two years in a row in the tap category!! We received platinum, the highest award given. I also received platinum for my tap solo "Shine It On!" I really enjoyed performing this solo and was asked to perform it at a fundraiser for my theater group.

I also enjoyed participating in our school concerts. One year I performed in a tap trio and the next year I performed in a jazz trio. Dance has provided many wonderful experiences and opportunities in theater, too. I danced in *The Nutcracker* ballet. I danced the lead part of Maria in *The Sound of Music*, and I was a dancer in *Joseph and the Amazing Technicolor Dreamcoat*. During rehearsal for *Joseph*, the director saw me performing pirouettes and she put them in an important scene in the play and the audience clapped really hard!

It's fun when people see me dance; it brings a warm feeling to my heart. I love dance so much that I'm absolutely proud to have dance as a part of my life.

Ana Elizabeth Cherry, Grade 4
Country Montessori School, CA

Taking Care of Animals

I love to study, play with, and take care of animals. I spend time and take care of two animals which are two dogs.

The first animal I take care of is a dog named Sebastian. Sebastian is a Rottweiler. His old family that had him abused him. My mom's friend Cindy found him at a fire station. He had a hurt paw. Now every time you lay down next to him he puts his paw on you. He is so protective so you have to watch how you play around with people he might mistake that you are in trouble. Every time you feed him you have to put medicine in his food. Every time I come over I play tug-o-war. When I am trying to beat him he is laying down.

The second animal is a dog, her name is Missy. Missy is a black Lab. Missy's last family abused her too. She was found at a gas station. Lucky for her she had no injuries. Missy now has a family she also lives with Sebastian. Sebastian and Missy get along very well. They treat each other like they are related. Missy also has tons of toys. There is one toy that she loves. We call that her baby. Missy is so funny. One thing that is funny is if you put lotion on her face or anywhere on your body she will lick and lick.

Aysia Bolanos, Grade 6
Isbell Middle School, CA

Differences

Everyone is different. That is what I like about us humans. All people have different personalities and that is what makes them so special. They are great in their own ways. It doesn't matter what country you are from or what your skin color is. You are still worth the same as everyone else. Everyone should have the same rights as everyone else.

I don't know why women and African Americans had less power and did not have as many rights as white men. They are humans too and they were born on the same planet with the same ancestors as everyone else. They should have the same rights. People probably never stopped to think and say "If I was a slave and I had to work all day, would I like it?" No matter where you're from, you have to know why some people say that boys are better and stronger than girls. Women are special too. Women fought for freedom and they got it.

Many African Americans and women have done many important things that we will remember. Martin Luther King fought for freedom and Harriet Tubman helped many slaves escape using the Underground Railroad. People shouldn't judge people by skin color or what country they are from. Everyone should be equally important and have as many rights as everyone else. Let people be independent and have FREEDOM.

Everyone is important.

Nahyun Park, Grade 5
La Mariposa Montessori School, NM

The Day I Grew Up

A year ago my dad's heart rate went up. Since his heart has been bad since birth and its beat was uneven, everyone was scared. Laying down a few basic rules, Mom rushed my dad to the hospital. I glanced at the clock, 8:30, my brother's bedtime. I read to Brett, my 6-year old brother, his story, trying to calm him down. Then I gave Brandon (my 8-year old brother) a book. By 9:00 I had them in bed and was down in the kitchen. I had just got a call from my mom telling me my aunt was coming. You have no idea how relieved I was that she was coming! When she showed up it was 9:30, my bedtime, so I headed upstairs and turned off the lights and turned on my radio. I listened until 10:00, then fell asleep. In the middle of the night, 1:30 to be exact, I was awoken. I stared into the deep brown reassuring eyes of my mother and instantly knew everything was going to be fine. While I was calming down a six-year old and reassuring an eight-year old, I was thinking of the bravery I had to direct into their hearts and how I had to be responsible and most of all how I had to judge how I and my brothers could stay safe. This is the day I grew up.

Kirsten Couch, Grade 6
Argyle Middle School, TX

Having Good Friends

I have lots of good friends. They share lots of things with me. Friends are an important part of your life. They keep you company. They help you with homework. Friends are your future. You shouldn't be left alone. Everybody should be in the group. I like my life because I have so many cool, wonderful friends. They always care about me when I fall down. They say are you okay and they invite me to their houses to play, eat, and watch television.

I always check my mail. If my friend mailed me then, I mail them back. You should care about them. Try not to get in an fight or blame it on them for no reason. Don't bully them. You should be fair with them. Don't steal anything. Only borrow the things. Be honest too. I even tell them very cool websites to go on. Any ways my friends are the best!

Sanjam Gill, Grade 6

My Favorite Place

Today I will tell you about my favorite place. It's at my Nana's house. She has a special room for me. It has my computer and TV for my video games. I have mats on the floor. I have this thing in there that I can climb on. It is always fun. There are two boys who live down the street. One boy is eleven and one boy is eight. They always come over and play with me. One time I was on my computer to find something new for the clubhouse. I found some light up shelves that I could hang some stuff up on the wall. I went outside because my friends were skateboarding. I am the best on my street. We ride out to the golf course. We ride on the golf cart sidewalk. We came back to my house and my shelves were in. We put them up on the wall and started hanging stuff up on them. It was so cool how they light up like that. So my Nana's house is my favorite place to go. I love her so much!

Dylan McCoy, Grade 4
Winona Elementary School, TX

Never Give Up

My grandpa was a nice, loving, and a kind man, but he went under surgery for parkinsons. After his surgery, he went out expecting to hit the golf ball three-hundred yards, but he couldn't and lost his swing. One day he asked us to play golf at Woodbridge Country Club, and we said yes. I couldn't hit the ball. I told him, "I want to give up." He said, "Never give up." I said, "What does that mean?" He said, "Did Tiger Woods give up after he lost the PGA tour?" And I said, "No." He said, "You are probably having an off day, or you aren't thinking positive." I started thinking positive, then I got a hole in one. After, he said, "Were you thinking positive?" I said, "Yes." And he said, "I have never gotten a hole in one in my life." The next day my dad and I went to Pebble Beach golf course, and he was having a rough day. He didn't hit the ball well, and I said, "You are not thinking positive." Then he shot a thirty-nine. I said, "Were you thinking positive?" And he said, "Yes."

Everett Vernon, Grade 6

The Wii

I wanted one gift for my birthday, the Wii video game system. It was really hard to find one at the local stores, so we expanded our search to Albuquerque. We couldn't find one for two weeks. I finally found one. I couldn't wait until my birthday, so I convinced my parents to let me open it a month early.

When I opened the Wii box, I was surprised at how small it is. It measures 1 3/4" wide and 7" tall and is the smallest game system that hooks up to a television. The Wii's most unique feature is the motion sensor. The motion sensor detects the accelerator in the Wii wireless controller. This technology links your movement with your character's movement.

The most fun part about the Wii is its interactive capability. Unlike other video game systems, the Wii lets you compete with your physical abilities, not just your fingers. The Wii gives you an opportunity to get off the sofa and work out. For example, the *Transformer* game, if you get close to the enemy you swing your arms to slash like in real-life sword fighting. Another example is in Wii sports boxing where you punch in real life, and your character punches in the game.

The Wii system is probably one of the best gaming systems ever made. It is the most popular system because it is affordable, it is very fun, and it plays other Nintendo system games. I can spend hours playing one game on the Wii.

Nate Odegard, Grade 5
La Mariposa Montessori School, NM

Hey, Batter Batter

"Hey, batter batter," is what I hear my teammates yelling in the outfield as I get ready to pitch the ball. Standing in the pitcher's circle, my hands are sweating as I am about to pitch. "Blue, what's the count," yells my coach. "Full count," shouts the umpire.

All of the fans, players, and coaches eyes are on me. I start getting nervous with everyone's eyes on me, but I keep focusing on the strike zone. Bam, the ball goes into the catcher's mitt. "STRIKE!" yells the umpire. I am so glad because we won the game. Our team is yelling and jumping up and down.

We still have one more game to play, so I will have to do it all over again. I know I can do it! If we win this game we will come in first place. Standing in the pitcher's circle, I hear my teammates again yelling like a crying cat. Bam, I pitch a strike. "STRIKE ONE, STRIKE TWO, STRIKE THREE!" the umpire shouts. That was the third out. Now it is our turn to bat. My friend, Taylor, is up to bat and she its a double. Here comes the second batter and she hits a single. I am the third batter and I hit a home run! My hit brings in three runs and those three runs put us in the lead. We win the game and are the champions. As one can see my favorite place is on the softball field.

Madison Strunk, Grade 5
Oak Crest Intermediate School, TX

What If There Was an Emergency

My emergency plan will help me escape from any danger in the house. I will be safe if I follow the plan.

In my emergency supply kit there are matches, a watch, flashlights, compass, money, batteries, walkie talkies, clothes, water bottles and canned foods. These things will be in every room in a back pack. There's two walkie talkies in my mail just in case we can't get the supplies in the house.

The escape route that we planned was to go to the backyard jump the fence and then jump an other fence to go to the street or go out any windows or doors.

If there was an emergency and we're in different rooms we wouldn't go to the same places so we would meet at the park or at the stop sign because it's not that close and not that far.

These are all of the safety plans that me and my family use in case of an emergency.

Francine Gonzalez, Grade 5
Liberty Elementary School, CA

Folded Ears

Have you ever seen a cat and wondered what kind it was? Did it have folded ears? If so, you've probably just seen a Scottish Fold. The Scottish Fold is a common house cat. In 1961 the first Scottish Fold was found. It was found in a farm near Coupar Angus, Scotland. It was named Susie.

There are two types of Scottish Folds; straight ear and folded ear. At three or four weeks old, the kitten's ears either start to fold or stay straight.

Scottish Folds are medium cats that are well-rounded and have a well-padded body. It has a short, resilient coat and has large, round, broadly-spaced eyes that are full of sweetness. It also has well-rounded whisker pads and a short nose with a gentle curve profile. They are hardy cats that adore human companionship. They have tiny voices and are not extremely vocal. They also have a very sweet expression.

They adjust to their surroundings very well and don't mind a room full of noisy children and dogs. They are very undemanding cats, which only require a clean environment, proper nutrition, and generous doses of love. The CFA disapproves declawing them though.

A few interesting facts are that now Scottish Folds have ears that range from one fold to three folds! If both the parents have folded ears the offspring will probably have joint problems. Scottish Folds can be long or short-haired and are recommended for families with young children because of their tolerance.

Next time you see a cat with folded ears, you can say, "That looks like a Scottish Fold."

Nick Miller, Grade 6
Isaac Newton Christian Academy, IA

Deadwood Reservoir

Have you ever been camping? My favorite camping place is Deadwood Reservoir. I go with our best friends the Millers. We have to boat across the lake to our camp spot. It's not an official camp ground, it's just a place in the wilderness where a few people have camped before. We camp by a wonderful cove where we swim in the blue-green lake.

One of my favorite things to do is wake up early in the morning, hop into the boat and find a great fishing hole. Boat rides are really fun too. Put your life vest on and push on the gas. We're on our way. On a really hot day, one of my favorite things to do is jump into the lake and take a relaxing swim. At the end of the day while the sun is hiding, we go down by the shore of the lake and look for slimy toads. They're usually hopping all over the moist ground.

When the moon is glowing, we sit around the toasty fire and share our favorite memories. Bedtime is one of my all-time favorite parts. Listening to the trees whistle in my ears is like a lullaby. When I get up I smell the refreshing aroma of biscuits and gravy roasting in the Dutch oven. Packing up is the worst part of all, but at least we'll be back next year. Those are some of my fondest memories of my trips to Deadwood Reservoir.

Claire Luger, Grade 6
Thomas Jefferson Charter School, ID

Get to Know Me!

My name is Libby Schnulo, I'm in Ms. Scott's fifth grade class at Wyandot Run Elementary. I've lived in Powell all my life.

I was born on October 6, 1996, at St. Anne's hospital at 6:00 p.m. I came home to a new house that my family built. I have an older brother named Alex. He is fifteen and in 10th grade at Liberty High School. I also have a thirteen year old sister named Katy and she is in 8th grade at Liberty Middle School. My mom is an interior designer and my dad an optometrist.

I love to be creative. A funny story about me is when I was a baby my brother brought home his school supplies and I crawled into his room, painted his floor, cut my hair and glued it to his carpet. When my mom finally found me, I was a mess. It took my parents weeks to get everything off the carpet!

I started playing sports when I was four years old. Some of the sports I have played or participated in are soccer, gymnastics, basketball and softball.

I LOVE to travel! I've been to twenty two different states and three different countries. Some of the places I've been are Washington D.C., the Bahamas, Canada and Mexico. When I went to the Bahamas with my family we went on a cruise ship.

This is just some of what I've done in the past years of my life.

Libby Schnulo, Grade 5
Wyandot Run Elementary School, OH

A Horrid House Fire

I am thankful for many things. Some of the things I am thankful for are my family, my sister Alex, Rock Point Church, and the people at my dad's work.

I am thankful for my family because they all love me. We all fight sometimes, but I love my family the most. We are the Bean family.

I love Alex because she saved our lives. We were all asleep and Alex was sleeping with my mom and kept kicking her. My mom got up and saw that the camper was on fire. Luckily, we all got out quickly and safely.

I am thankful for Rock Point Church because they took us into their church and welcomed us. Many people there gave us money, food, and clothes.

I am thankful for all the people at my dad's work because after the fire, they helped us move out our belongings out of the burnt house. Many people also donated stuff to us.

I am thankful for all those people in my life. They have all helped me in a certain way. I love all the people in my life. I am lucky to be thankful for so many things.

Austin Bean, Grade 4
Gateway Pointe Elementary School, AZ

Floridian Imax Museum

A couple of years ago my mom took me to an Imax with a museum in Ft. Lauderdale. The museum had bone digging and they are really hard to get out of the sand. It has fake bones of course. I think it was a T-rex.

There was also a giant tree house. There were slides, tunnels, and a mini arcade for the older kids! The slides go rapidly onto a soft, fluffy cushion. Next, are the tunnel slides where everything is dark and scary. Not many little kids want to go in it, but I was only three and I went four times. Then comes the regular tunnels. These go up, down, left, and right, even one that spins! In case of an emergency, there are five tunnels that lead to the outside of the plastic tree. The spinning tunnels are my favorite! Now the most amazing part is the mini arcade. It has racing, dancing, shooting, and you can step on bugs.

There is a huge arcade, too. It has magnet games. They also have a space ride. The magnets have a magnetic blast that stick to the blocks to make them magnetic, too. You can build with these, and if you do it right it will beep. The space ride is like a roller coaster, but you go left and right. At the end you crash into a rock.

In the best part, which is the Imax, there were giant glasses, a giant screen, and a soft chair. The glasses are huge, but they work. I was surprised they could fit my mom. I love the chair it is like sitting on four hundred fifty feathers. The screen was gigantic. It was like four giants.

Faakhira Aqueela Diljohn, Grade 4
Burchett Elementary School, TX

A Fine Day to Get Stuck

It was a fine day on the Teselle farm. My dad hurried in for breakfast. He was out the door before I had a chance to say "Hi." I asked my mom, "Why is dad leaving in such a hurry?"

She answered "He is going to fix a fence."

Later on that day my dad rushed in frantically. He shouted my name, "Nick!"

I ran over to the stairs, and he yelled, "I got stuck."

I knew what that meant, so I put my shoes on and ran out the door. It was a little nerve racking because when my dad gets stuck, he is really stuck.

We drove the ATV to the shop and stopped. As we entered the room, it sat in front of me. It was big, blue, and black. A TS130A tractor. This was the first time I was going to be allowed to drive it.

My dad and I climbed in the cab, started the motor and drove out of the shed. As we reached the field, I saw the stuck tractor. It was deep under the mud.

We drove in front of the stuck tractor so my dad could hook some chains to the front of it. We both got on our tractors, then I put my tractor in gear and pulled him out. My dad unhooked the chains. We drove back to the shop and went home for a nice long nap.

Nick TeSelle, Grade 6
Monforton School, MT

Veterinarian

Becoming a veterinarian has been a dream in my life. Education has played a big role in my life. It will help with my job. In my years of getting older, school will be more and more important in life, but it is also important now. At the right time I will need to go to college to achieve my goal in life. UC Davis medical school is where my dream college is. While in school I hope to get A.P. classes in high school. Needing to succeed is important and hopefully this time of academic achievement will help me with my job. In my time of getting older I want to change medical history. Vets are very important to me so that they can take care of our pets. We should know how to take care of our pets.

In my later years my goal is to make medical history and help the world. The president may even award me with the Nobel Peace prize. Also my greatest hopeful achievement is to make animals happy. This is why I want to be a vet. With being a boy scout and getting my veterinarian merit badge should also help with my dream job. Becoming an Eagle Scout will look good on my résumé for my job in life. This will teach me a lot for a vet. My chances of becoming a veterinarian are very good. Veterinarians have changed the world.

Ben Turner, Grade 6
Linfield Christian School, CA

My Key Chains

My key chains are like mini souvenirs. When my friends ask who got them for me, then I tell them how unique it is. I enjoy collecting them.

Each key chain has its own story. When I first see them, they will either remind me of something or someone, so I collect them to remember later. If somebody in my family goes somewhere, I ask them to get me a key chain. Then, I have an idea of where they went and what they saw.

So far, my collection is full of delight. It's a great feeling because I can look and touch them. Kids collect different things, like cards, dolls, and sometimes stuffed animals. We all like different things, and I'm proud of my key chain collection. It's very unique to me.

Skyla Alderman, Grade 5
Westview Elementary School, OH

Bros

My brothers are the most important people in my life. They love me a lot and I love them. They are there for me when I need help. Many people think that your mom and dad should be the most important people in your life, but I don't think so. My bros are the funniest and the weirdest people I have ever known. When we go to the beach they try to knock each other off their boards usually Josh wins, but sometimes Jeremiah does.

We would play beach football and whenever someone gets tackled Josh yells "dog pile!" It is a lot of fun. When I got my surf board Jeremiah tried to stand up on his boogey board and jump onto my board SPLASH! We both plunged into the water! When we're done playing in the water we sit around the campfire and sing songs, play games, and make s'mores. My brothers have helped me with so much it is hard to pay them back. My twin brother is more then just my brother; he's my best friend. Jeremiah and Josh will always be there for me no matter what happens, they will always be there for me.

Jacob Bailey, Grade 6
Linfield Christian School, CA

The Brat Sister

As you might already know by the title, I have a brat sister. Most people think not. She is also the most meanest three year old sister I've ever had, and I hope I never have another one. I have listed a few things she has done in the past year over and over again. She has bit me on the head, tripped me to the ground, slapped me in the face, kicked me on the leg, pinched me on the arm, and most of these things really hurt. If you were me, then you better hide from your sister before she gets to you. So that means if you have a brat sister like me, then watch out for all the mischievous things that could happen. So, keep an eye out because you never know what will happen to you next. And if your mom is having a baby boy or girl, be ready!

Joshua Ian Garcia, Grade 4
Burchett Elementary School, TX

Door of Faith

Door of Faith is important to me because I get to make many kids happy.

Door of Faith is an orphanage in Mexico about five miles from the beach. At Door of Faith there are many orphans. None of the kids have a mom or dad. At the orphanage, there is a big playground and many rooms with bunk beds. At the orphanage there is a school for all of the kids. All of the walls at Door of Faith are very colorful, and all the older kids play soccer. All of the younger kids want you to push them on the swings.

At Door of Faith there's a boy named Joel. Joel's four years old, and is my favorite boy at Door of Faith. Joel has three brothers at Door of Faith. One of his brothers is named Raul. Raul is my sister's favorite kid because the first time she went he ran up to her and wanted to play with her.

One time when we visited we took all of the boys to a soccer field. At the soccer field we played a game and they won 13 to 3. Another time I went, we took some kids to the beach. Whenever I go to Door of Faith I never want to leave because the kids will start crying and be upset. I love the kids at Door of Faith because they help me think about my life and be grateful for what I have.

Curtis Warner, Grade 6
Linfield Christian School, CA

Amber Eyes in the Jungle

Tigers are my favorite animals. I would like to tell you some interesting facts about them:

A tigress will care for her cubs until they're 18 months old. When they're 6 months old she will teach them how to hunt.

Back in Asian history a story was told about the tiger being the Spirit of the Jungle. People would worship the tiger. Every day people would put out meat for the tiger to eat. If you forgot you would have to feed twice as much the next day. If you forgot too many times, then the tiger was said to take your spirit away.

A male tiger will let tiger cubs eat first since they don't raise them. Male tigers will encourage the cubs to eat. One tiger was seen waiting for 10 hours for the tigress and the cubs to finish their share.

Tigers love to swim to cool them off. Tigers also like to live and hunt in ruins.

The tiger is endangered. The Javan Tiger became extinct in 1976. One reason is because princes were told to kill a tiger before age 12. Also it used to be considered a "sport."

Many people think tigers will kill people. Tigers only kill people it they're too weak, sick, hurt, old, or threatened. Now you know more about the tiger.

Quincee Kingston, Grade 6
Thomas Jefferson Charter School, ID

Stop Animal Testing

I think product testing on animals should stop. Tons of animals a year are in very great pain, some are even dying because they are being tested on. They are putting products everywhere on the animals' eyes, mouths, stomachs and the rest of their bodies just to make sure it's safe for people.

I think animal testing should stop because a lot of animals die because products infect their bodies. Almost all animals who have products tested on their bodies die. Some of the animals they test on are bunnies, mice, rats, guinea pigs, hamsters, and gerbils.

And so, in the end, I really think product testing should stop because it kills millions of animals. There are ways to make sure products are safe without animal testing. Products that do not use animal testing have the cruelty free symbol on them. You can help by looking for the cruelty free symbol on products and buying only products that do not use animal testing. If you want to help save animals you can do this.

Rachel Kirkpatrick, Grade 4
Lincoln Elementary School, WA

Witness of Global Warming

Global Warming is harming our one and only world. Global warming is an increase in the average temperature of the Earth's surface. The temperature has increased 0.5-1.5 since the late 1800's. Coal, oil, and natural gases are called fossil fuel. These are not good for the air. The heat of the ozone layer is melting. The ozone layer keeps oxygen in the Earth. I witnessed global warming at an aquarium in New York. The aquarium had bright colors everywhere. One of the activities was going on a boat ride to the bay. On the bay I saw a Frito's chip bag, candy wrappers, and other trash. There used to be pollution everywhere, but volunteers come and picked up trash every day. I hope that in the future, the bay will be clean and more beautiful. Other ways you can harm the Earth is using gas in vehicles, electric power plants, and using industrial factories. Changes in the temperature can effect rise in sea level, increased intensity of extreme weather, and changes to the amount and pattern of precipitation each year. Now you know why global warming is harming our one and only world.

Lexi Ehrenfreund, Grade 5
Desert Canyon Elementary School, AZ

Being a Competitive Athlete

I believe in being a competitive athlete, because if you don't do your best, you won't succeed. I say it's only 10% experience and 90% heart. If you put your mind to it, you can do anything.

Never give up, that's what I say, because if you quit, you know you're out. Keep trying. Who knows; you might win!

Being a competitive athlete is important, so you choose. Do you want to be the best you can be, or just give up? Go for it!

Cole Bachtel, Grade 5
Westview Elementary School, OH

New Year's Eve

Ding, Ding, Ding. The gigantic grandfather clock strikes at 12:00 midnight. All the children dance in joy and glee. Everyone is screaming and waiting for the very moment.

Boom! Bam! Crash! The fireworks are shooting up into the sky. For a slight moment, the anticipation grows even more still. Then the amazement begins. The fireworks cracked open and multicoloured fireworks blast out. The children are amazed and start applauding with joy and glee. Crackle by crackle, sparkle by sparkle. The fireworks slowly die out, which means New Year's Eve has passed by. The children still gaze at the dark black sky as if the joy is still in their hearts and as if the fireworks had never started.

Magically as if a magical fairy sprinkles fairy dust all around our cruel, but happy world. Lights turn on throughout our world and like a routine it's always January the first, beginning of a new year.

The fathers of the children slowly walk by to take away their amazed and shocked children. Grandpas, grandmas, mothers and fathers still staring at the clear, dark sky. They too are amazed and shocked as their children.

Everyone walks thoughtlessly back to their homes while parents carry their children through the doors and tuck them into their bedrooms.

They sigh in sadness as they would have to wait another year, anxious and waiting until New Year's Eve comes again. However, in everyone's dreams tonight the magic shall shine again.

Sandy Feng, Grade 6
Northwood Public School, ON

Things I Enjoy Doing

I love to do lots of things. My favorite thing to do is to play the drums. I love the sound of the drums! I teach my friends how to play basic beats on them.

My second favorite thing to do is street surf. I bet you that you don't know what street surfing is. Well, you ride on a Wave. It's not water; it's a type of skateboard with two wheels. People think that it is hard, but when you learn it, it is so easy and so exciting.

After that, I like to play with my best friend, Copper, my brother, and my sister. I love to play with my best friend in the whole wide world when I need to stay inside the house. Copper is so much fun and so cool. He likes to wrestle. Now, sometimes my brother (who is so hilarious) doesn't want to play. So, I play with my sister. She is really entertaining! Sometimes my sister gets a bit too rough. After that, I go and get a board game out and play with my family. It is so amusing! I love my family so much.

Now, like everyone else, I get to go to school. I have the coolest teacher, Mr. Sasaki. He makes everything fun. He is also funny. Once you're in his class, you can't forget about him.

These are just a few of the things I enjoy doing every day.

Chance Coon, Grade 6
Thomas Jefferson Charter School, ID

Scuba Diving

I love scuba diving. It lets you experience the underwater world. Scuba diving lets you breathe underwater and enjoy all underwater life. You can discover many unknown things.

I think that scuba diving is very fun. Scuba diving is very dangerous if you don't know how to do it. Everyone should do scuba diving.

When you go scuba diving you can see many different kinds of things. You can see octopi, sea stars, garibaldi and so much more. You can explore that underwater shipwrecks and caves. You can explore ice cold waters and tropical oceans.

Scuba diving is awesome. You can swim and make little water bubbles, you can make water rings as well. Doing practice in the pool is the most fun, because you can do flips in the water. You can do many things underwater.

Scuba diving is amazing. It is a mass of swirling bubbles as you breathe through your regulator. Your mask is a window to underwater life. Your fins are an accelerator that power you through the water. Your B.C is like your life force in which you can rise to the heavens or sink to the bottom of the ocean.

Nick Umphrey, Grade 6
La Mariposa Montessori School, NM

My Family

This is my family. I have 4 people in my family. I have 2 pets. They are both dogs. One is a Black Lab, her name is Shadow. My other dog is a Bichon Frise, her name is Lilly. I have a sister, her name is Hannah, and my parents' names are Amy and Chad.

My parents are awesome! My dad is a Belvedere Fire Fighter. My dad has an awesome job! My mom works at the Division of Specialized Care for Children, (DSCC) and my mom is a nurse. At the DSCC she helps kids that are really sick. I go to Jean McNair School in Winnebago, IL. I love to read. My sister Hannah is 8 years old, I'm 10 years old. Hannah goes to Simon Elementary in Winnebago, IL. My favorite subject is P.E. and math! I play guitar and a trumpet. In 5th grade you do band or chorus. I like band a lot better because I stink at singing. Ha! Ha!

My family moved to Winnebago 1 year ago. It was hard being a new kid. My whole family likes the Chicago Cubs. My mom likes the Chicago Bears, but my sister, me, and my dad like the Minnesota Vikings! Go Vikings. My family's house is 2 stories, it is huge. I love to play video games and sports. I have a PSP and a PS2. I play on a basketball, baseball, and football team. My favorite sport is football.

I'm happy my family moved to Winnebago. I think my family rocks!!!

Zach Cunningham, Grade 5
Jean McNair Elementary School, IL

What's Happening to Our Ocean

Have you ever heard of the expression, "There are plenty of fish in the sea?" Now that isn't exactly true.

Some methods of catching fish need improvement. Over the years fishermen have increased their catch by 400%. The 25% they can't use are thrown back but usually die. Sometimes fisheries don't have permits to catch a certain type of fish; when a fish population depletes, the fishermen move to a different species.

Problems arise because of the ways we catch and raise fish. Thanks to overfishing, the fish population has decreased. Because of the nets used, dolphins, whales, sea turtles, and seals can get caught and drown. Also, sea birds like albatrosses can get caught on baited hooks and drown. A good example is for every one ton of prawn or shrimp that are caught, there are three tons of other fish killed due to bycatch.

Some solutions are being introduced. In Australia and China they have banned fishing in some places with low populations. Fishermen have invented a device that lets sea turtles crawl out of nets. Fishing methods like longlining, hook-and-line, and trap fishing are habitat friendly.

Alternatives that we can use to help the ocean and ourselves are available. Eating farmed oysters, mussels, and clams don't harm people or the environment. Eating fish that are raised inland are healthier and environmentally friendly.

If we keep developing new alternatives and solutions, we can put a new meaning to, "There are plenty of fish in the sea."

Kathryn Anderson, Grade 6
Cheyenne-Eagle Butte Upper Elementary School, SD

Gettysburg

Last summer I went to Gettysburg, Pennsylvania. It was an experience to see all of the battle fields and the small town. We stayed at the Gettysburg Hotel. It was established in 1779. Across the street there is a building that Abraham Lincoln stayed in when he came to deliver the Gettysburg Address. On the second floor, third window from the left, there is still a faded area where Lincoln hung a banner flag under his window. This marks the room he stayed in.

Around the corner is a building where a cannonball is lodged between the bricks. It is now the Cannonball Ice Cream Parlor. All over the little town were gift shops with bullets, guns, uniforms, ammunition pouches, cannons, and cannonballs all from the Civil War.

We had a guide drive our car through the battlefields and tell us all about the war. They had a national cemetery with cannons lined all around it. My brother and I were taking pictures of the insides of the barrels and we found a cannonball inside one of the Ohio cannons.

We also saw where they think that Lincoln's speech was delivered, where the memorial stands, but our guide told us that the actual site was outside the premises.

Austin Lightle, Grade 5
Pike Christian Academy, OH

The Symbolic American Flag

The American flag means a lot to most Americans, including me. Every single detail on the American flag means something significant to the American history and to its people. It has thirteen equal, horizontal, red, and white stripes to symbolize the first thirteen colonial states that originally constituted the United States. Also, there are fifty small, white, five-pointed stars which represent the modern fifty states. These stars spread evenly over the upper, left, blue, rectangular corner. In addition, each color on the flag even has its own meanings. White stands for purity and innocence meaning the Americans are good people. Red shows for hardiness and valor to signify our founding fathers that fought and won the Independence War. Last of all, blue symbolizes vigilance and justice which translate to that all men are equal and should be treated equally.

Innocence, valor, and justice are the key ingredients to make this big melting pot of America, which I think is the best country in the world. Every time I see an American flag flying anywhere in the world, I feel very proud, and yet lucky to be an American.

Diamond Naga Siu, Grade 5

Deadly Storms

Cars flying, buildings collapsing, people dying. Those are only some of the things that come to mind when a hurricane roars in the direction of cities. It attacks without mercy or fear.

In various parts of the world they're acknowledged as twisters, in others, tropical storms. Whatever they're identified by, they're lethal. They're getting even more deadly. The reason is because of global warming.

Global warming is making our planet warmer each day. In the past, the climate was cooler than it is present day, especially in the past 10 years. In many cities, the temperature has broke previous records. In order to stop global warming, we must reduce, reuse, and recycle.

Hurricanes are attached to the clouds, and the winds can reach up to an average of 120 m/hr at the eye of the storm. The storm can reach up to 60-70 km/hr. The storm is also gray. It can change course at any time.

The difference between a hurricane and a tornado is that a hurricane forms on water and builds a tropical storm. A tornado starts on land and stays on land. Also, what a hurricane leaves behind, waves come in with extreme force and floods the area.

Next time someone tells you about a hurricane ask them do they know why they are getting more deadly? It's all because of global warming. People are not taking care of the Earth.

Karnvir Basra, Grade 6
Northwood Public School, ON

School!

SCHOOL! Summer was now over and school was back in. I was expecting for fifth grade to be hard, it isn't a walk in the park. Our newest subject, science, has also been hard while juggling math, reading, and social studies. I didn't like it, but I had to wake up from summer and start working.

The first day of school is always weird. It's almost as weird as dancing in front of people you don't know in your underpants! (Which is really awkward!) I was really nervous that day and didn't know what was going to happen. The first thing I did after unpacking was write the numbers I had in my books on some paper. Whew! A fresh and easy start. But as days grew, the work got even harder. Tests popped out of nowhere and more homework grew on. Studying the most and best I could every night was very essential. Although every test was going to be hard, I thought to myself, "This year is going to be hard! But I am going to pass! I am going to pass!" It was then clear that I was going to pass the fifth grade with my determination.

Nicholas Vallejo, Grade 5
Aloe Elementary School, TX

Catherine Bach

There are a lot of great people from South Dakota and one of them is Catherine Bach.

Catherine was born Catherine Bachman, in Ohio, March 1, 1954. She spent her high school years living with her father in Faith, South Dakota.

In 1976 she married David Shaw. In 1981 the two of them divorced. In August 1990 she married Peter Lopez. Sophia and Laura are their children.

After finishing high school and seeing her uncle, Tony Verdugoin, in a stage production, she flew to California to pursue an acting career she'd been dreaming about. Even with day jobs, she took dancing lessons, made auditions, and attained a few TV bits and movie roles. Her first screen appearance was, *The Midnight Man.* Her next role was Melody in the film *Thunderbolt and Lightfoot* in 1974. After *Dukes of Hazzard* she appeared in films such as *Canonball Run 2* and *Nutt House* and family channel series *African Skies* where she played Margo Dutton.

She is best known for playing Daisy Duke in *Dukes of Hazzard.* Unhappy with her wardrobe for Daisy Duke's character, she made short shorts from a pair of jeans. Short, cutoff denim shorts were named after Daisy Duke's character. On the show, *Dukes of Hazzard,* Catherine often wore cut off denim shorts. Over five million copies of Daisy Duke posters have been sold. She is a TV icon.

Catherine is really famous. She loves to act but she loves her family too.

Stephanie Longbrake, Grade 4
Cheyenne-Eagle Butte Upper Elementary School, SD

My Pet

Today there are so many things to write about, but today I'm only going to write one. I'm going to write about my pet dog named Max. He can be funny, bad, smart, and weird.

Max is my Golden Retriever. He is as funny as a clown! This is how to make him crash into walls. First, you throw a ball. Second, he runs after it. Third, he slides across the tile. Finally, he crashes into doors and walls!

Max might be cute, but he can also be a trouble maker! Sometimes he tears up the toilet paper. He also loves to chew on shoes and flip flops etc. One time he shredded my favorite Scooby-Doo Book. I got really angry when he did. So whatever you do, don't leave anything out!

Golden Retrievers are really smart dogs. Max happens to be really smart. Every time we eat, he literally goes to the bowl and eats! When he makes a mess he cleans it up all by himself! Is he a smart dog or what?

Max is weird because if he sees a cricket he tries to eat it! When we go swimming he gets thirsty and he drinks the pool water.

Like I said, so many things to write, but I can only write one! Max will always be funny, bad, smart, and weird!

Cheyenne Loew, Grade 4
Gateway Pointe Elementary School, AZ

My Team and I: Playing Basketball

Have you ever thought of playing a sport, but feared it would be too hard for you? That's what happened to me. When I was in third grade, I told my mom that there were basketball sign-ups.

She said, "You should sign up."

I answered, "I don't know how to play."

She replied, "You will learn. That's why you have a coach."

All my friends also started to encourage me, so I signed up. We had a coach named Mr. Ron, and he was really nice.

Nine players (plus myself) included Rheanna, Christian, Sabrina, Janessa, Nicole, and two players from the second grade named Rony and Montana. Once we started our practices, I loved it!

We practiced our passes, dibbling, shooting, and communication with the rest of the team. Before our first game, the coach handed out our uniforms. They were red, black, and yellow. My number was twenty-three. Luckily for me, I got my favorite number!

Our first fame was in the CYO gym versus St. Anne's. We were very nervous because it was our first game, and we had butterflies in our stomachs. We had all heard that St. Anne's was a very good team, but that didn't stop us from playing our best. We had started to play, everyone began cheering for us! And that gave us encouragement.

We all worked together as a team to win. I'll never forget my first basketball team at Corpus Christi School, here in San Francisco!

Alice Saidawi, Grade 6
Corpus Christi School, CA

A Woman Making History

In life, you can achieve your goals easier if you have a person you can look up to, your inspiration. Amelia Earhart had the abilities to become my inspiration. Amelia stood as one of the very first female pilots, who flew across the Atlantic Ocean alone and took part in the women's group the Ninety-Nine.

Her achievements in aviation have made her an inspiration to all women today. She inspired me when she improved women's status and stood up to the people who were against her. To help improve women's status, she helped in making the Ninety-Nine Association, which taught the very first women pilots how to fly. Helping this association made her a great inspiration to women.

Since Amelia worked hard, she was able to be successful and famous. People may think of her as an ordinary woman pilot, but to me she is my inspiration. Since I would like to become a pediatrician when I grow up, my parents tell me that perseverance and working hard are two ways that will make me successful. The way she worked hard to achieve her goals, teaches me how significant it is to believe in yourself and work hard. Without Amelia, I would have never understood why it is important to work hard.

Karishma Harry, Grade 6
Challenger School – Ardenwood, CA

A Right Inspiration

My inspiration is my beautiful, amusing, and wonderful mother. She has inspired me to study hard and be a wonderful person. The main points that I love about my mother is that she is intelligent and admirable. Today, my mother is my role model and my inspiration.

In my eyes, I have a superb feeling about my mother's intelligence. My mother was one out of two people in her high school eligible to go to college. She was one who had very high grades and studied every day. For science I had a question about the pancreas, I had no idea how to solve it. I asked my mom and she found a book that had all the information I needed because she used to work in medical fields.

A person who is marvelous is a wonderful inspiration. If we divided people into groups, my mother would be in the group who are outstanding. My mother went out to eat and ordered some spaghetti for lunch; however she did not eat it. Instead she saved it for me due to a trip to the dentist. I got a molar taken out and it was hard for me to chew. Since spaghetti is easy to chew she planned ahead and saved it for my dinner. One day my mom was extremely busy, she still came to pick me up for soccer practice. Do you think someone who is pleasant is the right inspiration?

Jessica Yang, Grade 6
Challenger School – Ardenwood, CA

The One And Only Torey!

The meaning of my name is victory, Goddess, and queen. It is Latin. My name reminds me of the color hot pink because it is bright, happy, and that is my favorite color. 21 is my favorite number and when I say my name it always pops up in my head. My name to me feels soft but rough because I can be nice and caring but tough and strong. I got my name, Torey, from my uncle, who's name is Tor. He is tall, smart, funny, and knows how to have fun. So far everyone likes my name and thinks it is pretty.

I know one person who has the same name as me but she is totally different. She is a big tomboy and I am a girly-girl. My name sounds like the ocean because it is peaceful and quiet. It reminds me of a roller coaster because they are fun and I love them. If I could change my name I would change it to Ashley because a lot of people say that I look like one and I think that name is pretty.

Torey Kay, Grade 6
North Oaks Middle School, TX

Who I Admire

I admire my uncle Angel because he is good at skateboarding. He is fast and good at the moves of skateboarding. He does crazy moves on the skateboard. He can beat people in skating and that's why I admire when he skates.

I also admire my uncle Angel because he is kind to people. He helps me with my homework sometimes. He lets me play video games. For an example, he also lets me play with his skateboard.

I also admire my uncle Angel because he is fun and cool. He sometimes just plays around. He can play around this month with me sometimes. He lets me be cool like him.

In conclusion, I think he is the best uncle I ever had. He treats me better than my other uncle. Who do you admire?

Kevin Lopez, Grade 5
Camellia Avenue Elementary School, CA

My Dog, My Hero

My dog is very important to me.

My dog brightens me up after a long hard day at school. I can just drop all my stuff and run to her! She is my hero! She is like a flag waving in the wind. When I am with her I feel like anything can happen. I trust her and I believe she trusts me. No matter what happens she will always be with me.

I believe that everyone should have a strong relationship with his or her pet. There is a lot more to having a pet than just feeding and making your pet a habitat. I believe everyone should treat his or her pet like part of the family.

My dog is a very big part of my family. She holds our family together. Without her, life wouldn't be as great. I love my dog very much and I always will. She will never leave my heart. My dog is very important to me.

Natalie Snyder, Grade 4
Addison Elementary School, CA

Imagination

Imagination is a great tool to have in everyday life. It helps me cheer myself up when I am feeling down and keeps me moving forward. Sometimes, when my mind is a jumble of thoughts and feeling, I just relax and think of another place that I could be. One of my favorite places to go to in my mind is somewhere remote and beautiful. I usually find myself on a mountain, by a stream, or by a river. Imagination definitely helps me to be more calm and easygoing. It also helps me make my friends feel better if they are having a rough day too. Imagination helps me when I write stories. Sometimes, when I have lots of ideas, I can hardly get them out onto the piece of paper because I am so excited. It is because of imagination that my friends say my stories are expressive and fun to read. They also say that my stories have great endings and are very descriptive. I sometimes find it difficult to stop writing or drawing once I get started. It is so hard that once in a while, my parents have to force me to stop writing or drawing in order to get some things done around the house. Imagination has definitely made a dramatic change in how I think, so thank you imagination.

Becca Smith, Grade 6
Tri-West Middle School, IN

I Think Bunnies Are So Cute!

I got a brown and white bunny named Cocoa one day with my sister. I've had that bunny for about 3 months now. My sister and I have learned much about our family rabbit. When taking care of our rabbit, there comes much responsibility. You have to feed a rabbit the correct food. Make sure you give a rabbit proper attention and love. Also, make sure the rabbit's cage is clean. Otherwise, it'll become messy and stinky.

Feeding a rabbit is a huge responsibility. You have to make sure you feed a rabbit the right food. Do not feed a rabbit pizza or candy taffy. You should feed a rabbit vegetables or special rabbit food at Wal-Mart. If you feed a rabbit other food it may get sick. My rabbit really enjoys eating lettuce.

Another responsibility is giving a rabbit much love and attention. I have a collar and leash for our rabbit. In time we'll build an outside playpen for it. We also like to have it run freely in our room for a short time. My rabbit likes to have her ears rubbed. You want to give a rabbit attention. I do not believe you want a mean, untamed rabbit. They need to know that you love them. If you do not love a rabbit he or she will not love you back.

Lastly, it's very important to clean a rabbit's cage on a regular basis. If you don't there'll be a stinky mess everywhere. That is why you must clean a rabbit's cage.

Wow, taking care of a rabbit's a big responsibility! Again, remember the correct food, plenty of attention, and a clean cage. This may seem like a lot of work, but I feel it's worth it. I love our bunny and it makes me happy!

Tatianna L. Brock, Grade 5
St Patrick's Catholic School, WA

Battle of the Alamo

In 1836, a battle arose where about 185 Texians fought 1,500 Mexican troops in San Antonio, Texas. This battle was called the Battle of the Alamo. The Alamo was a building armed with cannons and a hospital for the wounded during the battle.

On February 3, 1836, Lt. Col. William Barret Travis arrived at the Alamo with a handful of Texian troops. Soon, David Crockett and James Bowie were put in charge of our troops. These troops would soon fight in battle.

After a party, the Texians went back to the Alamo and got some rest and sleep. But little did they know that Mexican General Santa Anna sent out enemy troops to bombard the Alamo! Once the Texians realized what was going on, everybody got to their posts and started the battle. But once the battle started, Lt. Col. William Barret Travis had left the world forever (killed). A lot of important people died in battle, including James Bowie and David Crockett.

Once the battle was over, almost all the Texians died, and Mexico won. The Texians that survived were executed, and women and children were spared. What a terrible battle it was.

Texas had revenge and victory in another battle. This battle was called the Battle of San Jacinto. In this battle, Sam Houston led the Texas heroes, and Santa Anna led the Mexicans. We won easily. Santa Anna and his army surrendered. At some point in battle, Santa Anna disappeared. Afterward, Santa Anna's army evacuated Texas.

Justin Christoph, Grade 4
Burchett Elementary School, TX

Global Warming

What is global warming? Global warming is where pollution eats up the ozone layer of the Earth. Pollution is made up of bad gases (acid). The whole reason global warming is happening is because the harmful gases from cars have acid in the gases.

The icebergs in Antarctica are melting, because of the global warming. While the icebergs are melting, the polar bears and penguins are becoming extinct! These animals usually rest, play, and catch fish. But since the icebergs are melting, they can't do that anymore.

Well, if you don't like animals, here is another bad thing that is happening. The pollution from cars is rising up and eating away the ozone layer. Since this is happening, the layer over warmer places is even warmer than usual, and still rising.

So if you are an animal or Earth lover (or both), don't use cars so much. Please make the world a better place, for everyone's sake!

Mark Matas, Grade 5
Desert Canyon Elementary School, AZ

Sheila, My Grandmother

Grandma Sheila was born on November 17, 1942 in New York City, New York. She grew up with her parents in Miami Beach, Florida, which she moved to in the late 1940s.

Grandma Sheila went to high school at Miami Beach High School. For college she attended the University of Florida in Tallahassee and Moorhead State University in Minnesota.

My grandmother was very adventurous. She moved multiple times. Great Falls, Livingston, Big Timber, Laurel, and Billings are the places where she lived.

Grandma Sheila had many jobs. Some of her jobs include working for the Social Security Administration as a representative for 15 years. She is well known for her secretary skills in Billings because of her many years in working as a Legal Secretary.

Sheila Ann Tropp married Richard Sanders in 1962. Her name was changed to Sheila Ann Sanders. They were married for 12 years and then divorced.

On February 8, 1997, Sheila had a sudden asthma attack and died. It was a very sudden death. Many were sad and depressed. Grandma Sheila was 54 years, 2 months, and 21 days old when she died.

Grandma Sheila was buried in the Beth Aaron Cemetery in Billings. The service was held at the Beth Aaron Synagogue of Yellowstone, Montana. Her body is dead, but her soul will always live with us.

McKenna Gessner, Grade 5
The Shlenker School, TX

All About Koalas

Koalas are very complex animals. Most people call koalas koala bears, but they're just bear-like. Koalas are actually marsupials. Most koalas weight 20 pounds and have ash gray fur with some brown spots. When koalas are born, they are called joeys and weight about 0.5 grams. Breeding season is roughly from September through March. They are one of the only animals that can survive on eucalyptus leaves also known as gum leaves. Some animals are not very fascinating but I would say that koalas are very fascinating herbivores.

Just like the way humans communicate, it is also important for koalas to communicate. When males are signifying its social and physical position it uses a deep grunting bellow. Females don't bellow as often as males but they do bellow. Mothers and babies use a soft clicking, squeaking sound to communicate. They also use gentle humming and murmuring sounds. As you can see, it's just as important for koalas to communicate as it is for humans.

Do you know how humans like to live in homes? Koalas like to live in homes too! Most koalas are found in Queensland, New South Wales, Victoria, and South Australia usually living in trees. Koalas live in societies just like humans. They live all by their self. How lonely! From all of this information, I think you could agree that koalas are pretty complex animals.

Samantha Farmer, Grade 5
Ray E Kilmer Elementary School, CO

One by One

Have you ever wondered who inspires you the most? Well, I am here today to say who I look up to every single day of my life. The person who guides me through hardships is and will always be Najma. Why her? Who is she? I will answer these questions which remain unanswered.

Najma, my inspiration, is a miracle woman who has done many great things to help the Fremont and Oregon soccer community. First, she threw many exciting camps for teams. She taught coaches how to teach in a better way. Second, Najma taught kids a better understanding of the sport, soccer. She has taught to a large number of kids any age to gain skills. Najma inspired kids to do their best every time they set their foot on a field to play football, as they may call it. She strives for the best and led Oregon's soccer team to many victories. She taught kids to persevere and always have hope. Najma changes kids' lives one by one.

What are some of the many things she has done that are inspiring? She was an Olympic Development Player and received a scholarship in soccer and academics! She also remains the 22nd out of all the top women soccer players in the United States.

After meeting and training with her, I have done many great things. I achieved many of my goals as a soccer player. Najma, my role-model, will remain in my heart forever. She is the nicest friend!

Claudia Robinson, Grade 6

Friendship

There are four steps to have a great friendship with another person. Step one is how to be nice. Your friend will notice when you are nice if you treat them like you want to be treated. One other example is to call them names that are positive. That is the first step to friendship.

Moving on to number two, which is trust. If you trust someone you will tell many important details about your life. One other way to trust someone is to be kind and say joyful compliments. Trust is important in friendship.

Next, we have the third step, which is loyalty. A loyal friend is one who makes you happy when you are sad. Being loyal will help you in life to make friends. Loyalty holds friends together like glue from the beginning to the end. Loyal friends are everywhere to be found and you can be one of them.

Helpfulness is the final step. To be helpful you can assist a friend when he needs it the most. Then there is helpfulness by being a good sport to someone who you don't usually hang around with and saying, "Hey, I like your clothes." Or as simple as saying, "Hi, nice dress." Today is the day to be a fantastic friend.

Jennifer Bright, Grade 5
Covington Elementary School, NE

My Grandparents

I call my grandparents Patti and Thatha; they live in Madras, India. They live in a beautiful cottage by the Bay of Bengal. They visit me every year. When they visit me my grandma tells me stories about when she was young, when my mom was young and when I was a little baby. We like the same things such as beading, crafts, movies, Indian dresses, music and drawing portraits. My grandparents walk for at least an hour a day. My grandparents love to tell me stories about what's going on in India and about their travels.

When I go to different places near my house with my grandparents, I run and run and run all the way there and my grandparents try to run after me.

I play a lot of chess with my grandpa. He teaches me new strategies and I always win. My grandparents talk about when I was a little girl and I had my 6 year old birthday party. I talk to my grandparents about what 4th grade is like and how it's going. I also talk to them about what I'm going to do for my next birthday party. When school started, my grandpa walked with me to the bus stop every day to see me off.

My grandparents are fascinating subjects to write about. I love my grandparents. They are distinctive people. I look forward to seeing them whenever I can.

Aditi Krishnan, Grade 4
Indus Center for Academic Excellence, MI

Time

My time is what I need to stay alive. Much of my time on the weekdays is spent in school and sleeping. The other time is spent on sports and homework. I have the shortest amount of time for myself. Using that wisely is what I try to do. Most of my free time is spent on eating and playing with Legos. What I've been trying to do is read the Bible in the time I spend with playing toys. Now school takes up most of my day. School keeps my brain always working. My homework is either an assignment or studying for a test. Maybe even both, or if I'm lucky, none. Sleeping is my favorite hours of my day. It helps me relax and recharge. My sports occur after school. It's usually flag football and then I'm off to soccer practice.

The weekend is the best time of the week. Most of the time, my weekend is spent attending church, and having fun with my family. The other time is spent watching NASCAR and playing in soccer games. Going to church on Sunday is very important. I enjoy seeing my friends and learning about God. The second most important thing is playing board games, playing sports together, and going swimming with my family. Last but not least is watching NASCAR and playing in a soccer game. At the end of the week, I am always happy with what I did with my time.

Andrew Nagel, Grade 6
Linfield Christian School, CA

Relaxing Sensation

As I ran the bath water I was thinking of a relaxing sensation. That was to put bubbles and a fizz ball in my bath.

That was a good idea so I got started. I got the Skin So Soft bubbles and poured some of the creamy colored liquid in my bath water. It started to make bubbles and fizz. It's already looking relaxing. I looked through one of my drawers for the box that said Vanilla Ice cream flavored fizz balls. "I found them," I said aloud to myself. I took one ball out of the box and dropped it in the water. I got undressed and stepped into the water. It was a relaxing sensation. I bathed myself, laid my head on my bath pillow and soaked in the water until most of the bubbles were gone.

I unplugged the stopper out of the tub. I got my purple drying towel. I dried off, put on my pajamas, and brushed my teeth, and went to bed feeling squeaky clean.

Jalaina Douglas, Grade 5
Bang Elementary School, TX

Soccer

Soccer is one of my favorite sports. I have played soccer since I was 2 years old. To play soccer you have to be in shape and have a strong foot. Playing soccer is important to me because it is good exercise. It is a great sport and I think everyone should try playing soccer.

Being in shape is a major factor in soccer. You have to run on a field that is 108 yards long. Sometimes soccer players get out of shape because they don't exercise. Some people jog or ride a bike. Others go to the gym. That is why it is important to exercise.

Having a strong foot in soccer is excellent to get the ball high when you score a goal. Another reason to get the ball high is to pass so you can get the ball over the opponent's heads. I try to kick a ball 80-100 times a day.

Soccer is a very old sport. Scientists say it could have been played around 800 A.D.–500 B.C. Soccer is also the most played sport in the world. Soccer is my favorite sport.

Isaac Nelson, Grade 5
St Patrick's Catholic School, WA

Mount Vesuvius and Mount Cameroon

Most mountains are different in size and shape like Mount Vesuvius and Mount Cameroon. I wouldn't like to climb either of these because it would be a scary experience.

They are both active volcanoes and have no snow. They're probably over 8 thousand feet and they both have lava in them. They also have a rim around the top.

Mount Cameroon is in Guinea and near the Gulf of Guinea, but Mount Vesuvius is near the Roman cities of Pompeii and Herculaneum. On March 28, 1999 and May 28, 2000 Mount Cameron erupted and Mount Vesuvius, on the other hand, erupted in 79 AD.

I really like these mountains, and maybe someday I might climb one.

David Bair, Grade 5
Columbia County Christian School, OR

Inside Baseball Equipment

Have you ever wondered what's inside a baseball or maybe even a bat? And did you know there's illegal stuff that can be placed in a bat?

Did you know a baseball has compressed rubber in the middle shaped like a bouncy ball, and around it it has four windings of wool yarn? On the outside, its leather stitched with 108 red stitches. The middle is special because it helps the ball go farther. The insides been remade a lot, but the outside hasn't been changed at all. They fly farther than they used to because they are heavier. But they are still the same sphere size. A bat can be aluminum or wood, in the pros you can only use wood. There is illegal stuff you can put in your wooden bat like cork, foam, and other light materials. These are illegal because they make you hit farther. If you barely swing with these materials in your bat, you'll probably hit a hard grounder or hit it to the outfield.

Inside an aluminum bat there can be just metal or just aluminum. I guess hitting the baseball is 1/4 of bat, 1/4 of ball, 1/4 bat power, and 1/4 practice.

Kylin Washington, Grade 5
Oak Crest Intermediate School, TX

Hurricane Katrina

Hurricane Katrina was a devastating hurricane that took place on August 23, 2005, in the state of Louisiana. Many other states were also destroyed, and many lives were lost. The hurricane hit most of southern America.

The worst of the damage was in New Orleans. In New Orleans, the flood walls broke and the water flooded the city. The people tried to flee, but gas stations had run out of gas. People were unable to leave New Orleans before the flood walls broke.

On August 26, Hurricane Katrina strengthened to be a Category 3 storm in the Gulf of Mexico. President George W. Bush declared a state of emergency in Louisiana, Alabama, and Mississippi two days before Hurricane Katrina made landfall.

After Katrina passed, the recovery was chaotic. Many groups, including the Red Cross, tried to help, but the government said they had enough supplies, but it turned out that they didn't.

The highest winds of the hurricane were 175 mph. One thousand, eight hundred thirty six people died. It took 84 billion dollars to repair the damages. Many people who survived hurricane Katrina had to move to new houses, and had to move away from family and relatives, and lost many personal belongings.

Hurricane Katrina dissipated on August 31, 2005 but the sadness and repairing continued long after.

Molly Mingus, Grade 4
Norwoodville Elementary School, IA

George Henry Thomas, Civil War Hero

George Henry Thomas was an important person in the Civil War.

George was born in the South but fought for the North. He was born on a family farm in Virginia. When he was young, he gave Bible reading lessons to slaves.

George graduated at the U.S. Military Academy at West Point in 1840. He was active in the Civil War. He commanded independent troops in Eastern Kentucky. He won the first major Union victory of the war at Mill Springs. He served under Don Carlos Buell. When Buell was fired they offered George the chief command but he refused. At Nashville, in 1864, he inflicted the worst defeat sustained on either side during the war.

After the war he was a military governor of Kentucky and four other states.

Not a lot of people know about George Henry Thomas, but he was an important person in the Civil War.

Eric Traversie, Grade 5
Cheyenne-Eagle Butte Upper Elementary School, SD

Good Deeds

On September 11, 2001 many police and firemen died to save many people's lives. Now it is called "Good Deed Day." Some people do good deeds on that day, some people do not care about "Good Deed Day."

I think everybody needs to do a good deed on that day because if you are nice to other people, other people will be nice to you. You may also become a better person.

So to remember the police and firemen, we should all do a good deed on that day.

Khari Amos, Grade 5
Snake River Montessori School, ID

Pilots, Gymnastics, Wow!

Planes! Pilots! This is what I want to be in the future. When I am older, I want to be a commercial pilot. When I was younger, I would always want to fly in planes. Now, I'm studying in books about planes and knowing how planes take off, land, and how they fly. I also have been going on commercial planes. When I am older I want to fly, Delta Air, or maybe even fly United Air. When I grow up, I want to go to University of Minnesota and become a pilot from there. Maybe if I am lucky I can fly celebrities to their destination.

Also, when I am older, I might own my mom's gymnastics business. Since I will only have to fly three times a month, I will come here and have a part time membership. My mom's place is called Scega Gymnastics. It's awesome! If I stick with gymnastics it soon could stay #1 in the country. I know how to teach gymnastics because I compete. Two jobs may be a lot but, if I only fly three times a month, it's not that bad. Then I could go and coach gymnastics. I know I will be gone a lot, but I will have a lot of money. I hope soon in the future my dream jobs will come true.

Ron Strate, Grade 6
Linfield Christian School, CA

The Importance of Electricity

Electricity is important to modern people. It powers technology that some of us can't live without such as cell phones and gaming systems. Life would be difficult if we didn't have it.

Electricity also helps doctors with all their weird machines. It makes the operations quicker and less painful. Electricity also powers normal household appliances like toasters and microwaves. It chills refrigerators and freezers. Vacuums, I can live without, but it gets the job done quicker than a broom and a dustpan. Electricity powers your garage door too. I mean imagine, every morning before school helping your mom or dad lift up the garage, especially in the rain. No thank you!

What if you lived in New York in a tall apartment and didn't have an elevator? What would it be like in the summer if you didn't have an air conditioner? How would you go to Japan on vacation? You wouldn't be able to do much would you? I feel sorry for people that lived before electricity. Electricity is something I can't live without.

I don't know what I would do without electricity. In fact I wouldn't be typing this essay if it weren't for electricity.

Kaigetsu N. Simovich, Grade 4
Louise Foussat Elementary School, CA

My Hero

Terry Fox is my hero. He was born in Manitoba, Canada. During a car accident, he got a sore knee. But later in 1977, he felt sharp pain in his leg and diagnosed a cancer in his knee. Due to cancer, he lost his leg. As a handicapped person, he never gave up; ran for marathons, and played basketball. He had a big goal to achieve to raise money for cancer research. He wanted to run a "marathon of hope" across Canada to raise the money for cancer. During his marathon, unfortunately he was forced to stop at Ontario as he got pneumonia and he went into a coma. He died a day before his 26th birthday.

Arshdip Shahi, Grade 6
Micro Education and Consulting School, BC

Basic Soccer

Basic soccer is a series of sliding to the right, then left, and so on and on. When you have the ball and someone is coming at you from the left behind you, just slide to that side and do it 'til you're at your side of the goal. Pass it to the middle to get a clear shot at the goalie. If you are the goalie then practice catching the ball. When people are shouting at you, get a good defense to get the goal. Keep the other team from scoring. I will show you a secret move that I can only do myself. When someone is coming to get the ball fast, you slow down by tripping with one foot. Go left and right with another foot not touching it. When you're next to them you speed up and turn right really fast. This move is called the divine way. I made a move called the divine path.

Collin Keiser, Grade 4
Winona Elementary School, TX

My Inspiration

Ever had a person that inspires you? I do. My role model invented the light bulb, Thomas Alva Edison. Thomas Alva Edison accomplished numerous feats. For example, he invented the light bulb, phonograph, and improved the telegraph.

A reason why Thomas Edison inspires me is that he never gave up and no matter what anyone said he kept on working. He failed when he made the filament wrong and the bulb burst, but he still tried again. Then when people called him crazy and laughed at him, he ignored them. This has inspired me to make projects even though I might fail. Thomas also inspires me because he was a very social man. He attracted friends with his humor, storytelling, and fame. This made me want to make friends with humor and storytelling.

Thomas Edison, a scientist, constructed numerous inventions. Because of him I want to become a scientist and make new inventions. Thomas's famous quote is: "Genius is 1 percent inspiration and 99 percent perspiration." This means that to be smart all you have to do is work hard and use your brain to see results. Although Thomas Edison is no longer alive he remains in the hearts of many people including me.

Sidarth Shahri, Grade 6
Challenger School – Ardenwood, CA

Bravery

Bravery is a powerful thing everyone should have. I was not brave until I went skiing in New Mexico. Actually I wasn't even brave until I went to Six Flags that summer.

The summer after the ski trip, I went to Six Flags. It was my brother, my dad, and I. My brother and dad were pushing me to ride some roller coasters like the Titan, Mr. Freeze, and Batman. Well I decided that I would do Batman because I promised my brother that I would do it. I was crying on the 1st chain lift. But right when we started going down I forgot everything and started screaming with joy. I felt like I was actually brave when I finished it. But then my dad and brother kept pressuring me to ride Titan.

We went on the observation tower to look around. I had my eye on Titan the whole time. I still couldn't decide whether to ride it or not. But then my dad promised me Dippin' Dots! That made me almost change my mind instantly. I decided that I was gonna ride Titan for the Dippin' Dots. Then when we got on the ride I was sobbing and thought I was gonna die. Well it turns out I had a wonderful time and conquered my fears. I was so proud of myself! Try it and you'll never think of yourself the same again. That is what bravery is all about.

Cole McQuirk, Grade 6
Argyle Middle School, TX

Future Game Systems

I wonder what future game systems will be like.

I do have ideas of what they might come up with. My idea is a game system with a heavy duty camera that sees heat energy. Heat energy is a type of energy that shows as green when very cold, to red when very hot. I wonder who would think of that first? I hope Nintendo does. Who knows what Nintendo can think of? Of course there's Sega, which could come out with a system any time now. There's also X-Box and Play Station, which could come up with something like the Wii. Nintendo will probably stay ahead, though.

It makes you wonder.

What can people think of? Well, there's what ifs, like if Nintendo stops at the top of their game, or if Sega stops making Sonic. What happens? I know people would get mad, but what about E-Bay, the people that would sell Wii's would make a lot of money. If Nintendo doesn't stop, the people in it will make big money.

Nobody knows though. What can people think of? Anything can happen.

Max Kayser, Grade 5
Norwoodville Elementary School, IA

Good Deeds

One day in 2001, some planes were hijacked by some terrorists. The terrorists that hijacked the planes crashed them into the Twin Towers in New York City. Over 3,000 people died. The Twin Towers shattered and fell down. Now 6 years later, I do good deeds for the remembrance of the people that died.

I think that it is good to do good deeds in remembrance of the people that died that day, because when you do good deeds it makes people feel good. And if you do a good deed for someone, whose friend or relative died on 9/11, it will make them feel like someone cares about them and knows how sad they feel.

That's why I think we should do good deeds in remembrance of the people that died in the falling of the Twin Towers.

Kayla Stanley, Grade 4
Snake River Montessori School, ID

A Monstrous Reality

Let me tell you a story: There is an evil monster stalking the earth, murdering thousands of innocent children daily. One part of the world is protected from the creature and yet has the ability to weaken and eventually destroy the monster. But it doesn't — it is too selfish and lazy to make the small sacrifices necessary to solve the problem.

This story is a true one. And here is the horrifying truth: We, as Americans, do little to assist the victims of the cruel fiend which is poverty and hunger. Every three seconds, a child dies of starvation. And meanwhile in America we overeat and complain of the resulting health issues while the rest of the world cannot have the shelter, medicine, and food they need to survive.

The seldom heard pleas of these people have touched my heart. We can fix this appalling problem. How? Sacrifice. Be willing to give up some things that you want but don't need. For example, a family could give up junk food for a year and give that money to support those lacking basic necessities. Or, you could give up smoking or alcohol and so improve your own life and that of the underprivileged. Give to charities which help deprived children. Sponsor a child through a nonprofit organization such as World Vision.

Will you go on being an ordinary person and let life's opportunity to change the world pass you by? Or will you help defeat the monster?

Sierra McGovern, Grade 6
Home Schooled through Connecting Waters Charter School, CA

The Raccoon

We got a baby raccoon when he was about two weeks old. He was small and cute when we got him. We had got him out of a tree of eight raccoons. When my mom brought him home he was in a little cage for a dog. He was shy and sweet, but my mom said he would turn out mean if we didn't feed him and be nice to him. My mom thought of a name she said "His name is Velcro." When he was bad my mom would call him "Velcro" but usually we called him "baby" or "coon baby." A couple months later he got bigger so we had to get a different cage.

We had a cage from a dog that got too big for him so we let Velcro use it. He was very hesitant about everything in it and how big that cage was compared to his little cage. In the cage was a water bowl, a food dish, and a litter box. The litter box didn't work, he would splash his hands and then go in the litter box which would leave a mess. The wood pellets didn't work so we quit. My mom and I went to get a bigger cage. He is only ten pounds and seven months old now. He smacks when he eats bananas. He loves his teddy bear and he loves us a whole lot too.

Emily Shoemake, Grade 6
Argyle Middle School, TX

Science

Hi, my name is Dylan Brown and I am going to tell you about my favorite subject, Science. I don't know why I like Science so much. I guess I like it because it's fun.

I'm not really a big fan of reading science. I like doing it like in a lab. The reason I like doing Science in a lab better than reading it is because you can actually do the experiments. When you read Science you can only imagine them.

One of my favorite things to study in Science is explosives. The reason I like to study them is because of the chemical reactions they make.

Also, another area of Science I enjoy is the planets in space. The reason I like them is because they are so mysterious and we don't know a whole lot about them. I also want to be the one to find life on Mars.

I also love collecting fossils. I'm always finding cool fossils in my front yard. The reason I love them so much is because they hold a lot of history.

There are many things to learn in Science, but I like these three the most.

Dylan Brown, Grade 4
Scipio Elementary School, IN

Patriotism

"Give me liberty or give me death," is what Patrick Henry said on March 23, 1775.

That famous quote reminds you that Patrick Henry cared about our country and was patriotic. But over time, things slowly fade and people forget how many people sacrificed their life to make living in the United States a better place for us to live.

The United States has fought in many wars and many have died. In the Revolutionary War, 25,700 people died and 8,200 people were wounded all to fight for our freedom. In the Civil War 600,000 people died to fight against slavery. So we shouldn't forget what happened in the past and make a better future for generations to come.

I believe that the world can be a better place if we just remember the times of trouble and know that if we overcame the struggles of our patriotism and how some of us still kept our patriotism alive. Then we can help everyone else have their patriotism reborn. Some examples the World Trade Center, many people were injured but, that didn't destroy our patriotism.

No matter how much they try to bring our patriotism down they will never succeed. They can attack our airports, skyscrapers, and anything else, we still will stand strong. That's why I remind you we must keep our patriotism alive. We must stay strong! We must not give up!

Seth Jobes, Grade 5
Norwoodville Elementary School, IA

The Ones That I Love

Mom and Dad, they're the most important people to me. They always love me. My dad builds rockets for a business in San Diego. My dad was once in the Navy, so to me he's a super dad. My dad is completely concerned about my strength. Father-son time is doing push-ups in the living room. We have a blast. My dad and I love football. We watch it every time we get a chance. My dad was born in Wisconsin so we love the Packers. In the summer, we swim all the time. My dad is a very good surfer so we like to go to the beach. We also have a pool in our backyard. My brother and I love to swim with him. My brother's a freshman in high school, so he's busy with homework. I get to spend a lot of time with him. I love my dad.

My mom has always been the one who is looking out for me. When she's not teaching at Alta Murrieta, she's making sure I do my homework. Despite that, we have tons of fun. Our favorite game is darts. My mom is very active. We go bike riding, running and use the work-out machine. She reads a lot. She has a tub of books. Mom and Dad, I love them both.

Bailey Norris, Grade 6
Linfield Christian School, CA

Mary Edwards Walker, Civil War Hero

Mary Edwards Walker was a very important person in the Civil War.

Mary Walker was born on November 26, 1832, in Oswego NY. She grew up in rural New York.

Mary enrolled in the Syracuse Medical College in 1853. She graduated at age twenty-one in 1855. Mary was the second woman to graduate from medical school in the United States.

Mary Walker married a fellow classmate, Albert Miller, in 1856. She didn't follow the tradition and assume her husband's last name, so she stayed Mary Walker. The marriage ended in divorce in 1869.

Mary registered in the army as a volunteer surgeon because she was refused a position as an army surgeon. However, in 1863, she was promoted to army surgeon. She was the very first female army surgeon. Mary was captured by Confederate soldiers and sent to prison as a spy. After four months in prison, she was released in a trade for seventeen Confederate surgeons.

Mary was the first and only female Medal of Honor awardee. The medal was revoked in 1917 because Congress revised the standards to include only people who had engaged in actual combat with an enemy. Mary refused to return the medal. It was reinstated in 1977.

After the war, Mary began writing. Soon she was a published author. Mary Edwards Walker died on February 27, 1919 in her hometown of Oswego.

No one can disagree that the things Mary Edwards Walker did are important.

Katelyn Berndt, Grade 5
Cheyenne-Eagle Butte Upper Elementary School, SD

Stay Equal

Do you think a woman has the same rights, laws, or job choices as a man? No, they do not. As a boy, I think that a woman should have more rights and possibilities in job choices than they do now. I'll take you back in time and show you how it used to be.

Back a very long time ago, women had no rights. They could not vote, or even talk among the men to make decisions. Now-a-days, women eighteen and over get to vote. Pretty much all women will put their two cents in whenever they want to. Most women are very powerful in a sense of the word. They will work at home keeping their house clean. They will also hold down a job. Some have very good, well paying jobs and others don't. I'm not saying men don't have bad jobs, but honestly it's more common in women.

Women have probably always wanted to help make laws and be in high power in our country. Women have never done one thing that men have always done, and that is be President of the United States of America. They've been on the Supreme Court, and all that stuff, but they've never taken that president spot away from us guys. I have a feeling, though, that one of these days they will take the seat of power away from us.

So, in conclusion, women and men are even and uneven, but that could change.

Cody Stroud, Grade 6
Milltown Elementary School, IN

My Dad's First Time to SeaWorld

On Sunday my mom wanted to take my dad to SeaWorld because my dad had never gone. It was already 12:00 p.m. I told my mom that it was late, but she wanted to go any ways. She said we still had time, so we went. On our way to SeaWorld we were telling my dad about a big green ride called Journey to Atlantis and how scary it is. My brother and I had already gone on it before.

When we got there, we went straight to see the shows. The first show we saw was about seals. We were laughing because there was a seal that was talking on the phone with a girl. There was a big brown bucket that got us wet too. After that, we went to see the dolphin show. It was full of people so we had to stand up. Then, we went to see Shamu. That show got us soaked because Shamu was splashing water on us with his tale. The water was cold and salty. When the show ended we looked for the 4-D movie until we found it. It was scary because everything that happened in the movie also happened to us. After the movie we went to the pool. I only stayed in for five minutes then I got out because it was cold and windy. It started to rain so we went back home. My dad had fun even though he didn't go on the roller coaster.

Jacqueline Diego, Grade 6
Chapa Middle School, TX

What Is a Tornado

Today we are going to talk about what a tornado really is and some facts about tornadoes. Tornadoes are a strong power of wind and columns of winds spinning around the middle of low atmospheric pressure. Come with me, as we explore what a tornado really is and the meaning of a tornado.

First of all, the word thunder comes from the Latin word "tonare" meaning turn or twist. These are great descriptions of tornadoes, which are created by rotating and twisting air. A tornado is a violent column of oxygen that is in touch with the ground. Tornadoes take different creations. Some are large and ominous, while others are amazingly small and very hard to see. Tornadoes are capable of very large damages. Before thunderstorms are created, a change in wind create direction and an increase in wind power up with increasing heights make an invisible horizontal spinning affect in the lower atmosphere. Rising oxygen within the thunderstorm's updraft tilts the spinning air from horizontal to vertical. Moments later a powerful tornado has developed.

In conclusion, we have now explored what a tornado really is. It comes in many different sizes, big, medium, and even small but they are dangerous in different ways.

Nana Danso, Grade 4
Campbell Elementary School, CO

My Favorite Place

My favorite place is in the woods. When I go in the woods I go hunt with my pellet gun. I shot 5 squirrels and 8 doves. I killed them but it took me a long time to do that. I really enjoy going into the woods to go hunting. It is so fun. I want to go every single day but my dad says that I can't. Sometimes he takes me to get the twenty two. It stays at my grandpa's house until I am eighteen. When I'm eighteen I get to keep my dad's twenty gauge shot gun. Right now it will knock me down. When I get older it will not.

Dawson Rider, Grade 4
Winona Elementary School, TX

Mallard Ducks

One of the most human seen ducks is the Mallard. They live in North America and Eurasia. They are also found in park areas that have water. To tell a male from a female you can use these tips. All males have green heads and pale bodies. The females have dull brown all over.

Their year round range is mostly Northern United States. Their summer range is also a breeding area in southern Canada. Their winter area is in southern United States. Their food includes insects, aquatic invertebrates, seeds, acorns, aquatic vegetation, and grain.

The mallard is a hunted bird in the United States and Canada. In Europe it is not a legally hunted bird. Females usually lay eight to ten eggs. Hatchlings cannot fly until they are two weeks old.

Adam Hight, Grade 6
Franklin Phonetic Primary School, AZ

Napa Valley

Have you ever been on the top of a valley? Being on the cyma of a valley is an incredible experience. I enjoy the fresh breeze blowing on my face, smelling the pine trees, wild flowers and seeing the animals on the hills are remarkable. Napa Valley is located in Northern California. In Napa County Napa is the largest and best known valley. This valley is 30 miles long and ranges from one to five miles wide. The most important industries are, wine grape growing, wine productions and tourism.

One of the entertainments of the valley is the farmer market. Families come over to enjoy the fresh picked fruits and vegetables. Also, wine tasting is one of the most popular things to do since it's the main product of the industry. There are different kinds of wineries in Napa Valley, the most exquisite wines are produced in the region, making this place known internationally.

The copia is another tourist place to visit, in there important culinary events take place twice a year with famous chefs. They also have tours to show all kinds of fruits and rare plants located in the building. ON the other side of the copia, parents can find a little farm for their children to see.

In downtown Napa there are stores, restaurants and shopping centers where tourists can find their needs. Napa Valley is one of the most famous and known places in the world for its wine production.

Alondra Rodriguez, Grade 6
Our Lady of the Rosary School, CA

A Courageous Reporter

Once there was a lady who went undercover to discover news articles. Most men were not very happy with her working for them. But a few men allowed her to work for them. In those days, men thought that ladies had inferior brains.

Elizabeth Cochrane was born in 1867, in Pittsburgh, Pennsylvania; when she was reading Pittsburgh's main newspaper, she found an article called "What Girls Are Good For." In the article, it said that women had "inferior brains." She wrote a letter to the "dispatch" and did not sign it. The editor thought it was a man who sent the letter so he invited her to come because he thought "he" could write very well. He found out that it was an 18 year-old girl. He almost did not want to see her but she was such a persuasive talker so Madden the editor, hired her. Madden decided to protect Elizabeth and her family so he gave her a good reporter's name — Nellie Bly. Nellie's first article was about what happened inside rat infested factories. She pretended to be looking for a job. She was hired and set out to work in one of the darkest, oldest, and dirtiest workplaces. She wrote all about the horrible conditions and the news was a huge hit. Her next story was about the sad plight of insane people.

Nellie Bly died in New York City on Jan. 27, 1942. My hero was as courageous as a soldier on the field.

Jonothon Durodola, Grade 5
Montessori Learning Institute, TX

Good Health

Good health leads to a strong healthy body. A few things that you can do are exercise and eat right. If you do these things, you should be in good health.

Have you ever thought about how healthy you are? Well now is the time to find out. Start now, because when you are a kid it is easy to get into habits you might keep all of your life. Plus, keeping those habits in high school, could get you a sport scholarship or a job in sports.

Eating right also plays a big part in keeping your body physically fit. You should eat about 4 servings of fruits and vegetables. Also, you should eat about 3 servings of dairy and meat. Last but not least, you should have about 9 servings of grains. So if you would like to eat right you can follow a food diet or food pyramid.

Exercising also keeps you in good health, because it can keep you active and your heart healthy. Plus, when you work out you become stronger. So if you want to have that happen, do some of these exercises. You can run laps, do push ups and sit-ups. Now you know a few ways to work out.

As a result of keeping your body in good health, you have to exercise, eat right, and make a habit when you are young to keep your body in shape. As you can see, those things are the key to good health.

Katie Wictor, Grade 5
Covington Elementary School, NE

My Hamster, Ginger

My hamster's name is Ginger, and my name is Nicole. I got my hamster Ginger on December 6, 2006. Ginger was a baby when I got her, but now she is medium sized, about the size of a tennis ball. I got Ginger because I never had a hamster before and my mom wanted me to learn how to take care of one. I think hamsters are so cute and so adorable!

Ginger has a lot of pink body parts. She has a pink tail, nose, ears and a pink body underneath her fur. She has black eyes and brown fur. Ginger has big eyes and sharp nails too. Ginger eats beans, doughnuts, bananas, carrots and special hamster treats. I know how much to feed her because she finishes her food very fast. Ginger's cheeks get very fat when she tries to save her food and spits it out somewhere else.

When Ginger leaves her cage, sometimes she gets lost. The last time Ginger got lost, she did not come back for a long time, so I kept on crying and crying until Ginger came back. I was trying to look for her and I was crying at the same time! Ginger came back on the third day, and I was so glad that Ginger came back. No one taught me how to take care of a hamster before, but I just learned by trying and looked at pictures of hamsters that looked like Ginger.

Nicole Pillas, Grade 4
Holy Redeemer Catholic School, ON

My Disney World Trip

It was November 1st which is my birthday, and my friends and me were going on a trip to Disney World Florida. The people that were going was my friends Julie, Corina, Selina, Felicia, Kayla, Arlene, Samantha, Bryanna, Bob, Anays, Alex, my mom and me. We all met at my house and from there we left to the airport.

When we got to Florida we were all wide awake except my mom. She was already tired of the thought of taking care of 12 girls by herself. When we got to our hotel we went to our rooms. Then we saw that my mom had bought a master room for us. In the master room it had five humongous beds with the most comfortable pillows I have ever felt!

Right after we got everything settled in our rooms we went to dinner we went to a restaurant called BJs. Their food was so good, and their dessert was delicious. For dessert we had giant cookies with ice cream on top.

The next day we went to Disney World we went on at least 12 rides and we each bought something from the stores that we went to. The last thing that we went on was a roller coaster called extreme and on it Julie lost a hundred dollar bill!

Then we stayed in Florida for four more days and went to three more places. Then we finally went home from an excited trip.

Miranda Gonzales, Grade 6
Isbell Middle School, CA

Democracies, Ancient and Modern

I believe democracy is the best form of government. Both ancient Athenians and Americans have democracies, but they are somewhat different. However, they are both, "Rule by the People."

The qualifications of voters differs from Athenian to U.S. democracy. Only adults who have completed military training could vote in Athens. Anyone over eighteen who is a citizen may vote in the U.S.

The voting is different also. In Athens the voters had to be in attendance to vote. All men met every ten days. Each one could speak on a proposal. Every man there voted on it. In America, elected leaders make government decisions.

Both ancient Athens and America have three parts to the government. In the U.S. the three branches of government are executive, legislative, and judicial. All the three branches are very important to the country. They are elected by to represent the people.

In Athens the three parts were the assembly, the council of 500 and the court. Members of the assembly were not elected but, attended by right when and if they chose. The council of 500 members were selected by a lottery. A man over thirty years of age could serve on the council twice in his lifetime. Judges were also selected by lottery for one year.

All in all, the democracies of both ancient Athens and modern day USA are in the hands of the people.

Winston Gunville, Grade 6
Cheyenne-Eagle Butte Upper Elementary School, SD

Friends Forever

When it comes to being there for me, nobody is better then my friends. Sure, they can get on my nerves sometimes, but I know I can always count on them to pick me up when I fall down. Like once, when I was little I fell of a swing on the playground and nobody except my friend Dante saw me fall. Dante could've walked away and pretended not to notice, but did he? No, instead he immediately ran to get help, and from that moment on I knew I had a special friend that I can count on.

Over the years my friends have helped me more times than I could remember, and I have helped them too. Through this process, I have gained a lot of new friends. We have had to pull each other through some pretty tough times. Like the time when my friend Ben was disappointed about losing the school election, I tried to cheer him up. Or when I forgot my water bottle on a hot summer's day and my friend Chris let me drink some of his. During all those times, all of us have learned an important lesson: always value your friends, because they're something that you might never find again! So carry this lesson like I have, and remember when you are amongst people who help you through tough times, you are with some true friends.

Connor Vuong, Grade 5
Kyrene Monte Vista School, AZ

I Love Books

Books take me into other worlds. After school, I just unwind and read a good story. Whenever I start a new book, my eyes are instantly hooked. Strangely, that also happens when I watch TV.

Once I've started reading a book, there's no stopping. When a distraction hits me, the book shouts out, "Hey! Where do you think you're going?" The pages themselves seem to bring my brain closer and closer to the words, not stopping until I'm back in reading mode. Sometimes I think that I'll never stop reading a particular book. The hours go by as I turn into a block of ice, have massive hand cramps, and need to use the bathroom badly.

Books aren't always great. Every time I read a terrible book, my mind flip flops logic and I think all books were boring. The rest of the day I would just lie down in bed, staring blankly into space. But later I would be reading books again, forgetting everything that happened previously.

When I grow up, I want to be a famous writer like C.S Lewis. But every time I have a good story in mind, I just can't write. If I did start writing and looked back on what I wrote, I wouldn't think it was any good. I bet the trees sometimes hate me when I keep throwing away stories, wasting paper. Later, I'll keep trying. I won't give up. Not today.

Jasper Pacoli, Grade 6
Linfield Christian School, CA

My Tenth Birthday

I can't wait to see my presents! "Ding-dong." Someone's here. My hand reached out to the handle. I slowly opened the door. "Hi. Come in" I said. When I opened the door, the wind slowly blew in my face. "You can leave your presents here." I answered. I felt like my mouth was going to rip. When my guests came in, they plopped their presents on a hard surface. A couple of presents were in a bag with colorful tissue paper covering the present. The rest of the presents were wrapped up with wrapping paper.

My friends and I stampeded up the stairs and ran into my room. We watched movies and sang songs with my karaoke machine. For a second I tasted gifts, ready to be opened. I saw many presents lying on a hard surface.

We looked out in the backyard looking at a big tank of bubbling liquid. I saw the cloudy steam rising up in the air. We hopped in to our swimsuits. We splashed in the steaming tub. We held bubbly beverages. "Kids! Lunch!" my mom demanded.

We stepped out of the tub and took a blanket that dried us off. When we stepped in the house and I sat in a seat that was the color brown. I picked up a greasy lunch covered with cheese.

I heard one more doorbell. One by one, all my friends disappeared. This was a fun party!

Mary Kim, Grade 5
Dingeman Elementary School, CA

Summer

Summer is the finest season of the year. You get to go swimming, there's no school and you get to go to friends' houses.

Swimming is one of the fun activities to do in the summer. This summer I went to Hell Creek. Hell Creek is part of Fort Peck. At Hell Creek, you can swim, fish, boat, and do water sports. It's one of the most fun lakes to go to. Another fun place to swim is the Yellowstone River. It's the largest river I've ever seen and swam in. The Tongue River is also a lot of fun to swim in, even though it's not the biggest and widest river, it's still a lot of fun to swim in.

I think the all-time greatest thing about summer is there is NO SCHOOL. It's so cool. You can sleep in and the teachers aren't yelling at you for doing something dumb. You don't get to see your teachers for three months. Another thing is there is no school work for those three months.

Going to friends' houses is pretty cool. This one time I went to Jimmy Yeager's house and my brother Alec rode their one 50cc dirt bike. The most fun part though is going fishing, swimming and hunting the entire time.

See that's why summer is the best season ever!

Evan Haughian, Grade 5
Kinsey School, MT

Being Drug Free

Drugs! Drugs! Drugs! They are so unhealthy for you. They will eventually kill you. I would hate to die from doing drugs.

I would never do drugs because you could easily lose your family if the cops find out. It might just come down to keeping your family or your drugs. Which one would you want more? I would choose your family. Your family will love you forever and drugs won't.

Drugs are really unhealthy especially meth. If you do meth once, you will die from it. Drugs make you age sooner, you will die at a younger age, and they are just very unhealthy. If you start drugs it is very hard to stop.

Did you know drugs are against the law? If a cop finds drugs in your car you are going to jail. Then you are forced to quit. If you do drugs, you might as well kiss your fun good-bye. Drugs will also make you less attractive.

If you do too many drugs, it will kill you. I sure would hate to die over something so stupid. Many kids think it's cool to do drugs, but it's not. It's terrible.

So I hope you feel the same way about being drug free as I do. If you don't, please consider stopping drugs if you do them.

Haley Cox, Grade 6
Milltown Elementary School, IN

Unsung Hero, Lew Wallace

Lew Wallace played a big part in both the Civil War and the Mexican War. Some say he may have been more important than even Generals Grant or Lee in the outcome of the Civil War. I first learned about him when I visited the 1880 town in Kadoka, SD, so I enjoyed my research on Lew Wallace.

Wallace's military career started when he was a colonel in the Eleventh Indiana Infantry. He commanded the battle of Shiloh. He was the youngest general of his rank in the army and was something of a "golden boy." Battles such as Fort Donelson, Shiloh, Corinth and Monocracy Junction were led by Lew. He produced mixed results in the battle of Monocracy Junction. Lew Wallace was removed from command and from there he commanded the defenses of the department in Ohio.

Lew Wallace resigned from the army in November 1865.

Lew Wallace also had non military accomplishments such as being elected as a prosecutor of the First Congressional District. He was appointed state general in Indiana and helped raise troops. He participated in the military commission trail of the Lincoln assassination. He then served in the Mexican War from 1871 to 1885.

Lew Wallace died in Crawfordville, Indiana from cancer and was buried in Oak Hill in 1910.

In conclusion, Lew Wallace served well in the Civil War and as a military governor. He now and still is remembered as the "golden boy" of the Civil War.

Jett Peterson, Grade 5
Cheyenne-Eagle Butte Upper Elementary School, SD

My First Concert

On July 2nd 2006 was one of the happiest days of my life, I was so happy because my dad and my mom dressed me up and told me we were going to the Cricket Pavillion. I was so excited they were taking me to my very FIRST concert.

Once we got outside the Pavillion I could hear the music all the way from the truck since we were a little late from traffic. Going in they had us take off any chains we were wearing for safety reasons, we gave them our tickets and went inside. A lady working there asked me if this was my first concert and I told her, "yes" she asked where I was sitting and I told her, "Row RR seat 40," and then to our seats. I couldn't wait!

Cinderella was already on stage and they had long hair and lots of lights. After they played then the lady I spoke to came and gave me almost like an award paper that said "Ashly Duncan's Very First Concert!" with a place to glue my ticket stub too, for me to save. Then Poison came on and I liked them the best. I liked their songs and their style. They were fun to watch with all the lights flashing and all the fans were screaming long into the night.

I can't wait to go to another concert.

Ashly Duncan, Grade 6
Imagine Charter School at Rosefield, AZ

Nothing to Worry About

My moments in that car were spent on worrying. "What happens if I don't belong?" "Will I be the kid who sits alone at lunch?" Before I knew it we were there. "St. Matthew Catholic School" I sighed.

I walked through the halls quickly but took time to admire every corner and class. I found my homeroom and looked around to see a board covered with names and numbers. By the look of it I wasn't the only one late or the only Megan.

I found my name. Puzzled, I examined the room. Then a voice interrupted my thoughts. I turned, noticing that the teacher had seen me. Feeling embarrassed I said, "What…" I stopped, for the teacher was giving me instructions. "Find your name, then sit in the desk that has your number." Feeling as if she had read my mind, I walked away. I found my seat and saw a blonde-headed girl. I noticed the few items on her desk: a black pen, a spiral and a faded blue backpack with a hole in it. I stared at it for a while; suddenly the girl turned around and looked at me oddly as if I had intimidated her. Feeling sick I turned around. When all of a sudden she said "Hey, you're new." Struggling with shock I forced out "Yes." In the end I had a friend, Tiffany.

The rest of the day went by and before I knew it was the end of my first day.

Megan Rodriguez, Grade 6
St Matthew Catholic School, TX

My Long Trip

Last summer I went on a trip to Iowa. My family and I drove all the way to Iowa. We went to visit my grandmother and grandpa and all of my cousins. We drove for forty eight hours. It was boring. We passed through Nevada, Utah, Colorado and Nebraska. All I could see was grass. We drove and drove and finally got there. I was glad when we got to the end of the journey. We were glad to see our cousins and grandparents. We slept in my grandparents' house they had six rooms in their house. I slept with my cousin Jennifer.

The next day I rode on my uncle's horse, it was fun. We also went to a place called the World of Go-karts, we raced each other with go-karts, it was cool. My cousins and I also played video games. I beat them all. We went to sleep at eleven o'clock. The next day we woke up all tired. I couldn't get up that day.

The next day we went to eat in a restaurant, the food was delicious. We also went to my uncle's house, my cousin had a huge water slide. My cousins and I went on it, the slide was fun we were on it until night time. The next week we celebrated my aunt's birthday party, we bought her a cake, we sang happy birthday to her, we ate the cake, it was delicious.

The next week it was time to leave, we were sad to leave because we had stayed for two months and we had gone too many places with my cousins and grandparents and my family. We finally left I cannot wait until we come back to visit them again. I will miss my relatives in Iowa.

Raul Barbosa, Grade 6
Our Lady of the Rosary School, CA

My Dogs

My pets are really important to me because they're funny. For example, once one of my dogs, Roxie, was playing with my cat Tiger, who is much bigger than she is, and he just swiped her. Roxie is also funny because when she runs she puts her ears back and growls.

My dogs, River and Roxie are cute. Roxie is cute because she is only five pounds and she is a black Pomeranian with big ears. Then River, my other Pomeranian, he is ten pounds, his fur is a peach color, and his face looks like a grizzly bear.

My dogs are nice. They are nice because they do not bite when someone is holding them. But some dogs bite you.

A lot of dogs are helpful. My dogs are helpful because they will bark if someone is there, but sometimes they'll bark at the neighbors. Police dogs are helpful because they can search for drugs and missing people.

Every morning my dogs wake me up because they are barking because they want out of their cages. But sometimes it gets annoying, but I still love them with all my heart.

River is beautiful because he has a nice fluffy coat of fur. I like to cuddle with him and give him hugs because he is so soft. I like to cuddle with Roxie because her fur is thin and soft.

Veronica Hutchison, Grade 4
Santo Niño Regional Catholic School, NM

The Best Brother

The person I admire most is my brother Frankie. Who do you admire the most? I admire him because he listens to what I say. I like that he listens to my problems and my secrets. That's why I like sharing things with him.

My brother also loves and cares about me. He is always there when I need him. For example, he taught me how to ride a bike in two days. That's because I did not know how to ride one and he was there for me.

He takes me to watch movies at the theater when we need a little break from working. I really like when he takes me to go see movies because they're really funny. He does very funny things to cheer me up.

My brother helps me to get good grades on projects and homework. Right now he is in the university so he only helps me Saturdays and Sundays at home. I have two brothers. They both help, but it's mostly Frankie. I have no idea what I would do without my best brother.

Janette Rodriguez, Grade 5
Camellia Avenue Elementary School, CA

Flag Football

The Bobcats kick the ball. The other team runs it to the 50 yard line. They had bad snaps. The Bobcats gain 4 yards we gain 1 yard. We throw the ball pick off. The Defines runs on the field. We get through, we almost got them, we do that for the rest of the time. At the end of the game I scared the GB bad.

The reason I like football is it is fun. When you play football you will exercise your muscles. The game is fun for all. Sometimes you have glory other times you won't have any glory at all. The game is for fun, some will like it.

Boston Wright, Grade 6
Round Valley Elementary School, CA

My Visit to My Grandmother's House

In the summer I went to visit my grandma's house. She lives in Palestine. She was so surprised because the last time she saw me was five years ago when I was three. I had a very hard time talking to her because we spoke two different languages. She spoke Arabic and I spoke English. But she managed to give me love and I managed to feel it.

I would wake up and she would make me breakfast with fresh hot bread. She worked so hard to make me happy. One day, her back was hurting, so I gave her a massage to say thank you for your hard work. She felt relaxed after the massage.

We did a lot of fun things together. We played cards and I think she let me win a couple times.

I felt so sad when it was time to leave grandma's house and go back to America. It was very hard to say good-bye to her. We hugged and both of us were crying but I felt better when she said she is going to come to America in January. I can't wait until I see her again.

Leena Aggad, Grade 4
Salam Academy, NM

Signature Stamping

It was sweating hot and I was in Korea. "Today is the day," I thought. "Today is the day I get my stamp. I can't wait for my mom to buy me this present." My excitement was brewing inside of me. As I went into the store, someone told me to choose one from a basket. Inside the basket was a rainbow of all colors and shapes.

I chose a deep sea blue stamp with creamy white swirls of color. I also picked a lilac purple case with it. I gave it to a young lady. The lady transferred it to a rusty metallic cube to engrave my name. After she started it, I leaned against the wall, tapping my foot, waiting for the seconds to pass. Finally, it was ready. I snatched the stamp. The dust on the stamp was the same dust as the particles in the air. I can sign my name!

A gentle breeze flowed out of my mouth that scattered the dust about and away from the stamp. The lady took the stamp and dunked it into a red liquid substance. She pressed it on a scrap of paper. The words were flowing and connecting like water. It was perfect. As my family and I walked down the crowded street I thought, "I feel bigger now. Now I understand my mom didn't just buy it for a present, but as a congratulations gift. My mom found out I'm more mature."

Alice Kim, Grade 5
Dingeman Elementary School, CA

Everlasting Road Trip…

Two long sleeves — jacket, three pairs of jeans, socks, three T-shirts, two pairs of shorts — I think I have everything. I was going with my friend Savannah, her mom, and her three dogs. I've known her for four years, yet this will be the longest, greatest time I've ever spent with her.

My stomach filled with excitement and dread as I saw all of my family members lined up to bid me farewell. As soon as I stepped in the car I felt a variety of mixed feelings. I felt anxious — yet horrified because of the length of the trip. I felt anxious because I've never been away from my family for that long but excited at the same time to spend time with my friend and ride horses.

I drifted into sleep and woke up to Savannah banging on the dog cages screaming "wake up wake up." The dogs were placed in their comfy cages to sleep between Savannah and I, and there was a clothes dryer in the back. We were smushed! Before we left Savannah had mentioned that she had peanut butter crackers and she warned me that they spilled everywhere, which explains why she chose the opposite side of the car, leaving me sitting in the crumbs for 13 hours — 1 hour down — 12 remaining. Will the everlasting road trip ever end…?

Jessica Kozlovsky, Grade 6
Imagine Charter School at Rosefield, AZ

My Secret Place

My secret place is in my room. Under my bed I have a radio and some snacks I bring. My secret place is covered with blankets. I have a little night light under my bed for me to see. I have pillows so I can lay down there. I put a blanket in the middle so I can stay on one side and I put the food on the other side. I made it dark so at night no one can see me down there. I have pictures on the wall so I can look at them. I have one of the phones in my secret place. I vacuum under there so it can always be clean. When I am sad or mad I just go to my secret place, and stay there until I feel better. If I am bored I go to my secret place. I don't like it if it thunders so I go to my secret place. I get scared and so I turn on my light and go to sleep under there. My secret place is colorful. It has blue, red, orange, and purple. It is big and quiet, that is why I love my secret place.

Hazel Capetillo, Grade 4
Winona Elementary School, TX

My Dog Maggie

Maggie is my mom's and my dog that is now 1 1/2 years old. She is a Border Collie that can never make up her mind. For at least one week she was frightened and scared by everything.

The first day we had her was ridiculously funny because she acted weird and different than she does today. She would follow me everywhere. Maggie was so scared that she slept inside our house.

She is a pure bread Border Collie from Billings, Montana. I don't know the name of her mother. She is about 2 1/2 feet tall. She is a black and white dog that loves to eat. She is about 30 pounds and she is only 1 1/2 years old. What I think is very hilarious is that she can never make her mind up. She could be doing one thing then turn around start to walk then she will find something new to do for a couple of seconds then she will just go lay down.

Wyatt Foulger, Grade 6
Kinsey School, MT

My Big Crash

The snow under my ski's was crunchy as Juddy and I got off the ski lift. As I started down the hill, I went slowly until I got accustomed to being at the top of the mountain. Once we got to the end of the road, we were zooming down through the moguls into Jump City. Jump after jump we kept going until we got to the three biggest jumps at the bottom of Jump City. We always get about three feet of air.

Then we had the idea of doing a three hundred and sixty degree turn. So, one after another we were zipping down the hill. First my friend Juddy went down and got huge air but crashed. Then I went down, and when I went off of the jump, it felt like I was in slow motion. I was trying to turn but I didn't make it and crashed. It didn't hurt, so I go up and skied for the rest of the day.

Joe Swartz, Grade 6
Monforton School, MT

Anacondas

The Anaconda is one of the largest snakes in the world. They can grow over 29 feet long and weigh as much as 500 pounds! There are several types of Anacondas. One is the Green Anaconda. The Green Anaconda is dark green with black oval patches on its back, which help it blend into its thick habitat. Another interesting Anaconda is the Yellow Anaconda. It is mostly yellow with black spots. The yellow and black scales under the tail on these Anacondas have patterns, which are unique to each snake, just like our own fingerprints.

Usually, Anacondas eat large rodents, tapirs, deer, fish, turtles, birds, sheep, dogs, and other reptiles. They have been known to occasionally prey on jaguars and even attack humans! Human attacks are very rare though. The younger Anacondas feed on smaller animals like mice, rats, chicks, frogs, and fish.

Anacondas in the wild can live into their thirties. Anacondas are mainly found in South America and the Amazon. Usually they live in tropical forests, savannas, and grasslands. They prefer to be in water, but they do spend time on land in small caves or trees by the water to warm their bodies in the hot sun.

Anacondas are not poisonous, but they are dangerous and can definitely kill. Anacondas usually kill by squeezing their prey until it suffocates or is crushed to death or sometimes by drowning. That's definitely not a snake I want to mess with!

Anthony Taylor, Grade 6
Divine Infant Jesus School, IL

I Am Thankful For...

I'm thankful for my family because they produced me. They also help me, and provide me with the things that I need to live. I love them a lot because they have taken me to lots of fun places.

Every year all of my Kaiser side of the family gets together for Thanksgiving. We always take turns as to whose house we are going to go to. This year it is going to be at my auntie's house. My cousin Anna and I are going shopping together the day before we go! We are making cookies for the meal too! I love the turkey that comes out of the oven and the smell of it! Yum! Yum! Yum! It will be a lot of fun!

Every year the leaves turn different colors. I love to jump into the leaves. My brother Stephen and I have a big, big tree in our yard that the leaves fall down from. Even thought we are older now, we still like to jump into the leaves. Soon the weather turns cold, and the frost comes. I love fall!

These are all of the things that I am most thankful for this year. So this Thanksgiving, take some time to appreciate the good things in your own life. You will be glad that you did!

Allison Raitz, Grade 4
Linsford Park School, AB

Chincoteague Wild Ponies

Almost everyone knows the story of *Misty of Chincoteague* by Margaret Henry. Misty was a real horse from the island of Assateague, and today there are still ponies of the same breed roaming feral on the island of Assateague.

Every year there is a day called "Pony Penning Day" where the ponies on Assateague island are rounded up and they swim across the channel to Chincoteague island. Why do they do this? It started in 1924 when the volunteer fire department needed money to supply new equipment, so they created the Pony Penning Day and auctioned off the year's new foals. And the unsold ponies swim back to Assateague where they await next year's pony penning day. Except for 1942-1943 during the war, there has been a round up every year since then.

This is a great idea because it keeps the population of the ponies down because Assateague is a small island. Also, if trained right they make great children's ponies at just the right size and temperament. A Chincoteague pony is usually about 12-13 hands tall. (1 hand = 4 inches) These ponies often look fat or bloated because their island is surrounded by saltwater; most of the plants they eat are salty so they drink about twice as much fresh water as a regular domesticated horse.

This ends our exploration of the Chincoteague wild ponies.

Kathryn Sire, Grade 6
Cupertino Middle School, CA

God

God is the most important person in my life. He helps me with many problems such as if someone in my family dies. He is really the only one that can save us and the way for Him to save us is to ask Him. We all aren't perfect and sometimes we do bad things that are against God's laws. We can ask for forgiveness. God loves us all and I think it's good to go to church as often as I can. God can also help us in many ways. I read about a man in the newspaper that was on a $100 a day crack addiction and when someone told him about what God could do, he started to clean up his life. He got a job, and an apartment, and he's no longer getting high. I've never seen anyone not ask God to save him. You don't need to be at church to worship God, he is always with us everywhere we go. He will be there. John in the Bible said, "God loves every one even the worst sinner you know."

Never ever take God's name in vain or test God, it's one of God's BIGGEST rules. When your mom or dad tells you to clean your room, just do it! One of the Ten Commandments created is, "thou shalt honor thy mother and father." No matter how old you are always respect your mom and dad.

Robert Ward, Grade 6
Linfield Christian School, CA

My Favorite Place

My favorite place is over at my uncle's house. My uncle's house is fun because his girlfriend and her kids sometimes come over there and we get to go in the back room and play. Her kids' names are Jaeklyn, Rede, and Dashia. When I go over to my uncle's he takes us to the movies and out to eat and he takes us over to my aunts. We get to go swimming and we have fun. When we spend the night we watch cartoon with my cousin and stay up late. The reason I like to go over to my uncle's is because we have so much fun when we are with Miss Cleo and her kids. Me and my sister have so much fun when we go over to their house because we get to play with their little dog. I get to play with her Nintendo DS and we get to walk up and down the street. Sometimes we go to the mall. We buy perfume and other stuff. When we get back we usually walk the dogs around the block. We feed them. Then we watch TV. We went to play basketball at the gym and we had a lot of fun. When we left we went back to his house. We had a sundae. We took a nap and when we woke up it was time for me to go.

Kaelyn Robinson, Grade 4
Winona Elementary School, TX

My Crazy Teacher

I have an exceedingly crazy teacher named Mrs. Manning. Mrs. Manning is always doing something crazy, saying crazy things, dancing, and even making crazy things! Mrs. Manning is really funny and very nice most of the time! She's incredibly fun, but she's extraordinarily crazy!

During our class time with Mrs. Manning, everything is usually enlightening but very berserk! While she's teaching, she'll say things in abnormal ways, and make faces! Sometimes, she draws bizarre pictures for the lesson. During social studies especially is when she draws a great deal of examples. Mrs. Manning is an incredibly great teacher!

Sometimes, when Mrs. Manning is either very happy or very distressed, she'll do her "Dang Dance." When she actually does this, she says, "Dang" and dances! She doesn't care if she does it in front of us during class. We all know and love when Mrs. Manning does her "Dang Dance!"

Mrs. Manning is an unbelievable teacher! Right before I-STEP, Mrs. Manning dressed up as Hannah Montana and sang to a *Hannah Montana* song in front of the whole school! Most of the teachers dressed up, but almost everyone thought Mrs. Manning was the best! Everyone was laughing and so was she. That was hilarious to most everyone!

Everyone seems to love Mrs. Manning as a teacher. She does so many crazy things and loves to make us laugh! Mrs. Manning teaches things in fun ways! Mrs. Manning is very fun but can be extremely crazy!

Casey Smith, Grade 6
Southport 6th Grade Academy, IN

Going to a New School

I knew the day would come. Each time we drove to the construction site of my new house I knew I was one day closer to being at my new school. I didn't want to go to a new school because I didn't know anyone and I didn't know what it would be like. I knew I would probably never see some of my friends again. My mom said it was going to be a lot better but I liked the school I was at. I laid in bed the night before school started and I was so scared. I wished morning would never come.

When I walked through the doors of my new school the next morning I wanted to run back home as fast as I could. But my new school wasn't so bad after all. I met some new friends and my teacher was really nice. She was understanding to all of the kids. I had a great time.

I have now been at my new school for two years. It is awesome. I know everyone. We have so many opportunities at this school that my old school didn't have like Spanish and Art. At my old school, we had to eat in the gym and there was only one class in each grade! My new school is a lot bigger. I am so glad I came to this school.

Cole Thomas, Grade 4
Stilwell Elementary School, KS

A Beloved Man

A man whom I could trust and a respected person whom I count on; my grandpa filled my life with radiance. This hardworking man inspired me with his brilliance, his friendliness, and his morals. My grandpa has motivated me to lead an exceptional life.

I try to follow all the valuable lessons my grandpa taught me. He demonstrated many honorable and worthy values that all of us could benefit from. He never responded unless he fully thought the matter through. He would say, "Can I please think it through and then reply to you?" This helped secure our lives. He also never left a job unfinished. I remember a time when I visited him and he said to my dad, "Before we start, let me finish my work that is pending." I admire him for his industriousness and perseverance. This calm man is my true inspiration.

My intelligent grandpa will always remain close to my heart. This beloved man was someone I could trust. He taught me right from wrong, to use my time wisely, and work diligently. He told me to persevere no matter what happens. He told me to chase my dreams. I have taken action in all of his precious lessons. Because of him, I have changed and I strive to become a better person. His heart filled with warmth and passion, maintained kindness and love. Painful for me to say, my grandfather whom I truly admire, has unfortunately passed away.

Brinda B. Perumal, Grade 6
Challenger School – Ardenwood, CA

Red Pandas

A red panda is a lesser-known cousin of the giant black and white panda. Red pandas are slightly larger than house cats and weigh from 10-14 pounds. The top half of their body is red-brown colored and the lower half is a very dark brown, their tail has red-brown and brown stripes. The face of a red panda is red-brown except for its snout, nose, cheeks, and "eyebrows." The nose is black, but the cheeks, eyebrows and snout are white. Red pandas, like giant pandas have a "thumb" that helps them grip bamboo, the thumb is actually an extension of the wrist bone.

Unfortunately red pandas are an endangered species with less than 2,500 adults left. The reason they are endangered is that humans are cutting down the bamboo forest. The good news is that some zoos now are breeding red pandas and putting them in the wild, which has been successful.

Red pandas generally are herbivores, but if they cannot find other food they will eat meat. Red pandas mainly eat bamboo, which has little nutritional value so even with red pandas eating only certain bamboo they have little energy. Red pandas are crepuscular which means they are mainly active at dawn and dusk.

Red pandas have too many names to count but here are some: fire cat, lesser panda, bear cat, common panda, Himalayan raccoon, and the last I will name, fox bear. Red pandas live only in the Himalayan Mountains, in Southeastern Asia.

Blake Larson, Grade 6
Argyle Middle School, TX

A Smashing Success

My first glove for coach pitch was a Rawling's glove. It's very smooth. It's all leather. When I close it, it's like squeezing a pillow. The pocket of the glove looks like a quilt. Each time I go to get a ground ball or pop fly, in my head I always say I'm going to get it.

I play starting pitcher in my baseball games. I am obsessed with baseball, I play or watch baseball every day. One time in the burning hot summer it was my little league baseball team's last game of the season. Bases were loaded, I was up to bat. It was the bottom of the 7th. I needed to hit a grand slam. Sweat was pouring down my face like rain, the crowd was biting their nails right off. Everyone in the dugout was on their toes. Sam was on third, Kyle on second, and Tanner on first. Strike 1, Strike 2. It was down to the last strike…Bam there it went. Everyone back in their chairs, there was a long moment of silence. It's over, everyone screamed.

I love baseball because you never know what's going to happen. Baseball also makes you very burly. If you see people in the Major League Baseball, they are very big and strong to hit the ball very hard. My favorite baseball team is the Yankees. I love hitting the ball so you can try to hit a home run. Baseball is my favorite sport in the world!

Connor Grizzle, Grade 5
Dingeman Elementary School, CA

All About Me

This summer, I went to Palestine. When we were coming back, we had to ride in the airplane for 13 hours from Tel Aviv to Atlanta, Georgia. Then we had to wait 12 hours in the airport. Then we got in the airplane. It kept shaking and I felt like I was going to throw up. Then we got off and saw our dad.

My sister and I were going to sleep. And my sister, Leena was going crazy, so my other sister Seham carried her. Then, I started to massage Seham's back with my feet. Then, Seham said "What are you doing." Then Seham dropped Leena to the floor. Leena fell really hard but she just got right back up.

One day, my mom's back was hurting. She could not walk. She stayed in bed the whole day. She went to the hospital and they told her that she was going to have the baby soon. So, she stayed in the hospital and my aunt came to pick us up. After school, we went to go see my mom. Finally, she had the baby.

On our way to Palestine, the airplane kept shaking, but we still made it. My mom's back was hurting, but she still handled the baby. Things might seem difficult, but if you persevere, you can overcome anything.

Deena Aggad, Grade 5
Salam Academy, NM

Never Be a Sore Loser

One day on August 24, 2007 at Outdoor Adventures in cabin 26 in the living rooms me and my sister were playing Frequency. I was winning by 1 point it was the final round with 5 seconds left on the clock. Al Trashonna was on the drums and I was on the bass I had 3 wins and so did she. She got the last beat before I did then I started to call her a cheater then she started calling me a sore loser. I learned never to be a sore loser.

Brendan Adams, Grade 5
McMonagle Elementary School, MI

Leadership

Do you demonstrate leadership? Leadership is showing a positive example for children and others. We show leadership by guiding others in the right direction.

In school, we fifth graders demonstrate and are examples to younger students by not littering and taking care of our school. We also show them how to act in the halls and at assemblies. I help people and I am a leader by giving items or food to the local food pantry. I am a leader by using my manners in public and to others.

Many people like to help others by doing things the right way. Lewis and Clark helped other people by leading them to discover new lands. Martin Luther King, Jr. was a great leader for equality for all and stood up for injustices.

Leadership is a challenge, but a wonderful quality to have in life.

Miguel Valdivia, Grade 5
Covington Elementary School, NE

The Person I Admire

When thinking about how hard life seems and how impossible the odds are in accomplishing my goals, I sometimes get discouraged. But soon I shook off that attitude of defeat and think about Oprah Winfry. Oprah is a person who overcame seemingly insurmountable odds to become one of the most influential and famous personalities in television and the world. Her advice and opinion is admire and followed not only in America but, worldwide.

Oprah Winfry overcame an abusive childhood and poverty to become a great philanthropist. She did not allow poverty to stop her from achieving her goal.

"The big secret in life is that there is no big secret. You can set your goal to whatever it is that you want to do. You can reach your goal if you are willing to work." This is a famous quote from Oprah Winfry. She has always quoted that statement. So, Oprah Winfry is the person I admire because even though she suffered difficult situations in her childhood she continued to excel in her school work. And look at her now, famous and admired by all.

DeAngelo Townsend, Grade 5
Caledonia Elementary School, OH

Reading

Do you think reading is awesome? Reading is so amazing and cool. You can pass time, learn, and travel. Reading is awesome and I'll tell you why.

One way reading is great is because it passes time. Whenever you have nothing at all to do, you should read. Reading is a great way to get on with your day. One day, I was reading in the afternoon, and the next thing I knew, it was dinner time.

Another way reading is awesome is that it helps you learn new things. Did you know that a certain lizard can shoot blood 30 inches from its eye to scare off predators or that a gray bull shark can live in fresh water? I learned that from reading. Without reading, we couldn't write. We would learn from TVs.

The last reason why I think reading is so amazing and mind-blowing is because you can travel. When I read, I feel like I'm with the main character. If I'm so absorbed in the book, whenever someone dies in the story, I start to sob. If someone does something funny, I start to giggle. If I'm reading about the Civil War, I feel like I'm on the battlefield with my gun ready.

Reading is better than anything else in the world. Reading is one really great way to make time fly. Research, spelling, history all lead up to one thing: reading. Reading is like transporting to another realm. That's why reading is awesome.

Stefen Stransky, Grade 5
Joseph M Simas Elementary School, CA

Abigail

Abigail inspired my life in many ways, but the amazing thing is that she is no longer alive. When friends of ours, Kara and Steve, found out they were having a little girl they were thrilled, but they also found out they were having an anencephalic baby. that means that it can live while it is in its mom's stomach, but once out, it will not live long. It also means that it has no skull from the forehead up and has only a brain stem. Even though they knew their baby would not live, they always looked at it in a positive way. When the time came that Abigail was going to be born, I waited in the waiting room for fifteen hours. Every now and then Steve would let me see Kara. We were all sitting in the waiting room when a nurse came in and said that she was here and living. When it was my turn to see Abigail she had a pretty pink dress and hat on with her blue skin. She was so petite and sweet. Shortly after I left the hospital, she went into God's house. I was also amazed of how Kara and Steve still kept their faith in God. I will always remember what a precious thing Abigail was and how she impacted my life. Another amazing thing is how such a little baby could change so many people's lives.

Bailey Sutton, Grade 6
Argyle Middle School, TX

Bethany Hamilton

Who's your role model? My role model is Bethany Hamilton. Many people choose their role model because they're famous, or pretty, but I choose Bethany because she has an amazing story. Starting at the age of 7, Bethany started to surf without the help of her parents. By the age of 8, she won her first competition. On a morning like every other, Bethany went out to surf, but this time something would happen that changed Bethany and the way she surfed forever.

Bethany at the age of 13 went surfing off the coast of Key West, with her best friend Alana, Alana's dad, and her brother. Bethany was letting her arm float in the water, waiting for the surf to pick up, when she was conscious of a dark torpedo shaped object under her surfboard. Then she felt a tug on her left arm. She looked down only to realize that her whole left arm was gone! She calmly paddles over to where her friends were and told them her arm was bitten off by a shark. Then she started to head towards land, all the way shouting at swimmers and surfers that there was a shark nearby. When she finally reached land, she felt faint, losing over 60% of her blood.

After several surgeries Bethany was given the okay to start surfing again. She started to stretch regularly, and finally was given the chance to go out competitively again. Much to the surprise of everyone, Bethany didn't want to be treated special. She did the competition just like everyone else, and ended up taking 5th place!

Bethany still surfs. Despite only having one arm, she continues to be confident and strong. Bethany's my role model, and now you know why.

Taylor Hensley, Grade 6
Greendale Middle School, WI

Football

Football is my favorite sport in the world. Football is my favorite sport because it is a rough sport and most sports are not as rough as football. My favorite teams are the Carolina Panthers and the San Diego Chargers. My least favorite teams are the Broncos and the Raiders.

I play football for a team. I play for the Cowboys at my old school. I am running back. Running back is an offensive player, who is behind the quarterback and normally runs the ball. My favorite play is the tripod formation. That is when the two running backs go with the receiver. The full back is by the side lines. The tail back is in the middle. The receiver is closest to the offensive line. The receiver runs 5 yards and stops and tail back goes 10 yards and stops. Then the full back goes long and gets the ball. If it is a reverse, the receiver or tail back gets the ball. I love learning football plays.

Football is one of my favorite sports because my brother plays with me on the same team. I like to spend time with my brother at practice and games and playing football at home. Football teaches you that you must be loyal to your coach. I learn something every day from my coach. I especially like watching football with my dad and brothers on Sunday.

Football is a sport that has everything. It is exciting and fun on the field and off!

Manuel Hurtado, Grade 4
Santo Niño Regional Catholic School, NM

My Spleen

As I lay there limp on the ground I think of my family. I think of my brother and how he needs me to guide him through life, and my parents and how they need me to brighten up their day. I looked up dizzy as Isaiah rides past me. As soon as I feel the shocking pain I scream! The sound rushes out of me like water pouring, and dripping, falling as fast as it can. My aunt ran over trying to comfort me. "You're okay stop crying!" "No I'm not!"

On our way home I was lying in the car. So intoxicated by my tears I couldn't walk. I couldn't eat anything, I would sleep almost all day. I wouldn't watch TV, I wouldn't talk, I wouldn't do anything.

After 24 hours my mom rushed me to the Emergency Room! I got x-rays and something else. After all that the doctor said that I had "split my spleen." My mom asked how it happened. He said, "The spleen is near the stomach. I'm guessing her landing on the handle bars is what caused it." My mom started crying. I was in so much pain I couldn't cry. After about a week I healed. This event has changed the way I look at safety. Now when I even think of an injury I think of my family.

Indica Morgenstein, Grade 6
Round Valley Elementary School, CA

How Manu Ginobili Became a Star

Manu Ginobili is one of the most well known stars, but do you know how he got there? Do you know how he overcame the struggles of the first year in the NBA from his Argentinean years to the NBA champion of 2007 and star we know today?

Like his siblings, Manu was a late bloomer who grew ten inches in two years! But his coach never told Manu to shoot past the three point line. As he developed his strength, he was able to shoot farther. When he turned eighteen, he joined an Argentinean basketball club during the 1995-96 season. The next year, he used his athletic talent to lead his team in scoring. At that time, the Spurs GM saw him playing and was astonished at his ability to score. Manu, then, got the reward of being drafted by the San Antonio Spurs.

At the beginning of the 2003-04 season, Manu had to sit out because of an ankle and foot injury. Once healed, he earned Rookie of the Month and averaged 10.6 points in a game. As the Spurs got in the playoffs, they started dominating every team with the help of Manu. When they got to the Finals, they defeated the Nets with Manu receiving his first NBA championship!

As well as we know, he would later on win two more titles, but that doesn't matter much because we already know that Manu Ginobili is a star.

Jordan Rosales, Grade 5
Oak Crest Intermediate School, TX

Life as a Girl Scout!

I became a girl scout because I wanted to help people and the community.

When a tornado crashed through Marengo, it was horrible. Luckily, my girl scout troop and I offered to help the community by cleaning up the debris left behind. We came back every day we could so that we could help clean up. When they said we didn't have to help anymore, we still stayed to help clean up the town.

I helped the English play park by putting in new play equipment with the boy scouts. My troops and I also donated canned food to the shelter. At girl scout meetings, we talk about how we can help the community in different ways. We also sell cookies not for the prizes, but for the money, so we can donate it to a place that needs it most.

Some of my achievements in girl scouts have been helping people in need. I hold the door for the old and young alike. I can also help someone around their house if they need it. When someone needs help, I go and help them. One of the important rules is "Help others at all times" and I have lived up to that rule.

The reason I became a girl scout was to help people be able to do the things that they want to do in their life.

Amanda Morris, Grade 6
Milltown Elementary School, IN

Doing Drugs and Cutting

Drugs and cutting are very serious things. Why are they serious? Well, 1. they can kill you. 2. drugs are illegal, and 3. they blind you from the truth.

Cutting and doing drugs can kill you. Cutting is dangerous, one mistake cut, and you can slice open a vein in your wrist. Most people who cut say it won't happen, but it does. Drugs are extremely dangerous too. Drugs, when mixed with other substances, are lethal. When on drugs, it is easy to do dangerous things, and get killed.

Drugs are in the top ten reasons why prisons are full. If you are in possession, off to rehab and possibly prison you go. Doing drugs mean you could end up like Lindsay Lohan, cold, alone, suffering lawsuits, and jobless.

Doing drugs and cutting blind you from the truth, you need help. When on drugs you really wouldn't know that you've changed, or that you are not okay. When one cuts, you think it takes the emotional pain away, well it doesn't. Cutting doesn't solve emotional problems. It causes conflict with those who care about you.

Cutting and doing drugs are serious. They are things you really shouldn't do. Drugs do not solve problems, and neither does cutting. Both things can cause pain, grief, and trouble. Do the world a favor, don't be another "druggy" or "emo" person.

MacKenzie Olson, Grade 6
West Central Middle School, IL

Mike Miller, South Dakota Basketball Player

Mike Miller is a famous basketball player from South Dakota. There have been many famous people from South Dakota and Mike Miller is one of them. He is a professional basketball player.

Mike was born in Mitchell, South Dakota, February 19, 1980. His mom is a teacher and his dad is an assistant principal. He has an older brother named Ryan who played basketball at Northern State University. He has a sister named Chelsey, who played basketball at Mitchell High School.

Mike went to the University of Florida. His team won the 2002 NCAA championship. He even broke the Grizzlies NBA record! He made nine three pointers against the Golden State Warriors.

In his professional career, Mike played for Memphis Grizzlies and Orlando Magic. Honors he received are the Schick Rookie of the Year in 2001 and he won the Sixth Man of the Year Award in 2005-06.

Mike has a wife named Jen and two sons Mason and Maverick.

Patience and composure are Mike Miller's strengths. He has good leaping ability and a very good outside shot. He is a thinker and a creative player. To improve his weaknesses he needs to be more aggressive.

In conclusion Mike Miller is a very good basketball player from South Dakota.

Dawnee Keckler, Grade 4
Cheyenne-Eagle Butte Upper Elementary School, SD

My Father: An Inspiring Person

My father, the most inspiring person I have known, does everything he can to develop a bright and excellent future for me. A hard-working person is he, for he would not do anything wrong.

My father stays up day and night to finish what he needs to, even if it means not to sleep for three to four days. He would not procrastinate. He earns money so my brother and I will have a productive childhood, which he calls "Life's Golden Age," and then grow up to be a person just like him, who never complains, but keeps his focus on his work. He shows me that life is full of struggles, obstacles, failure, and success.

My father, a person who listens to everyone, runs a democracy in the family. He lets everyone participate in family decisions, no matter what they are. It can be as simple as what we want to eat for dinner or where we will vacation in the summer.

He can answer 95% of the questions I have for him. If he does not know the answer, then he would say something logical instead of saying "I don't know" and getting over with it before thinking about it. Sometimes I would not understand what he says due to his extensive vocabulary, scientific knowledge, and his knowledge of the outside world.

This is my father and much better. I will always try to be like him. I am proud of my father — an inspiring person.

Abhinav Prasad, Grade 6
Challenger School – Ardenwood, CA

The First Time I Went Fishing

October 12, 2007, the winds were blowing three mph. It didn't help much. I didn't even know how to throw the string in the pond. It took me about one hour to learn then I looked like a pro out there. Ssssss! the string went while diving in the pond. Plop! the pole started bending and I almost fell in the muddy stinky pond. Lola, my little sister had to come and help me yank this one out. Wow! Everyone was watching I got kinda nervous. They measured it and it weighted about six pounds six inches wide nine inches long. It was a long white Catfish. I was proud of myself because I had never been fishing before and I caught a fish.

Someone got me a big bucket to put the catfish in so it didn't just stay on the ground where people would step on it. Before you know it we had to go because the fishing contest was over and I was surprised that I won. But it was just a pond so no one expected to have a big fish there. I didn't like keeping a fish all locked up because if you think about their family down there and no one likes to be in a glass fish tank so I let it go. Finally we left and all I can remember was that I caught the biggest fish and that's all I needed.

Sina Krasniqi, Grade 6
Argyle Middle School, TX

What Is Football?

Football is a contact sport. It is played on a one hundred yard field with two end zones. There are four quarters. Each quarter is 15 minutes. After two quarters there's a half-time show.

There is a defense and an offense. On offense you're trying to make a touchdown. The offensive positions are: quarterbacks, halfbacks, fullbacks, wide receivers, center, offensive line, and tight end. On defense you're trying to prevent the offense from making a touchdown. The defensive positions are: safety, corner back, linebacker and defensive line. The offense and defense do different things.

Some things the defense do are: intercept the ball, recover a fumble, and get the ball by making the other team punt. You make them punt by not letting the other team get a first down for three downs. The person who receives the punt and kickoff is the punt and kickoff returner. The team with the most points at the end of the game wins. If it is a tie, they go into overtime and whoever scores a point first wins.

To decide who kicks off at over time, they flip a coin. The away team picks heads or tails. The winners choose if they want to kick or receive.

When the offense makes a touchdown, they go for an extra point. If they don't make it, they don't get the extra point.

If the coach of the team thinks the opposite of what the referee thinks, he can challenge the play. When they challenge the play the referee looks at an instant replay to see if he was right or wrong. That's what football is.

Trevor Giampaoli, Grade 5
St Victor Elementary School, CA

About Me

My name is Francine Lahoz. The Philippines, my family, and my school are all important to me. I was born on April 3rd, 1997. I was born in Cardinal Santos, Metro Manila which is in the Philippines. My dad was in San Francisco when I was born because he worked there.

I was born and raised in the Philippines. I lived there until I was 5 years old. My family moved to Washington in the summer of 2002. We first lived with my Aunt Cocot while we were looking for a house. My family moved to a new house near Tri-Cities Prep in 2005.

My family includes 5 people. I have one older sister in 8th grade. I also have one younger brother in 3rd grade. I am the middle child. I'm 10 years old.

I go to St. Patrick's School. St. Pat's is a private Catholic school. I'm in 5th grade. My brother and sister also go to St. Pats. There are 8 grades plus Kindergarten and Montessori. As you can see, I *love* my school!

Now you know that my name is Francine and that I'm a Filipino, and you know all about my family and school. One more thing I want you to know is that I really love soccer. I also really love gymnastics.

Francine Lahoz, Grade 5
St Patrick's Catholic School, WA

Japan

The Japanese place a high value on education. Modern schools began in Japan more than a century ago. After World War II, Japanese schools adopted a system similar to that of the United States of America [U.S.A.]. Nine years of schooling, [six primary school and three of middle school] are compulsory for Japanese children, and nearly all continue on to high school for three additional years. Higher education also resembles the four-year college system of the United States of America [U.S.A]. There are more than 450 colleges and universities in Japan, as well as many specialized schools and junior colleges.

Japan's geographical location has played an important role in its history. Japan lies close enough to the mainland of Asia to have been strongly influenced by China. At the same time, the waters surrounding the Japanese islands long serves as a barrier against invasion. After the first migrations of people from the mainland in the far distant past, Japan successfully resisted attempts at invasion until its defeat in World War II. This water barrier also encouraged the isolation that marks periods of Japanese history.

The Japanese call their country Nippon or Nihon. It means "base of the sun," suggesting that Japan, the eastern most country of Asia, is the land where the sun rises. The national flag depicts the sun — a red ball against a white background. The Japanese emperors traced their ancestry to a sun goddess, who in turn was descended from the god Izanagi.

Chandler Batey, Grade 5
West Elementary School, OH

Soccer Tryouts Gone Wrong

I was excited when my mom and I went to get the special gear I needed for soccer tryouts. Little did I know that I wouldn't need it. After all, I just knew I would make the quick and boisterous team. On the first grueling day of the tryouts, we ran a few long rigorous laps around the immense football field. We had to do innumerable exercises that weren't hard but they had to be done. Next came the ingenious drills that were difficult because I can't kick with my left foot. The next day was painful because we had to run and exercise harder.

The coach asked, "Who wants to try out for goalie?" I said, "I want to play goalie," but he said, "No!" Coach called for the goalies he had elected but I was sent to do the other drills. We had to kick the ball right away after the two assistant coaches kicked it to us. I did this three times. At first, the ball didn't really go anywhere. The second time, it shot into the left corner of the goal. Finally, I kicked it so hard that it flew over the goal post and into the ditch.

There wasn't much more to the tryouts but unfortunately, I didn't make the team. And the way I found out was by checking the computer that evening. No one bothered to talk to me in person and naturally I was really disappointed.

Michael Wood, Grade 6
St Matthew Catholic School, TX

The Titanic

The Titanic was one of the biggest ships in her day. She was more than 882 feet long. The captain of the titanic was Captain Edward J. Smith. Some of the richest people in the world traveled on the Titanic, and some not so rich people traveled on it too. But the richest people had a suite fit for a king. The rich people's tickets for a suite cost more money than a worker on the Titanic could earn in 18 years!

On the Titanic there were more than 1,000 passengers. Some passengers even brought their dogs. They kept the dogs in kennels and exercised them every day.

The life jackets that they had on the Titanic were made out of several floats about the size of a paperback book. The Titanic carried 20 lifeboats. It could have carried about 16 more but the owner did not want the ship to look crowded.

Nobody really knows how long the musicians on the Titanic played after the ship struck the iceberg, but they do know that the last song was "Nearer My God to Thee."

As the ship was sinking they shot off fireworks to get the attention of other boats around them. A ship that arrived to help, the Carpathia, brought many people to safety. The survivors of the Titanic gave the captain of the Carpathia a medal with a ship on it as a token of their appreciation.

Marcy Jimenez, Grade 5
Oakland Elementary School, CO

Sperm Whales

I love sperm whales. They are my favorite creatures on the Earth. I have a large sperm whale figurine. My goal one day is to go to Baja, California and pet a whale and its calf.

Sperm whales are the third largest of all whales. They grow up to be seventy feet long, and are also the largest toothed whales. They are the smartest animals on our planet, and have the largest brains, even bigger than the blue whale! Sperm whales are toothed whales, not baleen whales. Baleen is a material that is the same as our fingernails. It is thick and strong and catches small animals like krill.

Sperm whales eat squid. They eat giant squid the most. Giant squid are about fifty feet long, and are the perfect size for sperm whales. Wherever a lot of sperm whales are, there is most likely to be giant squid there.

In the 1600s whales were being killed all over the ocean. Sperm whales were the most common whales to hunt. Inside of a whale is a great supply of oil. Sperm whales have a great supply of oil. In the 1600s people were using whale oil for lighting lamps and many other things. At that time, many whales were getting killed. Some species of whales were even becoming endangered, like the humpback whale, but now people do not hunt whales anymore for oil. Whales are now protected so they can be enjoyed by everyone.

Abdelhakeem Wakil, Grade 4
Country Montessori School, CA

Armies of Hedgehogs or Alien Communication

In farmers' fields all across the world, everyone wants to know, "What on Earth is happening?" Or is it even of Earth? They have been called agroglyphs, phantasms, and even elaborate hoaxes. For most people, they are called simply "crop circles."

Although there are reports of possible crop circles dating back hundreds of years, the first modern agroglyphs appeared in 1975 in fields in England. Crop circles have mystified and intrigued people for decades. These mysterious formations are found in fields of tall crops or grasses, and are found most frequently near ancient sites such as Stonehenge. Since they first appeared, no one has proved how or why they are made.

Some ridiculous theories explaining circles are wind vortexes, lightning and even armies of hedgehogs! Although many crop circles are manmade hoaxes, scientists have discovered several ways to identify formations that could not possibly be made by humans. In authentic formations, the crops themselves are not damaged or merely bent over but are actually interwoven. The cells inside the crops have been exploded by exposure to microwaves; however the crops continue growing and in many cases grow even faster. The soil under some designs has been super heated to temperatures between 1,500 and 1,800 degrees. Some people believe this is an attempt to communicate with us from other planets.

Whether these designs are hoaxes or really something extraterrestrial, they will always intrigue and fascinate us. And perhaps someday, deciphering the truth could teach us more about the universe.

Ryan Roberson, Grade 6
Colorado Connections Academy, CO

Lucille Ball

One of the most famous actresses was born on August 6, 1911, her name is Lucille Ball. Everybody called her Lucy. Once Lucy was four her father died of a typhoid fever on the date of February 15, 1915. On her front door of her house it said "Keep out — health authorities."

Lucille's mother, DeDe, let Lucy drop out of school when she was sixteen for acting classes in New York City. She one day saw an advertisement for a musical called Rio Rita. When rehearsals started she got fired. Lucy didn't give up, she soon became a model.

One day Lucy was in a car accident. Her legs were getting weak, and at age twenty-one she had to learn how to walk again.

Now she has her own show called *I Love Lucy*, from Desilu Productions. After that she married her costar Desi Arnaz. They had two children. Desi and Lucy soon got divorced.

Many years after that Lucy had a heart attack and passed away. Many fans left flowers in her house in Beverly Hills.

Regina Quiroz, Grade 6
Isbell Middle School, CA

Diwali

Diwali is an Indian festival. It is also called the festival of lights. There are two main reasons why we celebrate Diwali: The South Indian version and the North Indian version. I will tell you about the South Indian version. It goes like this.

Vishnu, one of the three main Indian gods, the others being Shiva and Bramha, sent down a form of himself, named Lord Krishna. Krishna's mission on Earth was to destroy all evil. So one day, Krishna had just defeated one demon. The demon realized his sins, and asked Krishna to celebrate this day forever.

We celebrate Diwali by waking up early and praying to God. We get more fancy food than normal. We also get very yummy sweets. The sizzling and hissing comes from the kitchen. The food makes your mouth water. You will see kids running up and down the street, playing games. People also set off some really loud noise makers. When one goes off it goes KAA — BOOM! Your eardrums seem like they are going to burst at that moment. Also during the day people set little clay lamps all over the place to be lit at night. Finally, night arrives, clay lamps are lit and BOOM BOOM go the fireworks. What a day. I love Diwali!

Now you have learned about Diwali. Does any of your culture's religious days have a special tale and a special way to celebrate?

Anindit Gopalakrishnan, Grade 4
Butterfield School, IL

The North American Black Hawk

The North American Black Hawk is very swift, intelligent, powerful, graceful, committed and inspiring. Back in the day when Indians and cowboys fought until death, the black hawk owned the sky and watched the tyrants fight for no apparent reason. One of the leaders of an Indian tribe noticed the mighty black hawk in flight. He chose "Black Hawk" as his tribe's name, as did many others after he passed away. He has been greatly feared by other tribes and historically mentioned throughout the ages.

The North American Black Hawk is average for a hawk, reaching 20-23 inches long. It is grey and black all throughout its body except for a broad white band near the tail. The North American Black Hawk diets on wounded or freshly killed animals that are about ten to twelve inches long and if an animal such as a coyote, another bird or a fox is feasting on its prey, the hawk will swoop down without a second thought and fight the animal until death for the food.

The black hawk's habitat is on the United States and Mexican border in wooded water ways with water movement and many bugs to snack on. As you can see there are many different ways to love or fear a North American Black Hawk.

Dustin Jones, Grade 5
Ray E Kilmer Elementary School, CO

The Best Friend Ever in the World

My friend's name is Jennifer Birch. She is so awesome! Jennifer is really nice. She always helps me with my homework. Jennifer also plays with me all of the time. I think it's because she has no one else to play with at the time. Jennifer sometimes will get mad at me, but then the next morning she will say "That was yesterday, so forget about it! We all will have a good day today." Then after that I sometimes get a little confused, but I end up having a good day anyway. Jennifer will always have stuff in common with me. Jennifer is one of those friends that will be your best friend forever, but even better, your best friend ever in the whole world! Jennifer will always be there if I need her.

Jennifer will talk to me if she senses that something is wrong. Jennifer is a great help. I even remember when we got into the bus accident. She called my mom, so my mom could go to the hospital to pick me up. She took my backpack and gave it to me when I came home. I think that's more than a friend that will just talk to me, she's a best friend that cares about me and thinks about me. I thank Jennifer for all that she has done for me. That is my best friend!

Britney Clemens, Grade 6
Linfield Christian School, CA

Family

There is more to a family than what meets the eye. A family is a group of people in which the man and woman get married and the children are born from the same mother, unless they were adopted. All families do different things together, have different members with different personalities, and some are rich and some are poor.

Members in families have different personalities. For instance some families have really determined members and others have lazy members. In this world not all families have a lot of money. There are so many families living in poverty. A family is a family no matter who the members are or how much money they have.

Different families have different cultures. This can mean different holidays. It does not matter what their culture is or what their color is. Members of a family all love and care for each other. Everyone in a family and everyone in this world are equal.

A lot of families have hobbies they do together. Some families like to race cars, boat, or travel. When families can afford it they like to go on big trips with each other. Even if a family does not have enough money to do big things, they still do little activities together when they have a chance.

In a family it does not matter what color they are or what culture they belong to. They do activities together, and follow their culture. That is what makes a family.

Jacob Katz, Grade 5
The Academy, WI

My Favorite Place

My favorite place to go is to my Aunt Marilyn's house because she has twins. Their names are Audrey and Adrian. They are so cute. One of them looks like their mom and the other like their dad. I once have carried Audrey. Adrian is blond and Audrey is dark headed. They are very cute. One day they dressed like they came from Paris. They are so fabulous to me. Adrian cries a lot but she cries so cute. They are so gorgeous when they are in their baby crib. When we went to McDonald's they were in their baby carriage. They were dressed in pink but my aunt's favorite color is purple so when we went to her house they were dressed in purple. I love the twins!

Evelynn Mendoza, Grade 4
Winona Elementary School, TX

Sports

Hi I'm John David Longoria I play eight different kinds of sports. I play football, soccer, basketball, baseball, golf, tennis, swimming, and biking. I am really lucky to have parents who support me in all the sports I play. My favorite sport is baseball. My favorite team is the New York Yankees. I have three brothers I have two big brothers and one little brother. I am nine years old, I play soccer, football, basketball, and baseball at St. Luke's. I play fall baseball at North West Little League Fields. I play golf at Alamo Golf Center. The rest of the sports I play in my backyard with my brothers. I have lots of fun playing with my friends. My brothers' names are Joseph, Matthew, and Michael. My nickname is J.D. I like my teacher Mrs. Sparks. She is very nice. I get good grades so I get to play sports. It is really fun. I like it a lot. My brothers are very supportive to me.

John David Longoria, Grade 4
St Luke Catholic School, TX

Grady

I awoke to the sound of panting and felt drool on my hand. It turned out to be Grady, my dog, his bright yellow fur shone in the sunlight. The first thing people notice is that his figure is large. I've trained him to share, sit, lay down, roll over and get things. My greatest dislike is when he eats my stuff. In his current old age he mostly sleeps and lays around.

I can still remember when Grady was a pup and I was little. He would jump on me and never stopped kissing. Not so long ago with our new puppy's cage, he got his head stuck in the cage. He lifted his head, flailed around, and when the cage flew off it hit the ground a few feet away.

Grady is really smart about staying in our yard and barks when he has to go to the bathroom. My best memory is when he would bend his head and our new baby dog would climb onto him. Even though he's a pain at times and a nuisance, he's my dog and I love him. I hope this paper has helped you understand how I feel for my dog.

David Sturges, Grade 5
Barrington Elementary School, OH

A Day in a Soldier's Life

During World War II a soldier in camp was sometimes given breakfast. If you didn't finish the food on your plate, you had to lick the plate. The Lieutenant would yell and beat you every day. They would treat you like garbage or dirt.

In combat, if you lost your bag, you would be so desperate you would eat grass or bark on trees. Sometimes you would have to dig a trench or ditch with a shovel or even have to use your helmet. Remember there are no bathrooms in war either. If you were in a forest and were almost out of supplies you would have to cut down trees just to make a road for a couple of supply trucks to come. In a boat, the floor was so flat that when you hit a wave you would fly up in the air with your helmet flying up too.

You ate dinner when you could and when you had something to eat. Sometimes you would take hours trying to start a fire. Once you made a fire, you'd have to sleep in an old church or under a tree on the ground. Maybe you would have to share the same blanket with another soldier. Sometimes you used your helmet for a pillow. You try to go to sleep. When you wake in the morning, you start your rough day all over again.

Anton Gojcaj, Grade 5
Jefferson Elementary School, MI

Creatures of the Deep

"Wow! This snorkeling trip is great," I said, as I was on my way to plunge into the salty water. I would be careful not to touch the living coral. I wondered how much longer until I got to the reef. The tour guide gave a signal and I felt the boat slow down. It's snorkeling time.

I put on my equipment, which included flippers, face mask and a snorkel. Once geared up, I jumped over the side of the boat into the lively water. I wasn't sure how long I could hold my breath. The scene was beautiful, but I had to breathe. There were many fish and plant-like creatures. I explored the reef, looking for something interesting.

I found it, a real live shark. "Is it friendly?" I thought to myself. The guide was near the shark, so I inched forward to touch it. I jerked my hand back. The shark didn't bite me so I brushed it again. Its skin was so rough. The trip was exciting. I wondered what would happen next. Zoom! Something just swam past me! Was it the shark? No, it's a stingray! I couldn't believe it. I was swimming right next to fish that were deadly in books, but here they seemed harmless.

This being my first snorkeling trip, I'm impressed. I bet I could go again and again and never get tired of the tremendous things on the ocean floor. I love snorkeling with creatures of the deep.

William Fallon, Grade 6
St Matthew Catholic School, TX

What Happened in the Holocaust

The Holocaust was really real. Some people don't believe in the Holocaust. The Holocaust was a mass murder that began on January 20 of 1943 in Germany and Europe. Adolf Hitler and the Nazi Party were involved with the Holocaust. In history it was a major event.

In the Holocaust a lot of people were killed. 1.5 million children died. Over 5 million Catholics, gypsies, and homosexuals were killed. There were over 190 concentration camps during the Holocaust. Only 1,300 people survived and 5,000 to 7,000 children were killed as victims.

In the Holocaust, the women had a very hard time. They shaved the women's hair off. They made the women have forced labor. 1,526,500 Jews were killed between March of 1942 through November of 1943. They killed a lot of women by gas fans.

While the Holocaust was happening, they killed people by gas chambers. Austria, Belgium, Bohemia, Greece, Germany, Hungary, Lithuania, Netherlands, Poland, and Yugoslavia were very involved in the Holocaust. They killed people by having gas in showers and putting poison in the people's food. They would also starve them. When the people died they didn't bury them. They planted them in the ground. They killed too many people. That is why they planted them.

The types of people they killed were if you didn't have blue eyes you were killed. If you didn't have blonde hair you were killed. If you weren't white you were killed. If you weren't German you were killed. So there's the Holocaust.

Kelsey R. Stambaugh, Grade 6
Canaan Middle School, OH

Fencing

Fencing is a form of art that includes dancing with a sword. When people think of fencing, they think of an aggressive form of fighting, but fencing can be so much more than that. For example, when you fence you show a lot of inner emotion. The sword and you become one.

With fencing you also use your mind and body as one. Fencing also requires your focus and strength to become one. When you become one with your sword, you begin to look at everything differently.

When you fence you look at your opponent like a goal to achieve, and when you look at yourself, you are the sword. To fence you need to be one to correctly respond to your opponent. When you fence you don't feel one thing, you feel many things. You begin to feel very confident towards yourself. You also depend on the sword as your guide because you and the sword are becoming one.

Fencing will always be more than aggressive fighting. Fencing is the art of dance and to interact with your inner self. You have to learn to respond correctly to the sword. Fencing is a way to connect to yourself, to look at your opponent and know who you are.

Jessie Bodelson, Grade 6
La Mariposa Montessori School, NM

Rights in America

How many rights to do you think we have? Some of the rights are majority rules, representative democracy, and a right to say what you think about the government.

To start with, I will talk about the right of majority rules. Majority rules means the idea that half of a group or more can make a decision for the whole group. An example is when you vote on a new law the majority, which is 50% or more, decides if the law is passed or not. Second, the United States is a democracy, but citizens don't vote on every law. Believe it nor not, there are 267 million people in the USA! That many people can't meet in one place to make every law. Instead, citizens elect representatives or leaders to vote the way they would.

Last, if we didn't have the right of speech you would not be able to express your beliefs or what you think is right or wrong. There has been a lot of good changes in the world due to the right of speech, such as civil rights, animal rights, and children's rights. So you can see we have a lot of rights in the USA.

Alyssa Burd, Grade 4
Rohwer Elementary School, NE

Halloween

Ghosts, goblins, jack-o'-lanterns, and pumpkins on Halloween night kids will have a very big fright. Kids will dress up in costumes tonight just like ghosts, goblins, princesses, witches, and army girls. I love Halloween. I love the candy, I love the costumes, it's just so great. Pumpkins bats all the signs of Halloween! Trick or treat give me something good to eat!

On Halloween night we have a Halloween carnival at the school. Halloween is the best way to get candy it's so sweet. Army girls and boys, witches, doctors, even if you're nothing you should have fun. Halloween is the best holiday ever (in my opinion)! Thank you for reading my essay on Halloween.

Stefi Gonzalez, Grade 4
St Luke Catholic School, TX

Rain Storms

When it is storming outside, it is like drip, drop; every second a storm comes. Rain reminds me of little needles of water coming from that big, bad, black, gloomy, dark-black hole in the black sky. I like rain, because it makes me drowsy and makes me fall asleep right when I drop into my bed. Rain is neat, because it absorbs from the black clouds. When rain hits our car, it looks like a bucket of water. Rain feels good when it hits your cheeks. There is a reason why people like rain; it rains on the flowers so they get wet. And the grass gets wet and it gets all muddy. The best time to play football is in the rain, some people say. When I come inside from the rain, I put on some nice, warm, cozy pajamas and my mom makes chocolate chip cookies and hot cocoa when it is storming outside.

Carter Spindler, Grade 5
Greenwood Elementary School, MN

Better Than the Best

Many people in this world possess the ability to do extraordinary things, but how many do we know? I know one that stands out, even though you probably don't know her yet. Indu Bhavari Dornadula, a person I trust and admire, can be compared to no one. Excelling in tennis and karate, while still maintaining her grades, she lives a complex life.

Indu studies hard to maintain a 4.0 average. Once, she brought an assignment to a party and completed it there. As a result, Indu currently lives in a dormitory in Temple University, an outstanding medical school. Indu was awarded a scholarship worth over $100,000 because of her abilities in sports and academics. She made all the qualifications like straight A's, a strong sport, and confidence in what she states. Surprisingly, *everyone* enjoys her company.

I have set my boundaries with Indu's help and I now aim to attend a prestigious college, just like Indu, since I know that average people can succeed and not just the school's most brilliant geniuses. Indu gives me a general view of what to do, like find an enjoyable extracurricular activity and study tips. Indu gives me the confidence I need to carry on. I never doubt myself and if I hit a bump in the road, I think about Indu. She shows me the right way, step by step. Indu inspires me to do unimaginable deeds, and I shall succeed in reaching my goals with her guidance, advice, and support.

Harshini Chengareddy, Grade 6
Challenger School – Ardenwood, CA

Skate'n

Kickflip, ollie, casper manual, revert, pogo, caveman. I love to skateboard. I remember when I first got on: Slip! Oops! Splat! I was no expert when I started. It took me a while to even peddle on a board. Then I got the hang of it. I learned new tricks and got better and better.

My next door neighbor, an eight year old, taught me a lot about skate boarding. I remember when I could do my first ollie, I thought I was a pro. I guess I got too caught up in the moment and tried to do it off the curb. The board was fine, me on the other hand got hurt A LOT!!!!! I didn't give up. I tried smaller tricks and worked up from there, instead of trying big tricks and hurting myself. I received a Spiderman board for my seventh birthday. It was a good starter but I needed a better board. For my eleventh birthday I got a new green board. It was awesome! I still have my green board, it is a great board.

I love skate boarding with friends. It's fun to skate down to stores and other places. My next door neighbor has a half pipe and it's fun to use. My favorite skater is Rodney Mullen. He ROCKS!!! I have no idea how he does his tricks. He's inspired me a lot.

Noah Young, Grade 6
Linfield Christian School, CA

Swimming Is Fun!

I like swimming because it brings a lot of joy. I have been swimming for four years. I have been in competition for two years. In swimming, the races are called swim meets. I go to most of the swim meets. The meets are exciting because we get to cheer for each other. I also get to play with my friends. The best of all is getting medals and ribbons when I win the competitions.

I swim two hours every day except for Wednesday. My coach is Owen. He's amusing sometimes. He knows Zulu. It's a language in South Africa. Practices are playful because I get to race against my friends. Sometimes I get to do interesting things like corkscrew, where I spin around in the water alternating my strokes, from back stroke to free style. Another weird thing to do is backwards freestyle, where I do backstroke on my tummy. It's very difficult but it feels great to swim backward.

I have many cousins who are in competitive swim like I am. I was the first to swim in competitions and told them how much pleasure I have had. We sometimes swim together at my house. We race against each other. We play Sharks, Minnows, and Marco Polo games in the pool.

I sometimes show my 4-year old sister how to swim. I throw all the toys out into the pool. She has to get them all and bring them back to me. She loves swimming too.

Swimming is fun! I want to continue to swim for a long time.

Kevin Pham, Grade 5
Country Montessori School, CA

Going to Kansas City, Missouri

It was the day before going to Kansas City. My dad and I had to pick up a steam engine, pack and get coal for our first train trip.

The next morning was crazy! We strapped the steam engine down and left. The steam engine almost beat itself to death 3 hours before we got there. We kept adding straps until we had none left. That night we got there after about 12 hours of driving. We checked into our hotel, got into the room and fell fast asleep.

The next morning we got up bright and early to unload the steam engine and eat breakfast. We ate at the hotel because that was the fastest and easiest.

As soon as we were done eating we left to go to Pat's RR, called Big Creek and Southern RR. Once we got there we looked around. Pat said, "if you want to run on Gail Gish's Railroad you better run on it today because it's reserved for the 1 inch gauge trains tomorrow." So after we were there for a while and had looked around we decided to experience 2 railroads in 1 trip.

When we got there we unloaded right away to steam up. We ran the engine for a few hours before we left for Pat's Big Creek and Southern Railroad. On the last day we were there we ran out of coal and left for home.

Cooper Cash, Grade 5
Bang Elementary School, TX

My Favorite Place

My favorite place is Mrs. Hutson's classroom because it is lots of fun. I love writing stories and poems because I like to write with expression. Sometimes she even lets us play games and stuff. We get to taste an Oreo and write a story telling people about it. We even write poems and compositions. Then we enter them in contests. Last year I won in both contests. I was proud of myself. And when I write it makes me feel good. When I am sad I write about funny stuff. My poems I write make me laugh. When I'm mad I write about happy stuff. Sometimes my stories make Mrs. Hutson laugh too. When it rains, I write about sunny stuff. When it is sunny I write about summer or stuff that happens on sunny days; like weddings. I like to write about my dirt bike races. And I like to write notes to my teachers. Sometimes my teachers say I'm one of the best writers in fourth grade because I am a very good writer. I am a very good student, and writing is so fun for me. Some people don't like writing very much but I love it. I love the ideas Mrs. Hutson comes up with that we have to write. I especially love the language warm-up. I love correcting papers and I am going to be a writing teacher when I grow up. That is my favorite place.

Dakota Westbrook, Grade 4
Winona Elementary School, TX

Where Has America Gone?

America should NOT be a garbage disposal. Even though, sadly, it is. If you just throw your leftover trash right on the sidewalk, you are, right there, killing animals and the environment. Even one piece of trash could harm an animal. There are a lot of garbage cans around. Find one and toss your trash away. Even one little gum wrapper adds up to a lot! What if everyone just dropped one tiny piece of gum wrapper? It would add up to a humongous mess!!!

Lots of forest fires happen because of human carelessness. Sometimes, campers are not careful when they make campfires. Sometimes, people are smoking and just drop their cigarettes on the ground. We all need to be careful in order to protect our forests. Did you know, some scientists make forest fires on purpose? This actually can help the environment. In the ground, lots of seeds need the heat in order to pop open and grow. The scientists make sure they are doing it at the right time, though. If you are looking for firewood, look for fallen down branches. Do not cut a tree down!! We use trees every day in our lives!! We use them to breathe, for furniture, and even decorations. We should keep planting trees all year round.

Please do not drop your garbage on the ground and plant lots of trees to help keep America beautiful!

Mackenzie Ludin, Grade 5
Maple Avenue Elementary School, WI

Dreyfus Affair: Prologue to the Holocaust

The Holocaust is one of the most tragic events in the modern world. The Dreyfus Affair, a story of a French Jewish officer, is sometimes called the prologue to the Holocaust.

Alfred Dreyfus was born in a town in France, in 1859, into prosperous Jewish family. Alfred graduated from a military academy, and later specialized as an artillery officer. Soon after he made the General Staff, being the only Jew in such a high rank for the army. The French government began to suspect that a spy was giving Germany important information. Anti-Semitism was always strong in France, so when the Intelligence Office had a chance, it seized it to put blame on Dreyfus. In 1892, false letters were used to put Dreyfus into captivity. Even though there was no proof, he was sentenced to life imprisonment. In a few years, it was discovered that Dreyfus was innocent, and he returned to the office. He served there for the remainder of his life, until his death at the age of 75.

The part here that amazes me is this man's endurance and will. Even after the injustice he experienced, he stayed loyal to his country. This story is a horrid example of xenophobia. Alfred Dreyfus was wrongly accused of a terrible crime only because he was a Jew. Millions of people died in the Holocaust simply because they were different. To me, the Dreyfus Affair is not a biography of one man, but much more.

Mark Usatinsky, Grade 5
The Academy, WI

My Summer Vacation

Hi, it's me, Antonina Doucette. We had such a great time on the road. My family and I went to Marineland over the summer, and it was great! I heard that the dragon roller coaster is the fastest roller coaster in the world — it felt like it! We went on all of the rides in the whole amusement park! By that time, it got late, so we had dinner and ice cream. And then we watched part of a movie called *James Bond*.

We stayed up until one o'clock in the morning. We saw fireworks and there were 29 of them — I counted! My brother Donovan and I found the best seats because it had 5 seats, enough for all for us to sit on and watch the fireworks. After the fireworks were done, we went to bed. We stayed in Niagara Falls for two weeks. On the last days, Donovan and I went swimming for one hour each day. After we were done swimming, Donovan I went to A&W for lunch. We also had ice cream with sprinkles. Soon, it was time to go, so we packed our clothes in our suitcases with our toothbrushes and toothpaste and started the car.

My favourite part of the trip was going on all the roller coasters, but I really enjoyed spending time with my family. I hope I can go on another vacation like that again soon!

Antonina Doucette, Grade 4
Holy Redeemer Catholic School, ON

Teamwork

There are tons of great characteristics, such as friendship, honestly and responsibility, but I am going to inform you about teamwork. It is a cooperative effort to achieve a common goal. Harriet Tubman worked to flee many through the Underground Railroad and help them to freedom. George Washington displayed teamwork by working to win the War of Independence. People who are determined to do many things, work together to get it done.

There are numerous examples of teamwork. Many role models illustrated teamwork. Lewis and Clark tramped and sailed through the Missouri River to the glorious Pacific Ocean. Vince Lombardi, former coach of the Green Bay Packers said, "The achievements of an organization are the results of the combined effort of each individual." He also said, "Teams do not go physically flat, they go mentally stale." To me, Vince Lombardi is saying that if teams work together, the scoreboard is the results.

I challenge myself to express teamwork. The world sometimes lacks teamwork, but I can help. An example is when I worked together with my teammates to earn second place in the baseball districts. I have experienced that with teamwork the job gets done the majority of the time. But I have also hit many bumps in the road, such as disagreements and failures to get it done. I have observed that teamwork does work.

You can imagine that following these positive qualities isn't always as easy as it seems, but trying makes it a whole lot easier.

Casey Bright, Grade 5
Covington Elementary School, NE

Soccer

Soccer, the one sport I like the most, is very important to me. When I go to the field to play soccer, I feel happy. As I kick the ball, I have this great vibration in my leg. I find myself running with the ball in all directions. It is is fun to play soccer on a team and work together to score a goal. I enjoy playing soccer even if I don't know my teammates well. When I kick the ball and get a goal, I feel excited, and the whole team cheers because we have all had a part in gaining this point.

In a team sport like soccer, children like me learn to share by passing the ball and working together. By playing this game, I have made a lot of friends. They call me "Kareem-o-style" because I kick the ball very far and high. My teammates say I am a good goalie, but my favorite position is center or offense.

Soccer has other benefits, too. It is a good exercise for the heart and lungs. Because it is an international sport, people from different countries can also play and understand the game without speaking the same language. For all these reasons, I am happy that soccer is an important part of my life.

Kareem Taleb, Grade 4
Birchwood School, OH

Labrador Retrievers Are the Best Breed of Dogs

I think Labrador Retrievers are the best breed of dogs. I think they are good dogs because they have many good characteristics. To name a few, they are protective, good with children, and good natured.

To start, let me give you some examples of protective. One day I was swimming in the lake, playing and being loud. My Lab, Spice, thought something was wrong and jumped in to save me. Spice is very protective of me and my family.

Next, I will tell you why I think Labradors are good with children. They are good with children because my sister and I can do just about anything to Spice. We can sit on her, hug her, or even accidentally step on her or pull her tail, and she never snaps or growls at any of us.

Lastly, one of the best qualities of Labrador Retrievers is their good nature. In my family we also have a Chihuahua named Sophie. On Spice's birthday we gave her a rawhide bone and Spice chewed off the corner and gave it to Sophie. Most dogs would growl and snap at a puppy trying to get their bone.

These are only three of Labrador Retrievers' good characteristics; there are many, many more. This is why I believe that Labrador Retrievers are the best breed of dogs.

Dana Hohn, Grade 5
Spicewood Elementary School, TX

Small Idea, Big Return

On the day the tsunami hit, people were on the news for giving packages and presents to the victims. But, my mom thought of a totally different idea. She thought of making friendship bracelets, and selling them! I had my sister teach me how to make them.

The next day at school my mom got permission to sell them at our school store for a dollar! Our whole class made them and sales went well. After about three weeks the American Red Cross came in so they could get the check from us for three hundred dollars! Later the Ambassador of Indonesia came in to thank us and give us a speech. About one week later I got a letter in the mail asking if me and a family member would like to join him in Washington D.C. for an anniversary and retirement party!

Before I knew it I was on the plane with my dad, my friend, and her mother heading for D.C.! We landed and it was amazing! I had never seen such beautiful monuments in my life. It was the night of the big party! When we got to the embassy everybody wanted to take our picture. There were so many different people. After a while my friend and I had to go on stage so everybody could recognize us for the good we did. The Ambassador was so happy to see 9 year olds make a difference to people halfway across the globe.

Lexie Barnes, Grade 6
Charlevoix Middle School, MI

Tarantula

Jack is the coolest and most important person I've ever met. We do everything together. Just recently we made matching purple and red tie-dye shirts. They're really cool.

During that same exact day we went outside into the hot, humid air. There crawling on the ground was the biggest, hairiest, and ugliest tarantula we both had ever seen in our entire lifetime! So the creepy, horrifying battle began, I stoned the hideous monster, while Jack went inside to get an air soft gun from his brother Kelly. Crack! I broke its leg. It was limping into the bushes when Jack came running out. Bam! Jack shot its leg off. Boom! I shot another leg off. Bang! Jack had killed it. The tarantula curled up and bled to death. This may seem extremely cruel, but that was its third time crawling up to their house. Well, we don't have to worry about that hairy beast coming back.

Later that day we buried it. On the lump of dirt we put a wood tombstone and the B-B that killed it.

When we went back inside we were so scared that it would come back that we couldn't even sit down. The funny thing is that we put Jack's dog, Rocket, up to the tarantula, so it would try to kill it. Now we won't touch it. We call it the tarantula doggy.

My work with the creature is done.

Ian Humes, Grade 6
Linfield Christian School, CA

George H. Thomas Contributes to the Civil War

George H. Thomas played a big part in the Civil War.

George H. Thomas was born July 31, 1816 in Southampton County, VA. He was born in the South but fought for North.

George H. Thomas graduated from U.S. Military Academy at West Point.

George H. Thomas served the Union army in the Civil War under General Don Carlos Buell. He was offered Buell's regiment after Buell was fired but he refused chief commander. In 1864, George inflicted the worst defeat on the open field on either side during the war. He won the first major Union victory at Mill Springs in 1862.

George is known for many achievements. He had a wide-ranging secret service with a spy network, and the Civil War's most efficient hospital service. The first female doctor in the Civil War was hired by George. George established the Civil War's most efficient mess service for his troops and provided them with books and magazines. George H. Thomas didn't take a day of leave during the entire Civil War.

George Thomas continued to serve after the war. Toward the end of the war George was appointed military governor charge of states. George Thomas established in Mill Springs the first national military cemetery on a battlefield. George died in 1870 in San Francisco.

In conclusion, George H. Thomas played a big part in the Civil War.

Clay LaPlante, Grade 5
Cheyenne-Eagle Butte Upper Elementary School, SD

Raking Leaves

One Saturday morning my dad got everyone up early and said we had work to do. Our morning task was to rake up the yard as a family. Still half asleep I was handed a rake and we began our chore.

My brother, Matt, however was very good at convincing my parents of stuff and so he went off on his bike for some exercise.

Our yard is fairly large so it felt like the morning dragged on forever. Eventually, some neighbor friends came over to see if we could play. To their dismay they saw the work process and were dragged into helping. With their help the job went quicker and we started seeing some good piles.

My sister Sam, age nine, decided to hide in the pile and we devised a plan to scare the family. Just when we finished covering her Matt rides into the driveway. Ready to put the plan into action and hovered close to the pile, we point to the leaves and shout, "Look, look!"

Matt knew something was up and thought it was just a twig or something, so he rode his bike right over the pile of leaves and Sam. After we realized what happened, we screamed, "You killed her, you killed her!"

Sam jumped out of the leaves and we could see she had a tire track across her forehead and over her cheek. I will never forget that day and I don't think Sam will either.

Hannah Boyce, Grade 6
Concord Ox Bow Elementary School, IN

Count from 1 to 10 — Be Alcohol Free

Live on TV — a drunk driver weaving in and out of traffic. Police force the driver to pull over and count from 1 to 10. The driver starts at 5 and ends at 2. Every number is slurred and hard to understand. The breath analyzer is stuck close to the driver's mouth. He breathes into the meter. A moment later the driver is being handcuffed and pushed into the patrol car. He was busted for drunk driving.

Drinking is very harmful to you. It can affect your health, your job and your life. Too much alcohol hardens up the liver and destroys it. Alcohol will also ruin other organs.

Being an alcoholic could also mean loss of a job. Without an income, the family wouldn't be able to pay bills and could possibly lose their house. The kids wouldn't be able to afford college either.

The person who always gets drunk will not be well connected with the family. He or she will not be able to participate much. Their influence won't be a good one to the people around them.

The society will be in quite a lot of danger when a drunk driver comes zooming down the highway. 9 out of 10 times in alcohol related accidents, someone other than the driver will be injured.

Alcohol addiction will turn your life upside down. If you don't want that to happen, steer clear of alcohol and you'll be just fine.

Ashley Wong, Grade 5
Indus Center for Academic Excellence, MI

My Cool Mom

Who do you look up to or admire? Well, I admire my mom. I admire her because she is cool. She is cool to me because we do everything together. My mom is the best. I am so lucky to have her.

Secondly, she is very playful. Every day we go to the park to swing, swim and walk with Sunny (my puppy). My mom likes to tickle me when I'm sad or grumpy. My mom is playful now because her mom wasn't very playful with her. She is funny when she is playful too. She always makes me laugh.

My mom is also helpful and smart. She helps me whenever I get stuck on something like homework, word searches, and taking care of Sunny. I think she is smart because she knows everything I enjoy. Every time I give her a quiz on the things I like or enjoy she gets them all correct. She also knows how to press the numbers on the calculator without even looking at them. It's freaky. She does it so quick it looks like she has 100 fingers. Lastly, she is smart because she has common sense and she loves my whole family, herself and I. She is the best mom any kid could ever have!

That is why I think my mom is very talented in helping, playing, and smartness. I love you, Mom, very, very much! OXOX.

Stephanie Lopez, Grade 5
Camellia Avenue Elementary School, CA

What It Would Be Like Without Parents

If I had no parents I could do whatever I want. When I am in school I could talk and no one would call my parents. Then when I go home, I could jump on the bed and no one could stop me. I could eat everything I wanted without somebody saying "That's enough save some for later." I could stay up as late as I want and go to school whenever I want. I could call all of my friends over and they could stay as long as they want. I always wanted to be free, but not like this. I realize that without parents there would be no rules, but who would pay for the house and buy the food? Who would buy my clothes and tuck me in at night? Who would yell at me and say that's enough? Who will listen when I have problems and help me with my homework? Who will give me medicine when I am sick? And hold me when I am scared? Who will tell me "I love you" every day and comb my hair? It is so many things that I would miss, if I had no parents, so for this reason I change my mind and I want my parents to be there to see me grow up and give me support when needed. Who will hold me and tell me they love me? All the things parents do and I take for granted...

My parents.

Jasmine Sam, Grade 6
DeQueen Elementary School, TX

My Trip to Seagrove Beach

My trip to Seagrove Beach was very easy. At 5:00 am, we had to pack up and leave. I was very tired. My mom said that I could sleep in the car. It was a very long road trip. A lot of times I got bored, or sleepy. At 2:00 pm, we finally found a hotel that we could stay at. We unpacked and rested there.

The next morning we left. We stopped by Waffle House for breakfast. Till then, I was still asleep. At 4:30 pm, we got to the beach house. We unpacked again and we all took a nice nap. "Knock-knock!" I answered the door and there was a letter. I opened it up and it said,

"Dear Maddie,

Hey! It's me, your half-sister! I just wanted to tell you that I'm coming tomorrow. I'm soooo excited!

See you tomorrow!

Love,

Kimberly Solt"

I was so excited too! Three hours later, I ate dinner and went to bed. The next afternoon, I saw Kimberly! We played and played for the last eight days we were there. (And that was the best beach trip.)

Madeleine Solt, Grade 4
Montessori School of Downtown - Clear Lake, TX

Caring

Did you know that the definition of caring is to care about someone. The most caring boy in my house is my brother Eddie. When I was a little girl he took care of me by giving me food and tucking me to sleep at night. We also play together when we go to the pools. This shows me that he cares.

People in the world are caring too. Many of them help people when their in trouble. An example of when I helped other people was when their car got stuck somewhere. I was nice to the people that I didn't even know.

Being caring is being kind and helping others. Caring is a trait that everyone should have.

Silvia DeLeon, Grade 5
Covington Elementary School, NE

Stop Smoking

My name is Gabe Walker, and my essay is about why people should stop smoking. One reason why people should stop smoking is that it makes a greater risk of heart disease, cancer, emphysema and other chronic and acute diseases. Also scientific evidence shows tobacco smoking is often harmful to the smoker and to those inhaling the second hand smoke. Third, in a 2004 study showed that in New Jersey, bars and restaurants had more than nine times the normal amount of indoor air pollution. Last, researchers at the University of Dundee found improvements in the health of bar staff in the two months following the ban, so we should make a countrywide ban. I believe that we should stop smoking.

Gabe Walker, Grade 4
Lincoln Elementary School, WA

Honesty

Honesty is what makes the world a better place. It helps you be a good student in school because if you aren't honest about schoolwork there's no way you can learn. It also helps you in jobs because your boss is going to have to trust you when you call in sick. They can't come to your house and make sure you're sick.

Honesty helps you when you're a kid too. Your parents are going to trust you when you say you cleaned your room or made your bed. When you aren't honest to your parents or your boss, bad things are going to happen. Kids can't get fired from work, but they can get grounded.

When you're an adult worse things can happen. You can get fired at work or ruin a relationship when you lie. Then when you're fired or grounded you think to yourself, why did I lie? When you lie you get in trouble. When you lie you can lose the trust of your parents or boss and then you have less freedom.

The best thing to do is don't lie. If you do, fess up. You might get in trouble, but maybe a little less. Lying is what makes the world a not so good place. Most of the time when we lie we don't think about what we're doing. So do your part in the world and don't lie!

Katie Coy, Grade 5
Norwoodville Elementary School, IA

The Brain

The most complex thing on the Earth is the brain. The brain has many components and parts to it. Basically there are 3 main parts to the brain. They are the cerebrum, cerebellum, and the brain stem. Out of this 3 1/2 pound lump you have in your head, the biggest part is the cerebrum. The cerebrum controls basically all of your thinking. All of the math problems that you do are all controlled by your cerebrum. There is also one other part in your brain which is called your hypothalamus. It controls your hunger, thirst, anger, love, emotions, and all of that. Your brain controls different sides, so the left part controls right and right controls left. So people who are right-handed, their brain is most likely to be dominated in the left hemisphere and vice-versa. People who like math, science, and write detailed are dominated by their left hemisphere of the brain. People who like to draw and like to see the whole picture are dominated by the left hemisphere. Did you know that every time you learn something new, you get a wrinkle in your brain? The size of your brain is nothing more than an oversized walnut. That is how small it is. Now think of all the information in your head and think that all of that is in the size of a walnut. That is how amazing your brain is. So next time you think about a brain think of it as amazing.

Tanya Suri, Grade 6
Olentangy Shanahan Middle School, OH

Keeping Healthy

There are three ways of staying healthy. Being healthy starts with a lot of exercise, eating right and most of all never do drugs.

The first step of keeping yourself fit is to always exercise daily. Some ways of keeping yourself healthy is playing with friends or family like jogging, hiking, racing, jumping on your trampoline, or swimming. You can have fun all the time. If you don't know a game just make one up. Now you know all the ways of being active and staying fit.

The second way of staying healthy is eating right. You would have to eat daily. Do you know the important meal of the day? It is breakfast because it gives you energy for the day until lunch and dinner. You should always eat from the five food groups in the food pyramid. The groups are dairy, meat, veggies, fruit and wheat. That's the way to keep a good body.

The most important healthy step is never do drugs. Drugs can mess up you and your life. Cigarettes can give you lung cancer. So don't ever think about trying to light a cigarette, OK. The worst of all is beer. It has very dangerous mixings in it. Also it can kill or harm you. So never do drugs because they can mess up you and your life.

Now you know the three ways of keeping yourself healthy. So remember always stay fit, eat right and don't do drugs.

Valencia Primeaux, Grade 5
Covington Elementary School, NE

Rock Climbing Wall

"So what are we going to do at the party, mom?" I asked.

"Well, you are going to rock climb at Dicks," she replied. Great, I thought. I was afraid of heights. That meant that going up high wasn't my thing.

When I got to the birthday party it was a blast! Throwing water balloons and eating pizza and, of course, the prizes were fabulous! When it came time to go to the rock-climbing wall at Dick's. I remembered what my mom said before I left. Just go as high as you want, and when you want to come down just tell them that, and they'll bring you down.

I kept that thought in my head as I climbed. I got half way the first time. I came down. I knew that I wanted to go to the top. The second time, I went up with a plan! I got halfway there and probably a bit further. I asked if I could take a break, and looked down, whoo, scary. I kept going and was getting higher. I said to myself, "I am going to get to the top if I die doing so!" Ahh, my hand slipped. "See Megan, not that bad," I said to myself. When I rang that bell on the top, I felt like…incredible. Everyone was happy that I had conquered my fear. My family was more than excited. I am happy that I got over that fear!

Megan Jacobs, Grade 6
Haslett Middle School, MI

My Great Family

Wow this is one great family. My family has done a lot of great things. My mom is a great runner. She has ran 2 marathons. The first marathon she ran was the Chicago Marathon which she ran in 4:40 minutes. She ran another great marathon. The 2nd marathon was in Duluth, Minnesota. It was called the Grandma's Marathon. She did very great. My dad ran the Chicago and Grandma's marathon also, but he was behind my mom. He finished the Chicago Marathon in 4:52 minutes. He also does other things than running. He works at the Rockford Fire Station, Local 413. He works with most of the adults that live around our neighborhood.

We live in a subdivision with 10 other kids from my school. My school's name is Jean McNair Elementary. My old school that my little sister goes to now is called Simon Elementary. My older sister goes to the Winnebago Middle School. My mom teaches at Jackson Elementary and also attends a night class at NIU. I play baseball at Roy Gayle Ballpark for the summer. I am a very good pitcher and fielder. During the school year I play baseball for the Boys and Girls Club. My older sister plays 3rd base for the softball team during the summer. My little sister doesn't play any sports but she is a great artist and she loves crafts. This is the best family in the world!

Noah Walker, Grade 5
Jean McNair Elementary School, IL

Long Remodeling

It started a few months ago, when my hip, happenin' parents got the idea they wanted to "redecorate" the house. They wanted new wood flooring and new kitchen counters.

We began by going to Home Depot and waiting in a queue to place our orders. A few weeks later we received a call saying, "The new flooring you wanted has run out; it will take another 3-4 weeks for the shipment to come in." By now, it's near the end of June. Although the floor was not ready, we were able to get the shiny, black counters installed.

In July, we received a call saying, "Our shipment people who were supposed to deliver your wooden flooring were fired." We were not told why but were asked if we wanted a diversity of flooring. By now we were mad and decided not to use Home Depot. We hired a better, faster floor installation company. After another two, long weeks they started! We gloated on how much faster they were than Home Depot.

By August, most of the work was complete. So, do you think I'm done? Wrong. My mom spotted long, horrible indentations in the new wood flooring that she hoped was only an illusion. Unfortunately, the workers had to tear that scratched, ruined floor out and do it again.

Finally, the redecorating was complete. Everything looks great, and I've learned a good lesson: Do things right in the beginning, and you'll save a lot of energy and time.

David Elliott, Grade 6
St Matthew Catholic School, TX

Lucky

Hi, my name is Tiffany and I have a miniature horse named Lucky. The reason why we got him is because he was mistreated by his last owners.

He is a calm and gentle horse. He is a dark brown color and has blonde highlights in his tail. He eats pellets, oats and grass. In the morning when we let him out of his pen he will neigh at us. Then all day he will run and eat grass in the field. At night we put him up by coaxing him with pellets to his pen. Sometimes, he goes to the pen by himself at night without us taking him.

He is a very good and easy animal to work with. When you pet him he will put his head up like he is enjoying it. Something I noticed about him is that he is very thankful for the new home he has because he will eat every little crumb of food he has.

He is also happy. He is always doing cute things. Sometimes when we watch him an egret is next to him nipping at the bugs. He is a very loyal and kind animal.

When our friends come over to our house he will be friendly and let them pet him. Our neighbor next door has horses and he goes back there to the gate and looks at them.

Inside it makes me feel good that he knows he has a nice, beautiful home here with us.

Tiffany Munoz, Grade 5
Oak Crest Intermediate School, TX

My Little Devil

My little devil is my little brother Tony. He screams, yells and has temper tantrums.

It all happened on August 3, 2003. I was watching *The Simpsons*. It was very funny. "Time to go to bed," my dad said. My brother and I went to brush our teeth and go to bed. Three days later my parents left for the hospital and my grandparents came to our house to stay with us. Two days later, we went to the hospital. My grandparents took us through the hospital to see our parents in room 263.

We saw my brother Tony in my mom's arms with a blanket cuddled around him. Everyone took pictures and I got to touch him and he cried. After two hours at the hospital, my brother Derrik and I finally left from downtown Austin. My mom and dad stayed in the hospital for two more days with Tony.

When my mom and dad left the hospital, Tony was very sleepy. My grandparents gave him presents. He went to sleep in his new crib. It has been in my family for years.

The next few years he is screaming for toys he sees at the store, cries when he gets hurt, and yells when he wakes up. This is why my little brother is my little devil. But most of the time he is my parent's little angel.

Drake Touve, Grade 4
Menchaca Elementary School, TX

Helen Keller an Amazing Woman

Helen Keller was born June 21, 1880. She was born in Tuscubia, Alabama. In 1882, she was about nineteen months old, she got sick and lost her hearing. Her mother and father were worried. Helen never gave up and was a strong person. She learned how to communicate with other people.

In 1886 Helen and her father met Alexander Graham Bell. He helped Helen's family find her a good teacher. Her name was Annie Sullivan. People called Annie "the miracle worker" because she was able to help Helen see and hear the world. Annie taught Helen how to use sign language. She eventually learned how to write. In 1902 Helen wrote a book, it was called *The Story of My Life*.

Helen did not use sign language like everyone else. She used one hand to sign and one hand to feel what the other person was saying. Although Helen could not see, she could feel vibrations. She also could smell really good with her nose and her sense of taste was strong. Helen could recognize people by feeling their clothes and touching their faces.

Helen went to the Perkins Institution in Boston. She went on to Radcliffe College and graduated with honors. She was the first blind-deaf person to graduate in the United States. Helen became famous. She wanted to help people with disabilities. She traveled around the world.

Helen wrote a lot of books. Helen Keller was a wonderful person. She helped people understand more about what it was like to have a disability. She raised a lot of money for people with disabilities. She got a lot of awards for all of the great things that she did. Helen died from a heart attack in May 1968. She made a big difference in a lot of people's lives.

Ashton Gifford, Grade 5
The Arts Academy School, OH

Embarrassed in Fourth Grade

It was the last day of fourth grade. Everybody thought it was going to be a super and excellent day. I even thought that too, but we were all wrong, at least I was. We did reading as usual and math. Then came the worst part of the day, at least for me. It was lunch time, the cafeteria was full of people or students. It was a big mess and confusion. It was so loud that the principal came in and clapped 3 times, but no one heard her. So she shot the lights three times and left them off for 1 or 2 minutes. But in every class there has to be a boy who never pays attention about what is going on around him. When a teacher or a principal turns the lights off and claps 3 times we have to stop anything we are doing and face the person who is talking. He did not pay attention and dropped all his tray in my hair and clothes. I got so mad at him that I ran out straight to the nurse's office. I changed myself with the nurse's clothes. Even though I did change my clothes everybody in 5th, 3rd, 2nd, and 1st grade saw me. But I will remember that for the rest of my life.

Ana Meza, Grade 5
Aloe Elementary School, TX

Flagstaff

Have you ever been to Flagstaff? Have you ever made campfires and s'mores? All this and more happened to me. My brother and I stayed at my step dad's mom's cabin. More exciting things happen there.

At the cabin we, (my brother and I), rode a Ranger around the cabin. I drove my brother and my step dad's mom also. Both were frightened as I drove, because they thought I would crash into a tree. Quads are also available at the cabin. My brother likes to drive them, but I'm horrible at it!

Sometimes we go to different lakes by driving the Ranger or the quads. Zack (my brother) and I have rock skipping competitions. I always lose because I'm horrible at skipping rocks. Elk and deer are seen a lot at the lake they come to get a drink of water. I was amazed to see so much wildlife.

At the end of the day, we made a fire in the fire pit. Zack and I made s'mores with extra chocolate. Zack tried to roast a hotdog, but it fell into the fire pit. After that we had to put out the fire before we went to sleep. We finally went into the cabin and fell asleep.

We stayed at the cabin for 4 days and 3 nights. Zack and I learned how to drive a Ranger, which was fun. Animals are to be seen just about everywhere in Flagstaff. Many exciting things happened at our stay in Flagstaff!

Taylor Silva, Grade 6
Imagine Charter School at Rosefield, AZ

Our Chickens!

My family has the cutest chickens ever, and the noisiest. Our roosters crow *all the time!* We have 5 amazing chickens, and their names are: Cow (a rooster), Speckles (a rooster), Oreo (a hen), Thunder (a hen), and Penguin (Pengu for short; a hen).

Since late August, our chickens have been laying eggs. At first, we only got a brown egg a day. Then, we started getting 2 eggs, a brown and a white. Once we started getting three eggs (a brown and two whites), we got really excited. When our big German Shepherd/Rottweiler mix caught Pengu and ripped out her back feathers, I put Pengu in a pen and put some medicine on her wounds to make her feel better. When I came home from school the next day, there was a white egg in her pen! Now we knew she was one of the egg-layers!

Our family originally had 6 chickens (Cow, Oreo, Penguin, Hopie, Thunder, and Lightning, Thunder's twin). Then, we lost one (Lightning), adopted 2 (Speckles and Angel), adopted 2 more (E.T. and Wolf), then traded back the same 2, then released the 2 loudest roosters (Angel and Hopie).

My younger sister Emily and I are the ones who take care of the chickens. Sometimes I go outside just to play with the chickens. Usually, I do the water and Emily takes care of the food, but if she is gone, I can cover for her because it's so easy.

Matthew Hayden, Grade 6
Argyle Middle School, TX

Pets Are Amazing

Do you like pets? I love pets! I believe that all families should have some sort of a pet. A pet brings great joy and happiness. Yes, they are a big responsibility, but they are a lot of fun and will fill you with love.

There are many different types of pets. To name a few, you could have a dog, a cat, a rabbit, a bird, a hamster, and many others. Each animal will bring you joy in its own way.

I have a pet rabbit. His name is Sunny, and he is caramel colored with a white fluffy tail. I like to hold him and rub him between his ears. He gets excited when I bring him carrots, and also when I let him out of his cage for exercise. He lets me know when he wants attention by noisily tipping his food bowl over. I love Sunny, so taking care of him is not much of a chore.

Pets are a big responsibility. You have to make sure they have food and water every day. If they live in a cage, you should clean them out weekly. Some have to be brushed regularly. Of course, they need to be loved and given much attention as well.

Pets are so wonderful which is why I believe that everyone should own at least one. I hope that you will get a pet, so you can enjoy one too!

Anna Nisen, Grade 4
Concord Ox Bow Elementary School, IN

Picture Perfect

Looks are not everything. Beauty is not only skin deep. Sure, you look in magazines and see pretty models, but they are not the only ones who are. Many people judge others by the way they look, clothes; first impression. But that necessarily doesn't matter. It only matters what is on the inside.

At school you are judged "cool," or "uncool." But what is cool? Someone probably made up the word to count others out, like they have been excluded from all the fun. Well guess what? It is uncool to do that! It is cool to be your own person, your own boss. If you think pink hair is cool, then it is! If you think tank-tops in the winter are cool, then go right ahead (you might freeze!) because it does not matter what other people think. If they do not like you, do not worry.

Maybe at school picture day you put your hair in an original way, and people make fun of you. All you have to say is, "Tease all you want, because that will not change me." You are who you choose to be! Your thoughts count, too. Perhaps for lunch you have something exotic, and others make sick noises or move away. It is not nice to move away because it is different. Hey, how would you know if you like it or not if you have never tried it? So, live life. Be positive. Live who you want to be.

Maddie Wong, Grade 6

My Dogs

My dogs names are Pika and Cresta. They are both sisters, the same age, and Golden Retrievers. I love them both very much! They are now one year old. Pika and Cresta have very different personalities. First, Pika is calm and smart. Pika also has darker hair than Cresta. Secondly, Cresta is more outgoing than Pika.

My dogs are scared of stuff that is bigger than them. But, they can only go around my whole second floor and no other parts of my house. When we take them on walks we walk them up to our mailbox which is up the street a little bit. Whenever they want to run we take them to the park and let them run for a long time. When they come home they go in their crates and take a long nap.

Pika and Cresta love the snow. We go to the park when it snows and the dogs love it. I try to chase them but it makes me tired. They get soaking wet so we have to dry them off with towels. They also like to play and chew things up. I love my puppies.

Kirk Malm, Grade 4
Cheyenne Mountain Elementary School, CO

Bullying

To me bullying is when someone picks on you for no apparent reason. If you're playing kickball, and someone takes your ball and says you can't play, how do you feel? They picked on you for no apparent reason. That is bullying to me. Something should be done about it.

I believe that a bully picks on someone smaller than them. The reason they bully others is because something bad happened in their lives or they were bullied. It's sad that some people think that bullying others is a way to get revenge.

Sometimes a bully shows off when others are around. When people see others being bullied they gossip or don't tell a responsible adult or teacher. We should step up, and help others when they need us. I don't mean fight with fists, because there are many other ways to resolve problems. An adult needs to know about issues like this. If you're watching someone being bullied, then they were injured, how would you feel knowing that you could've helped them? Some things to do after being bullied are: stay away or talk to your family about it. Come up with good nonviolent resolutions.

Most of the time, a bully gets suspended and then they come right back and do it again. I think schools should try to get parents to talk to their children more. Our parents are our first teachers and they will always be our teachers. If we listen to what they say, we might be able to make a change in the world!

Bullies are just people that try to bring you down. I think they bully because they were bullied or something bad happened in their lives. There is nothing the school can do. Help others in nonviolent ways when they're being bullied.

Travis Maxwell, Grade 6
Starms Discovery Learning Center, WI

Why Kids Shouldn't Have Homework

I'm writing this letter to all the teachers out there. This is why kids shouldn't have homework. Reason #1: We're already in school 7 hours a day and we work hard enough. Why do we need to do more work at home too? Finally after 7 hours, kids just want to get home and not worry about homework.

My second reason kids shouldn't have homework is that we want some free time when we get home. We should be able to come home and rest. Kids like me want to come home and do other stuff, not homework. We have learned the stuff at school. Why do it more at home?

Reason #3: We have already learned the stuff at school. Why do it more at home? My final reason is we could miss activities. If we have too much homework we could miss sports and it puts stress on us, and we get bored when we have to sit in our rooms for an hour. Kids shouldn't have homework because we could be tired of doing school stuff and we could start not trying because were we're not getting other stuff to do. If teachers would even let us have less homework we would have some time to play or do whatever we want to do when we get home. That's why kids shouldn't have homework. So teachers the next time you think about giving us homework, think about this letter.

Adam West, Grade 6
Orchard Hill Elementary School, IA

Surprise

It was a beautiful Easter morning. I woke feeling so excited but I couldn't figure out why. As I was pacing down my stairs, I remembered hearing little peeps, lots of them. I bolted the rest of the way down the stairs to see what it was. My face lit up with excitement. I leaned over a huge cardboard box, and I saw lots of little tiny faces looking at me. They were baby chickens. That had reminded me that it was Easter.

There were chickens crowded in the box. They looked like tiny little furballs of yellow and black. They were pushing and shoving to get to the food bowl. I tried to count, but there were so many it was not possible. I tried to hold one, and it fit perfectly in my hand. Unfortunately, when I held them they pooped on me.

As they grew older, we figured out that there were three roosters. We had to get rid of them because they would fight with each other. We only found one of them a new home, and so we had to kill the other two. As the days went by my grandma and her dog came to visit, and the chickens were out of their kennel. One of my chickens went near the dog. All of a sudden the dog attacked and killed the chicken. It was so sad!!!

Gabi Golz, Grade 6
Monforton School, MT

My Special Tuesday

Every Tuesday morning and afternoon, I have to face zooming cars and many big and small people. This is Safety Patrol.

One day my teacher asked me if I would join Safety Patrol. I was nervous and worried at first but finally I joined. I knew from then on that it was the best choice I've ever made. I am glad that I can protect people from cars, like the real grown-ups do. I feel brave, different and even special. I also really like the uniforms that Safety Patrollers wear. The bright red T-shirt and clean white pants make me feel well organized and comfortable. Most of all, I am proud of myself that I can help my friends and their families.

Often a speedy car goes through the crosswalk while people are crossing. Also impatient people don't wait and just cross the street without guilt. It is so unbelievable that people do not obey the rules they learned in their childhood. I wish those people would be more mature and more patient.

Every Tuesday I have to wake up early and stay longer than any other students in school. But I don't mind because it's my duty. Sometimes I feel nervous that I will make a mistake. But in the end I feel really proud and happy to do this job. I think Safety Patrol will be the most important and special thing in my childhood.

SunWoo Kim, Grade 5
Dingeman Elementary School, CA

The Day I Got My Dog

One day my parents said that we are going to someone's house. I had no idea whose house it was. When we got there I said "Why are we at this house?" Once we got inside I said "puppies" and my mom said "surprise." My dog was the first dog to jump on me. We would be back on Thursday to pick up the dog. When I got home I was so excited and couldn't wait until Thursday to see my dog. I tried hard to remember his apricot ears.

On Thursday, I immediately saw the dog with the apricot ears. I was so excited as I knew he was mine. While he was in the car I heard a low noise and realized he was whining. I suddenly realized that although I was happy, he was scared and missed his family. But now we were his family.

Once we got home, I named him Mr. Snowflake. I remember that when we first got him he smelled like a warm bath. He was so warm and cozy and so, so soft.

Without realizing it, days, months, and years passed by. To this day I still remember the day I got my dog. Time has passed and he has gotten bigger and older. He is still doing well. I feed him, walk him, and of course play with him. As always he is happy, and sometimes annoying. But I still love him. Did I ever tell you that he is so cute?

Maya Elliott, Grade 4
Meadows Avenue Elementary School, CA

Animal Research

Adult small bay turtles have upper shells, or carapaces, that grow to about 5 inches in length, while the carapaces of the large gray's sliders can reach a length of 2 feet or more. Most pond turtles have at least a little webbing between their toes. The male is more colorful and has long thin front claws.

Pond turtles may eat meat, plants, or combination of meat and plants. Sometimes babies begin their lives as meat eaters but start to munch on plants as they grow older. The meat eaters may dine on such animals as fish, tadpoles, insects, worms, and slugs. Turtles that eat plants prefer grass, flowers, and berries. They also eat algae, or tiny plants.

Members of this family live in North and South America, Europe, Western Asia, and Northern Africa. New world pond turtles may live in tropical areas where it feels like summer all year or in cooler areas that have all four seasons. Many turtles spend almost their entire lives in or near ponds, lakes, and other fresh water areas, though some can live quite well in saltier waters. Other species live their lives mainly on land. Turtles have very bumpy shells. When a mean animal comes turtles hide under their shells or go into the water.

Many people have seen these turtles, because most of the animals in this family like to sunbathe, or "bask." Turtles that live in water typically climb up onto a rock or log sticking up above it.

Courtney Josetti, Grade 5
Mary Morgan Elementary School, IL

Canada Lynx

My paper is about the Canada Lynx. A Lynx is a medium sized cat that weighs 20 to 30 pounds and is located mainly in the northern part of North America.

The Canada Lynx lives in a habitat that consists of thick forest trees including bogs and swamps. They like the thick forest trees because it makes it easier for them to hunt. They also like to climb up on the trees and rest there too. It can capture 150 to 200 snowshoe hares a year. The male Lynx is larger than the female. The Canada Lynx eats snowshoe hares, and when there aren't any of those they eat medium sized mammals, and birds. When the Lynx cannot find food the Lynx populations go down. The Canada Lynx is not a fast runner so it captures, and ambushes it too. The Canada Lynx lives by itself and hunts every other night.

The Canada Lynx has light gray, scattered pale brown and blackish hairs. Their summer coat of fur is shorter than their winter coat. The Canada Lynx has a short tail that is tipped with black. It has a double pointed beard. The feet are large and have a lot of fur.

The Canada Lynx lives up to 15 years. The Canada Lynx gets pregnant for only 2 months, and have one to six kittens at a time. The female takes care of the babies all the time, and the male does not help out at all.

Jessica Swofford, Grade 4
Menchaca Elementary School, TX

Brian Urlacher

Crack, you have just been crushed by the Chicago Bears linebacker Brian Urlacher. You feel like you have just been mowed down by a race car going two hundred ten miles per hour. Then you realize it was only the five time Pro Bowler.

If you're a running back in the NFL and you see number 54 of the Chicago Bears bolting toward you, you know you're going to be hit. This 6'3" 245 pound monster may be the hardest hitter in the National Football League. Brian enjoys his 2000 NFL Defensive Rookie of the Year Award, but there is no way he is overconfident.

Other milestones of this awesome, fantastic, marvelous defender are 2005 NFL Defensive Player of the Year, four-time Defensive Player of the Week, 2000 Male Athlete of the Year, and last, but not least, NFL 2K3 cover man. What Urlacher concentrates on is his "smash mouth" defense. He hits like a freight train, and plays smart football.

This NFC North dominant linebacker receives much publicity. His commercial appearances include Nike, McDonald's, Dominoes Pizza, and Campbell's Soup. Being an NFL player really gets him the most publicity, though.

Brian Urlacher plays hard, is one of the most fierce players in the NFL, he is also popular off the field, because he is seen in commercials. I believe that Brian Urlacher is the best player in the NFL.

Nick Beach, Grade 5
La Costa Heights Elementary School, CA

Linfield

Linfield is the best school I have ever been to. I think It's so much fun, and I have made tons of friends here. I love how I can learn so much about God, and the way they teach here is fantastic! It is one of my favorite first experiences. I like the sports, and I'm looking forward to being on the soccer team. I like the Wednesdays here because we go down to the gym and have chapel, where we have announcements and sing songs. The campus is big and one night we get to play a fun game called "Night Crossing," where we run from the gym to the middle school without being caught by the teachers.

I got tired of sitting in one class for six hours, but now that I'm here at Linfield, I have to switch classes for seven hours (I don't know which one is better but I'll live with it). I like the electives because I can choose a new one each semester. One of my favorite classes is Bible, because the teacher plays the guitar to make a song for every single Bible verse we have, so it is easy to memorize. Linfield also has a high school that I am hoping to go to when I'm older. Linfield is the most fantastic school I have ever been to and I am planning to go here for many more years of my life!

Eric Drinhaus, Grade 6
Linfield Christian School, CA

The Questioner

'The Questioner', or better known as Albert Einstein, is thought to be the most unsurpassed physicist of all time. When Albert Einstein was a child he failed classes in language arts and social studies. His teachers would have never anticipated that he would become a superior mathematician. Albert Einstein is known for his intelligent theory of relativity. He was born in Germany, but when Nazi party came to power he moved to the United States.

Albert Einstein was born on March 14, 1879 in Wurttember, Germany. In school he was top in his science and math class. He was then sent to Switzerland to finish secondary school. In 1896 at age 17 he graduated from high school.

Albert Einstein's theory of relativity is his theory that explains gravitation as distortion of the structure of spacetime by matter, affecting the inertial motion of other matter.

In 1921 Albert Einstein received the Nobel Prize in the field of physics. When Adolf Hitler was appointed as Chancellor of Germany Albert Einstein's Nobel Prize was taken away along with his German citizenship. He then moved to the U.S.A.

On April 17, 1955 Albert Einstein experienced internal bleeding caused by an aortic aneurysm. On that day he wrote a speech that he was going to present on national television, but did not live long enough to present it. Now, if you ever travel to our nation's capitol, behind a row of trees, sits this great physicist with his notebook.

Ryan Shank, Grade 6
Concord Ox Bow Elementary School, IN

Miracle

I am writing about a USA Olympic hockey team who had performed something truly amazing. Some people say it was a miracle. For the 1980 season coach Herb Brooks was elected coach of this Olympic team. He had made it on the team in 1960 but was sent home, and didn't make the final roster. Herb planned a tryout that lasted a week but Herb picked the roster on the first day. They practiced nonstop for months, and he kept saying that they would be the best conditioned team. 3 days before the Olympics they played the best team in the world. They lost badly and worst of all their best offensive player Jack O'Callahan got injured. The trainer said he would be out for 1 or 2 weeks. That meant he wouldn't be able to play until the playoff round.

USA beat Czechoslovakia and Sweden in the first round and won both games. In the final round they played the Soviet Union again. In a miracle win they went on to the finals. There they had to play Finland. They came from behind and won the gold medal in the 1980 Olympics in Lake Placid, New York. They even made a movie about it. Herb Brooks died after filming the movie. He never saw it, but he was there. The name of the movie was *Miracle*.

Nathan Will, Grade 6
St Patrick School, IN

Friends

When people have something special that they want to tell someone, but not just to anyone, they tell a friend. A friend is a person who is close to you and can be trusted. Friends are an important factor in life. They let you release your inner-thoughts and have a little bit of fun while getting away from school and home.

Friends are usually people that take years-in-the-making. Most people meet someone, hang out with him or her for a day, and then call him or her a friend. That would not be a friend. That would be an acquaintance. With an acquaintance, people don't even know if they can be trusted or not.

A friend is someone that you would talk with about boyfriends, girlfriends, and all about the bratty girl that lives down the block. People discuss with friends what they don't want discussed with the entire student body.

Friends are like sisters. Friends will get into fights, but they will pull through it. Friends have things in common and they also have their differences. But overall, a good friend is someone that forgives your faults and likes you for being you.

Kelci Malloy, Grade 6

Can You Stop the Bullying?

Bullying is just wrong. My point is that the only reason kids bully is because they don't have a connection with their parents. They don't have an after school hobby or program to attend. About twenty-one percent of boys are bullied, as well as fourteen percent of girls. The bullies don't think about what they are doing, hopefully they will.

It is very wrong and immature to bully. Most people don't understand why children bully, but I know a reason. I feel that parents don't try to talk to their kids or help them with the problems they are having. Children have seen bullying, but are scared to tell. Don't be scared.

Some people have been bullied, are bullies, or have seen bullying. Well people have been cruel. Most people have learned that nobody's perfect. People are just cruel because they are having a bad day or week. Then there are some people that bully just because.

Some people bully because of what's going on at home or in the relationship between their parents. Do you know that about eighty percent of kids bully because they don't have a father or have a lot of anger? My point is that kids bully because they have issues. Everybody has a cruel day or week but bullies do this for years. They need to think sometimes. They may not know it, but the things they are doing wrong are going to come back to haunt them.

Some people have been cruel to others because they may have said something about them. I have been cruel because somebody started a rumor about me. Bullies should get over their anger, and listen to the sound in their heart. Can you stop the bullying? Or can you?

Damara Harrell, Grade 6
Starms Discovery Learning Center, WI

My Friend Katie

When it comes to best friends we are the closet. Katie is my best friend, we met at school in 4th grade. She was born in Wyster, Massachusetts in 1997. Katie moved to Arizona in 2002 we met in 2006. Thought for the first couple of days we kind of ignored each other we became the best of friends. We got in trouble a lot for talking to each other when we were not supposed to. All of our teachers get us mixed up because we always hang out together. Anytime we can we try to hang out together. She used to have a dog named Prancer back in Massachusetts, but unfortunately she passed away. Prancer was Katie's first and favorite dog. She has 2 brothers, a mom and a dad. One of her brothers is really annoying and sometimes entertaining. Nathan is 2 and sometimes annoying but also cute. Nathan is our little make-up doll because he lets us put make-up all over his face. Katie is addicted to books. If you try to take one away from her she will get really mad. She hates when people rip away books from her. As I said Katie's biggest attention is books/writing and fuzzy key chains from Claire's. She can always put a smile on my face and that is why we will stay friends forever.

Sarah Harris, Grade 5
Kyrene Monte Vista School, AZ

Working Hard

When working hard, you can do a lot of things in life. Here are some goals in life that you can have.

Having a great job is something every one would like to have. You would have to go through many things to get a good job. You would have to sign some contracts and many other things.

Working hard is also very important because you would want to take care of your family. Taking care of your family is important because you would have to buy food, clothes, and many other things they might need. These are ways you could take care of your family.

Another way working hard can help, is if you have a kid, you could save up money for his/her college. The reason you would save money is because you want your children to have a good education. One more thing about working hard is to be responsible. Being responsible is very important. The reason it is important is because you would have to wake yourself up on time, clean clothes, and be at work on time. If you are responsible you won't lose your job. But if you don't do this you're going to be sorry since you lost your job. This is how working hard can help you in life. You can take care of your family. you can also send your kids to college if you have a good job. But to do all this, you have to be responsible.

Todd Holeman, Grade 6
Milltown Elementary School, IN

Amelia Earhart

You and I both know that Amelia Earhart was famous for her spectacular flying, but did you know about some of the other things that she did?

I wonder how many people know that Earhart made and tested her own roller coaster as a kid. She also saw some of the early airplanes around my age at the St. Louis Worlds Fair. But her love of flight didn't come until much later. Also in her younger years, she was a nurse during WWI and went to college before and after that.

Earhart took her first flight one fateful day. It took place in Rogers Field. When she came down, her love of flight was born. She began setting records in great numbers. Not only that, but she designed her own line of clothing and wrote an article for *Cosmopolitan* magazine. Her clothes and article were all about aviation.

One day in summer of 1937, Earhart made a flight around the world in order to set another record. She was flying somewhere above the Pacific Ocean and she disappeared. Nobody knows why she disappeared, but I know we will never forget that brave, adventurous, independent woman who showed the world that even women can do amazing things.

Abigail Alwine, Grade 4
Concord Ox Bow Elementary School, IN

The Ghost Tornado

The tapping sound of the rain vibrated in the air. I lay in bed, staring up at the ceiling. I became wide awake as a flash of light appeared out my window. The rain died away as it was replaced by a pounding noise. I leapt out of bed and crept into the living room. I flipped the switch on the wall and the room was illuminated by two light bulbs attached to the ceiling.

As I sank into a sofa, the lights started to flicker. I noticed the light switch wasn't moving. The room went completely black, and lightning illuminated the night sky. A funnel was headed straight for my house!

It was advancing. I waited for the tornado to destroy my house, but the moment never came. I peered up again, just in time to see the funnel pass inches from my house.

The next morning there was no evidence of the funnel. So, I called it the Ghost Tornado.

Tornadoes are the deadliest, most powerful storms in the world. Their winds can reach stronger than 666 mph! They are rated by Geologists by the F-Scale. F0 is the least deadly, F1 is the second least powerful, F2 is moderate, F3 is considerable, F4 is powerful, F5 is devastating, and F6 is deadly, devastating, and powerful all put together. Usually, the smaller the tornado, the stronger its wind currents are. The strongest tornadoes usually form during super cell thunderstorms. These powerful tornadoes are called super cells.

Samantha Moore, Grade 4
Maple Avenue Elementary School, WI

American History of Wrestling

Wrestling is the most exciting sport I've been in so far. I have done a lot of sports, but if I had to pick one of them to do for the rest of my life I would pick wrestling. I have been wrestling for three years. The wrestling season hasn't started yet, so I am now playing football, but I plan to start wrestling soon. That is my experience with wrestling.

Wrestling began in ancient times. Nobody knows when people first started wrestling, but all people around the world wrestle in some way. Modern Olympic wrestling was first recorded in ancient Greece. The United States began participating in Olympic wrestling events in 1904 with the senior freestyle and Greco-Roman style. The U.S. team swept the medal events that year because they were the only team entered. The United States didn't begin seriously fielding teams until 1956.

Wrestling on television is entertainment. The most entertaining wrestling show in my opinion is the World Wrestling Entertainment or WWE. In the WWE there are three brands: Raw, Smack-Down, and Extreme Championship Wrestling. There are championships like the tag team, and the intercontinental championship, but the most important championships are the world heavyweight championship and the WWE championship. I have been watching wrestling for four years and what I have found is that this type of wrestling is indeed phony, but fun to watch.

Tyler Davis, Grade 5
Marcy Elementary School, WI

My Cool Parents!

My mom and dad are so cool. My mom's full name is Carolyn Marie Trammell, but her maiden name is Carolyn Marie Zirpolo. My dad's full name is Larry Michael Trammell. My mom rides horses, and my dad works in technology. My mom competes in a reining division, and my dad works at Techflow. My mom has brown hair, brown eyes, and she loves to spend time with her horses. My dad has grayish brown hair, blue eyes, and loves to spend time on his computer.

My mom and dad do so much with me. They are nice, caring, fun, cool, lovable, great, sweet, and awesome!!! They both make my life very fun. Every time I see them, it just lights up my day. They are always there if I need someone's shoulder to cry on. They also help me with things that I just don't understand. Also, they understand when I have a problem. They both do lots of nice things for me. They are great parents. If I'm sick, they are always there by my side to take care of me. I love my parents a lot. I thank God every day, that they are part of my life, and that it is a honor that I am part of their lives.

Kelly Trammell, Grade 6
Linfield Christian School, CA

The Life of Ciara

Ciara was born October 25, 1985, in Austin, Texas. After moving around to military bases (her mother was in the air force and her father was in the army), her family settled in Atlanta, Georgia. She says that by watching Destiny's Child on a day while home from school, she was inspired to pursue her music career. Ciara started her career off by being in a group called Hearsay, then became a solo artist. She met the famous producer (Jazze Pha) after graduating from Riverdale High School in Riverdale, Georgia in 2003. In 2004 Ciara came out with a top selling hit "Goodies" and soon came out with an album containing 3 more hit songs. Two years later Ciara came out with another album called The Evolution. She got her first Grammy Award for Missy Elliott's "Lose Control." In April 2006, Ciara was featured on Field Mobs billboard top single "So What." In May 2005, Ciara made her first acting debut in the MTV Films coming-of-age film *All You've Got*, and another film (upcoming) *Mama, I Want To Sing!* Ciara is playing a preacher's daughter in the church choir, who becomes a pop star.

Ciara has inspired my to go as far as I can with my dreams. Just watch where they take me!

Dahmone Bluford, Grade 6
Laraway School, IL

Siberian Tigers

What would you say about tigers, and not just any tiger a Siberian tiger? They're majestic, strong, and the biggest cat in the world! It's teeth are staggering, at almost 1 inch long. Imagine being bit by one. Ouch! A Siberian tiger's coat is one of the most elegant things you will ever see, but it's also the most wanted. People have been poaching the tigers for their fur for more than 50 years! Sadly, they're about to fall off the face of the Earth.

Poaching is illegal right? Let's just say people have gotten pretty sneaky over the years. Poachers don't even care if they're killing endangered animals to extinction. Illegally killing Siberian tigers is like the new fashion for poachers. It's simply horrible, mean, rude, whatever you want to call it. Put yourself in the tiger's place. Would you like to be poached to the brink of extinction just so these rich aristocrats can have their fur coats and accessories?

Zoos all over Russia have been trying to save this magnificent creature. They have programs for safe breeding, just to ensure every little tiger cub is healthy and safe. We could always use some tigers on this Earth. People like you and me can help keep this animal from vanishing by donating a small sum to funds in your area.

The Siberian tiger needs the world's help to keep it from vanishing…forever.

Ciara Hernandez, Grade 5
Oak Crest Intermediate School, TX

Supreme Court of the United States

Have you ever wondered about the judicial branch of our government? Well, the Supreme Court is at the top of the judicial branch. The Supreme Court is the highest court in the United States. That means the decision that they make is final. The Supreme Court has nine justices, one of which is the chief justice who is the top justice. These justices have all been hand selected by the President of the United States. Because they have these justices, there is no need for a jury or judge in the Supreme Court. The cases that our Supreme Court deals with are cases that go against the constitution. These cases usually do not only affect one person, but a large group of people.

There are three types of courts in the judicial branch. The lowest court is the district court. If the defendant is unhappy with the result of his or her case, they may appeal their case to a court of appeals. If they are unhappy with their result again, they can make another appeal to the Supreme Court. It is difficult to have your case selected because each justice receives thousands of cases a year, but only about 100 cases are selected to be taken to court. The Supreme Court is very important to our government and Americans because it helps us understand our constitution, our rights, and how to use them effectively.

Ben Irons, Grade 6
Argyle Middle School, TX

My Pet Dog Rex

The long awaited day arrived two years ago when we brought home a two-month-old Labrador Retriever puppy, I named Rex. At first he was nervous when we brought him home, but before long he spotted a new toy inside of a crate, and immediately the crate became his new home for the next year. Rex enjoyed the crate, it gave him a secure place to call home, but as he grew, the crate proved to be too small and the basement became his new home.

Rex liked to be trained and responded well to my commands. Calling him by his name to come to me was as important as any part of his training. With each new accomplishment, I always rewarded and praised my dog, and he responded by being eager to learn more and to please me.

Being an active two-year-old dog, Rex loves to play physical games and go for long walks. He loves to fetch balls and sticks and he has learned to play soccer. I enjoy taking him to the dog beach in Chicago, where he plays in the lake and can freely associate with other dogs. He has also become a very alert watchdog and is very protective of our family and home.

Rex has matured into a well-mannered and housebroken dog and is now allowed more freedom in our home. There is an old saying that "a dog is a man's best friend," that saying still holds true more than ever as my dog Rex remains my very best friend.

Jason Ebanks, Grade 6
Divine Infant Jesus School, IL

My Nana

Have you ever owned your own business? Have you ever had a tumor? Have you ever broken a hip? Well, my nana has done all of that, and much more.

My nana was born in Sudbury, 1936. She's 71 years old, lives in her own house and still drives. My nana owned 4 of her own businesses; two restaurants, and two clothing stores. One of the restaurants was called Northern Star and one of the clothing stores was called Garson Bargain Center. Too bad it burned down.

In 1991, she fell and broke her hip while finishing Christmas shopping. They had to operate and put a steel plate to fix her hip. But did this stop her? No. She was still home and made Christmas dinner for 5.

I guess you can say 2004 was a hard year for my nana. In January, my papa died after 49 years of marriage. She had to learn how to live alone and do things for herself. That same year, she had to have surgery to remove a tumor in her nose. Hopefully next year will be better.

In 2005, she brought me to bowling right after school. The owners forgot to put down sand on the ice and she fell and broke her other hip. That scared me, but she didn't push us around by saying "Can you get this, or that?" She tried to do everything herself.

She may not be a hero in your eyes, but in mine, she's the best.

Dante Foschia, Grade 6
St Francis School, ON

Daring to Try

On September 7, 2007, I went to Las Vegas. My grandpa is in charge of this convention that goes on every year, it is called the ABC Kids Expo. That means All Baby and Child Kids Expo. It was so much fun. I got to see a lot of people from my grandma's church.

One night after the expo I went out to dinner with a girl named Liz and her fiancee Justin. Liz is a reading specialist. She used to be a sixth grade teacher. We ate dinner at a Sushi restaurant. I wasn't going to get sushi because I didn't like the thought of eating raw fish. I was going to order an appetizer, it was raw meat and they brought out this extremely hot rock and I cooked it on the rock. I still ordered it. My mom, aunt, uncle, Liz, and Justin ordered sushi.

My mom told me to try some, I refused to try it and then Liz talked me into it. It was actually fantastic. I'm so glad I tried it. I think that more people should be as daring as I was to try sushi because you can discover new things that way. It's always worth trying something new, because you might really like it after all. No matter what it looks like! That is how I was daring to try sushi. NOW I LOVE IT!

Ariel Marin, Grade 5
Desert Canyon Elementary School, AZ

Being Drug Free!

There is one thing that kills overs one million people a year. Drugs. Drugs take control over your mind and body. It kills you.

Drugs kill you. Like a lot of things, after you try it, you are addicted. Some drugs, like meth, after a while it starts to eat your face and makes your hair uncontrollable. When you start doing drugs, you get addicted and they start to control your life, what you do, what you eat, everything. It is very sad to see little kids that get beaten, because their parents don't know what they are doing.

After one use, you lose at least one year of your life. Everyone who tries drugs says that you can't stop. That is all you think about. You feel like you can't live without them. It ruins your life.

Drugs are the most unhealthy thing on Earth. They will slowly kill you. Meth can eventually eat you. It can also make your organs shut down.

If you smoke tobacco, it ruins your lungs. You will probably get addicted to it, too. If you smoke most of your life, get second hand smoke, or work with tobacco, you have a bigger chance at lung cancer than a person who is never around smoke or does not smoke.

Drugs ruin your life. Some people think drugs are cool. Overcome them, because you're better than that.

Heather Little, Grade 6
Milltown Elementary School, IN

Jumping to Conclusions

There is this very important lesson I learned that I feel I must share: Never jump to conclusions. It might not seem like a very important one but you'll be surprised to see what kind on things it can destroy.

Every day, I dream of being a fashion designer. Whenever I had the time, I drew clothing designs on pieces of paper. Be it plain white paper or scratch paper. I even sketched on little pieces of paper! All of my friends say I draw really good, but deep down in my heart I knew that good wasn't enough.

One day I came up with a design that I thought was good, but my friends think that it was horrible. I kept asking them why, but they wouldn't tell me. Then they asked if they can take it home and examine it, and of course, I said yes, I mean what have I got to lose? They're my friends right? But I was wrong, and at the same time disappointed. The next day when I asked my friends to give me back my drawing, they played dumb. But over time I realize that my friends won't do such a thing, so I did a little investigating. The culprit turned out to be a shy girl who only wanted to copy my drawing. Surprising right?

Jumping to conclusions is bad. It can ruin friendship and so many things in life. So readers, never jump to conclusions!

Sherry Lin, Grade 6
Rita Ledesma Elementary School, CA

Dance

I love to dance. I dance everywhere. I also take dance lessons. I like to dance because it is fun, I like music, and it makes me feel good.

There are many different styles of dance, over one hundred and fifty. Almost every country and culture has its own style. There are three main categories of dancing: Social dance, Concert dance, and Competitive. Under Social dance there is Historical, which is a dance that tells a story, Folk dance, such as Irish Step dancing, Line dancing, and Square dancing. There is also Ballroom, Latin, Swing, and Street. Street dancing includes Hip Hop and Break dancing. Concert dancing includes Ballet, Belly dancing, Theatre dance including Jazz, Tap and Lyrical and finally there is Competitive dance, which includes many of the dances above.

Historians say dancing has been around as long as there have been humans. In India, cave drawings were found which showed people who appear to be dancing. This dated back to 5000-2000 BC. Dancing revolved around many social events such as births, deaths, weddings or sicknesses. Over the years there has been many changes and now dance is mainly for entertainment and pleasure.

In dance class I study Jazz, Tap, Lyrical and Hip Hop. My two favorites are Hip Hop and Jazz. I love the music in Hip Hop and you are able to act and have lots of attitude. I like Jazz because I also enjoy the music and there are a lot of fun steps. There is a style of dance for everyone and I think everyone should try it at least once.

No matter how young or old, it is healthy, it makes you feel good, but most of all it is fun.

Emily Carr, Grade 6
Hampton Middle School, NB

Follow Your Dreams

I say that everyone in this whole world can accomplish something if they work hard at it. I did, I got first in the county at cross country. I had to run a lot, but it was worth it.

If you have a dream and you really want it to come true, don't let someone tell you that you can't do it. Just keep working hard, and don't let someone tell you what your dreams are, because it's your life, not theirs.

It doesn't matter what you want to be, if it's a pro softball player, a nurse, or even a singer. You're the only one that knows what you want to be. So just keep working hard.

My sister is a great basketball player and she works really hard. She's been in AAU and Gym Rats and she's only in 8th grade, I think that's pretty good. My sister and I love to get awards at stuff that we work hard at.

Just think, if you try really hard you are able to get a trophy, or even a certificate. But if you work at your potential and you don't get an award it's okay, because you worked really hard. So always work hard.

Rachel Bolin, Grade 6
Milltown Elementary School, IN

My Summer Vacation

I woke up on Saturday morning, I was really excited. That day I was going to Washington.

When we arrived at my cousin's house, the first thing we heard was my cousin, Logan, shouting "They're here!" As we came inside, my cousin's dog, Lacy, attacked us. She is good at that.

On Wednesday we went to Seattle Aquarium. It was great. We saw starfish, seals, otters, jellyfish, an octopus and much, much more. However, I felt sorry for the octopus because it was in a very small cage.

The next day, my aunt took us to the zoo. It was really fun and you could hear birds everywhere. We saw a red panda that was hiding from everyone. A bush baby jumped at us, and a jaguar came right up to the glass of its cage, which I thought was really neat. I think it was the most fun I've ever had in Washington.

On my last full day in Washington we didn't do much except for going out to lunch with my grandma. My cousins, Lorrin and Logan, slept over at my grandma's house with my sister, Michaela, and me.

On our way home, the next day, there was a car crash. Seven cars were involved so the whole freeway was closed! It took us about three hours to get out of Seattle. Finally, after about seven and a half hours in the car, we made it home.

Rachel Rimmer, Grade 5
Eugene Christian School, OR

Roger Federer Inspires Me

Few people in the world are the best at their sport. Twenty-six-year-old Roger Federer is one of the best tennis players of all time. Roger has technique and focus, is far ahead of other players, and is a very attractive player.

Roger proves he can play by his technique and focus. Only focused players like him never take their eye off the ball. It is hard to be calm and aggressive at the same time. Roger never gets distracted. Federer always plays his best and never gives up.

Roger Federer also shows the big gap between him and other players. He has showed he is the best by winning twelve Grand Slam titles and plays like a champion. He makes people want to watch him by playing outstanding.

Why should you watch Roger Federer play? First of all, it thrills you to watch such admirable tennis. His skill and agility have been commendable. It also inspires some people to take up the sport. People who play sports, like me, will appreciate it when they lose and learn from their mistakes.

Roger Federer teaches me to be calm, play like a winner, and never give up. I hope he will inspire you in the same ways and you will learn to excel in your sport.

Rohan Ramakrishnan, Grade 6
Challenger School – Ardenwood, CA

Terry Fox

Do you know Terry Fox? At the age of 22 he became one of Canada's heroes. Did you know he was born in Winnipeg, Manitoba on July 28, 1958 and at the age of 18 he was diagnosed with osteosarcoma or bone cancer? And did you know that when he was 18 years old he had his right leg amputated in 1977?

Just because Terry had only one leg this did not stop him from running a cross-country marathon. He had a special leg called a prosthetic made and started to train for this marathon so that people would become aware of this disease. This marathon was called the Marathon of Hope.

He started at St. John's, Newfoundland and dipped his leg in the Atlantic Ocean on April 20, 1980 and wanted to finish by dipping it in the Pacific Ocean when he reached Victoria, British Columbia.

His plan was to run 42 km a day and no one has ever done anything like this. He was forced to end his marathon on September 1, 1980 when he was close to Thunder Bay, Ontario after he had run for 143 days. He was not feeling well and x-rays found a lump the size of a golf ball in his right lung and a lump the size of a lemon in his left lung. By now he had run 5,373 km and had gone through Newfoundland, Nova Scotia, Prince Edward Island, New Brunswick and Ontario.

Terry Fox died June 28,1981 after going into a coma after getting pneumonia.

Every year there is a Terry Fox Run in order to raise money for cancer research and remember the man who started it all.

Riley Boucher, Grade 6
St Francis School, ON

Sharks

They strike without warning. Patrolling the water waiting for a meal to come close to them. Sharks have been around 400 million years. Want to know their secret how they lived so long? Well, sharks survived the ice age by moving to different warmer water. Back then there was a colossus shark called the Megaladon. The behemoth shark could eat a killer whale. The Megaladon died because the food that it ate moved to different water. Sharks that live now are small compared to the Megaladon except the whale shark.

Sharks are fish but do not have any bones. Sharks' skin is make out of cartilage. No other animal is so misunderstood and feared than the sharks. A shark has 13 body parts. The fins keep the shark balanced. The 1st dorsal fin may look cool unless it's heading at you. Sharks have gills like fishes. The shark's gills help it breathe underwater. Also, they can smell blood from long distances. Sharks can see very, very well underwater. Sharks have rows of big jagged teeth. In fact, sharks have teeth on their skin. A shark is hard and tough.

Hugo Morales, Grade 5
Desert Trails Elementary School, CA

The Fun Has Begun

The whitish gray Mexicana plane swooped down into the land of the tropics, Mazatlan, Mexico. I was in the plane, sleeping until morning daylight. I felt the plane land and I gradually woke up, feeling a bit lightheaded.

Finally, I stumbled out of the plane, feeling drowsy like I woke up early in the morning (which I practically did). After stumbling, I walked normally (at last). As soon as I got out of the boarding alley, the humid air got into my lungs, making me almost choke! "I…can't…breath!" I gasped. Suddenly, the humid air disappeared like a wisp of fog in a sunny clearing. It felt relaxing for me to get used to this unusual air.

When I got to the checkout line, the boarding alley was like a stream of water, smoothly going down a slick a surface. I was leaning my head here and there. At the same time I was tapping my foot furiously. "Come on, come on!" I thought intensely. Suddenly, I hissed out, "I can't take this anymore!!!" The pressure filled my whole body, making me jump. The minutes passed slowly. The minutes felt like hours. Finally, our turn was here at last. My dad talked with him about the vacation agency that we're using and showed our passports. The man stamped each one. "Yes!" I exclaimed. At last we were on our way to have fun in the sun.

Jessica Ye, Grade 5
Dingeman Elementary School, CA

Dogs

Pets can change your life. They most definitely have changed mine. I have four dogs, two little dogs and two big dogs. My dogs have changed my life so much I can't even explain it. They have been there for me when there was something bad that happened. They have been my best friend when I really needed them, like when my friend and I got in a fight. They can tell when I am sick or not feeling well. I know that they can tell because they will not try to play with me or do anything to make me feel worse. They will cuddle up next to me and then I really know they care because they will stop doing anything that they are doing just to come up and make me feel better.

Dogs can change your life real easily. If you look into their eyes you can see that they actually care about you. They will beg for your attention which means that they want to be around you. Dogs love you unconditionally.

Dogs will get annoying sometimes. Your responsibility is to remember when they get annoying to try not to yell at them. Remember all the times they cheered you up and remember that you are the lucky one who got blessed with this dog. If you did not get blessed with that dog, then your life would not be the same.

Corbin Badger, Grade 6
Tri-West Middle School, IN

My Grandma

My grandma's name is Elizabeth Cervantes. She is a working machine. She was born on September 11. She is a big Cowboys fan; her favorite players were Emmit Smith and Troy Aikman. Now her favorite players are Tony Romo and Marion Barber. She watches every football game. She goes to the Ventura College 5 times a week, but she doesn't get homework. She hardly has any time to rest because she does so much for everyone. My grandma takes everyone everywhere. She takes me to soccer practice, sometimes my soccer games, and to school. She takes my brothers to school; takes my Tia Erica to school and to work, takes my other Tia to wherever she wants to go.

Her best friend's name was Judy, she passed away like a month ago in September. My grandma was really depressed; Judy was a good friend to my grandma. Sometimes I call my grandma, grandmother. She, well we really have a big family; probably all around California. She has a good life; I hope she will always have a good life.

Elena Vega, Grade 6
Isbell Middle School, CA

Hiking

One day I was camping with my dad, sister, and some friends. When we were getting ready to go to sleep my dad heard someone walking. My dad thought maybe it was one of my friends. Then he looked outside the tent and saw a bear.

When my dad saw the bear he came to wake me and my sister so we could go on a hike to see if there was a cave that had bears in it. When we got up we put our hiking shoes on and started to walk towards the mountains. While walking we found a whole bunch of animals.

We were walking through the woods making sure there weren't any dangerous animals around. We found a snake hole and we wanted to see what kind of snake lived in it but my dad said no because it might be poisonous. Then we continued our journey. Finally we found the cave and found a whole bunch of bears.

When we found the cave we went inside to look around. We found bones from people that were killed by the bears. My dad told us to stay behind his back just in case we ran into a bear. When my dad put us behind his back he saw a bear and told us to get ready to run. When we started to run the bear started to chase us. When we turned around we saw more than five bears behind us.

Then we finally saw a place where we could hide and get way from the bears. When we hid all of the bears went running straight ahead of us. When they left we went outside of the cave and back to our campsite and we were safe and sound.

Mandie López, Grade 6
Ranch Hills Elementary School, CA

Caring for the Next Generation: Make a Difference, Conserve!

It is imperative that we conserve energy! Conserving energy will help our environment not only for today, but for generations to come. Do you want our generation to be the reason the next generation dies early because of lack of energy? I don't want to hurt the next generation.

Oil is very rare and takes hundreds of millions of years to be formed by nature. Oil cannot be formed by man; this makes it a nonrenewable resource. Our vehicles are committing combustion. This is a burning of fossil fuels such as oil and trees. The exhaust from combustion is called carbon dioxide. With the burning of plants that use carbon dioxide in photosynthesis, the carbon increases. Too much carbon is poisonous to animals and humans. Do you realize that tons of carbon is released into the atmosphere yearly? We have to keep this under control! By doing so, we will be helping the carbon dioxide-oxygen cycle, ecosystem, etc. to become balanced again.

We can do many things to help conserve energy. We can ride bikes more. We can use energy star products. Many consumers tend to run their heating or cooling systems in an unhealthy way, by running it too high or low. This can lead to higher bills, breakdowns, or even lead to the release of harmful chemicals into the air, water, or ground. By conserving, we can help our country become even stronger, by becoming less dependent on imports. Let's make a difference.

Evelyn Thomas, Grade 5
Dishman Elementary School, TX

My Annoying Nephew

This essay is on my annoying nephew. The reason I call him annoying is because he bothers me too much and gets on my nerves. One of the reasons he's annoying to me is when I'm trying to do my homework and he'll keep on asking me to go outside. Most of the time, if I say no, he'll take my homework and hide it from me. So then I have to go outside with him for like 20 minutes. Then after we get done outside, we go inside and he'll give me my homework back.

So now another reason he's annoying is he cries a lot. Because I won't fill up his sippy cup. Also he'll cry if you tell him "No." So most of the time I say yes to go outside and only go out for like 5 minutes. A lot of times he cries for no reason to get attention.

A lot of times at night he'll wake me up to get him a drink. Also, he'll usually wake me up just to go outside at 11:00 P.M. to go play. When he wakes me up at night, that's when I get really mad because most of the time I have school. That's when I think he's most annoying, when he wakes me up. Also he'll wake me up to change him, but I never do it; I always tell him to ask his mom! So that is how my nephew is so annoying to me.

Jordan Dahl, Grade 6
Milltown Elementary School, IN

My Religion

My name is Jasmine Andrews. I am American, first my Muslim faith. Muslim means anyone who follows the religion of Islam. Being Muslim in America is not very easy. Sometimes when we go out people stare at us because of the way we dress. We dress this way because our tradition and our religion tells us. Dressing this way is called hijab. Hijab is a way to dress for a girl or a woman in order to cover herself. I think it is hard to dress this way because people think we are bad people and do bad things. Our bible is called the holy Quran. I have almost all the small scriptures memorized in Arabic. Islam is actually a religion of peace.

My grandfather actually is from Palestine. Palestine used to be very peaceful. It's a story about peaceful people, religions, and land. There are three different religions now that live on Palestine. They are: Islam, Christians, and the Jewish religion. In 1948, the holy wars began. The three religions all wanted this small land to be two different countries. Does it belong to Palestine or Israel?

Palestine has a lot of people who are hurting. There are people from all the religions who do now have a home, food or even water. I feel sad. When I get older I will help those kids and families of all religions and make sure that they have food and money. That is what my religion tells me to do.

Jasmine Andrews, Grade 5
The Arts Academy School, OH

The Greatest Family Ever

This is how the greatest family influences my life. Three other people make up the members in my unforgettable family. There is my sister, she is the best ever. I have an unbelievable mom and a super dad. Here is a little bit about them.

My sister, Chelsea, loves sports. She plays volleyball, basketball, and softball. She is extremely beautiful and nice. She is one of the most caring and loving people in the world! Chelsea is very energetic with everything she does. She helps me study and do my homework when my parents can not.

My mom, Marty, is extremely caring. She is the counselor at my school. She watches and comes to all my games. Marty helps Chelsea and I with our homework. She volunteers at my sister's and my school. She is very beautiful and always well dressed.

The super sports guy in my family is my dad, Ron. He helps me with all my sports. He is an athletic director at Decatur Middle School. Ron cares about my grades and health just like my mom. He is very athletic.

This is the greatest family. They are very supportive. Marty, Chelsea, and super dad have influenced me in my life a lot; I love them.

Bailey Brothers, Grade 6
Southport 6th Grade Academy, IN

The Big Game

My ears started to hurt from all the yelling. It was the Red River Shoot-out game happening at the Cotton Bowl. I am a huge Oklahoma fan, so I was rooting for the Sooners.

Since the Texas State Fair was happening right outside the stadium, we hung out there before the game. We went on a huge Ferris Wheel first. You could pretty much see all of Dallas from up there. After that, we went to the midway. I played some games and also rode more rides. I was having a blast so far.

We then grabbed something to eat and we saw there was a car show going on. The place was filled with cars and people. We got to sit in some of the cars.

After leaving the car show, we went into the stadium a little early to avoid the crowd entering the game. After watching the bands and the teams run onto the field, the game got underway. The first two drives, Oklahoma was forced to punt. Late in the first quarter, Oklahoma scored a touchdown and Texas had scored also. In the second quarter, Texas scored on a long pass, but OU answered with a tying score to make the game 14-14 at half time. In the second half, OU started to gain momentum and won the game 28-21. I left the stadium with a huge smile on my face.

Jack Graham, Grade 6
Argyle Middle School, TX

Kinnick Stadium

In my lifetime, I've watched and been to the University of Iowa's football games at Kinnick Stadium, located in Iowa City, Iowa.

Have you ever thought or wondered how Kinnick Stadium got its name? Well, it started with a man named Nile Kinnick. Nile Kinnick, a leader and hero to many people, opened the stadium, then known as Iowa Stadium in 1929. Then, on June 2, 1943, when his F4F crashed into the Gulf of Parcia, Nile Kinnick passed away. The stadium was renamed Kinnick Stadium; they will remember him because of the statue in front of the stadium showing Nile Kinnick as a student at the University of Iowa.

New stadiums are very nice, not just Kinnick Stadium, but all stadiums. The University's athletic director announced plans for the stadium between 1928 and 1929. Construction began the following spring. Horses and mules were used as heavy equipment movers. Animals that died during the process were buried under what is now the north end zone. Many Americans are proud of the workers who worked around the clock to complete the stadium. Kinnick Stadium, which has welcomed many people for decades, was completed in seven months.

Hundreds of people around the United States love Kinnick Stadium. What I know is I love the town, the people, the trees, the atmosphere and everything about it. It's so beautiful in the spring.

Emma Christensen, Grade 6
Nishna Valley Community School, IA

Panda Bears

The Panda Bear is probably the most famous endangered animal. The Panda lives in six small areas located in China. In China they call the Panda "Xiongmao" which means Giant Cat Bear. The Panda was believed to have magical powers that could ward off natural disasters and evil spirits. Writing about the Pandas can be traced back 3,000 years. They were even kept as pets by the Chinese Emperors. The Panda was first introduced to the western world in 1869 by a French missionary. He sent a pelt to a museum in Paris.

Panda Bears eat over fifteen different kinds of bamboo. Because of an inefficient intestinal system the Panda must feed for 12 to 16 hours a day, they can consume 22 to 40 pounds of bamboo each day. When they eat fresh bamboo shoots they eat about 84 pounds each day.

The Giant Panda Bear is black and white. In 1995 DNA tests prove that giant Pandas are more closely related to bears than raccoons. The mating time of the large Pandas fall into the month of March until May. It can come also to fights between the males for the mating privilege. The babies weigh only approximately 90 to 130 grams and are covered with pouring rem white skin. Like bears, giant pandas are basically heavy ponderous land creatures.

Madison Blazak, Grade 6
Rosefield Charter School, AZ

My Passion

My one true passion is dance. I like dance because it is fun and it makes you feel good inside. When I am bored I turn on some music and start making up a dance. There is a saying that says "Dance like nobody's watching!" When I don't feel like going to dance, I go and still have fun. Dance comes pretty easy to me. When I learn something new I stick it in my brain and work on it till I get it right. Every time I go to the dance studio I meet a new friend and they are always nice.

The dance studio I go to has a spring recital and a Christmas play called *A Gift for Emma*. Everybody is in the spring recital but not everybody is in *A Gift for Emma*. This is because the play is strictly ballet and modern. Some people are only in jazz or tap. Another reason is that you have to try out for certain parts and you have to be 11 or older. Everybody at the studio is nice and friendly. I am in ballet, jazz, tap, and pre-point. All the teachers are nice. The owner teaches some classes and she is really strict, but she can also be nice.

The dance studio is small compared to most dance studios. In this studio there are three main dance rooms. The fourth one is outside. My favorite studio is the biggest one because there is so much room to dance. I think it would be fun to be a professional dancer someday. I hope to stay with dance for a very long time and maybe do something with it when I get older.

Emily King, Grade 6
Argyle Middle School, TX

Basketball Ankle

I think it was ten o'clock when it happened. It was when I was in fifth grade.

The coach split us up into groups to play basketball. I was in a hurry to shoot the ball I jumped, and threw it, it missed. When I landed on my foot my ankle twisted sideways. I felt a pop. Then once I moved it a little I couldn't feel it. It didn't seem like anyone noticed I was in pain.

Then someone told me to get the ball. I stepped on my foot, and it felt like my heart skipped a beat it hurt so much. I tried to walk normal, but all I could do was limp. I was happy when my turn was over. I sat up against the wall, and took off my shoe. It looked okay, it was just a little pink. I walked up to the coach a few minutes later, and asked her if I could go to the nurse, because I didn't cry she told me to walk it off.

The reason I didn't cry is because my friends were watching. So I was limping in pain for three days. One day the teacher told me to go to the nurse. I had to get a splint because it was fractured. A couple of weeks later I got a cast.

Christina Parnell, Grade 6
Irma Marsh Middle School, TX

Pink Friends of Our Zoo Keepers

"Carol, I am afraid your test results are positive."

"What?" Carol asked in a confused voice. "Carol, the tests show you have breast cancer," replied Dr. Lad. There was a long silence and then Dr. Lad began describing Carol's treatment options. Carol barely heard a word he said. Her only thought was, "What about the animals?"

Carol Whits was the head zoo keeper at the New York City Zoo. Her favorite thing in the world was being with the animals. In many ways the animals were her family. She spent many hours with them talking, and even telling jokes. They responded as if they understood what she was saying. The regular visitors at the zoo also knew Carol and how well she cared for the animals.

The zoo manager and other workers decided to try to help Carol. They started a fund to help with Carol's medical bills. Pink signs and breast cancer information cards were posted throughout the zoo asking for help. Many people put money and cards in the pots placed with the signs.

Over time, Carol was able to make short visits to the zoo. The "Pink Friends of our Zoo Keeper" fund earned enough to cover Carol's medical expenses; educated many people about breast cancer; and had extra money to give to the American Breast Cancer Society. Each time Carol visited, the animals seemed happier and Carol grew stronger and finally came back to work.

Margaret Stein, Grade 6
Argyle Middle School, TX

Dakotah

My best friend is Dakotah Ferguson. She is like a sister to me. She's funny, nice, we do everything together, and we've known each other since forever.

First, she is funny because she says funny things. For example, one day we were watching a scary movie and someone called and she said, "Sorry I have to go, but what time is it?" We started cracking up and so did the person on the phone.

Next, she is nice. She does nice things for people like getting them stuff, holding their stuff, and waiting for you when you're behind. She comes to my softball games to cheer me on.

Third, we do everything together. We go shopping, roller-skating, and she spends the night at my house all the time. I spend the night at her house all the time too.

Last, she is my best friend because we've known each other since forever. Dakotah's dad and my dad are very good friends. We have a lot of fun together.

As you can see Dakotah is my best friend because she is funny, nice, we do everything together, and we've known each other since forever. She is like a sister to me. She is my best friend.

Savannah Pulse, Grade 6
West Central Middle School, IL

Saving the Wetlands

Saving the wetlands is of great importance. Eighty percent of wetlands are already gone. What will happen to the other 20%? Wet lands can be used to filter filth that enters them, however they are not cesspools. Roadway and sewer water run into wetlands where the debris will sink and remain. The water, however, carries on into our water sources. Go diving in a wetland and you might find that tennis ball you lost last month!

Wetlands do not only help keep our water sources clean, but also provide habitats for endangered or threatened plants and animals. Dragonflies, water bugs, fish, snails, leeches, snakes, turtles, frogs, ducks, birds, butterflies, deer, coyotes, foxes, owls, and beavers are just a few of the animals you might find in wetlands around Alberta. These animals depend on freshwater environments to survive.

A misunderstood sign of a healthy wetland is a dry wetland. Unfortunately they are filled in and things are built on them, like new houses. When the water returns the wetland does what it is designed to do and holds the water like a sponge. This is supposed to help with flood control of the environment but now that houses are there people find their basements flooding with water. Is that a good thing?

Hopefully, with this information, people will start to consider how important wetlands really are in our environment. They are wonderful places to visit, learn and experience life.

Brittany Dyck, Grade 5
Master's Academy and College, AB

My Marlin

So, here we are on our way to Cabo, I was so excited. The fishing was going to be awesome. We landed in Cabo, and on the way in we saw so may fishing boats on the water.

We were going to go fishing earlier in the holiday, but I had a breakout of asthma, so we waited a few days before going fishing. Eventually we went to a charter company and asked about going fishing. They were expensive but they were good.

About one hour the reel screamed, and the marlin took about 500ft of my line. I was in the chair and had the rod in my hand. He ran for about 2 minutes, and then finally stopped. This was my chance, a once in a lifetime opportunity. I saw him jump, he was huge. I had him at the top of the water. I started to reel hard, I was slowly gaining on him. I was getting line back. He was only 20m out now.

Then he started taking heaps again, he was going straight down. It was hard to get him back up. Finally I got him to the side of the boat and the deck hand, and the captain got him on board the boat. I posed for a few photos. The deck hand estimated the marling to be about 250lbs in weight, and 8ft long. We put him back after all, that's what fishing is all about.

Cullen O'Brien, Grade 6
Peoria Academy, IL

Believing

Believing in myself is the most important thing to me. This is because of everything I am going through. Believing has helped me a lot.

Believing in myself has helped me get awards. Just like last year, I got the award for the smartest 5th grade student. I got the award because I believed in my work and myself. Believing also is helping me get through my parents' divorce. Divorces are very hard to deal with.

Believing also helps me believe I can make new friends every day. It helps me believe that I will do better on my work the next time, as long as I keep going at it.

Believing in myself has helped me do a lot of things, and every time I finish what I start. Belief has helped me accomplish everyday tasks like playing games, doing work, and making friends.

Believing in myself has also helped me get good grades on my homework. This helps me get Honor Roll and then that makes my mom very happy.

Many miracles happen when you believe in yourself. Just like when I got a free bag because I believed I could. I got perfect attendance by believing I could go to school.

Many miracles happen by believing in yourself. That is what I want you to learn from my story.

Michelle Leigh Atwood, Grade 6
Milltown Elementary School, IN

Reilly, Michael, and I

Everybody has friends who fight, right? Well, I had a fight with my friend Reilly who went to my old school. We got into a fight over a hot boy for a year.

We were in the third grade and a hot boy was in my class. We both liked him. After school Reilly and I were talking about him. We were deciding who was going to get him. I suggested that I get him for two weeks and then she does the same. She yelled "No!" And then the fight began. We kept on fighting until Reilly said aloud that I like her brother. I ran in embarrassment.

A year later Reilly and I were playing softball, which we didn't know. Also we were on different teams. We were playing against each other, because I overheard her and she said that she played on the Diamond Backs. The team that we were playing was the Diamond Backs. So, we were playing them. I wasn't surprised. The game soon began.

Then something weird happened. Reilly was up to bat. As usual, she hit the ball to second base which I was playing. Then she stopped and asked if we wanted to hang out. It was weird, but I just said yes.

Now I guess we are friends again because we hang out a lot more. It turned out all right and guess what we are best friends. We never know if we are going to get in another fight.

McKenna Freiberg, Grade 6
Imagine Charter School at Rosefield, AZ

Full Count

The most important thing to me is baseball. I live baseball, I dream baseball, and I watch baseball. I am addicted to baseball. I prefer to watch the Dodgers, but if they aren't on, I don't care who I watch. I play baseball in the Pony League. I'm a really good hitter, but not as good as Stan Musial and Pete Rose.

My Dad got me into baseball. When I was five years old I thought my sport was basketball. I've played on a team for two years. My first coach was really nice and my second coach knows a lot about baseball. I play baseball for the Lord Jesus. It doesn't matter if I win or lose, I play baseball for fun. I made lots of friends on the team who are very nice, like Cameron, Haden, Austin, Drake, Mason, Taylor, Jared, Martian, and Reese. All of our team is really good. Usually the other team is better, but like I said it doesn't matter if we win or lose, I play to glorify Jesus.

My family has a record of playing baseball and softball. My Dad and sister both have played baseball and softball. I only play baseball, so I'm not very good at any other sport. I get my homework done before I play any games. Baseball is important to me because it keeps me active.

Christopher Jasien, Grade 6
Linfield Christian School, CA

Under the Big Trees

Every summer my grandparents fly over from China and we go on vacation together. This year we went to Sequoia. We chose Sequoia because it is one of the most famous National Parks and it features the ancient and giant Sequoia trees.

Our first destination was the visitor center. When we arrived, the morning sunlight was bright and the sky was blue without a whisper of cloud. The park ranger there told us we only have black bears in California. Black bears are smaller and less vicious than brown bears. They can be black, brown, or even white. Black bears are omnivores. They eat rodents, fruits, and nuts. It is important to put our food into a bear proof locker. We can protect bears by not letting them steal. When stealing, they become dangerous and aggressive, and will be destroyed.

Our second destination was the Big Tree Trail. The trail was a circular path around a meadow surrounded by giant Sequoias. There I learned water and sunlight help Sequoias grow. Wind helps the Sequoias spread their seeds. Fire helps cones to pop and release the seeds. The trail was my favorite place because I encountered a wild bear family there. The mother bear must have met humans before because she acted calmly when she saw us. I watched them for 15 minutes observing the mother never let the cubs out of her sight.

What a great day to start a great vacation!

James Wu, Grade 5
Ashley Falls Elementary School, CA

My Pets

I love pets. That is why I don't have only one, I have three. One of them is an orange and white tabby cat named Spotty. Another one of my pets is another cat but he is a gray cat that we found and his name is now Mister. One of last pets is a little black and brown dog named Lola. Taking care of them is very fun

I have a cat. Her name is Spotty. She is about three or four years old. She is also very playful. When she was little she stood out to me because she had a little spot on her nose. I thought that the little spot on her nose was so cute that out of a whole and entire litter of adorable baby kittens, I just had to keep her. Now she sleeps on my feet every night since I got her.

I also have another cat named Mister. We think he is an old cat. We actually didn't buy him, we found him. When my dad was going to work one day, he found a ran over cat pushed off to the side of the road next to the gutter. He is so cool.

Last but not least I have a little dog named Lola. She is a little trouble maker sometimes. She can be sweet, cute and playful. One of her favorite games is "FETCH." She loves to play tug-of-war too with her little beat up ugly rope.

Ashley Huff, Grade 6
Isbell Middle School, CA

My Family

My family is very nice to me. We sometimes fight but we get over it. I have ten relatives in my family. I am the eighth person in my family. I love my family in many ways. My mom is very nice. She loves and takes care of us. My dad loves me like my mom does. Hunter is very funny and nice. Damion is a little mean but I still love him because he is my big brother. Jazzlin is nice to me, too. Delton is nice to me but sometimes we fight. We all get over it in the morning. Everybody loves me the way I am and that will never change. I love my family as much as I love the world. Sometimes I get mad at my family. We all love each other. My family is the happiest family on Earth. I love my mommy, daddy, sisters, and my brothers. Harlin is sometimes a yeller and gets on our nerves but we still love her. My family has many friends. We love them like a part of our family. We make plenty of jokes, go swimming, and have fun.

I love my family and I hope I can stay with my family for a long time. My family and I are happy to be together. I hope my family can stay like this.

Juanita Coralyn Deese, Grade 4
Gateway Pointe Elementary School, AZ

Dogs

Dogs are man's best friend, and if you choose the right one you get a great companion. Domestic dogs come in a wide variety of shapes and colors. There are many types of dogs. Some are companion dogs, gun dogs, herding dogs, hounds, terriers, or working dogs.

An example of a companion dog is the bulldog. A bulldog received its name from English farmers who used it to wrangle bulls. They did this by grabbing the bull's neck and not letting go until the farmer ordered it to.

A gun dog would be a Golden Retriever. A Golden Retriever was bred from first a Flat Coated Retriever and Tweed Water Spaniel. Then Irish Setter, Labrador, and Bloodhound added later.

A herding dog would be a German Shepherd. German Shepherds were first seen at a dog show in Hanover, Germany in 1882 although its ancestry dates hundreds of years back.

A Dachshund would be in the hounds group. These dogs are descended from the Teckel.

An example of a terrier is a Miniature Schnauzer. A Miniature Schnauzer is a cross between a standard Schnauzer and an Affenpinschers. It was first seen in Britain in 1928. If you want a working dog, you should get a Swedish Elkhound. These dogs date back to the Scandinavian cavemen although it wasn't officially recognized until 1946.

If you're going to look for a dog, make sure it's the right one and you'll have a companion for life.

Chelsea Olson, Grade 5
Aloe Elementary School, TX

Ohio's Cedar Point

Have you ever been so excited you could just fall and scream? Well I did one day. I was so excited because I got to go to Cedar Point's Hallow Weekends. Hallow weekends is a month of scary things. Some things like a scary warped mummy popping out of the ground and pulling your feet down into a secret door that takes you to a secret ride with the mummy. The secret ride was a scary ride with the mummy. The ride was so scary they had to ban it from Ohio's Cedar Point. Another ride I got to go on was the four hundred feet, four hundred miles per hour Dragster. The Dragster is the biggest and fastest ride in all of Cedar Point. I was so scared I almost wet my pants. I also went on a ride a little smaller that the Dragster. It is the Atomic Force. The Atomic Force is three hundred miles per hour and has a ton of flips. That ride made me barf from all of the flips. I thought that was my last ride, but I stopped barfing, sat down for ten minutes, then got up and went to another ride. The next ride I went on was a train. The train rode through the woods so things popped out of the woods like the Texas Chain Saw Massacre. Stuff popped out because it was still Hallow Weekends. Man I sure loved Ohio's Scary Hallow Weekends.

Dennis Selmani, Grade 4
Jefferson Elementary School, MI

Martin Luther King

Martin Luther King worked for racial equality and civil rights in the United States of America. He was born on January 15, 1929, in Atlanta, Georgia. Martin's parents named him Michael but later on his name changed to Martin. He had one brother and one sister. Their names were Alfred and Chasten.

His dad was a minister, his mom a school teacher. Martin's mom taught him how to read. Later on after graduating Morse House College he married Correta Scott. Then he became a minister and he moved to Alabama. During the 1950s he became active in racial equality and civil rights.

He got his inspiration from Rosa Parks. He wanted to change many things for racial equality and civil rights. Martin Luther King wanted to change many things that white people were doing. He wanted to stop it, because it was wrong.

At that time black and white people could not drink from the same water fountain, or be in the same classroom. They couldn't even be on the same part of a public bus. Black people would get beaten for no reason.

Dr. King was awarded the Nobel prize. Martin was a spiritual man. He gave a speech called "I Have a Dream" it was very good. From that day on everything changed. Black and white people could do all kinds of things together. Then Martin was killed.

Felix Escamilla, Grade 5
Oak Crest Intermediate School, TX

Life with No Gangs or Violence

Life with no gangs would be great to me because people wouldn't get killed over a color. People do not want to stop gang banging, so I wish that they can come together all around the world, especially in California. No violence is better than no gangs because with violence, people just get killed and beat for nothing. Someone can be graduating from college, about to be going to the N.F.L. and all of a sudden someone kills them. I will never kill anyone or be in a gang even if my life depended on it. My cousin is a crip always claiming the East Side, always on the West Side, and always fighting. My other cousin has been to jail over five times for robbing people, drugs, running from the police, and playing with guns. I will never be like them. Life with no gangs or violence would be the best thing ever to me, I will never be in or do any of that stuff, like I said even if my life depended on it.

Javonta Jack, Grade 6
DeQueen Elementary School, TX

Love

Why are people in love? Love means intense affection and warm feelings for another. Synonyms include adoration, care, fondness, and cherish.

We can show love in different ways. First it is giving nice hugs and saying positive words to each other. It makes others feel happy and loved. We can also give things to others in need to show our love.

I can show love as well. At home I can be nice to my family and help with the chores. At school I can show love by saying nice things to classmates to cheer them up or help a classmate when they struggle on work.

Love is important in our world to show each day.

Karina Segundo, Grade 5
Covington Elementary School, NE

A Compelling Role Model

Have you ever heard about "$E = mc^2$?" A famous man known as Albert Einstein created this equation. Albert Einstein was gifted in math and science. His intellect proved to be so high that he studied at the Swiss Polytechnic Institute and became a member of the Institute for Advanced Study in New Jersey.

Einstein had many accomplishments such as his Theory of Relativity and advocacy of the production of atomic bombs. Einstein played the violin well and was very religious. He had no concern about money.

Einstein has influenced me to do well in school subjects, especially science and math. He makes my mind wonder about various things that I could discover with hard work. We have similarities because we both play the violin and are religious. The reason Einstein is my role model is because we both love science!

Adithya Shekhar, Grade 6
Challenger School – Ardenwood, CA

Leaving for Kentucky

One extremely hot day I went to my grandfather's house. I got to ride the four-wheeler. Then we were off for Kentucky to go to my Aunt Tammy's house. My cousin and I went out to the barn. She has so many animals. She has 150 sheep, 200 goats, 10 llamas, 3 ponds, 4 dogs, 8 birds, 20 to 30 horses, 50 cows, 3 pigs, and 5 to 10 fish in a tank. She had 50 rabbits, a turkey, 10 birds, and 3 raccoons, but she sold them. Then we ate some very good food. We had baked beans, hot dogs, hamburgers.

We had a great time eating and talking. After that, we went back to the barn and fed the other animals. Then we went fishing. My dad, he got the biggest fish. I caught a fish, but I caught the smallest. My great grandfather came over to see everybody. Then we went back in the back of the barn and saw the cows and llamas. They had 3 babies back there and 2 mother llamas. We had a great time and the day was almost over, but not yet. My dad said, "2 more hours." I said, "Ok," but really I did not want to go home.

Then we were on our way back to the truck. I said, "Bye," to every body. Well, the day is over at Aunt Tammy's house. Now we're on our way to my great grandmother's house.

Tristan Cummings, Grade 5
Lynnville Elementary School, IN

The Perfect Profession

What is the perfect profession? Every human being has different feelings about this topic. Here is how I have answered that question in the past:

When I was about three years old, I wanted to be the president of our country. I thought that by being the most important person around, I would be able to do anything I wanted. That idea sounds silly to me now, but at that time, I had not learned that everyone has to follow the law, including the president. As most four-year-olds feel when they board a fire truck, I once wanted to be a fireman. I still admire them, but I do not feel ready to risk my life. I like building and playing with my LEGO™ blocks, so I once wished to be a LEGO™ set designer. If I could design small-scale structures, why not go for the real ones? So, I thought I would like to be an architect, but when I found out that you have to draw all the time, I realized that I would not enjoy that career. If you ask me today, however, since I *love* to read so much, I would like to be a writer or an editor for a publishing company.

People like many different things, so they choose different professions. Answering my initial question, I believe that there is no *one* perfect profession, but there is *one's* perfect profession. I am still trying to find mine.

Mateo Garcia-Novelli, Grade 5
Dishman Elementary School, TX

Nervous Wreck?

Of course I am not scared to get up and perform on stage anymore. I used to be terrified though. Let me tell you how you get to the point of performing without being petrified.

The first thing you do is practice your dance technique for a couple of weeks. Before you actually dance, you must warm up your muscles. To warm up you must perform plies, tendues, degages, leg stretches and other ballet moves. Next, we go to the corner and perform combinations across the floor. You do all of these things in a practice class.

The first performance of the year my dance studio has is our Christmas show called *A Gift for Emma*. It is the same show every year, but the dances and costumes sometimes change. It is about a girl named Emma that learns the gift of dance. The dance classes work hard learning new dances for this show while still working on their technique. We run the dance until we are able to do it laying down, in our sleep backwards, underwater while spinning around!

After our Christmas show we start practicing for our spring show. We make up new dances and pick out new costumes. We practice our dances until our muscles can remember it. We call this muscle memory. After learning techniques and practicing dances over and over, I feel confident that I will perform well.

Of course I am not nervous. I am excited!

Erica Gonzalez, Grade 6
Argyle Middle School, TX

Books: My Past, Present, and Future

In *Blade of Fire,* the author brings me so far into the book that I never want to stop reading.

I could not imagine my life without books. If books didn't exist I would not have the close connection to Thirrin Lindenshield of the Icemark Chronicles, or Harry Potter. I wouldn't even know they exist! For instance, I would have missed Thirrin's courage and strength when she and her strange, yet helpful allies defeated the Polypontian army in a desperate battle to save the icemark. I would have missed the feeling of fighting beside her to win the war.

Books are important to me because they make me feel like I'm in the story with the characters, having the adventures that make my life more interesting. The author's words are so powerful that they ignite my imagination into a blaze that grows until my whole mind is set onto a smokeless fire and brings me into the world of the author's imagination.

Authors like Stuart Hill and J.K. Rowling have inspired me to become an author. I am writing a book called *The Mysterious and Mystical Journey of Mell.* It's about a girl named Mell, her friend Illena, and their trip to find Mell's father, Dr. Dillmound, who was lost on an expedition to the Bermuda Triangle. I would not have been able to start this book without ideas from other books I have read. My life would not be as happy or as fun without books.

Kayla Buss, Grade 6
Spring Creek Elementary School, WY

Gymnastics

Have you ever tried doing gymnastics? If you haven't, you should. Personally, I think it's even more fun than swimming (for girls) or football (for boys). I would rather do gymnastics than go to school and trust me, I like school a lot. It gives me something to do. In gymnastics, the bars are my favorite place. You can do all sorts of things on them. One of those things is a back-hip-circle. To do this trick you first need to get on the bars into a front support. A front support is where you have your hips on the bars and you are using straight arms to hold your body up. Then you swing 3 times keeping your body straight while taking your hips off the bar keeping your whole weight on your arms. Then you turn around the bar keeping your whole weight on your arms. Using the momentum, pull yourself into the bars. Using the momentum, pull yourself around 360 degrees or in other words, a full backwards circle around the bar.

You can also do a pull-over. To do a pull-over you need to start on the ground. You run up to the bars and, again, use the momentum to pull yourself into the bar should get you up to a front support. Go on. Give it a shot. See if God gave *you* the gift of gymnastics.

Rachel Rhoades, Grade 4
Kyrene Monte Vista School, AZ

One Step Closer

So you want to hear the best song by the best band? Well, you came to the right place. "One Step Closer" is one of the best songs by one of the best bands ever! It sold at least one million copies on the single song. The album "Hybrid Theory" sold more than just one million copies. The band is Linkin Park, other songs by Linkin Park are "Faint," "Crawling," and "Bleed It Out." But that is just my opinion. There are other good bands like, My Chemical Romance, and AC/DC. But that's my opinion, my friend Sam likes AC/DC but I don't like them. Anyway, the original title for "One Step Closer" is "Plaster." The band says they created "One Step Closer" while struggling on "Runway" the sixth track from "Hybrid Theory."

The single was released in 2001, achieving notable success in Australia, but moderate success in the U.K. and the U.S. There is a remix of "One Step Closer" on LD's remix album "Reanimation" (2002), titled "1 Stp Klosr," done by demo version of the remix (included as an Easter egg on Linkin Park DVD/frat party at the pankake festival).

Until 2007, Linkin Park has closed every concert to date with it, excluding live 8 from 2003 onwards, when "One Step Closer" is played live, it is extended. Like "With You" this song is always played live with parts from the version "Reanimation" after the chorus.

Casey Kisselbach, Grade 6
Imagine Charter School at Rosefield, AZ

Medieval Weapons and Armor

The middle ages began in the 5th century and ended in the 15th century. The land was full of knights and royalty. Their weapons and armor were early forms of technology. These times are exciting to learn about because of what took place.

Medieval armor was made from metals like bronze, iron, and steel. Leather armor, often worn by archers, was made from animal hide, like cow. Archers wore leather vamp braces on their forearms to protect them from skimming their arms with the arrows. Body armor was assembled to plate-like pieces. Metal plate armor weighed 40-60 lbs. on average! Shields and helmets were typically made from metal; shields could also be made with wood.

Knights carried a sword and knife worn around their waist. Daggers were small and could be hidden in armor for sudden attacks. Other weapons include axes, spears, and maces. Maces are long wooded sticks with a spiked metal end. Flails were wooden sticks with a spiked ball connected by a chain. Crossbows were preferred by archers over longbows. Crossbows too longer than longbows to load, but it took expertise to shoot an arrow out of a longbow as accurately and as far as a crossbow.

A large wooden weapon called a catapult was designed to propel large objects. Another large weapon was the battering ram. It was used to take down walls and gates. Cannons came later in the medieval period. This is an overview of medieval armor and weapons.

Clayton Vega, Grade 6
Imagine Charter School at Rosefield, AZ

Disaster Plan!

This essay is going to be about if I had an emergency in my house. I have like twenty first aid kits in my two story house.

Having supplies is important. I will have in my supply kit bandages, sanitizer cloths, and butterfly-bandages. We have can foods so they don't get rotten and 5-7 weeks of water, toilet paper, and blankets.

I have plenty of ways to escape if a really big emergency happened while we were doing something important. I have a lot of windows and doors and I could even escape through my front door and my sliding backdoor to my backyard to be safe.

There are plenty of ways we could meet if a real emergency happened. We would meet at Ralph's Market, the park, friend's house, a light pole, or at Stater Bros. I need to see which one my parents want to choose.

If we had a disaster or emergency this will be my disaster plan and be safe.

Alexis Leonard, Grade 5
Liberty Elementary School, CA

Is It a Bird…Or a Plane…? No. It's a Boxer Dog!!!!!

That is what I think about boxer dogs, Amazing! They are playful, loyal and great as guards. Most important, they are really active dogs. Boxer dogs stand out from all the rest.

Boxers are playful because they love to play tug-of-war and some boxers love to play Frisbee. They are loyal because they listen to people and they obey if they are trained. Boxers won't leave their owners, no matter what!

They are active dogs. They don't just sleep when you are not playing with them they exercise by themselves. Boxers love to take walks and run around the park. They need the exercise to stay healthy to live long lives. Boxer dogs have to go to the vet to have checkups. The way they eat is very important to stay healthy and active.

Boxer dogs are great guard dogs. They know when to bark and they are really protective of their homes. The word boxer describes how they protect themselves, by using their paws like a professional fighter.

When you put all that information together you can tell that boxer dogs are a very good breed to have as a pet. When I was scared of dogs, I never got near a dog, but when I got a boxer dog it made me feel, why do I have to be scared of dogs, so boxer dogs made me feel that I don't need to be scared of dogs. Next time you go to a pet store, ask to see about a boxer dog!

Mary Jane Sanchez, Grade 4
Louise Foussat Elementary School, CA

Cerberus

In Greek mythology, there's a creature who was the watchdog of the underworld, and no one could leave. This monstrous creature is Cerberus (sur'-bur-uhs). He guarded the gates for Hades, the ruler of the underworld. Cerberus had a serpent as a tail and three heads. But in the original myth, he had 50 heads. The best way to describe Cerberus is a monstrous creature who lies deep down in the underworld, guarding the gates for Hades.

Hades is the ruler of Cerberus. Hades has a helmet that makes him invisible. He's the god of wealth, because the earth carries a lot of metal. He's greedy for money. He was so greedy, he stole a goddess named Persephone (Purr-sef-foni) from her mother. So, she became the queen of the underworld.

Cerberus has an evil family. His father is named Typhon, who is really evil. Typhon had 100 horrible heads, and venom dripped from his eyes while lava poured from his mouths. Cerberus's mother is Echidna (e-kid'nah). Echidna has a beautiful nymph head, but the ugly body of a serpent.

A few mythological people ever were able to sneak past the watchdog by putting him to sleep. But mostly, Cerberus snarled with his three mouths at any spirit who dared to exit the underworld and at any living person who dared to pass through Hades' gates.

Conor Kruse, Grade 6
Isbell Middle School, CA

Global Warming

I mean, we hear about it everywhere, and we hear about how it can be stopped. So why aren't we doing anything about it? I mean, it's a serious issue and it's real, it's not just something to scare you, it's the real deal. It's caused by exhaust that comes from cars, buses and other vehicles. Global warming is wearing down your atmosphere. One way to stop it is to stop driving yourself everywhere and take the bus more often. I mean, the air may be beautiful here and in other places, but if you drive down towards San Francisco, Los Angeles, and around there, look at the difference in the air it's pretty scary. This is something that needs to be stopped immediately!

I picked this topic because I think that it is something that needs to be said. I know, I may be a kid and that not everyone will listen to me, but it's worth a try. I know if we all pitch in that we can make a difference and eventually stop global warming all together. We have to think about how much longer we have till global warming takes over. It's a very scary thought I know, I have thought about it. We have to think about what we all have done to help start global warming over the years, but since we helped start it we should have to help stop what we as people have started. But that's my opinion, thanks.

Caylan Johnson, Grade 6
Round Valley Elementary School, CA

Freedoms

Did you know you have all kinds of rights, responsibilities, and freedoms? Did you know that all of your rights, responsibilities, and freedoms are stated in the Constitution? Well they are!

Some of your freedoms are freedom of religion, freedom of speech, and freedom to work. So when you grow up you can choose your own job. Also you can have any religion. That means you can celebrate any holiday you want! You can give speeches in the town council.

A couple of rights you have are, you have the right to worship. The right to say what you want about the government. You also have the right to a fair trial so if you are blamed for a crime you didn't commit you can get things straightened out. This is a right that belongs to you.

You also have different responsibilities. Some of them are laws some of them are just things you do by choice. You have to obey traffic signs so nobody gets hurt. Most people vote for president, governors, and mayors. You want to treat others fairly.

These are some of your rights, responsibilities, and freedoms we all share in America. Got to go to practice voting so I'm ready when I grow up.

Sheridan Macy, Grade 4
Rohwer Elementary School, NE

The Real World Trade Center

On September 11, 2001 the spotlight was New York City 4,000 people died. Hijackers are what caused this. Hijackers are people who steal planes in flight. Flight 175 and 11 caused many tragic deaths. They crashed into the World Trade Center in early morning hours. Yet, 2 courageous men, P.A.P.D. Sergeant John McLoughin, and Will Jimeno survived the attack.

John McLoughin, Will Jimeno, and three other officers entered the World Trade Center to help evacuate the tower, when all of a sudden lights started flickering. Then, "WHOOSH!" The South Tower started falling like upside down dominos. Next thing you know only three men were struggling for survival. John was the farthest in the debris. Luckily only his legs were covered. Will was on top with the other officer. Dominik Pezzulo, the 3rd officer, was able to break free. He tried to help Will but couldn't. All of a sudden a second layer of debris fell which killed Dominik. A few hours later Dominik's broken firearm started firing wildly, bouncing off the walls of metal.

On the 12th hour, Will was rescued by marines Jason Thomas and Dave Karnes and other rescue teams. Ten hours later John was rescued. John was in a coma for 6 weeks and went through 27 surgeries. Today they're still recovering but living a happy life. After retirement both received a Medal of Honor from the Port Authority Police Department.

Do you have a rescue story?

Brianna Delgado, Grade 5
Oak Crest Intermediate School, TX

In the Heavens Above

I couldn't believe it. This could have never happened. I felt as if I would never see daylight again. My great grandfather was dead.

I was so depressed. I didn't think I could take it. I was hoping he would get better but, unfortunately he didn't.

Mother explained "His cancer was too strong. The doctor didn't see it until it was too late." We couldn't do anything.

I got all dressed up for his funeral. I wore a long black skirt and a maroon shirt with high heels. I left my hair down and pulled some of it over to the side with a barrette.

I went to the church. I though I wasn't going to make it. Then I saw his dead body.

I told mom, "That is not him."

Mom softly said "That is him. People look different after they die."

I cried my eyes out. I just couldn't believe it. Then grandma came over to me and said that he went to a better place. She also said that he was now in heaven and he wasn't in pain anymore.

I still miss him a whole bunch. Now I understand that it was time for him to move on. He will be there in the heavens above.

Teresa West, Grade 6
Nancy Hanks Elementary School, IN

Reading

I love to read. Books are my free time. Fantasy, realistic fiction, and historical fiction are my favorite subjects. I like fantasy because I love to imagine what it would be like if we had magic in this world. I like realistic fiction because I can usually relate to the main character. I like historical fiction because I like learning about ordinary people during hard times and what they went through.

When I read, I'm not thinking about how much homework I have, or that I have to practice the piano, or anything else. All I'm thinking about is what's going to happen next. I don't really listen to anybody, and my body signals just shut down. I'm not tired, I'm not hungry or thirsty, until I stop to think about myself.

My father gets mad at me, telling me to, "take my nose out of that book." I won't listen to him, but keep reading anyway. I never get any work done if I'm in the middle of a good book, especially if it's exciting. I like to read books that challenge me a little, so they're not totally tedious. I also like to reread books, because I notice things that I wouldn't have noticed before. I always take recommendations for good books.

Books are the reason I know so many random facts and have such a wide vocabulary. I love books of any kind.

Karla Rondon, Grade 6
Colorado Academy, CO

A Wolf Community

A fantastic thing I've discovered about wolves is that they have a society not very different from ours. Wolves love, hate, and enjoy different things.

Wolves have leaders and seconds-in-command. The leaders of the pack are referred to as the alpha male and alpha female. Vice-presidents are beta. Alphas get to eat first when the pack makes a kill. Alphas are normally the only wolves in the pack allowed to breed. This is so the pups have the best genes.

Pups are usually born in March. The mother wolf can give birth to between one and eleven pups in a litter. When born, wolf pups weigh about one pound and are both blind and deaf. After three weeks of living on their mother's milk, they can see and hear and also eat meat. An interesting fact is that a fighting wolf "bully" will protect and care for pups. This applies to all wolves. They all have a soft spot for pups.

Another important issue is food. Different packs prefer different meat. For some packs, elk is the choice meat. For others, caribou is the best thing on the menu. When there isn't enough elk or caribou, wolves will eat small rodents.

Wolves are amazing and intelligent animals that must be preserved and protected. Without our help, the entire wolf race could die out. They almost did. We need to make sure this never happens again. Let's not allow wolves to become a thing of the past.

Matthew Arvedson, Grade 6
Whittier Elementary School, WI

Shooting

The sweat drips from my brow. My stomach lurches. I am hungry for the words, "Shooter ready! Fire!" Every time I go shooting with my dad, our bond grows stronger. Nothing tops the smell of gunpowder and the anxious feeling I have as I wonder if I hit my target.

I love shooting with my dad. There's a special feeling that happens to me when we are together at the range. My desire to shoot like him and our growing friendship unite to form a great manly feeling.

I love that strong smell of smoke that surrounds me when entering Safer Arms Shooting Range, and the soft chime of the doorbell as we push the door open.

A feeling of power overcomes me when gently squeezing the trigger. I look forward to the anxiety I feel as I check my target; and at the same time, I almost feel as if I don't want to check it for fear I missed!

Bonding with my dad, the smell of gunpowder, and the anxiety that comes with target practice all work together to make this a sport I really enjoy!

Jackson Chinchay, Grade 5
Chinchay Christian Academy, CA

Walt Disney

Walt Disney was a brilliantly talented man. He was born on December 5, 1901, in Chicago, Illinois. He didn't attend school until he was seven years old. Walk had four siblings named Roy, Ruth, Herb, and Ray.

The summer before high school, Walt applied for a job as a New Butcher on the railroad. While in high school, Walt began taking classes at the Academy of Fine Arts, where he sketched live models. Several of Walt's teachers predicted that he would someday become a newspaper cartoonist.

Walt's brother Roy returned home from war when Walt was sixteen. Walt then joined the military with his brother. He used his artistic talent to paint medals on the marines jackets. He came home to tell his parents of his desire to become an artist. His father wanted no part of this and wouldn't even listen to another word about it.

Walt moved to Kansas City and found a job as a cartoonist, which paid $50 a month. There he met a young artist named Ub Iwerks. Ub and Walt joined forces and started a business called Laugh-O-Grams. They raised over $15,000 even though New York never paid them for a single idea that they used.

Walt soon had enough money to leave Kansas City and move to Hollywood where his brother Roy was in the hospital. Before long, Disneyland was created.

Sadly, Walt Disney died on December 15, 1966. He was 65 years old.

Megan Ruiz, Grade 4
La Costa Heights Elementary School, CA

Underground Animals

Meerkats, prairie dogs, and groundhogs are unique. They dig burrows, eat interesting foods, and have other unusual abilities.

Groundhogs are common mammals in northwest Ontario and parts of the United States. They are very shy and seldom venture far from their burrows. Groundhogs are grazers and eat the succulent parts of plants, including dandelion greens, clover, plantain, and grasses. In their burrow is a special room for hibernation throughout the winter. Females produce one to nine offspring each year.

Meerkats are members of the mongoose family. They live in the Kalahari Desert in Africa. Their burrows are grass-lined and shared with ground squirrels and yellow mongooses. Martial eagles and jackals are their primary predators. Meerkats' main diet includes beetles, spider, centipedes, millipedes, worms, crickets, and scorpions. Their life span reaches to 12 to 14 years and their litter size is 2 to 5 babies. They live in groups of five to thirty, called "mob" or a "gang."

Prairie dogs are robust rodents and closely related to squirrels. Their habitats are in waterproof burrows located in grass prairies and plateaus of the American West. A prairie dog's diet consists of a variety of grasses, roots, weeds, forbs, and blossoms. There are five species of prairie dogs: the Black Tailed, White Tailed, Gunnison's, Mexican, and Utah. One litter is born to a female consisting of three to five pups yearly.

There is much alike about these underground animals, yet all are distinctly different. That's what makes them interesting and amazing!

Megan LaLone, Grade 5
Concord Ox Bow Elementary School, IN

McDowell Mountain vs Goodyear

This summer I was in a baseball tournament in Gilbert, Arizona. My team was called the McDowell Mtn All-Stars. There were two brackets of seven teams. We went 5-1 which was the best record in our bracket. My favorite part of the tournament was the semifinals against Goodyear. Although we lost 3-2 it was an amazing experience.

I hit a ball into the right-center field gap with a runner on first. The runner was tagged out at third base. The score was 2-1 my team in the bottom of the sixth inning. The first batter hit a double to left field. The next batter struck out, but then the next batter singled to center field and that made it runners on first and third. Then the next batter struck out. We were one out away from the finals when it happened. The batter laid down the bunt, it rolled toward Michael and me. We both hesitated and that was our downfall. Both runners scored, because our catcher wasn't behind the plate. He was far down the first base line. Although my team lost it will be one of the most memorable baseball experiences of my life for now.

Drew LaSalle, Grade 5

Cats

Do you have a favorite animal? I do! My favorite animal is a cat. Cats are possibly the most graceful and beautiful of all animals. The domestic cat is one of the most popular pets because it is loving, intelligent, and playful.

All cats like to hunt. Lions can break a bone in half with one bite of its strong jaws. Tigers are night hunters, preying on animals smaller than itself. When cats hunt it takes up a lot of their energy. Cats like to stalk their prey, then pounce and ambush them! Their hunts may be successful, sometimes they are not.

There are two cats that are different than other cats. One of them is a cheetah. The cheetah is a running cat, the rest of the cats are leaping cats. The cheetah is also different because it does not have sheaths over its claws. The other cat is the clouded leopard. The clouded leopard is big, yet it does not roar and groom itself.

Cats have lots of slick fur. Fur has tons of uses. Fur keeps the cat warm during the winter time. In the summer, the cat sheds its fur, so it is not so hot. Fur is also a good camouflage for cats. It is useful for hunting, so cats can sneak up on their prey, without being seen.

I also like tons of other animals, but cats are my favorite. I think cats are very interesting. Do you have a favorite animal now?

Megan Dialogue, Grade 6
Thomas Jefferson Charter School, ID

Disaster

This essay states what you should do if there is a disaster. It tells where you can meet, escape and what goes in an emergency kit and where to keep it.

Some items you should keep in an emergency kit are 5-7 days' worth of water and 3-5 days' worth of food. You should also keep Band-Aids, walkie-talkies, batteries and a flashlight. But in case of a fire you should have a fire extinguisher. (You shouldn't just have one emergency kit.)

Most houses should have an escape route to get out of a disaster. If you are trapped in a fire you should jump even if it's high because it is better to break a few bones than burn. You could also go through a window. If your window doesn't open then kick it open. But if you have a chance it might be better to go through a door.

You and your family can discuss where your meeting place is. It can be at the stop sign or across the street. It just needs to be somewhere safe.

In conclusion this essay tells what to do in case of a disaster. But it is also a good lesson. I would recommend this to people because you never know when a disaster will hit.

Michael Alvarado, Grade 5
Liberty Elementary School, CA

Middle School Fears!!!

Beep, beep, beep, went my alarm clock. I was scared to death about middle school. I had millions of questions racing through my mind. Such as, am I going to be able to get my locker open, what if I walk into the wrong class, and what if I don't make it on time? I had butterflies in my stomach. "Should I be scared about middle school?"

I had arrived. After all the begging I did, my mom came into the school with me. I couldn't get my locker open!! I started to panic. "Oh shush dear, just ask a teacher" ah ha that was my solution, ask a teacher and try to memorize your locker combination. I was ready to go into a classroom. "Oh wait, is this the right one?" I gasped. "No, whew," that was a close one. I went to my correct class. Also, try to memorize your class schedule. The starting bell rang, "Oh great, the bell rang," I said disappointed. One way to make sure you're on time is to wear a watch.

As I was lying in my bed I thought middle school wasn't so bad. I have nice teachers. I found a solution to almost all of my problems, I can open my locker now, I memorized all of my class schedules, and I'm also on time. Now I think, "What was I scared about?" Middle school is going to go by in a flash.

Nicole Boulier, Grade 6
St Clair Middle School, MI

How Do I Get Out of Here

Mazes and labyrinths are multi-taskers. If you've ever solved a maze on paper, or found your way through a hedge **or corn** maze, you know that they are great fun. But did you **know** that mazes can be used for protection, are relaxing, and are also used in science?

In ancient times, the definition of mazes and labyrinths was "a confusing path of passageways with many dead ends." They were mostly used for protection of people or objects. For example, the maze in the city of Knossos on the island of Crete was supposed to protect people from the mythical Minotaur.

Today, the definition of mazes is the same as in ancient times, but labyrinths are now usually defined as "a single passageway curved into a spiral with a dead end in the center." Now mazes and labyrinths are not commonly used for protection. There are books filled with mazes for puzzlers to solve as recreation. Some churches and parks have labyrinths for people to follow, thinking or praying as they walk, which provides relaxation. Lab animals are put through mazes repeatedly to test how they learn under various conditions, and to test their memories.

Mazes have filled many roles for thousands of years. They have been used for protection, relaxation, and science. Don't forget to have fun with them too!

Adam Klager, Grade 5

Somebody Important

Do you have someone in your life that is important to you? A person in my life that is important to me is my mom. Anybody can feed me, but only my mom knows what my favorite foods are and will make them for me. When my mom makes my favorite foods I feel like she really cares for me.

I like to play soccer and my mom drives me to my practices and games. My mom supports me, cheers me on and encourages me during my games. I know that my mom is watching me and is trying to make me play hard.

When I am sick, my mom takes care of me. I would rather have my mom take care of me than a doctor. Even though a doctor knows medical treatments, my mom knows more about me and loves me. I feel a little bit better when my mom takes care of me.

My mom helps me with schoolwork. Homework and studying for tests are two things my mom helps with. I like it when my mom assists me with schoolwork because then I can get good grades. When I get good grades I feel proud because I know I have tried my best.

These are not all of the reasons why my mom is important, these are just some. At times I may feel there are more important things than my mom, but then I remember that my mom is more important than anything else.

Colleen Coady, Grade 4
Maple Avenue Elementary School, WI

My Trip to Disney World

My favorite vacation was when I went to Disney World. We rented a villa which was located near Magic Kingdom. We went over Presidents' Day weekend. We went with my family and my cousins. The villa had three bedrooms, a kitchen and a pull out couch. We all got to stay together and it was a lot of fun.

The first day we went to Magic Kingdom, I got sick that night. I went to a very crowded emergency room full of really sick people. Finally, I went to a smaller doctor's office at 1:00 in the morning. I had an eye infection and an ear infection. By the next day after taking the medicine, I felt better.

The next morning after breakfast, we headed to Frontierland to ride Thunder Mountain Railroad. It was our favorite ride. We rode it over and over and over again. After lunch we headed to MGM Studios. We all rode the Great Movie Ride. That night we went to see Fantasmic. It was a spectacular light and water show.

After the show, we went to Main Street USA. We saw an electric parade. We ended the night by watching fireworks over Cinderella's Castle.

We stayed at Disney World for five days. We went on a lot of rides and saw some great shows. It is a wonderful place to go with your family. I can't wait to visit there again real soon.

Gianna Figueroa, Grade 6
Divine Infant Jesus School, IL

Argyle Red

I love football. My football team is Argyle Red and we are really good. We are 8-0 right now, which means we are undefeated. This week is our first playoff game. We are going to start playing pretty good teams now, so we've got to get ready. I am starting fullback and starting middle linebacker, so I've got two very important jobs on offense and defense. The fullback runs the ball, and they're usually bigger and stronger than the halfback. The middle linebacker is on defense and he is behind the defensive line, watching the ball the whole time.

What I love about my team the most is that we are really all leaders. We don't play selfish and we give it our best effort. My favorite play is on our armband and it's called Black 4. It's where I get to run the ball around the end and up the field. I love running because I get to run people over with my power and velocity. There's nothing better than hitting hard and scoring touchdowns.

Football is not only fun, but it's taught me a lot about life. What I've learned the most is that if you don't give up your best effort, you won't turn out as good as you hope. My coaches say I'm a great leader, and on the field, they say I'm like an entirely different person. I also love my friends and we have a lot of fun playing.

That's my football team!

Christian Hackney, Grade 6
Argyle Middle School, TX

My Pets!

I am very grateful for my pets because when I am sad I know I can depend on them. I have a dog named Gracie who is a Yorkie; she has a beautiful black and brown coat. Sometimes I dress her up in Build-A-Bear clothes. Gracie loves going to the park and meeting new friends. Gracie greets me when I get home; she is the sweetest dog ever.

I also have a cat named Peepers. Peepers just showed up one day on our back porch, hungry, tired, and homeless. Now, he is a troublemaker. He gets into all kinds of mischief. He loves to kill lizards and birds! One day he brought a dead baby bird to the house and I had to bury it. I was mad at him for days until I realized that a cat killing a bird is just a fact of life. We named him Peepers because he is always peeping in windows and doors.

I am also lucky enough to have two African spurred tortoises whose names are Bubba and Bubbles, one is a girl and the other one is a boy. The funny thing about the turtles is that they like to watch TV! Who knew animals could watch TV? One of them is a girl and she will lay 20 eggs every year! Now that is a lot of eggs! One thing I know for sure is that I love my pets and they love me!

Addison Miller, Grade 4
Gateway Pointe Elementary School, AZ

Football 24

Football is important to me because I can play with my friends and family, and it also allows me to make new friends. My brother played in 7th and 8th grade, and now he's going to be playing in high school. My brother helps me a lot with running, catching, passing, and hitting. My brother and I play this game together where either he kicks the football off to me, or throws it to me, or I kick it off to him or throw the football to him. The returner has to get past the defender and score a touchdown. There are fumbles and safeties too! A touchdown is worth one point in this game, and we play until we reach ten points. In order to win you have to win by two points. My dad helps me very much! He was the one who taught me how to hit, catch, pass, and he even taught me how to run! He coaches me also. My dad, my brother, and I play this game where one person is the receiver and one person is the DB and we run pass plays for fun. My mom and grandpa are always at my games to support me. I've played tackle football two years, one in Pop Warner and now as a 6th grader I'm playing on the Middle School Linfield Lions!

Jack Dickson, Grade 6
Linfield Christian School, CA

A Violin Genius

Thundering applause filled the theater as Mindy Chen finished playing and left the stage. Mindy, at only eleven years old, had already won an international competition, and received a scholarship to the best music school. She even owns a dog that she earned by winning a competition.

Mindy, my friend, is someone I admire. Hardworking, friendly, and talented, she won many competitions. When she fails, she keeps on trying.

Ever since she was four, she has been practicing violin for four hours every day. She never had much time for games, but her future beckons her. As soon as she becomes of age, she can enter the best music school available with her scholarship.

Whenever she enters a competition, Mindy returns with new friends. Once she walked into a bathroom, and met a woman, the judge of her competition, and they became friends. Also, because she is talkative and humorous, she makes friends quickly.

At the age of four, Mindy started to play violin. Learning from her father, she soon became an excellent player. Every time someone had a birthday party and she arrived, the hosts persuaded her to play for us during the party, and our parents would tell us to learn from her because she competed with people older than her and won.

I admire Mindy because she is diligent, sociable and brilliant. Now, I try to follow her by working hard, acting friendly, and playing my best in flute. I want to follow her footsteps.

Sara Gong, Grade 6
Challenger School – Ardenwood, CA

Tragic Bridge Collapse

Screams of horror! BOOM! BOOM! BOOM! Cars crashing. Dust flying up as if birds were flying up to the clouds. Police sirens. People crying. Tear drops on their seat. As they fall, people screaming for help! And then silence. Except for the people who survived. They were in shock. The police are trying to find the other survivors. But it looks like many people survived. They were in shock. They were so lucky. Half of the people drowned. The other half got crushed. I was at home when this happened. My mom said to me the bridge had collapsed…I was amazed! But she amazed me even more because someone we knew was on the bridge! My dad was talking to her on the phone fifteen minutes before she dropped down into the cold, fast flowing water while pounds of cement blocks were crashing down on top of her. I was still in shock days after. The woman was our friend's girlfriend. We were all so sad when she passed away and we will never forget Christina and all the other victims that were on the 35W bridge.

Kaylee Smith, Grade 5
Greenwood Elementary School, MN

My Dog Blue

My dog Blue and I like to go hunting. Blue and I are best friends, one time we were walking in the channel with my friend Jordan. I saw a black bird and then I shot it with a BB gun and it started to run. Blue chased it down and finished it off. Blue is always with me and we will always hunt together. Blue and I also like to swim. Our house is right next to the river so we swim all the time. The only problem is he is always trying to save me. I like to make him chase me up stream. Blue is a great water dog.

We also like to take walks. On our walks we like to run and play. We always see deer, rabbits, and squirrels. When we walk by the river we see carp feeding and gold eye jumping in the rapids. Then we run around and smell the rain from the morning. That is what Blue and I like to do.

Bridger Doeden, Grade 6
Kinsey School, MT

Environmental Issues

The environment is very important. If we don't take care of the environment we could lose lots of important foods, plants, animals and other important things. Some of these include bananas, rubber, polar bears, medicines, herbs and many more important things. If we all work together we could change what could happen in the future. Here are some things we can do to save the environment:

1. Buy things with less packaging.
2. Reduce the amount of garbage you throw out each week.
3. Don't litter.
4. Grow a garden to help produce more oxygen.
5. Drive less, walk or bike more.

Whitney Benoit, Grade 5
Forest Hill Public School, ON

Air Soft War

On one Sunday afternoon my friends Danny, Timmy, Will, my dad, and I have an air soft war at my dad's warehouse. The teams are Will, Timmy, and I against my dad and Danny. The other team has the advantage of setting up first and has smoke bombs.

As I scout ahead I see a swift throw of a smoke grenade followed by bursts of fire. "Take cover" I yell, running back to our stronghold at a half finished wall. As we are throwing down fire they try to advance but from their cover to ours is too wide open so they peel back.

Just as we have the upper hand I run out, so I have to reload my HK. But as I do so, they take advantage of this and have a swift attack and kidnap Timmy. We think everything is lost when they run out. They keep Timmy in a death grip while they run to the next room to reload. When this happens we advance to closer cover by the door. After they reload they come busting through the door! When this happens I feel like I am in the Vietnam War because I just stick my gun over my head and fire rapid, Will does the same thing as well.

Finally I hear a yell, I pop my head up only to see I shot my dad 1 centimeter under his glasses. Because of this the war is over. We win!

Coleson Carmell, Grade 5
Barrington Elementary School, OH

My Summer Vacation

On my summer vacation I went to Long Beach. We stayed at the Coast Long Beach Hotel. After we checked in, we took a water taxi to Shoreline Village. We found a pirate store and it was cool. For Dinner we went to Bubba Gumps Shrimp Company. It was delicious.

On the second day, we went to the Aquarium of the Pacific. I saw lots of sea animals and I got to pet a sting ray and a baby shark. I also got to feed nectar to birds. That night I went to a restaurant called GameWorks. It had lots of games. It was really fun.

On the third day, we went whale watching. We saw saw three blue whales. I was sea sick and almost threw up, but the day was exciting. Later that night, we went to a restaurant called, Tokyo Wako and had Japanese food. We saw the chef cook in front of us and it was cool.

On the fourth day, we woke up early and went fishing. We didn't catch any fish, but I had fun. We went to the Queen Mary and took a tour, then went on a Russian submarine. I got to look in a periscope. It was very cramped. We ate at the hotel restaurant that night, but it wasn't very good.

I swam every night and had a great vacation. I didn't want to go home.

Kevin McCarty, Grade 6
Isbell Middle School, CA

Ah! A Nightmare Waiting to Happen

In the early evening, somewhere in the middle of a favorite cartoon being watched by a child, a commercial comes on. It is about the latest movie coming to theaters. Sure, it's supposed to be a good action film, but it is violent too. It starts to play and he is thrown from in front of the television set to under the nearest sofa. The poor kid had to suffer three of these commercials and his parents were very angry when they had to pry him out from under the couch. As this kid demonstrated, some commercials were too scary for kids, including eleven-year-olds like me, and shouldn't be shown when they are usually watching. I'm sure the child's parents would agree with me.

Obviously, these commercials are frightening for children. Many other people say that these commercials are one of the greatest things on TV, but I would disagree. Many times they cause nightmares and create fear in many children and even adults. The commercials expose children to things that aren't age appropriate.

Next, these commercials can promote violent behavior. They show bad examples of violent behavior and can make the children want to try out the violence. The commercials also make violence seem acceptable, when in reality, it isn't acceptable at all. What they see on TV isn't always true, but most kids think it is always correct.

Additionally, these commercials sometimes have bad language. They promote the use of the unacceptable language by children. Children get the impression from such commercials that the bad language is acceptable by society, when it is not.

In conclusion, some commercials are frightening to children. Many commercials also promote violent behavior and the use of foul language. All of these shouldn't be shown during typical hours that children view TV.

Madisyn Yaron, Grade 6
Beacon Country Day School, CO

I Am Thankful

Giving thanks and being thankful is hard to accept and/or appreciate for many families. I have a family for which I am extremely grateful.

As a family, we do many things together. My dad and mom both have jobs which support us. My mom works part time which allows her to pick my sister and I up after school. She is there to help us with our homework and have supper ready when my dad comes home from work. There aren't many children who have that opportunity to come home after school. After a long day at work, Dad comes home and takes me to baseball practice. He also helps coach my team.

Going to baseball and hockey games, floating and camping on the river, attending church on Sundays, and talking out situations makes our family strong and close. Therefore, I am thankful for my family.

Lain Hermes, Grade 5
Aloe Elementary School, TX

Trilobites

Trilobites are creatures that lived before the Dinosaurs ruled the Earth. Trilobites are now fossils that you can collect or buy. Some of them are fake and most people get tricked and sometimes they end up buying them for five hundred dollars. All trilobites had antennae and legs. Their legs and antennae were their soft bodied parts and it is really rare if they are preserved. Trilobites lived underwater so they either swam or walked on the bottom of the water and some of them did both. Trilobites are really related to roly-polys because they both have antennae and legs. Both trilobites and roly-polys each roll up into round balls to protect themselves. Some trilobites grew to be two feet! Mainly all trilobites have very long names like the trilobite Dicranurus Hamatus and that is my favorite trilobite.

I have fifty-nine real trilobites and four fake ones. My brother has four real trilobites and zero fake ones. I have no idea how many trilobites my dad has because he has over seven hundred! My dad is known all over the world for his fossils and especially his trilobites he is known in books and mainly the world wide web. I have a trilobite that is five-hundred dollars! My dad knows almost half of the trilobites names and there are over thirty-five thousand trilobites. Some trilobites have really big eyes and some have none. My dad's the best fossil collector that I know.

Coleman Durney, Grade 4
Menchaca Elementary School, TX

My Dad in Iraq

My dad Jeff Green has worked in the Navy for eleven years. He has worked on three ships. Their names are USS O'Bannon, the USS Constellation, and the USS Nitze. My dad's job in the Navy is Fire Controlman. He is responsible for weapon systems and air defense of the ship. He did something different after a couple of years. He volunteered to go to Iraq. My dad had to do three months of combat training. He then left for camp victory in Baghdad. My dad took air defense weapon systems and installed them on land instead of on ships. My dad was in charge of operating and fixing them if they broke. He lived in a giant tent with forty other people. My dad had to drink at least two gallons of water a day, and man it gets hot out there. It gets up to 120° F. When the bad guys shoot rockets at the base, they track the rockets down with radar and shoot them out of the sky, protecting the whole base. My dad also got to visit Saddam Hussein's palace. I am positive the best part is when he came home. We met him at the airport to show him welcome home signs and later the same day we went out to breakfast. We talked the whole time about how we missed each other. That was my dad in Iraq.

Spencer Green, Grade 4
Burchett Elementary School, TX

The Day at Geauga Lake

A few months ago, my sister, my aunts, my cousins, my mother, and I went to Geauga Lake (an amusement park). My aunt got all the tickets from her job, because it was Family Day. We got a discount, the tickets were only seven dollars, so that was not too much. The regular tickets are $35.00.

We got up really early and left the house at 10:00 because we had to pick up a lot of people. We waited for everybody on the side of the road until everybody who was going got there. Once everyone was there we left to go to Geauga Lake.

When we got there, there was so many people, and the parking lot was filled up! We were so happy to get there, when we got in, straight to the Thunder Tank we ran. I thought it was going to be scary, but it wasn't. Then we got on the Twister, the Batman, and the Ville. The Ville was the scariest ride of all.

After having so much fun on the rides, we went to the pool, and the water rides. All the lines for the rides were long. We got in the pool and cooled off. We had fun splashing water and jumping into the pool. After swimming we went to the Big Buck. Then we went home. On the way home we got lost. But everybody was talking about the good time we had.

Jamar O'Neal, Grade 6
Prospect Elementary School, OH

The First Woman

Hillary Rodham Clinton, the wife of former President Bill Clinton, recently decided to run for President after George W. Bush. Mrs. Clinton, born in Chicago, Illinois, received her law degree from Yale University in 1973. Later, she became a distinguished lawyer and gifted speaker. When Bill Clinton was elected President, she was recognized as the most active first lady in the world. I think that Hillary should win the presidency because she holds the main qualities a person needs to govern our great nation.

Hillary remains the one woman who inspires me to achieve my goals. This outstanding role model inspires me for the reason that she is absolutely hardworking and confident about her job. Also, one of her best qualities seems to be excellent leadership skills. She believes women can achieve anything they strive for. Mrs. Clinton, being the first lady to run for President, has worked her best to be successful.

What have I done to follow Hillary's example? I believe in myself, and have tried my best to retain good grades. Also, I ran for Activities Coordinator on student council to gain leadership qualities as this fantastic lady has done in her life. She stands today as the most encouraging role for any young girl like me.

Kamya Arora, Grade 6
Challenger School – Ardenwood, CA

The Mystery at the Bottom of the Ocean

The Mariana Trench is the deepest known underwater trench. Its maximum depth 6.8 miles deep and, as part of the Hadal Zone, is in total darkness 24 hours a day. The Mariana Trench is the deepest location on the Earth's crust. Located near the Mariana Islands, it is the boundary between two tectonic plates. At its deepest, it is farther below sea level than Mt. Everest is above. On the bottom, its atmospheric pressure is 1,000 times that at sea level.

There is very little life in the Mariana Trench due to the pressure, lack of food, and most of all, darkness. Most of the life seen there are 1-foot long soles or flounder and small shrimp.

"The bottom appeared light and clear, a waste of firm diatomaceous ooze." — Explorer Jacques Piccard

Few people have explored the Mariana Trench, but it has been explored. In 1951 the Royal Navy vessel *Challenger* explored it for the first time, reporting a depth of 35,760 feet. In a unexpected dive, the U.S. Navy's *Trieste* got to the bottom with Lieutenant Don Walsh and Jacques Piccard on board. They reported a depth of 37,799 feet, but later changed it to 35, 813 feet.

Despite those three explorations, the Mariana Trench remains the mystery at the bottom of the ocean.

Allison D. Gant, Grade 6

Stories in the Sky

As I stared up at the bright stars that blanked the night sky I wondered when the fireworks show would begin. It was a hot evening on the Fourth of July and I was sitting in my grandparent's backyard with my grandparents, my parents and my little sister, Gianna.

"Look!" said my grandmother, pointing above us. "I see the constellation, Scorpius."

"What's a constellation?" I asked.

"A constellation is a cluster of stars that form the shape of an object." My eyes traveled to where my grandmother was pointing. "I see it!" Scorpius' 16 bright stars were perfectly clear.

My grandmother explained that there were a total of 88 constellations. She also taught me that Scorpius is a zodiac sign along with Leo, Cancer, Gemini and many more and that every person has a zodiac sign according to the month of their birthday.

"If my birthday is in December, what would my zodiac sign be?" I asked her. Sagittarius was her reply.

The last thing my grandmother explained was that people who live south of the equator see the constellations upside down from people in the Northern Hemisphere.

After a brilliant fireworks show, I thought about how the constellations will appear the same way as I grow old and how I'll be able to tell *my* grandchildren the same stories in the sky.

Alexa Agostinelli, Grade 5
Desert Canyon Elementary School, AZ

Family Is Important

Why is your family important? I'll tell you why. Even if you don't get along with your family, they'll always love you. Besides, where would we be without them?

Living with your family may be tough but, it's doable. Every family has its ups and downs, their good and bad points. But no matter what, they're your family anyway and they love you.

Sometimes those downs lead to family fights. Family fights are not good. A common thought is, "It's all my fault!" But believe me, it's not your fault, no matter what a sibling says or does that makes you think that.

Do you have a night dedicated to your family? It's a common tradition. During family night, you can get to learn about your family more and have fun doing it by playing games and watching movies. If you don't have family night, try to plan one out.

Family is a great thing. We should cherish them forever. Remember, family is very important. We wouldn't be here without our mom or dad. We would be bored without our siblings, and we should always be there for our family. Your family is always there for you.

Anna Hubbard, Grade 6
Orchard Hill Elementary School, IA

Imagine If…

Imagine you were drifting away on a cloud. All of your worries would go away. Imagine if you were trapped in a cave by a hungry bear. Your heart rate would beat even faster than before. Imagination can make you feel anything: happy, scared, worried, great and even sometimes like you need to laugh out loud. It is one of the keys to enjoying life.

Imagining things is important because you can imagine anywhere anytime about anything. I think imagination makes you think outside the box. It helps your creativity build up. If you imagine it could help you understand about more difficult things. Another reason why imagination is important is because it can help you in life. Imagination is a huge part of my life. Mostly I do it when I'm in the car and I'm getting bored. Whenever I think about something I imagine it to be something else for example: if I think about my cats I imagine that they talk when I'm not around. Also when I'm playing with a toy or something I imagine what its house would look like or imagine what it would be saying to me. Some people probably think that they don't really imagine things but, they actually do. I think everybody imagines about something sometime in their life.

I love to imagine things. It's fun. That's one of the reasons why I like to do it so much. It makes you think differently about something.

Catherine Read, Grade 6
Argyle Middle School, TX

Canada Lynx

I researched an endangered animal. Canada Lynx are found in Canada, western Montana, and in Idaho and Washington. The Canada Lynx lives in forests, rocky areas or tundra. The head-body length is between 670 and 1,067 mm and the tail length is 50 to 130 mm. The female Lynx lives for about 21 months and the male lives for about 33 months. The Lynx lives more in captivity than in the wild. It has good hearing. The Canada Lynx is endangered in Michigan. Canada Lynx are short tailed, long legged wildcats. The Canada Lynx weighs 20 to 30 pounds. The Canada Lynx has a black tipped tail and a gray-brown face. In the winter, the Canada Lynx's feet act like snowshoes.

The Canada Lynx is nocturnal. Snowshoe hares are its primary meat. Canada Lynx also eat small mammals, red squirrel, and some birds and fish. They also eat larger animals that died from other causes. The Lynx eats about 150-200 hares a year.

A male Lynx's territories are in range of 56-94 square miles. Canada Lynx are one of the rare mammals in which the DNR collects: information.

The female gives birth to four kittens in a den. The kittens are blind until ten days old. The Lynx's predators have not been found. The young are scared of larger carnivores, like wolves and bears. In the winter the Lynx will kill deer and other large animals. The Canada Lynx eats at night.

Ashlee Liu, Grade 4
Menchaca Elementary School, TX

My Role Model

My role model is Raven-Symoné Christina Pearman. She has played in so many movies and shows. Her birthplace is in Atlanta, Georgia. Her D.O.B. is December 10, 1985. She's been acting since she was three years old when she made her first debut on *The Cosby Show*. She was even an actress before she could even read.

Every single movie and show she has ever played in, is the best! The movies she has played in are *Cheetah Girls*, *Cheetah Girls 2*, *Zenon*, *Dr. Dolittle* and *Dr. Dolittle 2*. The shows she has played in are *That's So Raven*, *Kim Possible*, *The Cosby Show*, *Mother's Prayer*, and *Hangin' with Mr. Cooper*. They are all brilliant.

Raven is a fashion designer, singer, actress, and a great model! She is a great role model for young girls, also for little toddler girls. She is my role model because she played the best parts on television. I've liked her since I was a young girl.

I love Raven-Symoné Christina Pearman, and she is the best woman celebrity that I've ever known of! She is the best actress ever! I knew that she would be a role model for me. I hope I follow my dreams and become something like her someday. She makes people want to become like her and fulfill their dreams. I hope she never stops.

Chayani Ayers, Grade 5
Desert Trails Elementary School, CA

Camp Luwisomo

Camp Luwisomo is an exciting place to visit. You can make new friends as well as spend time with the people you know.

You're never stuck in your cabin because there are always spectacular activities to do. You can go swimming with Barracuda (she's the lifeguard with the pink hair). You can also try to hit the headless weasel in archery class. Kayaking, canoeing, and paddle boating on the lake is a great way to spend time with your friends.

Make sure you bring your camera. If you don't, you will miss all the great pictures you will someday cherish.

At Camp Luwisomo it gets crazy! One day at breakfast, a guy named Fluzzy drank a whole bottle of syrup. He was sick the rest of the day. When you meet Doc he will tell you he eats anything, so offer him some mud and see what he does with it. My counselor, Pepper can sleep through anything and we have pictures to prove it!

You can shop in the canteen for yummy treats like ice cream bars, candy, and soda. All the great things your parents love you to eat!

After 5 days your parents come get you, and then the party is over. Camp Luwisomo is an exciting adventure, so if you need some time away from your parents Camp Luwisomo is there for you.

Noelle Koepp, Grade 5
Trinity Lutheran School, WI

My Pets

My pets are Thunder, a dog, and Marvin, a goldfish. They are very friendly and I love them both.

Thunder is a four-year-old black labrador retriever. I got him when I was six-years-old. Thunder really likes food. In fact, it may be his favorite thing in the whole world. His second favorite thing would either be playtime (tug-of-war), the Dog Park, or his nightly walk. I love Thunder so much. He loves to swim because he learned when he was just a puppy!

Marvin is my other pet. He is a goldfish. I'm not sure how old he is because we won him at the Fun Fair last February. Marvin had to go on eating sesame seeds for the first two weeks until we bought him some real fish flakes.

After a while, we bought a nice big fish tank and things to put inside it. I love the way that Marvin glistens whenever he sways his tail back and forth as he swims.

Even though I love them so much, there are a couple negative things about pets. For instance, when you're trying to work, you may hear barking and it won't stop. Sometimes when you forget to feed Marvin he starts trying to swim through the glass.

But there is nothing like hearing the pitter-patter of dog paws when you yell, "Thunder!", or when the fish darts to the top of the fish tank when you come.

Haley Schueler, Grade 5
Butterfield School, IL

Skateboarding

Skateboarding is one of the world's most popular sports. Billions of people skateboard around the world.

There are multiple styles of skate boarding, my style is simple or novice. Many people think skate boarders are inconsiderate jerks, but they're not. They set a standard to live up to.

There are many pro-skaters on earth, each of them works hard, eats healthy, and sets a standard to live up to. They never give up even when they get bashed up. They know what it takes to be good at skateboarding. Pro-skateboarders start out just as normal people, but work hard and became pros at it.

In order to not get killed while skateboarding, you wear loads of pads. The most common pads are elbow pads, knee pads, and of course a helmet. There are also wrist pads, which protect the wrists and hands, and butt pads, which protect the lower spine, butt, and thighs. You also need gear to fix your board and to customize your board, which also makes it easier to skate.

I have introduced the topic of skateboarding, talked about pro-skaters, and told you what gear you need to skateboard. Now I will end my paper with some words from a great skateboarder named Michael. "Michael, what does it take to skateboard?" His reply was, "It takes practice, focus, and discipline." Skate boarding is the best!

Ragnar VanZante, Grade 6
Franklin Phonetic Primary School, AZ

Cute Kitty Cats

One morning, I was surprised by how extraordinary I felt. I felt jaunty and excited to go to school. I got to school and finished my day with extremely hard homework in every subject. When the bus dropped me off at home, my dad's Dodge truck was parked in the narrow driveway. Since my brother was inside before me, I emphatically shut the door. The second I set my schoolbags down, John (my father) screamed, "We're getting kittens!" The way he said it was quite endearing. One minute later, our mother called and talked to each and every one of us. The first thing I said when it was my turn was, "What do they look like?" She said that one was black and one was tiger striped. The lady who rescued them inferred that they were brothers. I sat on the couch to continue to talk to her when it began to rain. I began to lose her when we finished talking. The rain was so dense that you couldn't see a thing. I worried about her getting home for the next thirty minutes. When she did get home, I was outside waiting. The noise I heard next was the most touching moment of my life. It was the *meow* of the kittens. "I'm home!" she screamed at the top of her lungs.

Matthew Goodpaster, Grade 6
Argyle Middle School, TX

Trees Are Important

In the world there are things that give us oxygen, those are trees. Trees suck in carbon dioxide and breathe out oxygen.

Instead of just throwing away paper, why not recycle? It helps save trees if you recycle. It can change things if you just recycle and reuse! You can reuse paper over and over again until it's just a little, tiny scrap of paper, then you can throw it in the garbage! Yes trees may give us pencils, paper and Kleenex but cutting down trees for nothing? NOT USEFUL!! That's why there are such things as recycling bins!

Cutting down trees, destroys animal habitats and homes. If all trees were gone, there would be no life on earth! People love to see wild life all over the world. Trees provide a lot of needs in this world. Trees provide food for people and shelter, if a tree is dead then yes you may chop it down. Destroying animal habitats could kill animals and they will all be extinct!

Almost everything depends on trees and vegetation. On websites they say "Every second in the world a tree from somewhere disappears." And it's pretty true, people say it, too. Also "Every 5 seconds a tree from the rain forest disappears." That's pretty bad.

If you want to help trees, then you can plant new trees! I'm trying to make a difference; everybody is trying, and YOU CAN TRY AND MAKE A DIFFERENCE TOO!

Adrienne Ng, Grade 5
Park Meadows School, AB

No War

War should not happen. People should have freedom. Nobody wants to be invaded. People have different opinions.

War makes people feel sick inside and sad or makes them depressed. War makes some people feel good but to me it just doesn't feel right, good or safe. War is about a lot of things such as countries, oil, freedom, and many other things. I think they should just ask for something without fighting.

Everyone should have freedom. If someone wants freedom they should be allowed to have freedom. It's not fair if someone asks for freedom and their enemy puts them in jail, for example Nelson Mandela.

Nobody wants to be invaded because let's say one day you're in the ice cream shop and you hear a bomb explode and next thing you know your life changes instantly. I bet in all the wars we have had the other countries didn't want to be invaded. Some people don't realize the other countries just care about themselves.

Everyone has different opinions. Some people want war, but others don't. People want to fight, but others don't. My opinion is no war.

War shouldn't happen. People don't have to get along but they don't have to have war. People can ask, not fight. NO WAR!

Tristan Gonzales, Grade 6
La Mariposa Montessori School, NM

Imagination!

Imagination can be a good thing if you use it in the right way. I like to pretend that my stuffed animals and I are piloting a plane. Imagination has been known to get people in trouble or make them scared. If it is really windy at night, I think that a tree is going to fall on our house.

In some *Adventures in Odyssey Radio Drama* episodes presented by Focus on the Family, some kids got carried away with their imaginations. For example, "The Boy Who Cried Destructo" is about a boy named Lawrence who tricked people by accidentally making them think that what he was imagining was real. Gradually people stopped believing him, and when he really needed them, at first they didn't believe him. That is an example of how not to use your imagination.

Books like *Anne of Green Gables* are a good way to spark your imagination, because it looks like the characters have a lot of fun with their imaginations.

In this essay, I have shown you how to use and not use your imagination, and some sources to spark your imagination. Even though there are many other things I could tell you about, I would like you to imagine them for yourself!

Laura Schwartz, Grade 4
Schwartz Home School, MN

A True Gem

I believe that Hillary Rodham Clinton contains the potential to earn the distinguished title of America's Most Talented Woman. She has pointed out many of the problems associated with childcare and America's public school system. This gifted speaker delivered an extraordinary speech about women's rights and their role in our social community. In addition, Mrs. Clinton wrote a book called *It Takes a Village* to call for community participation in helping children grow and develop. She and her magnificent ideas drive me every morning to start another day and live up to my personal expectations.

Furthermore, my inspiration lies in this amazing woman who I look up to and support. I try to perform the best I can in hopes that one day I will be as phenomenal, strong, and hardworking as she appears to be. She has inspired me to help with charity fundraisers, feed the homeless, watch over my nieces, and donate to St. Edward's Church every Sunday. Her famous speech "Women's Rights are Human Rights," contains superb ideas about human rights I had never dreamed about. I also believe that we children should be protected as the next generation and the successors of our elders. My inspiration gives me hope that we can make the world better. Without a doubt, Hillary Clinton remains my inspiration, and she, in every aspect, is a true gem.

Stephanie Nguyen, Grade 6
Challenger School – Ardenwood, CA

Grizzly Bear

I read about the grizzly bear and here is what I learned.

The grizzly bear lives mainly high in mountain wilderness. Grizzly bears have fat bodies with strong legs. They have very big heads, short tail, and small rounded ears. This bear has a big muscular shoulder hump, and the hook like claws on the head paws are huge and strong for catching fish. The grizzly bear got the name grizzly from the silver tipped grizzly hair they get when they are older.

This bear is usually peaceful. They try to avoid a fight and flee from danger, but they are very short tempered and get mad quickly.

Their diet consists of berries, grasses, herbs, nuts of all kinds, honey, animal carcasses, fish, marine animals, elk, and bison. Grizzly bears will eat up to 80 to 90 pounds of food a day.

The mating season for the grizzly bear happens in June and July. They are ready to breed at the age of 5. A pregnant female will give birth 4 to 5 months after she has mated. This bear is very protective. The mother bear will fiercely protect her cubs from adult males and other predators. Bears have a life span of 15 years or more.

The grizzly bear is endangered because farmers will kill the bear when they see it near the livestock, and hunters are interested in their teeth, fur, and claws. The bear has long been an American symbol of strength and courage.

Paul Jarrell, Grade 4
Menchaca Elementary School, TX

Freedom

Freedom! I love freedom! We have all types of freedoms; everyone has freedoms, they're awesome!

First, we have four different types of freedom: freedom to work, freedom to worship, freedom of speech, and freedom to vote. Do you know any more? If you do, great! If you don't, well…that's okay!

Next, I'll tell you about your first freedom. This freedom is important for earning money, helping others, and even helping your whole country! You share this freedom; it goes all around the world. This freedom is…freedom to work!!!

Then, you also have another very important freedom; freedom to worship! Some people bow their head, fold their hands, and close their eyes as a way to worship. You also have the freedom of speech. This freedom enables you to be able to speak the language you want, to say things about the government, and to learn any language you please.

Last, freedom is a very important thing in our lives. So, your last freedom is…freedom to vote! We vote when we are electing a new mayor, governor, or president. So enjoy all your freedom!!!

Ashlyn Johnson, Grade 4
Rohwer Elementary School, NE

My Secret Place

My secret place is in my clubhouse. It has shelter and it has a table with a bowl of fruit in the middle of the table. I have a laptop on another table. I got a mirror in there. I got two lamps in my clubhouse. I got a nest because I made four birdhouses. I put flowers on the top of the four birdhouses. In my clubhouse I painted the walls with flowers. I got four chairs. I love the door. It's red. It's terrific. The outside door is red and white. I put something on the outside, I put spray paint. I wrote Ariana's Clubhouse! I drew a heart and colored it red. I have a jacket holder. Sometimes my sister and brother come and cut my flowers. I get so, so mad. One time when I had a friend over in my tree house my brother and sister were putting spray paint. They spelled — This is a stupid clubhouse! I had to wash my clubhouse with water. My friend helped me clean the spray paint off. I love my clubhouse. I play games on my laptop. Sometimes I read to my friend. Sometimes I do math and writing on my board. Me and my friend play tic-tac-toe. She wins most of the time. I love my tree house and that's my secret place.

Ariana Avila, Grade 4
Winona Elementary School, TX

Halloween

Halloween was originally referred to as "All Hallows' Eve," or "Hallowe'en" or even "Nos Galen-gaeof" but in today's English, it is spelled and said as "Halloween." Halloween is on October thirty-first.

Dressing up for Halloween was originally started as a ritual and has been passed down through the centuries. In many of the festivals people would dress up in skins of animals, and in others, people would dress up as Saints, Angels, and Devils.

Jack-O-Lanterns were originally started as folk tale in Ireland about a trickster named Jack who is said to have died and his soul went to the devil, so Irish people carved faces in turnips but as it migrated into North America, it turned into carving Pumpkins.

No one really knows when witches were first introduced. In ancient times to test if a woman was a witch or not a council would dunk her in a tank of water. If she floated, she was claimed to be a witch, if she drowned, she was innocent. Here is an example of a spell:

"Double, double toil and trouble;
Fire burn and cauldron bubble.
Eye of newt, toe of frog,
Wool of bat and tongue of dog,
Adder's fork and blind worm's sting,
lizard's leg and howlet's wing."

Halloween is an inspirational holiday for all ages. Halloween is fun, creative, and really scary occasionally. Halloween is the most fun holiday to some people.

Happy Halloween! Trick or Treat!

Alexis Montpas, Grade 5
McMonagle Elementary School, MI

Books

Books can open up your imagination and take you on an adventure. They can take you to other worlds, or to the past. They can take you to medieval times, or to a world war, or to different places of the world in recent times. The books you read can be scary, funny, or dramatic. They can be about adventure, laziness, history or they can be an autobiography. Books can be just about anything, even sadness. Books can be helpful for when you are studying, or they can be read for fun. Books can range from a few pages to thousands of pages long. Books can be the cheats to a video game, or an instruction manual. Books can usually teach you an important lesson. Books can be an audio book or a paper book, it does not really matter. Books date back to B.C. in the form of tablets and scrolls. Books can be for people of all ages, just as long as you can read or have someone else to read to you. The good thing about books is that they are not computerized or anything like that, they are actually fun and educational and can open up your mind for an adventure. Trust me, I know, I love reading. One more thing, never judge a book by its cover; it does not always have good consequences, and you might not get to read a good book because of it.

Kyle Varney, Grade 5
Kyrene Monte Vista School, AZ

Hawaii

You won't believe this mouth-watering experience as I introduce you to the beginning of my summer.

It all began the day I started to pack my bags. I was very delighted to come to realize that I had my own luggage. My sister and I made a checklist to make sure we had everything that we needed. I was glad that my packing was finished, which meant that I was now hassle free.

Hawaii! As we reached our hotel, our room was on the 14th floor, I was afraid because I was always scared of heights. While we were going to our room I was not looking down, I was SUPER scared. I was happy when we reached our room. It was gorgeous! Right by the ocean! As we finished unpacking we went straight to the beach. As I went rushing in I came rushing back out because the water was super cold. It took me a while to get used to the water, but I got used to it. In Maui, I got to see a beautiful sunset which was on a mountain. As 3 more days went, today was the day I was going on a submarine. I doubted that there would be a shark, but who knows. In the submarine there were oval shaped windows to look through. We got to go 110 ft in the ocean. It was awesome.

Thanks to my parents, I had a never-forgetting trip to Hawaii.

Shivani Ghadia, Grade 5
Dishman Elementary School, TX

Why I Think Wiener Dogs Are the Best Dogs in the World

I think wiener dogs are the best dogs in the world. Besides the fact that wiener dogs chew up stuff, they are the best dogs for pets. They are good camping dogs because they will not run away that often. But their fur is very slick and they can get out of your backyard sometimes. They are very sweet but they may bark at the thunder if there is a thunderstorm. They may also bark at your friends when they come over to play.

A fun thing to do with wiener dogs is to go to the Buda Wiener Dog Races. Any dog can be in the parade, not just wiener dogs, but only wiener dogs can race. In the parade, dogs wear funny or cool costumes. Some wiener dogs are really fast, but some are funny to watch because they will run off to the side and look at the people watching the race.

My wiener dog, Scooter, is very sweet and he sleeps with me because I won't roll over on him like my mom does. Also, Scooter will dance around three times if you hold food above his head. Sometimes, he won't go outside in the backyard unless you give him a treat. We call it a "treat-treat" and he gets all excited. We love Scooter and we think he is cool and that's why we think wiener dogs are the best dogs in the world.

Casey Follis, Grade 4
Menchaca Elementary School, TX

Penguins

Penguins may not look like birds, but penguins are really birds. They have all of the components a bird has. Like birds, penguins have feathers around its body, penguins are also warm-blooded which means their body temperature never changes, and lastly penguins are born from an egg like birds. Not all penguins only have white and black feathers. Some penguins have bright colors to recognize their species.

There are eighteen types of penguins. Scientists believe that the closest relative is the sea bird such as albatross and shear-water. If you didn't know penguins have a very poor sense of smell. For penguins' protection they use their razor sharp beaks. Scientists think that penguins could see better under water than on land. Also most birds have hollow bones to help them fly, but a penguin has solid bones that allow it to dive into water.

Penguins live on the coast of Antarctica, South Africa, New Zealand, Australia, Chile, Peru and the Galapagos Islands. These places are all south of the equator. Many penguins live in Antarctica where the land is covered in ice and snow. Always remember penguins do not live in the arctic.

A penguin's mouth, throat, and stomach stretch, allowing it to swallow its prey whole. A penguin can swallow prey that is almost as big as itself! Penguins' enemies include orcas, sea lions and leopard seals.

Penguins are really great animals, never forget that.

Armando Raya, Grade 5
Desert Trails Elementary School, CA

My Army Friend

At the beginning of my 5th grade year, my class wrote letters to the army in Iraq. At almost the end of the year I got a letter back from William Leshack. When I got his letter, my teacher, Mrs. Garretson handed it to me. She told me right away that it had come, so I could read it to her. As I read it, Mrs. Garretson started to tear up because she thought it was beautiful. Then she told me that I should read it in front of the class sometime that day.

Wow, what a good and glorious day! After the day was over and my homework was done, I got the letter out of my backpack and started to write William back. Guess what! I got a letter back about a week later. He then said that he would like to be my friend and that we could be pen pals. He has a nickname too, B.T. (Billy the third). I am his friend so I can call him that.

William told me that he has a family too. He has two children and a wife who all live on a base in Kansas. He told me so many cool things about where he is and what he does, like if there are women working where he is or who his other friends are. It is really awesome. For now I wait for my army friend's next letter.

Kaytlin Hall, Grade 6
Imagine Charter School at Rosefield, AZ

The Benefits of Computers

Computers have really improved our civilization. Financial business, research, and communication are all faster and more efficient thanks to computers. We are definitely better off with our computers than without them.

These days our banking systems, money, and purchasing are all computer based. You can now use online banking systems for paying bills and keeping track of your accounts. Now that we have computers, it's easier to buy things like clothes, cars, or toys with online catalogs and have items shipped straight to your door. Cashiers in stores use computers to scan your card, scan bar codes on items and also figure out your change.

More and more schools and students have been getting Internet connections for studying and information purposes. We are able to communicate with each other even around the world using computers. You can keep in contact with friends and family by using e-mail and Instant Messenger. With these programs you can even share your favorite photos and videos with far away friends and relatives for no extra cost, unlike expensive long distance phone calls.

Furthermore, computers have really changed our world. What would our world be like without them? I can't imagine. We share information faster and more efficiently than any pony express rider had ever dreamed. Whether you are using a computer at home, for your jobs, at school, or play and entertainment, we are constantly relying on computers. We are absolutely better off with computers!

Kathleen Bragg, Grade 5
Liberty Ranch Christian School, NM

My Gift

My gift is gymnastics. I give ideas to other people about my gift. When I give ideas it helps others get fit, healthy, and strong. Gymnastics is my terrific gift the Holy Spirits from above gave me. So, I want to say, "Thank you Holy Spirits."

When I do gymnastics, I give to others. I do gymnastics and people look up to me. They also want to be like me. If it helps them to get fit and be healthy, then this is a way that I can give to them.

When I do gymnastics, I help others. I help others by giving them ideas about doing gymnastics so they can stay fit. When people do gymnastics, they want to watch their health and what they eat. If they eat too much, they might not be able to lift themselves during all the gymnastics skills. I can help others by being a good example.

When I do gymnastics, I practice. I have to practice a lot in order to be good. In each practice I have to do a lot of strength exercises to be strong.

When I do gymnastics, I believe in myself. As long as I believe in myself, I can do it!

My gift is gymnastics. I give ideas to others. When I give ideas, I help others get fit, be healthy and be strong. Gymnastics is my terrific gift the Holy Spirits from above gave to me. So, I want to say, "Thank you Holy Spirits!"

Quin Malm, Grade 6
Cheyenne Mountain Elementary School, CO

Epilepsy

Hi! My name is Laura. I'm a person living with epilepsy.

Epilepsy is a seizure disorder. A seizure is when my brain does something it's not supposed to do.

There are two big categories of seizures: generalized seizures and partial seizures. Generalized seizures start from both sides of the brain at the same time. Partial seizures start at one part of the brain.

My epilepsy is a partial seizure disorder. My epilepsy is kind of rare. It is called Autosomal Dominant Nocturnal Frontal Lobe Epilepsy (ADNFLE). That is a lot of words. (I don't know how to pronounce it.)

I don't really know what happens during my seizure because I'm asleep at night. But people have told me that either my whole body, or different muscles jerk. The seizures make me very tired.

About 65% of epileptic people can get rid of their seizures by taking medicine.

The rest of us have to get operations, a seizure alert dog (like my dog, Chip), or just deal with them.

So, now you know about epilepsy. Remember, you can't catch epilepsy, and I can do pretty much the same things as you!

Laura Hamilton, Grade 6
Daniel Wright Jr High School, IL

Hero

My brother is a very loving brother. He is a great role model for me because he usually does what is right. Occasionally he gets angry. He is a very funny, silly, and brave guy.

He is chivalrous like a knight of the round table. When I need him, my bro's there to comfort me. He is always willing to do something to help. I think my bro is the best in the world. If I could think of a color to describe him it would be a rainbow. If you look at him hard, I think you could see the light of caring shining through him as if he were a messenger, delivering love and care to those who need it.

He is like a great teacher, who is full of glee and love. He has taught me to be a fair athlete in any sport I try, to never cheat or be a bad sport. He strongly encourages me to not fight and do my chores and homework.

My bro has taught me all the fun things about video games, even though they are not important, they are still fun. If I do something wrong or break something he forgives me. He is the most involved person in my life. I want to be just like him in his good ways not the bad.

Connor Busby, Grade 6
Round Valley Elementary School, CA

Tattoos Don't Change — You Will

People shouldn't get tattoos because they can be dangerous, can affect your career, and they are permanent.

You can get diseases from tattoos if the needles aren't clean. Diseases can include, but are not limited to, Hepatitis and AIDS. These are serious diseases that can end your life or alter it significantly.

Tattoos can affect the way people think about you, particularly in the workplace. Some people might think you are less responsible. Many people don't believe they are appropriate in the workplace. It may prevent you from pursuing certain careers like politics, law, and other professions. Even as a teenager it might affect your ability to earn money. Many parents wouldn't want to hire a baby-sitter with tattoos.

People who get tattoos might argue that it's their body and they have the right to express themselves however they want. There are safer ways to express yourself. People could use signs, T-shirts, bumper stickers, etc. These methods of expression are not permanent.

The fact that tattoos don't change is the biggest problem about having a tattoo. Many tattoos express a person's beliefs or thoughts. If you change your thoughts or beliefs the tattoo won't change with you. For example, let's say you're dating Mary, and you get a tattoo saying "I love Mary." If you break up with Mary, the tattoo will still be there.

People shouldn't get tattoos because things might change in your life. You might not want a reminder of the past ruining your future.

Drew Gannon, Grade 6
Beacon Country Day School, CO

Model Railroading

"What does model railroading mean to you?" Model railroading is a lifelong hobby because you are never finished. Also, there are so many companies to choose from.

When people think of train sets, they think of giving them as gifts for Christmas or for birthday presents. In fact train sets make good gifts for any occasion. Model railroading is the best hobby because you can always change things. Also, you can take apart your track and make a new track plan. One of the most fun things to do is to buy more train cars and to try to make your layout look real with scenery and buildings.

Like I said before, there are so many companies to choose from. One of these companies is Lionel. Lionel makes O gage trains that run on a three rail track. Then there is American flyer. American flyer makes S gage trains that run on a two rail track. Sadly enough American Flyer was bought out by Lionel. Another one is Marklin. Marklin makes HO gage trains that run on a track with a center stud system. Then there is Bachman. Bachman makes HO gage trains that run on two rail track.

Like most people, I got started with a train set. Train sets usually include a transformer, some track, a train, a couple of train cars, and sometimes a couple of accessories. I hope you will get started in this lifelong hobby.

Joseph Kosmicki, Grade 6
Orchard Hill Elementary School, IA

The Giant Squid

Have you ever seen a creature that can grow as big as a school bus and attack sperm whales? The giant squid is a carnivorous mollusk that has a long torpedo-shaped body. Above the tentacles, the largest eye in the world sits. A giant squid's eye is about the size of a dinner plate.

For years, scientists tried to capture pictures of a giant squid in its natural habitat: the deep sea. In 2002, a team of Japanese scientists led by Tsunemi Kubudera and Kyoichi Mori succeeded during an expedition to the Pacific Ocean some 600 miles south of Tokyo. The squid they photographed was approximately 46 feet long. Scientists have long argued whether the great squid was snailish and passive or active and aggressive. The pictures these scientists took seem to settle the issue as they show the squid viciously attacking bait on a line and only backing off after one of its own tentacles was torn off by the hook.

Giant squid live in the deep depths of the ocean at about 10,560 feet. The temperature affects a squid's buoyancy system. In warmer water, a squid will rise to the top and if it can't get back down, the squid will suffocate.

The giant squid is still a big mystery to many. Maybe we will learn more about the animal in the future.

Adam Roenker, Grade 5

Shopping at the Mall

Shopping is so much fun. I love to shop. I love fashions. I love cute clothes. I like to shop at the mall. I buy all kinds of things when I am shopping. Sometimes I take a break to buy my favorite ice cream. Ice cream helps me think of things that are cute. Sometimes I think that I'm as cute as an ice cream sundae.

Shopping at the mall is so much fun because there is so many things to do and see. One day I went to the mall to buy a dress. I was going to a party and I needed a new cute dress. I went to a few stores like Jump, the Gap, Sears and finally to Rainbow. I found the cutest dress in Rainbow. Then I had to look for shoes to match. I found the cutest shoes to match my dress. Then I went to Rogers Jewelers store, to buy some earrings, a necklace, and a ring. Everything matched my dress. I was going to be so cute for the party. Before I left the mall, I bought a double chocolate smoothie. It was good! I had a little time before the party started so I took a nap for two hours. When I awoke I got a call saying that the party was canceled. So, I called my friend and asked her if she wanted to go to the mall.

Cherish Chapman, Grade 5
Prospect Elementary School, OH

Miley Cyrus

Destiny Hope Cyrus, also known as Miley Cyrus, was born on November 23, 1992. She was raised and loved by Billy Ray Cyrus and Leticia "Tish" Cyrus. Miley is the fourth child of six, all of who were raised in Tennessee. She was named Destiny Hope because her parents thought that she would be very successful. Her name "Miley" was used because she smiled a lot ("Smiley").

Miley became interested in acting at the age of nine when the family lived in Toronto, Ontario, Canada. In 2003, she became "Young Ruthie" in *Big Fish* and was credited as Destiny Cyrus. She was also featured in Rhonda Vincent's music video for "If Heartaches Have Wings," and appeared on *Colgate Country Showdown* with her father, Billy Ray Cyrus. Miley was 11 years old when she originally auditioned for Disney for the part of the "best friend," Disney Channel executives then judged her for being too small, after all Miley was determined in her desire to be part of the show, so Disney called her back for auditions when she was twelve. Miley was chosen for Hannah Montana because of her energy and lively performance and was seen as a person who "loves every minute of life." Later in an amazing twist, Miley had to audition Billy Ray Cyrus, to see if he would fit the role of Hannah's dad. Miley currently stars as the lead character Miley Stewart. Miley also performs for albums and concerts. Miley is my personal favourite actress! YEAH!!

Johanna Pineda, Grade 5
St Gerard School, MB

Be Drug Free

I don't want to do drugs. I don't want to do drugs because they harm you. I don't like drugs because they change you. If you smoke your lungs will turn black. Your finger tips will turn yellow. Smoke can harm the person beside you, if you are smoking. Alcohol can harm your brain cells. Alcohol can make you crazy. Alcohol can harm you. Wine can change you. Wine can change the way you act. Drugs can harm you.

I don't want to do drugs. If you do drugs it can change your life. I'm doing the right thing. I hope you are.

Jeniece Helms, Grade 4
Lynnville Elementary School, IN

My Summer Vacation

For my summer vacation I went to Arkansas. My cousins live there. It was a very long 8 1/2 hour ride there. When we got there, their house was for sale!

The next day we went boating. The lake we went on was called Beaver Lake. It was 180 feet deep. It was crystal clear, and in one spot it was as clear as the Kingsley swimming pool.

When we got back to their house we played Xbox 360; my uncle won it at his work.

The next day we went to Devil's Den. There we took a long hike. We climbed on rocks too! It was really hot, so we found a waterfall to get wet in.

Then we found the Icebox. It was nice and cool in there. We also found two caves. The first cave was very hard to climb out of. The second cave was very fun! It was slippery and there were bats.

The next day we looked at houses that they were thinking about buying. One was absolutely huge! Both of the houses had theater rooms. One house had a small kitchen upstairs! There was a bathroom in each bedroom except the guest room. The ceiling in the living room was 30 feet tall!

After that we went rock climbing. My mom and cousin made it to the top and rung the bell! I didn't make it, neither did my other cousin or my brother.

We went back to their house, and the next day we went home happy!

McKenze Carlson, Grade 4
Kingsley-Pierson Community School, IA

Mom and Dad

My parents are the best things in my life. They always tell me, "Have good manners and respect others."

First, there is my mom, who loves me, no matter what I do. So does my dad, and, he is funny and fun to play with. They give me all I need, like clothes, food and water. They give me a comfy bed to sleep in.

My mom has two other children, but I am the baby. I love my parents so much, I couldn't ask for better folks.

Hannah Muncy, Grade 5
Westview Elementary School, OH

My Trip to Las Vegas

Almost every couple months we go to Las Vegas to see our aunt, uncle, and two cousins, Dylan and Sydney. At their house we would usually stay two or three days until it's time for us to go. The trip takes about four hours but it's pretty fun when my brother and I are just watching a movie in the back of the car.

When we arrive there we are welcomed by two hugs by my two little cousins Dylan and Sydney. In the afternoon we will usually go swimming in their pool or just take care of Dylan and Sydney. Sometimes we all bake chocolate chip cookies together. At night we would go to a place called Excalibur and we would just hang around the arcade. When we go to Excalibur we would win a lot of prizes which we would give to the little cousins.

When we are done and ready to go back to my aunt's house we would go for a stop at Jack N the Box to eat because we would be starving. By the time we're at my aunt's house Dylan and Sydney are sound asleep. Then we would probably watch a movie while the kids are sleeping.

When it is time for us to go back home we would get two big bear hugs from both Dylan and Sydney. So you can see that these are most of the fun things I do when I go to Las Vegas with my family.

Kayla Sison, Grade 6
Ranch Hills Elementary School, CA

Bears

What do bears eat?

Some bears are hungry all the time! But some bears eat different kinds of food depending on their diet. A grizzly bear for example eats grass and roots. It also likes to eat fish that are in the water. It can also eat bigger animals like young deer. They can also eat small animals that are in the ground. Grizzly bears eat about 35 pounds of food every day. They eat a lot because they are so big. A grizzly can grow longer than a sofa. It can weigh as much as 10 grown-ups!

Another type of bear is called a polar bear. A polar bear is different from a grizzly. A polar bear lives where it is cold. They eat a lot of food. That is how they stay warm. They mostly eat seals. They also eat whales or fish that have died. They sometimes hunt for walruses.

How do bears find food? All bears have a nose called a snout. Their nose gives them a sense of smell. That is how they find food. Even some bears can smell a person from a mile away! They may also smell an animal that is dead from 12 miles! Bears have to travel very far to find something to eat. Bears can stand on two legs to make themselves bigger. This may help their enemies stay away. Bears can be very fast runners. Those are some facts about bears.

Jennifer Hernandez, Grade 5
Desert Trails Elementary School, CA

Max Is My Hero

Twelve years ago, when I lived in Tucson, Arizona, my family found a sad, lonely, scared puppy in the desert. We decided to name him Max.

He has a disease but that doesn't stop him. He is a light brown cocker spaniel. Max is very old but he is also very wise. Whenever he is awake, he is always in a cheerful mood. His nose looks like a teddy bear's but also, guides his body through the jungle of the neighborhood. His vision is very cloudy, therefore makes him cautious. His ears are long and shaggy but very in tune like a satellite searching for a signal.

Max has experienced many things in his life. He's been camping a lot and loves riding in the car. He always likes to play with neighborhood dogs and their owners, especially me! He has a friend that is a Chihuahua and his name is Moose. Moose is a light brown dog and weighs 6 pounds. He is also good company for Max whenever we can't be home with him. Max can't go camping anymore because of his disease.

Max's disease is hard on my family because he looks very different and ill. His disease is Cushing disease. This disease gives him many problems. Max gets bloating in the stomach and dizziness all the time. He has liver and kidney problems, too. He doesn't eat much either.

Max is my first dog and I will miss him greatly.

Cullen Williams, Grade 6
Spring Creek Elementary School, WY

All Nine of Us

My family is awesome! I have four brothers and two sisters that are great. I am the second youngest, so I don't remember when my brothers were growing up. But I do know that they love me, because of all the birthday cards, baseball games, and playing "house" with me.

I am glad to be one of the youngest in the family because I get to watch all the fun times we have together. I still get piggy back rides, pushes on the swings, toying with their possessions.

My oldest brother got married this summer to an extraordinary woman named Hollie. She is just like an older sister to me.

Two other people in my family, which I could never, ever forget about, are my mom and dad. They are there when I need them, and give me space when I want to be alone. They are kind but firm and brought us all up to be kind, caring, Christian people. I love them so much!

Garrett, Trenton, Nolan, Kayla, Logan, and Brooke are more than brothers and sisters. They are my heroes, counselors, playmates, someone to have giggle attacks with or to cry with. I look up to and respect every one of them. I have been blessed greatly by having such a large and loving family. All nine of us have greatly appreciated one another.

Krista Hovland, Grade 6
North Iowa Community School, IA

My Trip

Have you ever wished that you could just get away from your normal everyday life? Well, that's exactly what my friend Hannah and I did. I was ecstatic!! Wouldn't you be if you just found out that you were going to a five star resort with one of your best friends? After I hung up the phone, I rushed to Hannah's house.

When I got there we packed the car and left. Hannah and I laughed hysterically at expressions of the people in back of us, as we waved at them joyfully in her car.

As soon as we walked in the doors of the resort we stared in awe. It was magnificent!!! There was a fountain right in the middle of the lobby. Then I turned and saw exotic flowers in elegant vases.

After we looked inside of the resort we rushed outside to see the pool. It was enormous!! But then, I looked around and saw even more. There were water slides and a lazy river too. First Hannah and I went in the pool. Then we went tubing down the lazy river, trying to hide from her sisters in the sea of people. Finally we went on a water slide. The water slide was my favorite part. It was very slippery!!

When we were done in the pool we went to eat dinner. It was delicious!! After we ate dinner it started to rain so we went inside. I can't wait until tomorrow!!!

Kayla Rolland, Grade 6
Imagine Charter School at Rosefield, AZ

The Woman Who Cares

Hardworking, wise, and caring are characteristics of many people. Oprah Winfrey is the one who fits the description. She even has a big heart.

Oprah Winfrey lived a hard life. Before the *Oprah* show started, Oprah received a job on the radio. After she got fired for making too many mistakes, she appeared on the news. Using all the money she earned, she started her own production company. Her company later bought the news show and turned it into *The Oprah Winfrey Show*. A characteristic that inspires me is that even after failing numerous times, she still never gave up.

Wise and caring, she used her money to build a school in the place where her heart belongs, Africa. This school was built for poor girls who have been raped in their life or who have family and wealth issues. This school can be found away from the cities so the girls have to live in the school. Oprah has spent 1.1 million dollars on the school and its uniforms. Oprah used her money to not only build a school, but also supplied them with a better life by giving them a better education.

It is just amazing to know that Oprah cares about the life of these girls in Africa. Oprah inspires me to never give up even if I fail numerous times and to also not to spend too much money because other people will cherish every cent that we spend on unnecessary things.

Sana Allam, Grade 6
Challenger School – Ardenwood, CA

Honey Bee

Of the 10,000 types of bees, I'll be writing about the honeybee. There are three types of bees in the hive, the worker bee, who has many types of jobs such as honey gathering, fanners, and guards. Worker bees are always females. The second type of bee is the drone. A drone is a male bee whose job is to mate with the queen. After a drone mates, he will die. If he does not mate the worker bees will most likely kill him in the fall. The queen is the last type of bee. The queen is an egg-laying machine. Her only occasions to leave the hive are mating and swarming. Honeybees eat pollen and nectar, which is honey. Bees get their food by going from flower to flower sucking nectar through their tongue. As a bee goes collecting nectar the worker bee will pick up pollen. As the bee travels from flower to flower the pollen will brush off, as more clings to the bee's legs. This will pollinate each flower. A beehive that is made by man has five main parts. The first part is the bottom board, which is used as a landing space. Second is a space where the queen will lay her eggs which is called the brood chamber. Third is a queen excluder. This keeps the queen from coming into the honey storage comb, which is the fourth part. Last is the cover. Honeybees are incredible insects to learn about. I love honeybees!

Heidi Galster, Grade 5
Mary Morgan Elementary School, IL

Cross Country

I have been in cross country all year. It has been really fun, but sometimes our coach makes us run way too hard and way too far!

Last week on Thursday, Coach made us run five to six miles, without stopping! We ran 4 miles to the hill on a dirt road. As soon as we got there, we were all glad to stop, but then she told us to run up and down the hill five times! I was so exhausted!

The day before that we had a race and I got second place. I was so happy I got a seven up!

In the cross country meets, it's enjoyable because it's exciting to run and I don't give up. If I do well I get rewarded. Even if I don't do well, my mom is still proud of me! But when I'm done with the race my face is all cherry red and I can hear myself breathing loud. In the race I can hear people screaming, sometimes for me, and I see lots of fog and dew, but I run through it like it's not even there. I try as hard as I can to beat my friends and other school because I want to be great!

I love cross country and hope to do it next year too because I learned a lot from it. I learned to never give up and always try. Cross country truly is a healthy thing to do!

Kelsey Wilbur, Grade 6
Haslett Middle School, MI

Bullying

I used to get bullied when I was younger. It was not a good feeling. One day I stood up to my bully. She continued taking my things. I got really upset and fought my bully. That is not a good thing, fighting, but I had no other choice.

Bullying is when someone messes with another person younger than them. Bullying is the meanest thing anybody can do. It's just wrong. When you hear about it you just become so angry and you become sick and want to fight the bully.

When teachers and parents ask who gets bullied we say little kids. The little kids that get bullied cry and they get things taken away. The people who do the bullying are older kids. Some older kids bully because they want to see little kids cry. It's just not right.

If I ever get bullied I would handle it myself. I would tell the teacher. If I ever witness a kid getting bullied I will break it up myself. If the bully took anything they will give back what they took. If schools want to stop bullying I feel that they should suspend the one who's doing the bullying. Otherwise the principal should suspend them and call for a meeting with their parents. At school there should not be a bully everyone is there to learn not to get bullied on.

Deja Hood, Grade 6
Starms Discovery Learning Center, WI

Tony Parker's Journey to the NBA

Tony Parker is an extraordinary basketball player for the San Antonio Spurs, but have you ever wondered how he came over the tough obstacles and journey to fame?

Before Tony Parker enjoyed playing basketball, he enjoyed playing soccer. Then one day, he saw Michael Jordan play as a global basketball superstar, which changed his life. As Parker perfected his skill, he decided he would play point guard on-court, based on his speed, size, and potential in the game. Because Parker had two brothers, he would enjoy playing a few basketball games with them perfecting his skills.

As Parker grew older, he was offered many great opportunities, such as attending the National Institute for Sports and Physical Education in Paris. His performance caused a recruiting war at several colleges, including UCLA and Georgia Tech. In 1999 Parker agreed to play professional and signed with Paris Basketball Racing. In the summer of 2000, Parker left Paris because he was invited to the Nike Hoops Summit in Indianapolis. While participating, he challenged a few pro scouts to see how advanced he really was. Once the Nike Hoops Summit was completed, Parker traveled back to competing in the French Championship before the 2001 NBA Draft.

Throughout Tony Parker's career, he has been extremely successful, but we should still remember how he got this far in the NBA. Tony Parker defines a real role model due to his character and dedication.

Colin Trainer, Grade 5
Oak Crest Intermediate School, TX

Amanita Phalloides

Amanita phalloides, also known as the "death cap," is a toxic basidiomycete fungus that is commonly found in Europe. There are reports of it being found further east in Asia, but they are unconfirmed. The death cap has a large epigeous fruiting body which appears in the summer and autumn, and its greenish cap is generally five to fifteen centimeters across. Its stipe and gills (the underside of the cap) are white.

One of the reasons that A. phalloides is potentially dangerous is its resemblance to many species of mushrooms commonly consumed by humans, such as Volvariella volvacea, making it responsible for a large number of mushroom poisonings worldwide. It is estimated that only about thirty grams (one ounce) is enough to cause death. Additionally, the toxicity is not reduced by cooking, freezing or drying. No definite antidote is known, but benzylpenicillin, or penicillin G, has been known to help.

Its two main toxins are the amatoxins alpha-amanitin, which damages the liver and kidneys, and beta-amanitin, which adds to the toxic effects. In fact, alpha-amanitin is considered by many to be the deadliest of all known amatoxins.

Some early symptoms of death cap consumption may include abdominal pain, vomiting, and diarrhea. These usually stop after two to three days. However, some life-threatening symptoms may develop, such as damage to the brain, pancreas, kidneys, and heart. Death usually occurs six to sixteen days after poisoning. Consumption of the death cap is considered a medical emergency requiring hospitalization and a liver transplant.

Keith Favre, Grade 5
Dishman Elementary School, TX

Taipans

Slipping through bushes, slithering sneakily across the ground, the one and only taipan! Did you ever wonder about taipans? Why are people so scared of them, what is their favorite food, and where do they hide? I have the answers to all those questions.

People are really scared of taipans because they are really big; some people believe they are the most venomous snakes ever.

Taipans are actually super scared of humans; they hide in grass and dark places to get away from predators and us people.

The last and final thing I will tell you is that taipans favorite foods are rodents such as rats, mice, hamsters, and guinea pigs.

Now you know a little about a taipan.

Sean Brogan, Grade 6
Pomerene School, AZ

The Extravaganza Fun Ship

I think one of the most memorable events of my life is when I went on a Carnival Cruise. Everything was absolutely incredible on that ship, everything was in tiptop shape. Also, everything was fancy, from the dining room to the hallways, from the cups to the chairs; absolutely everything was shiny, beautiful, and attractive. But I think the best part is when my brother, Kyle, my cousin, John, and I stayed with each other and just had fun the whole time.

Kyle is tall and skinny and always had a curious look on his face and John is short, skinny and lean. We played golf and ate all the food we could eat, we also went swimming and rode terrific dune-buggies.

The place where we hung out the most was probably the arcade room. There were 14 games in that room. Kyle would spend all of his money on one game, which was called *Soul Caliber 2*. John and I would just go crazy and play every game in that room. It was fantastic because the game room was hidden behind support beams and fake plants that were tall and extremely wide so we got the room all to ourselves.

One thing I always liked is after everything we would do, Kyle would say, "Let's go get something to eat and then get some ice cream." We would say "No no no! We're tired of ice cream and pizza!"

When the cruise was over, we said our good-byes and went home, it really is the greatest trip ever!

Mitchell Keith Earwood, Grade 6
Faith Academy of Marble Falls, TX

How Bad Is It?

Many people in our world don't realize how bad smoking or taking drugs is. But I do. Smoking turns our lungs pitch black. I went to a body museum and I saw it. It is vulgar. You might as well be living in a house full of smoke if you are going to smoke. Many people think it is "cool" to smoke. An outrageous number of people smoke just in L.A.

And drugs. I don't know which is worse now. Drugs destroy your life so easily. They can give you brain damage and make you go crazy. Many people say, "I just want to try it." Before you know it they become addicted after "trying" it so much. A ridiculous number of actresses take drugs or smoke because they feel pressured to do a spectacular job in their career. I think that's why *a lot* of people take drugs. Because they feel pressured. So if you ever feel pressured to do something that's bad, please don't do it. Many people have the power to say NO but sometimes they don't use their power.

All I'm saying is that if you smoke or take drugs, then it will diminish your life span. Remember, you have the power.

Bronwyn Stephenson, Grade 6
Round Valley Elementary School, CA

Thanksgiving

Thanksgiving is a great time for families to get together. Last year my whole family went to my auntie's and it was so much fun! My auntie recently had a baby boy and his birthday is the day after Thanksgiving so it was a big party. Everybody brought their trailers. All of the parents sat around the fire and talked for the whole weekend, while the kids were running around and playing tag. I hope that we can do it again some year!

Thanksgiving is a wonderful holiday! This year our whole family is coming to my house and they are all supposed to bring their dirt bikes and quads. I can hardly wait and I hope that the weather will be really nice! This Thanksgiving weekend is going to be the absolute best!

For my family's Thanksgiving we also have a humungous supper. Last year I felt like I was two hundred fifty six pounds after eating all of that food. After dinner it was time for dessert, but all of the kids were smart enough to push their plates away. I hope that I don't stuff my face again this year but I guess that is a big part of Thanksgiving. Food, family and fun times, that is what Thanksgiving means to me!

Shaylee Fillenberg, Grade 4
Linsford Park School, AB

My Pets

Do you ever think your pets have anything to say? Do you ever wonder why they do certain things to get your attention? Well my pets talk to me. They talk to me not with words or voices, but with body language.

Gabby was a little fuzzy ball of spunk when we got her. She'd act as if she was the queen of our house and pranced around the hall meowing and clawing at our doors as if she was ordering us to open up or face the wrath of her. She has grown up now and gotten bigger but she is still the same. She still meows as if she's queen of the house, but not as much since we got the new kitten.

Gabby acts jealous since we got Oreo. I'll never forget the day when we got Oreo. You see Oreo was an injured street kitten that was going to die if my sister didn't find her and take her home. When Gabby saw Oreo she hissed and growled then ran off. Every time Gabby ran into Oreo she'd do the same thing and sometimes throw in a paw.

She acted as if she was hurting in her heart and thought Oreo was replacing her. Gabby hid for about a week and avoided the family. She wouldn't let anyone pet her. Finally she stopped acting like she was being replaced and ignored Oreo. Oreo then would try to annoy Gabby by following her but Gabby would see her and hiss at her.

Gabby still acts this way but she tries to ignore Oreo. Gabby will probably have this personality for the rest of her life. She'll meow and claw if she wants to because she'll always think she's the queen of the house. She's a very good cat but she can be a big pain sometimes.

Selena Macias, Grade 6
Ranch Hills Elementary School, CA

Not So Perfect

Sometimes we are not born perfect and may have challenges. Some of the challenges we could have could be a bad heart, trouble breathing or bad eye sight, that make doing things harder. But having a challenge is not that bad, how I know it's not that bad because I have one. I was born with "club feet" and if you don't know what that means; I was born with no heels and I would not be able to walk. But I was lucky to have a great doctor.

My doctor is Richard Shindell and he has been my doctor for 10 years and I like him very much. I had to be in casts since I was one week old and had to wear them for two years. I never needed to wear shoes because I always had casts on my feet. But this didn't stop me from crawling around everywhere. My mom said that I even learned to dance in my casts. I soon learned how to walk in my casts, it was cool. After I had my casts taken off I had to have many surgeries on my heels and feet. I stayed in the hospital for two days and one night. I am thankful for my doctor and my family that they have been there for me when I had my surgeries. I was so happy when they let me go home.

Antonio Calleros, Grade 4
Gateway Pointe Elementary School, AZ

Ladianian Tomlinson

Ladianian was born in June 23, 1979 in Rosebud, Texas. Waco University High School named him Most Valuable Player. Ladianian attended Texas Christian College where he was the second player in college football history to rush for 2000 yards in one season and 5000 yards in his college career. During college he was named two-time WAC Offensive Player of the Year, three times Conference Player of the Year and named Player of the Week 11 times. Texas Christian honored him by retiring his number.

In 2001 he was a first round draft pick by the San Diego Chargers as a running back. Included in his numerous achievements are MVP, Man of the Year, and helped the Chargers to their first ever Associated Press MVP in 2006. He is the first player in team history to win the leagues rushing title with 1815 yards, got 6 new team records and set a total of 13 AFL records.

Ladianian also demonstrates excellence off the field through his charity work. With the help of his mom and wife, he oversees the Tomlinson Touching Lives Foundation. The foundation gives kids school supplies, scholarship funds, football camps, holiday dinners and takes 21 kids to every home game.

I admire Ladianian because he is a good model of what an athlete should be. He doesn't try to be flashy, get in trouble with the law and works hard on and off the field.

Zack Broeg, Grade 6
Thomas Jefferson Charter School, ID

Jane Goodall

Have you ever heard of a woman named Jane Goodall? If you haven't, then I hope that after you've finished reading this you'll understand some of the struggles and sacrifices Jane Goodall made for chimpanzees.

Jane Goodall was born on April 3, 1934 in Tanzania, England. She is one of the world's leading influences on chimpanzees.

In the Gombe Game Reserve in Africa jungles, she spent all of her time gaining the chimps' confidence. Many of her phenomenal observations and discoveries are well known around the world. Her research and writings have made a difference in the scientific thinking concerning the evolution of humans.

Dr. Goodall received her Ph.D. from Cambridge University in 1965. In 1984, Jane received many awards for helping millions of people understand the significance of wildlife preservation on this planet.

In 1985, Jane Goodall's twenty-five years of anthropological research was published, helping us all better understand the relationship between all creatures. She has devoted over thirty years to her assignment, and is still living. She dedicates her years of service to her mother, author Uahne Goodall.

Jane continues her duties by teaching and encouraging young people to appreciate the conversation of chimpanzees and all animals great and small.

She lectures, writes, and teaches to continue her numerous projects including the Chimpanzee Guardian Project.

These are only some of the facts about Jane Goodall and how she has enhanced our Earth's knowledge of chimpanzees. I hope you've enjoyed learning about her as much as I have.

Haley Huxford, Grade 6
Concord Ox Bow Elementary School, IN

Art by Van Gogh

Vincent Van Gogh was a famous artist. He made the famous picture, "Starry Night" and he lived before my time. He was the only one who used color in a different way.

Van Gogh was born on March 31, 1853 in Grootzundert, Holland, "way before my time." He was born by Theodorus and Anna Cornelia.

Van Gogh's most famous picture was "Starry Night." Starry Night is still recognized by kids at Pershing Elementary School in Mrs. Plachers class.

Van Gogh used colors in a different way than all of his artist friends. He mixed color and swirled them and did everything he could with them. That's why he became famous.

In conclusion, Vincent Van Gogh was famous for colors, his pictures, and he lived before my time.

Raytoria Richardson, Grade 6
Laraway School, IL

A Wonderful Mom!!

It was November 10, 1995, my mom was in the hospital. She was going to have a baby. My mom was in pain, but happy at the same time. She was glad because the baby was already here. When the doctor asked what is the baby's name, and my mom said "Her name is Jocelyn." We then went home and fell asleep.

It's now November 10, 1998. I was now turning three that year. My mom was taking good care of me, and getting my birthday ready for me. Then one year passed, and I was starting pre-k. My class and I went on a field trip to the zoo and science museum. My mom would always go on the field trips with me.

A few years went by I was now seven years old. My mom was now teaching me how to ride my bike. I then learned, and told my mom that I was glad that she taught me.

Four more years passed, and I was now starting sixth grade. My mom would tell me that she remembers when I was just a little baby. One day my mom told me that I was growing up so fast, but I then told her that I will still be your little girl. I then said that "I love my mom, I think she is beautiful, awesome, and a helpful mom." My mom is a wonderful mom.

Jocelyn Pena, Grade 6
Irma Marsh Middle School, TX

My Broken Arm

Monday, July 25, 2006. Remember what you did that night at 9:02 P.M.? I sure do. I was rushed to the hospital in a copper-colored truck. I had completely shattered my arm in half. It literally looked like the letter Z.

When I arrived, I immediately went in the E.R. in the West Wing at Ingham Medical Hospital in downtown Lansing M.I. They put me to sleep and started setting it. "It's okay son," my dad whispered, "It's okay." "Sir are you okay?" a nurse asked. "Yeah I'm fine," he said back. Then he fainted right there in the E.R. "Push the chair under him." another nurse said. "It won't work," Dr. Detraziac said worriedly, "The bones keep on slipping."

Tuesday, July 26, 2006. 7:30 P.M. I was taken to the E.R. again for open arm surgery. "Okay. Do this thing," I said. So they put me to sleep.

I'm awakened by a nurse hovering over my head. "Wake up Isaiah. Come on wake up," she said calmly.

My arm ached as I sat up, "Ouch. My arm stings," I said.

"It's okay. I'll get you more morphine," she whispered.

"Thanks can you get me some dinner? I haven't eaten since my surgery. I'm starving."

"Do you mean breakfast? It's 8:00 A.M."

"Wow. Can you also put on a movie?"

"Sure," the nurse said. I was released out of the hospital. It was pouring outside. I was glad, because when I got home, I was surprised to see my grandma.

Isaiah Peterson, Grade 6
Haslett Middle School, MI

My Dog: Scout

My dog's name is Scout. He is an English Springer Spaniel. Scout is two years old. His birthday is October 10, which is four days before my birthday.

Scout's fur is very nice. His fur is black, white, and his eyebrows are brown. Scout's ears are long and floppy with long hair. Scout's nose is cold and wet. He has a very short tail which is about two and one-half inches long. Scout is twenty-five inches tall from the ground to his shoulders. Scout is a hunting dog; I take him rabbit and squirrel hunting.

Scout is sometimes annoying. He likes to steal things from me and then he hides behind the couch. Scout likes to chase my sister's cat. He also takes pleasure in eating the cat's food. Scout likes to steal my food. I think it is funny when he steals my sister's things.

Scout is smart; he goes to the bathroom outside. He learned some things that I didn't even try to teach him. Scout knows that I will give him a bath when I get the hose out. He usually runs away when I get the hose out.

In conclusion, my dog is annoying, funny, and smart. He is annoying because when he steals my things. Scout is smart because he does some tricks. He is funny when he steals my sister's things. I really like my dog.

Austin Schneider, Grade 6
West Central Middle School, IL

Physical Fitness

Did you know that not being physically fit can affect you in many ways? If you don't, I am going to tell you how it does affect you.

First of all, you need to know what health problems you could have. If you are overweight you could have a heart attack possibly. If you are lazy you could gain weight. Also, you could have diabetes.

Eating good can lead to good fitness. Vegetables and fruits are the best. Milk and protein helps you. They might help you lose weight if you're overweight. If you have high metabolism, it helps your physical fitness.

Did you know that you don't have to be big to be out of shape? I myself have seen people real skinny and they are out of shape. You should always have a good breakfast.

Getting yourself motivated to start doing this is what you're going to have to start doing. Make a schedule of what you need to do to get used to your routine.

People think that you have to do the hardest things to get in shape. Well you don't. You could start out with something simple, like throwing a football, riding your bike, or doing whatever you want that helps you get fit.

To stay fit when you are — stay in that mode.

Tyler Holeman, Grade 6
Milltown Elementary School, IN

Friends

Friends are people who care about you, play with you, and talk to you. They would play and laugh all day long. My good friends treat me the way they want to be treated. We go to the mall, sit together at our lunch table, and play together at recess. If they need help on something in school I would help them. I help them on math problems, science experiments, social studies worksheets, on reading a book and things like that.

Being nice is how you make pals. An example of this happened when I was a new student to Covington in South Sioux City. I was shy when it was my first day of school. My classmates were nice to me and showed me around the building. My friends today are Alicia and Val. They are good friends and we are always nice to each other. Friends are kids who can laugh together and be funny with each other. Teachers can be friends, too. Today is a great day to make a new friend by being helpful, nice, and laughing.

Jennifer Almarez, Grade 5
Covington Elementary School, NE

About Orphans

Orphans miss out on not having a family to love them. Orphans miss out on not having a dad to play football with. Orphans also miss out on not having a brother to play video games with or a sister to paint nails with. Orphans miss out on not being able to bake with Mom.

Back then, orphans would get on a train. The train is called the orphan train. The train would stop in different cities and the children or child would get out of the train. People would select which child they wanted. Some farmers were looking for a farm hand.

An orphan is a child whose mom and dad died or put them up for adoption because they could not afford to take care of them.

Kara Gillenwater, Grade 5
West Elementary School, OH

Gravity

Sometimes we don't appreciate gravity. Think, without gravity, we would die. Either being too close or too far is bad. If we were too close, we would burn up. If we were too far, we would freeze. Without gravity, we couldn't walk. Like the astronauts we would have to jump instead of walk, and if we jump, we would float into the atmosphere and burn up. Everything would float out to the atmosphere. The water would disintegrate because it would float into the atmosphere. There wouldn't be any plants or trees because there would be no water, and we couldn't breathe because there would be no plants or trees, and there wouldn't be very much color because the plants would be dead. The planets wouldn't orbit the sun. We wouldn't have the moon, the stars, or any light. You see, God made gravity for a good reason.

Sable Kessler, Grade 6

Black Death

In the early 1350s to the 1380s a strange sickness raced across Europe. This sickness was called the Black Death and it came in three basic forms Bubonic, Pneumonic, and Septicemic. It was called the Black Death because of the pustules on the skin named Buboes which came from the Greek word groin and is where the buboes appeared the most. Doctors were baffled by the way it spread so quickly.

People who caught the Bubonic plague didn't get it from human to human contact. They contracted it from the rat flea, a flea that can carry bacteria. People who got the Pneumonic plague contracted it from the air and died of lung failure. The Septicemic plague was contracted from contact and was the deadliest and rarest. Even today there isn't a cure. The Black Death was named for the spots that appeared on the skin caused by septicemia.

The mortality rate during the plague was an average of 70%-93%. A third of the Jewish population died because of the first holocaust because the English thought that they were causing the sickness. After the plague ended 75 million had been killed. Two thirds died from the plague and a fourth died from panic.

The Black Death was the worst sickness ever. No one could stop its horrible rampage through the world. Even today it's a mystery to disease experts. The Black Death left a permanent scar on the world forever.

Zack Campbell, Grade 6
Southport 6th Grade Academy, IN

The Japanese Culture

I have looked up about the Japanese cultures and how much it has changed over the years. Its original cultures to what it is now. The culture has been picked up by Pacific immigrants and Chinese people. The people who lived in Japan were isolated from the people who lived outside of Japan. This was because of Japan being islands. With the arrival o the Black Ships and the Meijiera they were not longer by themselves.

I have researched about the language. It is small but it has pitch accent system. Their language is mainly spoken in Japan and by immigrants. The earliest time it was spoken was around 252 A.D. Japanese is written in three different ways. It is written in Kanji, Hiragana, and Kata Kana.

Art is a big thing in Japan. Their sculptures are from old legends. They like to paint by blending colors and using stroke speed. They also use the texture for an extra touch.

Japan's most popular food is seafood. They sell millions of fish each year. They like to eat sushi, which is raw fish. Japan has a healthy food diet which is why they have a long life span.

Reneé Mounts, Grade 6
The Arts Academy School, OH

The Best Dog Ever

Last August, we had a cat named Cookie. She grew up on a farm in North Dakota. One day when we opened the front door, she ran out and didn't come back.

A few days later my dad was coming home from Tae Kwon Do and saw her body on the side of the road. I missed her a lot. Three months later we were trying to figure out what pet we were getting next, a cat or dog? My mom's friend had to find her dog a better home because she worked long hours away from home. We said we would take him. His name is Oz and he is a Shih Tzu breed and is white with brown spots and has a curled tail.

Oz had a lot of problems. He took my nerf ball and tore it up. I started chasing him but he hid behind a chair. If you reached your hand behind the chair, he would bite you. My brother went outside and rang the doorbell. He got out from behind the chair and started barking at the front door. While he was doing that, I got the football and put it upstairs. We tried to teach him to go to the bathroom outside. Eventually, he got it. A few months later, he had no more problems. He loved getting groomed and barking at other dogs. We love Oz very much.

Michael Kolember, Grade 6
Argyle Middle School, TX

What Are We Thinking?

What are we doing? What are we thinking? Do we even care? Care about what you ask. Animals, all kinds of animals. Big, small, endangered, non endangered, and in this case, I'm talking about panda bears. Again, you might ask, "Why do I have to care about panda bears?" You don't have to care about them, but I think you should at least not like what is happening to them and their habitat. We can't walk around and not care about what's happening. We should do something.

Being one of the most popular animals in the world, it is also one of the most endangered animals, too, due to poaching and habitat fragmentation. By estimation, there are only about 1,600 panda bears left in the wild.

Now, we are sort of helping the panda bears with putting some of them in zoo's, but we can't have all the panda's in zoo's. Don't you think the panda's would rather be in the wild where they can roam free without the worries of poaching? Here are some ways we can help: donate money to the World Wildlife Federation, support your local zoos, or raise awareness in your school by making posters or talking to your teacher about having a special class period to educate the students on endangered animals.

It would be my honor to help the pandas survive, and with your help, I'm sure we could make a difference.

Alyse Haven, Grade 5
Marcy Elementary School, WI

Comparing Talk

Believe it or not kids talk a lot! Not just girls though. When you're in 6th grade boys talk a lot too, but both genders talk about WAY different things. That's why I'm comparing! So get ready to be filled in on the chitchat in 6th grade.

The girl's side of "talk" is VERY emotional, most of the time. For me, I stay out of the "crying" emotional as much as I can. The feelings come out when gals talk about: teachers, boys, gossip, school, friends/enemies etc. It really comes out on topics of things girls dislike. Girls BARELY talk about games, but occasionally we do.

Now guys, that's a different story. My info may not be exactly what guys talk about, but at least it's accurate. Of course I'm not going to know "for sure" what guys talk about, I'm a girl!

Relying partly on my little brother's actions with friends, boys like to talk about sports, like upcoming practices and bowls. Guys also talk about out of the blue things that pop out from nowhere. Older boys talk about: girls, disliking certain teachers, and people. Boys have an obsessed habit to talk about games. Not just handheld, but Playstation, Xbox, Wii, and more. Most guys like to talk about bands, guys talk about it, girls dislike it. All ages of boys talk about TV and gross things.

As you can see, girls and boys are very, VERY different. Especially when we talk to our peeps and pals.

Madeline Todd, Grade 6
Imagine Charter School at Rosefield, AZ

My Summer Vacation 2007

Spanish camp: I flew from Portland to Minnesota for Spanish Camp, it took four hours. When we got there, we drove four more hours to the camp. In the winter, this camp is a ski resort. I learned some songs and dances in Spanish, ate some Spanish food, and made some good friends. I hope to go back next year.

Family Reunion: We had a family reunion in Sun River with all our cousins. It was nice to see our cousins from North Carolina. It's funny because our cousins don't speak in an accent but our aunt does and you can barely understand her. While the cousins were still with us, we went boating. On the first day my dad ruined the propeller, he got it fixed the next day. At the end of the day my cousin gave me a scary, bone thrilling wild ride.

Trip to California: My whole family went to California for a family wedding. It took ten hours to drive to California. The ceremony was one hour long under the hot burning sun. It was probably 100 degrees!

Swim Team: I was on swim team for Eugene Swim and Tennis Club. My favorite swim stroke is Breast stroke. I don't know why it's my favorite but I think it's the easiest.

I had a great summer!

Joseph Jacobson, Grade 5
Eugene Christian School, OR

1964 Ford Mustang

You may not know this, but before 1964, American cars weren't one of the cars to have. All of this changed in 1964 when the first Ford Mustang came along. The Ford Mustang was powerful, stylish, and fast.

There were three models available. The body styles included a coupe, convertible, and a fastback. All 3 models offered a side scoop, and at the back end, there was a vertical chrome bar with 3 horizontal bars extending along the back sides. They also had 3 vertical taillights. Along with body styles, there were engine choices which ranged from 101 horsepower to 271 horsepower V8s. These engines were pretty impressive for the time. The suspension was conventional Detroit hardware. Manual three and four speeds were most popular with automatic transmissions also available. The stock brakes were drums all around, with front disc brakes as another option.

These new additions were very popular with the public. The sale of these cars boosted profits for the Ford Company. The mustang continues to be popular and is now considered a classic.

Dalton Zigmond, Grade 5
Oak Crest Intermediate School, TX

Soccer Rocks

The thing I enjoy doing the most is soccer.

In soccer, timing is very important because you have to beat a defender at the right time, finish the ball at the right time, or pass the ball to the right place at the right time. Soccer is cool because you need fast feet. My favorite move is the stepover because I can make them think that I will go one way but I really go another way.

Soccer can be challenging because it can have bigger, better, stronger, and faster opponents. For soccer you need to have a healthy body. It is important to have lots of endurance, speed, fast feet, and a hydrated body because your opponents will have an advantage if you don't have those things.

I enjoy watching soccer because it is fascinating and I can learn stuff from it. It is entertaining because I can watch soccer teams from around the world. It is entertaining because I can try doing what I see on TV or at a game. I like reading about and watching soccer because I can learn about the sport and its rules. My favorite soccer players are: Cesc Fabregas and Kolo Toure for Arsenal F.C., Brian McBride and Clint Dempsey for Fulham F.C., David Beckham for L.A. Galaxy, Tim Howard for Everton F.C., Carlos Tevez for Manchester United, Hernan Crespo for Inter Milan, and Thierry Henry for Barcelona F.C.

That's why soccer ROCKS!

Matthew Nevels, Grade 4
Gateway Pointe Elementary School, AZ

A Whale of a Fish

The emerald green grass and the chocolate brown dirt surrounded the turquoise blue water. I was with my dad at the Bidwell Ranch. We pulled into pond two and set up our vermilion tent. We got out our long, flexible fishing rods. I felt ecstatic.

I walked over to the still, shiny water and dropped my red and white bobber in the water. Little ripples formed on the cool, unmoving surface of the water. I waited and waited. I just got bored. Then "Bam!" a whale of a fish was on my hook! I pulled my long rod up and reeled in the fish. "Dad!" I screamed. He came running over and put the fishing net in the water and around the fish. We pulled the fish in and brought it back to camp. I couldn't believe it! We started peeling off the small, slimy scales with a long sharp knife. We made a long incision in the fish's stomach and disgustingly ripped out its guts. I wanted to barf.

We put the bright colored rainbow trout and some broccoli, which looked like little green trees, on the barbecue grill. In what seemed like hours, I started to smell the mouthwatering aroma of cooked fish and steamed broccoli. I could almost taste the food. My Dad finally put the masterpiece on my Buzz Lightyear plate. I put the bright silver silverware on the cherry wood table.

"This is great Dad!" I exclaimed with my mouth stuffed. "Thank you." replied my Dad. That's when I finally realized that I had caught my first ever fish.

Joey Coulter, Grade 5
Dingeman Elementary School, CA

The Rabbit Show

It started at 5:45 in the morning. My grandpa was coming to pick my brother and me up. I was ready to go because I got some things together the night before for the 2 hour drive. My mom and dad were coming up with my grandma. We were taking 13 rabbits to the show. This was my brother's first show. He was taking 6 rabbits. I was taking 7 rabbits.

When we got there, my grandpa had to fill out 13 entry forms! It was $2 per rabbit and we took 13 rabbits. It was finally time to show them! I showed the Satins first. I got Best of Breed and Best Opposite Sex! My brother and I both showed after that. He beat me on Florida White and California. In New Zealand, he got Best of Breed and Best Opposite Sex! After that we went to show the rest of the rabbits. Then we were ready for the Best of Show! My brother nor I won the Best of Show. We had a great time! We won three vases.

Then it was time for the raffle drawing. I won two rabbits. One Fuzzy Lop and one Satin. We are friends with the judge's wife. She won one Lion Head and asked the man that won the other Lion Head if she could have it. He said yes. She gave them to us. It was the best time of my life!

Amanda Straeffer, Grade 6
Fort Branch Community School, IN

My Life

Love, fun, and joy, what else do I need? One important thing to me is my family because they love and support me with soccer, singing and anything else I want to do at that moment. My family is like no other family in the world!! My mom is the only mom that says F.U.N, when I'm playing soccer, and my dad is just crazy on soccer day, and my sister is just different!

My friends are important to me too! They make me smile and laugh with the exciting, stupid, amusing activities we do. God has made my life so wonderful because of my relationship with Him. He helps me believe I can do anything because I know that through Christ, I can. God has blessed me to have a beautiful singing voice. I speak my own opinions and thoughts, all of the time. Singing is really important to me because I hope it will be my career in the future.

What would I do without my imagination? In my opinion, imagination leads to intelligence. Also, I think that we would have no personalities without our imagination. My life is very important to me too! I love my life because, I'm on a traveling soccer team (the best one!) Temecula United, I have an enormous amount of love from the people around me, I live in a fabulous house, and I go to a wonderful school, what else do I need? I love my life!

Cadie Bates, Grade 6
Linfield Christian School, CA

My Favorite Family Members

I like practically everyone in my family, and most of them live in China. On my mom's side, I like my granduncles, grandaunts, and their children if they have them. On my dad's side, I like everyone. (Some of my family members smoke.)

One of my granduncles lives in Tong Hua, which is in the province of Jilin, China. I like his family because their house is big, they're nice, they own a lot of cool stuff, and they're pretty rich. I can't tell you their English name because they don't have one.

One of my other favorite family members lives in Mei He, which is also located in Jilin. She is one of my grandaunts. Her house is big and she is the richest in my family. I also like her son, who is in college.

On my dad's side, I have 5 cousins. I always like to visit them in the summer for various reasons. One reason is that their homes are big and they have computers with Internet connection. Another reason is that they're nice and used to the way people live in America.

Those are my favorite family members in China. The most important people in my family are my parents, little sister, and grandparents who are in China too. I have many other family members that I consider "relatively favorite" because they are kind but do something unhealthy, like smoking.

Fred Zhu, Grade 6
North Oaks Middle School, TX

Horse Care

In God's infinite animal kingdom, there are many animals. In my opinion, the horse is the greatest of them all. There are many responsibilities to owning a horse. The "mane" key points in caring for a horse are brushing, saddling and riding. It is important to know how to do these safely.

Brushing a horse has benefits for both horse and rider. For a horse, this helps to keep the dust from caking under the saddle while it sweats, and keeps the horse from itching. Brushing also helps to keep the saddle in place for the rider. It also helps to keep the horse from trying to lie down and roll.

Saddling a horse is very important. Riding without a saddle is fun, but it isn't the safest thing to do. The saddle has a handle to hold on to called the saddle horn. A saddle helps to give me a better sense of balance.

In order to mount a horse, I place my left foot in the saddle and swing myself up. When I tap the horse's sides, it will take off. The feel of the wind in my hair and the sensation of power between my legs is a thrill like no other. Finally, I believe riding a horse is the best excitement of all.

Whether I am brushing, saddling, or riding a horse, I enjoy each of the responsibilities in caring for the greatest animal of all.

Maddie Chinchay, Grade 6
Chinchay Christian Academy, CA

Our God

One thing that's true is there is a God, that's one thing you can believe in. God is made of three parts, Holy Spirit, Jesus, and well God. The Holy Spirit is what lives in you. So really God lives in you.

God is everywhere at once. He is on a rollercoaster with you, He is out having fun with you and He is with you when you are sad! Jesus is my main man. He came and died for us on the cross to save us from going to Hell. While He was on the cross, people made fun of Him, spit on Him and they gambled for His clothes. Three days later He was alive and well and people believed in Him!

Jesus did many miracles. He would heal the blind and deaf, and lots of other cases. Jesus was and is the only perfect person who ever walked the earth.

Prayer is a way you can talk to God privately. You don't have to use impressive words it can be short and simple or long, whatever you want to do. God will always listen to what you have to say!

The only person I want to impress is God. I want to live for God and no one else. He is the one that created me, not monkeys or whatever weird thing you think created us. I choose to believe in God, I don't know about you!

Laurie Beth Chalk, Grade 6
Argyle Middle School, TX

Snickers

Do you like chocolate or peanuts? Are you allergic to any of those ingredients, but want to know what they taste like? Do you want to know more about Franklin Mars? Well…go on, READ!

Franklin Mars was 19 when he started to sell candy. Then he met a lady named Ethel Healy and they got married. In 1911 they started a chocolate company in Tacoma, Washington. They made a chocolate that was filled with caramel, peanuts, and outlined in chocolate.

Frank was known to love cattle, horses, and owned a ranch called Milky Way. He had a very special horse named Snickers! Guess where he got the name for the chocolate…that's right, he got the name from his horse, Snickers.

The business was going great, so they decided to move to Chicago to start a new plant. Then in 1940 the first wrapping machine was used, which increased business a lot! Workers could work better, faster, and they didn't have sore hands, but what's even better is they sponsored the "Howdy Doody Show." It was one of the first TV shows. In 6 years time the business went from $69,00 to $26,700,000.

Sadly, though, in 1940 Frank died. Just because he died doesn't mean the company died. No, the company strived, and now Snickers is one of the most famous chocolate bars.

So, does that answer all your questions? I hope it does. Now when you eat snickers you'll think of Franklin Mars.

Rebecca Martinez, Grade 5
Oak Crest Intermediate School, TX

My First Deer Hunt

Since I was a little girl, I have always wanted to go deer hunting with my dad. Last November, I finally got the chance. We were at my grandparents' ranch in east Texas. They have a lot of woods filled with wild animals. It was Saturday afternoon, and my dad was about to go hunting when I asked if I could go with him. He said I could go, and he said I could even shoot a buck if we saw one. I was excited.

We headed out into the woods riding in my grandfather's Kawasaki Mule, which is an all-terrain vehicle. My dad even let me drive. We had driven about a mile through the woods, across three creeks and up a big hill. We then came out into the open, and there stood a very large 8-point buck. He was only about 40 yards away, and was standing broadside. My dad quietly handed me the rifle and I propped it against the steering wheel of the Mule, aiming at the buck. I had him in the crosshairs of the rifle scope, and he just stood there looking at me. After a few seconds, my dad said to gently squeeze the trigger whenever I was ready.

As I thought about shooting the buck, my lips started quivering, and tears filled my eyes. I could not shoot that animal. Finally, he ran off, and I am glad that he did. My dad was proud of me.

Laine Lowry, Grade 6
Argyle Middle School, TX

The Month of Ramadan

My religion's main event is Ramadan. In the Month of Ramadan all Muslims over the age of 12 have to fast. In order to perform a fast you wake up at 4:00. You can eat from 4:00 to 5:50. The time changes every morning. Right after the fast you have to pray. From then on you can't eat, drink or put anything in your mouth. If you do you are forced to break your fast.

While you are fasting you can read the Holy Qur'an. You would have to read the five prayers daily. You have to pray them daily through the year anyway but it is more important in the Month of Ramadan. If you are too sick to fast you can have someone fasting for you. If you have missed some fasts, you have the ability to complete the fasts of Ramadan by fasting the amount of the fasts you have missed after Eid.

Some people think that it must be hard to perform a fast. It is hard at first but it's easy once you get the hang of it. For my family, on the last day of Ramadan we take out new clothes to wear on the next day. We wake up early the next morning, get dressed, and go to a mosque to pray the Eid prayer. There are two prayers you could chose from. One is early and the other's at 9:30 am. Ramadan is my favourite event.

Aishah Mohammed, Grade 6
Dr F D Sinclair Elementary School, BC

Sandy, the Loved One

Have you ever had a dog that you love? I do. Her name is Sandy. Let me tell you how I got her.

It all started at Traders Village. While I was drinking my Coke, I heard barking. "Daddy, can we go look at the puppies?" I said. "Sure!" he said. You should have seen all the breeds! Then I saw a puppy that caught my eye.

She was a sandy color, with a pink nose. My mom was in a bad mood that day. "Don't even ask me. You are not getting a puppy." she said. But then my dad started talking to my mom. "Amanda, you may get a puppy because you did well in school." my mom said. After that I gave my parents a big hug.

The lady at the store asked, "Are you going to buy a puppy?" "Yes!" I yelled. I quickly showed her which puppy I wanted, and she let me hold her while my parents signed papers.

While we were driving home I thought of a name, Sandy. "Mom, Dad I'm going to name my dog, Sandy." I said. When we got home I made Sandy a bed, and I gave her food. After that I got on my computer to research puppies and how to take care of them.

I hope you enjoyed my story. If you don't have a dog that you want, keep believing.

Amanda Rodriguez, Grade 5
Bang Elementary School, TX

Saving My Brother Brennan

My family and I were on a road trip to my last wrestling tournament of the year, the State Finals. We were going to stay in a hotel named Amerihost in Battle Creek. I located the pool and we went into the hotel to check in. My brothers and I rushed right through the hallway to our room, and put our swimsuits on before our parents even came through the door. We ran all the way to the pool area, swiped our card in the slot and got in. My brother Brennan forgot his lifejacket. When we were swimming, we splashed each other and did tricks in the water. Finally, my parents came in to swim. Suddenly my brother was gone! I thought he finally realized he didn't have a lifejacket on so he went to go get it. I started swimming again. I swam over to the deep end and saw a shape in the water. It was moving like it needed air. "BRENNAN!" I said aloud. I dove in as fast as I could. I got a hold of his arm and pulled him up for air. My dad came over and pulled Brennan out of the water. He was safe and alive because of me!

I was scared, but we all have our scary days. I just put all that aside. I was finally happy again because I saved my brother's life. That happiness put me in first place in the State Finals.

Corbin Simzak, Grade 6
Haslett Middle School, MI

Having Fun

We had fun cleaning up because we found many unusual things. Using the pinchers to clean up was a lot more fun than I thought it would be. My little sister kept bugging me about using them, though. One thing happened that wasn't fun. One of my friends accidentally stepped in a cactus, but she was brave and didn't cry. There was also a park were we got to play. A girl named Lilly played with me, while a girl named Deja played with another girl. They play Harry Potter. Lilly and I played that Lilly was a crook and I was trying to catch her. There was a set of monkey bars on the play ground, a set of swings (two swings), a little bridge that rattled when we walked on it, a slide, and many other different strange things.

I think I can tell you what we found. A diaper is one thing, I think we found a glass beer bottle and for sure we found many beer cans. We also found many pull tabs for beer cans. Here's another thing we found: a pack rat's nest with his own address! ADDRESS: #7 Coyote Trail, Cochiti Lake, New Mexico.

Unfortunately, we didn't find evidence of a zip code. For safety, his house (hole) was built on a cactus. Not by a cactus, on a cactus. At least he/she has (or had) slick and thick fur so he doesn't get hurt.

Zanzia Eklund, Grade 4
Santo Niño Regional Catholic School, NM

Ernest Shackleton

In 1908, Ernest Henry Shackleton was the first man to come within one hundred miles of the South Pole. He was a world famous explorer, a hero for his efforts. But Shackleton wanted to go to the South Pole again.

Shackleton set a new goal: to cross the southern continent of Antarctica from one side to another.

The Endurance started off from Pearl Harbor! The medium-sized ship drifted off into the ocean. For the rest of December, the Endurance picked her way through ice.

A huge iceberg loomed ahead, like the Great Wall of China. The ship had become stuck in the ice because the water was frozen around the ship. So the crew had to wait until the iceberg cracked.

Shackleton and his crew hunted for seals to eat. They worked thirteen hours a day to survive. In 1915, the Endurance was crushed by ice. Luckily the crew had managed to survive by camping under row boats.

One day in the early morning the iceberg cracked! The men knew what to do. They packed up and split into groups. They rowed, only stopping to camp on icebergs.

Days seemed like weeks, weeks like years! Finally, they reached dry land in England!

The crew had traveled for over eight hundred miles. Shackleton did not reach his goal; however, he was the first successful person in the world to go within fifty miles of the South Pole!

Angela Li, Grade 4
La Costa Heights Elementary School, CA

The Life and Times of Abe Lincoln

In 1809, in a humble cabin in Kentucky, Nancy Hanks Lincoln was having a baby, Abraham. As Abe grew up he found out that they were poor farmers, but Abe still worked hard. Abe was a boy that loved to read.

He went to college for law. In 1834 Lincoln was elected legislator. Abraham in 1854 emerged into politics again. He then became a republican in 1856. He wanted to run for president in 1860. Abraham Lincoln and Steven A. Douglas were about to have debates. On March 1861 Abraham Lincoln became the 16th president of the United States of America. When Abe was elected he received a letter from someone who suggested him to grow a beard, so he did.

Abe then had to fight his way through the Civil War. In January 1863 he issued the Emancipation Proclamation. It said that slaves in the southern states were free. In November 1863, Lincoln gave his famous speech the Gettysburg Address. In 1864 Abe was elected president again.

On April 14, in 1865 Abe and Mrs. Lincoln attended a play called, *Our American Cousin* at Fords Theater. An actor, John Wilkes Booth, shot Lincoln in the head. The next day he died at 7:22 a.m. The United States had lost Honest Abe.

Sean Schaefer, Grade 5
Nancy Hanks Elementary School, IN

Monday at the Cabin

Last Monday my whole family went to my cousins' cabin for family night up in the Big Horn Mountains. It was a long drive there but it was okay. When we arrived my two cousins, my sister, and I went to headquarters (the tree house that we found), to play Harry Potter and explore the forest. We found tons of things but nothing important. Then we went back to the cabin to eat and we had a barbecue with hot dogs, chips, water and beans.

After dinner, we all went inside the cabin and messed around on the balcony. Later we went back outside, roasted marshmallows, made s'mores, and told stories by the campfire. After all of that we still had about 30 minutes before it was time to go home, so we went back to the tree house and wandered off into the mysterious woods, farther than we have ever been. We decided to head back to the cabin but we couldn't find it. We were lost. Finally, we came to a stream we knew and crossed it. Suddenly, the sound of elk calls made us start running. We chased the sound but found out it was only my uncle using his bugle. So we walked back to the cabin and sat down inside for about 10 minutes talking. Finally, we had to go home because it was a school night. The drive was very long but we all had a great time.

Jacob Price, Grade 6
Lovell Middle School, WY

My Brother the Golfer

My brother Anthony is a great golfer and he is also very nice and loving. Anthony was not always a golfer. He used to be a champion skateboarder from age 9-12 years old.

When Anthony was 12 years old he tried golf. He loved his new sport so much, that he gave up skateboarding.

Anthony is a natural golfer, he only had a few golf lessons and became an excellent golfer right away. My family and I go with Anthony to many tournaments for school, CJGA, Ace, etc., and he usually wins. Anthony is a senior in high school now and is the number one player on his team. He just won the Regional Tournament!

The whole family is getting ready to go to Denver to watch Anthony play in the State Tournament. I believe that Anthony will win State. I also believe that some day he will play against Tiger Woods and Phil Mickelson and win!

Anthony's passion is golf and he will get a scholarship to a great school because of his talent and love of the game. I know he will be the next "big golfer."

Even though Anthony and I fight sometimes, we still love each other and he is my inspiration and hero. I look forward to the State Tournament and doing many things with him, including golf! Anthony is my brother, the golfer.

Christina Leggett, Grade 6
Colorado Connections Academy, CO

Spartan to Cardinal

It was finally the day! I was in my fashionable uniform carrying my weightless backpack, walking to class. I was so nervous and my heart was beating so fast!

I stepped in the large sized door to the class room, I saw all these new people. I saw Trevor of course the tallest one. He said, "Hey Marisol what's up?" That day I made a lot of new friends.

I was glad I came to this large amazing school! I felt sad that I had to leave my friends behind from my old school Rolling Hills Academy. My old school's mascot was the Spartan and now my new school's mascot is the Cardinal! My old school was fun, but this school is a lot better, it's awesome!

We have a football team and cheerleaders and all this fun stuff to do! We have awesome pep rallies, we also have a school band! This would happen to be the best school I have ever went to in my whole entire life! I made a lot of new friends that year!

And I'm still making more to this day! Everyone here has been really awesome! I like these uniforms way better than my old school uniforms! I've always gone to Catholic schools and it's really nice to just wear one thing almost every day and I'm glad this school has cool uniforms!

And that's how I became a Spartan to Cardinal.

Marisol Luna, Grade 6
St Matthew Catholic School, TX

My Super Special Pets

My essay is about my pets. Pets are a lot of fun and are most people's best friends. I am lucky because my parents let me have lots of pets.

First, I have a ferret named Jeffery. He runs everywhere and loves to aggravate my dogs. Jeffery is really small, long and skinny. He is cute but stinks really bad! The most interesting thing about Jeffery is that he can lay himself flat and squeeze underneath doors.

Then there are my dogs, Little Dog and Chloe. They bark loudly to let us know when people are at our house. Chloe loves to take rides in my baby stroller, she is very funny. Little Dog and Chloe love to play dress up. I dress them up in all my clothes and sometimes I put sunglasses and hats on them, they are funny. Chloe is a Toy Poodle and is 3 years old, and Little Dog who is long and black must be 100 in dog years.

Last but not least are my cats named Tiger and Sierra. Tiger is gray and Sierra is a calico. Tiger is a crybaby; all he does is meow, meow, meow all the time. Then there is Sierra. She is a special cat because she has been through three hurricanes and is perfectly fine.

All my pets are special and are a lot of fun. If you don't have a special pet, you should get one because they will keep you laughing.

Emily Booth, Grade 5
Aloe Elementary School, TX

Camping

It was hot, sunny, and there was a warm breeze. Me and my dad were so bored. In the morning we decided to go fishing. I was so excited, I forgot to pack! We went to go buy the equipment for camping and fishing. When we got home we started packing. I never went fishing, but my dad went millions of times with his dad. Now all we needed was a map to find a forest to camp. When my dad found a good camping place, we hit the road.

When we got there we started putting the tent up and I got tangled. We brought lots of firewood so we could cook fish, YUM! We set our little boat in the water, or we tried to get it in the water but it was too hard because there was a big rock on the way. When we finely got the boat into the water, I accidentally fell in the giant river. My legs were feeling funny. When I looked in the water, I saw a baby turtle biting my feet. We caught a lot of fish. Well, my dad got the most he got two fish and I only got one. When we cooked the fish, well not yet cook, I tried to make the fire with two sticks but it was too hard so I quit. So my dad said, "Let me do it." He got a match and made the fire. My mouth was open; I spent two whole hours trying to make the fire with sticks!!!! Then I found out that he brought matches!! Now that was a rip-off!

Nahum Hernandez, Grade 6
Chapa Middle School, TX

Mother and Child

Off the Kenyan Coast, a baby hippo named Owen struggles out of the water. Owen has faced a lot in his short life; first being swept down the Sabaki River, then pushed into the Indian Ocean. Earlier that week one of the biggest tsunamis hit Kenya and many other countries and continents. The big, thrashing waves forced Owen back to shore, where wildlife rangers later rescued him. Rangers then took Owen to Haller Park in Mombasa, Kenya. While there Owen embraced a giant tortoise named Mzee to be his new "mother." While there were many other animals inside the enclosure with Owen, Mzee had eyes only for him. They both became attached to each other forming a strong bond. Owen protected Mzee like its biological mother. Conservation workers added a female hippo name Cleo to join the pair, not knowing how either would react. The threesome got moved into their own enclosure. Cleo and Owen had a dividing fence between them, sniffing each other from time to time. Eventually the fence was removed and the two hippos got along. Workers at Haller Park say that every day Cleo and Owen's friendship grew stronger. Sometimes Cleo was getting too rough with Mzee, and the old tortoise was removed from the space. Though Owen and Mzee's friendship was over, many people recovering from the aftermath of the tsunami heard the story and their hearts were warmed at the thought of a tortoise and a hippo, becoming a mother and child pair.

Benjamin Love, Grade 5
Mary Morgan Elementary School, IL

Watervale 2006

I was so bored, I was in the car going to Watervale, Michigan in 2006. Every year my family goes to Watervale and stays for a week. Last year we went and our cousins couldn't come so our friends came. We drove separately so it was really boring and such a long drive. It is eight hours, and eight hours back.

Our cabin is right near the lake and we swim every day. Sometimes we swim, and then hang out in the cabin, get our suits on, and go take a shower in the lake! It is fun!

Also, our cabin is kind of small and hard to fit everyone. There are different rooms in our cabin. Sarah and I sleep in the small room, my brother and David sleep in the porch room, my mom and dad sleep in the back room, and Mr. and Mrs. Moore sleep in the room next to me and Sarah's room. It is crowded. Also, my aunts stay in a different cabin.

Every year we go to a huge hill that I think is thirty or thirty-five feet high. It is called Baldie. But, we don't walk up the front of it, we walk the back way. It is through a forest. When we look down from the top, there is Lake Michigan at the bottom. My favorite part is when you run down!

Watervale 2006 was so much fun! It is one of my favorite parts of summer every year!

Alex Hoey, Grade 5
Barrington Elementary School, OH

The Exciting All-Star Game

McDowell Mountain All-Stars went undefeated in the District tournament and won their first 3 games in the State Tournament. The fourth game that we played was exciting, but it did not turn out as a Cinderella story. The McDowell Mountain All-Star team played Continental. The score was 6-2 in the bottom of the fifth. We were losing. The first batter grounded out. The second batter struck out. Then I came up.

The first pitch the umpire called a ball. The next two pitches he called strikes. I thought the first one was eight feet outside and the second pitch was eight feet inside. I knew that if the next pitch were close, I would have to swing. The next pitch came and I hit it over the center fielder's head. When he picked up the ball I was rounding second going to third. I realized that the third baseman was about to catch the ball so I jumped over the kid, overslid the base, reached back, touched the base, and I was safe.

Sadly we did not win the game, but at least we did not get shut out. I started the momentum for my team to score two more runs. The ending score turned out to be 6-4. The McDowell Mountain Little League had a great run. We had a lot of exciting games and for some reason I decided to tell you this one.

Creighton Morfitt, Grade 5
Desert Canyon Elementary School, AZ

The Holocaust

The holocaust started around 1933, when Adolf Hitler got the political power in Germany. Adolf Hitler was born on April 20, 1889, in a small Austrian town called Braunau near the German border. At about 1908, he developed a hatred of Jews, also known as anti-Semitism. He later then made a group called the Nazis. The Nazis were some of the people who worshiped Hitler. The only people Hitler did not kill were people with blonde hair and blue eyes.

Many Jews went into hiding, but if they were found, they were taken to a concentration camp. At a concentration camp, they had the people first shave off all of their hair. Next, they would send them to a room with bunk beds that were stiff and uncomfortable. Hitler also took kids thirteen and under, pregnant women, and people who he thought couldn't do any labor (work). When he took them, he told them that they were going to go to a better place, but he really took them somewhere else, lined them up, got out his shot gun, and shot them all one by one. He would also tell people to take a shower, and instead of water, it would be acid and it would burn their skin. When they killed someone, they would hide the evidence by putting them on a metal board and burn them to ashes. Adolf Hitler died from suicide on April 30, 1945. The holocaust was a very painful time for everybody.

Erica Zuniga, Grade 6
Croghan Elementary School, OH

Fact vs Fiction

Many times in history people have made mistakes and tried to learn form them. I have recalled one or two or maybe even three or four, but sometimes we make those mistakes again. I have a *big* example of one of those times.

In the 1600s in Salem Village there were many accusations for witchcraft. Many innocent people were accused of this because the government was basing it on the girl's words.

Many historians believe that there were no witches at all. They believe that a group of girls were pretending to get people into trouble. Why they did this you might ask? No one knows for sure.

This example of falsely accused people and many other times brought the saying, "Innocent until proven guilty."

We now base our evidence on hard facts not just people's words. The government still makes this mistake, though.

We have a family friend who was falsely accused and sentenced to jail just a few years ago. We don't know why they did this if they didn't have any hard facts on what happened, but we shall just get over it.

Don't think that making mistakes is horrible, it's a part of life. All we need to do is to try to be better next time and move on.

Kaylee Allred, Grade 6
Thomas Jefferson Charter School, ID

My Hero

Hero, that's the thought I have about my mom. She is a real hero because she is encouraging. I was frightened to get braces. The whole time though she was there encouraging me.

She is also kind and loving. She is loving for a lot of reasons. I will tell two reasons. First reason is she is always there for me when I'm not feeling well. Another reason was when my cat got ran over she was really loving.

My mom is also understanding. She is always by my side when I have an argument I need help settling. Secondly is when the family has a bad day at school she will try and work it out with us.

One of my favorite memories that tells how my mom is caring was a few winters ago. It was a snow day and I kept getting snow in my boots. So I went inside. She let me help make hot chocolate and get warm.

After that we called everyone in for lunch and some nice, creamy hot chocolate. There are so many exquisite times I have had with my mom. She is always trying to help us become hard workers. She is great at making anyone feel wonderful about themselves. That is why my mom is my hero.

Jessica Thurgood, Grade 6
Thomas Jefferson Charter School, ID

My Outrageous Birthday Shopping Spree

As soon as I walked in, I saw hundreds of stores. I looked at all the clothes and smelled all the fragrances. When I turned around, my jaw dropped. It was my favorite store. My aunt and I walked under the 10 foot door. The shirts had sparkles on it, so shiny that it could blind you in the sun. Almost all the shirts were blue, which reminded me of the sky.

Guess what the store was? Limited Too! Was it the fabulous sign or the clothes that made me like it so much? It was great being there, but on to the next one. Claires. The store was filled with glamorous earrings and necklaces.

When I went in, I heard earrings rattling together, and saw necklaces and earrings dangling. The circled shiny earrings were awesome!

"I bought dangly earrings, necklaces and a fake crown with all the rhinestones and colors on it. I had to buy it!" I cried.

I started to think to myself, "I'm hungry," so I went to go eat Cinnabons. They smelled like they were fresh out of the oven. They looked creamy and very mouth watering. I felt like biting into a soft pillow. After that day, I felt old and it was time to go back home. As I walked outside a cold breeze brushed my face. It was the best birthday at the mall!

Angelina Rodriguez, Grade 5
Dingeman Elementary School, CA

My Extraordinary Imagination

One day I walked up on stage for American Idol. I sang the best I had ever sung in my life. The next thing I knew, I was voted the next American Idol. I became famous and traveled around the world. But it was just my imagination.

I enjoy my imagination because it is wild, interesting, funny and sometimes serious. You never know what you will get out of me. I also want everyone to imagine so they can open up their dreams and hopes and think whatever it is they want to think. Imagination can bring you a whole different world. You can imagine anything.

Imagination is also a good way to reach your goals and do what you put your mind to. Don't let anyone tell you that your imagination is weird or wrong, because you can think what you want to think. You can dream and believe in something because it is what you imagined. Imagination does not mean that you are lying. It means that you are telling the truth, because you imagined it and you believe in yourself.

Dream what you want to dream. It doesn't matter what you believe in or what you dream, your imagination is special. Remember to reach your goals, you should imagine what you want to imagine!

Jada Fernandez, Grade 4
Gateway Pointe Elementary School, AZ

The Family Jetliner

Being from a very large Indian family, I have relatives scattered all around the world. It would be impossible for me to see the people I love if it were not for the modern jetliner. Most kids my age can simply jump in a car for a few hours to visit their family. Whereas, I have to ride in a Boeing 747 and cross the Pacific and Indian Oceans in order to see mine.

As you can see, I think of the jet as being like our family car. Granted, most people don't have cars that travel 600 mph and carry 400 people! However, my world would be very lonely without the ability to quickly travel halfway around the world. Sure, you can always call faraway family members on the telephone or send them an email, but there's nothing like a big hug from someone you love.

I love to fly! From the minute we arrive in the airport I feel the excitement of a big adventure waiting for me. There are always so many people involved in preparing our jet for its big journey. There's NOTHING like the thrill of being on a jetliner during takeoff! You can feel the incredible surge of power from the four jet engines as they push you back in your seat!

Soon our 'family jetliner' will deliver us safely overseas to India. And so concludes a trek that would otherwise have been impossible without the modern miracle of jet travel.

Venkatesh Varada, Grade 6
Enterprise Middle School, WA

Israel

Israel is a small country in southwest Asia. The estimated current population of Israel is 7.2 million people. Israel is bordered in the north by Lebanon. Syria is to Israel's east and also to the east is Jordan. On the southwest border of Israel is Egypt. Israel has a variety of geographic features including the Negev Desert in the south and mountain ranges in the north. Israel is approximately 10,700 square miles, of which very little is water.

Israel's national anthem is "The Hope." The capital city of Israel is Jerusalem, which is also the biggest city. People in Israel speak Hebrew and/or Arabic, though most Israelis speak English fairly well.

Israel has an interesting system of government. There is a president whose duties are largely ceremonial, meaning he doesn't have any real power. The current President is Shimon Peres. The Prime Minister runs the country and is the head of the government. Israel's Prime Minister is Ehud Olmert. The Israeli government is made up of 120 members of Parliament called the Knesset.

There are a lot of cities in Israel besides Jerusalem. Tel-Aviv, the second largest city, was founded in 1909 by David Ben Gurion. The current mayor of Tel-Aviv is Ron Huldai. Because Israel's population is always growing, new cities are popping up all over. For example, the city of Modi'in was founded in 1993 and the population is already 68,000 people.

Israel is a country with interesting geography, government and people.

Ariella Lerer, Grade 5
The Academy, WI

Courage

Do you know what courage is? Here is my opinion of courage. To me it is the quality of no fear. Some synonyms include bravery, boldness, valor, and gallantry.

Here are a few examples of courage. Writers have courage to let others read and criticize their books. Albert Einstein once said, "Great spirits have always found violent opposition from mediocre minds. The latter cannot understand it when a man does not thoughtlessly submit to hereditary prejudices but honestly and courageously uses his intelligence." This means it would take courage to go somewhere different, strange, dangerous, violent, and scary to learn something or experience it. This is true about our military people.

I have done some courageous things. For example, testing for my black belt was very scary and took lots of courage to accomplish. Another time I used courage when I was not afraid to show my feelings when I was frustrated with my siblings. I didn't argue or fight back.

Courage is not easy to live, but well-worth it in the end.

Corey Beekman, Grade 5
Covington Elementary School, NE

Music

Music is very important to me because it helps me show my feelings toward someone or something. God gave me a great voice, so I can express myself with songs and music. Some songs have meanings about how life affects everyone's life. It lets one see something in a different light. Without music we would all be a little different. We wouldn't be able to understand our feelings. With my voice, I hope to share the meaning of life. The song "It Makes Me Happy" has a good meaning to it. It talks about how much he appreciates life ever since he was in a car accident and almost didn't make it.

One can tell how another is feeling with music. Music gives me an incentive to do something helpful. It can cheer me up if I'm not feeling well. If something bad happened, music takes my mind off of it and helps me think of the good times. Any kind of music is great because they're all different. There's rock, pop, country, and a lot of others types. Music is wonderful, it's one of my favorite past times.

I want to express my feelings with music; it really touches my heart and helps me understand more about people. Music affects a lot of people's lives. I love the fact that music is all over the world so everyone can sing or listen to any music, and we all have something in common.

Savannah Rogers, Grade 6
Linfield Christian School, CA

Take Me Home Country Road

Only one more day before the recital! Practicing and practicing the song gets stuck in my head. All this intense pressure is killing me. After dinner I pray to the Lord…

"Oh Lord, help me to do my best for the recital. Let my nervousness flow away. I love you. Amen."

Finally after a goodnight's rest the moment has come. I'm so excited that as I get into the car, I almost cry! Mom drives into the parking space so I get ready. The guests arrive; the recital begins!

My turn edges closer. I get out my John Denver book and my guitar. The woman who's in charge announces, "Emma Malik with her acoustic guitar." At that second I knew the moment had come.

Steadily I walked across the room next to Mr. Ken (my teacher). Then I began to pluck out the melody of "Take Me Home Country Road" while Mr. Ken did the harmony. My confidence grows as we strum along. Will I succeed? I carry on and finish with only two mistakes! Yippee!

That night after dinner…

"Oh God, thank you for letting me succeed. You've given me a great day. I love you. Amen."

And I really meant it!

Emma Malik, Grade 5
Seminole Academy, MI

Loyalty

There are many ways to show loyalty. First it means to be faithful to others or causes. My friend is loyal to her family by helping around the house. I am loyal to my mom when she gets home exhausted, I help her with her bags and work. Taekwondo students are loyal to their teachers by doing what they say. Students are loyal to their teacher by listening to directions in class and completing their work.

You can live in loyalty by helping in your community. You can help clean up your neighborhood. You can also help others to solve their problems. I can be loyal by helping my family with chores, homework, or projects. I often am helpful to fold clothes. I help my friend with her baby-sitting by playing a game with the kids or cleaning up messes.

These are some things about loyalty you might want to do.

Carmen Morales, Grade 5
Covington Elementary School, NE

Friend's Party

On September 7, 2007 I was going to Jake Buckle's house for his birthday party. He is my best friend. Yes he is that kind of a friend. I had to wait till school was out but that was a testy day. We had three tests we had Math, Spelling, and History and the day went real slow. We only had ten minutes left; I was sweating so bad I could just taste getting out on this stormy day. The bell rang; ding, ding, ding and I darted out the door!

My mom Ronda picked me up from school. So we went to the address from the invitation, Deer Lane Road. I got him a twenty dollar gift card. We got to his door and rang the door bell, ding dong. Jake said, "Hello, Chris buddy." I said, "Hello, Jake buddy." My mom and brother left, we darted upstairs and four more people darted their names were Joseph, Tristan, Kordell, and Adam. We all played Halo Two. I was the nine and I beat them all.

Then we ate ice cream and Jake had a WWE birthday. Then we all left for Lazer Tag. When we got there my code name was Omega. I came in first place. Then we stopped at a pizza place, but we took it back to his house and ate outside. We wrestled and I was so hot I fainted. The last thing I remember I was at home in my bed.

Christopher Gates, Grade 5
Lynnville Elementary School, IN

My Life Without My Parents

If I didn't have my parents my life would really be empty. I would not have anyone to love or talk to about important life things. Who would I have to share fun times with, if my parents were dead or just not around.

I don't think I could find the courage to play anymore. I cherish them and adore my parents so much, that I would do nothing but sit around the house doing nothing.

Travontae Fontenette, Grade 5
DeQueen Elementary School, TX

Greece

People know Greece as the place where many myths originated. Several myths state that Greece was made up of a handful of rocks that were left over from after the Earth had formed. This is probably because Greece is rocky and mountainous.

Greece was started by many tribes from Asia and other countries and islands surrounding it. Historians cannot be positive that all tribes came from the same culture, though they had the same language and origin.

In Greece women and men had very different expectations. When the men were boys they had to go to a school that only taught them how to prepare for war. The unbelievable thing is that they started going to this school at the age of eight. There they would learn how to fight and tackle, unlike schools from America that only teach reading, writing, and arithmetic. It was sort of like football camp only thousands of years ago.

The women on the other hand stayed home for a while to learn common household chores. A few years after they learned those things, they attended school. When they did attend school, it was like finishing school to learn etiquette and manners. Can you imagine young women from Greece wrestling? The school also provided an area for sports that included wrestling. It is hard to believe, but some of the girls enjoyed this.

From myths to schooling, Greece is a truly amazing country.

Emma Nicoson, Grade 6

Smoking Is Poison

When I was five, my Grandma Arline was diagnosed with Lung Cancer. I didn't understand because I was too young. My Grandma and I would do many things together. She had a pool and I would swim at her house all summer. She also was a great cook and baker. She made the best pasta I've ever had. I never even knew that she smoked until my mom told me. She had quit 25 years prior to getting cancer. One year after being diagnosed, she died. I really didn't understand why she still could have died after not smoking for 25 years. Even if you quit, some people still get cancer. I really could not believe it. I will never smoke!

Smoking is poison! It gradually attacks your system over many years of use. Quitting is very difficult because it is an addiction. Smoking harms just about every organ in your body. You're also harming other people around you by smoking. Their lungs are breathing in your secondhand smoke. So, not only are you harming yourself, but you are putting your family and friends' health in danger as well.

I feel very lucky to have this opportunity to share my story. I don't want anyone else to lose someone as special as my Grandma Arline.

Mikey Ollmann, Grade 4
Woodside Elementary School, WI

Dreams

Dreams are magical, mystical, and mysterious. If you hop onto the train of dreams, the roller coaster of your life begins. Dreams are the things that help you through life and answer many questions. Dream big and shoot for the moon because the worst you can do is fall into the stars. Always follow your dreams and don't let anybody stand in your way, or tell you that you can't follow your dreams. It's your dream, and nobody can take that away from you. When you dream it's kind of like a fairy tale land that you control. You do whatever you want whenever you want, and there are no limitations.

But sometimes, dreams show our fears in the strangest ways. For example, if you're about to have a surgery that could change your life and you are scared to death, the chances are that you're probably going to have a nightmare about it. One thing that you should always remember is that, no matter how much you dream or what happens in your dreams, it is worth nothing unless you try to make your dreams come true. Then not only will your dreams come true, you will also achieve in making the world a better place. Also no matter how much you go through in life, you always have your friends, family, and your dreams to comfort you in your times of need.

Veena Agusala, Grade 5
Trinity School of Midland, TX

Bamby the Deer

It was 1996. Gram C. had enough goat milk saved for four mouths! She lived in the country and had a few milking goats. She made lots of things with that milk: butter, cheese, yogurt, and goat-milk soap.

"I'm going to town for some goat feed. I'll be back later," Gram told my grandfather, Grump.

A couple hours later she had picked up the feed and was on her way back from town when she saw a doe deer had been hit by a car. Just as Gram was about to drive away she heard a cry from the forest. She stepped out and looked around and saw something moving! She creeped up and…it was a baby deer. It still had its spots! She put the little buck deer in the front of the truck and drove off!

"Fred," she said to Grampy, "Look." As she held out the deer you could see he was happier. "We should give him some goats milk. It's easier to digest. We'll put him in the hay barn."

Gram filled a baby's bottle with goat milk and the deer drank his fill. "I'll call you Bamby!" She fed Bamby every four hours, as she would a baby goat.

A few months later, the latch on the hay barn unlatched and Bamby escaped once again!

Taylor L. Burke, Grade 6
Hampton Middle School, NB

Feeling Like a Queen

So there I was on the immense Air France plane to Europe, excited, I could barely keep still. I got off the plane and could barely believe I was in the famous Paris.

I felt my inflammatory heart pumping as if I had run one million marathons. All this excitement built up inside of me on our way to our mysterious hotel.

When we arrived to our unerring hotel, I started exploring like a nimble intensive archaeologist. I kept saying, "Ooh what's this, look at that."

Walking up at this ingenious hotel, I thought "It looks incalculable." Its first titanic impression was that it was the size of the world's largest skyscraper. Its second impression was that it looked like a famous landmark. And its third impression was it was worth 1 trillion European dollars. I couldn't get over the thrill in this French world. Inside the hotel, I see myself surrounded with fancy furniture, beautiful paintings, and intricate murals. I feel like a queen walking around my palace.

Now in our bedroom, it was smaller than I thought it would be, nevertheless, the thrill was still inside me. Right before my eyes were two soft beds with celestial pillows and a soft, serene comforter, fancy, dimmed lamps and a beige, rough carpet.

We have a balcony with an amazing view of the famous Sacre Coeur Basilica. The Basilica lit up in indigo color at night. From the balcony, I feel like a queen overlooking Paris.

Megan Sia, Grade 6
St Matthew Catholic School, TX

Dirt Bike Racing

It was the first day of thirty two weeks of racing. Dirt bike and I were racing my rival Kevin Burlington. He has been beating my team for a long time and this time I was going to stop his winning streak.

When he picked a race, he picked a motor cross race. I was fixing my bike when he walked up behind me and kicked me and said, "That was for bad luck." I told his manager and he almost got fired for bad sportsmanship.

When we got on the track he tried to do something with my engine so I kicked his bike over and said, "Don't touch the bike." When he got back up we started the race.

I kicked my bike into first gear and took off; when I got to second gear I was going 80 miles an hour. When we got to the finish line we both lost because both of our bikes ran out of gas right before the finish line, so neither of us won.

This was my last chance to beat him. It was the last day and my gas was full to the top and guess what, he did not even bother to fill his gas tank. So when we started the race, he did not move. At the end of the race I won $500,000 to buy new bikes for the team. That is how I beat Kevin!!!

Christopher Thomas, Grade 5
Bang Elementary School, TX

Disasters

What would you do if you were in a disaster? You would need many supplies to keep you alive. Think over a plan with your family like an escape route and a meeting place.

In your supply kit you will need Band-Aids in case somebody gets hurt and walkie talkies to contact your family in case you get separated. Toothpaste and toothbrushes are needed to take care of your teeth. You also need a hair brush, flashlight, blankets, pillows, food, water and extra clothes.

There also needs to be an escape route. An escape route is a plan to get out of your house the fastest and safest way. You can go through the nearest doors or windows. I could go through the family room door, my parents' door and the front door. These are the windows I can go through. I can go through the dining room, my brother's room, the sitting room and my room. I can also go through my garage sometimes.

Then we have to make a meeting place to meet when the disaster happens. We can meet at the corner of our street, a mailbox a couple houses down and I could go to my neighbor's house if a fire was happening. You have to go to the meeting place so you can see if your family is okay. If they never show up in forty minutes go for help.

I learned to always be prepared for a disaster. Always try to be safe.

Michelle Mole, Grade 5
Liberty Elementary School, CA

Horikawa Elementary School

This summer, I went to a new school, Horikawa Elementary School in Japan. Since I had lived in Japan before, the language change was not hard for me. I learned lots of new things. What I liked best was Social Studies. We learned about fishermen and the population of fish in the sea by Japan.

That was my favorite lesson. I like the swimming lessons we had for school in the summer. We had getting into the water, which was the hardest part, getting used to the water, which was not hard, and free time, the time I and my friends enjoyed the most. Recess is very different than the recess at my school now. You can go outside or stay inside. You can go to the library at recess too. This was my favorite part because we don't get to go to the library at recess in Byron. I think those things are the best things about the school I visited.

On the first day, I was lucky. I met Fumika and Yuri, two very nice girls. We played a lot together. It was really sad saying good-bye to them on the last day. I miss them very much.

Aya Bridgeland, Grade 5
Mary Morgan Elementary School, IL

The Amazing Wonders of the Ocean

Do you like the ocean? Well you should. It gives us many resources such as water and food. The ocean covers 70% of the earth and we are very lucky to have it. The oceans help us a lot and they even affect our weather and temperature. Our oceans used to be all connected until the year 2000. There were four recognized oceans: the Pacific, Atlantic, Indian, and Arctic. Did you know that the Pacific Ocean is 15,215 feet deep and that is just the average depth? Have you ever wondered why the ocean is blue? Well now I'm going to tell you. Sunlight is made up of the same colors of the rainbow: red, orange, yellow, green, blue, and violet. Some of the sunlight bounces off the surface of the water, and reflects the color of the sky.

Did you know that the Pacific Ocean is the largest ocean? Its name may sound peaceful but it can also be fierce. Now I will tell you about Tsunamis. Tsunamis are caused by an underwater earthquake, volcanic eruption or more rarely by an asteroid or meteoroid crashing into the water from space. The biggest Tsunami was on July, 9 1958. A HUGE earthquake happened and that triggered a HUGE landslide at Lltuya Bay. The first and biggest wave was 516 metres high. Wow, that's huge! So now that I told you all I know about the ocean, do you like it?

Asfand Faisal, Grade 6
Dr F D Sinclair Elementary School, BC

Argentina

I went on a trip to Argentina this past summer. I got a chance to see a lot of interesting things.

When I got to Argentina, I smelled a lot of good food and I also heard a lot of Spanish people talking. In Argentina the food tasted good.

There was a lot of stuff in Argentina that you would not want to touch, like sewage in the streets, stray dogs, and dead animals.

I had a really fun time in Argentina because I met new people and got to see new sights. In Argentina, their favorite sport is soccer.

In Argentina, the church we went to was called Longchamps. The service was only about 10 minutes long. The place we stayed at was very cold and sometimes the toilets didn't work. We also went to a children's' museum. I also made new friends, Junior, Benjamin, Becca, Cameron, and Kaleb. Junior was very funny. Kaleb, Cameron, and Becca were my very best friends.

When we were leaving home from Argentina, our plane ride was very long. Our first plane took 2 hours, our second plane took 4 hours, and the third plane ride was 10 hours. It was a fun trip and I would like to go back some day.

Kyle Schwin, Grade 5
Eugene Christian School, OR

The Fascinating World of…Sharks

Have you ever known much about sharks? You're about to enter the shark world! You're in luck, because I am an expert on sharks. Enough about me, let's get started on sharks!

People are still wondering if the Megaladon is still living in the ocean. Some people say they've seen it with their very eyes. Other people say it became extinct thousands of years ago. We may never know.

Sharks have been around since the dinosaur ages. I can't believe they were able to live that long. The dinosaurs failed to live that long. It's probably because the dinosaurs ate each other. Sharks don't do that unless they're VERY hungry. There's lots of fish in the ocean for them to eat, so I don't think eating each other will be a problem.

Braces would be very, very expensive for sharks. They can have up to FOUR rows of teeth! The reason they have so many is because when they're eating, their prey's flesh is hard, so some of the shark's teeth fall out! Sharks can lose hundreds of teeth each year. They grow in fast, but sharks always need those back up teeth!

The ocean is the shark's territory. Sharks live in all depths of the ocean — even as shallow as 5 feet! Great Whites, Oceanic Whitetips, and Bull sharks only come up that shallow when they're hungry.

Hopefully, you are now a shark expert.

Peggy Morgan, Grade 4
Ossian Elementary School, IN

Cats, the Magnificent Creatures of the World

Cats are very smart animals. The mother takes care of her young and lets them go at about one year to one year, four months old. The mother may attack her young if they stay. In some cases, one of her young may force the mother out of her territory. Pet cats tend to be hungrier. The reason is usually that the owners spoil their pets by giving them too many treats. (Although you can't blame a guy for being too nice; who could resist just giving a cute little cat another treat?)

Some people think cats are the cutest things on Earth. Other people think cats are dark and evil. Cats are very sneaky and have very, very sharp claws. Unlike Garfield, cats cannot walk on their hind legs and they usually will not steal your chicken. In the wild they do not have anything to cook their meat on so they don't like fried chicken.

Cats belong to a scientific group called felines. Dogs are canines. Canines have really large canine teeth. (I think that is how scientists named them!) I personally think they evolved from the same animal — the long dead saber-toothed tiger.

Cats are very nice and they are fun to study. I hope a lot of people grow up to study cats.

Timothy Wang, Grade 4
Addison Elementary School, CA

Hawaii

Hawaii is wonderful and beautiful, nice and small state from the dark blue oceans to the seas, to the lovely dancing and dark green palm trees. From my point of view, Hawaii is the one of the most beautiful places. The ocean is light blue, with the nice big waves, with dark blue shells under you sandy feet. The ocean has dark green rocks here and there, but the waves, the blue waves lift me up into the sky.

There is a light blue sky with the red and black birds flying high and chirping when the clear rain falls. The sand, the soft yellow sand is lovely, great to walk through and nice to lay in. As the yellow sand touches my tanned feet, it reminds me why I love it so much here, in Hawaii. The lovely hula dancing filled with joy and happiness brings out the best of Hawaii. From the colorful costumes to the great music, it gives joy to all of us. How they show their wonderful culture is heart warming, as their amazing music as well.

Hawaii is gorgeous, stunning and spectacular island. Hawaii is an island-paradise and I hope it will always be. The blue ocean, the amazing dancers and green palm trees warm my heart. I hope they warm everybody's. Hawaii is a wonderful state of USA and everybody should have a pleasure to visit there.

Angelica Poversky, Grade 4
Tomekichi Homma Elementary School, BC

Will Smith

Will Smith is a talented actor. He was born September 25, 1968 in Philadelphia, Pennsylvania. His full name is Willard Christopher Smith Jr. People know him as the Fresh Prince. He got that name in high school. They used to call him Prince.

He is now 39. He has a wife named Jada Pinkett Smith. She is an actress. They have 2 children. His son's names is Jaden Smith and his daughter's name is Willow Camille Reign Smith. Jaden is 9 and Willow is 7.

In 2001, Will Smith was awarded best actor. He is also a rapper. He was in many movies. Some of the movies he's been in are *Men in Black, Bad Boys, Hitch, I Robot,* and *The Pursuit of Happyness.* He was in *The Pursuit of Happyness* with his son Jaden.

Will Smith and his wife created the show *All of Us* on UPN. He also was Will on *The Fresh Prince of Bel-Air.* He and his wife created *All of Us* based on their life. He got the role of Willy Wonka on *Charlie and the Chocolate Factory.* He also hosted Kids Choice Awards on Nickelodeon.

That is a biography on Will Smith. I chose him because he is a great actor. He is an inspiration on me. He is so cool. I hope he keeps acting. He is an interesting man. I hope he keeps up the good work.

Imani Day, Grade 5
The Arts Academy School, OH

ATM Football Team

The ATM football team is from College Station in Texas. It was founded in 1876. The colors of the team are maroon and white. The stadium is called Kyle Field and its capacity is 82,600. The coach of the team is Dennis Franchione.

The Aggies quarterback's name is Stephen McGee who has 737 yards passing and 412 yards rushing for the 2007 season. Did I mention that Stephen McGee has a backup quarterback named Jerrod Johnson? Jerrod is a very good quarterback and can assist the Aggies in comebacks to win the game.

ATM ranks last in the big 12 in passing but first in rushing. They are overall ranked 11th in the big 12 conference football standings. They are getting better and better as the years go by.

Some of the Aggie players have won 3 big awards. The first one was in 1957 for the Heisman Memorial Trophy Award for John David Crow. The second one was in 1998 for Dat Nguyen for the Chuck Bednarik Award. Finally, the third award was also in 1998 for Dat Nguyen but for the Vince Lombardi/Rotary Awards. I think the Aggies are the best college team in the world and should win more awards.

As you can see, the Aggies are ranked high for the year 2007. In my opinion, the Aggies are way better than the Longhorns. The Aggies will make a comeback and get better each year. So Gig Em Aggies!

Garrett Covert, Grade 5
Oak Crest Intermediate School, TX

Discover Italy

This summer my family and I (21 of us) were gifted with a wonderful trip to Italy from my generous grandmother. My family heritage was rooted in Italy. My great-grandfather died somewhere in Italy after being shot in World War II. My grandmother wanted all of us to experience some of Italy's culture and their way of life.

Italy is shaped like a boot and surrounded by the western part of the Mediterranean Sea. The largest Islands that surround it are Sicily and Sardinia. Its population is about 58,147,733 people, and Rome is their capital and largest city. Their language is Italian, German and Slovene speaking minorities. Their largest religion is Roman Catholic, but 90% is Protestant, Jewish, and Islamic. Until the 3rd century, the Etruscan civilization ruled but was then taken over by the Romans.

The Italians are almost just like us because they use cell phones and eat good food just like we do. Even though they speak a different language and eat different food, they still have an amazing country and background. I hope to visit Italy some day with my children and grandchildren as my grandmother did. I hope to keep alive our Italian culture, and am able to have them experience it as I did.

Elizabeth Bayer, Grade 6
St Gertrude School, OH

The Colts

"Manning pump-fakes, touchdown!" Peyton Manning is the quarterback (QB) of the Indianapolis Colts. The Colts are in the AFC South and have dominated that division for the last 5 years. This is mainly because of Peyton. After the Colts' Super Bowl title last year, the Colts have gotten a lot more credit for their hard work. So far this season, the Colts are 5-0 and there are talks about an undefeated season. The only thing standing in their way is the New England Patriots.

One of the best players on the Colts is Marvin Harrison. He is one of the great wide receivers (WR) on the Colts' squad. Peyton and Marvin have connected on touchdowns 104 times, which is the most from a QB to a WR in the history of the NFL. There will be a lot more of them this season and seasons to come.

The other Colts receiver is Reggie Wayne. Since he is number two to Marvin Harrison, he isn't as popular. But Colts fans love him. His best play was in Super Bowl XLI when he was wide open and scored a touchdown. Reggie has scored a lot more touchdowns like that, but people remember that one because it was in the Super Bowl.

Altogether, the Colts have the best lineup in football. I haven't even named players like Bob Sanders, Joseph Addai and Kenton Keith. These are the players who make the Colts the Colts.

Chris Stasiewski, Grade 6
Greendale Middle School, WI

How My Family Celebrates Christmas

My family celebrates Christmas by putting up a Christmas tree, giving presents to each other and having a special dinner with relatives. In my country, we have two Christmases. We have one on December 25th and the other is on January 7th.

Our dinner is turkey, mashed potato, salad, stuffing and that's all I know. We sometimes invite guest and relatives so they can share the meal too. Last year on Christmas I had a lot of presents. So on Christmas Eve, Christmas and Thanksgiving we have that special dinner and boy do I enjoy it!

Sometimes, close to Christmas I make a wish list using a Sears Wish Book. First I look in what I am interested in then cut it out with scissors. Then glue it on a piece of paper then I show it to my parents or gramparents and then they go shopping for my presents. This year I started making it in September. I made it by using a piece of newspaper by covering it all with blank paper then in front of it I wrote Wish List. On the next page I glue on my wishes. Mostly I get the things I want but sometimes, what I pick is too expensive. I am usually the one who gets more things on Christmas. I guess when I'm the youngest, I get more.

Emma Blagojevic, Grade 5
Dr F D Sinclair Elementary School, BC

My Life's Lesson

This is not the first essay I've written for this contest. There's an old saying, "Sticks and stones may break my bones, but words will never hurt me." I found out the hard way that this is not true. Sometimes it's not the words that are said or written down on paper that hurt, it's the words that aren't spoken or forgotten.

The first essay I wrote hurt somebody I love very, very, very much. It almost killed me to see how sad and upset she was; she even cried! My paper was about my family and how much they mean to me. However, I accidentally left two of the most important people in the world out of my first essay.

This mistake has taught me a very valuable lesson. I'm glad it happened to me now; because if I was older my loved ones may not have been here to know how sorry I am. I love them both with all of my heart. I hope Granny and Papa will be able to forgive me.

I will always think about the words I use and write. For words can leave a lasting impression. I will always remember the look on her face and the hurt I have caused them. I hope after reading my essay you'll learn from my mistake so you, too, don't hurt someone that you love. Be very careful with your words and don't miss an opportunity to tell your family that you love them.

Nicole Nelson, Grade 5
Bridgewater Elementary School, MN

Save the Koala Bears!

Koala bears are very important to Australia and many more places. Unfortunately, if people keep moving into their habitats, they will soon be extinct.

Some reasons the koala population is dropping is because men hunt them and dogs attack them. If we stop hunting koalas, they would be seen a lot more in the world. You don't see them killing *us* for things like skin, so why should we kill *them* for their fur?

Another reason koalas are becoming rare is because they are being pushed out of their natural habitats. A lot of people don't think about it when they build a new house or a new neighborhood in Australia, but if koalas live there, you are killing a big part of their population, and that's just not right! I bet you didn't know that in the last decade, 90% of the koala population has dropped. That is unbelievable! So, stop! Take a minute and think if that happened to us!

Maybe you could do something to help koala bears. Some people are raising money; others are donating money. I bet if we swapped positions with the koalas, they would help *us*. If enough people helped out koala bears, they would become more populated in the world.

So next time you see or read about a koala, please stop and think about this wonderful animal being killed to extinction. Do something to help the koala!

Madison Simon, Grade 5

Imagination

What is imagination? It is something you hold tight throughout your life not knowing when you will need it the most. Some use it more than others, but we all have an imagination. It is what separates us from each other. Imagination is what pushed some of the greatest creators to make some part of what we call the modern age. The telephone, the plane, were all in just someone's imagination until they opened their wings and let themselves fly.

My imagination is leading me into a new life and new world that not many people may know of. Everyone has their own world. It leads me with no end. Only I say when it ends, but not yet; my wings aren't open yet.

You might have some crazy idea that you think no one will ever believe in and everyone criticizes you for believing in yourself. Some people may not want you to try and make your imagination real. Many have been told this and listened. But if you opened your wings, you might find that your imagination can help you fly and help form the future.

Try and open your wings make the world some place better, spread your wings. Let your imagination soar throughout the sky; you may learn that imagination is something that no one can steal. You make it in your heart; isn't it about time you spread your wings? I think so.

Alexandra Scott, Grade 6
Mendocino Middle School, CA

Painful Accident

The bright orange crisp of sun covered part of the sky. My cousin, aunt, and my cousin's friends went swimming. I watched. In my colorful tank top, I, put my dry feet in the ice cold pool. My cousin screamed, "Briana come here!"

"Why?" I answered, not amused.

"I found a piece of gold!" he exclaimed. I ran over, but didn't realize my feet were wet. My cousin was near the edge of the concrete where it lowered and there was a canyon-like area with cacti.

"Awww!" I squeaked. I fell and slipped. Pain slivered all over my body. I stayed still. "Molly!" I cried, scared with fear. Cactus covered my whole body. Molly carried me and carefully clutched me in a ball up the bumpy hill where my mom was. Bump, bump, bump.

I remember my mom trying to get some needles out, then a car to the emergency room. I laid on an uncomfortable bed. It was a regular grey room that had a big light. Several doctors surrounded me with masks and caps and gloves with only their eyes showing. I slowly fell asleep, with only a sliver of my eyes open. They finally shut.

The next time I woke up, I didn't feel anything. I just felt like a lazy, tired bee in my bed at the quiet hotel. Now whenever I see a cactus, a constant freeze surrounds my body like the ice cold pool on that horrible day.

Briana Powell, Grade 5
Dingeman Elementary School, CA

Follow Your Dreams

Never let anyone boss you around. Be yourself. Don't be someone you're not. Follow your dreams. Use your imagination to help you create what is inside of you.

Never do anything you do not want to do. People cannot make you do things. Stick up for yourself. Be strong. Show people that you have courage in you, and be brave. Never give up on what you believe in. If it's being a doctor, nurse, chef, a school teacher, librarian, cook, acrobat, or a maid. Anything you set your mind to, you can do it.

Never give up on what you believe in, whether it is Christian or any other religion, It may even be a good citizen, a volunteer, a good education, or a good friend, and not just being two-faced.

Imagination is the best key for following your dreams. If you did not have an imagination you would not have any dreams at all. Or you would not have any dreams, you might just have little figures in your head. And you write them down on paper.

Following your dreams is mostly about thinking of a thing, and keeping it in your head and going for it in your life while you are an adult.

Shelly Jenkins, Grade 6
Milltown Elementary School, IN

My Patchwork Quilt

The people that are most important to me are my mom, dad, step dad and step mom. Even though we are separated, we still love each other very much.

My mom and I moved to Arizona two months ago, after my mom and step dad got married. I had to leave my dad, step mom and the rest of my family back in Pennsylvania.

I love being here in Arizona. My mom is very understanding and patient. She helps me with my homework, answers my difficult questions and loves me to the moon and back! My step dad is a lot of fun! He acts like a big kid. He tells funny jokes, acts silly with me and we play music together.

I go back to Pennsylvania to spend time with my dad and step mom during the school breaks and summers.

My step mom is so cool! We do so much. We love to cook, shop and go walking. My dad is fun-loving and goofy. We watch our favorite TV shows together and he cooks my favorite garlic chicken better than anyone else.

It may be difficult at times to be separated from my family, but my mom always tells me that a family is like a patchwork quilt. It takes many pieces sewn together to make one beautiful quilt. You have this quilt with you when you need comfort, warmth, security and love. I carry my patchwork quilt everywhere I go. It is always in my heart!

Gabrielle Zeiss, Grade 4
Gateway Pointe Elementary School, AZ

Friendship

There are many values to follow in life, but showing friendship is important. Friendship is the condition of being friends. Albert Camus once said, "Do not walk in front of me, I may not follow. Do not walk behind me, I may not lead. Walk beside me and be my friend." To me this means one person is not the leader, but they are equal.

Here are a couple of ideas to learn about friendship. Other words associated to friendship include harmony, fondness, and understanding. Two examples to show friendship to everyone are to have a good attitude and be kind.

These are some ways you can show friendship. If your friend makes a mistake you can still be their friend. Another way is to talk to a new kid in school and make them feel welcome.

In conclusion, these are some important details you need to know to be a friend.

Brooke Heinemann, Grade 5
Covington Elementary School, NE

Metamorphosis

"He hath made everything beautiful in His time." Eccl. 3:11a

The life cycle of a Monarch Butterfly is a beautiful example of God's handiwork. It includes a complete change of form called metamorphosis.

In the first stage, the eggs are laid by the females during spring and summer months. The football-shaped eggs are about the size of a pinhead. They are found on the underside of milkweed leaves.

Secondly, caterpillars hatch from the eggs, and are no thicker than a strand of hair! The caterpillars eat their egg cases, then feed on milkweed leaves. They grow to a maximum length of two inches. Their yellow, black, and white bands easily identify them as Monarch Caterpillars.

The third stage is the chrysalis stage. During this stage, the caterpillar spins a silk pad on a twig or leaf. It hangs head down in the shape of a 'J'. The caterpillar sheds its skin, revealing the beautiful green chrysalis. In the chrysalis is when the caterpillar changes into a butterfly.

After about two weeks, the mature butterfly emerges — the fourth stage. It is a wet and crumpled butterfly with a large abdomen. Immediately it begins to pump fluid from its abdomen into its wings to expand them. The butterfly remains unable to fly until its wings are completely dry.

As fall approaches, the butterflies make huge migrations south to escape cold winter temperatures. Although the Monarchs may be gone for the season, you can be sure they will be back next spring!

Abby Rubsam, Grade 6
Isaac Newton Christian Academy, IA

Who's Special to Me

Who's special to me? Out of everyone I know, my mom is special in many ways to me. She has been there for me all my life. She feeds me and washes my clothes. She lets me help her cook Christmas and Thanksgiving dinner. She takes me to get my clothes for school and to get bathing suits. She is one of my two favorite people in the world. She's my mom. I love her a lot. No matter what, she lets me go places with her and she lets me get stuff that I want sometimes. My mom likes and watches my favorite tv show with me. It's *Reba*. My mom wakes me up and tells me to get ready for school. She respects what I think of stuff. Sometimes she takes me to the mall. She's special because she raised me to be good and smart. My mom is fun, smart and nice. She's special to me because I love her for who she is and I think she is the best mom. I will always have her as my special person. I had fun telling how my mom is special to me. If it wasn't for my mom I wouldn't be here today.

Diamond Garcia, Grade 4

Honesty

Do you know what honesty is? It's the quality or state of being honest. Some synonyms for honesty are frankness, sincerity, and trustworthiness.

People can be honest if they tell the truth. They can also be honest at their work by doing what their suppose to do. I'm always honest with my homework and to my parents. I'm honest with my homework because I do what is expected and do it correctly on my own. I'm honest with my parents because I always tell them the truth when they ask me questions.

All in all, this is what it means to be honest and how I show honesty on a daily basis.

Rubby Simite, Grade 5
Covington Elementary School, NE

My Favorite Mountains of the Northwest

I live by two interesting mountains; My St. Helens and Mt. Rainier. I have been to Mt. St. Helens and Mt. Rainier. I like Mt. Rainier best because it has more life.

Mt. Rainier and Mt. St. Helens are located in the state of Washington. They are over 8,000 feet tall.

Unlike Mt. Rainier, which was originally known as "Talol" or "Tahoma" from the Lushootseed language meaning "mother of waters," spoken by the Puyallup, Mt. St. Helens is named after the British Diplomat Lord St. Helens. Mt. Rainier is 14,410 feet tall, however, Mt. St. Helens is only 8,365 feet tall. Mt. St. Helens is an active volcano. Mt. Rainier is a strato volcano, which means layered volcano.

You can sometimes see Mt. St. Helens and Mt. Rainier flying into Portland, and on sunny days while you are driving in your car.

Jacob Swatman, Grade 5
Columbia County Christian School, OR

The Computer

Too many people are using the computer for crime. I think that the computer is great! But a lot of people abuse their rights on the computer.

I like the computer because you can message people and have conversations to people from all over the world. Also, you can keep in touch with your friends from other towns. Messaging can also be bad too, because people spread rumors about someone else or a group of people. Rumors can be very hurtful and maybe the rumor isn't even true, but people still believe it.

There are a lot of great people on the computer. There are also bad people like stalkers that act like someone who they really aren't so they can try to meet you. People give out fake prizes just to try to get your address. Never give out your address or personal information without your parent's approval.

People who make website games are putting bad pictures or violence on the site and letting any age play it. This is making them think that it is all right to use violence.

Also, obesity is a big problem. Kids and adults who play computer games a lot get addicted and play it all the time so they don't get outside to get exercise. They turn obese. So be careful when you're on the computer.

Ross Pierschbacher, Grade 6

LeBron James

As you know LeBron James is a high-flying superstar who plays for the Cleveland Cavaliers. He was born in Akron in 1984. He had no dad. His mom was 16 when he was born. When Lebron was a kid he was poor and lived in very scary neighborhoods. Then he went to live with extended family while his mom went to college. When LeBron was in middle school people already knew he was a great athlete.

When LeBron was a freshman in high school he played football. He was a wide receiver and he was great. He was the best player on his team. St. Vincent High School got all the way to the national basketball championship. They played Oak Hill, the best team. They beat them by ten points, 53-63. LeBron had 24 points. They won their first 12 games. Then they played Oak Hill. They lost 64-63. Lebron had 30 points that game. They made it again to the championship. Then they played Oak Hill again. They won by 6 points, 75-69. Their record in two years was 53-1. In his junior year they made it to the semifinals. In LeBron's senior year he won the Mr. Basketball award for MVP that year.

He was a lottery pick in '04. He was sent to the Cleveland Cavaliers. He got second in MVP in '05. They made it to the playoffs that year. But they got knocked out in the first round. This year they lost in the championship to the Spurs.

Max Bechtel, Grade 5
Barrington Elementary School, OH

My Loving Friends and Family

My friends and family are important to me because I know I can lean on them when I need help. My mom and dad would do anything for me. I know they would be willing to go to the edge of the earth for me. Without my parents I wouldn't know Jesus. I know I can trust them. My parents are the absolute best!

Colton, Connor, and Paige are my siblings. We all care about each other and I love to be with them. I can trust in them. Everyone in my family believes in God and I'm so proud of that. We go to church most Sundays as a family. When a member of my family is in a game, my whole family will go and cheer for whoever is playing.

My best friends are Kelly, Kelsey, Kylie, and Nicole. It is important to me to have friends so I can talk to someone else besides my siblings. They can be goofy, but I know I can trust them with anything. They all believe in God and that is so important to me and them.

My friends and family cheer me up when I'm down. Without my friends and family I don't know what I would do. I love my friends and family so much. My family and friends are more than I could ever ask for. I know God loves me because it's a miracle that I was given everyone around me.

Faith Brandt, Grade 6
Linfield Christian School, CA

A Big Wave to Microwaves

Have you ever wondered how microwave ovens heat food? Inside of a microwave oven, a magnetron makes a beam of microwaves. Microwaves are very short radio waves. Before the microwaves go into the cooking space, the microwaves go through a stirrer. A stirrer is like a spinning metal fan that spreads the microwaves out evenly. The microwaves are absorbed by water in the food causing the water molecules to rapidly vibrate. The vibration causes heat which warms up your food. Microwave ovens cook moist food faster than dry food because there is more water to absorb the microwaves.

Microwaves can go through glass, paper, ceramics, and plastics, making containers made from those materials better to microwave foods in. Metal containers should not be used. They reflect microwaves and keep food from cooking. They sometimes reflect microwaves into the magnetron and ruin it.

The use of microwaves to cook food was accidentally discovered by Percy L. Spencer in 1945. He was testing a magnetron intended to create short radio waves for a radar system. He was standing close to the magnetron and realized that a candy bar in his pocket melted, although he did not feel any heat. He invented the first microwave oven, originally called a Radarange, in the early 1950s.

Percy L. Spencer made a very helpful discovery. The next time you use your microwave oven, remember how accidents are not always bad; they can improve your life!

Carolyn Stone, Grade 6
Isaac Newton Christian Academy, IA

My Family Zoo

I have two dogs, two cats, one snake and one rat. My first dog is named Sasha, my second dog is named Maggie. My cats' names are Midnight and Zippy. My snake's name is Striker. My rat's name is Gizmo.

I like running around with my dog, she is a Boxer, and she is big. Maggie is old, fat, and clumsy.

My cat Midnight is black, he is a scaredy cat. For some reason he only comes to me, he does not like my dad or my brother. He does not even go toward them. Zippy is gray, he is fat and he likes everyone except my brother. He likes to wake everyone up by jumping on their stomach.

My snake Striker is smooth and pretty. My mom does not like him. He doesn't bite. He eats mice. First he strangles them, then he eats them. It is cool to watch.

My rat Gizmo is getting old and skinny. He is two years old, almost three. He likes to run on his wheel and he loves to eat.

I like having my animals, they are all fun to play with. All six of them make my family zoo complete. I wouldn't have it any other way.

Brody Kelly, Grade 4
Gateway Pointe Elementary School, AZ

United Flight 93

September 11, 2001 was a sad day for all of America. Two planes crashed into the Twin Towers (the World Trade Center), one plane crashed into the Pentagon, and one plane was supposed to crash into the White House. This essay is about that plane.

United Flight 93 was late, after pushing off from the gate at 8:01 a.m. Flight 93 took off at 8:41 a.m., 40 minutes behind schedule. There was a "light load" that morning; only 37 of the plane's 182 seats were occupied. Minutes later at 8:38 a.m., air-traffic controllers heard a man speaking in a thick accent saying, "This is your captain. There is a bomb on board. We are returning to the airport." The hijacker was speaking accidentally in the cockpit microphone; the one the air-traffic controllers could hear.

The hijackers herded the people to the back of the plane. Some people began to call their loved ones and tell them that they were being hijacked. A few people called the FBI.

The passengers on Flight 93 decided to do something about the hijackers. They first took out the hijacker who was claiming to have the bomb. Then the passengers stormed into the cockpit. The last transmission recorded someone, probably a hijacker, screaming, "Get out of here! Get out of here!" Then grunting, screaming, and scuffling. Then silence.

Flight 93 crashed into a field outside of Shanksville, Pennsylvania instead of our nation's capitol. The passengers of United Flight 93 are heroes.

Rylee Green, Grade 6
Kingsley-Pierson Community School, IA

Halt!

Did you know that one acre of Brazilian rainforest is destroyed every nine seconds? All of Central America was once covered with forest, too, but now only a small portion of that richness remains. If people do not act to change these tragic facts, all rainforests on Earth will soon disappear.

A rainforest is a very damp place with many kinds of plants and animals. Ranging from inch-long ants to beautiful orchids, a rainforest has lots of biodiversity. We do not want any species to become extinct. Even though rainforests occupy only six percent of the Earth's surface, they support more than half of the world's plant and animal species!

By destroying the rainforests, we are allowing the level of carbon dioxide to increase, since plants use carbon dioxide. Cutting down trees and rainforests thus increases global warming.

How can we help? We should use cloth cleaning rags, not paper towels. We can and should stop using paper cups and plates. We should also recycle paper and wood materials so that we do not need to cut as many trees. Providing recycling boxes for our homes, classrooms, and communities is another way we can get involved in preserving the Earth's rainforests. Finally, we can start planting programs that will add many more trees to our rainforests and fill the Earth's surface with green plants. These steps will help to halt the destruction of the rainforests, a resource that is vital to our existence.

Kavya Ravichandran, Grade 4
Birchwood School, OH

McDowell vs Goodyear

It was the semi finals, McDowell Mtn. was going head to head with Goodyear in the semi finals at McQueen Park in Chandler. Pitching for McDowell, Creighton Morfitt. Behind the plate, Drake Sadosky. Michael Ksobiech at short. Tommy Olsen at third. Ethan Hyman at second. Mickey Horne at first David Ksobiech, Jack Brancheau, and Jack Baker in the outfield. Up to bat, a boy with long hair.

McDowell was at the *Arizona State Tournament* for the first time. McDowell scored two scrappy runs in the first inning and held Goodyear, until the fifth inning.

Creighton gave up two runs due to fielding mistakes. Then in the top of the sixth, Drake Sadosky got a huge one run double off of the fence to put McDowell up by one.

Michael came into pitch in the bottom of the sixth. He struck out the first batter and hit the second batter. The next batter laid down a perfect bunt and scored two runs. Goodyear won. Goodyear went on to win the State Tournament. *But just wait until next year. Don't count us out.*

Drake Sadosky, Grade 5
Desert Canyon Elementary School, AZ

Green Diesels Are Best

When it comes to being green, clean burning diesel engines are the answer rather than electric-gasoline hybrids. Although there is a lot of attention being given to hybrids and less attention to diesels, proof shows that the diesels are more environmentally friendly.

Diesel engines are more efficient than electric-gasoline engines. Diesel is 20-40% more efficient than gasoline. Hybrids use conventional gasoline for propulsion. So, diesels will get better gas mileage when driving at mid to high speeds. By improving fuel economy, you will be helping the environment.

People claim hybrids are environmentally friendly. In truth, hybrids cause environmental harm. Hybrid batteries are made with nickel. Nickel mining devastates the mining area and it is left barren where nothing can grow. The batteries in hybrids have to be fully replaced approximately every 6 years. Again, causing harm to the environment both by the manufacturing of the batteries as well as the disposal.

Diesel engines are made to last longer than hybrids. The diesel engines last well past 150,000 miles. The manufacturing of new cars causes pollution. If you are required to replace a car more often, then you are aiding in harming the environment.

Taking these factors into consideration, you would be a better friend to the environment if you were to buy a clean burning diesel engine rather than an electric-gasoline hybrid engine. There is less pollution in the manufacturing of clean burning diesels and they get better gas mileage than hybrids.

Kyle Smith, Grade 6
Beacon Country Day School, CO

Who I Respect

Do you respect someone? Well, I do. His name is Manuel but we call him Cezar.

When I was five he taught me how to play soccer. He made me one of the best goalies of all my friends in my apartment. When we got older we both got better and better. Now he plays attack and I play goalie still. I'm better than him at being goalie but he is better at attack.

He also taught me how to play basketball. He is really good. He can do slam dunks at Sun Valley Middle School. I can make three pointers. He once made ten half court shots in a row. Then I shot ten also but did not make them. Then I only made five, but not in a row.

The last thing he taught me was baseball. He is really good at catching and hitting. I am not that good. I always get lucky because they throw foul balls to me, or fast balls. Five times I hit really hard. We lost the ball. He has done that lots of times.

In conclusion, he taught me soccer, basketball, and baseball.

Chris Soto, Grade 5
Camellia Avenue Elementary School, CA

My Life Goals

Everyone has goals for life. I will tell you about some of mine.

Ever since I can remember I've been singing. I sing in my spare time or when I'm working on homework or cleaning my room or especially when I'm in the shower.

Singing is my life. This is my second year in voice lessons. Every year we have a showcase in July. There is competition in almost every type of music; and there is your recital which you get either excellent or superior.

The first year in voice lessons (January of 2006) I sang my recital song and a duet competition song. I sang "Inter Plant Janet," from School House Rock, with my friend, Linnea. My recital song was "Fireflies," by Faith Hill.

This past July (2007) I sang three other songs. I sang two competition songs. One of my songs was a Broadway song "Beauty and the Beast." My other competition song was for a fundraiser called Christmas in July, I sang "Christmas Cookies," by George Strait. My recital song was "Juke Box Blues," by June Carter Cash. I got a superior on that.

Someday I wish to meet my idol, George Strait. He is my idol because he has sung over fifty #1 hit songs.

In the future I plan to go on to American Idol when I turn sixteen.

Those are a few of my life goals.

Molly K. Byerly, Grade 6
Thomas Jefferson Charter School, ID

The Best Job for Me

If you know what you want to be when you grow up, it is a goal worth trying for. I know what I want to be…a veterinarian. I think it is the best job in the world!

I think that being a veterinarian is the best job in the world because you get to help hurt animals. You can help them by telling owners what to feed them and how to take care of them when they are sick or are going to have a baby. You can also tell owners what kind of medicine would be best for them.

Veterinarians are helpful because they help baby animals being born. You can tell owners which foods are best for the baby and how to care for it when it arrives. It must be fun seeing a new baby animal being born.

Veterinarians can help stop animal cruelty by helping other people spread the word about how to spot it. Vets can also spread the word about animal abuse by giving speeches themselves to stop it from happening again.

No matter who you are, everyone can help animals one way or another. That is why I want to be a veterinarian. I think it is the best job in the world because you get to help animals one way or another.

Isabel Guerrero, Grade 6
Holy Family Catholic School, IL

Friends

Friends are like heroes to me, ready to sweep me off my feet, ready to pick me up when I am down. My friends are important to me.

I enjoy thinking of my friends like prized possessions; I would never want to lose them. Day after day after day, I have friends I've known since kindergarten or 1st grade. Even this year I've made 2 new friends. Once in a while my friends and I will get in a little fight, but the next day we find paths on how to get around the problem. If you know someone that you think is your friend, and they judge you or treat you badly, maybe they're not your friend.

I think it's better to have more than one friend, more people to support you when you're struggling through a hard time. You can never have enough friends.

It's also ok to have one specific friend to always share your secrets with and you know you can trust them, or just someone to look up to. A brother or a sister can be like a friend or a friend can be like a brother or sister. Sometimes you and your BFF (best friends forever) will drift apart, or you'll stick together like magnets! Remember friends are heroes.

Madeline Spencer, Grade 5
Kyrene Monte Vista School, AZ

Be Healthy

"Today, 10% of 2-5 year olds and more than 15% of children between the ages of 6 and 19 are overweight." Overweight kids are at risk for getting diabetes, high blood pressure, and other diseases. All kids should be fit to fight obesity.

Being fit is important to my whole family. My dad lifts weights and coaches my baseball team. My mom likes to run. When I was little, she ran and I rode my bike next to her. My little sister is a gymnast and exercises five days a week.

I'm lucky because, unlike some of my friends, I've never been overweight. There are a lot of things I like to do to stay fit. First, in fall, I play football five times a week. In winter, I play baseball twice a week. In summer, I play baseball three times a week. I also exercise at NX Level with Joe Panos from the Philadelphia Eagles. The trainers teach me the right way to exercise so I don't get hurt. Second, while I like to play my Nintendo DS, I make sure to exercise the same amount I play the game. If I play the DS for an hour, I exercise for an hour by riding my bike or playing outside with my friends. Finally, my family eats right. While we like treats, we make sure to not eat too much.

All kids should choose exercises they like so they can stay fit and be healthy.

Jacob Hagmayer, Grade 6
Greendale Middle School, WI

Casey Tibbs, South Dakota Legend

Casey Tibbs was a champion bronc rider from South Dakota. I was interested in learning more about him because I enjoy competing in rodeos.

Casey Tibbs was born March 5, 1929. He lived five miles northwest of Fort Pierre. Casey grew up in a log cabin. His parents were John and Florence Tibbs. He went to school at Orton Flat. 8th grade was his last year.

Tibbs started riding broncs when he was 14 in SD. He was trailing bucking stock with SD producer Bud Annis. In 1949 at age 19 he won the National Saddle Bronc Championship. He was the youngest to win this title.

Casey wrote and produced and starred in movies. *Born to Buck* was made in South Dakota, his home state. He also made a movie called *The Young Rounders* in South Dakota. There were people from Ft. Pierre and Eagle Butte, SD in the movie. He was awarded the Golden Boot from the motion picture and Television Relief Fund for his contribution to the industry.

Casey wrote a newspaper column called, "Let'er Buck."

Casey loved children. He visited children in hospitals. He produced a rodeo in Fort Pierre each August. The proceeds were given to 4-H.

Truly, Casey Tibbs was a good character. He was a good bronc rider and also participated in movies.

Dylan Lemmon, Grade 4
Cheyenne-Eagle Butte Upper Elementary School, SD

What Is Horse Tack and How to Use It

Horses are fun to ride. Tack is what you use to ride horses. I will explain what tack is and how to use it.

The bridle/halter is used right when you take the horse out of the stall. The grooming box is used for grooming the horse. A normal grooming box includes: body brush, face brush, rag, curry comb, hoof pick, and a tail and mane brush. The reins are used to steer and can be a lead rope. The bareback saddle pad is put on before the saddle. It protects the saddle from: sweat, lice, ticks and hair. The whip is really only used in championship races and makes the horse go faster. The helmet protects your head in case of a fall. The saddle gives you a more comfortable seat while riding. The stirrups just give you an easier way to get on and dismount properly. Fly spray is spray that you spray on a horse's legs so it does not get bit during riding. A fly net is used for when it is very buggy. You Velcro it on its face to stay safe.

That is all the tack that is used to ride a horse. Riding horses is a lot of fun when you start. I am very happy to be riding horses. Now every day I think on what I will learn next and how to improve on my skills.

I hope you had fun reading this essay because I was really elated writing it!

Theo Bender, Grade 4
Louise Foussat Elementary School, CA

What Did You Do Last Summer?

I taught my mom how to swim. When my brothers and sisters and I were in the swimming pool, we asked our mom to come in the swimming pool with us. She said "No Way." I don't know how to swim. She said she was going to drown. I told my mom that "I could teach you how to swim." She got her bathing suit and got in with us. My mom said it was too cold, I said "Come in, you'll get used to it." It was so funny because I was holding my mom by the waist and I told her "No, you have to do it this way." My brothers and sisters were laughing so hard. My mom was laughing too, she almost drowned from laughing so hard. It was so much fun on the first day my mom went swimming in our pool.

The next day, we asked out mom to come to the pool again, but this time we told her to put on our little sister's floaties so she wouldn't drown. She put on her floaties and she couldn't believe how much they really worked. My mom almost learned how to swim, but summer was too short. Maybe she can learn how to swim better next year. I'll always remember how we helped teach our mom to swim. It was the best day ever.

Valentina Gojcaj, Grade 4
Jefferson Elementary School, MI

An Amazing Solo Flight

I can't explain how scared I am. I'm flying *alone* to visit my sister, Rena, in New York!

I'm on the plane and everything seems okay, but then the judicious pilot announces, "A plane has broken down at JFK Airport." Oh man! That's where I'm headed. We can't take off for forty-five incalculable minutes until JFK is cleared.

My unlucky, miserable flight wasn't going so well. We finally take off. The pilot says, "Because of bad weather we're going to have to circle before continuing to JFK." We circle for over an hour because the rigorous rain wouldn't calm down. I try to fall asleep but I can't. I want to hear what the amiable pilot says.

I'm flying Jet Blue, so I'm able to watch satellite TV. Thank goodness! Finally, we land. The crowded gates are full because of the annoying delays. We sit in the crowded, stuffy plane for another half hour. I land three hours late, at 1:00 a.m.

Finally, a gate opens and our plane pulls up to it. The applause sounds. Since I was an unaccompanied minor I'm allowed to get off the immense plane first. Right when I arrive in the airport I see my wonderful sister. I run up to her and give her the biggest, loving bear hug. We get my hefty luggage, then catch a cab and head to her apartment. Getting into that nice soft bed of hers is the end of the biggest, unforgettable adventure I've ever been through.

Ray Cortez, Grade 6
St Matthew Catholic School, TX

The Accidental Picture

"Look at it! It's going over there to that camp site!" someone whispered.

Arff! Arff! Arff! My grandparents' dogs were barking like maniacs.

"What's going on?" my cousin Walt groaned as he got out of bed.

"I think there is something outside," I answered.

Walt walked over to the back window. People were taking pictures outside with open mouths.

"Walt! Taylor!" my grandpa shouted, "Look at this bear!"

"W…W…Walt," I stammered looking out the front door, "C…c…come over h…h…here."

He walked across the fuzzy floor, anxious to see what had made my mouth drop to my chest. When he got to the door, he saw what had made me freeze. We stared at the gigantic beast, breathlessly. It's teeth were triple the size of my front teeth and its claws were half the size of my index finger. About three yards away from us lying on the ground was a huge, full-grown, dusty brown bear who was almost the size of a VW Bug.

My grandpa went outside and slowly moved closer and closer with his camera.

Suddenly the bear growled as loud as an avalanche tumbling down a slippery slope. My grandpa was so startled, he jumped up and accidentally took a picture of his hand. The people that were taking pictures from a distance stood in awe while my grandpa ran away from the bear.

From that mouth dropping moment, I have learned never to get too close to a wild bear!

Taylor Anne Becknell, Grade 5
Dingeman Elementary School, CA

What's in Your Pencil?

Do you know what's in your pencil that makes it write? It's not lead if that's what you're thinking, and there's a good reason why.

Lead is a poisonous metal that can severely harm people. Before the 1950s, lead paint was used on houses and buildings. This was a big problem. The pain could chip off, and a young child could become terribly sick. Some pre-1950 structures are still standing today, so people need to be careful.

Lead also can be found in soil near roads, since gasoline used to contain lead. In addition, drinking water sometimes contains lead. This happens when the pipes in sinks start to break down. Also, lead can be found in old toys that were imported to the United States from other countries.

Lead poisoning has been, and will continue to be, a huge problem. That is, unless it is addressed. Young children between the ages of one and five are most susceptible to lead poisoning, but everyone needs to be careful.

MacKenzie Druecke, Grade 6
Big Bend Elementary School, WI

Dogs with Beards

Did you know that there is a dog that has a beard? They are called Schnauzers and they are from Germany. Schnauzers make great pets. Taking care of a dog is very hard work but is rewarding. You will be learning interesting facts about Schnauzers and how they make good companions.

Schnauzers date back to the 1800s in Germany. There are three sizes; giant, standard and miniature. I have a Miniature Schnauzer named Pepper. They are part terrier and love to chase mice and ground squirrels.

Schnauzers are very loving so they would make a great pet. They also protect the house by barking at unfamiliar guests. These dogs also are very easy to house train. If you don't like to be alone then this dog is right for you, because they are always by your side.

God created these amazing animals for us to love and take care of. Their basic needs are to be fed, have fresh water, and walked daily. You need to brush their beards often, but they may not like it because mine does not. Dogs like lots of attention. Pepper likes to be chased and have his belly rubbed.

If you would like to have a dog you should get a Schnauzer. They are loving, playful and look cute with their beards. I love owning a Schnauzer and you will too!

Hannah Laird, Grade 6
Isaac Newton Christian Academy, IA

Devoted to Our Earth

The environment is our home. The environment is our nature. Our environment has everything we actually NEED to survive. It's fairly simple, although you'd be surprised how many people DON'T know that.

I knew little about the environment and nature at the age of 6. The teachers would always teach us about electricity, but nothing to do with the earth's power. I only paid attention to things being taught, not even always that. Like all the other students near the end of grade 4, I had to take the Otis Lennon test. After a few tests, and months, I was labeled "gifted." Nearly 8 months later I was learning (and thriving) about the facts of our nourishing earth. The small musty curtains hiding the broken window that I once was oblivious to, had opened up. A new world was outside that window, and the view grew to be my passion. This was a new feeling — something had to be done when our earth was in trouble. As my awareness grew, so did my theories and facts. Our earth is going to die faster than we know it. Global warming is something that grows as the pollution does. It melts the glaciers, causing polar bears to die. Soon we'll all have to move to Mars, literally! But I'm one kid, and the only way I can save the world is if the rest of it is willing to devote their lives to saving life, too.

Liah Wallace, Grade 6
Charles Beaudoin Public School, ON

American Bison

I researched the American Bison for my endangered animal project.

I found that the American Bison live in the Great Plains of the United States and Canada in big groups called herds. They range from the Great Slave Lake in Canada way up north, to Mexico to the south. They also range from eastern Oregon all the way close to the Atlantic Ocean. It has two main subspecies, one is called the Plains Bison. They are noticeable by the tiny size and also more rounded hump on their back. The Wood Bison is more noticeable by their bigger size, and more taller and square hump on its back.

The American Bison likes to graze near a heated spring in Yellowstone National Park. They eat mostly vegetation and drink water. Bison can be one of the most dangerous animals to United States citizens or Canadian people.

The American bison have mating habits. The male bison is called a bull. The bull has many wives. It takes 285 days to have a baby calf. The American bison's mating season is in the middle summer to late summer. Sometimes the mating season can last to September, but only in the northern ranges.

In some states bison hunting today is legal. The wolf is one of the bison's few predators. The wolf would mostly just kill the females and the calves, instead of going to the stronger males.

This is what I learned about the American Bison.

Amanda Livingston, Grade 4
Menchaca Elementary School, TX

Cross-Country

I've always loved running. This year I decided to do cross-country. Running cross-country helped me to get faster and it taught me a lot of life skills. All the people on the team were really nice. They didn't care about how fast I was or what I looked like. They just liked me for who I was. When we first started running, I wasn't as fast as most of the people on the team. My coach and my team kept cheering me on. By the end of the season I improved a lot and was able to keep up with my friends. Some meets I didn't do very well. Everyone cheered me on anyway. So when one of my friends had a bad meet I would remember how it felt and would cheer them on. I built great friendships with my team. At practice when we felt like we could barely go any farther we would do things to distract ourselves. We would sing at the top of our lungs. One day my friend tucked her shirt in and pulled her shorts up really high and ran that way. She got a lot of funny looks. Running has taught me about working together as a team, improvement takes practice, and a sense of humor goes a long way. Running cross-country was a great experience and I'm looking forward to next season.

Josie Knapp, Grade 6
Tri-West Middle School, IN

Rosa Parks

Rosa Parks was born on February 4, 1913. Rosa Parks was born in Tuskegee, Alabama. In Rosa Park's life they thought that African Americans had no rights. Rosa was married to Raymond Parks and that day was great. Every time she got on the bus she sat in the back.

One day Rosa Parks went on the bus and there was an empty front seat. She went over and sat there but Africans were not supposed to sit in the front. When three people came on the bus, the bus driver told her to move and she did not move. That day the bus driver called the police and Rosa Parks was arrested. A lot of people remembered that day.

Later, Raymond came and picked Rosa up from jail. She told Raymond she had to drink out of a certain water fountain. Rosa always dreamed of freedom. Rosa Parks standing up made such a change. Hardly anyone was on the bus.

There was a boycott and it was a success. Later Rosa started to ride the bus again. When she went to get on the bus it was closed from the boycott. She was surprised at how much it affected the world.

Rosa Parks died on October 25, 2005 at the age of ninety two years old. I think that she was a great person. My family looks up to her. She gave a lot of African Americans a chance to have rights. I really like her spirit.

Jada Robinson, Grade 5
The Arts Academy School, OH

Be Brave, Stand Up

Have you ever wondered how our government was made? It was made by people who weren't afraid of losing. They were brave enough to stand up and fight for freedom and democracy. In a democracy people can express their feelings in many different ways, like protesters. They can write editorials in the newspaper and say what they think. You can even write a letter to the President!

We need to fight! We fight wars because we don't like another country or we think they are plotting against us, but maybe they are misunderstood. People are brave when they stand up and speak out for their beliefs! If you never do it then you'll never know what might have happened or who could have benefited. Look at the people who stood up to fight and make the United States. What about the women who stood up for voting rights? If they had not done that, I might not be able to vote when I turn 18. We need to remember the lives that were lost at the Tiananmen Square protest in China. They were brave to stand up but the government shouldn't have killed so many of the students.

Does America know, if being brave is right or wrong? Sometimes it seems what we do may not be right. Will we ever know? History will tell us. So, will people stand up?

Katie Hinh, Grade 6
Southport 6th Grade Academy, IN

Sea World

In fifth grade our school went to Sea World. We drove big charter buses. I sat with my best friend Laine. We took lots of pictures. We also played mash and lots of other games. When we arrived we unloaded our things where we were sleeping. We slept on the most beautiful coral reefs. The next day we say Shamu, but there isn't just one Shamu there are seven! We had to get up really early. Later that day they let us ride roller-coasters. I'd never been on a rollercoaster. I had a lot of butterflies in my stomach. My first ride was with my best friend Lindsey. The ride was called Great White.

After riding that eight times in a row, we went and road the Steal Ell. It was seventy-six stories high. It was a blast but on that ride my conscious kicked in, telling me not to do it. But I did it.

My school only planned on going for two days so my mom and Mrs. Eckert drove down here to stay a couple extra days with me and Lindsey. While we were there we swam with beluga whales. It was amazing watching the beautiful creatures move smoothly and gracefully right before our eyes and touching their soft slimly skin. It was a life changing experience. They were pretty, sweet, and very playful. Lindsey and I had a blast except for those wet suites. Boy I'm glad I am out of those.

Whitney Sanders, Grade 6
Argyle Middle School, TX

My Farm

My farm is my most favorite place to be. I love to go there and relax, especially on the weekends. And I really like to take my friends with me. It has been in my family for fifteen years, longer than I have been alive. I think the farm is thirty acres of fun.

One reason why I love to go to the farm is that we have a group of vehicles that we get to play with. We have a four wheeler, two go-carts, lawnmowers, and a gorilla/small motorcycle. They are all fun to drive especially the gorilla. When my friends go with me we race each other and we go really fast.

Another thing I love about the farm is the fishing. We have two ponds to choose from. I like to fish at the older pond because there are about sixteen catfish as long as my leg. They are hard to catch because of how smart they are. We also have a goldfish bigger than my head. I have caught him a few times.

Another thing I love about the farm is the creek. I love to explore and find what I think are fossils. I have found crawdads, Geodes, salamanders, a turtle shell, and lots of interesting rocks. I once found something iron, shaped like a gun and the bones of a deer. Those are just a few of the reasons why I love the farm so much.

Billy Cross, Grade 6
Southport 6th Grade Academy, IN

Swimming Pool

Did you know that you can do more than swim laps in a swimming pool? There are a lot of things that you can do to have fun in a swimming pool, and swimming laps is not the only thing!

While you can definitely spend a great amount of time in the swimming pool, swimming laps around the pool, there are so many other things that you can do while enjoying your time in the pool. I have found a way to work on my handstands while relaxing in the pool. I try to do one-handed handstands, two-handed handstands and even handstands with my legs crossed.

In addition to handstands, I like to dive for objects. There are a lot of different types of objects that you can dive for, from rings, to torpedoes, to just about anything. The ones that float, or should I say sink to the bottom are the most fun. When I am swimming with friends or family, we usually have a competition on who can retrieve the most objects in one dive.

In conclusion, there are several ways to enjoy yourself in a swimming pool! Think about the exercise that you get from doing these different things, wow!

Jennifer Peterson, Grade 4
Louise Foussat Elementary School, CA

Nature Being Destroyed

We are destroying our own home because of our actions. Mother Nature says that we are creating the cause that this land is becoming a waste dump. We use some items too much.

Have you heard of global warming? You have probably heard of this on television. This is happening because of our cars. Cars need gasoline for power but what a lot of people don't know is that the car gives off harmful gases made from the gasoline. Those harmful gases could poison us. The same goes for airplanes, helicopters, and motorcycles. Just one fluorescent light bulb could be like taking 7.5 million cars off the road. Or you could ride bikes, carpool, or walk.

Some people are very lazy. They usually throw their trash on the ground and litter. That is causing the waste dumps. If you throw your trash in the ocean, the animals there will suffer because they might get caught in oil or trash. The animals in the water are Mother Nature's gifts too. If we can't take care of them who will?

People who eat meat are okay but they should at least not eat meat once in a while. If they keep on eating it, there will not be any more meat left to eat and we will starve to death without protein for strength. Protein is important so we have strength to be active. Plants are edible but they're nature so don't eat plants a lot.

Rommel Ballesteros, Grade 5
St Victor Elementary School, CA

Time of Death

The world does not feel as much hatred as I do toward the Nazis. Hitler was the cruelest man on earth, and he was the one who started World War II and the Holocaust. The worst part of everything he did was the evil death camps. They truly meant it when they said death. People died by the millions. Over six million Jews died in World War II.

The worst death camp of them all was Auschwitz. Auschwitz was located in Poland. The most horrid part of Auschwitz was the gas chambers and the acid showers. When people first walked in they thought they were taking a shower. They were taking one, just not with water. They would take an acid shower. The acid was actually called Zyklon-B; it was designed to eat the people alive.

After the people were killed they were stripped of everything. Their skin was used for chandeliers, their hair was used for blankets, and their clothes and jewelry became the property of the Germans. After the people were rid of everything they had they were cooked in a human-sized stove.

Most people do not feel the same way about the Holocaust as I do. Most people don't even care about the holocaust. I care because I am myself a Jew. I care so much because if I lived at the time of the Holocaust I would not be here today for I would probably be dead.

Ariel Pershman, Grade 5

My Family

My family is one of a kind. It seems like we never get along. See, there is my hardheaded dad, my nice mom, my older sister Allison, my other older sister Alyssa, me Alaena, and my little spoiled brother Alan-Jacob (but we call him Jacob for short). My family fights, we yell at each other, we tell jokes, we swim together, and of course, we eat together.

Allison went to college in San Diego and is staying with my aunt Faith. We have a house near my school. It's a light brown house with a pool and a trampoline. We have few neighbors because we have a small cul-de-sac neighborhood. Our house is kind of big but we love it. There are 4 rooms and two bathrooms. Our family is not rich but we don't need a lot of money since we have each other.

We're a family from many places. Allison was born in Washington like Alyssa. I was born in Sasebo, Japan. Jacob was born in San Diego. My mom and dad were born in the same city and state, Salano, Nueva Vizcaya. We all were born in different places but that makes us a different family than any other I know. We came back to California for good in 2005 from the Philippines. It was hard getting used to a new home but it builds your character. A year later we found a house for sale and it was near my school. A month later we found out we got the house. So we've been living in this house for almost a year. After we moved in we still fight but that means we're just like a regular family like yours.

Alaena Logan, Grade 4
Joseph M Simas Elementary School, CA

Foul Ball

"Dad, do you think we're going to get a foul ball?" I asked.

My dad answered, "Maybe."

When we got in the stadium I could smell my hotdog with ketchup and relish. My nachos were as spicy as the sun. My drink was as cold as fresh snow. My hot chocolate was warmer than the sun. Then we went to our freezing seats. They were singing "Oh Beautiful." It was the first game I had been to this whole season. It was the Padres vs. the Rockies.

In the fifth inning, Khalil Greene hit the ball, it hits the wall behind me and lands in the crack between my seat and my dad's seat. This other kid goes for it and my dad squeezes his hand. It drops down the crack and I grab it. I scream while holding it up in the air. I had a game ball! In the seventh inning, I dropped it and it rolled down the stairs. My dad had to go get it.

The Padres lost four to three. I told my dad I should have brought my glove. I fell asleep in the car playing video games. I woke up when I got home and I took out my souvenir. I put it in my new case and placed it on my dresser. I put on my pajamas and fell asleep on my couch. It was the best day ever!

Andrew Almond, Grade 5
Dingeman Elementary School, CA

What I Admire About Miley Cyrus

I wonder if I will ever meet Miley Cyrus? What would I say to her? What would I ask her? Those are the questions that I wonder about! She is such an awesome role model for girls that are ages 9 and up. The reason why she is an admirable role model is because she sings appropriate songs for kids and teens. I really admire that about MIley because she is very true to herself as a person. She is also a talented singer!

Did you know Miley's real name is Destiny Hope Cyrus, not Miley! You're probably shocked, me too! Anyway, Miley is a really kind person and that's why she is famous. Let me tell you a few facts about Miley Cyrus.

Did you know that when she was little she always wanted to act like her dad? So with a little help from her dad, she developed her skills as an actress. She played the little girl, Kylie, on her Dad's show. This gave her the ability to practice her acting and singing skills. Her dream was that she always wanted to act and sing. She accomplished her dream by working hard.

I want to do the same thing, which is follow my dream! My dream is to be a doctor and I know that I will accomplish this because I will work hard just like Miley did, to make my dream come true.

Ala'a Mashal, Grade 6
Northwood Public School, ON

Arc de Triomphe

Long ago, Emperor Napoleon of Paris, France ordered Jean Chalgan to design him the most wonderful arch in the world. He wanted to do this for his imperial armies. He wanted to remember his troops so he chose to make a huge arch.

When Jean was summoned to his presence, Napoleon ordered him to make it 172 feet tall. Jean searched the world to find a perfect design for this enormous arch. After searching and searching, he finally found the arch of Titus in Rome, Italy. It had just the right amount of support and balance.

He went back to Paris to tell Napoleon the wondrous design he had found. Jean ordered his builders to build this magnificent Arc de Triomphe. Napoleon became anxious. It took a total of 30 years to build. Of course, Napoleon did not live to see his arch completed. After he died, the Paris government changed. They decided that it would be much more logical to go along with the other European countries and make their ruler a king.

Under the power of King Louis Phillip, the arch was completed in 1836. In the year 1920, an unknown body of a soldier was placed under the arch as a remembrance of the soldiers who gave their lives in World War I and World War II. To honor them, an eternal flame was lit.

I would love to see the arch some day. In the meantime I will just have to learn about it!

Kaitlyn Sheppard, Grade 5
St John of the Cross Parish School, IL

My Fat Cat

The story you are about to read is about my cat and his life. I lost my black kitten and I wanted a new kitten but my mom said no! Since my mom said no I just followed her around the house begging and pleading but she kept on saying no. She finally said yes only because I annoyed her so much. I was so happy I was getting a new kitten.

When we went to the pet store, I finally found the perfect kitten. He was white with orange spots everywhere. He was a gorgeous kitten but very very skinny. My mom tried to talk me out of getting him but I said no, I want this kitten, he may be skinny but he is going to be mine!

My mom bought the kitten and with him we bought some kitty toys. Rusty is going to have a great new house, a great new family, and a great new place to sleep. When we got home I sat Rusty on the couch so he could get used to his surroundings. After that I started playing with him. He looked so cute playing with his new toys I just knew he was going to love it here.

After about six months Rusty started getting fatter and fatter. Then he got bigger and bigger now is 18 lbs and very lazy but Rusty is a very sweet cat.

Erin Brown, Grade 5
Bang Elementary School, TX

Brodi

Brodi came to my family when he was less than a year old, but he was still as big as he was going to get. Brodi is a blue-silver miniature Yorkshire terrier, and is 10 inches tall and 1 1/2 feet long. When we got him he was around 4 1/2 pounds, but now he is around 5 pounds.

Brodi was my cousin's dog, but she wasn't taking care of him because she had just started college in Seattle and had too much to do. When she had to give Brodi away, my dad (who had already met Brodi) said we would have him. My dad had to fly to Seattle for business anyway, so on the way home he brought Brodi.

When Brodi came home he was a little shy and kept turning around because of his blind eye. Brodi is blind in one eye because when he was a puppy, one of his littermates scratched his cornea. He soon discovered Lady and Shadow our 2 large female dogs and even though they are 5 times his size, he is really protective towards them and my family.

Now, two years later, Brodi is still the joyful, protective, and an adorable dog. He has made a lot of happiness in our house, and when he is not being noticed, he barks so that we know he is there. I am glad Brodi was brought into my family's lives because he is a great pet.

Monica Cañizares, Grade 6
Argyle Middle School, TX

Conservation and Preservation

Did you know that conservation and preservation are synonymous? They both mean to protect and keep safe.

This summer I had the opportunity to become a member of a conservation camp. Our Oakland Park Conservation Club pledge is, "I give my pledge as an American, to save and faithfully to defend, from waste, the natural resources of my country, its forests, waters and wildlife."

By preserving the air, we can't burn styrofoam, rubber, or plastic, because it will be harmful to people and wildlife.

To protect our soil we plant new trees and flowers. This is good for birds, butterflies, bees, and other insects. We cannot chop down trees, break limbs, or pick flowers because birds and insects need them. This helps our forests.

After fishing tournaments, we collect soda cans to recycle, which also keeps the environment clean.

I help protect our lakes because of the aquatic life such as fish, snakes, turtles, vegetation, and frogs. We don't use three-sided hooks because they will kill fish. We use special kinds of hooks which will dissolve quickly and won't stay in the fish long. There is a catch and release policy.

In order to protect wildlife, we don't tame or feed animals or birds, because they will become dependent on us. This winter, when we're not there to feed them, they will starve.

I'm glad I learned about conservation and preservation. It's fun to be part of such a good thing.

Brittanie Thompson, Grade 5
Westview Elementary School, OH

My Disaster Plan!

The reason on why I'm doing this essay is so I can be prepared for a disaster. Everything you need for a disaster drill should be ready and packed.

For a disaster whether it's a small or big disaster you would need an emergency supply kit, what's in an emergency supply kit are gallons of water, sacks of food, blankets and so much more. In my very own house there are supply kits all over the place like my parents' room, garage and the kitchen and different places too so my family and I can be safe.

If my city would ever have a terrible disaster or my home, one of the doors I would get out of is my kitchen sliding door or my garage door just to be safe.

By any chance I would get out of my house I would have to have a meeting place, where my family can meet. My meeting places would be State Bros., Circle K or at Liberty Park. I chose these stores and this park because they are right by my house and they're easy to go to.

Here are some ways to be aware of a disaster and to be ready step by step.

Naomi Valdivia, Grade 5
Liberty Elementary School, CA

Being Drug-Free

My topic for the essay contest is being drug-free. I believe it is important to be drug-free because people who do drugs usually have many severe health problems. Drugs include smoking, taking pills (not for sickness), tobacco, and many others. Some are illegal in the United States while others are sold all over the world. I believe that we should make a good choice and try to influence the younger generation to do so as well.

Smoking is usually considered doing drugs and is something you can become easily addicted to if you are not careful. Many diseases are caused by smoking including lung disease. When you smoke your lungs start to turn black and don't work as well as if you don't smoke. Sometimes you have to get your lungs replaced because they don't operate very well. Your teeth can turn yellow and brown. Your voice might sound weak if you smoke. There are many reasons not to smoke.

When some people do drugs, they sometimes take pills to get a reaction. Some are illegal, but some are just pills you take when you get sick. These people just take too many. Pills can be very addicting.

Doing drugs is a very bad habit and can be very dangerous to others. Maybe you can try to influence others to be drug-free too! Try saying something to friends, family, and maybe even your classmates about making the decision not to do drugs.

Tricia Sutton, Grade 6
Olentangy Shanahan Middle School, OH

Quit Smoking

There are many good reasons to stop smoking. First, once you do, you will have cleaner air around you. This will help you and the people with you to have better health. You can easily get addicted to smoking. Addiction means that when you have one cigarette, you soon have to have another one, and you cannot stop smoking one after another. If this continues, you may develop lung cancer, have a heart attack, have sick babies and children in your home, and have ugly yellow teeth and fingernails.

My great-grandfather smoked, and he had a heart attack. One day my great-grandmother found him dead in his basement workshop with a cigarette in his mouth. This tragic scene could have been prevented if he had never decided to smoke.

Some people are forced to smoke even when they do not want to. Secondhand smoking is when people smoke, and others breathe the smoky air in. They can develop the same diseases as the smokers. Children who live with smokers can have asthma and other health problems.

If someone asks you to have a cigarette, don't take any chances. Refuse to even try that dangerous substance. If you already smoke, quit! If you can't quit, go to your doctor. Help is available to assist you in recovering your health.

Cameron A. Stewart, Grade 4
Birchwood School, OH

My Grandparents

My grandparents are one of the best people in my family. I always go everywhere with my grandma she calls me, "her little man." My grandpa always calls me, "monkey man." Every day when he comes home from work I always help him get out his lunch box and his mug. Whenever I spend the night at a friend's house and come back in the morning they are happy to see me.

I go everywhere with them. They even took me on a cruise to Russia. We even got a piece of the Berlin Wall. We took a big ship and it was a lot of fun. We knew everybody that worked for the ship and they all liked my family. But there was one guy Eddie who liked me the most. He gave me tokens to the game room and then hung out with my grandparents. One of the scariest times was the sea storm but we all made it.

The next morning I woke up and the sea storm was all over. My grandpa and I went out and played tennis and my grandpa hit a ball overboard and it disappeared in about five seconds.

The next place we went was Copenhagen, Denmark. We stayed in a hotel right across from an amusement park where I rode my first roller coaster with my grandpa.

We stayed there for about five days and then we started heading home and I hope we can go there again.

Dan Andreas, Grade 6
Round Valley Elementary School, CA

My Trip to New York

"Yes! We get to go to New York City," I said, talking to my parents. I had been bugging my parents to go to New York City and we finally got to go! We were already going to be on the east coast visiting my mom's family in Maryland. We were on our way! We stayed for four days. The first day we traveled there, so we really did not do anything that day. But, the next day was amazing! We got on the bus and went to the subway station where I got on my first ever subway that took us to downtown New York. I remember the first thing we did was shop! I got a hat that said "New York Princess." Then we went to the Empire State Building and went to the top! It was so cool looking at the city of New York. We went to Times Square, where there's a huge Toys "R" Us with a ferris wheel in it that was awesome! While we were in Times Square we went and ate at the ESPN Zone. It was so cool to watch all of those TVs. The second day we went to see the Statue of Liberty, and Ground Zero. We also went to the church right next to Ground Zero, it was pretty sad. We then went to Wall Street and saw the New York Stock Exchange building. The whole trip was an extremely fun experience.

Alyssa Bruton, Grade 6
Argyle Middle School, TX

Never Giving Up

"Failure is only a fact when you give up. Everyone gets knocked down, the question is: will you get back up?"

Never giving up, what does this mean? When you give up you are done trying, you quit, you stop, and you're done.

What if Christopher Columbus had given up and didn't sail over the sea? What if Abraham Lincoln had given up and didn't save all those slaves? What if Thomas Jefferson didn't invent the light bulb? We would be sitting in the dark. Or what if the firefighters from 9/11 had given up and didn't save the people in the Twin Towers? What if everyone gave up?

If everyone gave up, what would our society be? That is why we have to keep trying and keep working at everything we do. You have to think about everything you know.

Sometimes people give up too easily and don't think about what they are capable of doing. You can really do anything you want to, you just have to remember that life has all sorts of obstacles. When life gives you lemons, make lemonade!

When you think about the word, 'achieving' what do you think of?

You should think of succeeding, and letting nothing get in your way.

You need to believe in yourself and good things will happen.

Now let me ask you something, if you get knocked down, will you get back up??? Never Give Up!

Brooklyn Allgood, Grade 5
Norwoodville Elementary School, IA

Bringing Home a Kitten

Bringing home a kitten — how exciting! To think, one day it will be a great cat! But you need to know how to take care of your cat in order for that to happen.

When you're getting your kitten, make sure it's eight weeks or older. If you bring it home any sooner, it may not grow properly. Another thing is to look to see if its fur is soft and smooth, it has clean ears and a clean bottom, soft damp nose and bright eyes. If the kitten has all that then it's probably in good health.

When you bring home your kitten, it might hide at first. Don't pull it out of its hiding place. It'll come out on its own. When you pick up your kitten put one hand under its bottom, the other under its front paws. The first three weeks are the most important. Treat your kitten with love and respect, and your kitten will learn to trust and love you.

Scoop out your kitten's waste every day. Once a week, dump out all the litter and wash it with hot soapy water. Always wash your hands after cleaning your cat's litter box.

You also have to be willing to play with your cat for about half an hour every day. Having a kitten will cost $350 or more if your kitten needs special treatment.

Have fun with your kitten!

Michelle Brooke, Grade 5
Forest Hill Public School, ON

Sport-oholic

I play a lot of sports and I'm going to tell you about a few.

First hockey. I like hockey because of the constant rush, back and forth, back and forth. I have 2 favorite hockey players, one is retired and his name is Wayne Gretzky; the other is a goalie and still plays, his name is Martin Brodeur. Hockey means a lot to me, I love the game.

Golf is the next, it may take time but it rocks, and I'm pretty good. It feels awesome when you shoot par or get a low score, I love that feeling. Now I'm talking about Tiger Woods — the best golfer in my opinion, he has the skills, and I want to be as good as him some day. Sometimes you hit a good shot, sometimes you hit a bad shot, and you have to learn that if you want to play golf.

Soccer is the next of the seven sports. If you play soccer then you know the feeling I'm talking about. It is a feeling that you get when you score a goal or make an astonishing save, you get the feeling that you did something…something that helps your team. My coach is spectacular, he can shoot really hard and put a ton of spin on it, punt it really high, and he's nice too. Soccer is one of the biggest (meaning most watched and played) sports in the world.

A simple summary, I play tons of sports — this is only three.

Graham Anderson, Grade 5
Barrington Elementary School, OH

Ancient and Modern Olympics

Both ancient and modern Olympics are athletic games, but they are not completely the same.

The purposes of the games are different. The ancient games purpose was because of the Greek god, Zeus, held on the Plain of Olympic in Greece. The first Greek games were in 776 BC. It was only one day but it changed to three days, then five days in the fifth century. They were held every year.

Modern games are held for fun athletic competition. The first was in France, but now they are held in a different city every time. It takes several days. Winter and Summer Olympics alternate every two years.

The competitors are different. In ancient games, only men from Greece competed. They raced in the nude. Women were not allowed to compete or watch. In modern games women and men from many countries compete.

Winners are honored differently. Ancient Greek winners got an olive branch wreath to wear. Second place got nothing. They could have a statue of themselves set up in Olympia. Modern winners get medals for the first three places. Both had parties to honor champions.

Events have changed. They only had a spring 102 meters long, then fifty years later they added the pentathlon with wrestling, boxing, single horse and four horse chariot races. In modern Olympics there are women's and men's competitions. Summer Olympics have 25 events and Winter Olympics have 16 events.

Ancient and modern Olympics are athletic competitions but differ in purpose, competitors and event.

Ryan Cook, Grade 6
Cheyenne-Eagle Butte Upper Elementary School, SD

When My Sister Was Born

When my sister was born I had new responsibilities. Like I would have to watch my sister, and feed her, too. The first time I saw my sister, I thought she was so pretty. The first time I held my sister she was really light. I was glad to have a baby sister. When we got to go home, I was glad to leave the hospital. When we got to our house I waited a few minutes to ask if I could hold my sister. When I finally asked to hold my sister my mom gave her to me. She felt the same as the first time I held her at the hospital. After a few minutes my dad asked to hold my sister and then he talked to her in baby talk.

The next day I had to go to school. I felt sad because I wanted to stay home with my sister and my mom. When I got home from school I asked my mom if I could hold my baby sister. She said, "No, son, she's asleep." When she woke up, I played with her and it was fun. Every day I got home I asked to hold my sister. I always asked if I could hold my sister because I love her so much and because she is so fun to play with. That's the story of when my sister was born.

Michael Gonzales, Grade 4
Menchaca Elementary School, TX

Auntie's So Young

Auntie Brooke come here! I'm lucky to experience the feeling of having a niece and a nephew so young. I feel like I've never loved somebody as much as I love them. Jadyn is my niece, she's four years old. Joey's my nephew, he's one year old. They are both unique in their own ways.

One thing that pops in my mind when I look at Jadyn is the beautiful twinkle in her eyes. It is as if I am looking at the stars. Whenever I'm sad, or crying all Jadyn has to do is smile and say "I love you" and I'm no longer sad.

Now, Joey on the other hand, he has the cutest little smile. Every morning I am not woken up with an alarm clock, I arise with my nephew's joyful smile and his love. He is the one who gets me joyful for school.

I've got a binder full of pictures of Joey and Jadyn. Whenever I'm sad at school I look at my binder and I get a smile on my face. If I see either of them crying it breaks my heart. One thing I love doing is helping Joey walk. He's so close he's just lazy. Another thing I love is when Jadyn comes up to me with her cute voice and asks, "Auntie Brooke will you do my hair?" I always say yes. I'm so thankful for family.

Brooke Hayes, Grade 6
Linfield Christian School, CA

An Inspiring Hero

A real hero is someone who fights for something, whether it's extremely frightening, dangerous, or something difficult. Hero's are someone who believes in hope; tries as hard as they can to reach their goals. That's a well told description of Terry Fox! His goals were to fight cancer, raise money for a cure, by running across Canada.

Terry was loved by many Canadians; he was first diagnosed with cancer after he was in an accident. He smashed into a truck. He survived but had a sore knee, which lead doctors to diagnose the cancer.

Terry was diagnosed with Osteosarcoma it affected his knee, and then spread throughout his body. It affects men more often than women. He ended up losing his leg over this tragic disease.

Terry then decided he wanted to do something, he decided to run across Canada to raise money to help find a cure for cancer. Terry started his run by dipping his leg into the Atlantic Ocean and was hoping to dip that same leg into the Pacific. Terry's run was cut short. He made it to Thunder Bay. Throughout his run he was very sick but, kept trying to make it. Terry was so ill that he could not continue his run for cancer. Terry soon after passed away from cancer.

What Terry did was inspiring; he fought cancer and ran no matter how hard or sick he was. He fought a good fight. His run was named the Marathon of Hope.

Rebecca Wells, Grade 6
St Francis School, ON

My Baseball League

When I first went to play in the baseball league I was nervous, because I never played on a team before; never batted with a pitching machine. I was nervous to make new friends. When I started playing it was fun. I was catching fly balls and batting well. I got hit in the face with a hard baseball by accident. It hurt me so much I didn't want to play baseball ever again. Then I gave it another try.

One Saturday my dad brought me to the batting cage. When I was batting, the ball hit my index finger. It hurt a lot. I was angry at the man who made the pitching machine, and mad at my dad for taking me there. I wanted to quit playing baseball. I had to put ice on my finger to cool it down and to help decrease the swelling. We splinted the finger until I could see a doctor.

My mom took me to the doctor Monday. She examined my finger and took x-rays. It was broken. Then the doctor put a splint on my index finger to keep it straight and protect it.

I couldn't play sports or practice my violin and piano for three weeks. I watched my team's baseball games and practices. I practiced what my teammates were doing on the other field. I practiced doing agility drills with my dad so I'd stay in good shape. Baseball seemed to be more fun now. I didn't feel nervous anymore.

My team, the Jay Hawks, haven't won a game yet. When my finger feels better I hope to help my team win at least one game. It's important to have fun with your friends, learn how to play the game well, and keep trying even if you get hurt.

Nicholas Hasapes, Grade 4
Montessori School of Downtown - Clear Lake, TX

My Days at Isbell

When it was the first day of school I was scared. Isbell is a school that goes up to 6th-8th grade. I was scared because I thought my teachers were mean. People said that there were fights every day. Isbell seemed scary.

When it was the first day of school I was scared. I thought I was going to get pushed around. My sister said I will be ok. I felt safe with my sister. Isbell seemed fun.

Isbell was a school that went up to 6th-8th grade. Isbell is a school known for, kids getting in fights. But everyone thought wrong. Isbell is a wonderful school. So never listen to people when they say your school is bad.

When I got my schedule I was scared. All the teachers I got were nice. A few weeks later I got switched to honor classes. My teacher's names are Mrs. Philips, Mrs. Lidig, Mr. Lopez, and Mrs. Hicks.

Isbell seemed scary. But during the few weeks of school I made new friends and got to see things at Isbell School. I am so glad I went to Isbell School.

Franchesca Espino, Grade 6
Isbell Middle School, CA

Hiding for Life

Have you ever played the game Hide 'N' Go Seek? The purpose of the game is for a few people to hide and then one person to seek. But did you know that in the early 1930's through the late 1940's, some people were hiding and nervously hoping that nobody would seek them out?

One of the families that were hiding was the Franks. The Franks were a Jewish family living in one of the worst times in history, World War II. In Germany, a wicked man named Adolf Hitler, was ruling the country. He disliked Jews so much that he thought that all the Jews should be killed. Many Jews left Germany; the Franks went to Holland. They left all their belongings and even their cat Moortje.

Anneliese, also known as Anne, was one of the Frank's daughters. Anne loved to tell jokes and often joked around. On Anne's thirteenth birthday, she received something that is now one of the most famous possessions from the Holocaust, her diary. She loved to write in her diary whenever she had a special feeling. Anne kept writing in her diary until the day when the Nazis found the Franks.

Anne died at a concentration camp, but her diary didn't die in the horrible war. Instead it became a huge success.

Gabriela Fuhriman, Grade 5
Maple Avenue Elementary School, WI

Black Widows, Danger in South Dakota

There has been an increase of black widow spiders in South Dakota. People need to look out for them.

Black widows can be recognized by their look. The females have a shiny, jet black, spherical abdomen with two triangles on the underside which form an hourglass. The male usually has red spots down the middle. Adult female northern black widows are a shiny black or brown-black with a row of red spots on the abdomen.

Black widow's mating takes place in the summer. A common misconception is that the female usually consumes the male after mating. The females lay eggs in a silken sac that is globular shaped. Each sac contains 25 to 250 eggs. The spiderlings hatch and shed their one time inside the sac. It takes 2 to 4 months for them to grow up.

The black widow is a cobweb builder whose silk is very strong. When the female black widow sleeps, she sits belly upward on the center of the web.

The black widow is the most venomous spider in North America. A female injects such a small dose of venom into a human, it rarely causes death. The bite of a black may go unnoticed.

The black widow is a very dangerous species. South Dakota, you better look out for them. Do not and try not to be bitten by them. Make the increase stop; step on them, get them out of your house, do whatever it takes to stop them from increasing.

Grant Chavez, Grade 6
Cheyenne-Eagle Butte Upper Elementary School, SD

My Backyard

My backyard is not like most people's backyards. I live in the country, and my backyard is big! I have acres of timber to play in. The timber is full of cottonwood trees, big oak trees, and cedars. There are lots of weeds in the summer, not to mention all the poison ivy! Luckily I haven't gotten tangled up with any. In the fall the timber is full of colorful leaves. Winter is my favorite time to play in my backyard. When it snows and blows, I can make some real cool snow forts. I like watching the animals in the spring.

My favorite place in the backyard is the creek. My brother and I have built several different bridges. Some have worked and many have failed to serve their purpose, getting us across the water without getting wet! The creek is also my dogs' favorite place to play. They are always wet and muddy.

A lot of kids might think that it's boring to play outside. I think there is more to do outside than there is inside. Can you shoot a bow and arrow in the house? Can you play with a paint ball gun inside? Can you roast marshmallows over an open fire in your house? I wouldn't recommend it.

So if my mom and dad say, "Go outside and play." I don't think of it as a punishment. A little fresh air and exercise is just what a kid needs.

Gabe Barney, Grade 5
Nishna Valley Community School, IA

Papa

My Papa was David Wantoch. My Papa died on April 28th, 1998 from a brain aneurysm; that's when a blood vessel pops. I didn't know him very well; I was only two years old. But that made him all the more special, because at least I got to know him.

I have a favorite picture with Papa and me. He had just gotten a new tractor with a cab so he wouldn't have dust in his eyes when he was in the field. He was excited. So when Mama, Dad and I went to my grandparents' farm, I got a ride on Papa's tractor with him.

In the picture, Papa was letting me push and pull the gears and I was waving to Mama. That was one of the last pictures Papa was in, and the last both of us were in together.

My Papa had a funny mustache and glasses. He was busy, a lot of the times helping people. He also loved computers, cameras, and tractors. Papa was a pack rat too. When he died, Grandma found thirty-year old receipts in his shed!

My Papa was special. Maybe not to you, but that's because you probably don't know him. My Papa was special to *me* and I loved him. We miss him, but we know that he is up in the stars and heavens with Jesus.

I wouldn't be surprised at all, if you have a special someone who's not with you anymore. I'm not worried about mine.

Sydney Edens, Grade 6

Antarctica!!

Antarctica is a magnificent continent; also known as the White Continent or South Pole. The name Antarctica comes from the Greek word antarktikos meaning the opposite of the arctic. Antarctica is an ice cap stretching 14.4 million square km; almost twice the size of Australia. The ice is approximately 1.6 km thick and covers 98% of Antarctica. Winter temperatures range from -75 to -90 degrees Celsius and summer temperatures can rise as high as 15 degrees Celsius. Winds can exceed 300 km an hour throughout the year. Antarctica is actually a desert! It receives less precipitation than the Sahara Desert.

Getting there is difficult. Fly 11,000 km from Toronto to Ushuaia, Argentina, the most southern point of South America. Then board a ship to sail 640 km over two days through the Drake Passage, also known as the Drake Shake for its rough waters.

Life is sparse in Antarctica. Plant life consists of moss and lichens. Sea birds such as skuas, albatross and petrels share the landscape with emperor, gentoo and chinstrap penguins. Ocean mammals include crabeater and leopard seals along with humpback, minke and pilot whales. People live there only temporarily in research stations.

The White Continent has 90% of the world's ice and 70% of the world's fresh water. If all of the ice melted due to global warming the sea level would rise 200 feet and would cause flooding around the world! We have to be responsible and preserve this amazing part of the world for the future!

Gregory Taylor, Grade 6
Sir William Osler Elementary School, ON

Being Drug Free

Do you ever wonder what drugs can do to you? Have you ever thought of using drugs? Well I feel that using drugs are a really terrible thing to do. Most people that use drugs think that it is really cool. But, they don't understand in real life, it can really harm you. You may think that you are impressing your friends, but really you are not. When you use drugs not only do you hurt yourself, but you hurt other people. The problem with drugs has become a major issue today.

Most places have put laws in place in regards to that situation. People just choose to ignore them. There are protests against drugs, because drugs are affecting our cities, this problem is spreading all over the world. If we didn't have drugs in our community it would be a better place to live. Not only should parents stay away from drugs but children should as well. Being drug free is good for everyone. Careless people try drugs and don't bother to think of the effects. I strongly feel that drugs are affecting too many cities and that one day something horrifying will happen. The next time you think of doing drugs think of not only what it can do to you, but how it will hurt or affect the ones you love.

Jackie Orellana, Grade 6
Westwind Intermediate School, AZ

Anne Frank

Anne frank was one of the most popular and remembered girls from World War II. She was born in 1929. She had one sister, her name was Margot. Margot was three years older than Anne. Anne says that Margot was more proper.

Have you ever played hide and seek and you don't know when the seeker is coming, or if they even will come? Well I can tell you I haven't. But, Anne Frank has. During the war, the Nazis invaded a bunch of countries. It was very dangerous to go into hiding. Anne Frank went into hiding on July 16, 1942. Anne went into hiding with four other people not including her family of four. All eight people were hiding in a secret annex above some offices. There was not much room in the annex. Of course, nobody got their own room. Anne shared a room with Fritz Pfeffer.

Anne's days in the secret annex were not very fun. Most of the time she did her school work. Other times she would write in her diary or do anything else that was quiet. Every night all eight people would hear planes and other aircraft machines. That caused lack of sleep. That means that during the day, the eight would sometimes be tired. Anne had good and bad times in the annex.

Now the secret annex is a public museum. In all this tragedy Anne's diary is not lost; it was published in fifty-five languages.

Erin Russell, Grade 5
Maple Avenue Elementary School, WI

The Man with Coaching Abilities

Many table-tennis coaches in the world have tried to teach their students with his technique. Many want to learn to coach like him, but there is only one Masaki Tajima. He has won many tournaments and coached many champions. He has been the number one coach in Butterfly, a ping-pong company, for the past three years.

He taught me how to eat healthy and retain my strength. Showing me the right technique to hit the ball, Masaki helps me win the hard matches. Also he inspires me with the way he explains perseverance. You have to work hard to reach your goals. He puts emphasis on being a good sportsman. How to show incredible sportsmanship, where to show it, and anything else you can think about the way to have this amazing effort. The most important thing he says, "enjoy the game."

I follow his advice because I know it works. I eat healthy food and I run half a mile, at least, every week. I try to keep my health in balance so I will not stop playing for a short time. I show good sportsmanship when I win or lose and I enjoy the game. Masaki Tajima and his coaching has really inspired me.

Arjun Desai, Grade 6
Challenger School – Ardenwood, CA

Protecting Animals

All animals are special in their own ways. There are no animals that are exactly alike. For example, a cheetah is the only animal that can run up to 70 miles per hour or a penguin is a bird that does not fly. We are surrounded by these wonderful creatures. They, however, could be gone if their environment gets interrupted.

Currently there are a few problems we need to be aware of. Pollution is one of them. There are people who are too careless or lazy to put their trash in the trash bins. They let their trash lay around on the ground. There are also some business companies that throw away their harmful chemicals in nature. Animals can be hurt or killed by them.

Rising temperature is another problem. Temperatures in some areas are getting higher and the animals are not used to it. Their lives can be affected. In addition, there are companies that keep cutting trees down for papers, boxes and different kinds of products. The animals have fewer trees to hide and sleep in and food to eat.

Very soon the animals will go away or become extinct. If we want to protect the animals, we need to recycle and take care of the environment.

Hannah Bulow, Grade 5
Dishman Elementary School, TX

Pick the Right Friends

I remember a time when I didn't pick the right friends, and I learned a lesson from that. It was July 24 and it was getting dark, and I was getting ready to go to my cousin Courtney's slumber party. We were arriving and I saw a lot of people at the party. When I went in the house and got settled, a little girl named Chionne asked if I wanted to be her friend? And I said "yeah." So we were having fun, and we were all playing together. We did each other's nails and drew pictures of each other too. Then my cousin Courtney said, "I'm getting tired, I'm going to sleep." Then everyone made their pallets and went to sleep. In the middle of the night my cousin's friend Chionne that she invited, had got my phone and put my phone in her belongings. That morning I was very upset because I couldn't find my phone. Then I asked everyone had they seen my phone and everyone said "No." Then my auntie said, "Call it." And I did and I found it in Chionne's belongings. When I found it she was afraid, scared, and shy because I was looking very upset. She knew she had it all along the way I was looking for it. When I found out she had it I told her it's not right to steal from other people. And that's when I found out that she was not a good friend to hang out with a lot. She said, "sorry," and I forgave her, but it was time to leave the party.

The lesson I learned was to pick the right friends.

Dazjah Bowman, Grade 5
McMonagle Elementary School, MI

Reaching Kids for Christ

Do you know what Awana means? Does it mean a-wan-a ice cream? Is it an Indian word for fish? No, it's a club where boys and girls can go to learn about Christ.

Awana means, "approved workmen are not ashamed." It comes from the Bible in 2 Timothy 2:15, "Do your best to present yourself to God as one approved, a workman who does not need to be ashamed and who correctly handles the word of truth."

You learn scripture verses, play games, and have council time. When you learn scripture, you say verses to your leader from your handbook. There are fun activities in your handbook too. When you go to council time you listen to Bible stories. These stories are true, they actually happened. You also listen to more scripture verses.

Awana is a very fun atmosphere. It has changed my life in so many ways. I have become closer to God by being in Awana. I've also learned to share my faith with others.

Awana is a place where kids can come to know the Lord. If it changed my life, it will change yours.

Quentin Gaeta, Grade 6
Isaac Newton Christian Academy, IA

Hold Your Horses...Close to Your Heart

When my pony and I won the championships, I knew he was special. But, unfortunately, special wasn't good enough to keep my parents from selling him. The day Rebecca Mercer hauled him off in her trailer was the day I said good-bye to our team forever. Crying wouldn't bring him back. My happy life seemed to have ended...until Timmy came.

We'd been looking at horses for my mom and myself to ride. My parents said they'd surprise me, and, oh man, they did!

I woke up on a Saturday morning and jumped out of bed. I grabbed a pair of jeans, pulled them on, and headed downstairs for breakfast. My dad was taking me to riding! We drove to the Maple Valley Safeway, strolled inside, and hopped in line. The lady in front of us was taking her sweet time ordering. Honestly, the lady would not quit. As soon as we ordered, they were ready. We jumped in the car and took off! When I got to the barn I headed straight for my tack trunk. As I was getting ready, I saw a small, bay, skinny, frisky horse trotting around the ring. There was a small circular sticker on his back end. My father came down to check on me, and to tell me that my best friend, Max Connell, had arrived. I strapped my helmet on, and ran up the slope to the barn. I got to my friend, and he finally said something: "good luck!" Soon I realized why everybody was here. The horse in the ring was...was...was mine! All I could do was laugh! I ran into the ring and threw my arms around him. I thanked my mom and dad, and since that day we've been a great team!

Maddie Morton, Grade 6
Tahoma Middle School, WA

My Summer

My family and I and twelve people from our church went to Mexico. It took about 24-hours to get there. We left at 5:00 PM, so we got there at 5:00 PM the next day. We got to spend the night in the car. It was so fun.

When we got there, we finally got to get out of the car. My legs felt like Jell-O. When it was dinnertime, we went to a place called Happy Chicken.

The next day we helped an orphanage cover their playground with gravel, which was hard work. We also helped them paint their houses. That part was fun.

When we were driving back, we stopped in San Diego and stayed at the beach for a couple days. The first day we were there my brother Aaron and I dug a big hole. It was really fun, and then when it was lunch time we had a chicken sandwich, which was really good.

Then we drove over to Disneyland. My favorite ride was Splash Mountain. It was so fun when we went off a fifty foot drop. Then we got pizza at Down Town Disney. It was just right. The last thing we did was watch the fireworks. They were awesome.

My summer was so fun!!!!!!!!!

Jonathan Shedrick, Grade 5
Eugene Christian School, OR

The Unsinkable Ship

On April 10, 1912 the Titanic left England for America. It was an enormous ship! It was as long as three football fields, and was 11 stories tall. They made it in compartments, so if four compartments filled up with water it would still stay afloat. That is how everyone thought it was unsinkable.

It took three thousand men three years to build the Titanic. Its construction included sixteen watertight compartments that included steel doors that were supposed to shut in 25 seconds or less; this was to enclose any water that might have threatened the safety of the ship and her passengers. It was supposed to be the safest ship on the ocean.

The Titanic was a beautiful ship, too. Passengers could sail 1st, 2nd, and 3rd class. 1st class was the most elegant, so the costs of the tickets were high. One first class ticket back in 1912 would have cost $4,700. Nowadays, it would cost $50,000.

On April 14, 1912 at 11:40 p.m. the Titanic struck an iceberg. The iceberg ripped a 12 foot opening into the hull allowing water inside the ship. The ship was going to sink. The first lifeboat to leave the Titanic carried only 28 of the 64 that it could have held. Three hours later, the ship sank. The Carpathia rescued the lifeboats. Out of 2,208 people 705 were alive the next morning. Today 6 are still alive.

Hannah Higgins, Grade 6
Irma Marsh Middle School, TX

My Two Very Treasured Girls!

My two very treasured girls are a man's best friend, my dogs. The old one's name is Bailey Darrow. Bailey is a shaggy haired Wheaten Terrier. Her unique colored hair is light brown and white. When I first spotted Bailey at the puppy store in the mall I felt as if I were hitting a grand slam to win the World Series! I could tell she was the certain dog we were looking for. My mom asked a worker if we could look at her, and that's exactly what we did. When everyone was staring at her the first name that popped into mind was Bailey. My brother and I wanted to name her Princess. We got her when I was four years old and she was four months old. I love Bailey so much!

My other very treasured girl is a cute dog named Lucie. She is a puppy with short blond hair. She is mixed with a Jack Russell, Chihuahua, and a Miniature Pincher. She has long legs and she is very fast. How we got her is a weird story. I was on my way to the skate park but it was closed. So we went back to our house, but on the way I saw people selling puppies. I yelled "PUPPIES." There's not much to say about her because she is gone. Lucie and Bailey are my two very treasured girls!!

Logan Darrow, Grade 5
Desert Canyon Elementary School, AZ

Walt Disney World

For fall break 2006, my family and I went to Walt Disney World in Orlando, Florida. We stayed for a week. In that week we went to Magic Kingdom, Animal Kingdom, MGM Studios, and Epcot. I loved every park. We saw and rode a lot of rides and shows.

In the parks I heard lots of screams and talking, especially on the scary rides. I saw lots of rides, food stands, and water. I felt excitement, awe, and amazement. It was the best feeling in the world! All of my family felt the same.

The themes for Magic Kingdom were exploration and magic. The themes for Animal Kingdom were animals and habitats. The themes for MGM Studios were movies and inventions. The theme for Epcot was the fascinating world around you.

We saw Mickey, Minnie, and Goofy. We even got a picture with Tigger! Some of my favorite rides were Expedition Everest at Animal Kingdom, Tower of Terror at MGM Studios, and Aerosmith Rockin' Roller Coaster at MGM Studios. On Expedition Everest, my favorite part was when we rode backwards in the dark. On Tower of Terror, my favorite part was dropping up and down on the broken elevator. In Aerosmith Rockin' Roller Coaster, my favorite part was the loop the loop at the beginning while going really fast!

Out of all the theme parks I've been to, Walt Disney World has been the best. My trip was an awesome experience. I hope I can do it again sometime soon.

Brad Beasley, Grade 5
Desert Canyon Elementary School, AZ

My Family

My family is important to me because we all love each other. I care for my family because they love me and treat me with respect. They treat each other with love and kindness. I love my family very much because we get along great as a family of mostly boys. I kind of like my family being boys 'cause they toughen me up. I think when boys are around I do get toughened up.

My family is mostly boys so I get toughened up a lot by my cousins. I love my cousins as they were my brothers. I love them very much because they protect me. They love me very much too. They pay attention to me and I pay attention to them. We are a great team.

We are such a good family. I love my family very much and they love me. We work together. We are a perfect family. I wish we all lived together. I love them.

Paulette Griego, Grade 4
Santo Niño Regional Catholic School, NM

Skunk Alert

I was sprinting through big bushes with my dad. We were looking for antelope. We heard rustling in the long grass. As my dad's friend was getting ready to shoot, my dad heard screaming. He whipped his head around, and he saw my friend and me bolting back through our tracks and shrieking as loud as possible. Something black and white was following us. My dad focused in a little closer and he saw it, the skunk. All of the sudden the skunk glared its eyes at me and his tail flew up. Guess what that skunk did to me? Yes, you're right. It drenched me. I reeked so badly.

When we got home, we buried my clothes in the soil of our garden so the odor would go away. After a year or so, we took my clothes out of the dirt of our garden. They still had the fragrance of a skunk. So then we trashed them. That story was a smelly situation. I got sprayed with the essence of skunk.

Maddy Fisher, Grade 6
Monforton School, MT

Ouch!

It was my first time snowboarding, and I was five years old. My brother, Sean, and I were going to Bridger Bowl together. We started out at Snowflake. We rode on the lift to the top of the hill. My brother taught me the basics of snowboarding, but he forgot to teach me how to stop. I went flying down the hill not knowing how to stop or how to slow down. People jumped out of my way as I went straight into the brick wall of the lounge. My brother came down the hill to check on me as I was laying there with a big bump on my forehead. My brother helped me up, and we went into the lounge and rested for a minute. Then we went back outside, and he taught me how to stop.

Nate Duffy, Grade 6
Monforton School, MT

You Are What You Eat

I often hear complaints: "I lost my appetite for lunch," "My teeth hurt," "I can't focus on my work," "I find it hard to catch my breath when I run." These are common ailments from gorging on junk food and not enough exercise.

Junk food is low in nutritional value. It has no vitamins or minerals which are essential for our growth and development. Junk food spoils our appetite for healthy meals. Without a proper diet, we will get tired easily. Then we won't have the energy to study or exercise.

Junk food is high in calories. This might cause obesity if we don't exercise frequently. Obesity may lead to a lack of self esteem, diabetes, heart failure, and hypertension. 26% of Canadian kids, according to a Parliamentary Health Committee, are overweight and obesity among children has almost tripled over the past three decades.

A recent study of almost 9,000 TV ads targeted at kids show that 44% are for junk food, 28% are for cereal, and only 5% for dairy products and juices. Perhaps we could create our ad to promote healthy eating and help children choose a healthy diet.

Poor eating habits are very hard to kick. We should develop good eating habits when we are young. We are not supposed to pollute our environment and we shouldn't pollute our bodies with junk food. Learn to treat our bodies with respect, and we will be rewarded with good health and long life.

Brennan Wong, Grade 5
Crosby Heights Public School, ON

Dealing with Friends

You know how sometimes friends talk about other people, well that's what this story is about.

One day I asked my friend why she talked about people so much. Well she said that she doesn't talk about other people, but she does.

One morning I was on the bus and going to school and I heard her not only talk about someone, but I heard that she was going to tell my best friend something I did not say, which ended up making my best friend mad at me. That day at school I felt like telling her best friend something she did not say, but I made the right decision to not act that way.

At lunch my friend saw me walk by her and she gave me a note that said, "If you want to be my friend then do not talk behind my back," and I circled ok.

After lunch I went up to my friend and told her I did not say that and she did not believe me, but we just forgot about the whole thing and started playing.

So, if you talk about other people STOP, put yourself in that person's shoes and see how you feel.

Brooke Ventresca, Grade 5
P H Greene Elementary School, TX

Global Warming

The global average air temperature near the earth's surface rose 0.74 Celsius or 1.33 Fahrenheit during the last one hundred years. The Intergovernmental Panel on Climate Change (IPCC) concludes, "most of the observed increase in anthropogenic greenhouse gas concentrations are via the greenhouse effect."

Natural phenomena such as solar variation combined with volcanoes probably had a small warming effect from pre-industrial times to 1950 and a small cooling effect from 1950 onward. These basic conclusions have been endorsed by at least thirty scientific societies and academies of science, including all of the national academies of science of the major industrialized countries. However, a few individual scientists disagree with some of the main conclusions of the IPCC.

Climate models referenced by the IPCC project that global surface temperatures are likely to increase by 1.1 to 6.4 degrees Celsius (2.0 to 11.5 degrees Fahrenheit) between 1990 and 2100. The range of values results from the use of differing scenarios of future greenhouse gas emissions as well as models with differing climate sensitivity. Although most studies focus on the period up to 2100, warming and sea level rise are expected to continue for more than a millennium even if greenhouse gas levels are stabilized. This reflects the large heat capacity of the oceans. All in all, we should work together to stop global warming.

Joey Baladez, Grade 4
Lincoln Elementary School, WA

Fall

Fall is such a terrific time of year. There is so much to be satisfied about when summer ends. The air starts to cool off after what seems like ages, and the leaves start to shift colors. It's such a charming sight, the vibrant deep shades of orange, yellow, and red. The earth seems so lively at this time of year; all the different colors flashing like a color collage up to your face. Then, soon after the season begins, Halloween excitement spreads across the town rapidly. When Halloween does finally come around you feel like the fattest person in the world for a week. Uuggh! When the cheer does slow down that's the end of fall fun, right? Wrong. Then comes football! For about another 4 weeks the sport of football keeps me occupied. There's so much to it! You can watch football, play football, I could write another essay on football! Football, okay you aren't into it, maybe you're more of a TV person. Well guess what? Fall is when all the new shows begin. Yes, you probably don't believe me. That's okay, but just so you know, I'm telling the truth. Okay so now we're moving into late fall and Thanksgiving is right around the corner. Fall is coming to an end, but that's okay; now it's time to play in the snow!

Ryan Jackson, Grade 5
Butterfield School, IL

My Pet

My dog's name is Weiser. He was a Christmas gift to my dad from my uncle. My dad picked the name Weiser because he liked it. Weiser is a Chocolate Labrador with a pretty brown coat that is nice and fluffy. He has been in our family for eight years. He is almost as old as me in human years.

Weiser has qualities that make him special. He is cute and lovable. He makes the cutest puppy dog face when he is hungry, and he is very huggable. He is a friend to me when I am lonely and need someone to talk to. He always listens and responds with a bark.

Weiser is very fun to play with. When my family plays baseball he always runs after the ball, catches it, and slobbers on it. This makes me, and my sisters crazy! He likes to go on long walks with me and my mom.

Weiser is not always a gentle dog. He sometimes chases after bike riders. He practically knocks me, and my sisters down trying to get into the house when it is about to rain. He is afraid of thunder and lightning.

I love my dog Weiser. He is great. He is funny. He is the best dog ever.

Mariana Padilla, Grade 4
Santo Niño Regional Catholic School, NM

Trash or Treasure

Our world is a beautiful place. Islands, oceans, mountains, and plains are only some of its features. But how do we treat the Earth? We cut down trees and don't recycle things we make from them. We pollute our oceans and create a large hole in the ozone layer. By doing these things, we're killing our planet!

What can we do to keep the Earth clean and healthy? We can plant trees, recycle, conserve gas and water, and much more! Did you know that when we take two seconds to turn off a light when we're finished in a room, we're helping to save the world?

Another thing we do is kill animals when we don't need to. I know we *will* keep doing this, but could we at least do it less? Perhaps we could start by not destroying elephants, gorillas, or pandas. This is poaching. We need to save those animals in particular because otherwise they will soon be extinct. Animals are an important part of our world, and we should treasure them. I am positive we will soon come to our senses and stop poaching.

Our grandkids should see the elephants, gorillas, and all the other animals, too. I want them to see the great forests such as the Amazon, wetlands like the Everglades, and miraculous natural monuments such as Niagara Falls. It is important to care for the wonderful natural sites, plants, and animals this world has.

Katelyn Vlastaris, Grade 4
Birchwood School, OH

Billy Mills, Olympic Champion

Billy Mills was the first Indian to win an Olympic gold medal. I read about him in third grade and wanted to know more about him. Billy was born on the Pine Ridge Reservation in South Dakota, June 30, 1938. He is an Oglala Lakota Sioux.

Billy graduated from the University of Kansas. He was one of three Kansas track legends.

An Olympic gold medal was Billy's fortune. Billy was unknown before the NCAA, All-American Cross Country Championship. In 1964 everyone knew him. Billy won the 10,000 meter run gold medal, in the Tokyo Olympics. He is the only American to win this race. He set an Olympic record of twenty-eight minutes and twenty-four seconds.

After the Olympics, Billy continued to achieve. He became a marine lieutenant. After leaving the marines, he made a movie called, "Running Brave," about his life. He became a runner again.

I live in Eagle Butte, South Dakota, where there is a youth center known as, "The Main." Billy contributed a lot of money and his time to this center and they named it after him. I enjoyed learning more about Billy Mills.

Irish Dupris, Grade 4
Cheyenne-Eagle Butte Upper Elementary School, SD

Terry Fox

Terry Fox was born in Winnipeg, Canada. A few years later his family moved to Port Coquitlam, B.C. As a kid Terry was always enthusiastic about sports. A teacher encouraged him for cross country running, which he had little interest. In 1977, when his knee pain got worse, he went to the hospital. He was diagnosed as having Osteogenic Sarcoma, a form of bone cancer. As a result his right leg got amputated. He had hard time in the hospital and pushed himself to learn to walk again.

During his stayed time in hospital, he found out that little money is spent on cancer research in Canada. So, he decided to run across Canada in order to raise money for cancer research. On April 12, 1980 he was Marathoner of Hope from St. John's and ran each day in all kinds of weather. He couldn't finish dream marathon because of bad health. He died on June 28, 1981. Terry became a source of inspiration for lot of people suffering with cancer and others too. Even today Terry Fox runs are held annually all over Canadian cities in schools, parks during which millions of dollars are raised. Terry represented everything that is good, inspiring, generous, selfless and decent to whole world. I hope if all the people work together one day, we will be able to find a cure for all kinds of cancer and Terry's dream will come true.

Manvir Gill, Grade 5
Micro Education and Consulting School, BC

Great Buddies, Great Times

When a friend moves away, you have a lot on your mind. That's what happened to me. My friends, Julia and Heidi, moved away. I was very sad, as anyone would be, but they moved all the way to Finland, which is in Europe.

Julia and Heidi were sisters and always kind and sweet. Every time I saw them, I thought how pretty they looked. They were always polite to everyone and happy. We still keep in touch through letters and emails, but I hope to see them again one day. Not a day passes without me thinking of them.

I think we would all agree that our favorite memory together would be splashing and laughing in their pool. Sometimes we could play, be swimming around, or be stroking and kicking at high speeds, bursting through the clear blue water, racing, or just float in what seemed to be an endless array of calming water. We could swim for hours or just a little while and still have smiles on our faces. As long as we were together we felt as if we could be together until the sun went down.

No one can simply "just forget" something that had a big impact on them. I know they live so far away, but there is still a friendship between us. I can't "just forget" when my friends moved away, it really impacted me. It truly did.

Ashley Epps, Grade 5
Dingeman Elementary School, CA

Heroes

Some people have the wrong ideas about heroes. Sure, Superman is a hero but have you ever thought about someone else being a hero? Have you ever thought about who your hero is?

Heroes don't have to be Superman or Wonder Woman. My dad isn't Spiderman and the man down the street isn't going to transform into the Hulk but that doesn't mean they're not heroes. Heroes are all around, you just have to look for them.

My heroes? My heroes are my mom, dad, grandparents, great-grandparents and my teachers. They are my heroes because they love me. Who are all the people who love you and are your heroes?

Heroes don't have to have super powers or save your life. All heroes have to do is make you smile or brighten your day. They can show an act of bravery like holding your hand during the scary parts of a movie or comforting you when you can't sleep at night. Real heroes are the people who are there when you have the chicken pox.

Sure, not all heroes can pick up a car with one hand or have laser vision, but they are still real heroes because they love and care for you. You know if they could instantly freeze a monstrous villain they would. They do it because they know you would do the same for them. *Now* who is your hero?

Kelsey Newhouse, Grade 6
Southport 6th Grade Academy, IN

Camping

Have you ever been camping? Well I have many times. I always go camping with my grandparents. One time my mom and dad came. My aunts Kourtnie and Chris always come. My brother and sister like to go camping with us, too. We all love to go camping except for my dad.

BEES! Have you ever been stung? I haven't but my sister has. Once we were getting ready to go home and my sister, Clarissa, started screaming. So we asked her what happened and she screamed, "I think I was stung by a bee!" So we took her to my grandparents camp and my grandma put baking soda on it.

I love it when there is low water! There are frogs and you can swim farther out, too. Frogs are awesome! They are my favorite amphibian. It is so fun to catch frogs. Once when we went camping my brother caught a frog. He was going back to the campground to show my grandma, and he got lost. So we started to look for him and we prayed we would find him. Eventually we found him but it was still scary.

These are some reasons I love to go camping.

Ashley Fairbank, Grade 6
Thomas Jefferson Charter School, ID

Black Rhino

Charging with their giant horn. Eating on the savannas. Scaring off all other animals. That is the ability of the enormous black rhino. Have you ever wondered about the black rhino's amazing horn or had any questions? Well hopefully, I will answer your questions. So let's keep on reading!

Black rhino horns are gigantic. The front horn ranges from one foot eight inches to four feet four inches long. The back horn can get from one inch to twenty-two inches long. That is pretty impressive.

They not only use their horns for combat. They use them to defend themselves and their young as well. Wait, there is more! That's still not all they do with it. It goes from digging up tough roots for food to digging in waterbeds to finding water.

Have you ever wondered what their fierce horns are made of? Some people believe it's made of bone. That is so far from the truth. It's made of keratin (the stuff that's in your fingernails) and compacted hair. Just think of something so powerful, strong, with the use of so many things, and only made of fingernail and hair.

You now know some interesting facts about the black rhino. I challenge you to share them with other people. Be sure to tell them that there are only about three thousand, six hundred of them left. The Black Rhino and the four other species of rhinos are really close to extinction.

Dallas Dastrup, Grade 6
Pomerene School, AZ

Pearl Harbor

December 7, 1941, a brutal force of Japanese fighters bombarded Pearl Harbor. Without mercy, several ships were sunk including a much bigger battleship, the Arizona. Fighters on the land had to be quick to help the people on the battleships, unfortunately they were too late. Many people tried to pull over the Arizona but it failed. Weapons used on Pearl Harbor were a 50 caliber machine gun or a pistol. Pearl Harbor affected Japan greatly because now they could move their battleships in, and take out America's Navy. Little did they know that America's bombers were on their way to bomb some airfields.

On land they had ways of tricking the Japanese, like black broom poles to look like machine guns, to scare away patrols. The reason for this was, the bombers were too heavy to get off the battleship, so they lightened the load and had 1 gun and very little ammo. They all hit their targets but most crashed or ran out of gas and crashed right next to Japanese patrols. The Americans fought bravely, but were taken prisoner. The Japanese weapons were called car 98's, they were effective because they were a 1-shot reload, so it did not do much compared to the ballistic automatic rifle (B.A.R.) which fired long bursts of bullets which put out a wall of lead. They were effective in cases like this one, but unfortunately they did not have one, and that's what happened in Pearl Harbor.

Michael Wright, Grade 6
Northwood Public School, ON

My Dad

My dad would be the one because he's gone through everything I have. Even though his death was a tragedy everyone still loves him, he knew so many people that cared about him. He is loved and still remembered, he will never leave my heart. Some people say it's just another loss, and others say God bless him. He was everybody's friend. He made some mistakes but fixed them. He even made friends out of enemies. He was kind to all, he never said mean things about people, and people never said mean things about him. Our family visits his grave every chance we can we say a prayer to him and write a letter. We love him and always will. He would care for everyone and everything. We are all very sad we would cry in our pillows every night besides if someone's at our house. My sister just got married most of us cried because he wasn't there. He died on *May 18, 2003.* My mom pulled me out of school and drove me home, two of our neighbors were there, and when I heard the words *"Your dad passed away"* I nearly passed out, but I started crying my eyes out, they comforted me until I stopped. I couldn't stop crying for three days straight. Then I couldn't cry any more for some reason I was still very sad. Why did I stop crying?

Allison Morton, Grade 6
Round Valley Elementary School, CA

Family

There are five people in my family including me. There is my mom Norma, my dad Rocendo, my older sister Roxanna she's 19, my other sister Malenna she's 17, me Mariah I am 11, and my dog Nemo he is one. My family is caring, and loving. They are always caring about me, ask how I'm doing every day, they never let me down. They buy me what I need, sometimes what I want.

My dad is the most loving person, he thinks about his family before he thinks about himself. Like one Monday we were bored, my dad came in and said we should go to the movies or go to eat. I said we had no money. Then he said that he would give us some so we could go. It was like one Sunday when he took the whole family out to eat then we went to see the Game Plan. I thought it was so much fun.

My mom and dad both didn't go to college but my sister Roxanna is going to college now, while she is balancing a job at Answer America, my sister Malenna is a Junior in High School while balancing a job at Pizza Hut. My dad works with concrete, he drives the big truck. My mom has two jobs at Joy James Elementary, and Lane Bryant clothing store. I just love my family a whole lot. I wouldn't trade them for anything.

Mariah Garcia, Grade 6
Irma Marsh Middle School, TX

Imagination

One of Albert Einstein's famous sayings was, "Imagination is more important than knowledge." I agree. Imagination is a very important thing.

Without imagination, I would say that many of our most helpful inventions would not have been invented. For instance, without imagination no one would have invented the car. I say this because no one would have thought that they'd come in handy in the future.

If people didn't have any imagination, then they wouldn't be thinking about their future. They wouldn't be prepared at all for the things ahead. They'd maybe even fail school.

With imagination, people could think of wonderful things making them feel happy all the time. Say someone had been in a fight and was very depressed. He could think of good things that would make him feel better. Or someone could cheer someone else up with his imagination.

Imagination can also lead to a funny life because you can make up jokes with it. If this was not possible, then life would be very boring after a while and stay like that. I don't think anyone at all would want to live a boring life.

I also think that if people didn't use their imaginations then there wouldn't be any cures for many or any diseases. I say this because no one would have even bothered to wonder if it was possible for a human to do that. That is why imagination is important in life.

Joseph Morris, Grade 6
Southport 6th Grade Academy, IN

Individuality

Individuality can be a great way to go through life, but in some cases it could become harmful. "Emo," just short for being extra *emo*tional, is a situation where someone is depressed because of the way they are. They may also try to hurt themselves in abnormal ways like cutting their wrists.

Many more girls are influenced by friends to do this even if they're not actually over-emotional. It's very hurtful to cut because of the chance that you will strike an artery or hurt your friend who is trying to help out.

Girls who do this should get some help to straighten things out with a counselor or social worker. Exercises like writing in a journal and talking everything out prevent cutting to ever happen again. If you're friends with someone who is secretly doing something similar to this, you should tell someone right away. She will most likely be mad when she finds out that you gave away her problem, but if you just hang in there she'll realize that why you did it was just to keep her safe.

There are lots of emo styles with clothes, music, and makeup, so just because you wear those kind of things doesn't automatically make you a "cutter."

Emo has become more common in the past few years, so everybody will probably have to make a choice between your instincts and your friends. When you choose to hurt yourself over your friends, you end up worse than you started.

Kaiti Reid, Grade 6
West Central Middle School, IL

The Recovery

One night my parents left in the middle of the night. They went to see my grandpa. He fell out of bed. When my mom and dad came home they told both me and my sister that one of grandpa's blood clots in his brain popped. So the next day my mom was bursting into tears and I think I was too! A few days later we were going to San Francisco to see him. When I stepped into his room he looked nothing like he did before it made me feel scared. I held his hand he smiled at me. Then my mom asked him if he knew my name, he said "Julianna." But it wasn't clear because he had a breathing tube and feeding tube. But even though it wasn't clear I knew he remembered me and loved me.

Now it has been about two months since his accident and he's already out and back home from the hospital. He is still going to speech therapy and all that stuff. I go over every now and then, he gets mad at me when I sit in his wheel chair. Then he just laughs at me. My Nonie on the other hand is doing ok but still a little sad, she always has a smile on her face when I'm over. I love them and wish they would live forever.

Julianna McIntosh, Grade 6
St Anne School, CA

How Golf Became a Sport

Golf was started in 1421, near the east coast in Scotland. Players used a stick to hit a pebble in a rabbit track at the sand dunes. A few years later they got bored and wanted something more exciting than hitting a pebble on a track, that's when they created the hole. Golf later became popular because of King Charles and Queen Mary introduced it to France where she studied.

In the 18th century golf came to the United States. A Scotsman named John Reid first built a three hole course in New York where he lived. Later that year John formed the first golf club, St. Andrews Club of Yonkers. By the next century there were 1000 golf clubs in North America.

The first golf equipment was the club, made in 1603 by William Mayne. The clubs were pretty heavy because they were made from solid wood. Next, was the golf ball, which was hand stitched and filled with feathers.

In today's world, golf is a well-known sport and has improved since then. Golf clubs are made of iron and golf balls are made of hard molded plastic. Each year, new golf equipment is being made and new golf courses are being built.

Golfers today, like Tiger Woods should thank the people in the east coast. Because of them thinking of hitting a pebble with a stick is what we know today, as golf!

Seleste Griego, Grade 5
Oak Crest Intermediate School, TX

My Secret Place

At my house we have a secret place. It is in the woods. We hide there a lot. We hide there when we play hide and seek, tag, or just exploring. We used to explore with my cousin who lived at our house. We watched him play games too. We hide there all the time. But if my parents came out and saw us we would have to go inside. We still go there to our secret hiding place. It is fun. I hate it when we have to go inside. I used to climb trees and hide there but my dad had to cut the tree down. We have a fun hiding place.

Jacob Gray, Grade 4

Caring

Have you ever been caring to someone? Well I have and this is what I know. First, I know that being caring is a person who is nice an helpful, and about how they give you a hand. Another thing I know about being caring is how someone helps you with something. This shows that they care. For example, my brother can't open the door because his hands are full, so I help by opening it.

Caring about my family is important to me because they are caring to me back. I also care for my friends by not letting other people call them names. All in all, that's what I know about the word caring.

Any Martinez, Grade 5
Covington Elementary School, NE

First Time

Thank you for listening to my speech… clap, clap, clap!

It was going to be my first time saying a speech. I was so nervous that my teacher might pick my name. Everybody who didn't go yet was looking for who was going to go next!

Then it happened… she called my name. Slowly I got out of my seat, and walked up to the front. Everybody was looking at me! My heart was beating fast, my hands were shaking. My class was looking at me, waiting for me to start.

The topic of my speech was about my favorite book. I was extra nervous because the principal and some other teachers were sitting at the back of the class. So I started reading, during my speech, I had to stop and look down on my cue cards because I forgot a part of my speech.

Whenever I looked up to take another pause I could see faces looking at me… waiting for me to start again. When I finished I hurried back to my seat. I was sure that I was going to have a bad mark, but when I got my mark back I knew that I was wrong! I got a B on my speech and I felt proud because I did it!

Kathie Luk, Grade 6
Northwood Public School, ON

My Pet

"Wow! I didn't know you could do that! You deserve two bones!" Poppy did some pretty amazing things I didn't know he could do.

Poppy, my dog, has black hair and also has webbed feet. He kind of looks like a muskrat, except bigger. Whenever he lies down, his ears flip inside out and he can hear a lot easier.

One day, two people came to our door with a cage, with something scratching inside. They said they had found him out in the woods abandoned. They already had two dogs so they gave him to us.

Poppy loves to run in and out of the dog door. He also likes to chase our cats inside or out. but what he loves most of all is swimming.

He is very intelligent. He can sit, lie down, rollover, jump, and shake hands. I didn't know he could do all this, but someone told me that labs are very intelligent.

We also love to swim in the creek. Once I got in the water, he would get in too. We always have a lot of fun playing tag in the creek. Once, I almost drowned, because I fell in a hole, but he saved me. I will always love my dog for that.

Clearly, you can see that I love my dog dearly and will always. Don't forget that dogs are a lot of fun and could save your life someday. Most importantly is to never doubt a cool dog!

Nate Woods, Grade 6
Milltown Elementary School, IN

My Incredible Summer Vacation

The air was fresh and amazing. The smell was refreshing as cold, cool, lemonade on a hot summer day. The sun was as bright as a new born baby's butt. It was perfect for swimming and that was what we did. The waves crashing into me like a car crashing into a wall. I was about 8 years old so I couldn't go far into the deep water. I collected a lot of shells on the beach. When we finished swimming we went to a hotel. I think it was a 5 star hotel because it had cable TV, hot tub, swimming pool, and great food. What didn't I do at the hotel? I did everything. I even got amazing dessert. Oh man, I could remember it melting in my mouth. Then I went into the pool with other people. Man, talk about huge pool! I couldn't find my sister or brother. Then I found them in the hot tub. When I went in I was in heaven, and when I went out I was sleepy. So I went to sleep with the TV on. I was watching and sleeping. Wow! what a fun day, and when I woke up we fished for crabs, my favorite seafood. We fished for 25 crabs at least. Then we bought gifts but then we had to leave (crying). It was fun and all but now I will tell you where I went. The one and only Galveston beach, or was it a bay?

Stewart Cao, Grade 6
North Oaks Middle School, TX

Trip to Mexico

This year on July 26, I went to Playa Del Carmen with my family. Playa Del Carmen is by Cancun. While I was there I went to Xcaret, and Grande Porto Real. Grande Porto Real was my family's hotel. Xcaret is basically a zoo with an aquarium and you can swim.

The plane ride to Mexico took two hours. Me and my mom played cards and slept on the plane ride down there. When we took a ride to our hotel it took forty-five minutes. You know the name of our hotel, so I'll tell you about the rest of the hotel. It had five bars, and five restaurants. Our hotel room was really nice and had a view of the ocean and beach. My family's hotel room had three beds, one huge bathroom, ad a medium sized closet, and a balcony. We had a TV, Internet connection, and a mini bar.

The third day we went to Xcaret which is a zoo that you can swim in. When we got to Xcaret we had to go through this river that was 68 degrees. The only reason we went through the river was because that was the only way to go.

When we got out of the river we got chairs then went snorkeling and saw a bunch of different fish colorful, striped, camouflaged, and plain. We saw the same fish in the aquarium.

That was my trip to Mexico. I wish I could come back to Mexico.

Colton Hinnrichs, Grade 6
Argyle Middle School, TX

Cavies

What is a cavy?

A cavy is a scientific word for a guinea pig. The first thing I'm going to talk about are the breeds of cavies. There are 13 breeds of cavies that fall into two categories: long hairs which are Coronets, Texel, Peruvian, Peruvian Satin, Silkie, Silkie Satin, and short hairs, which are White Crested, Teddy, Teddy Satin, Abyssinian, Abyssinian Satin, American, and American Satin.

Cavies need love and care. They need food, which has vitamin C in it, and tap water (not bottled water). Cavies need their cages cleaned once per week. Lastly, they need a bath once every two months.

Cavies aren't just loved for pets. Cavies are also used for showing. To get a cavy ready for a show, you register them for a show, get an ear tag in the left ear, trim their toenails, and give them a bath. Sometimes at shows, cavies get disqualified, which means they can't be shown. When cavies are judged at shows, they are given points; 100 points is the most possible your cavy can receive.

Today, I taught you about the breeds, care, and about showing cavies. Here are some facts that might come in handy someday:

Did you know cavies have 28 teeth?

Did you know baby cavies are called pups?

Finally, did you know cavies are from Peru?

Carrie Nolan, Grade 5
St Patrick's Catholic School, WA

My Day on the Lake

Whee! I'm on a tube going 30 mph over waves. I did a double back flip off the tube. My cousins and I are on the tube in Tennessee. They are both boys but I have fun with Seth. We do toilet flushers all the time. It's when the boat keeps going in circles with you and then the boat goes right through the waves, which makes us go 5 feet in the air.

There are few houses where the dock has a roof and we jump off of it. It's probably about 24 feet high. It was fun. It was very thrilling.

By our dock where we swim, it is very rocky and bumpy. My friend swam with her sunglasses on and they sank. But I jumped down and got them, and she was very excited.

For dinner we boated to the restaurant. When we got back we roasted smores and did fireworks but I love sparklers. We had tons of sparklers.

At night time we played a game where you bet on who was going to win. And if that person won you got poker chips. I wasn't very good at it.

There was a huge couch where everyone slept, well at least the kids. There were two pullout couches. I got a lot of room. It was comfortable. Then the day came when we had to go back from Tennessee to Ohio.

Meredith Grilliot, Grade 5
Barrington Elementary School, OH

Family

The most important thing to me is my family. They're always there for me if I'm down. Everyone cares for each other a lot. If something is wrong, we work it out together. We call ourselves Team Vanek. We work as a team in everything we do. My dog cares a lot for us too. If anyone is sad she comes in and cheers them up. If you're sick she tries to make you feel better. We call her Nurse Buffy. She's a big part of Team Vanek also.

My grandma lives in Washington. We love it when we travel to go see her. She's 92, so she can't do much anymore, like coming down to visit us, but she always calls to check on everyone and make sure we're ok. We love her a lot.

People have their strengths and weaknesses, but combine your strengths and reduce your weaknesses. In our family, my little brother Brock has Cerebral Palsy and sometimes that means I have to do extra work around the house. I don't mind too much because I know something bad could happen to me or anyone else in my family. If you love someone you don't mind doing something extra for them to make them happy. When I say my prayers at night I thank Jesus for everything He's given me especially my family. That's why family is so important to me.

Lauren Vanek, Grade 6
Linfield Christian School, CA

Having a Good Education

Having a good education, you're able to play sports, after school activities, and good grades, tryout for cheerleading, basketball, track, even cross country.

If you get good grades and don't get a F on your report card, then you can stay in sports, and do good. Lots of people get good grades in school, or are good at sports, and a good runner. Like me for example, I get A's and B's on my report card and I'm good at basketball, softball, and cross country. I hope it stays like that.

Hey, don't forget, don't drop out of school. Be smart. Because if you don't stay in school you can't be good at sports. If you do you won't get a good education. People who do drop out of school are stupid. They make bad mistakes or they go to jail. Don't make the same mistakes that lots of people do. Be in school and be good at anything you can.

If you have to get a tutor, if your friends laugh at you, it doesn't matter, you will get a good education, and they won't. Just try your hardest, and if you're not good in school or sports, don't give up.

So, if I was you, stay in school, get good grades, do good in sports. Have a good year. And never give up, try your hardest.

Karissa Hensley, Grade 6
Milltown Elementary School, IN

The Hershey Process

Have you ever wondered how Hershey bars are made? I mean, how can you get a cocoa bean and change it into a chocolate bar? It's not like you magically poof it into a chocolate bar!

Milton S. Hershey made the first chocolate bar in the 1900s. But what's the process?

First, people go to places like Africa, South America, and tropical regions near the equator to cut down cocoa beans from trees. They export them to Hershey, Pennsylvania where the main Hershey company is located.

Milk and sugar are really important in this process without it there wouldn't be Hershey bars. Here's the main process. The beans are put in a chamber until needed. When they are needed, they clean the beans and sort them by regions. Any unwanted things are removed.

After they are cleaned, the beans are roasted to enhance their flavor. They break the bean shell to get the inside, nib, which is used to make chocolate liquor.

Next, they pour butter into the chocolate liquor to make the chocolate softer. They remove the butter, then they cool, pulverize and mend them to make the cocoa powder. Finally, they put the butter back in and mix it all up.

Did you know that thousands of cows supply two million pounds of milk a day? Did you also know that one million pounds of chocolate is made each day? Mmm, who is hungry for chocolate now?

Courtney Paige Henserling, Grade 5
Oak Crest Intermediate School, TX

The Coolest Thing Ever

My family and I were going on a trip to see my aunt and uncle in Seattle. When we got to the city, we saw really tall buildings that were like skyscrapers. We saw the Space Needle and really big boats and cruise ships. We found the house my aunt and uncle live in which was really nice.

The next day we went to the science building which was huge. There were bugs in cages, but the best thing was the butterfly exhibit. There was a big dome building and huge butterflies everywhere. Many of them had colorful wings. After being in the enclosure for thirty minutes, we were checked so we didn't bring any out on our clothes.

The next day we got to go in the science building for free, and we saw a forty minute movie in 3D. It was pretty good. After that we went to the aquarium. Out of all the things that we got to see and do, the aquarium was the best. There was a huge glass wall full of fish which we got to see being fed. After that we saw a spot where you could touch starfish and see plants. We got to see an octopus. There was a glass tube that attached to two cages. When the octopus went through the tube, you could see its mouth and suction cups. When he disappeared we left.

Jacob Schott, Grade 6
Monforton School, MT

Wolf Protectors

Wolves have been here since cave people were here. A couple of years ago wolves were an endangered species because of humans. In some states money would be awarded to anyone who brought in a dead wolf.

Wolves are in many ways similar to people. Wolf packs have one wolf that stays back while others go out to hunt. This wolf "baby sits" the new born pups.

Wolves once had no reason for scientist to study them until they sent some protester scientists out to see what they would find. They were amazed at what they found. Only the alpha wolfs (or leaders) get to produce offspring (or pups). Wolves bury dead pups that don't make it out in the world. In packs only the alpha male can lift his tail high and hold his chin up. This body language tells the other wolves "I am the leader around here." If another wolf lifts its tail too high it is an immediate challenge for power. The scientists also found that the main reason wolves were being killed was that they were blamed for killing cows. This was false! Actually, wolves rarely eat human cattle unless sick. Wolves prefer deer, rabbit, moose, and beaver.

With this evidence, killing wolves was now illegal. Even with new laws made, some people still illegally hunt wolves. People have not lost hope. Wolves have made a big come back since their hunting days. People are still doing what they can to help them.

Breanna McGeorge, Grade 5
Marcy Elementary School, WI

My Grandma

A hero is someone who cares for people, a hero is someone who doesn't let you down, and someone who believes in what's right. They don't need super powers to do what's good, just believe in that person. So I think that person is my grandma. I think my grandma is a hero because she had a hip injury and had to suffer from cancer and she believed in what's right and wrong and showed me to believe in myself!

My grandma is a hero to me because she never let me down and showed me to believe in myself. She always said "Keep your head up high and stand strong," and that's now my motto!

Three years ago she fell and she needed to get a hip replacement. So she was in the hospital for a year.

Two years after her hip replacement she found out she had terminal cancer and five weeks later she passed away on September 30, 2006 and she was 70 years old.

When she was in the hospital with cancer she knew there wasn't much time left and you could tell from her voice and eyes she was terrified! But she still kept her head up high! She always did and she always will, and that's bravery to me!

That's my FANTASTIC hero!!!

Amy Beauchamp, Grade 6
St Francis School, ON

The Creepy House on "Standwood"

I have never, ever seen a house like this before. It had a broken down door that looked like somebody had just thrown a wrecking ball through it. The door was so rusty and creepy that it looked as if a witch or goblin would come flying out at any moment. The roof was so old and broken down that it looked as if the whole house was going to fall down. The house had a lot of vines and plants hanging from it and growing all around it and the fence. The roof had so many holes and patches in it that it looked like somebody could set up a whole math problem and then solve it. The most scariest part about the house is the name of the street it was on. "Standwood." Think about "Standwood," what kind of name is that? It sounds like a secret code for something.

Most of my people and friends know that I am not a scary kind of person, I am just me! But the color of the house scares me. That house was the color of horror, blood, and fear. It had a little touch of white and tan. The vines on the house made it look even more frightening. It was the creepiest house I ever saw, that house on "Standwood."

Tajhnique Gholston, Grade 6
Caledonia Elementary School, OH

A True Hard Worker

"And the winner is…" Sarah and her opponent anxiously waited to find out the winner for 'Star for a Night,' a singing contest, "Sarah Geronimo!" shouted the host. For some people, they would think she is my idol just because of her voice but it is because of her determination and perseverance.

The Geronimos started as a poor family. Sarah, the third of the four children, started her singing class when she was two years old. She has been working ever since she was a kid like being part of juvenile shows, but between her auditions, she performs at shopping malls and hotel lounges. 'Star for a Night' brought Sarah to stardom. At the age of fourteen she emerged as the grand champion of the Philippine's version of American Idol. She won one million pesos and a managerial contract after all her hard work. She spent the money not only for herself but for her eldest sister's operation. After this turning she started to have concert tours, her own CD albums, shows and fans.

Sarah Geronimo has inspired me because if you practice and strive hard enough, you can accomplish more than expected. Since Sarah has strived hard, she has inspired me to do other activities such as swimming, gymnastics, and kung-fu and I have been accepted to join contests for those sports. In conclusion, she has inspired me to do a lot better on my sports and activities and to follow my dreams of becoming an active person.

Eizyl Tanedo, Grade 6
Challenger School – Ardenwood, CA

My Best Friend and I

Hi my name is Selina and my best friend is a girl named Julie. I met her on the first day of school. We have been like sisters ever since. We do everything we possibly can together. We go to the park, shopping and many more places together. I don't know what I would do without her. If we did get separated we would keep in touch.

When we go to the park we have so much fun. We mess around on the big toy and push each other on the swings. Sometimes when we go our other friends are there we hang out with them and talk about the boys we think are cute or like. When we were really bored we make up dances and do flips. I love hanging out with Julie because we always find something fun to do.

The first time we ever went to the mall together we went straight to Hollister. That is our favorite store ever. We like Abercrombie & Fitch too but it smells disgusting in there. After a while shopping we went to the food court to eat because we were dying of starvation. I can't wait to go back with her. We are going to be friends for a long time.

Selina Martinez, Grade 6
Isbell Middle School, CA

Hiking in the Alps

Every summer break, my parents plan something fun and exciting for us to do. This year, we took a two and a half week trip to Europe. On this trip, we visited many beautiful cities such as Prague, Budapest and Salzburg. However, the most memorable part of the trip for me was our stay in the beautiful Swiss Alps.

We stayed at a cozy lodge in a quaint little village called Wengen located in a valley wedged between two mountain peaks. Every morning, we hiked up the lush green hills dotted with colorful wildflowers. The air was so pure, brisk and fragrant. Along the hiking tail, the cows were peacefully grazing and their cowbells made the loveliest music I ever heard. The views of the mountain peaks above and the valleys below were breathtaking! There were hiking trails everywhere descending and ascending through clouds linking village to village. After our hikes, we relaxed at local restaurants enjoying homemade hearty meals. My favorite food was a local specialty called Raclette which is melted cheese served on jacket potatoes.

One of my favorite hikes was the one when we walked down through misty clouds to the sunny valley below. It was magical. On the way, we saw a little hut that reminded me of the house that Heidi's grandfather lived in, in the Alps. Cows got really close to our trail. Their big eyes with long lashes blinked at us curiously. It seemed to me that their milk udders were ready to burst after eating all that juicy grass.

I will never forget this once in a lifetime experience hiking in the beautiful Alps.

Brigitte Schrunk, Grade 5
Country Montessori School, CA

Peyton

Mahwah! I know, I know, you're not supposed to kiss a dog, but I do it anyway. I just can't resist those big puppy dog eyes staring at me.

Well my dog's name is Peyton. He's a Yorkie Terrier, and his name tells it all! He's very spoiled, he gets anything he wants and needs. To top things off he even has a winter vest. If he could talk, I bet he would ask for a bed and a blanket. He loves to give kisses and hugs! You say the word and the next thing you know you have three pounds on your leg trying to give you a kiss. Peyton loves babies. He will lie down right by one and stick out his paws to give a hug. That's really weird, I know. When Makaylee and I are outside and we are doing really silly stuff, he will *try* to do the same! He looks very hilarious.

Zoom, zoom, zoom! "Peyton stop!" yelled Michelle. Peyton was going around in circles. He was giving us a headache. Peyton really looked like a boomerang flying around the house, except he rarely comes back.

Peyton and I have lots of fun together. He makes me laugh, and sometimes makes me mad. In the end I love Peyton and I never want to lose him.

Derian Scales, Grade 5
Nancy Hanks Elementary School, IN

Skateboarding

There are a few different kinds of equipment that you need to get started skateboarding. A rail, ramp, helmet, knee pads, wrist braces and skateboarding shoes are some of the things you need. The helmet is very important because you could damage your skull. The ramp and rail are meant for tricks.

A skateboard is made up of 5 parts. They are the deck, wheels, trucks, bearings, and grip tape. The grip tape is one top of the deck. The trucks are on the bottom of the deck. The wheels and bearings are put on in one piece. The four wheels are put on the trucks.

There are over 50 brands of skateboarding, here are a few: Zero, Girl, CCS, Element and Bam. You can get a skateboard with two brands put together such as Element and Bam. There are a lot of tricks such as ollie, kickflip, heelflip and manual. To ollie you slide your foot up and kick. To heelflip and kickflip you ollie but for a heelflip you kick to the left. To kickflip you ollie and kick to the right. To manual you ride on two wheels. There are some rail tricks like darkslide, 50-50, and a boardslide.

I love to skateboard and I have been skateboarding for seven years. This is a sport that I would like to do as a profession. When and if I become a professional I would teach people how to skateboard.

Christopher Craig, Grade 6
Imagine Charter School at Rosefield, AZ

All About Monkeys

Monkeys are the clowns and acrobats of the world of animals. Most monkeys are all grown up in seven years. Capuchin monkeys have very large brains for their size. Capuchin monkeys can use their tails for lots of different things like climbing, swinging, and for grabbing stuff like fruits and nuts. These tails are called prehensile tails. A prehensile tail can hold up a monkey's whole weight. Spider monkeys are the largest of all new world monkeys. There are six different types of howler monkeys. The uakari monkey might be the most weird of all the new world monkeys because of its strange looking face. Mandrill monkeys are large and usually mistaken for baboons. There are 19 different species of macaque monkeys. Some macaque groups are as big as 1,000 monkeys. Colobine monkeys have very sharp molars to shred tough leaves into pieces before swallowing. Colobines have two stomachs for eating leaves and slowly digesting them. Colobine monkeys from Asia are called leaf monkeys or langurs. Hindu people believe that hanuman langurs or temple monkeys are sacred. Monkeys communicate lots of things with their faces. Monkeys use hands and teeth to pick and comb through each others hair.

Johnathan Moore, Grade 4
Sunny Slope Elementary School, NE

How My Family Celebrates Eid

Eid is a special reunion in my religion. You have to fast for a month and if you see the moon on a special day it means Eid is coming.

Eid is a time where you celebrate because you feel the way poor people live. Eid is a process of losing weight too. If you fast for a whole month all your sins go away. You can fast when you're younger than eleven, but when you turn eleven, you have to fast. On Eid people wear very fancy clothes, and lots of jewelry. They can put on henna the day of Eid.

You play lots of different types of instruments like drums. You play music on the day of Eid and you invite family and friends over to your house or throw a party in a hall. You have to pray to god in a Mosque, which is a place where Muslim people pray in, because you get good luck and destiny in your life. Also you pray because you get god's forgiveness and you get self-control.

On Eid you cook good food and have a cake. If you're celebrating Eid in your house, you usually decorate it with balloons and ribbons too.

Eid is a holiday my family celebrates. I know a lot about it. For Eid I'm going to wear green clothes because in our religion green clothes are for a happy day. On Eid I'm going to visit four different houses!

Zainab Bokhari, Grade 5
Dr F D Sinclair Elementary School, BC

In a Box

They matched our surroundings perfectly. Snow, crystal white. The only way you could tell the precious puppies were there was because of the dusty, brown cardboard box, where they were closely huddled together.

I took one in my arms. The sign on the box looked old and dirty but I could read "FREE" in bold red letters. I put him down and ran down the block to my warm house.

Enthusiastically, I told my mother which one I wanted and planned everything. She agreed, so I jogged to the box and ignored the icy-sweat that was sliding down my neck.

I had fallen in love with him, the puppy with the hundreds of layers of soft, beautiful fur. The one with the doll eyes, black and shiny as if he were crying. The only one with the wettest, cutest nose and the tiniest. The absolutely bite-size puppy overjoyed when my promise of coming back for him had come true.

When I lifted him once more into my arms and hugged him making him feel loved, I smiled big and held him high letting everyone around me know that although I was trying to catch my breath and couldn't, my nose felt so cold it would freeze, and although I didn't know what will come next and how he would be, I was happy.

The miracle in my arms on that hideously, cold winter day would be named Spike, a special friend that has warmed my heart ever since.

Amarainie Marquez, Grade 6
Irma Marsh Middle School, TX

Philippines

The Philippines is such an interesting place. The reason I am so interested is because my mom used to live there, in the city of Bataan. She lived with her mother, father, and seven brothers and sisters. The Philippines is a very poor country and my mother's family didn't have a bunch of money so they lived in a hut with only one room, and two windows. In order to make the hut you would take two bamboo sticks push it up and the bamboo sticks would hold it up. The floor was made of bamboo, it was smooth like wood. Bamboo is really common in the Philippines and helps a lot. They didn't have an oven either so they would make a fire to cook their food.

Her school wasn't like our school now, it only had two classrooms. First and second graders in one classroom and third and fourth graders in the other. Fifth and sixth was in a totally different school. High school is only four years, so school didn't last that long. Also, Mom's school only lasted half of the time we spend at our school. She only stayed until about 12:30, I wish I went to her school.

So life in the Philippines wasn't that easy, as you can see. My mom always says she liked how she lived there, but it wasn't easy living there all the time!

Isabelle Soto, Grade 5
Oak Crest Intermediate School, TX

At My Nana and Papa's House

I couldn't believe it, I was about 30 seconds away from my nana's and papa's house! The reason I wanted to get to their house so bad was because I had never seen their house. I also just wanted to see their dog Hogie. If Hogie wants you to pet him he'll roll over on his back and make you rub his belly. When I got there my family and I said hi to Hogie and my nana and papa. I couldn't believe what I saw, my papa must've gotten a boat and not told me. Right after I saw the boat the first thing I said to my papa was, "Can we go fishing?" My papa said we could go later that afternoon. I went to go play on my papa's swing with my brother and we were trying to see who could jump off the swing farthest. I won though it was pretty close.

When it was time to go fishing we got the fishing nets and went to the dock. When we got to the dock we went to go buy some worm bait. I had never fished before so I was practicing my cast. All of a sudden a fish had caught on to the hook and I didn't even have bait on! I pulled and pulled until I finally caught the fish. We all went home and ate fish and my family went to our home.

Adam Ivey, Grade 4
Menchaca Elementary School, TX

Blow Pops

Blow Pops aren't only for children, they are for grown ups and teenagers too. Blow Pops are lollipops that can get you pumped up because of its flavor and the center part of the lollipop that is always a surprise.

Blow Pops are like no other lollipop because they combine a hard flavored candy shell with a large bubble gum center. Blow Pops come in all kinds of fruit flavors like cherry, sour apple, strawberry, watermelon, and grape. Many people love Blow Pops because they are both a lollipop and a piece of gum combined together to form a sweet and unique treat.

Blow Pops were originally produced by the Charms Company. Many people in this world today think that Blow Pops are cool because they can be bought individually. Blow Pops began to get popular around the 1900s. Blow Pops were soon produced in New York, and then in Chicago. Blow Pops are now produced everywhere in the United States.

My opinion about Blow Pops is that they are a tasty treat. The best thing about Blow Pops is the fruit flavor and the center. Yummy, I can just taste that fruit flavor and the big chunk of juicy gum in my mouth as I speak.

Blow Pops are found in candy stores, gas stations, and shopping stores (Wal-Mart) today in life. If you have never ever tasted a Blow Pop take a risk and try one for yourself. You will probably love it.

Christie Cosper, Grade 5
Oak Crest Intermediate School, TX

Friendship

Friendship, it is a need for almost every human being. Wanting to know someone will be there for you no matter what. Having someone to go to when you're in need of help. It is a great feeling when you know there is someone there that you can trust, a true friend who will never let you down when you need them most. It always gives you a good feeling when you know you can talk freely about whatever is on your mind. Relieving us of our troubles, sharing good news, or just telling a goofy joke to see if they thought it was funny. A true friend would laugh even if they really didn't think it was funny, just to make you feel good. That is the great thing about true friends, they don't care how you look, how smart you are, or however many goofy ideas your mind comes up with. They want to be your friend because they see the real you, not what other people say you are, but for who you really are. They judge you by your heart, not how you look. Friendship gives a person a feeling of acceptance, a feeling of hope that people will see them for who they truly are. I believe friendship is one of the best gifts you can give another person; it is a wonderful gift that brings them joy, a gift that could last them a lifetime. Acceptance, love, happiness, trust, that is true friendship.

Kathryn Harrington, Grade 6
Argyle Middle School, TX

The One That Got Away

The mighty sun was almost down. It was the hottest season I'd ever felt. I was happy we didn't have school, but it wasn't going to last long. That summer, I was as tall as my dad's knees and I was going into first grade. When my dad stopped the car, I was smiling because I knew that we were there.

I felt misty fog. It was all green around the shiny pond. We took the fishing poles down to the muddy ground because it was the only place to go fishing. I was jumping up and down with excitement.

I took the fishing pole back behind my shoulder, then pressed the button to bring it forward. The line flew like a plane over the clear pond. My heart was pounding. I was hoping to get a grass green fish as big as a truck. The hook landed in the water.

Suddenly, it jerked, but it didn't pull, so it wasn't a fish. What could it be? We looked over. I had captured a plant! Dad and I had a frown. I was shaking. Am I going to lose the fishing line? With jerking motions of the fishing pole, the hook became free. I smiled, because I did not break the fishing line.

We fished for five more minutes, then quit. We still had all the lures, because we never got a fish. On the way home, we got some delicious ice cream. It was a fantastic fishing day!

Conner Kubis, Grade 5
Dingeman Elementary School, CA

Six Traits to Being a Great Writer

Do you want to be a fantastic writer? If you do, just keep the following traits of writing in mind. The first trait is ideas. Have a message that the reader can find easily. Have purpose, stay on the topic, and don't wander off!

The second trait is organization. To make sure your writing is organized, make it easy to follow. Like for example, if you were writing about the giant panda, then you started writing about your trip to California, the reader would be lost. You also have to have a beginning, middle, and end. It has to be in that order! If it's not and you wrote the end first, the beginning in the middle, and the middle last, it would be confusing.

The third trait is voice. Add your opinions and what you like to say. If your writing doesn't have any voice it would be boring!

The fourth trait is word choice. Your writing has to have strong words. It'll be more interesting. Strong verbs and adjectives are key!

The fifth trait is sentence fluency. Make sure some of your sentences are long and some are short. A story with all short sentences or all long sentences wouldn't be as fun to read.

The last trait is conventions. Your writing has to have good grammar, capitals, punctuation, and spelling. You wouldn't want a never ending sentence, bad grammar, or misspelled words. If you follow these steps you'll be a great writer.

Julie Campbell, Grade 5
Scenic Elementary School, CO

The Big News

What was the news? I wanted to know so much. My parents said I would know at 5:00 p.m. As the clock was at 4:59 my parents walked up and sat down with me. Then my dad said, "If we were to move would you be okay?" I said, "YES!" Then I remembered a Girl Scout song, "Make new friends but keep the old, one is silver and the other is gold."

It took about a year to figure out where we would live. Then my mom said, "It was time." So some of my family came up to Austin to help us move.

We had to wait for our house to be built so we stayed with my aunt and uncle for a few months. I went to St. Matthew Catholic School. My second grade teacher was Mrs. Ingram. After those four months I moved into a small apartment. I felt small in an apartment.

At school I had lots of friends. After those six months I finally moved into my house. Three people from my school lived on my street.

This year my teacher is Mrs. Patterson and she is a great teacher. I will always remember all my friends and all the great times I had with them. The best part about moving is that I am with family!

Samantha Ritchie, Grade 6

Iraqi Solution

I'm a kid whose friends' parents are in the military. When my friends only have one parent at home, their family falls apart. On the news, I see there are people mad at President Bush because he won't pull the troops back. He is sending even more troops.

I think there's no one correct way to end it. Sometimes, the best way to do things is not clear. My mom thinks we started the war and should end it. I think we should pull out of Iraq and let them finish their civil war.

When we had our Civil War, no one helped us end it. I think that's why we have a better country now. If we pull out of Iraq and defend our country, we will be happy. In the end there will be no war in Iraq because one side will take over.

My best friend's dad is military. Whenever he spends the night at my house, he has to go home. He gets scared; he feels sick. If we pulled out of Iraq, maybe we could have a decent sleepover. I'm not going to be able to have a slumber party for my birthday because he won't stay and I can't just tell everyone that my party is at his house.

I really hope that soon, either President Bush will come to his senses, or the new president will know that we need to leave Iraq.

Matthew Thompson, Grade 6
Fairview Public School, NE

Snickers

Some days, dogs seem like they have no brain — *whatsoever*. Take one day last June. I was playing with my friend and my dog, and I threw my dog's ball high into the air. It hit my friend's thigh and ricocheted right back into my lap. Snickers, hearing the slight *thwump*, came bounding back to me. She obviously didn't see the brick wall, and hit it head-on. She took no notice, staggered around the wall, and hit her head on the air conditioner. Yet again, no signs of pain just pure excitement. I threw the ball back to her to keep her from hitting the swing set.

Other days, she's pretty sly. Yes, I know. An overgrown Labradoodle with wobbly legs, *still* even at age one, be *sly*? Tell me about it. But seriously, she has some fox blood in her. So, here Snickers comes trotting up to Kylie's mini table. Kylie had spilled taco meat, and Snickers had a glint in her eye, particularly on a big hunk of meat. She came by casually, and scooped up the meat when she thought nobody was watching. Although Mom and I were watching, and started laughing hard, Snickers put on her "Who me?" expression which made us laugh harder.

Through experiences like these I will always stick with my dog. I dread the day I know is coming. The death of my puppy. She truly is my puppy. She proves it every day.

Caitlin George, Grade 6
Argyle Middle School, TX

Flying Time

Time flies by way too quickly. One moment it's Friday, you're making plans for the weekend, and the next moment it's Monday, waking up early in the morning groaning. Time is very important to me. It's crazy how many people take time for granted. Yet sadly, I'm one of them. Sometimes when I have a "Lazy day" and I'm bored to death, slowly melting, I realize I could be spending time with my family. Watching a movie or hanging out, those are the times I'm going to remember. I don't know how to explain time but I know it is very valuable. Most people don't realize how important time is, I am just noticing it myself. A lot of kids want to grow up too quickly, but right now, I just want to sit back and relax.

Every day and every moment, time is moving. I don't really notice it because I am busy with every possible thing I can think of, sports, school, chores, and then somehow I have to find time to spend time with my family. My mom always told me I have a long time to live, take my time, enjoy life. I agree with that, but anything can happen to me or my family and I don't notice how fast time goes until I don't have any left. So with that, time is very important to me because of how little we have of it.

Anna Rocco, Grade 6
Linfield Christian School, CA

The Memories of My Loving Uncle Dwayne

My Uncle Dwayne died last June just two weeks after his 47th birthday. He was an amazing person. If you were in a bad mood, he would make you laugh and make you forget about how upset you were. He enjoyed every minute of life and his happiness was contagious.

In addition to celebrating life, he was the biggest Sidney Lanier High School fan and celebrated every victory the team had! No matter rain or shine, win or lose, Dwayne would go to the games and show his support. His favorite game was the Chili Bowl. If you have ever gone to a game, you know the fans show their spirit with the blue and red apparel they wear to support their team.

At the funeral, his coffin was besieged with blue and white flowers. After the funeral, my mom had the ingenious idea for the cars to honk their horns in honor of Dwayne since this was a tradition of Lanier when they won a game. It was sad and funny at the same time because we must have shocked the neighborhood with the incomprehensible scene we created.

My Uncle Dwayne was an extraordinary person and everyone he was introduced to became lifelong friends. He taught things like how to laugh even if something is not going the way you want it. He always said, "Laughter is the best medicine for the soul." I miss him immensely but I will always have the memories of my loving Uncle Dwayne.

Megan Lozano, Grade 6
St Matthew Catholic School, TX

Friendship

A true friend is a person you like. A true friend is someone who is always there to help you. A true friend is anyone who will always listen to what you say, no matter what you are saying. True friends may argue, but they won't hate each other after the argument is over. I like my friends even when they are not with me. But I like them better when we are together.

The true meaning of friendship is everything that I have mentioned. And there are a lot of things about friendship that I don't know yet.

I have some friends in fifth grade. Here is what I said about the true meaning of friendship. That is because we argue at the end of first recess. Sometimes we get into a small fight, but that does not happen after every first recess. If you have a friend you might share an idea or two. Maybe also a part of your personalities. If this is true, then you might become better friends. If I am right, then you might even become best friends.

Best friends are people you trust the most. What I mean by trust is you tell them a secret and they won't give it away. Now that I am coming to the end, I want you to go outside and pick a friend for yourself so you will not be a lonely person.

Alex Gursky, Grade 5
The Academy, WI

King Tutankhamun — Believe It or Not!

King Tutankhamun, or mainly known as King Tut, is largely known for the immense treasures that were buried with him. But have you ever wondered what his life was like or how he died? If so, please read on.

No one is sure who King Tut's parents were, but scientist believe that he was the son of Amenhotep III or the son of Amenhotep III's son, Akhenaten. They believe that King Tutankhamun was probably the son Akhenaten around the year 1342 BC. King Tut was married to the attractive Ankhesenpaaten which could also possibly have been his sister.

At the age of nine, he was appointed to be Pharaoh, ruler of the great Egypt. He was the ruler until he died at the age of eighteen. Some people believe that he was murdered and others insist that he died in battle against the Romans.

On March 8, 2005, Egyptian archaeologist, Zahi Hawass, revealed the amazing results from a CT scan performed on King Tut's mummy. The scan answered the heated debate of how the young pharaoh died. Scientists now believe that King Tutankhamun died from an incurable infection in his broken leg which was most likely caused in a chariot collision. When he returned to his palace, his open wound festered horribly and he died a slow, painful death.

Grace Lofgren, Grade 6

The Miracle

It was a simple rock like thing, no bigger than a pebble. It was buried under moist, black, soil, and nourished for every day. It was given water and its own place on the windowsill. After a week, a small, vivid, green sprout sprung out of the rock look alike. It was beautiful, and I could almost sense a tiny heartbeat within it. In a few days, it was a couple centimeters tall and it made me feel delighted to witness a life.

Of course, now you know it is a plant, but as you are pondering its type, I set her down to earth and she continues to grow. Actually, she grows quite rapidly and in four weeks is almost a meter tall. Three days later, she starts blooming small bright yellow flowers. Then as more flowers bloom, a little green ball replaces the older flowers. The green sphere grows fast, and slowly, but surely, it starts turning orange.

Obviously, you can guess it is a tomato plant, but my story does not end here. As she grows larger, the tomatoes get redder, and finally, after months of strained patience, I pluck a tomato off its stem, and carefully slice it in two.

Can you guess what I saw? Hundreds of seeds just like the one I planted. Many scientists today are going about with their fancy computers looking for the miracles of life. Well, I have just witnessed a miracle of life.

Chris Zhang, Grade 6
Crosby Heights Public School, ON

My Family

My family is like a group of loving bears. There is the gentle but protective mother. There are the playful brothers that always like to take things apart and put them together again. Also there is the father bear with the love of being the coach of many sports. I can never forget the happiness that our wonderful pets have given us. There are the dogs, cats, chinchilla, and the very small hamster. The dogs are the special bit of the family with the peppy Gracie, the quiet Aspen, and the playful Jrake. The cats are a joy to have like Dollybear, the very quiet but full of spirit kitten and, most of all, Kitty-Kitty the special one that sleeps a lot. The chinchilla that likes to bite, along with the hamster, are only a small portion of this family. The chinchilla's name is Delilah. The hamster's name is Lola and I got her on my birthday. I am the friendly part of the family. I keep us together with love and extra hugs! Altogether we are a loving and happy family of bears. We care for each other and we love to play with each other. Everyone has a special part in the family and we all love each other. All of our pets have a great place in our heart and mean a lot to us. Everyone has their own pet and mine is Dollybear and Lola. I love my animals and everyone in my family.

Nicole Frances King, Grade 6
Spring Creek Elementary School, WY

The Heroic Invasion

D-Day took place on June 6, 1944. It was going to be a day that would go down in history. On the beaches of Normandy, France more than 150,000 U.S., British and Canadian soldiers stormed. They were to establish five beachheads. The invasion was nearly called off due to bad weather but Commander-in-Chief Dwight D. Eisenhower took a risky decision to go ahead.

To get to the beaches, ships bombarded while the troops went in on small carriers. When they got there they tried to take hold of the beaches but this was not easy because the Germans were set up with bunkers, barricades and many other challenging hazards.

The Germans had been expecting the invasion more to the east so they had set up there. As it turned out General Eisenhower's decision was a good one. The invasion was a success. This was the beginning of the end for Germany.

I believe that if we would not have won World War II then Hitler and his beliefs would have been shared across the world. He believed that Jewish people were an inferior race, and those with blond hair and blue eyes were the best race. Since we won the war, countries are now free to decide their leaders and make their own decisions. I don't care what race or religion people are. I just care about people.

Jack Rieder, Grade 5
Marcy Elementary School, WI

Go Green

Reducing the pollution and saving natural resources has to be more than a trend, because it's changing the planet. Everyone can help by doing one thing.

My mom's work is trying to help the environment by putting barrels of worms in their business. The worms help to cut down on the waste. Worms eat up banana peels, egg shells, apple cores, tea bags, bread, and coffee grinds. Once the worms eat this up it turns into a natural soil that can be used to make plants grow.

We can try making less trash by using reusable grocery bags. Recycle your plastic bottles, paper, cans, glass bottles, batteries, and electronics. Electronic devices have lead and mercury which can get into the groundwater. We have the computer take back program, where you can give your computer away and not put them in the trash.

Planting a tree can help by cutting sound and cooling your home. It will help by cutting down the use of air conditioning and saving energy from power plants. They also eat carbon dioxide, a main greenhouse gas. If every family planted a single new tree, the amount of carbon dioxide in the air would be cut down by a billion pounds a year. You can get a free tree from the city, thanks to the mayor of Los Angeles. All you need to do is e-mail milliontrees@hbteam.com. Please go green and save our planet.

Jacob De Haro, Grade 5
Cameron Elementary School, CA

Someone I Know

Can you think of someone who never lies, gossips, or is selfish? Someone who doesn't cheat or steal? Well, I know someone. He's very close to me. He has never done those things. In fact, He's perfect! He is always there for me. When I am sad, He comforts me. When I'm bad, He punishes me. When I am good, He says He's proud of me. He even knew me before I was born.

When I was born, He had a plan for me. His plan was for me and my sister to be adopted! I'm so thankful He gave me Christian, loving parents. So my sister and I went to a new country: America. Learning English and new things were hard, but He helped us through it. He gave us new friends and Christian schools to go to.

He made the seasons: colorful fall, snowy and cold winter, beautiful spring, and the hot summer. He controls the weather, the waters, and much more. He created the mountains, rivers, and lakes. He wants you to know and believe in Him too. He died on the cross for the wrongs we've done. Who is this you may ask? He is our creator. He is our God!

Malia Rickards, Grade 6
Linfield Christian School, CA

The Heroes of 9-11

Have you ever risked your life just to save someone else's? Have you ever ventured into a burning building, getting third degree burns just to save someone? Have you ever donated your home to complete strangers just so they could have food and shelter? Well, the 9-11 heroes have experienced this and have completed these heroic tasks.

This essay is dedicated to all of the brave souls, survivors, heroes, helpers, and the ones who have passed, all during the fatal experiences of 9-11. All of the victims and helpers of 9-11 are true heroes.

Most of the people who were in the area of the Twin Towers as they fell were trapped, crushed, and killed and a small fraction escaped. A lot of the survivors' homes were crushed so the loyal citizens of Newfoundland donated their homes to these complete strangers.

Firefighters, rescue workers, doctors, nurses, police officers, helping citizens, survivors and victims are all heroes to me and I believe that it does not only take one hero but many heroes to have been able to save some 9-11 victims. That is why I am not only writing about one hero but about all of the heroes of 9-11.

Each person who has been through such a tragic, horrific and terrible experience is a hero. These people have risked their own lives for the sake of others; they are loyal and are true heroes in my book!

Vanessa Bulfon, Grade 6
St Francis School, ON

Chicago

The city of Chicago is best known as *The Windy City*, and one of the most exciting places to visit. It's well known for its *Magnificent Mile* of shopping. Chicago has some of the most famous architecture. In Millennium Park, they have the Bean. You can go under it and see your reflection. The Chicago skyline has unique architecture, such as the John Hancock building and The Sears Tower. The Sears Tower is over 1,000 ft. high. It is one of the tallest buildings in the world.

Chicago has many attractions. It is home to Navy Pier, a dock that is fun-filled with many activities such as boat rides. The city also offers museums to visit, and many stores too! Many designer stores are located on Michigan Ave. Now stores aren't the only attraction, food is too. On Rush St. or in just about any part of the city, you'll find many restaurants from steak houses to Italian cuisine! There are endless possibilities of restaurants to eat at!

Chicago is home of the Bears football team, the Cubs, and the White Sox baseball teams. It also has the Blackhawks hockey team and Chicago Fire soccer team. The city has become bigger and better, and a lot of people enjoy it, I know I do!! When you enter the city there is a beautiful fountain that welcomes you and at night, its lights glisten through the water. These are some of the things that make Chicago an exciting place to visit.

Alyssa DeBartolo, Grade 6
Divine Infant Jesus School, IL

Dealing with Friendships

Friendship is hard, and I have learned that everywhere I have ever lived.

It hurts when you have a really close friend and they dump you just to be popular or because they have found a new friend. But now I have a group of friends who stick by me through everything. Last year we had some trouble and it was mostly my fault, I left them with another friend because we thought they were being "mean" to us. It was one of the worst decisions I have ever made. Friends are really important in my life, because they can help me through things other people can't. I could not imagine life without them. Some days I still have doubts and just want to leave but I know I could not survive without them by my side.

I think being a girl is tough sometimes because we are all a little too sensitive. But I also think being a girl is great because you can learn a lot from fights, make-ups, and getting to be friends with others. Something I have learned is to just go with the flow and to try to always be there for others. I know being a girl is hard, but so many other girls have gone through it that so can you. Stand up for what you believe in, and hold on to your friends; you'll never know when they could leave.

Sarah Mount, Grade 6
St Gertrude School, OH

Why I Like Hunting

Have you ever been hunting? It is really fun.

To get ready for hunting we get our clothes and equipment together. If it's hot we get a long sleeve shirt and jeans no matter what. If it's cold we put on underarmour and maybe a coat on top. We always bring orange hats so other hunters can see us. We pack our guns and bring food and drinks, like eggs, sausage, snacks, water and Gatorade. Then we're on our way.

We hunt turkey, pheasant and quail. It feels really good when you shoot a bird. I really hope I can shoot one every time we go. That doesn't always happen, but it is still fun walking the fields. I feel happy hanging out with my friends. Sometimes people make jokes that are hurtful, but I try to ignore that.

The first safety rule is never point a gun at someone. Also, when you don't need your gun, unload it. Don't shoot towards houses and only go hunting where you have permission or on a friend's land.

Besides hunting, we play football, with one of the older kids as all time quarterback. It is really fun. We practice with our guns using cans and bottles. Sometimes we walk around the cabin and shoot stuff with BB-guns. We also eat in our spare time and play catch with a football or baseball.

That's why I like hunting. Maybe you should go sometime.

Lucas Mace, Grade 5
St Robert Bellarmine School, NE

Mummies, the Where, What, and How

Often, when people think of mummies, they think of the Ancient Egyptians. Mummification is how the Egyptians buried their dead.

Egyptian pharaohs are usually buried in the Valley of the Kings. Mummies can be found in many countries however. I've always thought they were fascinating.

Pharaohs aren't found every day. One of the most famous is King Tut. His tomb was discovered in November 1922 by Howard Carter. In the tomb was many riches for the young king in the afterlife, (life after death). Inside four to five sarcophagus' was the body of the young king, perfectly preserved. How did they do it?

King Tut's mummy was perfectly preserved, and so are other mummies in the world.

After someone died, their bodies were laid in salt for several days. Then, the organs were removed and placed in Canopic jars. The heart was left in place, for it was believed to be the main function of the body. The brain was removed through the nose! The body was then wrapped in linen bandages, put in the coffin and buried.

The mummification was complete, the body was preserved.

Grace Barr, Grade 5
St Mary Parish Catholic School, KS

Deep Sea Fish

My essay is about deep sea fish. There are many deep sea fish and one of the fascinating characteristics about these fish is that some of the parts of the fish shed neon light. The neon glow is caused by special bacteria in certain areas of their body. This bacteria is very helpful to the fish. For example, the deep sea Angler fish uses it to lure prey with the top of its antenna. Their antenna sways back and forth until a fish comes, then it SNAPS at it no matter how large, because food is scarce there.

Another amazing fish is the Hatchet fish. After millions of years of evolution, the Hatchet fish has developed a different type of bacteria on its belly. If a predator is beneath it, its belly turns blue so it completely blends in. Still another remarkable fish that lives very very far down is the Gulper Eel. The Gulper Eel has a very long skinny tail and a very large head, it has one of the largest jaws in the world. Its large jaws help it to swallow large prey. Food is very scarce deep in the ocean, so when a large carcass falls down to the ocean floor, thousands of fish feast on it. If the carcass is some sort of whale, the fish can feast for more than eight weeks on the same body! For all these reasons and many more, I think fish are awesome!

Tyler Breske, Grade 6
Webster Middle School, SD

Baby Aaleyah

I was having one of those happy-nervous-scared-anxious kinds of feelings during those two hours I was waiting in the waiting room. I was sitting with my Maw Maw (my mom's mom) and my grandma Suzanne (Aaron, my step dad's mom). We were waiting for my mom to get done with her surgery. She was having a baby! I couldn't wait to see my baby sister! Her name is Aaleyah, Ali for short.

Finally Aaron came in and told us to follow him. He brought us up to the nursery. He said to me, "See the one with the pink little hat and the blue blanket?" "Yes." I said. "That's your baby sister!" I screamed in excitement! She started to cry. She is loud, I tell you loud! I could hear her all the way outside the glass!

A few hours later my mom was done, and they brought her up to her room. I was happy to see her. I stayed in the room with her for a little while. Later, they brought Ali in the room. I got to hold her. She is so adorable! She has chubby cheeks and beautiful blue eyes. But one thing that I don't understand is that my mom and Aaron have brown eyes and she has blue eyes. Weird isn't it?

A couple days later we left and went home. Now Aaleyah is eight months old and she is very cute! I love my baby sister!

Meredith Wingate, Grade 5
Bang Elementary School, TX

Skateboard

Hi I'm Michael Torrescano. My favorite sport is skateboarding. I like skateboarding because my whole family does it. I have a lot of role models. I like skateboarding because it is hard. I love it when I fall. It feels cool when I'm going off a jump.

I love the wind in my face when I go down a ramp. Skateboarding is a lot of fun until you fall. It will hurt, but only for a little while. It is so much fun once you know how to do it. I love how it freaks me out.

If you want to skateboard you will have to know angles. It will be fun learning angles; it looks easy but it is not. Once you learn about angles you can ride. Next you need to know jumps.

Jumping is the hardest thing out of all of them. First thing you have to do is ollie. That means to kick your board in the air. It is so cool when you go in the air. You must know angles before you can jump. You must know how to land.

Wow, skateboarding is so much fun. There is a lot to learn about skateboarding. When you go to the skateboard park you must wear a helmet and pads. We'll see you at the skate park.

Michael Torrescano, Grade 5
St Patrick's Catholic School, WA

Frank Gore: My Inspiration

As running back for the 49ers, Frank Gore has stood in the end zone eleven times in the two years he has played football professionally. He undoubtedly is the most superb runningback in the NFL. Gore has inspired me to have perseverance, work harder, and be more friendly.

Gore has been persevering and hardworking through his years on and off the football field. In football games, he received many injuries, but he has not given up. As soon as his doctors announced he could play, Gore continued playing as though he had never gotten injured. Because his mother was sick with cancer when he was in high school, Gore consequently had to work twice as hard. Despite this hardship, he still played on his high school football team although most people in his circumstance would have quit.

Although he is a famous player, Frank Gore is friendly in person and does not boast about his talent. Most fantastic football players never sign autographs for their fans. Instead, they wave and leave.

He has inspired me to play football and strive to do my best. He has also taught me to have perseverance and keep going no matter how bad your circumstances. If Gore quit playing football in high school, he would never have became prosperous. Lastly, he has taught me that if I ever become famous, I should not boast, but be friendly. Because of Frank Gore, I am inspired to be just like him and hopefully go to the NFL.

Amar Agasaveeran, Grade 6
Challenger School – Ardenwood, CA

My NXT

My name is Damion and I like to play with my NXT! A NXT is a Lego robot that you can program. I got my NXT last Christmas. It was like a dream come true! I had been telling people about it for 6 months straight. Why don't I tell you more about the NXT.

The NXT has a disk that you can download into your computer. When you do, you can use your USB cable and download a program into your NXT. You can even go to Lego.com and download programs that people have posted. If you want people to see your programs, you can post them but you have to become a member. It's easy!

Also, the disk features 4 cool programs to build. They are Spike, Roboarm T-56, Alphrex and finally, Tribot. Spike does not roll, it walks and it looks like a scorpion. Roboarm T-56 can tell the color of a ball. Alphrex is slow but can see good. Tribot can be programmed to follow a line. If you ask how it can hear, see, feel and see light, it has 4 sensors and 3 motors that come with it. Also the NXT has Bluetooth but I can't figure out how to use it.

Once I made a toilet paper shooter and it made a big mess. Also, I made Spike and it stung my sister because it is a scorpion. It was funny! I like my NXT because I can make robots!

Damion Mounts, Grade 4
Gateway Pointe Elementary School, AZ

Jelly Bellys!

I just love Jelly Bellys! Do you know what Jelly Bellys are? If you can't remember, they are the number 1 producer of jelly beans! Let me tell you some more about them, come on!

I'm not the only one that likes Jelly Bellys, more than half of America loves them! Believe it or not, they sent Jelly Bellys to space to surprise the astronauts on the Challenger in 1983! They also created some wacky Jelly Belly vehicles. They called a few out of many, the Bean Machines! This is the choice of bean for people who want some real flavor!

In 1976 they only had 8 flavors! Can you believe that? They may have had only 8 flavors in 1976, but now they have 50 flavors for us to savor and enjoy! I can't believe they have so many flavors!

Did you know that they have another kind of bean? These are called Bertie Bot's Every Flavor Beans. These are some that I thought were the most disgusting: Booger, Earthworm, Vomit, Rotten Egg, Sausage, Grass, Dirt, and many more. If I was forced to eat one I'd pick Dirt.

When I heard about Jelly Belly I didn't think much of them, but when I was researching I found out that Jelly Bellys are quite interesting. And as I was saying, I just love Jelly Bellys!

Jordan Lukasik, Grade 5
Oak Crest Intermediate School, TX

A Big Heart of Love

It started on the day of January 9, 1996 at 2:12 a.m. "It's a girl." My new mom Bernice and my new amiable dad Fernando "Fernie" Munoz said, "Isn't she the most beautiful baby in the whole world?" I smiled looking at my dad as if I knew him forever. Automatically, looking at my smile you can tell that I was a daddy's girl.

After I turned one, we moved to Colorado since my dad had joined the martial U.S. Army to serve his country. A Hispanic, brown eyes, brown hair, tall, big smile, and a big wholesome hearted man. My dad worked on the AH-64 Apache helicopter which is still used in Iraq today. In the year 2001, he chose to quit his work in the military, because of me. He says that he missed me so much.

He came home with tears, a smile, and most importantly open arms to me. Since 2004, he was the head coach of the Superstar's volleyball team. He was a great coach.

Whatever sport I was in, he was there watching or on the court helping the girls and me. On June 6th he and our volleyball team went to Chester's to celebrate our last practice. Sadly, the next day he went to be with God at the age of 31. He had an enlargement of the heart, which is too big of a heart. I always say he had a big heart because, he cared for many people especially his volleyball team and me.

Martha Munoz, Grade 6
St Matthew Catholic School, TX

The Colosseum

If I visited the Colosseum in Rome, Italy I would love to learn more about it and actually see it up close. Although it is a beautiful sight on the computer, I am sure that it would be even more beautiful up close in person. There is a picture with the Colosseum in the background when my brother went to Europe. It was amazing and so beautiful. I am shocked that the Colosseum is still standing from 70 to 82 A.D. years ago an earthquake destroyed many sections of it.

The Flavian emperors built the Colosseum, in the first century A.D. as a gift to the Roman citizens! It was built where a previous emperor had built his residence, the Domus Aurea. What I thought was a little different, is, we don't know the names of the builders! It remains as proof of both the grandeur and the cruelty of the Roman world.

There are a few things I would definitely want to do if I went to Rome, Italy. First I would try some exotic looking and unusually named food. I would see all the beautiful lights everywhere in the evening on my way to see museums. I love to go to museums and learn about history. I would walk around and see the Colosseum and after I have seen the Colosseum I would understand more by actually experiencing it.

Maggie Ryan, Grade 5
St John of the Cross Parish School, IL

The 18th Century Voyageurs

The eighteenth century voyageurs traded with the Indians for skins. They traveled in birch bark canoes with a trade bale.

The trade bale was a bunch of items that the voyageurs traded to the Indians for furs. If they came to a fallen tree or a waterfall they had to unload their canoe, carry it until they could set the canoe back in the water, reload their canoe and be on their way.

They were required to carry two eighty pound trade bales. Their sash held in their stomachs so they wouldn't get a hernia, the number one death of voyageurs.

In the trade bale there were traps, large copper kettles, small kettles, tincle cones, brass thimbles, brass arrowheads, knives, awls, onion bottles full of Brandy, burning glasses, and a lot of other items. The voyageurs wore a touque, knee britches or a breech cloth, knee socks, a shirt, shoes or moccasins, and a sash.

Anything in the trade bale that had value was based on the beaver. The beaver was the currency of the day and it has been the currency for a century and a half. If the Indians wanted to buy a trap they would have to give the voyageurs five beaver furs or fifty muskrat furs. If the Indians wanted a large kettle they would have to give the voyageurs seven beaver furs or seventy muskrat furs.

The voyageurs were not given paddles, they had to make their own. I hope you learned about the 18th Century French Voyageurs.

Drew Berens, Grade 6
Hopkins Middle School, MI

Behind the Scenes

During the summer my grandma said, "Let's go to Ashland to the Shakespeare Festival." I was thrilled!

When we got to Ashland, we checked into a hotel and went to have dinner. Then we went to *The Taming of the Shrew* at the Elizabethan Theater. The play is a comedy.

The next morning we went on a backstage tour of the theater. Our guide showed us where the actors wait before they go on stage. There are speakers backstage so the actors can hear their cues. The guide told us that they had to be able to get their costumes off quickly, so an elegant tuxedo would have Velcro down the middle so the people helping him with the costume could just rip it off the actor and help him into another costume. He said sometimes it takes people 45 seconds to change costumes.

Our guide showed us a light. Technicians could slip a red plastic sheet over the light to make it red like an actual sunset. It was fascinating.

The following day, we went to the Theater to see *Romeo and Juliet*. I didn't want to leave Ashland; not that I would want to live there, but I had a great time!

Tamara Benedict, Grade 5
Eugene Christian School, OR

The City That Never Stops

After 2 1/2 hours, I was finally in New York City. I could get off the train and see what this city was all about. I grabbed my bags and stepped off the train. I took in all the sights and sounds. I was thrilled to see all the people. My first look at New York City was exactly like the picture in my head.

We walked to catch a taxi, and suddenly we heard a thump noise. I could not believe it! A man getting hit by a taxi, he quickly gets up, the taxi moves on, and the city never stopped. I thought to myself, "Only in New York City." After a taxi ride, we made it to the hotel. With my heart still pounding, I got out of the taxi and looked around. The skyline was beautiful, tall buildings surrounded me. I felt like I was in another world.

We did so many things, but my favorite had to be the American Girl store. I idolized this place. I also experienced the Statue of Liberty, the Empire State Building, the World Trade Center site, the subway system, the Today show and saw the musical *Grease* on Broadway. I experienced it all.

As I was on the train back home, I remembered all the sites and sounds of New York City. I realized then, New York City was exactly how I imagined, a city that never stops.

Ashley Chakales, Grade 6

My Dad

Did you ever have a person who inspired you to do many deeds? I have that special person and that person is my dad. First of all, my dad is an excellent engineer. He works with computers and other routers. This all helps to improve technology. Nowadays, we have video cameras, so we can see the person we are talking to (when we are both are in different places) on the computer. When we try doing it now in my dad's office, there is a big screen on which it appears as if everyone is sitting at different ends of one conference table. So it feels as if the person who you are talking to is sitting right next to you. When my dad helps improve this type of technology, it inspires me to do the same thing as him. My dad also inspires me to get high grades, since I want to work the same profession as my dad. When my dad was the same age as me, he always used to get high grades. This all led up to him being a wonderful engineer. My dad also inspires me to become an honest person. He never lies about anything, which is also a part of his success. If people strive for honesty and intelligence, then they would also be successful. In conclusion, my dad inspires me to be an honest person, always get high grades, and to always do my very best!! My dad inspires me and I will apply all these morals in my life to become a better person.

Shivani Vaidya, Grade 6
Challenger School – Ardenwood, CA

The Person I Admire

My dad is so cool, that's why I chose to write about him. He cares about the environment. Although he hunts, he only takes what he needs, and teaches me lessons like, "Take what you need and leave some for seed."

I admire him because he's strong. He had a blood clot in his leg from a hit in hockey and had to get surgery on it but he wouldn't quit — he even went to B.C. and still played. He broke his nose 9 times but that didn't stop him either. I hope I'll be strong like him.

He's very loyal to his friends, old teammates, and his family. When he played hockey, he won the most sportsmanlike award three years in a row. When I have a bad game, he just works on it with me. One time I crashed into the generator house — it broke, and he didn't even get mad!

Now he's settled. He used to play hockey, hunt, and that was it. His family was a wife and a dog. My dad was very independent until he married my mom. He settled down, and was instantly a dad to me. Then they had Jerzi, my little sister. Now they're having another baby…see how things change?

I hope you understand how I feel about my dad. My dad's amazing. I wouldn't change him for the world. It's incredible how much I love him.

Hunter Leishman, Grade 6
JW Walker Public School, ON

Genius George Washington Carver

There are not many times when you'll be able to meet a genius, but if I you had ever met George Washington Carver then you would have met a genius. If there ever was an award for the most resourceful person in the world then George would win!

George was born July 12, 1864 in Diamond Grove, Missouri. At an early age, Carver's mother was kidnapped by night raiders. How sad! George never even met his father because he was also a slave at another plantation! Lucky for George the Carver's cared for him like he was one of their own children. George desired an education so he went to high school and was accepted at Simpson College in Indianola, Iowa. He transferred to Iowa State Agricultural College at Ames, Iowa in 1891.

When the little boll weevil ventured from Mexico to the United States and started eating all of the farmer's cotton, George had a simple solution: alternate growing peanuts and cotton in rows and the bug will die. Carver's idea worked and he became a hero!

George Washington Carver died in 1943 at the age of 78. George is still remembered today whenever we eat a peanut butter and jelly sandwich, and although he wasn't recognized at first, he will be remembered forever. Like I said, the people who knew him met a real genius!

Meridith Balbach, Grade 5
Nancy Hanks Elementary School, IN

Mega Jawbreaker

I have a jawbreaker that weighs 10 pounds. It smells like sugar. It tastes sweet like sugar and a little sour like lemon. It is smooth and bumpy. The jawbreaker sounds like a rock hitting the floor. My jawbreaker is round and looks like a sphere. The colors of it are orange, pink and white. The jawbreaker is also known as the jawcrusher. The jawbreaker I have might last me the rest of the year. I like jawcrushers because they are sweet and delicious!! I would rather have a mega jawcrusher than any other candy, except for gum. The jawcrusher makes no mess when you eat it. I liked writing this essay because jawcrushers are the best candy I would ever want, when I want something sweet.

Amber Trenck, Grade 4
Burchett Elementary School, TX

Mocha

Mocha is a brown, furry, cute Labrador. She was my first dog. I loved her and everything about her. Sadly, she died August 8, 2007. I cried for her and I thought nothing could ever help me. I knew this was really happening. I wanted to go back and help her. I wanted to prevent it. Luckily I had great memories. When she was happy she would run around like crazy. When I was angry or sad she had a way of understanding every word I said. I loved taking long evening naps with her. We played fetch a lot. She could jump up and catch the ball when I threw it really high. I never realized that she might die.

Through all of my sorrow Judy, my neighbor, took my hand and helped me through it. We had sleepovers a lot. Then one day she told me I was too depressed and needed to get over it. I got really mad at her. Mocha was not a dog I could just get over. I missed her sweet bright smile. I realized Mocha would be disappointed if I were mad at Judy. Mocha knew Judy well. I really hope dogs go to heaven because Mocha deserves it. I miss my dog Mocha.

Katie Love, Grade 6
Linfield Christian School, CA

My Favorite Place

Most people think going to Louisiana or Six Flags is a favorite place. I do not think so. My favorite place is Club Brayden. It is made of wood. I made it myself so I would have somewhere to be alone, to do my homework, and play around with my Gameboy. I do lots of fun things. I am still making accessories, like I am putting a TV in there so I'll have more fun. I will get maybe a pet to go in there and play with me. It will be the best club ever. My friend and me are always having sleepovers out there. We tell ghost stories in the clubhouse. It was a full moon. We get scared. I went and got a big rectangle board and put it against the clubhouse. The club is all right.

Brayden Smith, Grade 4
Winona Elementary School, TX

The Achiever

My grandfather, born in New York City in 1924, lived to be a great doctor. He may not be world famous or even famous in this country, but he still stands as my inspiration. Coming from an immigrant family, he had to pay for college and medical school with his own money. He forced himself to work just a few more hours to pay the exceedingly expensive bills from college. Later on, even after college and medical school, he worked long hours, day after day, until he was satisfied with his important, often lifesaving, work. Thanks to his powerful influence, my aunt is a nurse and my mother is a physician, and in the future, possibly I will be too.

Growing up during America's Great Depression, many hardships arose and a few people my grandfather knew simply ran out of money. Luckily, Grandpa Paul did not turn into one of these people.

My grandfather died in 2002, but he still remains inspirational to me. Despite all the obstacles that stood in his path, he broke through them all and graduated from medical school. He inspires me to do my best, because I know that only the best students are accepted into medical school. Maybe these efforts will prove themselves useful, so that maybe one day I, too, will become a doctor, just like him.

Hannah Sternberg, Grade 6
Challenger School – Ardenwood, CA

The Best Brother

Do you have someone you admire? Well, I do. His name is Gustavo and he is my big brother.

He is very helpful with my school projects. Last year, in 4th grade, we had to do a project on a mission. My mission was San Francisco de Asis. It was due in one week but my brother told me to buy the kit of the mission, so I did. When my dad bought me the kit, me and my brother started right away.

Another reason I admire him is because he is very fun. Yesterday when I came from school we went outside to play soccer. We were having a lot of fun. When I was goalie he was shooting the ball hard. But I didn't mind. I am going to be a soccer player someday.

The other reason I admire Gustavo is because he is very smart. On Wednesday when I had to look up a song for my New York project, I kept on looking on Google but I couldn't find it. Then my brother came in and changed for his soccer practice. Before he started to change I asked him, "Gus, can you help me find the song, "I Love New York"?" Then he said, "Yes!" So he started looking through the web and he finally found that song for me.

Those are all the three reasons I like my brother. He is helpful, fun, and smart.

Leonel Sibrian-Curiel, Grade 5
Camellia Avenue Elementary School, CA

Lacrosse

Lacrosse is one of my favorite sports and now this is my second year playing it. In 2007 I was on Ohio State. We had an undefeated season.

Our team looked pretty bad at our first practice, but we kept on getting better and better each practice. At our first game we did really good. I scored two goals! It was really exciting to win our first game.

Our coach played for the Virginia Pirates in college. He graduated in 2003 and lives near me now. Some of our better players are Matthew Holidinak, Ryan Query, Danny Logan, and Jack Party.

We practiced on Wednesdays and Saturdays. Our game days were on Sunday afternoons. As the season went on, the drills got harder and harder.

At the end of the season we had a tournament. This is four, 15 minute games. The first game we played was Georgetown and we won by a lot of goals. Then we played Denver. They almost beat us. We won by five points. Next, we played Maryland. Again we won. At the end of the game we tackled the goalie because we won. Finally, we played Loyola. That game was really close, but we won by 1 point. The next day at school the Loyola people said that they won, but that wasn't true, their coaches were trying to make them feel better.

At the end of the season our team had a pizza party. I am hoping to do lacrosse next spring because it is really fun and I feel I'm really good.

Clayton Harkey, Grade 5
Barrington Elementary School, OH

My Homecoming Hero…My Mom

My hero is my mom because she was so supportive of me during homecoming. She made me a mum that was huge, shiny, and was all about softball. My mom let me wear my mum to school, to the parade, and to the LYSA dance. My mom was also supportive by giving me advice on what to wear to the LYSA dance, so I could look like a princess. She also took me shopping for shoes. She also was being supportive by going to the homecoming game and parade for our lions.

My mum looked beautiful, it had softballs hot glued here and there. It had strands of beads from one side of the flower to the other side of the flower. In the middle of the mum it said "homecoming" in red glittery letters and to the left it said "Casey." In the middle it had this big softball with my softball number, 7, on it. At the parade I saw some of my friends who I played softball with. At the game a transformer blew out, and a football player got injured, and one of the band players passed out. That is why my mom is my hero because she is always there for me and I love her for being there all the time.

Casey Wellington, Grade 6
Irma Marsh Middle School, TX

The Four Faces

This summer we visited the four faces, also know as Mount Rushmore in South Dakota. I learned several interesting facts about Mount Rushmore. Gutzum Borglum wanted to sculpt something out of rock. Mount Rushmore is the rock he chose to sculpt. Ninety percent of the mountain was carved with dynamite. There were 400 men that worked on the sculpture. Through the 14 years of carving there were no deaths. The construction of this masterpiece lasted from 1927 to 1941. Gutzum Borglum died in the early part of 1941. His son, Lincoln Borglum, continued the project until they ran out of money later that year.

Mount Rushmore is a sculpture of four of America's past Presidents; George Washington, Thomas Jefferson, Theodore Roosevelt and Abraham Lincoln. Each contributed in a unique way to our country. We saw the lighting ceremony of the president's faces. We also saw the Avenue of flags which has a flag of each of the fifty states. There was a fascinating movie about the making of Mount Rushmore. We learned and saw many things on our trip to Mount Rushmore. The best part of all was seeing it in person. We had an exhilarating time on our visit to the four faces!

Zachary Colton, Grade 5
Heritage Christian School, CA

Star Wars Episode IV: The Story Behind It

Star Wars didn't just happen overnight. It was a very hard film to make in the 1970s. George Lucas made the script in a year. To get Fox's approval, they needed something huge. Lucas hired concept artist Ralph McQuarrie whose drawings blew them away. Then they started casting. Results came up in this order. Luke = Mark Hamill, Leia = Carrie Fisher, Han = Harrison Ford, Chewbacca = Peter Mayhew, R2-D2 = Kenny Baker, C-3PO = Anthony Daniels, and Darth Vader = David Prowse. They then started filming in Tunisia, a desert country. The first day of shooting was delayed because of rainfall. When they finished filming there, they moved to London. The big sets were finally finished in London.

When they finished there they needed a special effects company (which was hard to find). Lucas founded ILM, Industrial Light and Magic. They created the special effects. Lucas then needed a musical score. In came John Williams. His music with the London Symphony Orchestra was amazing. The finished movie aired May 25, 1977 in 35 theaters. By the end of the summer it was in over 100. It was the first movie in a long time to make a crowd cry, cheer, and applaud. The fans were amazing. It inspired young directors and helped the country. Now it is the year of the 30th anniversary and we must celebrate. So good bye for now, and may the force be with you!

Stan Zalewski, Grade 6
Stanton Middle School, OH

Basketball Story

I am going to tell you about my favorite sport and why I like it. My favorite sport is basketball. I like basketball because I can play as a team and also alone.

To play a basketball game, you must have a team of five players. Two guards, two forwards and one center. The team with the most points wins the game. Every game has four quarters, except college basketball. College basketball has two halves.

To play the game of basketball you must be able to dribble the ball and shoot in the hoop. You should also know how to play offense and defense. Every position is important. If you are not strong in your position, the other team will get past you and may score.

Some of the rules in basketball are:

1. You can't push anyone on the court,

2. You can't stay on your side of the court when you have the ball for more than thirty seconds,

3. You can only have four fouls in each game, if you have five you can no longer play the game,

4. If you make a basket in the wrong hoop, the other team gets the points.

I like basketball because I have been playing it for a long time. I hope you like it too.

Andrew Griego, Grade 4
Santo Niño Regional Catholic School, NM

Bald Eagle

The Bald Eagle is our national bird. Back then the word "bald" meant white. There are two different kinds of Bald Eagles. The southern Bald Eagle is found in the Gulf States from Texas to Baja California across to South Carolina and Florida. The other one is the northern Bald Eagle. The largest numbers of northern Bald Eagles are in the Northwest. The northern Bald Eagle is bigger then the southern Bald Eagle. The northern Bald Eagles fly into the southern states and Mexico. The southern Bald Eagles fly north into Canada.

Bald Eagles were declared an endangered species in 1967. On June 28, 2007 the interior department took the American Bald eagle off the endangered species list. It is protected by a law. It is against the law to collect eagle parts, nest, or eggs.

The bald eagle is a bird of prey. It is found in North American and is recognized as the symbol of the United States. The bald Eagle is a large bird with a body length of 71-96 cm. The adult bird has a brown body, a white head, and a white tail. It catches fish by swooping down into the water. Sometimes big fish take them into the water and they drown. Eagles will fight for food with coyotes, vultures and gulls.

It is a sacred bird in North American cultures. They are messengers between gods and humans. Many dancers use eagle claw. That's what I learned about this bird.

Danny Cruz, Grade 4
Menchaca Elementary School, TX

Mathew Brady, Civil War Photographer

When people think of the Civil War they think of the soldiers. Mathew Brady was very important even though he wasn't a soldier. He had an influence on the activities of the war as a photographer.

Mathew Brady arrived in the city of New York at the age of sixteen. In the year of 1844, Mathew Brady had his own photography studio in the city of New York. Then in the year of 1856, he opened a studio in Washington D.C. to photograph the nation's leaders and foreign dignitaries.

Brady was best known for his photography. Brady planned to document the Civil War. The people of New York City told Brady not to go, but he said, "My feet told me to go and I went." After he left the city of New York, he got a group of photographers and went off to war. In the year of 1862, Brady shocked America by displaying his photographs of the battlefield corpses. He showed how bad the war was.

After the Civil War, Brady fell into bankruptcy, because they were not interested in the photographs any more. He died in the year of 1895.

Mathew Brady was a photographer who took pictures of the Civil War battlefields. He influenced how people felt about the war.

Kirby Peterson, Grade 5
Cheyenne-Eagle Butte Upper Elementary School, SD

My Classroom

My classroom is my favorite place. One reason my classroom is my favorite place is it has vivid colors of posters on the wall. The blackboard is filled with writing. Also, there are a lot of desks where kids are learning or studying. And my teacher Mrs. Allison sits at her big desk and looks over us like God does the world.

I can look out the window and see the playground. So calm, so peaceful, so lifeless. The big white puffy clouds peer down at us softer than the moon does. Behind the playground the sun peeks through the great oak trees. A cardinal chirps frantically, the wind whispers through the trees. They sway to the wind's deep voice. The dragonflies chase each other; the squirrels jump tree to tree. The grass is a dull color of green and is freshly cut. The swings also dance to the wind's music. But then the bell rings. I hear fourth graders going out for their second recess. My body springs with jealousy. They were going outside; I was not. Now the playground is full of children laughing, playing, having fun. The playground is not empty. Now it is full of life. The wind is singing, the birds are chirping.

In my classroom I learn, and it is fun. It is a place I will cherish forever.

Katie Louise Solomon, Grade 5
Neosho Heights Elementary School, KS

Playing Football and Spraining My Ankle

Two Saturdays ago we were playing in our football game. It was time for half time. Thomas, one of our coaches, put me in as the second running back. I was nervous. I played running back that game but I wasn't very good at it. I fumbled once, went to the wrong place and Cody tried to run but he got punished.

Last Monday I learned all the run plays. It was fun. Then all us football guys went to eat together, and after we ate we were playing tag and I fell and sprained my ankle. When I sprained my ankle, felt like I was going to throw up. I just sat there and one of my friend's mom asked if I was okay. I got up and went inside and told my mom. I could barely walk at all because of my ankle. We put ice on it that night and we decided I wouldn't go to school the next day or two. The next morning I had to drag myself on the floor to get around. My uncle told me I should keep moving my foot or it would become stiff and that would be it for my foot. I went to school Thursday and Friday but it was hard to get around. That Monday the doctor said it is a pulled tendon.

Aden Wheat, Grade 6
Irma Marsh Middle School, TX

My Family

My dad is very loving to me and loves me very much and my dad loves as much as he can. I really love him for the way he treats me and he really protects me from my bullies and stuff that hurts my feelings. He just loves to care about my family and that's why I love him and I'm glad he's my dad. Whenever I need help with something he helps me. My dad likes going swimming with us and we usually have a blast!

My mom is important to me because she really cares about me. My mom loves me and helps me with my homework. She cares about me as much as she does with everyone else. Sometimes she takes us to fun places. She loves to care about people. My brother's named Bryce and when he wants his baba he says "Jesse baba." I go and get him a baba and he says "Please Jesse." And he is just a little character. He loves doing stuff that makes me laugh. Bryce loves to say night-night and jumps in bed with someone.

My sister is important to me because she loves me. My sister really cares about me! My sister loves to take me on her motor scooter and when we go swimming we usually play a mermaid game and usually have a blast with her!

My brother is important to me because he is nice. Me and him love to play the computer! Me and my brother like going swimming and we play Pizza Hut and we bake pizza for four dollars and we sell pepperoni, cheese and combos and that's all. They love me for who I am. And I love them for who they are and that's my life as Jessica Donston!

Jessica Donston, Grade 4
Gateway Pointe Elementary School, AZ

Sixth Sense?

Sight, smell, hearing, taste and touch are the five senses. Is there a sixth one? Scientists are suggesting that there might be a sixth sense that can predict the future. It is still under research and investigation to see whether it exists.

So what if there is a sixth sense, will anything change in our lifetime?

There is a chance that our lives will stay the same even if it exists because the sixth sense is so rare and weak that it is very unlikely to provide a meaningful impact. On the other hand, it could have radical applications to our daily lives. Studies show that the sixth sense could change the way that an illness healing process is going to be through so called "retroactive intentional influence." It could also lead to early warning systems. For example, future aircraft might have heart-monitoring systems, which could detect when an emotional event is about to happen. This could save people's lives.

In the way I see the sixth sense, it is just an extraordinary coincidence and/or imagination. Even if the sixth sense does exist, not everyone will have the same strength with it. In some people, their sixth sense is hidden and not as powerful as others. In other cases, the sixth sense has a significant presence and could be put into use. Therefore, in a likely scenario, the sixth sense isn't a very reliable ability to count on like the other five senses we have.

Joyce Chen, Grade 5
Marcy Elementary School, WI

The Real Meaning of Life

Life brings to you many obstacles but with a family you can overcome them together. I once read a quote about families that I believe to be true. The quote was "You don't choose your family. They are God's gift to you as you are to them." I believe that family is three things: a place to lay your head, love, and inspiration.

At the end of the day, I know that I can come home to my family. My family always makes me feel welcome and safe. I feel very fortunate that I have a place to lay my head at night and a family that loves me no matter what.

Love is number one in my family. Without the love of my family, mom, dad, and sisters, it would be hard to make it through the day. The love of my family is like a big pile of pillows that I can fall back on for comfort.

My family inspires me to believe in myself. They are always there to lend a hand or share words of wisdom. They are always there with an encouraging smile. They inspire me to always do my best.

My family has always been there for me and I always want to be there for them. A family is a place of comfort, love, and inspiration. These are three things you can get nowhere else. That is what family means to me.

Madison Hardy, Grade 6
Argyle Middle School, TX

Michel De Nostradamus

I saw an interesting show on Discovery Channel about a man named Michel De Nostradamus, and I had to write about him. Michel De Nostradamus was born on December 14, 1503 in St. Remy, France. He came from a long line of Jewish doctors and scholars. I think he was very interesting because he made predictions that became true. He studied medicine, herbalism, and astrology. He made a lot of quatrain (poems with four lines) predictions. One of his most famous ones was about the Twin Towers. It was in his almanac called Century 10 (listed in Roman numerals) and was quatrain #72. His words were, *"The year 1999, seventh month, from the sky will come a great King of Terror; To bring back to life the great King of the Mongols, before and after Mars to reign by good luck."* Many believed he predicted the Twin Towers were going to fall in 1999 in July. He began to write his quatrains in the city of Salon in 1554. They are like almanacs. They were published in 1555 and 1558. During his time the bubonic plaque wiped out a quarter of Europe. His treatment to cure it involved removal of the infected corpses, fresh air and unpolluted water for the healthy.

Nostradamus is said to have predicted his own death. When his assistant wished him goodnight on July 1, 1566, Nostradamus reputedly pronounced, "You will not find me alive at sunrise." He was found dead on July 2, 1566.

Drew Rodriguez, Grade 5
St Robert Bellarmine School, NE

The Best Moment Ever

I stood on the deep blue line of the free-throw. The pressure was on. The teams, the coaches, and the whole crowd were staring, no, glaring straight at me. The referee passed me the basketball. It almost slipped out of my sweaty hands. I dragged my hands against my shorts. I let the ball flip off my fingertips. The ball was airborne.

It was spinning as fast as it could, just an orange-black blur. The ball hit the rim of the basket. It plummeted into the net. The crowd went ballistic. I made it. That was the only thing in my mind. The time on the scoreboard started to tick away. I snatched the ball from the other opponent, but number 21 tripped me again.

I stood on that cold blue line once again. It was welcoming me back. If I made this I would be the MVP of the game, but if I missed I wouldn't be able to show my face for that team ever again.

I bent my knees and dribbled. I positioned my hands to the perfect angle and squared up to the basket. The referee blew his whistle. I looked at the hoop; it stared just like everyone else and egged me on to miss. I took the ball and I shot. I clamped my eyes shut afraid of the results. I saw my parents, teammates, and coach's faces gleaming with pride. I won the game!

Britt Todd, Grade 6
Monforton School, MT

Presidents Have Them, Shouldn't Congress — Term Limits

I believe Congress should have term limits of around eight years because, in my opinion, after that long individuals start to become too influenced. In this essay I will explain the reasons I think Congress should have term limits.

First, I think they get disconnected from real issues. They get too powerful after awhile and forget the real issues. They start to focus on their own needs, rather than focusing their time on the people. They just want to stay in power longer.

Next, some people disagree with this theory. They believe it is better to have people there longer so they are more experienced. In my opinion, if they switch in shifts at different times, then there will always be experienced people.

Also, there is something I have heard people refer to as the "Good Ol' Boy's Club." This means that someone gets so powerful that he/she can substitute qualified workers around themselves with friends or family. So then they are able to hide all scandals that might possibly occur.

Some people may argue that they are all qualified people and they are only family because they are sure of their capabilities.

I believe that in my essay, I have portrayed why Congress should have term limits. Still, some people may argue, but through this essay, I have found, and now believe strongly, Congress should have term limits and I hope when reading or hearing this, you do also.

Zander Boisse, Grade 6
Beacon Country Day School, CO

Ramadan

You might of heard of the Islamic month Ramadan. Ramadan is when Muslims fast from sunrise to sunset. Fasting is not just not eating or drinking. While fasting Muslims try to be nicer to others. Muslims also try to set goals for themselves to improve on their attitudes.

Ramadan is the month our god Allah sent the first revelation of the holy Quran to prophet Muhmad pbuh (peace be upon him). That is how Islam started.

In Ramadan there is a special night called lylatul kadir (the night of power). Laylattul kadir is when prophet Muhmad (pbuh) got the first revelation of the holy Quran in the cave of Hira.

I think Ramadan is a very special month. It teaches me to be patient and to give a lot of charity to others. After Ramadan comes Eid. I love Eid because I get presents, money and candy. I've worked so hard to achieve my goals during Ramadan. Eid is the time to celebrate our hard work. Check out your local library for books on Ramadan and/or Eid.

Omar Abdul-Hafiz Asfour, Grade 6
Northwood Public School, ON

Surprise?

"Look Dad! A horse!" When I first walked into Helen Woodward's Animal Society, I knew I would find the perfect pet for me. "Let's go to the dog section," I said. "Ok." Dad answered. We saw squirmy fluffy little puffs that we guessed were guinea pigs, cats with white and orange bodies, and even rats that had pale worm tails that had black furry bodies.

Suddenly, I saw a yellow tan dog that had brown crystal eyes. Dumbo. I noticed his tail was tucked in between his legs, which I guessed he was scared. "Dad can we get him?" I pleaded. "Please?" "Hold on," my dad responded, "Let's look at the other dogs first." "Ok." I answered sadly. When we passed Dumbo, I almost fainted because of the sad glare that glinted into my eyes. I couldn't find any dog that could match Dumbo's cuteness and personality. He was one handsome dog. "Let's take Dumbo out." my dad said. "Yay!" I thought.

"If Dumbo is a good dog can we have him?" He thought about it and replied, "Maybe." "Here he is!" the dog trainer said. Dumbo was squirming out of his arms. He dropped him on me and Dumbo started nibbling on my finger. I gave him to dad and made a "please" face. "Ok," my dad said smiling. My face looked as if it was going to explode with happiness.

Dumbo is a great dog and I love him very much!

Ellen Hee, Grade 5
Dingeman Elementary School, CA

Seeing the Farm Animals

Have you ever gone to the fair to see the farm animals? I have, and if you ask me, I'd say viewing the farm animals is the best part of the fair. I went on Thursday night with my Dad, Mom, and toddler sister.

It felt so right walking into farm territory. I knew people were getting a lot of stress because of the competitions. We went to go see the pigs and chickens first. You would not believe how cute those little eyes are. The moment you would set your eyes on one you would just faint! After that we went to see the pigs. My little sister said the most adorable thing! When we saw the pigs she yelled, "Disgusting!" and to tell you the truth they were disgusting, all muddy and smelly.

The horses were in the barn next door. Even though the horses were gorgeous, they still scared me. Every dang time I would walk past a horse I thought it would kick me and I'd go soaring through the roof. I was pretty pleased to leave the horse barn.

I suggested going to the 4-H binders. I found one filled with nothing but 2007 Super Bowl pictures. It was AMAZING!

In the end it was a fantastic moment in my life. Oh yeah! I'm still afraid of those horses!

Bruce Bell, Grade 5
James R Watson Elementary School, IN

Franky

Before my mom had me or even my older brother, my dad and mom "adopted" a young kitten named Franky. Franky's story is unique and makes me grateful to have him around every day of my life. When my parents had been married about three years they moved to Euless, Texas. My parents' neighbor was a single mother with a daughter. Their neighbor decided to adopt an orange tabby kitten for her little five year old girl. It was spring time with April showers day and night. The single mother turned out to be highly allergic to Franky, so she had to give him away no matter what. All my mom could think was, "Poor Franky," when she would see the defenseless kitten. One day my mother had had enough seeing Franky all hungry and wet. The neighbor did not put any food or water out for him. So my mom decided to give Franky a new, better home! My parents were ecstatic to start their new life with Franky and the three moved to Arlington, Texas. Franky became the sweetest and most loving cat ever. Two years later, my older brother Devon was born. After they moved to Keller, Texas, my parents had me and a year later my sister Vanessa was born. A few years later we found our two other cats, Glory and Krystal. Had my parents not "adopted" Franky, my life probably would not have been the same without my nineteen year old cat, Franky.

Nicole Zielinski, Grade 6
Argyle Middle School, TX

Drugs

Have you ever thought about trying drugs? Have you ever tried them? I have never tried drugs and have never thought about trying drugs. More and more people in the United States of all ages are taking drugs, not knowing that they are killing their own bodies. People take drugs thinking it will make them feel better or that it will fix their problems. The reality is that drugs don't fix anything. Drugs can only make things worse. Using drugs doesn't only affect your body; the effects of using drugs can harm those who care about you.

Since some drugs are legal in the United States it's easier for people to consume them. Some things that are legal are alcohol, prescription medications, tranquilizers, and cigarettes. With legal access to these things, there is a possibility to become addicted. It is so easy to stay drug free, but still people are lured into trying drugs. It is better to be drug free as opposed to slowly destroying your body or dying.

It's so simple; don't listen to your friends if they say it's cool to try drugs. Enjoy your life, it is the only one you have. Don't throw it away by using drugs. Drugs destroy dreams and your entire life. Being drug free will benefit you. you'll be much happier, healthier and better off. So be drug free. You won't regret it!!!

Marie Lopez, Grade 6
Westwind Intermediate School, AZ

The Best Friend Ever

My mom and I have a really great relationship. She is the best thing that ever happened to me or vice-versa. My mom is 26, beautiful and young. She is a good business women and recently applied at the Tarbell Relator School. She will be starting in October. My mom is my inspiration because she helps me understand things in life. We do everything together: clothes shopping, the movies, mall you name it (except roller coasters we hate them!) My mom brings joy into the house every time when we are feeling down. She also makes the best of things. Sometimes I don't think of her as my mom, but a big sister. My mom and I make a good team. Sometimes when it is just her and me, we get something comfortable on to wear, grab biscottis, milk, and our favorite show, Gilmore Girls. It reminds us of ourselves. She is the mom and I am the daughter. The mom and my mom had daughters as a teen (15). The mom is also a good business women, and the daughter is a bookworm like me. I love my mommy so much! I hope everyone has a good relationship like my mom's and mine.

Michelle Killingsworth, Grade 6
Linfield Christian School, CA

Stewardship

This week I asked four people what stewardship meant to them. I asked my mom, dad, grandma, and ten-year-old sister. I also looked it up in the dictionary.

First, I looked in the dictionary. The definition is "One actively concerned in the direction of the affairs of an organization." This is what stewardship means to me, giving your time, talent, and treasure to help the church and community.

You don't have to be an adult to be a good steward. To be a steward you have to be giving, kind, and thoughtful. You can be any age for that.

My mom and dad said the same thing. I asked my mom what stewardship meant to her. She said, "Giving generously of time, talent and treasure. Also sharing your gifts with God and your community." My Dad said that stewardship was "Giving your time, talent and treasure trustingly to God."

Then I asked my grandma. She said, "A steward was someone who provides financial support through the church." Next, I asked my sister. She said, "Stewardship means volunteering."

Stewardship isn't just giving time, talent, and treasure. It's being honest, generous, kind, willing to give up time, and things that are important to us in order to help others. Anyone can say that they can do it or that they did it, but for it to really be stewardship we have to actually do it. You can talk the talk but can you walk the walk?

Ethan Barr, Grade 6
St Mary Parish Catholic School, KS

L.T.

I am passionate about many things, especially football. It is amazing! Of course like most people, I have a favorite team, the Chargers! I also have a favorite player. His name is Ladainian Tomlinson or as most fans call him, L.T. L.T. is a great running back for the Chargers. I really like him because of what he does in the community and on the field. In Tomlinson's 2006 season, he did many great things. L.T. rushed for 31 touchdowns, breaking the all-time record for most rushing touchdowns in a season. When off the field, Tomlinson helps people in need. For example, this one kid's house burned down in a fire. The kid was really bummed because he lost his football signed by L.T. Somehow, L.T. found out and gave him a new one in person. He also has donated thousands of dollars to charity, therefore helping his community. Charity wasn't the only thing he helped. He helped the Chargers too. Tomlinson won many of the Charger's games. In one, L.T. got hit really hard. But that's not what he hurt. L.T. busted up his jaw. He just laid there for a minute, holding his mouth, but he got up and continued playing. I admire L.T.'s courage. He is braver than anyone I know. To some people, he might be an ordinary running back. But to me, he's my hero!

Sam Carleton, Grade 6
Linfield Christian School, CA

Miriah the Nicest Friend Ever

"Mom, can we go yet?" I cried. "Everyone is probably there."

"Honey you just got home from school." Mom exclaimed.

"But I want to go to Miriah's birthday party." I begged.

Well you probably don't know who Miriah is or what she looks like. She is about five feet tall. She is as skinny as a stick and she has long, brown, soft hair. Her smile is as bright as sunshine, and her eyes look like the dark brown fudge on a hot fudge sundae.

Miriah's favorite sports are soccer, volleyball, softball, and basketball. Miriah is really good at softball. In softball she can really hit the ball and she plays first base. In volleyball Miriah is just learning. We went to a camp not too long ago and played for fun.

Miriah is the nicest best friend ever because she includes me in everything. She makes sure no one is left out. One time another of Miriah's friends, Lauren, wanted to just have Miriah play with her. She told me that I was too mean to play with her. Miriah stood up for me and said "I play with C.J. all the time so I guess I am too mean to play with you." I love that!!! Miriah has much self-confidence and she is a loyal friend.

Miriah is a very good friend. She is always sharing. Also she is as joyful as a cat with a string. That's what makes her the nicest best friend.

C.J. Nance, Grade 5
Nancy Hanks Elementary School, IN

Why Can't We Watch a Lot of TV?

Derek I love you, click, gozila.a.a.a.a.a, click, you're watching tree house, click, welcome back to AFV. Much better. Boom! The TV broke! Why does this happen to me?

Did you do your homework? Ah yes mom. Then why are you holding the remote? This is not the remote it's a writing tool stick thing… a pencil. Yeah, a pencil disguised as the remote. Why can't our parents let us watch lots of TV whenever we want? It's unfair! They always say go outside or play a game while they get to stay up and watch TV. It stinks!

On Discovery channel they teach important skills and science experiments plus car shows demonstrate what is inside a car engine and how it works. Wait a minute!

I just remembered in a book I read that if people watch too much TV they need glasses. Also their brain starts to shrink. So that's why mom told me to stop watching TV because she wants me to be healthy when I grow up.

In conclusion, we should be careful not to watch too much TV. TV should be like a fast food restaurant. We only need to watch a certain amount of TV. Then maybe we would be even more healthy, wealthy, and happier.

Kuchak Shahbazi, Grade 6
Northwood Public School, ON

When the Lights Go Out!

Electricity is everywhere! Electricity is in our homes and even outside. You will find electricity in the kitchen pulsing through the radio, stove, oven and microwave. It can even be found outside pouring out of hydro dams. One fact is sure, electricity is a very important part of our everyday lives.

Imagine what life would be like if we didn't have electricity. This form of energy helps us to make tasty meals for families, makes it easier to heat and cool our homes, and gives us ways to communicate or make contact with each other. Think about how difficult these things would have been in pioneer days. Over 1.5 billion people in the world still lack access to electricity today.

Since we use so much electricity every day, we also need to conserve this energy. Simple ways to do this include always turning off the lights after using them, shutting off the electronic devices you are not using and putting on an extra sweater instead of cranking up the heat. When we conserve energy we are also being respectful to the environment.

In conclusion, with billions of people flicking on computers, televisions, phones and lights the demand for electricity rises phenomenally. With electricity our lifestyle has become super comfortable. When demands are so high we need to save electricity at home, at school, at work and even with friends. So next time the lights go out, think about how valuable electricity is to you.

Connor Laleff, Grade 6
Tosorontio Central Public School, ON

Imagination

Imagination is a very strong word. Imagination can take you so far. From an enormous castle, to a monkey in a bathing suit. Imagination gives you the crisp feeling of happiness and enjoyment. Imagination can take you from a day that is boring and unpleasant, to a day that is one of your best days ever. But, sometimes imagination can take you too far. If you can keep it under control, you should be fine.

The cool thing about imagination is that you can go anywhere and be anybody. There are no limits. You could be from a rock star to a football player, from a ballerina to an artist. Or you can go from Paris, France to New York City or from China to Italy. It's amazing what imagination can do for you.

I think it's very important to have imagination. It's a big part of your character. Whether you're 10 years old or 100 years old. Plus, if you ever want to be a writer or an artist, you have to have imagination. Speaking of writers, writers have to use a lot of imagination, especially if you are a fiction writer.

So as you can see a lot of things require imagination. Even though imagination can lead you off to day dreaming, having imagination is a very important thing.

Maddie Moseley, Grade 6
Argyle Middle School, TX

A Compassionate Lady

My hero was born in 1820 and passed away in 1913. She was born a slave in Bucktown, Maryland. She had such a difficult childhood but she was a very hard worker.

When my hero was seven, she started to work. She had ten brothers and sisters, a mom, a dad, a grandmother, and a grandfather. When she was a teenager, an overseer accidentally hit her in the head with a rock. That gave her brain damage and a huge scare. In 1844, she married a free man named John Tubman. She left him in 1849 when she became afraid that her husband would report her. She made her escape to Philadelphia, but she missed her relatives so she went back. By 1850, the Underground Railroad was created to help the slaves escape to freedom. Harriet had saved enough money to make her nineteen trips back to the South. She hid during the day and she traveled at night to help the slaves escape to freedom. She rescued three hundred slaves. Once she had to hold a slave at gunpoint. No slave was ever caught following her to the North. Some people put a reward for her capture at three thousand dollars. She was never caught. During the Civil War, she served as a spy to the Union. She was a cook and a nurse. She found shelter behind the lines. She cooked for the African American people.

Harriet Tubman was as brave as a cougar. I admire her strength.

Paul Andrew Ingram, Grade 5
Montessori Learning Institute, TX

All Stars

I got chosen to be an all-star in baseball. We got to go to Gresham, Oregon and play baseball. We also got to stay in a hotel; it was fun swimming in the hotel's outdoor swimming pool after our games.

We were the very first team to play in State on the cool field in Gresham. When we walked on the field it smelled like brand new dirt and grass.

Our first game was against Pendleton, Oregon. We lost 18-0.

Our second game was against Murray Hill. Their team went to the Little League World Series last year. We lost 16-0 because our hitting and fielding wasn't good.

The teams we played were so much more disciplined and good at baseball. I would say Pendleton was the team there to beat. We ended up losing the whole thing, but that was all right because I got to play state baseball in Gresham and meet new friends and players. It was cool because we could hear our names being called like, for example, "Will Stewart number 32" and hear people cheer for us. But it was also sad; we were all crying after the final game at night against Murray Hill. Then we all went home.

Will Stewart, Grade 5
Eugene Christian School, OR

The Luckiest Man

In the summer of 1904 a special man was born who set an example of courage. His name was Lou Gehrig!

Lou's parents were very poor and had bad health. His mother was a laundress. She and her husband had to feed their two children. Sophie, Lou's little sister, died when she was almost two years old. Now there was only Lou to care for.

In college, as he was getting an engineering degree, Lou played in sports. The manager of the New York Yankees baseball team watched Lou play. He was impressed and asked Lou to play for the Yankees.

Lou played for the Yankees with Babe Ruth. They won the 1927 World Series in a four game sweep. Lou Gehrig was the highest paid baseball player in 1938, earning 39,000.00 that year.

In his career he was at bat 8,001 times, hit the ball 2,271 times and hit in 1,995 runs.

Lou was getting worse at hitting the ball. He felt fine, but Lou's muscles weren't working right. He went to the Mayo Clinic in Rochester, Minnesota. The doctors could do nothing to cure him. Lou announced at a Yankee's game that he would not be playing baseball anymore. He said, "I am the luckiest man on the face of the Earth."

Monday, June 2, 1941, Lou fell into a coma and died.

I will always remember my idol, Lou Gehrig, because he showed courage when he was sick.

Kristie Patterson, Grade 6
Thomas Jefferson Charter School, ID

Rawhide Ranch

I am in the car and I am on my way to a camp called Rawhide Ranch where I will be with two of my friends having the time of our lives; a whole week to ourselves.

We all go to sleep. The next morning we head off to our breakfast. When we get inside I see the food, and I say to myself "That looks gross." I get my food, I sit down, and I take a bite. To my surprise it is really good.

Following breakfast my friends and I go to the worst thing ever; animal cleaning. We have horse duty! It's the most disgusting thing ever. After that we go swimming, have arts and crafts, horseback riding, animal studies, and vaulting. This is our schedule for seven days.

The end of the week was finally here and we have a big show. I am doing vaulting with my friend, Kelsey, and my other friend, Julia, is doing sheep riding. Everybody does great and I did the best out of the three. I got second place and my friends didn't place. Oh well it was fun.

Finally, I was reunited with my loving and caring family. We rode home and I said hi and went to bed dreaming about my big trip.

Haley Dickerson, Grade 5
Country Montessori School, CA

Frustrating Fun

"But I don't want to!" I complained.

"Fine you don't have to take lessons, I'll teach you," my dad replied.

"Okay," I answered happily. As I rushed up to what looked like a cloud white snow cone upside down, my eyes focused on the elegant trees and scenery.

When I got to the top, I shouted "I'm gonna try!" I was actually on a snowboard.

As my dad's voice faded away, I cried, "How do you stop this?" My dad played Follow the Leader with me down the hill, but I was flat on the ground.

"I think I need butt pads!" I said sarcastically.

My dad asked, "Are you okay?"

"Yes," I said while I went up the mountain with confidence.

"I'm going to try again," I announced with a grumble. I repeated this many times throughout the day.

The sun was about to set, I finally got on the slope with my board, it felt like I was going for twenty minutes at one hundred miles per hour rushing past people and trees. I was invincible! My lips and teeth were shaped in a smile as the wind was blowing my face. I was at the bottom of the slope, almost there, then… I was flat on my back. My dad showed up with a grin and a ton of happiness. I was all steamed up. My dad tried to cheer me up. The next day, I had done it!

Nathan Khuu, Grade 5
Dingeman Elementary School, CA

Diving

When I first went to Elite I was nervous, but when they said I made it I was so excited. At U.S. Elite we'd go to the diving gym they have at their office. At the gym they have diving boards that are not going into water. There's a big mat under it and you attach bungee cords to you and do all kinds of tricks with them attached to you.

After we're done at the gym we go to Ohio State's diving center. They have a 7 meter platform, a 5 meter platform, and a 10 meter platform. The platforms have no spring. There is also a spring board, they have a 1 meter and a 3 meter. I normally do spring board, but sometimes I go off the platform but I can't do any flips.

YES! Today we found out if we get to go to Oxford for the Junior Olympics I get to go.

I was so sore the next day, but I was too excited to think about the soreness. I had to get ready fast because my ride was here, so I jumped into the car and we were on our way. I tried to go to bed, but my friend's arm was on top of me.

Finally we were there. I had to get dressed fast because my session was up next. "Anna Cecutti will be doing a front dive pike," the announcer said. I got this funny feeling up in my stomach, but I knew I had to go so I went. Scores 6, 6, 6 1/2, 6, those scores are good for my league.

Competition was over and it was time for team awards. In first place, U.S. Elite. I was so EXCITED, I knew I wanted to keep doing it!

Anna Cecutti, Grade 5
Barrington Elementary School, OH

African Elephant

The African elephants are the largest land mammals on Earth. It has two big ears to communicate, two small eyes that blend in with its skin, large trunks used for smelling around, drinking water, picking food, breaking branches and fighting. They have two big teeth that are called the tusk and four large teeth that are called the grinding teeth.

Adult elephants eat up to three hundred to four hundred pounds of food per day. They eat grass, leaves, bamboo, bark and roots. The also eat crops like bananas and sugarcanes that are grown by farmers nearby.

The big land mammal's population is an estimate of 450,000 to 700,000. Today elephants are in danger because of the poaching problem. Poachers kill the elephants for their tusks. The elephants tusk is made out of ivory. Ivory's nickname is "white gold" because of the money you can make. You can sell it for $300,000 or more. They live in Africa, near rivers, wet muddy lands, or farms. Sometimes they eat farmer's crops like bananas, sweet sugar canes and more. They eat human foods like eggs, carrots, lettuces, and peanuts. They get mad when they lose their baby or if someone steals their baby. They pick a fight with anybody.

Isabel Rosales, Grade 4
Menchaca Elementary School, TX

It's Important to Read

Can you imagine a world without books? That would mean no more going to McDonald's, or going to school so you would not be able to learn. Without books the world would only be forest, and people would live in huts, that would be pretty bad.

Books are very important; they help make the world what it is today. Think about it for a minute if you couldn't read you would not be sitting here right now.

So do you still think reading is that horrible? Well do you have a favorite movie? The actors have to learn their lines. Reading is not that bad when you think about it in the long run.

So next time you think reading is horrible think again! For some people reading is not a problem. They're really good because they read at home. If you read at home you build up your endurance making you a better reader. That's not so bad is it? In my opinion I love reading. The great thing about reading is you get better every day you read. Let me give you an example. One day your friend tells you a joke and you don't get it. You go home and read a book. The next day he tells you the same joke and you get it. See every time you read your brain gets smarter. Still think reading is awful? Then you will never be good in school. Well, I can't help you.

Taylor Beimborn, Grade 4

Video Games

My first video game was *Mario Golf*. It was made for one system called a Game Boy Colour. Now it works on three systems, Game Boy Colour, Game Boy Advance, and Game Boy Advance SP.

I had a Game Boy Colour, now I have a Game Boy Advance. Before I had a game called *Pokemon Silver* and *Gold*, but now I have a game called *Pokemon Leaf Green*.

I like video games because they are fun and exciting. The basic idea of *Pokemon Leaf Green* is to beat people in battles and catch Pokemon. I also know two other games on the computer. One of the games' names is *Maple Story* and the other game is called *Shining Force*. The point of the game *Maple Story* is to battle monsters and get famous for it. It is also about getting items and money. You can trade or sell the items you get; you can buy items and party with other people in the game. Partying means to join other people's team. The part that makes the game interesting is that anything can happen. What makes it fun is that it is funny.

The point of the game *Shining Force* is to help people in their cities, and defeat monsters like Golems or Zombies. When you defeat all the monsters in one city, you can go to the next. It is an adventurous game and I like it very much.

Donovan Doucette, Grade 5
Holy Redeemer Catholic School, ON

Friendly Spirits of the Sea

The moment I saw those magnificent creatures, I knew I was in love! I was in love with beluga whales of course!

I was at SeaWorld San Antonio having the time of my life. These sea mammals had snub noses that looked like they had been punched. Their long, fat, white bodies made them look as if they had been bleached. They seemed social and friendly, making as much noise as teenage girls talking on the phone. It's amazing how they mimic a variety of different sounds. The sun reflected off their pearly white skin, making them look like spirits of the sea.

After our trip I went to the library to learn more about them. I was surprised to find out that they are not born white, but gray or brown. They turn white around the age of five. I also learned that their necks are so flexible that they can move their heads in all directions.

They live in the coastal waters of the Arctic Ocean. Beluga whales eat worms, fish, and crustaceans. They are twenty to thirty feet long, weigh two thousand to three thousand pounds, and have no dorsal fins. Beluga whales live in small groups called pods. I kept thinking about how smart they were because of the way they responded to the trainers at SeaWorld.

I love the beluga whales. I hope these friendly spirits of the sea stay with us forever.

Sana Kidwai, Grade 5
Lee Elementary School, TX

My Dog, Hunter

What's your pet? My pet is a dog. It's a yellow lab named Hunter. He'll be three on October 10, 2007. He's very skinny but he weighs about 90 pounds. He loves attention. He knows how to sit, stay, lie down, retrieve and a few other things. We were training him to hunt ducks, but the only problem is we can't find a place for him to hunt. Something funny my dog does is when he's in shallow water, he raises his feet out of the water to walk. The only thing I don't like about him is he whines a lot. He's very playful. If you pet him, he'll roll on his back and ask you to rub his tummy. I remember when we first got him. It was almost three years ago. He was so sweet! Whenever we go camping we take him with us. I remember two things that happened. One was when we went on a walk and there was a cattle guard. Since my dog couldn't get through, we found a barb wire fence nearby and he went underneath it. The other time was when we were driving to our campsite; our dog was in the back in the kennel. We put a pillow in his kennel so he'd be cozy. When we got him out he had chewed up the pillow. We threw it away and haven't put anything in his kennel again. I love my dog, my friend.

Alyssa Andrew, Grade 4
Concord Ox Bow Elementary School, IN

Camp

Camp Eshquagama is located in St. Louis County, Minnesota.

There are ten cabins at camp Eshquagama: south porch, south lodge, center, north lodge, north porch, cabin 1, cabin 2, cabin 3, cabin 4, and cabin 5.

At camp Eshquagama there is so much to do! With a counselor you can do archery, riflery, boating, H2O, arts and crafts, nature and land sports.

During free-time some popular activities are tether ball, free swim, and field and courts. Almost every night we have a special activity like capture the flag, Mexican festival, and a camp fire.

There are no electronics allowed at all.

The thing I love the most about camp Eshquagama is archery and riflery. I'm not any good at riflery but I am pretty good at archery but not good enough to make it to the silver bullet or the black arrow.

We wake up at 7:00 in the morning every day then we have flag rising, breakfast, cabin cleaning, first activity, free time, lunch, siesta, second activity, third activity, free-time, dinner, free-time, flag lowering, special activity, then we go to bed.

Tiffany Nixon, Grade 6
Rosemount Middle School, MN

Comparing Humans and Fish

Although people think that all fish are dumb, my angelfish proved that they are smarter than what people think. When I first found out that they laid eggs, I watched them very closely. The two angelfish always watched the eggs or stayed real close to the eggs while mouthing the eggs, fertilizing them; they took a lot of responsibility. I watched it with fascination while the two angelfish took turns guarding the eggs. It was soooo cool; whenever we gave them food, they would not eat but would guard the eggs from the other fish we had. Finally we separated the fish. As the days passed on, the eggs hatched into a wiggling fish and the two angelfish would put these baby fish in safe places. They would get mad if I get too close or they would suck the fish in their mouths and put them someplace else.

As the fish formed eyes and grew a bit by bit, the parents still kept them safe and sound. Some fishes died along the way, but the angelfish checked to see if it was dead and if it was, then they would leave it alone and focus more on the live ones.

I think we should learn from this experience, I mean people who always fuss with things they don't have are always miserable, but people who are happy with what they have might have a happy life. These fish have taught me many things, not by words but by action; could we do that? I know words are easy, but action is very hard.

Seung La, Grade 6
Cupertino Middle School, CA

Things That Are Important to Me!

I am Thankful that I don't use drugs. Drugs are bad for you because, they make you become unhealthy, like damaging your brain and your body. If you use drugs you will not get a good job and you might even have to go to jail. I want to be healthy and get a good job, so I will not take drugs.

School is important because you learn a lot of information. The teachers teach you a lot of subjects like math, science, language arts, social studies, writing, reading and we go to gym and have recess too. School is fun because you get to see all your friends and play with them at recess.

My dog is important to me because she protects me. She guards the house while we sleep, and while we are away from the house. If someone is walking down the sidewalk she will bark to let us know someone is close to the house. It is nice to know she is looking out for our family. My dog Hailey is fun to play with also, she does tricks like rolling over, giving five, and she can stand up for a few minutes. Some people think she is mean when she is showing her teeth, but she is just smiling. Hailey is a Catahoula Leopard dog, she is a rare breed of dogs. My family and I adopted her in Florida from the Humane Society.

Dillon Vanderwell, Grade 4
Gateway Pointe Elementary School, AZ

My Fat, Lazy Cat

Fez is a couple of things and neither of them are good. He is fat and he is lazy. He thinks he owns the house. You should see the weird and annoying things he does. It is pretty funny actually.

Fat, lazy Fez lies down when he eats. He spends the day eating, pooping, and sleeping. Fez, not a cat for speed, will chase a mouse, get tired, and lie down.

Fez owns the house. He'll sit on your chair, table, and homework. Fez is the only cat in the house that gets to go in the basement. If not, he'll sit by the door and caterwaul. Fez's strut stands out most of all. He shows no fear when getting in our way to get what he wants. His only care is that he gets his way.

Fez does weird, annoying things. Fez uses cardboard boxes for boxing practice. Fez doesn't sit like regular cats. He'll find a chair and lean his back against it with his legs sticking out. It's similar to how humans sit. Fez doesn't like the boundaries of the house. He'll sit by the door and, when you open the door, he'll run outside.

Fez is really funny. This fat, lazy cat thinks he owns the house. He does some pretty weird stuff. You should get a cat like Fez. If you already have a cat ask yourself something. Is your cat like Fez or is it like all of those other plain, old, and boring cats?

Tommy Lewis, Grade 6
West Central Middle School, IL

Our Arctic

Beautiful scenery in the Arctic is dazzling, but wait, the polar cap is melting. Countries are claiming the natural resources underneath the sea. Do you think that's right? This summer about five nations claim the natural resources that are underneath the Arctic. Global warming is making it easier to explore the Arctic, but it is killing the natural beauty. When we burn fossil fuels like oil and natural gases, the fuels release carbon dioxide in the air that put a heat-trapping blanket around earth, which melts the ice! If all this ice keeps melting, then there will be a passage for our ships. Countries don't want whales or fur anymore. They want minerals like gold, diamond, uranium and gas.

We don't realize that all of the gas we release is polluting the air and causing global warming. It is dangerous for our plants and animals out in the wild. If there's too much pollution in the air, one day it will affect us too. Some things we can do to help the environment is recycle. That will help save our trees. Walk, ride a bike, carpool are ways we will release less gas in the air. The arctic is melting and it's up to us to save it, so one person can make a difference! We can save our arctic and make the world a healthier and safer place to live. Little things you do to help can change everything.

Puja Shah, Grade 6
Prairie Park Elementary School, KS

The Arctic Fox

Did you know that the female arctic fox has an astonishing weight of only 6.7 pounds, which is smaller than my cat, Isabella!! The average head and body length of an arctic fox is 21" and the tail length averages 12". An average male only weighs 8.2 lbs — that is so tiny!! The adorable arctic fox has smaller rounded ears and the feet are furrier than other foxes. This fox occurs in two distinct color morphs: blue and white. The "blue" morph comprises less than 1% of the population! A female arctic fox gives birth to about twelve young.

Arctic foxes have some amazing adaptations and they have evolved to live in the most frigid climates! In the snow, you can barely see the arctic fox. Deep thick fur, a system of countercurrent heat exchanges in its paws, and a good supply of body fat helps keep it from freezing. It can also cover its nose and face with its bushy tail!

This fox will eat almost any meat it can find. Their favorite is lemming, a fat furry hamster-like creature. A family of arctic foxes can eat dozens of lemmings each day! When normal prey is scarce it might scavenge the leftover scraps of a polar bear's dinner even though the arctic fox is prey of the polar bear!!

Because the arctic fox is so tiny and cute and can manage to live in such cold climates, I think it is an amazing animal.

Hailey Holder, Grade 5
Mary Morgan Elementary School, IL

Autism

Autism is a sad disease where someone is in their "own world" and don't have the social skills most people possess. Autistic children do not react to a lot of situations the same way you or me might. They don't start using hand gestures at the age most people do.

Autism can affect the parents or siblings of the child. It might make them appreciate more, set higher or lower goals, or even make them feel depressed.

Child Protective Services used to take autistic children away; they thought they had to sink into themselves because they couldn't go to their parents for love or attention. But now they do not take children away for being autistic; which, in my opinion is a good thing.

Having an autistic child makes life a lot harder on the parents; they have to figure out what is wrong how they can help etc. etc. If the child has a mild case of autism they take everything literally.

Samantha Murray, Grade 5
Oak Crest Intermediate School, TX

Heroes of World War II

On the morning of D-Day, Pvt. Barrett, landing in the front of extremely heavy enemy fire, was forced to wade ashore in neck deep water. Disregarding his personal danger, he returned to the surf again and again to save his comrades. Refusing to stay pinned down he saved many lives by carrying casualties to an evacuation boat lying offshore.

John Ellsworth Asmussen was a pilot in the Air Force. He finished his training with the 569th Squadron. The 390th Bomb Group arrived in Framingham, England and began what would be over three hundred missions. On October 20th enemy fire split the aircraft in two. Two crewman were killed, one escaped, the rest were captured. He was the one who escaped.

Ken Doran was the first flight lieutenant to receive the Flying Cross. James Stewart's quick thinking and courage on a mission saved an entire bomb group from total destruction.

The words of the men themselves:

"Soldiers dying, calling for their mothers…that was the hardest part, laying there all night hearing them moan and groan, beg for help, beg for their mama, and you were so tired, exhausted, dehydrated. It's not very glamorous, no sir, it isn't…but then it's consistent with war." — Clarence Sasser

"Most of them (the recipients of the Medal of Honor) feel that they received it for others and that their own actions were not especially heroic." — Senator Bob Kerrey

I think these men are perfect role models. I deeply respect these men for what they did.

Kyle Hoback, Grade 6
Isaac Newton Christian Academy, IA

Casie

My name is Ashley Sweet and I have a rabbit named Casie. She is an English spot rabbit. Her fur color is white and has brown spots. Her ears are up sometimes, and sometimes they're down. She weighs nine pounds. Casie has a wide waist, but she is still adorable.

Her age is three years. My Dad adopted her from the House Rabbit Society. My Mom found her on a website, and I said yes to her. The website had other rabbits, but I wanted Casie.

Casie likes to sit under our air vent when it is hot outside. Also, she hates to be cradled. My Mom and Dad have to clip her nails every few weeks, and actually I don't know if she likes to be cradled while getting her nails clipped all the time. I think it would be hard to clip her nails because she kicks sometimes.

She is the cutest thing, but she can be grouchy. We have to feed her pellets in the morning and salad at night. Her food bowl for her pellets is pink with different colored polka dots. Casie has to have water too of course. Her water bowl is gray and black. The black dots are spots. She doesn't have one of those cups with the straws like guinea pigs have.

Do you think rabbits are trouble? Well, they are, and remember, they live longer inside than out. So go rescue a rabbit for a pet!

Ashley Sweet, Grade 4
Scipio Elementary School, IN

My Family and Friends

My family is so amazing! They encourage me so much. They've helped me by supporting me, leading me in the right direction, loving me, and so much more.

My sister, Chelsea talks to me when I need it. I've learned so much from her. A while ago she rode horses, and then she started drama. From her doing those I started them; I've been in 17 plays and have been riding for six years! I've got a dog named Peanut, he is crazy! But he is such a big help when I'm sad.

My friends are so much fun. They cheer me up when I'm sad and helped me through my grandfather's death. I've been with some of them since I was a baby! I love spending time with them. We've been in the BIGGEST fights, but we are always best friends in a week or two. My friends at school help me stay on time and stop from freaking out over a test.

My family and friends are so important to me. I love them all so much! I don't know what I would do without them. They've all helped me get over something more than once. I love all of them and I know that God has a plan for all of them! They all shoot for the moon, and even if they miss, they land on the stars!

Chloe Howard, Grade 6
Linfield Christian School, CA

Animals Are Beautiful People

Animals have been important to me for as long as I can remember. When I realized that some animals were close to the edge of the waterfall of extinction, and some had already perished on the sharp rocks below, I knew that we had to do something. That night, when I was about five, I asked mom to help me look up the list of endangered species. Now I am eleven, since then many animals have been taken off the list but many more have gone off into oblivion, never to be seen again.

Animals have always been of great interest to me. Another creature with intelligence. Another creature that seems to understand. Eyes that seem to know more about you than you do.

When you kill an animal, the last of its species, it's like taking the alphabet block out of the middle of your tower. Animals are disappearing and if too many go, our world, as we know it, will crumble.

Think about it. Would you save the animals? "With all your power, what would you do?" (The Flaming Lips, 2004)

Billie Scambler, Grade 6
Spring Creek Elementary School, WY

Bullying

Bullies bully on smart kids. Would you do something about it, or try to stop a bully form bullying on a smart kid? Well you should if you see it happening to someone. Bullying is very sickening. It's not right to bully others.

Bullying needs to be destroyed. Sometimes bullies bully on people for no reason. The main people they pick on or bully are smart kids. They bully on them because they are weak and they don't ever stand up to them.

In addition to what I was saying about bullying, it's just not right. If you were being bullied what would you do? I would stand up to the bullies and tell them to leave me alone. If that didn't work I'd tell an adult so they can do something about it.

If someone was being bullied I would try to help them. First I will tell the bully to leave them alone. If the bully keeps bullying then I will go tell an adult.

Schools should start a no bullying program for bullies. All bullies should go to the program. It will teach them how to be a respectful person. The program is for victims of bullying, as well as the bullies.

Keviana Caffey, Grade 6
Starms Discovery Learning Center, WI

Index

Author Autograph Page

Author Autograph Page

Author Autograph Page

Author Autograph Page

Author Autograph Page

Author Autograph Page